The Human Operator in Process Control

The Human Operator in
Process Control

Edited by

Elwyn Edwards
Department of Ergonomics and Cybernetics, Loughborough University of Technology

Frank P. Lees
Department of Chemical Engineering, Loughborough University of Technology

Taylor & Francis Ltd · London

Halsted Press
a division of John Wiley & Sons Inc
New York–Toronto

1974

First published 1974 by Taylor & Francis Ltd,
London and Halsted Press (division of John
Wiley & Sons Inc) New York.

© 1974 Taylor & Francis Ltd.

All rights reserved. No part of this publication
may be reproduced, stored in a retrieval system
or transmitted, in any form or by any means,
electronic, mechanical, photocopying,
recording or otherwise without the prior
permission of the Copyright owner.

Taylor & Francis ISBN 0 85066 069 6

Printed and bound in Great Britain by
Taylor & Francis Ltd, 10/14 Macklin Street,
London WC2B 5NF.

Library of Congress Cataloging in Publication Data
Edwards, Elwyn,   comp.
   The human operator in process control.
   Bibliography: p.
   1. Man-machine systems. 2. Electronic data processing --
Process control. I. Lees, Frank P., joint comp.
II. Title.
T59.7.E38   1974   658.5   74-19204
ISBN 0-470-23335-4

By the same authors:

Man and Computer in Process Control
(1973, Institution of Chemical Engineers, London).

" We're creepin' on wi' each new rig—less weight an' larger power;
There'll be loco-boiler next an' thirty mile an hour!
Thirty an' more.   What I ha' seen since ocean-steam began
Leaves me na doot for the machine: but what about the man ? "

RUDYARD KIPLING
(McAndrew's Hymn, 1893)

Preface

Early in 1970 the Institution of Chemical Engineers approached the editors with a request that they should undertake a joint Industrial Research Fellowship on the interaction between the process computer and its users, which was eventually entitled "Man-Computer Interaction in Process Control". The report arising from this Fellowship was published in book form under the title *Man and Computer in Process Control* in 1973.

One section of the book comprises a review of the studies which have been carried out on the process operator. From this several points emerged. First, the number of studies of the process operator is appreciable; perhaps some 30–40, depending on the definition used. Second, the majority of these have been carried out from the environment of a university-based research team, beginning with the pioneering work of Professor E. R. F. W. Crossman and his collaborators. Third, many of the key studies are relatively inaccessible. They include material in university theses, internal reports, out-of-print or occasional publications, papers in symposia, proceedings and journals which cover such a wide range that they are unlikely to be seen by one individual and are often difficult to obtain. Fourth, familiarity with the work is patchy among ergonomists generally and is often non-existent among engineers.

It seemed, therefore, a worthwhile enterprise to make available in a single volume a selection of some of the principal, and often classic, studies of the process operator. This is what the present collection attempts to do.

Some comments on the criteria of selection are appropriate. Most of the papers describe actual experimental work on the process operator. The majority are concerned with field studies, though some laboratory, simulation and design studies are also included. It has been necessary to exclude entirely the very large amount of work in experimental psychology which is potentially applicable to the process operator. This includes work in such areas as vigilance, decision-making, manual control, interface design, training. It includes many types of model of the human operator. And it also includes studies of other human operators whose jobs have similarity with that of the process operator, such as air traffic controllers.

A summary of the papers in the collection and of the subjects with which they are primarily concerned is given in Table 1. This is inevitably only a rough guide, since many papers touch on a variety of topics and there are many possible principles of classification. The papers have been chosen to give a

Table 1. Features of the studies of the process operator in this collection.

Paper	Type of study of process operator							Methodology of study of process operator						
	Review	Laboratory study	Simulation study	In-plant study	Design study	Computer control	Type of process	Observation and activity sampling	Interview/questionnaire	Verbal protocol	Simulation	Manual control assessment	Dynamic modelling of operator	Investigation of operator's mental models
Crossman (1960a)	X			X			Various (1)	X	X					
Crossman, Cooke and Beishon (1964)		X		X			Papermill	X				X		
Crossman and Cooke (1962)		X		X			Water bath		X	X			X	X	X
Spencer (1962)				X			Liquid washing plant	X	X			X		
Beishon (1969)				X			Baking ovens	X	X	X				X
Bainbridge, Beishon, Hemming and Splaine (1968)			X				Electric arc furnaces			X	X	X		X
Kitchin and Graham (1961)				X			Chemical plants	X						
Attwood (1970)		X		X		X	Papermills	X	X				X	X
Kragt and Landeweerd (1974)		X		X			Chemical plants		X				X	X
Bainbridge (1974)			X				Electric arc furnaces				X	X		X
Daniel, Puffler and Striženec (1971)				X			Chemical plants (2)	X	X					
Striženec (1967b)	X						N/A							
Towill (1974)				X			Chemical plant, steel mill						X	
Department of Labor (1970)				X		X	Various (3)		X					
de Jong and Köster (1971)				X		X	Refinery plants	X						
West and Clark (1974)				X		X	Pilot plant	X		X		X		
Rasmussen (1968a)	X					X	Nuclear reactor							
Anyakora and Lees (1972a)				X		X	Chemical plants							
Crawley (1968)					X	X	LD furnace							
Ketteringham and O'Brien (1974)			X		X	X	Soaking pits				X	X		
Duncan (1974b)			X	X			Acid purification plant	X		X	X			X
Munro, Martin and Roberts (1968)			X		X		Refinery plant							
City and Guilds Institute (1972)							N/A							
Central Electricity Generating Board (1966)					X	X	Nuclear reactor							
Engelstad (1970)			X				Papermill							
Lees (1974b)	X					X	N/A							

(1) Including **oxygen** and solvents plants and board mill.
(2) Including **distillation**, pyrolysis, **gas** separation and polyethylene plants.
(3) Including **petroleum**, chemical, cement and electrical power plants, steel works and papermills.

	Principal type of behaviour studied							Principal system aspect studied							
General process control	Vigilance, monitoring, signal detection	Information sampling	Manual control, tracking	Decision-making, strategy development, scheduling	Fault detection, diagnosis and correction	Learning	Allocation of function	Interface and control room design	Information display	Prototype production	Task analysis	Job design	Training	Man-computer interaction	Organizational and social factors
X															
	X	X	X						X						
			X		X										
			X												
			X	X											
				X		X									
X			X								X				
		X	X		X			X					X		
		X		X	X										
			X												
X															
			X												
						X									
X							X					X			X
	X	X			X		X								
	X	X	X	X	X	X		X	X					X	
	X			X			X	X						X	
				X			X	X						X	
							X	X	X					X	
			X					X	X					X	
			X	X	X						X		X		
												X			
													X		
							X	X	X						
X															X

representative sample in terms of the workers in the field, the types of investigations conducted, the methodology of the studies and the processes and control systems and the problems studied and to give a balance between pure investigation and system design.

The first sustained work on the process operator dates from the late 1950's. These studies were largely pioneered by Professor E. R. F. W. Crossman and the collection opens with three classic papers by this author. The first (Paper 1) is an extract from the pamphlet *Automation and Skill*, which describes the jobs of several types of industrial operator; the material given consists primarily of those sections which are concerned with the process operator.

A central concern of this work is the definition of the skill involved in process control. Considerable success had already been achieved in the application of ergonomics techniques to observable skills, but the perceptual and cognitive features of such skills as that of process control are less readily amenable to observation. There arise, therefore, problems of the methodology of studying the operator, of the operator's mental processes and models, and of the modelling of the operator.

These early studies of the process operator were initiated against a background of active interest, in related areas of human factors, in attempts to quantify human performance in tasks such as information sampling and tracking. The second paper by Crossman, Cooke and Beishon (Paper 2) represents the exploration of the applicability of current ideas on information theory to the problem of information sampling in process control. Both laboratory experiments and in-plant investigations in a papermill are described.

The third paper by Crossman and Cooke (Paper 3) examines the problem as one concerned with the manual control of a slow-response system, and preserves the orientation of earlier work on tracking performance. The paper describes the now well-known ' water bath ' laboratory experiment on manual control.

Although substantial contributions, these are only a fraction of the 20-odd papers written by Crossman on process control and related skills during this period.

Further industrial studies of particular process control tasks are given in the papers by Spencer (Paper 4) and by Beishon (Paper 5) on a liquid washing plant and a baking ovens plant respectively. Both deal with manual control, but the latter is also concerned with scheduling. And both raise the problem of the methodology of studying the operator.

Beishon's paper is also concerned with the operator's thought processes in executing his scheduling function. This problem is pursued further in the paper by Bainbridge, Beishon, Hemming and Splaine (Paper 6) which describes a simulation study of an electric arc furnace scheduling task. The mental processes of the operators are made manifest by means of a running commentary, or ' verbal protocol ', and are then subjected to detailed analysis. This also illustrates the use of simulation as a half-way stage between laboratory and field studies.

The work described above consists essentially of academic studies undertaken in order to learn more about the skills involved in process control. At the same time a number of investigations were made of the ergonomics of man–machine interfaces in control rooms. These included the work of Sell, Crossman and Box (1962) on a hot strip mill; of Sinclair, Sell, Beishon and Bainbridge (1966) on an LD waste heat boiler; and of Sell and Pulsford (1967) on the National Grid. None of these papers is given, but this type of investigation is represented by the Central Electricity Generating Board (C.E.G.B.) study described below.

A large-scale investigation conducted by industry itself on the mental load involved in some 50 process control tasks is described in the paper by Kitchin and Graham (Paper 7). A single index is defined which is based on the decision-taking load and which comprehends factors such as information acquisition and control actions and takes account of frequency of occurrence.

The foregoing papers represent some of the principal investigations of the process operator in the first decade, ending in, say, 1968. Sometime about this point appears to represent a watershed. The original investigators are no longer so active, but a number of others make their appearance. The diffusion of ergonomics knowledge into industry begins to result in studies which are more oriented towards system design. The advent of the process computer constitutes a fundamental change in the control system available to the operator. And control engineers, having spent the decade digesting computer control, are now ready, and indeed feel the need, to look afresh at the problems of the process operator.

Investigations of process control skill continue. Further studies of manual tracking are described in the papers by Attwood (Paper 8) and by Kragt and Landeweerd (Paper 9). Attwood gives an account of 'water bath' laboratory experiments on tracking, including some which involve the use of a control computer interface. Again the context is that of papermill control. Kragt and Landeweerd describe both laboratory experiments on tracking and on mental models and field experiments on a chemical plant on mental models.

Detailed analyses of the verbal protocols obtained in the electric arc furnace simulation have been made by Bainbridge. The paper given (Paper 10) is representative of her recent work in this area. It suggests that the protocol technique may have an important rôle in the methodology of operator studies.

The paper by Daniel, Puffler and Stríženec (Paper 11) gives profiles of four process control tasks obtained from field studies. It is therefore to some extent complementary to that of Kitchin and Graham.

A review of work on decision-making, particularly in scheduling tasks, is given in the paper by Stríženec (Paper 12). The investigations of control tasks considered include those in process control, such as the work of Cristian and Zbăganu (1964) on electrical power dispatchers, and those in other areas, such as the study of Leplat and Bisseret (1965) on air traffic controllers.

There is a large literature on the modelling of the human operator in control tasks, particularly tracking, e.g. North (1952), Sheridan (1960), Bekey (1962b). However, there has been little application of this work to process control; the paper by Crossman and Cooke perhaps comes nearest to this. Nevertheless, it did seem desirable to include a paper illustrative of techniques of modelling the operator. This aspect is therefore represented by the paper by Towill (Paper 13), which describes the modelling of a rather different feature of operator performance, namely learning.

The 1960's were the decade of the computer in process control. By the end of this period the technology was relatively mature. Although the majority of new control systems still do not include a computer, the proportion which do is growing rapidly, particularly on large plants. A study of the impact of computers, with special reference to the effects on employment, has been conducted by the U.S. Department of Labor and is published under the title *Outlook for Computer Process Control*. An extract from this booklet (Paper 14), consisting of those sections which are primarily devoted to the process operator, is reproduced.

Several workers have discussed the task of the process operator and the allocation of function between man and machine in plants with computer control, *e.g.* J. J. de Jong (1964, 1965), Rasmussen (1968c), Lees (1970). This is also the central theme of the full-length study by Edwards and Lees (1973).

The paper by de Jong and Köster (Paper 15) describes the conclusions drawn from field studies of process operators in a computer-controlled refinery. As the degree of automation increases the rôle of the operator is increasingly to give the system a self-repairing capability. Thus the monitoring function of the operator and the alarm systems with which he is provided are of growing importance. The authors emphasize the motivation of the operator and its relevance to allocation of function. The sampling of information from chart recorders is discussed in detail. This latter work is complementary to that of Crossman, Cooke and Beishon.

An experimental study of the process operator in a computer-controlled laboratory pilot plant is described in the paper by West and Clark (Paper 16). Some of the problems considered in this study are the learning process of the operator and his development of strategies; his handling of fault conditions; and the relative merits for these purposes of conventional control panel and computer console displays.

As the operation of the process under normal conditions becomes more automated, attention is increasingly focused on the administration of fault conditions. The paper by Rasmussen (Paper 17) discusses the basic philosophy which should underly computer-based facilities such as alarm analysis and fault correction and highlights some of the pitfalls in these areas. The paper by Anyakora and Lees (Paper 18) gives a detailed account, based on field studies of operator reporting of instrument failures, of the types of check which the process operator makes to determine whether an instrument has failed.

Most of the remaining papers are rather more oriented towards system design: allocation of function, interface design, task analysis, job design, training, system assessment. Thus the central theme of the paper by Crawley (Paper 19) on the design of an LD converter control system is the allocation of function between man and computer.

The design of a control interface is described in the paper by Ketteringham and O'Brien (Paper 20). This gives an account of a simulation study of an interactive, game-playing facility, based on a touchwire interface, for the scheduling of steel mill soaking pits.

Rational design of a control interface or of a training scheme requires careful definition of the operator's task. This is the function of task analysis. There have been a number of studies of task analysis in process control, *e.g.* Annett, Duncan, Stammers and Gray (1971), Duncan (1972). A representative and thorough treatment of this work is given in the paper on analytical techniques in training design by Duncan (Paper 21), in which an investigation of the task of the operator on an acid purification plant is described.

Job design for the operator requires the integration of individual tasks into a complete job, with attention paid to aspects such as operator loading and job satisfaction. The paper by Munro, Martin and Roberts (Paper 22) illustrates the use of Monte Carlo simulation to determine operator loading and plant availability for a refinery tank farm.

Training of the process operator has two aspects: general education in process technology and training for a specific process control job. Formal education for process operators is available in the U.K. in the form of the Chemical Technician's course of the City and Guilds Institute. This course is quite comprehensive and quite widely used. An extract from the syllabus (Paper 23) is given, consisting primarily of those sections which are relevant for the process operator.

Training the operator for a specific task is the subject of the paper by Duncan (Paper 21) already mentioned, which gives a fundamental discussion of the philosophy of training for tasks such as process control. The approach suggested is based on detailed task analysis. Numerous problems which arise in training are considered, such as the utilization of algorithmic aids, the use of simulators, and the order of presentation of material.

When a control system is operational it may be evaluated. Mention was made above of a number of studies of control rooms. This type of investigation is represented by the paper by the C.E.G.B. (Paper 24) on the control system at a nuclear power station.

Finally, it is necessary to take account of the organizational and social environment in which the process operator does his job. This is the subject of the paper by Engelstad (Paper 25), which describes an investigation in a papermill of the effect on the process system of the initial organizational situation and of changes made to this.

It will be apparent from the foregoing that since about 1960 there has been a considerable amount of work on the process operator. The original initiative came from the effort of ergonomists to apply human factors principles to this task, but there is now an increasing interest from engineers. The latter are no longer quite so preoccupied with the sheer mechanics of computer control and have become rather more aware of the problems of the process operator, which emerge more clearly as the degree of automation increases.

There is clearly a need, therefore, for a critical review of the work done so far on the process operator and of the directions in which future research might go. This has been attempted by one of the editors *faute de mieux* in the last paper (Paper 26).

It will be obvious that the present volume does not provide any kind of general introduction to human factors. This is available in a number of standard texts, *e.g.* Fogel (1963), McCormick (1964), Chapanis (1965), Murrell (1965), Kelley (1968), De Greene (1970a). Short accounts of human factors relevant to process control are given by Edwards (1973) and Edwards and Lees (1973). The latter also give an extensive bibliography of some 3300 references classified under 170 heads.

Several of the papers are contributions invited specifically for this volume based in part on work already published by the authors. The contributions concerned and the corresponding published work are as follows:

Kragt and Landeweerd (Paper 9)	Kragt (1971); Landeweerd (1968)
Bainbridge (Paper 10)	Bainbridge (1969)
Towill (Paper 13)	Towill (1973b)
West and Clark (Paper 16)	Clark (1972)
Ketteringham and O'Brien (Paper 20)	Ketteringham, O'Brien and Cole (1970)
Duncan (Paper 21)	Duncan (1974a)

The affiliations and footnotes in the papers are those given in the original. Thus these affiliations often no longer apply, particularly in the case of less recent papers.

We would like to thank for their encouragement in this project Professor D. C. Freshwater and Professor B. Shackel and our publishers, particularly Mr. S. A. Lewis. We are grateful to the authors of the papers for allowing their work to be reproduced and, in several cases, for writing a paper specifically for this collection. Our thanks are also due to those who have assisted us in the work of publication, and especially to Mr. J. Messenger who re-drew all the figures.

ELWYN EDWARDS
FRANK P. LEES

Loughborough.
January, 1974.

Acknowledgments and Sources

For permission to reproduce the papers in this collection the editors would like to acknowledge the respective authors and in addition the following:

Paper	Publication details	Additional acknowledgments
1	E. R. F. W. Crossman (1960) (London: H.M. Stationery Office)	The Controller, H.M. Stationery Office, London
2	E. R. F. W. Crossman, J. E. Cooke and R. J. Beishon (1964) *Univ. of California, Berkeley, Calif., Human Factors in Technology Res. Gp. Rep.* HFT–64–11–7	—
3	E. R. F. W. Crossman and J. E. Cooke (1962) *Int. Cong. on Human Factors in Electronics, Long Beach, Calif.*	—
4	J. Spencer (1961) *Occup. Psychol.*, **36 (1–2)**, 30	National Institute of Industrial Psychology, London
5	R. J. Beishon (1969) In *The Simulation of Human Behaviour* (Edited by F. Bresson and M. de Montmollin) (Paris: Dunod)	Dunod, Paris
6	L. Bainbridge, J. Beishon, J. H. Hemming and M. Splaine (1968) *Opl. Res. Quart.*, **19,** *Special Issue*, p. 91	Operational Research Society, London

Paper	Publication details	Additional acknowledgments
7	J. B. Kitchin and A. Graham (1961) *Ergonomics*, **4**, 1	Ergonomics Research Society, London Imperial Chemical Industries Ltd., London
8	D. Attwood (1970) In *Paper-Making Systems and their Control* (Edited by F. Bolam) (London: Br. Paper and Board Makers Ass.), p. 69.	British Paper and Board Makers Association, London
9	H. Kragt and J. A. Landeweerd (1974) *This volume*	—
10	L. Bainbridge (1974) *This volume*	—
11	J. Daniel, F. Puffler and M. Stríženec (1971) *Studia Psychologica*, **13**, 326	The Editor, Studia Psychologica
12	M. Stríženec (1967) *Studia Psychologica*, **9**, 3	The Editor, Studia Psychologica
13	D. R. Towill (1974) *This volume*	—
14	Department of Labor (1970) *Outlook for Computer Process Control* (Washington, D.C.: U.S. Govt. Printing Office)	Department of Labor, Washington
15	J. J. de Jong and E. P. Köster (1971) *World Petroleum Cong., Moscow*	World Petroleum Congresses, London
16	B. West and J. A. Clark (1974) *This volume*	—
17	J. Rasmussen (1968) *Atomic Energy Commission Res. Est., Risö, Denmark, Rep.* Risö–M–686	—

Paper	Publication details	Additional acknowledgments
18	S. N. Anyakora and F. P. Lees (1972) *Chem. Engr., Lond.*, **264,** 304	—
19	J. E. Crawley (1968) *Proc. B.I.S.R.A. Symp. on Steelmaking*	B.I.S.R.A.—The Corporate Laboratories, British Steel Corporation, London
20	P. J. A. Ketteringham and D. D. O'Brien (1974) *This volume*	B.I.S.R.A.—The Corporate Laboratories, British Steel Corporation, London
21	K. D. Duncan (1974) *This volume*	Taylor and Francis, London B.P. Chemicals Ltd., London (Figures 5 and 11)
22	H. P. Munro, F. W. Martin and M. C. Roberts (1968) *Chem. Engr., Lond.*, **222,** 355	—
23	City and Guilds Institute (1972) *086 Chemical Technicians Certificate* (London)	City and Guilds Institute, London
24	Central Electricity Generating Board (1966) *Report*	Central Electricity Generating Board, Cheltenham
25	P. H. Engelstad (1970) In *Paper-Making Systems and their Control* (Edited by F. Bolam) (London: Br. Paper and Board Makers Ass.), p. 91	British Paper and Board Makers Association, London

Foreword

Between now and the beginning of the twenty-first century, the rapid advance of technological change will create a phenomenal disturbance in the lives of millions of people.

During the next quarter of a century, the working populations of certainly the industrialized nations of the world will find themselves up against the most painful speed of change that has ever occurred in the history of civilization. Many people refer to these years as the second industrial revolution, but Sir George Thompson, the British physicist and Nobel Prize Winner, suggests that the nearest historical parallel with today is not the industrial revolution, but rather " the invention of agriculture in the neolithic age ".

Mr. John Diebold, the American automation expert, warns that " the effects of the technological revolution we are now living through will be deeper than any social change we have experienced before ", and Sir Leon Bagrit, so well known in this country for his work in relation to computers, has said that automation by itself will represent " the greatest change in the whole history of mankind ".

All those who have been in industries and services already affected by the use of the computer understand full well what changes have already been made and the prospects of change in the years to come. The need today is for a very much wider understanding by the public of these changes and of the requirements that technological changes will further impose upon people.

One of the greatest events that has happened in the world has passed by almost unnoticed. It is that for the first time in history in the United States of America more people who are gainfully employed, are employed in servicing wealth, rather than producing it. In Great Britain the numbers creating wealth are being reduced year by year and in due course we, too, will find a larger proportion of the population engaged in servicing, rather than creating, wealth. This means that, in the area of manufacture and production, enormous changes have already taken place in method and in technology, and with these have arisen tremendous problems in relation to those who are responsible for operating the most sophisticated plants that the world has ever known.

These great changes, both in industry and in office, are not only affecting productivity, but are affecting methods of organization and this, in turn, is making changed demands on individual men and women. The use of transfer machines and automatic handling with automatic process control in factories and workshops and of electronic computers in offices requires new skills on the part of those who are responsible for operating automatic plants and computers. Change will continue as the technology changes, and this means a continuous training process; certainly not a single training for the rest of an operator's life, but training which is continuous in order to keep pace with the new technology as it develops.

Whilst all around physical labour is being and will be substantially reduced, and in some cases totally eliminated, the mental skills will require to be increasingly dominant. Information processing and decision-making become of growing importance.

There was a time in the 1950's and the 1960's when automation was something of a dream, based upon some modest experiments, and people talked about plants which would be fully automated and where labour would not be required at all. This, of course, has been shown to be a myth and it will be many, many years before the completely automated factory is operating. Meanwhile, the development of automation goes on and this means that for many years yet there will have to be increasing reliance upon the human operator and the attitudes to his task. It is the human operator who will be responsible for discovering the malfunctions of the system he operates, and indeed for proposing to the backroom boys changes in design, based upon his day-to-day experience. Fast development of automation will depend more and more upon the training and the use of the skills of the human operator in process control. That is why this book is a 'must' to all those who have responsibility for higher management, because it has brought together between two covers a whole wealth of knowledge and information based on case studies, without which the future development of adequate training of the process operator is not possible.

The speed of change today is somewhat unreal. New knowledge is gained every day and the baby born today will, during its life-time, be surrounded by new knowledge far greater than the whole of the world's knowledge during civilization to date. It is speed of change which causes great problems for people, because they are not trained mentally to accept it, or attuned to deal with it.

These studies into human behaviour, therefore, point the way we must go in providing the right education and training to enable mankind to face the future of the speeding rate of change without fear, and indeed maximize the advantage of technological change to the human race.

ROBENS OF WOLDINGHAM

May, 1974.

Contents

Paper	Page	
	vii	Preface
	xv	Acknowledgments and Sources
	xix	Foreword Lord Robens
1	1	Automation and skill (extract) E. R. F. W. Crossman
2	25	Visual attention and the sampling of displayed information in process control E. R. F. W. Crossman, J. E. Cooke and R. J. Beishon
3	51	Manual control of slow-response systems E. R. F. W. Crossman and J. E. Cooke
4	67	An investigation of process control skill J. Spencer
5	79	An analysis and simulation of an operator's behaviour in controlling continuous baking ovens R. J. Beishon
6	91	A study of real-time decision-making using a plant simulator L. Bainbridge, J. Beishon, J. H. Hemming and M. Splaine
7	105	Mental loading of process operators: an attempt to devise a method of analysis and assessment J. B. Kitchin and A. Graham
8	120	The interaction between human and automatic control D. Attwood
9	135	Mental skills in process control H. Kragt and J. A. Landeweerd
10	146	Analysis of verbal protocols from a process control task L. Bainbridge
11	159	Analysis of operator's work at various levels of automated production J. Daniel, F. Puffler and M. Stříženec
12	165	On research into operator's thinking and decision-making M. Stříženec

Paper	Page	
13	178	A model for describing process operator performance D. R. Towill
14	186	Outlook for computer process control (extract) Department of Labor
15	196	The human operator in the computer-controlled refinery J. J. de Jong and E. P. Köster
16	206	Operator interaction with a computer-controlled distillation column B. West and J. A. Clark
17	222	On the communication between operators and instrumentation in automatic process plants J. Rasmussen
18	238	Detection of instrument malfunction by the process operator S. N. Anyakora and F. P. Lees
19	249	The present and future contribution of the human operator to the control of LD steelmaking J. E. Crawley
20	260	A simulation study of computer-aided soaking pit scheduling P. J. A. Ketteringham and D. D. O'Brien (with an Appendix by P. G. Cole)
21	283	Analytical techniques in training design K. D. Duncan
22	320	How to use simulation techniques to determine optimum manning levels for continuous process plants H. P. Munro, F. W. Martin and M. C. Roberts
23	327	Chemical Technician's Certificate of the City and Guilds Institute: Syllabus (extract) City and Guilds Institute
24	348	Study of operators information requirements at Trawsfynydd (extract) Operational Research Section and Nuclear Plant Design Branch, Central Electricity Generating Board
25	367	Socio-technical approach to problems of process control P. H. Engelstad
26	386	Research on the process operator F. P. Lees
	426	References
	447	Author Index
	455	Subject Index

Automation and Skill

By E. R. F. W. CROSSMAN

[*The following is an extract. The original numbering of chapters, figures and tables is retained. Some photographs of processes given in the original are omitted.*]

Introduction

The spread of automatic methods in industry and offices greatly affects not only productivity and methods of organization, but also the demands made by work on individual men and women.

A brief outline of changes in operative skills was given in the D.S.I.R. report on Automation (D.S.I.R. 1956), where a common trend was noted " towards supervision rather than direct manipulation of the process, and towards skill based on knowledge of plant and equipment ". The emphasis was shifting from manual skills to those based on " the ability to take in information and to organize and interpret it for action ".

Little was known then about the precise nature of these new skills, how far they would be of general or specific application in industry, and what effect they would have on selection and training. To find answers to these problems, D.S.I.R. sponsored a study, and this booklet is a summary of some of its results.

Industrial Survey

The study was based on visits to factories and plants representing different types of technical advance. They included factories manufacturing motor-cars, valves, cigarettes, textiles, instruments, electrical equipment for motor-cars, heavy electrical equipment, paint, biscuits, margarine, a heavy chemical plant, an oil refinery, a board mill, a steel works, a liquid oxygen plant, a brewery, electricity generating stations, an electricity distribution centre, a railway electrical control room, and an electronic computer in business use. The visits were mostly short, but on a few of them it was possible to spend some hours recording operators' activities and discussing their work with them. Shift or departmental managers provided most of the information about plant operation and its demands on the operator.

The work and skills were studied from the standpoint of an experimental psychologist, rather than that of an industrial manager: interest was directed at the present abilities and performance of operators, and how they achieve their results, rather than at their formal training and experience. Psychologists use the term ' skill ' for any particular ability, from dexterities and knacks to complex decision-making; whereas when industrialists talk of a ' skilled man ', they usually mean one who has undergone a certain training or apprenticeship which is needed for the job in question. The industrial reader should bear this important distinction in mind.

1. Three Types of Automation

The starting point for the survey was the threefold classification of automatic techniques adopted in the D.S.I.R. report—transfer machines and automatic handling; automatic process control; and electronic computers in offices. While this breakdown is useful in relation to technology, it proves inadequate from the standpoint of the demands on the operator; the following breakdown is more helpful:

(1) *Continuous-flow production.* Transfer machines and automatically-controlled processes have been grouped together. Though technologically very different, they both represent a similar advanced level of industrial development. The skills needed by the operators in these very different industries are surprisingly alike, though several sub-patterns (which will be discussed later) can be identified within the broad picture.

(2) *Program machines.* Computers in offices stand alone, not so much because they are fast and automatic, and produce information rather than goods, as because they are very flexible. They can be made to do quite different classes of work in quick succession by inserting different ' programs '. Electronically-controlled machine tools also have this flexibility. They seem likely to make broadly similar demands on operators, though at present these are difficult to assess because there are still very few of these machines in everyday use.

(3) *Centralized remote control.* Centralized remote control is typified by the modern railway control centre. Such centres are of growing importance in public services such as transport and communication, and may well become important in manufacturing. Their common characteristic is that the operations being controlled are inaccessible to the operator and so must be handled in an artificial setting.

Remote control is also found on continuous-flow production, for instance, in process control rooms and continuous strip mills, but, as the operator can view these operations directly, the demands are less severe.

In the following chapters an attempt is made to outline the essential features of work and skill under these headings; to provide a framework of thought for those whose job it is to select, train and employ workers in automatic industry; and to forecast some of the future developments to be expected. While the emphasis is on individual skills, brief mention is made of responsibility and of the working environment.

2. Continuous-Flow Production

It has been pointed out (Woodward 1958) that manufacturing methods in an industry usually pass through three stages of technical advance: first, small-batch and ' unit ' (*i.e.* one-off) production, where craftsmen predominate; second, large-batch and ' mass ' production, with many semi-skilled workers; and, third, continuous-flow or ' process ' production. Different industries reach the stages earlier or later according to the severity of their technical problems.

Flow production was first achieved some time ago in the so-called ' process ' industries, such as chemicals and oil, where the raw materials are particularly suitable for continuous handling and processing. More recently the difficult technical problems of mechanical handling and automatic processing have been solved for the making of separate articles, for example pistons, cylinder blocks, glass bulbs, cigarettes, cardboard boxes and so on. As a result it has become possible to manufacture them automatically, *i.e.* without needing an operator to start each cycle of the production process. This is automatic *operation* and should not be confused with automatic *control*, which is a later development.

The change to automatic operation brings a considerable change in the demands on the operator from those made by the repetitive work characteristic of ' mass ' production. But the jobs, though new in their context, closely resemble process work as performed in a conventional chemical factory, for the operator has to monitor and adjust a continuously-running process, making no direct contribution to its sequence of operations and speed of action.

Although production can continue without him for a time, the operator's presence is still essential. His job is to maintain quality and avoid breakdowns, a function which was carried out piecemeal when the various operations were done on separate machines, but which in the new plant is handled by one man, whose actions affect the quality of a much larger output. In short, he is a ' controller ', rather than a ' producer '.

All observers agree that manual skills needing co-ordination of hand and eye (often called ' sensorimotor ' skills) are much less important under automation, and the findings of the survey endorse this view. Some observers say that they are replaced by conceptual skills, meaning that operators who monitor larger and more complex machines have more difficult observation and thinking to do in proportion to their physical effort. But others claim that the new processes require virtually no skill, and that the operator is simply a ' machine-minder ', kept on the plant to record instrument readings and call for help in emergency. Both types of situation were seen during the survey, for the variety of monitoring, machine-minding, and process-operating jobs in automatic industry is almost as great as the variety of manual operations in conventional factories.

Table 1 shows the main distinguishing characteristics of the various continuous-flow processes seen during the survey.

While, in principle, the characteristics shown in the table can be combined in many ways, most of the plants seen during the survey fall into only four groups:
   (1) Large manually-controlled plants* making a continuous product by a predominantly chemical or physical process. There are several operators, each in charge of a fairly small part of the plant, and success depends not only on the ability of each operator but also on the co-ordination of the team as a whole. Individuals have a good deal of detailed control work to do, but few complex decisions to make.
   (2) Plants similar to (1) but with automatic *control*. Individuals have much less detailed control work, but usually more complex decisions to make.

---

* These plants are not commonly included under the heading of automation, but the demands for skill made by the other groups can best be understood in relation to them.

Table 1. Classification of automatic plant

Relative size	
Large	Several operators to one plant. (For example: board mill, chemicals, oil, electricity, *etc*.)
Small	One operator to one or more machines. (For example: cigarette-making, weaving, automatic lathes, *etc*.)
Product	
Continuous	Materials *flow* through the plant; it is usually wasteful to stop and restart the process. (For example: board mill, chemicals, oil, electricity, many foodstuffs, paint, glass, *etc*.)
Separate articles	Materials transported mechanically; the process can usually be stopped and restarted easily. (For example: transfer lines for cylinder blocks and pistons, packing machines, printing presses, *etc*.)
Control	
Manual	The operator directly controls the process and is responsible for making all running adjustments. (For example: board mill, older atomic energy plant, weaving, printing, *etc*.)
Automatic	The operator sets desired running conditions and automatic devices ensure that they are maintained. (For example: new chemical and atomic energy plant, oil refineries, newer boilers, *etc*.)
Type of process	
Mechanical	The process consists of mechanical actions such as cutting and shaping; the operator can easily visualize what is happening. (For example: transfer machines, final stage of glass-bulb making, packing, knitting, *etc*.)
Non-mechanical	Chemical, physical or other processes where the operator cannot easily visualize what is happening. (For example: chemical, electricity, plastics, some foodstuffs, *etc*.)

(3) Transfer lines—sequences of mechanical operations such as cutting and forming, performed by self-acting machine tools with a regular cycle of operations, and automatic transfer from one to the next. Operators are there principally to feed in workpieces, maintain control of dimensions, and repair breakdowns.

(4) Relatively small continuously-running machines that can be controlled by one operator. Usually a number are grouped together, and one operator may be given charge of several machines.

The demands of each of the four groups on the operators will now be described in more detail with several examples. The general characteristics of continuous-flow plants will be outlined in relation to the first group, and the special characteristics of the other three will then be taken in turn.

Large Plant under Manual Control

The first group comprises the large process plants, automatic in operation but not automatically controlled, where the work is typical ' process work '. The first example comes from a long-established process industry which would not ordinarily be regarded as having ' automation ', and where recent technical change does not distort the picture. It does, however, represent a very high level of technical development in large-scale production.

Case 1. The column-operator in a liquid oxygen plant

To make liquid oxygen, air is drawn from the atmosphere, compressed and liquefied by an expansion engine. The oxygen and nitrogen are then separated in a distillation column at temperatures around $-180°C$. The nitrogen returns to the atmosphere and the oxygen runs into an insulated storage tank. Rare gases—argon, neon and krypton—can also be obtained from the distillation column if required.

A plant producing liquid oxygen equivalent to some 15 000 cubic feet of gas an hour is controlled by two men, the compressor- and the column-operators, and it is run continuously on a four-shift system. The column-operator's job is to control the column to give liquid oxygen at least 99·5% pure, with the minimum waste of oxygen gas to the atmosphere; he may sometimes be asked to produce rare gases. He must be able to start up the plant, and shut it down in emergency or for maintenance, without causing permanent damage or undue waste of material or power.

The column-operator cannot see the process he is controlling, and relies on some 20 pressure, temperature and flow gauges for a knowledge of its behaviour. He can also draw off a sample of the product and analyze it for purity, which he usually does every hour. He has some ten valves for controlling flow, pressure, and temperature at different points. During normal running he logs instrument readings every hour. He also has some routine maintenance to perform.

In the factory visited there were several plants of different size and age; the operators knew them all, were able to switch from one to another, and quite often did so. A shift foreman had charge of four pairs of operators and there was a works foreman on the day shift. There were also several maintenance craftsmen and some labourers on each shift.

The work of the process operator

The process operator's duties on a typical continuous-flow plant fall into four categories, as illustrated by this example:

(i) *Control*. He must monitor the various gauges, attend to the signs coming from the plant itself, such as noises, smells and vibration, and occasionally carry out special tests on the product. According to his interpretation of these indications, he must adjust the controls when necessary so as to keep the product within specification, and correct any chance disturbance or drift. Apart from the 'official' controls, there are often special ways of influencing the process, such as propping doors open to give greater cooling, or tapping pipes to loosen deposits.

Most processes require several more or less independent variables to be controlled at once, so the operator usually has to divide his attention between several activities, and he generally carries out a regular patrol of the various indicators, making adjustments where necessary.

The components of the control task may vary widely in difficulty. At one end of the scale is the simple task of keeping a single variable at a desired value by means of a direct control, *e.g.* maintaining a flow by opening or closing a valve. At the other end, an operator may have to maintain a combination of qualities in the product by a complex balance of conflicting requirements, as in the board-making plant described on page 9. The amount of work presented by a given control task varies widely, depending mainly on the degree of spontaneous variation in the running of the plant, together with the fineness of the control required.

In many plants, the product is changed from time to time without stopping the process, and then the operator must quickly readjust the process to the new specification so as to waste as little raw material as possible in a substandard product.

Control duty also requires the operator to be on the lookout for early signs of trouble to come, so that he can take preventive action. An acute operator may save large amounts of material and money by this means alone.

(ii) *Special procedures and drills.* There are usually set sequences of manipulation to be carried out when starting up or shutting down the plant or in particular emergencies. They are often rapid and complicated manual operations, interspersed with some control activity.

(iii) *Routine maintenance.* This may include oiling pumps, keeping the machine stocked with secondary materials, and cleaning inside vessels when they become clogged.

(iv) *Recording and reporting.* The readings of important indicators and gauges, control settings, and the results of special measurements are logged at regular intervals, and any disturbances or changed conditions are noted when they occur.

Apart from keeping written records, operators must also pass on information to their colleagues and to management by word of mouth. This is important in order to co-ordinate the operation of the various sections of a large plant.

COMPARISON WITH WORK IN BATCH OR MASS PRODUCTION FACTORIES

Production workers in non-automatic factories usually work to a set cycle, with occasional ancillary jobs. They carry out definite operations on recognizable workpieces, and the results of their actions are immediately apparent. Speed is of primary importance since it directly governs output.

By contrast, in automatic factories:

(i) There is no definite work cycle, usually little need for physical exertion and no emphasis on speed. The operator acts as and when he judges it to be necessary. In many cases he is free to move about the plant much of the time, but he can never leave it unattended for long at a time; he needs a relief for meals, and in case of sickness.

(ii) On the other hand, there are occasional periods of intense effort, for instance on startup, or shutdown, or when breakdowns have to be repaired.

(iii) Each supervisor has charge of fewer operators, yet there is often less direct supervision because of the greater distances between workplaces.

(iv) The operator has more contact with technical staff and managers. He is more often asked for information about his plant, and is treated more as a member of a team than his counterpart in non-automatic workshops.

(v) Shift work (either three shifts on plant running five days a week, or four shifts continuous) is very much more common because of the high capital cost of plant and/or of waste of materials involved in shutting it down. This means more responsibility for the operator on evening and night shifts when there are fewer engineering staff on call.

(vi) Financial incentive schemes based on work measurement ('piecework') are rarely applied in continuous-flow plants, whereas they are common elsewhere in industry.

(vii) Employment tends to be more stable, because production is planned for years ahead. Hence there is a greater sense of security.

(viii) Women are rarely employed in automatic plant. This is mainly because of shift working but also partly because control work seems to be more suited to men.

Despite these differences operators of automatic plant usually have a background similar to that of semi-skilled men employed on mass production. They are recruited from the general pool of unskilled labour and have no more than a minimum of formal education. On the whole they are paid about the same, though there is little opportunity on continuous flow plant for the occasional very high earnings made on piecework.

Process operator skills

The skills exercised by a process operator are not obvious. It is impossible to gain an impression of them from a few minutes' observation, as one can with a semi-skilled worker. One can see very little going on in some plants; the operator watches his gauges or inspects the plant, makes an adjustment from time to time, and occasionally talks to a colleague or a manager. There is no means of assessing his skill from these activities alone.

To gain a proper perspective, one must first ask the question, what is the operator trying to achieve—or, perhaps better, what does management want him to achieve? There are five possible answers to the second question, according to the type of plant or process:

(i) Keep the process running as nearly as possible at a given condition. (*Regulation or Stabilization*.)

(ii) Adjust the process to give the best results according to certain criteria, *e.g.* yield, quality, minimum use of power, least lost time. (*Optimization*.)

(iii) Make changes from one product to another quickly and economically. (*Changeover*.)

(iv) Avoid breakdowns as far as possible.

(v) If a breakdown should occur, regain normal running as soon as possible, and minimize loss of material or risk of serious damage.

It may be possible to assess an operator's skill in these respects from plant records, but many other factors besides his performance affect the operating results in most practical cases, and a complicated statistical analysis is needed to single out the operator's effect on them, be it favourable or non-favourable.

However, it seems clear from subjective assessments, that individual operators do differ widely both in their speed of learning new control jobs and in their final level of ability. An individual who is good on one criterion tends to be good on all, so there does seem to be a common factor or *control* skill underlying all of them (except possibly speed of repairing breakdowns). Without resorting to statistics, an individual's control skill on a given process can perhaps best be assessed by observing the speed and smoothness (or otherwise) of changeover from one running condition to another. Operators seem usually to acquire control skill on one plant or process only and cannot transfer to another without re-learning; the skill is *specific* to the situation in which it was acquired.

Analytic study suggests that a specific control skill comprises five components:

(i) *Sensing*—the ability to detect the signs and indications such as noises, smells and appearance, which indicate how the plant is running.

(ii) *Perceiving*—the ability to interpret these signs and the instrument readings in relation to one another, and to infer what is happening.

(iii) *Prediction*—of what is likely to happen in a given situation if the controls are left alone.

(iv) *Familiarity with the controls*—knowing what means can be used to influence the process, what their effects are, and how they interact with others.

(v) *Decision*—the ability to select the control action most likely to achieve the desired result in the given circumstances or to avert unfavourable developments when they threaten.

This last item, decision-making, is the central feature of the skill. It can be carried out in several ways:

(i) The operator may follow a 'rule-of-thumb'—doing what has always been done in a given situation, or what worked last time; but this allows little flexibility.

(ii) He may use a 'mental model' or idea of the process, on which he can try out the different possible control actions in his imagination and pick the best bet. A good operator seems to 'feel' his way into the process, becoming *intuitively* aware of what is going on and what to do about it.

(iii) The operator may use a logical approach and consciously reason out the meaning of things, analyze the situation, and come to a *rational* decision.

On the whole, discussions with operators have suggested that the first, or 'rule-of-thumb', method is common among the less good operators, and the second, or 'intuitive', method is often characteristic of the better ones. But few operators seem to use a fully rational or conceptual approach. So it is a little misleading, as has been suggested (D.S.I.R. 1956), to regard control skills as 'conceptual', if conceptual is taken to imply conscious reference to general principles; they are perhaps better described as '*intuitive*'. But further study may modify this conclusion.

A plant operator needs to know a good deal about the plant and its nomenclature, the raw materials and products, the rules for its operation, and so on. These can be taught 'off the job', whereas the control skill itself cannot. While an operator can soon learn to control a plant by following rules, the intuitive understanding which enables him to deal with subtle changes and unusual situations seems to come with experience alone.

DIFFICULTY OF CONTROL JOBS

It is particularly difficult to control processes

(i) where several display and control variables depend on one another;

(ii) where the process has a long 'time constant'—that is, takes a relatively long time (minutes, hours or even days) to settle down after a disturbance or alteration of control settings;

(iii) where important variables have to be estimated by the operator rather than measured by an instrument;
(iv) where the readings of instruments at widely separated points have to be collated; and the operator has to remember one while going to another ('short-term memory');
(v) where the operator gets imperfect knowledge of the results of his performance, or where the knowledge arrives late (this is a very common condition);
(vi) where the basic process is either difficult to visualize, for example chemical reactions, or contradicts 'commonsense' assumptions, or is too complicated to be held in mind at one time.

Status of process operators

Many process plant operators appear to exercise more influence in the factory than their formal training would warrant. This seems to be because they form an essential part of a fairly small operating team. The management relies on them for information about the plant, and they have to co-operate closely with maintenance and laboratory staff, as well as their superiors, on topics related to the process. (Figure 1 shows this diagrammatically.)

Perhaps because of this, they have a more responsible attitude to the job than is usually found among semi-skilled workers. They seem to recognize that 'the plant must be kept running at all costs'. A sense of responsibility is also fostered by the greater stability of employment in highly mechanized industry.

Case 2. The machine-man in a board mill

Another example of a large plant under manual control is a board mill, where very little automatic control has been introduced. This serves to illustrate a somewhat different kind of control work—where a large plant has many variables, but the process is largely visible and obeys commonsense mechanical principles. The major difficulty arises from the lack of a direct measure for important process variables, and from the delay of several minutes in getting information on the results of control actions.

Cardboard is formed from a suspension of wood fibres in water by several 'moulds'. Each mould is a rotating drum made of stainless steel mesh, and it deposits a thin layer of fibre on an endless band of felt. The wet board is removed from the felt as a continuous sheet, pressed, dried by passing through heated rolls, and reeled. A typical board mill runs at 150–400 feet a minute, producing three to eight tons of board an hour. The whole process is supervised by a foreman and about 22 men on each shift, roughly half of them being employed in the 'beaterhouse' preparing the stock from waste paper and wood pulp, and the other half on the 'making' machine and its auxiliaries. When running normally the machine itself is controlled by a 'machine-man' and his assistant, the 'felt-boy', who control the 'wet end' where the board is formed, and a 'dryer-man' on the 'dry end'.

The machine-man's job is to keep the 'making' process going, which requires that the board should adhere to the felt, and should not break under the traction between the rollers of the successive presses. The board leaving the machine must meet a given specification of weight, thickness, moisture,

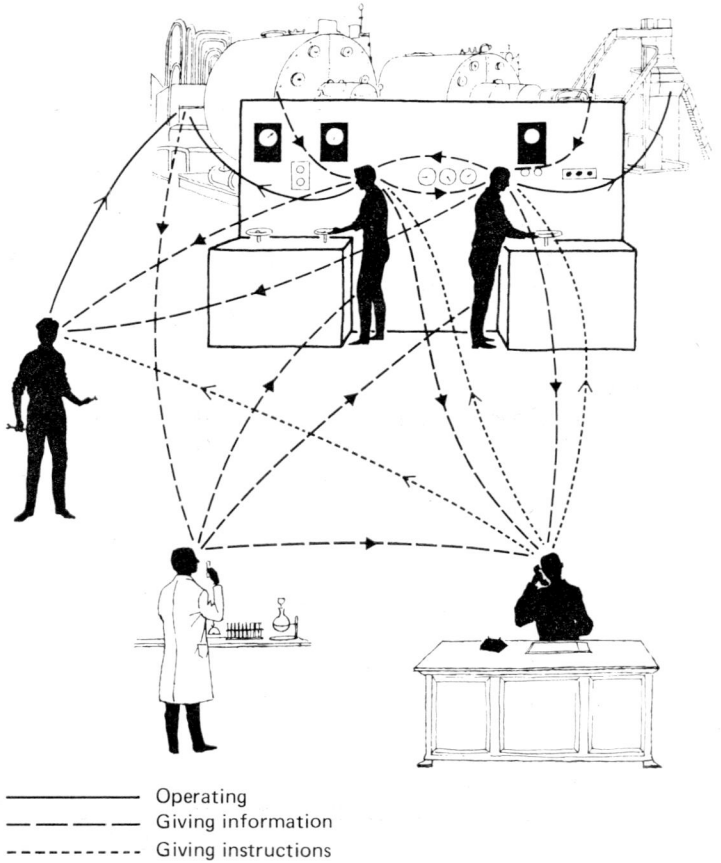

———— Operating
— — — Giving information
- - - - - - Giving instructions

The operators study the plant, and operate its controls. They pass information to the management, to maintenance workers and to one another; they receive reports from the laboratory. The managers collect information from operators and from direct inspection; they issue instructions to operators and to the maintenance staff, who carry out repairs. The laboratory staff collect samples from the process and pass their results to the operators and to management. Thus plant operators are near the centre of the communication system, providing the only direct continuous link between the plant and its various services.

Figure 1. Communication between members of the operating team in a highly mechanized plant.

strength, and appearance, and economical operation of the mill demands that the speed should be as high as is consistent with quality. This means that special care is needed to avoid frequent breakdowns.

The machine-man exercises control by adjusting the stock flow, stock depth and suction on each mould, the machine speed, pressure and 'draw' between rolls and so on (about 100 controls in all). His principal sources of information are the appearance of the liquid in the 'making' vats and the manner in which the board runs between the rollers, though there are altogether some 50 dial indicators and seven graphic recorders on the plant. Measurements of the weight, thickness and moisture of the finished board become available about six to ten minutes after its formation, and they are the final criteria of quality. The difficulty of the machine-man's job depends partly on the quality of the liquid stock arriving at the machine from the beaterhouse.

On completion of an order, the machine is kept running and must be readjusted to specification for the next order as quickly as possible. Speed is essential as the board produced during readjustment has to be scrapped. If a break should occur at any time, the board goes to waste while it has been re-threaded through several hundred feet of drying rolls. The mill runs six days a week, and the Monday morning shift has to start it up from cold.

Large Plant with Automatic Control

The introduction of automatic control over process variables reduces the amount of routine control work to be done by the operator, but considerably complicates the decisions he must take.

In modern process plants overall control is achieved by installing a recorder/controller to stabilize each important variable, such as flow rate and temperature, at different parts of the plant. The controller gets its information from a sensing device which registers it on a graphic recorder and activates a control element (valve, heating element, *etc.*). The operator sets the required value (setpoint) by adjusting a second needle on the graphic recorder, and thereafter, whenever the quantity departs from the set value, the controller operates to bring it back again. The operator sets up a combination of setpoints according to previous instructions or to his own judgment, and he has then only to check the recordings occasionally to ensure that the automatic controls are working correctly.

Case 3. Organic chemical works: solvents unit

The current use of automatic control may be illustrated by reference to a plant producing solvents in an organic chemical factory. Over the last five years this plant has been improved by the progressive introduction of automatic controls for temperature, pressure and level in various plant elements. These controls have now been installed in a central control room where 70–80% of the process operator's work can be performed.

The raw material for the unit is vaporized, superheated and then passed through a catalytic reaction chamber in an oil- or gas-fired furnace, where it is converted into the main product (the solvent), a permanent gas and several other by-products. The gas is separated, scrubbed free of residual organic material and passed into a gas main for subsequent use in other parts of the factory. The solvent, together with the other by-products, is then passed through a series of distillation and washing columns, which separate the various constituents, leaving a pure product, which is finally pumped into bulk storage tanks.

This plant is managed by a team of four process operators on each of three eight-hour shifts. The team comprises a leading hand, who is a working chargehand and supervisor of the complete unit, and three process operators, each of whom is responsible for one section of the plant. The leading hand is the co-ordinator of the system and is informed by the other operators whenever different sections run into difficulties. An important subsidiary activity of the leading hand is to train new operators in plant operation.

One man, termed the furnace-man, looks after the furnaces and is responsible for adjusting their temperatures to an optimum, which varies with the state of the catalyst and with the throughput of raw material. He also takes care of shutdowns, furnace relighting, periodical reactivation of the catalyst, and changes of fuel. The furnace temperature is adjusted by altering the set-point of the appropriate recorder/controller, and by adjusting dampers in the flue gas streams. He is expected to regulate the furnace temperature by hand if the recorder/controller develops a fault. Each furnace has two other recorder/controllers which the furnace-man adjusts as required. One controls the vapour feed to the catalyst chamber, and the other the flow of water to the gas scrubber. There are also about ten indicators for other plant variables on the furnace-man's panel.

Another man, known as the 'still-man', is responsible for the solvent distillation section of the plant. This consists of a number of distillation columns and washing columns, with their heat exchangers and intermediate tankage. The distillation columns are controlled by several recorder/controllers for each column, governing, among other items, the feed to the column, the rate of reflux and the temperatures at various points. The still-man adjusts the setpoints of these instruments to achieve steady operation within specified limits. He is also expected to operate the plant manually if an automatic controller becomes unserviceable. An important part of his job is to patrol the plant and check it for visible faults, such as fluid leaks and blocked steam traps. He also has about 30 instruments indicating various plant conditions on his panel in the control room. There are few manually-operated controls on the plant itself.

Laboratory analyses of plant products are carried out at two-hourly intervals and the results are reported to the process team. More than 20 different variables are measured and the leading hand can ask for a repeat analysis of any item that differs from expectation or that he wants specially checked, perhaps because of an alteration made to the setting of the plant. Every effort is made to see that results of the analyses are not more than an hour old when they are reported to the process team.

Important process variables are recorded by the appropriate hand every hour. The hands keep a diary of abnormal conditions and an 'unserviceability book' in which they note the occurrence of any fault and subsequent action taken.

Work of the process operator

Automatic control is usually introduced to maintain more accurate and stable conditions in a plant, rather than to save labour, though it may occasionally replace a man on a very routine control job. However, automatic control has made it possible to operate some processes which could not be run by unaided human control.

The instruments themselves are usually located in a central control room. The operator has to collate readings on instruments in the control room with conditions in the plant outside. This tends to complicate the work, though the physical conditions are improved. Further he must understand the operation of the sensing devices and control mechanisms as well as the process itself. The adjustments themselves, though they demand less frequent attention, require a higher level of thought since the effects of recorder/controllers, as well as process variables, must be considered when attempting to diagnose a fault or account for a departure from specification. In a sense one may say that his work is carried out at two removes from the actual materials being processed (see Figure 2) rather than at one remove, as in a manually-controlled plant.

In those few cases where the action of the plant has been fully analyzed and planned by engineers, the need for control skill has been virtually abolished; but in many cases this point has not yet been realized and the operator can

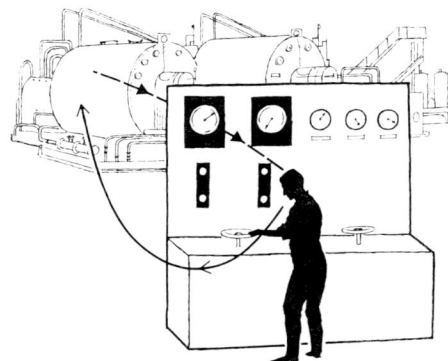

The operator receives information about the process directly and from instruments; he maintains correct adjustment by operating the controls—he ' closes the loop ', adapting his mode of control to the current situation.

In taking control decisions, he must consider the action of instruments and controls together with the plant itself.

(a) Manual control.

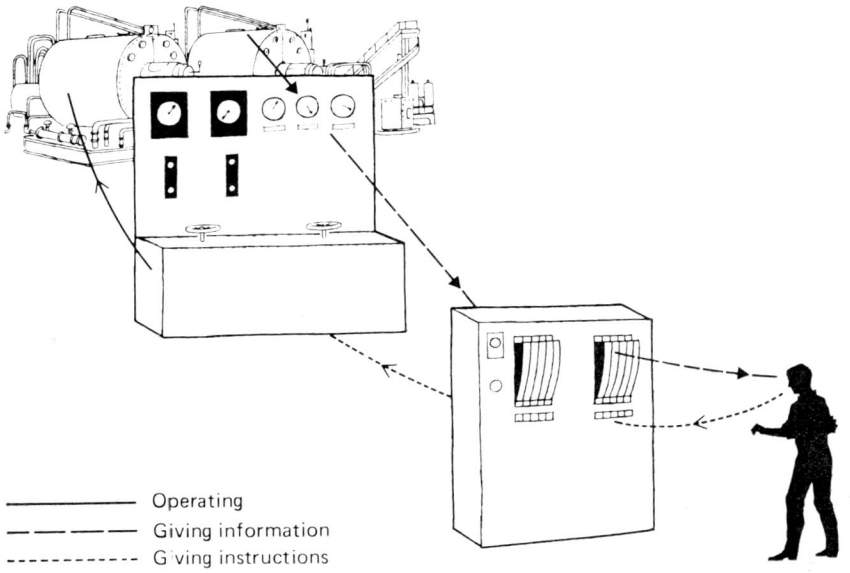

——————— Operating
— — — — — Giving information
------------- Giving instructions

The ' loop ' is now closed by an automatic controller which keeps the process in a set condition. The operator monitors the result produced by the controller, adjusts its setpoint as required, and may ' trim ' the control characteristics for optimum efficiency.

In taking decisions he must consider the sensing devices and controls, the plant itself, and the action of the automatic controller.

(b) Automatic control.

Figure 2. Direct and indirect control in highly mechanized plants.

still make an important contribution to efficiency. Contrary to what is often believed, the level of vigilance required is not unusually high, as safety devices and alarms are always fitted to cater for all potentially dangerous contingencies. Other duties include keeping records, maintenance, and the use of startup, shutdown and emergency procedures.

In the larger automatically-controlled plants in the oil industry, as in this example, each member of a team of several operators, the ' oil-man ', ' cat-man ', *etc.*, is responsible for one section of plant under a ' still-man ', who combines the functions of process operator for the whole unit and chargehand. The operators act as his assistants, checking the instruments and plant to ensure that the settings decided on are maintained, and detecting faults such as steam leaks, mechanical failures and variations in feed stock to either the plant or its furnaces. They do not often have to make adjustments on their own initiative. In case of emergency they work as a team under his leadership.

[*There here follow further sections of Chapter 2 on transfer lines for machining of separate articles, smaller machines operating automatically, and other jobs in flow production, and Chapter 3 on program machines (digital computers).*]

4. Centralized Remote Control

Advances in communication techniques, especially pulse code signalling and the introduction of reliable ' slave ' mechanisms like the dial telephone exchange, mean that the control of widely separated equipment, previously carried out at a number of places, can be now centralized in a ' control room '. The ordinary railway signal box is an early example of this trend.

The most impressive applications of centralized remote control are found in those public services which operate over a wide area, such as electricity supply, railways, air transport, and telephones, but similar systems are also found within factories for directing the flow of materials, the organization of maintenance effort and so on. The work of a control operator in a railway electricity supply system will be described by way of example.

Case 7. Control operator in a railway electrical control room

The 600 volt direct current required for electric trains working on the third-rail system is supplied by converters drawing power from the National Grid at 33 000 volt a.c. Owing to conduction losses, a single converter station can only supply some four miles of track, and so a number of them are needed to supply a complete railway. The older converters were rotary machines. An attendant had to be on the spot to start and stop them; he also operated the switches when necessary, but his time was only partly occupied. The newer mercury arc converters can be left unattended and can be controlled by remotely-operated switchgear. Some 20–30 of the new converters, with 100–150 associated switches, are now under the control of a single controller and his assistant located in a control room at the centre of a railway district.

The remote switches and indicators, which are connected to those in the sub-stations through an automatic transmission system like a telephone exchange, are laid out in a schematic map on the control room wall. The controller's desk, provided with meters indicating line voltages, ordinary telephones and a log book, is placed facing the wall map. The controller's job is to ensure that all tracks are supplied with current when there is traffic, and isolated when idle or when maintenance teams are at work. In case of converter failure, he can cross-connect lines to replace the lost supply from elsewhere. Each converter is protected from overload by an automatic cut-out. When this happens, as it does perhaps two or three times a day in the whole area, the controller has to take quick action. The cause may be a momentary overload from a train starting up, or a chance short-circuit (in one instance a hoop thrown onto the line by children) or, just possibly, a serious accident. The normal procedure is to replace the cut-out twice, and if it still fails to stay in the controller has to find out why. This he usually does by making telephone enquiries to someone on the spot.

There is normally an engineer on duty in the building, and his advice can quickly be sought in an emergency, so the operator does not carry long-term responsibility for judgment in difficult situations; but a simple mistake or oversight on his part can cause serious damage or even loss of life.

The work of the remote control operator

As can be seen from the example, the control operator generally has three duties to perform:

(i) *Carrying out scheduled control and working operations.* The demand for public services, such as electricity or transport, follows a more or less regular curve of rise and fall through the day, week, month and year, and this often dictates the pattern of work in a control room. The operator (or his superior) follows a schedule catering for each expected change in demand, observes what the situation is at the time and then makes further changes if the actual position differs from what was expected.

(ii) *Meeting chance demands in his area in the most advantageous way.* Remote control mechanism limits the operator's scope in dealing with chance demands. This means usually he has a much smaller range of choice than someone on the spot would have. It also limits the amount of information available to him. Thus, when making a control decision, he has to select one out of a very few alternative actions, according to the limited information about the actual situation given to him by symbolic indicators, such as lights and pointers. If the operator wants more complicated information or action than the remote control equipment can provide, he has to use the telephone.

(iii) *Keeping a log.* Control actions and any unusual events are recorded and if necessary reported verbally to the engineer.

Skill at remote control

The remote control operator is not a skilled craftsman, he does not exercise sensorimotor skill or control skill of the type needed to run a plant. The main requirement is ability to interpret arrays of indicators, relating them to one another and to the outside situation and to take quick decisions. While he could do this by following fixed rules, there will be far more flexibility if his decisions are based on actual knowledge and understanding of the system being controlled. In the example quoted, the controller appeared to adopt the latter approach, though he dealt with some situations by rule. As a controller cannot build up the necessary mental picture of the equipment, and how it works, from experience in the control room alone, he must acquire it beforehand. Control operators are therefore often recruited from operators or maintenance workers with experience in the same organization. This is also useful from the social standpoint, as the controller finds it helpful if he is personally acquainted with some of the people with whom he has to deal by telephone.

This type of ability may be described as 'information handling' skill. Its possessor can quickly evaluate coded information and make decisions between well-defined alternatives within an artificial system.

The skill seems to comprise:
  (i) *Selective vigilance*—being receptive to particular signals in the presence of other distracting ones.
  (ii) *Translation of data*—relating the symbolic information from remote indicators to the real world.
  (iii) *Decision*—reviewing the possible control actions and their consequences and selecting the best for the given circumstances by predicting the consequences of each. Decision could degenerate into a habitual response, but a skilled operator will not be guided solely by habit.
  (iv) *Short-term memory*—being able to remember recent instructions, events and conditions relevant to a given decision and, perhaps equally important, to forget them when out of date.

As yet there is little indication of how far individuals differ in information handling skill, or what conditions favour its acquisition.

Strain of remote control work

Apart from skill and knowledge, the power to resist anxiety is important in control room work. If an operator makes a mistake, it can easily cause injury or loss of life. Yet he must take his decisions rapidly in a highly artificial situation, deprived of the numerous cues which combine to prevent error in the more natural and direct situations of everyday life. Wrong interpretation of signals, lapse of memory, failure to notice a signal, or misunderstanding of instructions, may have serious results. Yet all human beings are prone to make such errors occasionally. If an operator consciously or unconsciously dwells on the possible consequences of a mistake, he may become chronically 'anxious', developing digestive or other bodily symptoms, even though he never actually does make a mistake. Unfortunately, it seems that the most conscientious and efficient operators are the most prone to this disorder.

Other Control Room Work

A clear distinction must be drawn between the work of centralized remote control operators, as discussed above, and that of plant operators, though the latter may also spend a large part of their time in a control room. The difference is that the plant operator frequently visits and inspects all the equipment under remote control. He can thus both maintain an accurate idea of the situation being controlled and supplement the instrumental indications by direct inspection. A further point of difference is that plant operators are usually concerned with the fine adjustments to a single complete process, whereas remote control operators tend to carry out discrete switching or signalling actions at various separate places.

REMOTE HANDLING WITH DIRECT VIEWING

Another type of remote control is found, for instance, in the continuous strip mill of a steel works, where the roughing mill pulpit operator's job is to pass slabs of red-hot steel back and forth between pairs of rollers by operating the electrical controls of the roller transporter. He sits at a control panel above the mill, and all his actions are guided by vision, together with verbal messages from other parts of the mill. He exercises remote control over the machinery; his skill is essentially a sensorimotor one, as the expert learns to use the machinery without conscious thought—as if it were an extension of his own body. In this respect the job, and others like it, have much in common with driving cranes or even motorcars.

Operating a continuous strip mill also requires process control skill as described on page 7. The key job, carried out by the 'roller-man' and his assistant, is controlling the width and gauge of the strip.

5. Maintenance Work in Automatic Plants

While the proportion of maintenance staff to production workers rises steeply as automation progresses, there does not seem to be any marked change yet in the balance of craft skills except that rather more electronic technicians and instrument mechanics are needed to service the increased amount of electrical control gear (see Table 2).

Preventive Maintenance

As plants increase in size and reliability, the balance of maintenance effort is altered by the widespread introduction of 'preventive' or 'planned' maintenance. Its purpose is to minimize the risk of interruption to the smooth flow of production, and this is achieved by inspecting all parts subject to wear and, if necessary, refitting or replacing during planned shutdown periods, rather than waiting until they fail in operation. The maintenance work can then be better organized than during unforeseen stoppages.

Table 2. Number of process and maintenance workers in a modern oil refinery

	Process workers	Maintenance workers	Total	Percentage of total number of employees
On shift work	752	64	816	36·3
On day work	114	1319 (622 skilled 697 others)	1433	63·7
Total	866	1383	2249	
Percentage of total number of employees	38·5	61·5		

Under this system of maintenance the staff are divided into:

(i) *The day work force* which is responsible for major overhauls. These overhauls may be carried out entirely by skilled craftsmen, but in some cases it has been found possible to divide the work into a series of more or less repetitive operations resembling semi-skilled work in batch production, and thus save skilled effort for the more critical items. Incentive schemes based on work measurement have been applied to this type of maintenance work.

The day work force is also responsible for some routine maintenance on plant during production. While it is on site, it may be called on to tackle unforeseen breakdowns and to make running repairs.

(ii) *The shift maintenance staff or ' crash gang '* has some responsibility for routine maintenance, but its major function is to tackle unforeseen breakdowns occurring on the evening and night shifts. Speed is essential here, for shutdown time may be very expensive; if necessary, the team may call for special support from the management, or even call out members of the day work force.

Shift maintenance staff co-operate closely with shift process operators, but they usually belong to a different department. In an oil refinery, for example, the shift maintenance force (under the shift engineer) belongs to the mechanical department, whereas the operators (under the shift superintendent) belong to the process department.

The day work force usually numbers far more than the shift maintenance staff. In an oil refinery, for example, there were only 16 on night shift, compared with 1319 on day work.

Diagnostic skill

It is important, especially during production runs on large plant but also in other critical situations, that the ' crash gang ' should make speedy repairs to unforeseen breakdowns. This means that they need to be especially good at diagnosing the cause of faults and resourceful in curing them. Several strategies can be adopted in tracking down a fault, which are based on a more or less systematic elimination of the various possibilities. One is to test for faults in order of likelihood, and another to eliminate half the remaining possibilities at a time by properly chosen tests. Diagnostic skill probably consists partly in sensitivity to the clues which may be important, partly in interpreting them effectively in relation to the situation, and partly in selecting the most efficient testing strategy.

There appears to be considerable difference in diagnostic skill between individuals, even among those with the same level of technical knowledge.

New Types of Craft Skill

It seems likely that two new craft skills will soon emerge, and new apprenticeship schemes may be needed in the near future to cater for them.

' POLYVALENT ' CRAFTSMEN

The traditional division between mechanic and electrician is becoming a hindrance in servicing some modern equipment. For example, in the unit head used on transfer lines in the motor car industry, the electrical and mechanical parts are closely interlocked, and the craftsman servicing it needs a grasp of both electrical and mechanical practice. Conventional craft apprenticeships provide a man with one skill or the other but not both. Apprenticed electricians can be trained in the mechanical side, or *vice versa*, but for proper balance a mixed or ' electro-mechanical ' training will probably be found essential. In France, where the development has already taken place, the term ' polyvalent ' is applied to craftsmen with more than one field of competence.

CONTROL TECHNICIAN

Though servo-mechanisms for automatic plant may be actuated by electrical, pneumatic, hydraulic or mechanical means, according to convenience, a common theory of feedback and control underlies them all. At present instrument mechanics usually deal with them as an extension of their proper field, as there is no recognized qualification in servo-mechanisms as such. Control engineering has recently been established as a distinct discipline at graduate level in the Battersea College of Technology and elsewhere, and a similar innovation may be expected at technician level.

The 'control technician', as he might be called, should have a grounding in the theory of servo-mechanisms and control, in electrical and electronic principles, and in the various practical methods. He should be able to set up and service all the automatic controls and instrumentation on a plant and to diagnose operating faults due to disturbance within control loops.

At the present time it is sometimes not possible to recruit instrument fitters as such; for example, at Britain's largest oil refinery electricans and mechanical fitters are recruited in about equal numbers and are then given intensive training in electronics and the basis of instrumentation. This appears to be a tacit recognition of a new trade on the lines described above.

6. Working Conditions

Through instrumentation and remote control the plant operator is enabled to work away from the actual plant. This is a great advantage when, as in the chemical, food and metallurgical industries, the plant is hot, steamy and emits smoke or fumes. However, operators must often inspect the plant itself, and then they are exposed to adverse conditions. Even simple applications of automatic control, such as thermostats for ovens and constant-head devices, improve the working environment, not by eliminating harsh conditions but by reducing the time of exposure to them.

Isolation

Workers are often more widely spaced apart in automatic plants than in conventional factories (though the reverse is true in control rooms), yet this *physical* isolation does not necessarily mean social isolation. The job usually entails communicating with various people at frequent intervals, and the operator can often leave smoothly running plant for brief periods. Automatic control helps by reducing the frequency of adjustment and so confers still more freedom. The most serious cases of social isolation seen on the survey were due to noise so loud that people could not talk intelligibly to one another, even at close quarters; this was particularly true of workshops with many smaller automatic machines, such as automatic looms. Noise may also have an adverse effect on work if it hinders essential communication between members of a team. In some situations this may well present a serious problem, to which little attention has so far been paid.

Monotony

Process-operating on continuous-flow plants is often thought to be very monotonous, but few complaints were heard on this score. Not many automatic plants are so tightly controlled that nothing at all happens for long periods, and even if this is so the operator is free within certain limits to move about and do as he likes, knowing that automatic warning devices such as hooters and lights will recall him in an emergency. The most monotonous work is found where simple but important process variables are under manual control, for then the operator may have to keep his attention permanently on the job, though the job is not difficult enough to engage his full mental powers.

7. Supervision

The survey covered mainly work and skills at operator level, but it also included observations concerning supervision. Previous writers have pointed out that the foreman's rôle changes with automation, and the survey endorsed this view. While the exact position varies widely, it is usually true to say that automation reduces the number of workers supervised by a given foreman, so that this side of his function diminishes in importance. But a more fundamental change stems from the nature of the work being supervised. The worker need no longer exert continuous physical effort to maintain output; instead he monitors a continuous process and, in doing so, seems to acquire a sense of responsibility towards the plant itself and an attitude of mind quite different from that of the semi-skilled worker in mass production work. He is largely self-supervising, but there is a good deal of indirect supervision as he is in close touch with management, reporting the plant's behaviour and so on. So the need for direct supervision of his work is very much reduced.

The foreman's position tends to become equivocal. If he possesses sufficient technical skill and knowledge, he may act as a roving technical adviser; and if he has also the necessary personal qualities, he may become the accepted leader of an integrated team. But, however good he is at managing men, unless he has extensive technical knowledge and experience, he is apt to find himself a fish out of water, merely keeping records and arranging rotas. Where there is a qualified engineer on each shift, it is doubtful whether there is a place for him at all.

In short, the evidence from the survey suggests that the place and purpose of first-line supervision in automatic plant needs further study and rethinking.

8. Responsibility and Social Skills

Responsibility

Most managers of automatic plants visited during the survey stated that their plant operators must be 'responsible' men, but it was not always clear just what they meant. As applied to the production worker the term 'responsible' seems to have one or more of the following meanings:

(1) *Responsible*—able to make satisfactory judgments on matters of discretion, so that his work does not need frequent checking by superiors. (One research worker (Jacques 1956) has proposed that the 'time span' elapsing before work is checked is a good measure of the 'level' of responsibility.)

(2) *Conscientious*—ready to take extra trouble and care, without direct instructions, when the situation demands it.

(3) *Reliable*—never making mistakes, forgetting instructions, overlooking important indications, *etc.*, or otherwise failing in his prescribed duties.

(4) *Trustworthy*—honest and truthful in reporting to superiors; not concealing the facts when his own actions may have had adverse effects.

These traits are by no means always found together; for instance, a stable personality of low intelligence may be ' reliable ' but not ' responsible '. On the whole, it seems that ' trustworthiness ' and ' conscientiousness ' are most sought after for the lower grades of process operator, but ' responsibility ' and ' conscientiousness ' for the higher grades.

Program machine operators need good judgment (responsibility). Remote-controllers must be ' reliable ' since a single mistake may be disastrous.

Managers also very frequently mentioned that their operators were chosen partly for their interest in the job. It seems that without this quality, which provides an incentive to find out what is happening and why, the operator would be much slower in learning the job.

Social skills

Although workers in an automatic plant seem at first sight to be isolated, closer study reveals a surprising amount of inter-communication between individuals operating the machinery. Each member of the team—operators, maintenance men, engineers and laboratory staff—frequently gives and receives information or instructions about the plant from the others, by word of mouth, in writing and even sometimes by hand signals. It seems that the efficient running of a plant depends a great deal on the effectiveness of these interchanges. Therefore, each member of the team must be able to communicate easily with his fellows, understand their points of view and put his own across. In other words, they must exercise *social skills*. As yet no serious attempt has been made to identify or analyze these skills further, but perhaps it is significant that management want their operators to be ' good mixers '; for personal acceptance and friendship ease communication at work. There is no place in an automatic plant for the ' No talking ' rule; in fact the more talking, within limits, the better.

9. Some Personnel Problems for Management

Selection of operators

Labour turnover is low in automatic plant, because relatively few operators are needed and because the jobs are often desirable. Numerically, therefore, personnel selection presents only a small problem. But the jobs are key ones and a mistaken first choice of a recruit may prove disproportionally troublesome later on. At present most managers select promising men from the firm's labour pool and put them on the plant as trainees for a trial period. Even so, it is difficult to assess a potential operator's real aptitude for control work, still less the hidden factors in his personality.

Psychological aptitude tests have had some success in other fields and they could presumably help to assess aptitude for control work and capacity for responsibility, as defined above, so forming the basis for a more scientific approach. So far none of the existing tests has been proved valid for this purpose, except that a minimum level of general intelligence can be laid down for many classes of job. The first step in the right direction would be to administer a number of the standard tests to operators on various control jobs and find out which gave the best agreement with their measured performance or with supervisor's ratings. New tests would then need to be developed to fill in the gaps, and a 'battery' of tests assembled which would enable employers to predict a recruit's future performance.

Training

A recent survey (N.I.I.P. 1956) has shown that systematic operator training is exceptional even in non-automatic plants in this country; in automatic plants it is rarer still, probably because the processes need fewer new operators. It is often set up when new plant is being commissioned, but tends to lapse soon afterwards for lack of demand. Elsewhere basic courses for process operators are run at infrequent intervals. Such schemes usually provide formal instruction on the process, nomenclature, elementary science, safety and so on, but hardly any attempt has been made to inculcate working skills as described above, and in practice these are invariably acquired on the job by working alongside experienced operators. While this procedure can be fairly satisfactory, it leaves much to chance, and many costly breakdowns may be attributed to inadequate training of operators.

Since the last war a strikingly successful method of training for repetitive skills has been developed in this country (Seymour 1959). The first step in this method is to make a careful analysis of the experienced worker's performance; then sections of the job are practised, using the experienced worker's method and making his speed a 'target time' for the trainee; the separate sections are then combined progressively to make a complete cycle, performed at the experienced worker's speed. The method, known as 'specialized operator training', cannot be applied as it stands to control jobs because the work is neither manual nor repetitive.* But a similar analytic approach may well lead to an effective method of training for the new skills, if a substitute can be found for practice by progressive combination of parts of the job. This poses problems for future research. Work is also needed on methods of retraining older workers made redundant by changing technology (Clay 1960).

Payment and incentives

Financial incentive schemes based on time study are widely applied in unit and mass production industry, and some managers have sought to apply them to plant operation. However, the stop-watch is of little use, because the time spent in physical work is so small. Conventional incentive schemes cannot be used, as the operator's effectiveness is not at all closely related to high speed or effort. Yet plant operators may feel unfairly treated when they compare their moderate flat-rate pay with the high piece-rate wages that some semi-skilled operators or labourers can earn on the plant.

A different approach, known as the multi-factor incentive scheme, is to measure performance in terms of yield, quality and other factors, combining them into a single index, weighted according to importance, and then to pay a bonus according to the index figure achieved each week. The operator then has a direct incentive to do better at his job. But the difficulties of assessment and weighting are so great that very few such schemes have been applied and these have achieved mediocre results.

---

* A recent study (King 1960) sponsored by the European Productivity Agency deals more fully with training for automatic processes.

Two other systems of payment are in use, but neither of them is based on direct measurement of work done. The first—merit rating—gives bonus pay according to the supervisor's assessment of performance, and the second—job evaluation—allows basic rates to vary with the difficulty of the job, giving operators on more difficult plant a higher rate. Both of these systems depend on subjective judgments of merit or difficulty, and disputes about whose judgment is right are apt to arise. Attempts have recently been made to put job evaluation for control work on a more objective footing. If they succeed, they may well provide a satisfactory solution. However, the whole problem may be superseded if, as seems at least possible, piece-rates are gradually abandoned throughout industry in favour of high time-rates.

10. Conclusions

The most impressive finding of the survey concerned continuous-flow production plants. Although the term 'automation' has only been applied to some of them, notably transfer machines and automatically-controlled plant in the oil industry, they have a common pattern of work and skill. The work comprises *control*—monitoring and making adjustments to secure good yield and quality—and *communication*—logging instrumental readings and reporting to other members of the operating team.

The first of these elements requires 'control skill', which is usually specific to one situation and can only be acquired by experience. Its chief component is decision—selecting the best control action for each combination of circumstances that arises. The less good operators tend to work by 'rule-of-thumb', the better ones by an intuitive appreciation of the state of affairs, possibly using a mental 'working model' of the process. Logical thinking seems to be less common than might be expected. While the trained engineer may use logical thinking to solve plant problems, the ordinary operator appears to behave more intuitively. Yet oddly enough the operator can sometimes achieve better results than the engineer. This can probably be put down to his ability, derived from intimate experience of the plant, to take into account the many ill-understood factors which affect most plants' running but which he cannot communicate to his engineer. It seems that the rational approach cannot adequately handle complicated events and intuition must take over.

Repetitive manual jobs, though virtually abolished in production, tend to reappear in the guise of planned maintenance. Hence the difference between the type of work done by *day work* and *shift* maintenance staffs is growing steadily wider. The latter must be able to deal rapidly with unforeseen breakdowns and may need 'diagnostic' skills as well as their regular craft training. New maintenance skills will probably emerge—the 'electro-mechanical' fitter for servicing modern types of machine tool, and the 'control technician' for servo-mechanisms and control devices.

Lack of information precludes a proper estimate of the numbers in each type of occupation mentioned here. Plant operators in continuous-flow production are certainly the biggest group, but even in the most advanced process industries (and allowing for shift working) they do not amount to a half of the total labour force (see Table 2, page 17).

The introduction of automatic methods leads to an increase in output per head, and to a reduction in the number of direct production workers. However, as the changeover from conventional to automatic methods is made in stages over a period of time, and is accompanied by an overall rise in production, redundancy does not present as serious a problem as is sometimes feared.

Taking the country as a whole, only a tiny fraction of the labour force is employed on operating automatic plant, though the plant itself forms a relatively large part of the country's productive capital equipment. Thus the efficiency of these few operators has an economic importance disproportionate to their numbers and it would seem worthwhile to intensify study of the factors affecting it. Subjects particularly worth studying are: methods of personnel selection; training techniques for specific control skills; principles of equipment design for effective human use; and types of social organization, team structure and leadership most fitted to operate different kinds of process.

This short report can only sketch the outlines of a picture. It glosses over many subtle differences of work and skill within the categories described and the industrial reader will undoubtedly question from his particular experience the content and emphasis of some of the statements made. Since there is as yet little accredited knowledge on the subject, the survey can be counted a success if his questionings lead the reader to fruitful discussion and further investigation.

Visual Attention and the Sampling of Displayed Information in Process Control

By E. R. F. W. Crossman, J. E. Cooke and R. J. Beishon

Institute of Experimental Psychology, Oxford University

1. Introduction

When designing displays one tends to assume that the operator will attend to them continuously or at frequent intervals because he needs all the information that they can provide and that the main problem is ensuring that their data are conveyed as quickly and as accurately as possible. But in real life operators ignore displayed data for long periods without ill effect, and they can often manage perfectly well with very poor instruments, as a brief visit to almost any factory will show. Evidently the operator must be getting superfluous data and this implies that the designer could economize on display facilities, if he knew exactly how often and with what accuracy data are really needed to meet a specified performance requirement. He could then design the displays to provide just the right information, but to do this he needs to have a clear appreciation of the role played by display information in task performance and of the quantitative laws governing its gain and use, particularly those concerning the frequency and duration of attention to displays. The present paper sets out some empirical results and theory on this point, together with tentative principles for an improved design procedure.

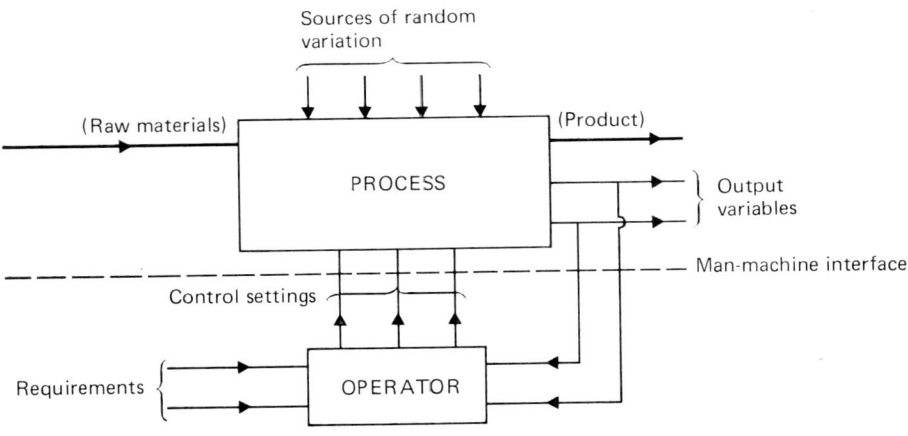

Figure 1. Manual process control.

The paper deals mainly with visually-displayed information used in the control of continuous processes such as occur in the chemical, oil and steel industries (Crossman 1960a, Spencer 1962, Sell, Crossman and Box 1962), though its conclusions are also applicable to such fast tasks as vehicle control and to management, where data may be presented in any sensory mode. The process control task situation is shown diagrammatically in Figure 1. In general the process or *machine* is an autonomous 'self-propelled' system and the operator's job is to keep it running and maintain a specified product quality, which he does by observing the output and making suitable adjustments to settings and controls. The paper-making plant described in Section 5 below is a paradigm case; here production can continue for an hour or two with the operating team away, but the product will slowly drift off specification, and the process will ultimately break down unless corrected. Similarly, a workshop or office may operate normally for a considerable time without its manager but his attention is ultimately needed to resolve accumulated difficulties and to ensure that the desired results are being achieved. While the diagram shows only a few modes of interaction between man and machine, most real-life systems are far more complex. However, it is usually possible to resolve a complete system into a number of subsystems partly or wholly independent of one another and hence to break the operator's total task down into a number of subtasks by taking each characteristic of the product, or *output variable*, separately and inquiring into which *internal variables* affect it.

Our concern is with the transfer of information across the *interface* from machine to man. Normally much more information is available from the various displays and sources of data constituting the interface than the man needs or can use at any one time, and he filters or selects what he requires by directing his attention to different parts of the display in turn, 'sampling' the various sources of information in some more or less regular pattern, as shown for instance by studies of visual fixation in landing aircraft (Fitts, Jones and Milton 1950). Each subtask concerned with the control of a single variable such as heading, air speed and height in flying, requires periodic attention and the operator therefore performs a number of interleaved sequences of sampling actions, or observations, each sequence providing information about the variables relevant to one subtask. In other words, the operator handles the subtasks in rotation using a single information processing channel by time-sharing (see Craik 1947, Crossman 1964c). Process control usually requires little physical work so that the maintenance of an adequate pattern of sampling behaviour constitutes the major part of a process operator's work load; since there has hitherto been no objective means of assessing this load and no criterion of its effective performance, serious problems have arisen in this connection for work measurement and job evaluation (Kitchin and Graham 1961) as well as in design.

2. Visual Detection of Rare Signals and the Observing Response

One can approach the sampling problem, as this research area may be termed, empirically by studying how operators distribute their attention when more data are displayed than they really need, or theoretically by analyzing the sampling policies that could be adopted to gain the information needed to perform a specified task. Ideally, theory and observation should then converge in establishing that the behaviour of an actual operator conforms more or less closely to a given theoretical model, or perhaps to different ones in different circumstances.

The major difficulty with the empirical approach has been to identify and record instantaneous focus of attention and until quite recently the only technique in use depended on studying successive eye fixations on a known visual field (see Mackworth and Thomas 1962). One set of results has been reported on the relative frequency and duration of attention to instruments in the process control task of landing aircraft (Fitts, Jones and Milton 1950), but otherwise the method has only been applied to search tasks where more or less rare signals appear against a blank or repetitive background as in the classical studies on watchkeeping and vigilance (Mackworth 1950, Ford, White and Lichtenstein 1959, White and Ford 1960). Broadly speaking, in these cases the eye has been found to sample spatial areas in a quasi-random manner, with inefficient matching between patterns of sampling and distribution of signals, though some improvement is shown when a strong visual frame of reference is provided as by grid lines or other markings.

Crossman and Smith (Crossman 1961a) studied the effect of information*-per-signal (*i.e.* rarity of signals to be detected) on visual scanning by recording eye movements in a proofreading task. They found that with low discriminability, where exact fixation was required to detect the signals, their information content had little effect on scan pattern or on fixation time over the range 3–9 bits, whereas when discriminability was increased so that signals could be detected in peripheral vision the area covered per fixation and hence the number of potential signals inspected per unit time, increased steadily with rarity up to a point where the chance of detecting the very rare signals when they occurred was only 25%; at this point the scanning pattern used was a distinctly inefficient means of gathering information. Thus the well-known phenomenon of missed signals in vigilance may at least in part be explained by the fact that operators use inefficient sampling policies and in some cases it can be eradicated by designing displays in such a way that efficient scanning patterns are encouraged or even enforced by the display itself.

Another experimental technique for studying the distribution of attention has recently been introduced as an offshoot from the operant conditioning studies of animal behaviour due to B. F. Skinner. It is based on requiring subjects to make an 'observing response' by pressing a key or lever when they wish to view a display or a selected portion of one; this behaviour can easily be recorded and using a vigilance task Holland (1958) found that its rate could be controlled by changing the schedule of presentation of signals. He claimed that human observing responses obey the same laws of reinforcement as do the pecking responses of pigeons with food reward, and that the signals themselves act as reinforcing agents. However, Jerison and Wing (1963a) have argued that it is not signals but *detections* that provide reinforcement and hence control the rate of observing responses. Adams (1961) has criticized the observing response technique on the grounds that key-pressing is artificial compared with 'just looking at' a display; this point may have some weight in purely visual tasks such as radar watchkeeping, but overt observing responses such as walking to a panel or switching on a light are by no means rare in industry, and in general the 'observing response' technique seems to be a very promising one.

---

* The terms *information* and *entropy* are used hereafter in the technical senses defined in Shannon's classical work on the mathematical theory of communication (Shannon and Weaver 1949). Thus:

Information in a signal $= -\log_2$ (probability of that signal).
Entropy of a signal source $=$ average information in all possible signals.

The task of searching for rare signals in an otherwise featureless environment is not very common in practical life, and it should not be thought too surprising if human beings perform it inefficiently. Theoretically the best sampling policy in a binary detection task is to devote just enough attention to each area of display so that a signal will be detected if it is present and if this policy is adopted the scanning pattern will depend, not on the *probability* of a signal being present, but solely on its *visibility*. Most of the inefficiency found in human search performance appears to arise from a tendency for the attention devoted to a given locus to decrease with the probability of a signal appearing at it, presumably because of the reduced rate of reward from detections. Expressed in information-theoretic terms, as signals becomes progressively rarer the information gained from each rises but the average information or *entropy* per item or per unit area of a search field falls off steeply, as shown in Figure 2; it seems that as this happens operators unconsciously attempt to maintain the same average rate of information intake by increasing the area covered per fixation or reducing fixation time, as happens in ordinary visual tasks such as reading, and this causes the signals that do appear to fall below

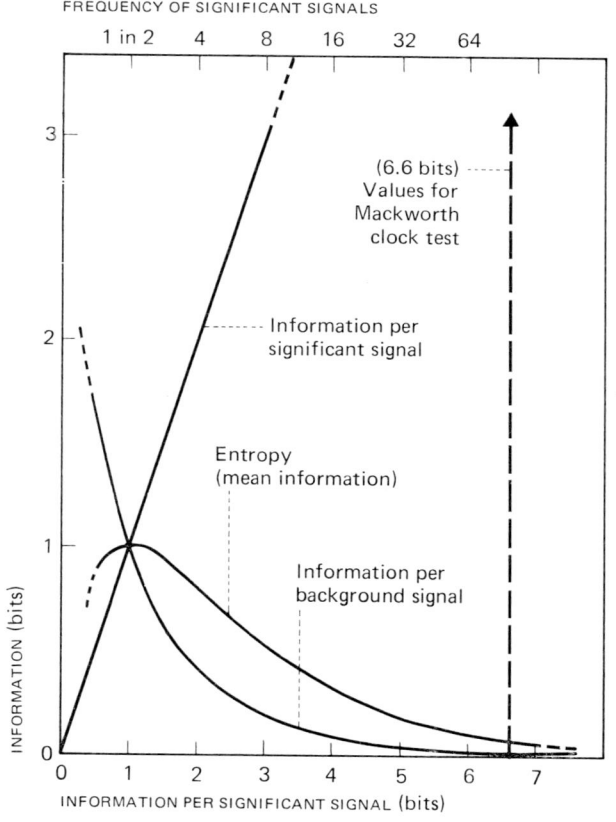

The operator is assumed to examine a sequence of objects or signals each of which may or may not be significant. The abscissa is the logarithmic probability of occurrence of the significant items and the ordinates are information in bits.

Figure 2. Information gain per signal in binary search tasks.

the threshold of visibility. The peculiar difficulty of controlling attention in binary vigilance or search tasks can be summed up by saying that nearly all the time the operator gains nearly no information about his environment, and he finds this a very unrewarding use for his perceptual capacity.

3. Senders' Application of the Shannon-Wiener Sampling Theorem

The more normal use of human vision evidently is to create and maintain an internal image, map or model of the environment, from which information can be abstracted to determine future action. If the environment were static, one complete observation would suffice for all time, as with an aerial photograph, but since it changes, more or less frequent observations or 'samples' are required to keep the internal model up to date, and the question then arises of how frequently samples are needed to maintain the representation at a desired level of accuracy.

In process control the process itself is the 'environment' and it has a fixed structure within which only certain variables change; thus sampling consists in ascertaining the values of relatively few quantities in a known framework and using them to up-date an otherwise static model. Such a set of values or readings describing the system at a particular time is called a *system state* and fairly obviously we may expect that the sampling frequency required for accurate representation of system behaviour will depend on the rate at which the system state can change. J. W. Senders (1955b) first pointed out that the Shannon-Wiener sampling theorem (see Shannon and Weaver 1949) applies to this problem, setting a minimum permissible rate of $2W$ samples per second for fixed-interval sampling of a random variable with bandwidth W cycles per second. At this sampling rate, if the variable has power (*i.e.* mean square variability) Q, and needs to be known with accuracy (*i.e.* mean square error) N, the information gained per sample is $\frac{1}{2} \log_2 (Q/N)$ bits; Senders suggested that these two quantities determine respectively the frequency and duration with which an operator should attend to a given displayed quantity.

He later tested this theoretical prediction by having operators monitor a bank of four instruments whose readings varied randomly with different bandwidths, asking them to report deviations beyond specified limits. Their eye fixations were recorded and it was found that the frequency and duration of attention given to each dial depended appropriately on bandwidth, range of variation and permissible error (Senders 1964). These pioneer studies, though incomplete, provide a clear lead towards a satisfactory theoretical treatment of of sampling behaviour, and they deserve to be more widely known.

However, Senders' experimental arrangement still required the observer to *detect* relatively rare events (excess deviations) rather than to *record* or report system states through time as the Shannon–Wiener theorem implies and in a somewhat similar experiment on detecting deviations in which operators had to press buttons to illuminate one of three dials at a time, Blair and Kaufman (1959) obtained opposite results. The deviations in question were sudden stepwise movements from an arbitrary zero, occurring at random with rates up to 60 signals per 15 minutes and while the pattern of results was complicated, the distribution of attention between dials did *not* appear to be affected by the relative frequency of signals. However, this finding is actually consistent with the theory for while in Senders' experiment the pointers were in constant slow random motion, and observing that a certain pointer was near the middle of its range would enable the observer to be confident that no excess deviation could occur for some time ahead, in Blair and Kaufman's case deviations occurred suddenly and quite unpredictably. Since bandwidth is related to the maximum possible rate of change of reading, which varied between the different dials in Senders' experiment but not in Blair and Kaufman's, rather than to the *frequency* of a given deviation, which varied in both, straightforward application of the sampling theorem would predict equally high sampling rates for all three meters in the latter case but not the former, as was actually found. The contrast between these two experiments indeed highlights the essential difference between binary detection or vigilance tasks, and recording, monitoring or control of continuous processes. In vigilance tasks the system has wide bandwidth, since there are sudden changes of system state and hence a high maximum information rate, but the mean information rate is low since such changes are rare; whereas in continuous control both mean and maximum information rates are in strict proportion to the bandwidth and hence to one another. There is not, of course, a sharp dividing line between the two situations but the distinction is a useful one to bear in mind.

The sampling theorem has also been applied to manual pursuit tracking of a fast randomly-moving target. Here Crossman (1960c) found that with courses of bandwidth greater than about 2 cycles per second operators made discrete motions aimed at the successive peaks or turning points of the course, a mode of behaviour which was in almost exact agreement with the theoretically optimum sampling policy under the given conditions. However, in this experiment the course had a rather special mixed-harmonic waveform which would facilitate this particular behaviour and the agreement between behaviour and theory may have been fortuitous. Discontinuities which could correspond to intermittent display sampling have been found in many other tracking studies (see *e.g.* Craik 1947) but those authors reporting the phenomenon have not considered the sampling rate in relation to course bandwidth, and have usually interpreted the discontinuity as the outcome of a fixed action lag or periodicity inherent in the human perceptual-motor mechanism (Hick 1948): indeed a sampled-data model of the human operator with a fixed sampling rate around 3 per second *un*related to course bandwidth now seems to command general acceptance among workers on fast manual control (Bekey 1962a). There is a field for further investigation here.

4. Sampling and the Growth of Uncertainty

The sampling theorem certainly sets the minimum permissible fixed-interval sampling rate for recording a random signal. In process control the signal of most interest is usually the system output whose bandwidth is determined by overall system response. This parameter can easily be estimated from the shortest time required for a significant change to occur and the corresponding sampling rate predicts operator behaviour with sufficient accuracy to assess the work load arising from a given control task or subtask (Linquist and Gross 1958) and for various other design purposes. But the theory is evidently incomplete, since it takes no account of (1) the operator's own controlling activity, (2) the desired accuracy of control, (3) the 'cost' attached to errors of control, (4) the uncertainty of sample readings themselves, (5) the operator's prior knowledge of system behaviour other than its bandwidth, (6) the nature of other concurrent activities. Our observations in process plants have shown that each of these factors has an effect on sampling rate and ideally they should all be reflected in the theoretical analysis. To cater for them and to predict the short-term fluctuations in sampling rate which occur during a period of controlling or monitoring (see Section 5 below) we need a more detailed theory of how single sample intervals are determined and we propose that this should be based on analyzing how information gained in sampling offsets the operator's uncertainty of process behaviour. It is not our purpose in this paper to develop a full theoretical analysis along these lines, but the following qualitative scheme will serve as a conceptual framework for the empirical studies to be reported.

Consider an operator who has just ascertained that process A is running exactly on specification and who has turned his attention to activity B—say reading the newspaper. As time passes he will become progressively less certain just what state A is in (see Figure 3a), and since he expects to incur a penalty of some kind if the process goes off specification, he experiences an increasing uneasiness which can be roughly quantified as the subjective probability that process A is off specification multiplied by the penalty for being off. But looking to see that all is well will 'cost' something—perhaps only the time taken away from activity B—and at intervals the operator mentally evaluates the payoff to be expected from sampling, which is the difference between the gain from reduction of uncertainty and the loss from the 'cost' of sampling; as soon as the expected payoff becomes positive he will take a sample, when his uncertainty reverts to zero and the cycle starts again (see Figure 3b).

On this elementary model, the length of a given sampling interval is determined jointly by (1) the rate of growth of uncertainty, (2) the penalty attached to error, and (3) the (non-zero) cost attached to sampling. Each of these factors is subject to a number of influences and a full theoretical treatment would be cumbersome, but it will be useful to consider now certain aspects which are particularly important in practice.

4.1. *Random Fluctuations and the System Time Constant*

In the absence of any deliberate correction, all processes drift more or less unpredictably with time, and it is this random variation or 'noise' which causes the steady rise of uncertainty between samples. The successive values of a given variable usually form a random series like a one-dimensional Brownian motion or 'drunkard's walk', so that its expected distance from a known starting point increases approximately as the square root of time, and entropy increases linearly with time. However, the operator knows that nothing can have happened within a period less than, say, 1/10 of the system time constant after sampling, and he is also aware that even after several time constants the variable must still be within a given range so his uncertainty will tend towards a maximum (see Figure 3c). Thus the sampling interval should normally lie within a relatively narrow range centred on the system time constant; this is another less precise way of stating the sampling theorem. But not all fluctuations create uncertainty, for the operator can predict and discount some in advance, such as steady drifts due to known causes, and others, such as high-frequency 'noise' in instrument readings, can be eliminated by averaging. Thus it is not always obvious which disturbances and time constants actually do enter into the determination of sampling interval. There is no general answer to this question, and it must be solved in practical cases by analyzing the sources of uncertainty 'seen' by the operator.

4.2. *Control Changes*

Suppose that on taking a sample the system is found to be in a given state outside the desired range. A correction is required and using his knowledge of system behaviour the operator decides on a suitable adjustment. Ideally, if its effect were precisely predictable, no extra uncertainty would be introduced by the correction and the next sampling interval would remain unaffected. But in practice the operator does not know what the precise effects of his

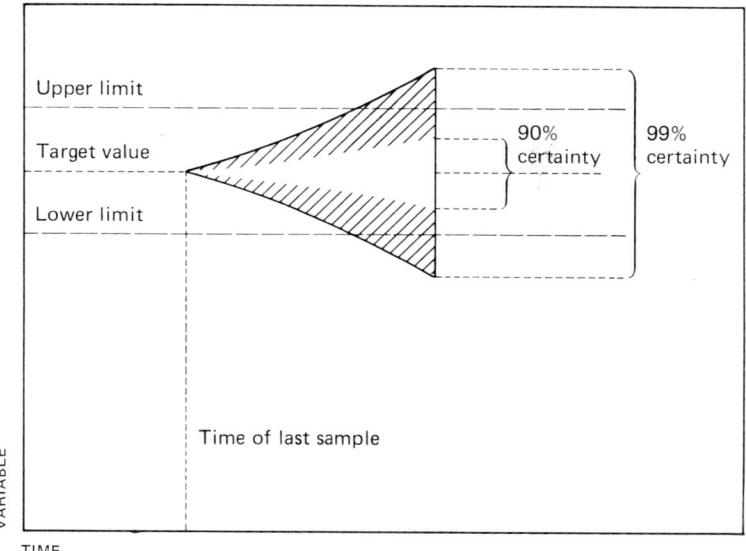

Two different fiducial limits are indicated, defining the high-probability region within which the variable should lie.

(*a*) Range of uncertainty as a function of time since last known position.

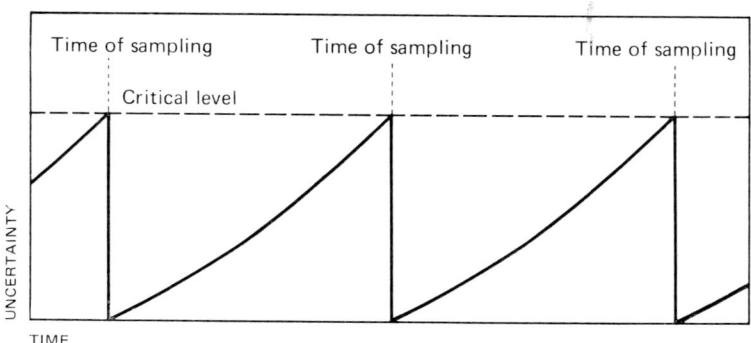

(*b*) Uncertainty plotted against time with repeated sampling.

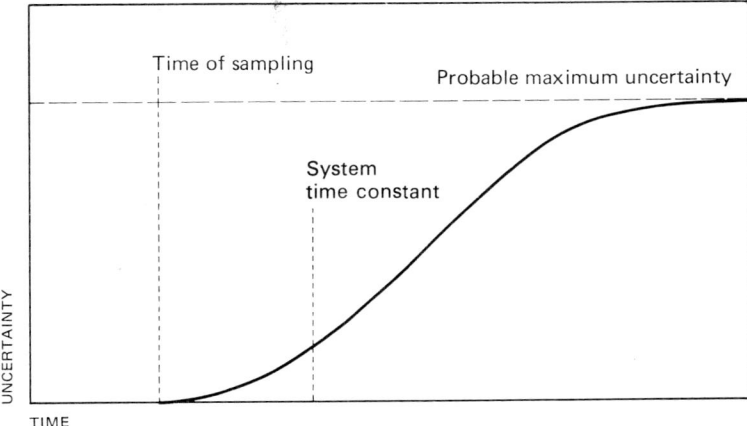

(c) Hypothetical time pattern growth of uncertainty for a system with exponential lag and a limited total range of variation.

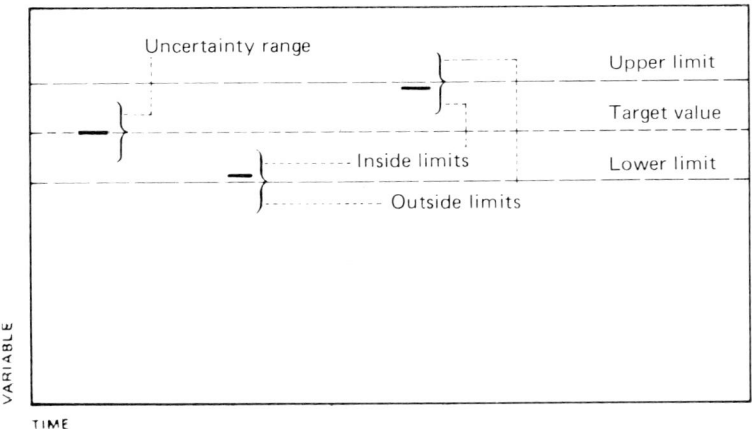

(d) Placement of uncertainty range in relation to control limits.

Figure 3. Growth of uncertainty after sampling for a single system state variable.

control action will be and the uncertainty due to this ignorance is added to the existing background uncertainty due to random disturbance, which causes the subsequent sampling intervals to be reduced until the expected effects of the control change have worn off; thus any control change should cause a temporary increase in sampling rate. It is also worth noting that uncertainty of the results of control action prevents exact control and causes two or more successive control changes of decreasing size to be used where one would suffice for a given correction, thereby further prolonging the transient rise in sampling rate.

4.3. *Tolerance Limits and the Effect of Increased Accuracy Requirement*

While uncertainty of the exact state of a system may cause the operator uneasiness when it is in the middle of its permitted range, actual penalties only arise from going outside assigned limits and corrections are not normally made until a variable is near the edge of its tolerance band. So the lesser uncertainty contained in the question whether or not the variable is within specification (and hence whether or not an adjustment is required), tends to carry more weight in determining the payoff from sampling than the greater one of exactly where it is (see Figure 3d). One can infer from this that sampling rate should rise when a variable is known to be near its tolerance limits. Greater accuracy means that the limits are set closer together, and the overall mean sampling rate should rise in proportion. Hence greater accuracy entails more sampling.

4.4. *Operator's Knowledge of System Behaviour*

Since the experienced operator can draw on more stored information to predict system behaviour and is therefore less uncertain of its movements, he should sample less frequently than the beginner. But the opposite effect can also occur, for the beginner may be unaware of possible system states, experience less uncertainty than he should, and hence use a lower sampling rate than the expert.

4.5. *Forgetting*

Uncertainty and hence sampling rate will evidently be increased if the operator forgets system states, or indeed any other data relevant to a given subtask. As recent studies by Yntema and his colleagues have shown (Yntema 1963), this is particularly likely to happen where the operator has to remember the states of a number of variables at the same time and they are expressed in the same symbolism, a situation frequently met with in process control. Even with only a single value to be remembered there is likely to be some increase in uncertainty due to memory decay during a sampling interval though actual errors may be rare. For this reason a human operator's sampling rate is probably always greater than the theoretically-required minimum.

These qualitative inferences from the uncertainty analysis could be expressed more precisely in the mathematical language of communication theory, and we hope to do this in a later paper. However, our present objective is to test their validity against field and laboratory data, before proceeding with more exact analysis.

5. Sampling Behaviour in the Control of Basis Weight in a Papermill

We were first stimulated to undertake the foregoing uncertainty analysis of the sampling problem by observations made during industrial field studies of process operator behaviour and skill from which one rather clear case will be cited by way of illustration. It concerns the machineman's task of controlling the basis weight of paper being made in a modern high-quality mill; a full account of the process and of the machineman's job has been given elsewhere (Beishon 1963).

The weight of a given area of paper, or 'basis weight', is specified in each customer's order and it must be held to within ± 1 lb of a nominal value lying between 15 and 30 lb per demy during a production run which may last several hours or even days. Its current value can be obtained either by removing and weighing a sample, a procedure which can only be carried out during a reel change, or (less precisely) by means of a beta-ray gauge situated at the 'dry end' of the machine; and it is controlled by means of a 'stuff valve' which controls the flow of pulp into the 'wet end' of the machine. Its value also changes with the overall speed of the machine. One of the machineman's subtasks, then, is to adjust basis weight to the desired value for each successive order and monitor it during production to ensure that it remains within the specified limits until the order is completed.

The paper-making machine is a complicated system, containing many interacting variables and sources of chance variation, but broadly speaking it gives a proportional response of basis weight to small alterations both of stuff valve and of speed setting. Stuff valve changes are subject to a total lag of the order of 5 minutes, made up as follows: first there is an exponential lag with time constant about 3 minutes because an increased (or decreased) pulp flow must change the concentration of pulp in a large volume of circulating water before it can begin to produce heavier or lighter paper, and second there is a transmission lag because paper emerging from the 'wet end' takes some 0·9 minutes to pass through the drying train to the 'dry end' where its basis

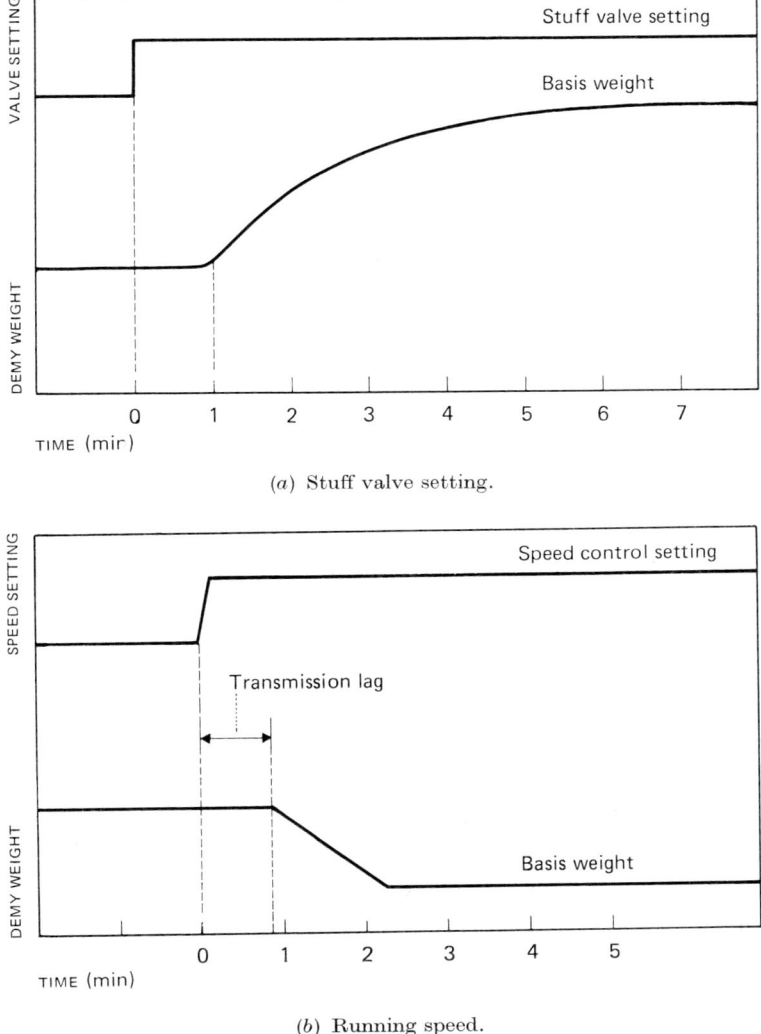

Figure 4. Idealized dynamic response of basis weight to various changes in a papermill.

weight can be ascertained. If a physical sample of paper is taken, the cutting and weighing operations require a further 2 minutes approximately, and thus 5 to 7 minutes elapse between a stuff valve change and its final result in a measured change of output basis weight (see Figure 4a). The speed control has a more rapid effect, following approximately a ramp function of time (see Figure 4b).

5.1. *Sampling during Long Production Runs*

The time course of basis weight fluctuation was recorded by virtually continuous observation of the beta-ray gauge through 6 hours of a typical day's run following the change to a new order, and is shown in Figure 5a together with the times at which the machineman inspected the beta-ray gauge or weighed a sample, adjusted the speed or stuff valve, and at which reel changes were made. The sampling interval, that is the interval between occasions on which the operator noted the current basis weight, had a mean value through

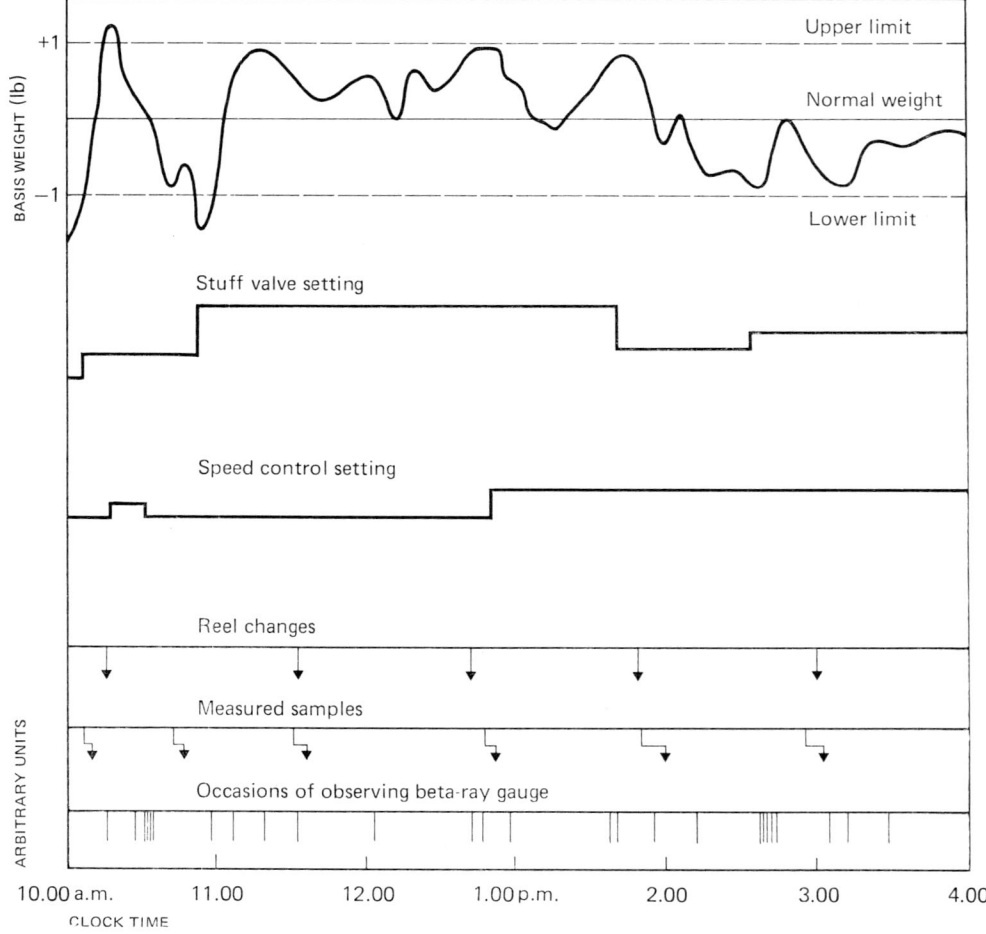

(*a*) Record of basis weight, control changes, and samples taken through a 6-hour period.

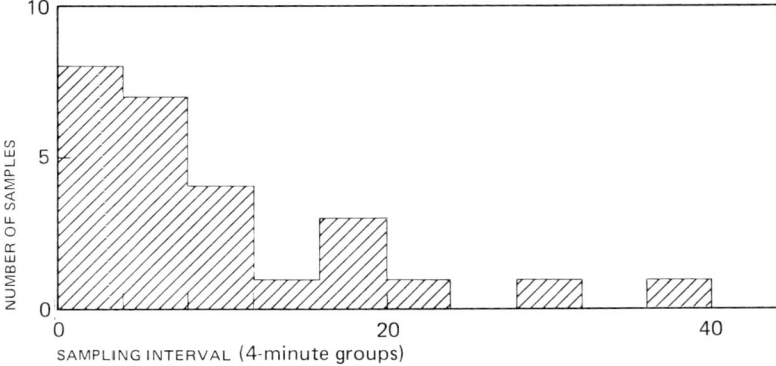

(b) Distribution of all sampling intervals during the period.

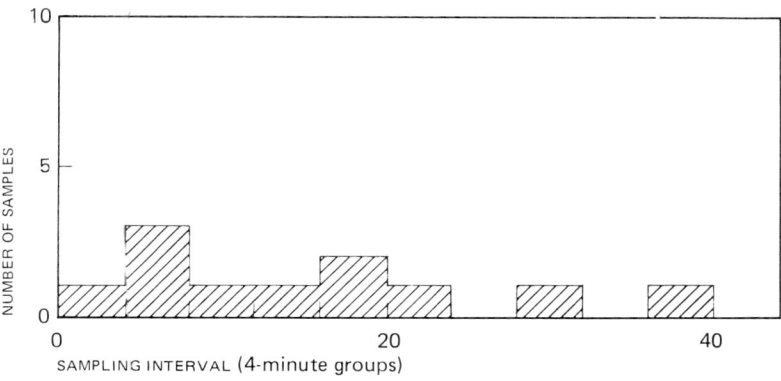

(c) Distribution of sampling intervals excluding those within 10 minutes of a control change.

Figure 5. Sampling during a long period of steady running at a single nominal basis weight in a papermill.

the day of 8·5 minutes (s.d. = 7, $n = 25$) with a highly skewed, almost exponential distribution (see Figure 5b). There were two periods of very frequent inspection at 34 and 284 minutes from start during which sampling intervals could not be recorded, both occurring shortly after control changes. However, after excluding periods within 10 minutes of any adjustment (Figure 5c) the mean sampling interval was found to be 14·1 minutes (s.d. = 11·0, $n = 12$); and when reel changes which in effect produced forced samples were also excluded the mean interval was 24·8 minutes (s.d. = 8·0, $n = 5$). The background sampling rate thus seems to have been about 2 per hour, which would correspond on Senders' analysis (see Section 3) to a bandwidth of 1 cycle per hour. The actual bandwidth was obviously greater than this, since basis weight drifted up and down significantly over periods of only a few minutes, but the amplitude of these relatively high-frequency disturbances was small in relation to the permitted tolerance range. It seems that the operator was aware of this fact and used it in determining his sampling rate which suggests that when applying Senders' formula the proper bandwidth figure to use is the *highest frequency component of random fluctuation having a peak amplitude greater than the assigned tolerance*. Using this 'effective bandwidth' to calculate the proper

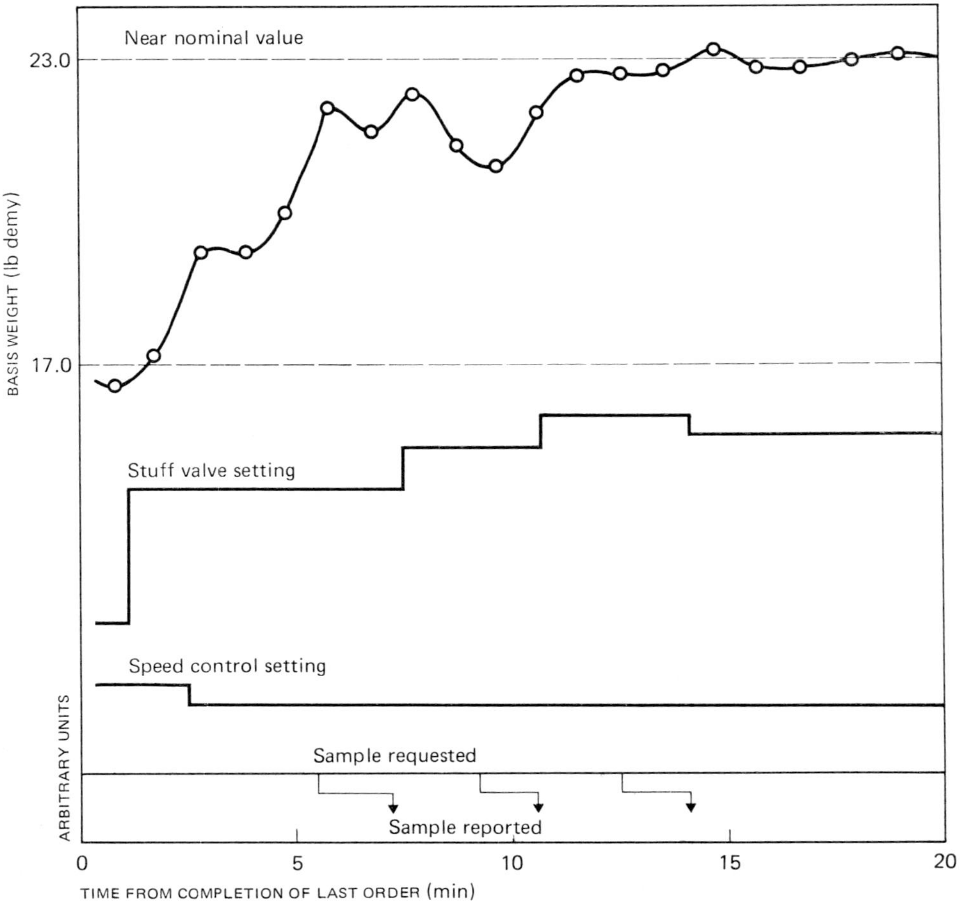

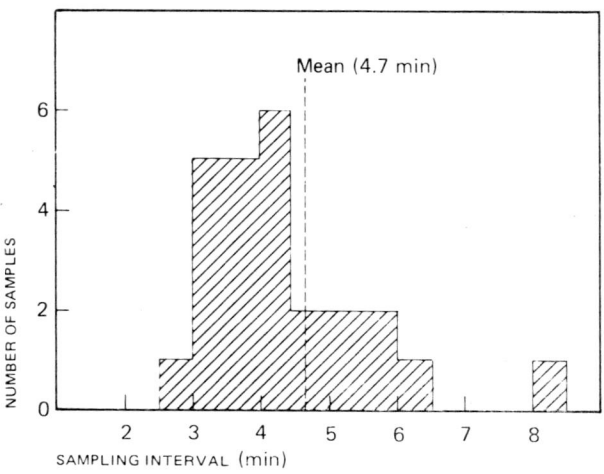

(a) Typical record of basis weight during a change.

(b) Distribution of sampling intervals during 20 changes made by 3 operators.

Figure 6. Sampling while readjusting to a new nominal basis weight in a papermill.

sampling rate makes the latter depend on required accuracy, as the uncertainty analysis suggests that it should. There were also irregular long-term drifts in the beta-gauge record, correlated with small control changes made at about hourly intervals. Indeed the complete day's record of basis weight shows an extremely slow oscillatory approach to a central stationary state, and it is possible that the sampling rate would subsequently have dropped to a much lower level, say once per two or three hours. Further observations extending over very long production runs will be needed to test this prediction.

5.2. *Sampling after Major Control Changes*

The pattern of control adjustment and sampling was also recorded during several occasions of readjusting basis weight to the next required value after finishing an order (see Figure 6a). The beta-ray gauge was off scale during this period, but the paper produced until the correct new basis weight had been achieved went to waste, so that pieces could be torn off and weighed at any time on a signal from the machineman to the dryerman. The mean interval between such sampling actions was found to be 4·7 minutes (s.d. = 2·5, $n = 25$) with a distribution more nearly symmetrical than that found during long runs (see Figure 6b). This interval is nearly equal to the lag in the stuff valve system measured to 80% of final response, as shown in Figure 4a, and it seems that, as might reasonably be expected, *the next sampling interval after a control change is equal to the lag in system response to the particular disturbance applied.* Most basis weight changes were achieved by making a sequence of 2–5 diminishing control adjustments resulting in a monotonic approach to the desired value, one sample being taken per adjustment.

The accuracy with which the operator's sampling behaviour matched the system lag was particularly striking since the men had many other things to do and there was no conveniently placed clock that they could refer to, nor did they use their watches. When questioned, operators gave widely differing estimates (from 1 to 8 minutes) of the time within which they would expect a given control change to be effective and it seems that their actual behaviour did not depend on explicit estimates of clock time but on an internal ' feeling ' for system behaviour.

These findings have been repeated in several other factory studies, to be reported elsewhere, and it seems clear that in industrial process operation bandwidth alone does not suffice to predict operators' sampling behaviour. Quite extensive knowledge of the factors contributing to uncertainty is needed to form even approximately realistic estimates.

6. **An Experimental Study of Sampling in Water Bath Temperature Control**

The industrial studies did not permit us to study the effect of practice on sampling rate in a newly encountered task nor the detailed relationship between sampling interval and system state, both of which should have definite effects according to the uncertainty analysis outlined above. We therefore undertook a laboratory study using the simple but realistic task of water bath control in a chemical plant (Crossman and Spencer 1960) and more fully described elsewhere (Crossman and Cooke 1962). In the usual version of this task the operator had to control the temperature of one litre of water in a brass tank by means of an electric immersion heater connected to a variable-voltage transformer (Variac) with a linear scale 0–200 volts. Temperature was displayed on a mercury-in-glass thermometer calibrated in degrees and tenths (5 mm per degree Centigrade) suspended in 20 ml of water inside a glass boiling-tube in the main vessel. For studying sampling the thermometer and voltage control were screened from view and each could be seen only on lifting a small inspection flap connected to an event recorder. Continuous records were also taken of temperature and control setting.

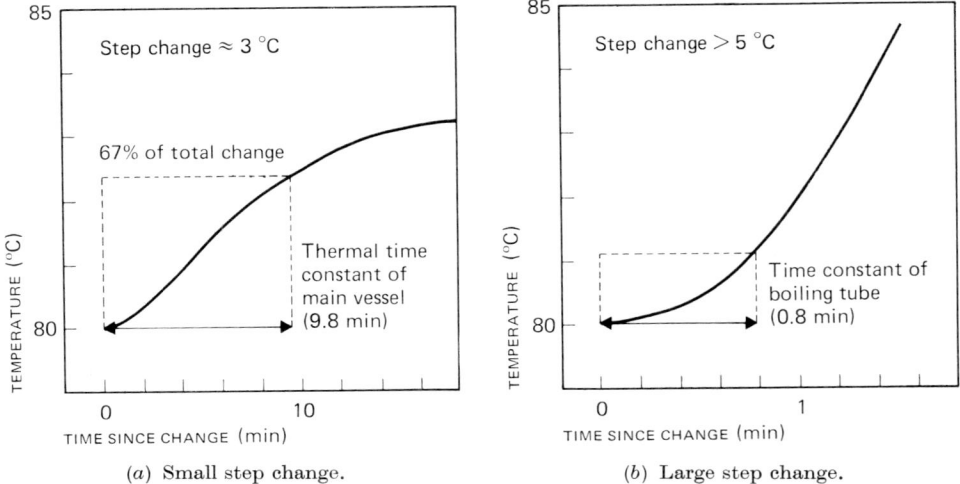

Figure 7. Water bath experiment I. Measured dynamic response of temperature to voltage setting.

The balance between gains and losses of heat together with the heat capacity of the water in the main vessel and boiling tube resulted in a very roughly proportional response of indicated temperature to voltage setting over the middle range of 80–120 volts and 70–95°C. Within this range the response was subject to two tandem exponential lags, one of time constant 9·8 minutes due to the main vessel (see Figure 7a) and the other of 0·8 minutes due to the boiling tube (see Figure 7b). Over the linear range, therefore, the system gave proportional control with second-order lag. But the operator's task was to bring the temperature up from an initial steady 70°C to 85°C as quickly as possible and keep it within ±0·5°C for the 30 minutes duration of the trial. This could not be done within the linear range, and during the initial phase of getting onto target, lasting about 5 minutes, the voltage setting was treated as a first-order control with first-order lag having upper and lower limits on possible control settings and hence on the maximum rates of rise or fall of temperature. Once on target, temperature was subject to a steady drift due to loss of water by evaporation and to small irregular drifts caused by fluctuations of supply voltage and ambient temperature. The effects of these chance variations, analogous to the types of disturbance met with in industrial processes, were small in relation to the allowed temperature tolerance.

This type of task where the operator controls an actual physical process that he can see and understand offers the crucial advantage over a conventional 'black box' arrangement using an analogue computer, that the operator experiences no uncertainty of *what* the system he is controlling will do, only of *how much* and *how fast*. Another task with similar dynamic properties where only the display and control were visible and not the process itself gave quite different and less consistent results (Beishon 1964).

Some results on the frequency of observations in this task have previously been reported (Crossman and Cooke 1962); the mean sampling rate showed a marked decline with practice to a minimum of about 1 observation per 3 minutes. The present experiments were undertaken to obtain better controlled data in essentially the same situation.

6.1. *Practice and Free Sampling Rate (Experiment I)*

Each of six student subjects performed three trials, no restriction or cost being placed on the use of the inspection flaps other than the effort involved in lifting them, and with no other current activity. Under these conditions, with low sampling cost, operators might be expected to sample very frequently, as they did. However, the mean interval when the flap was left closed between observations increased significantly both within and between trials (see Table 1). Differences within trials reflect the initial stepwise approach to target that occurred in the first few minutes of each trial and the decrease of sampling rate in the first 15 minutes over trials was probably due to reduced uncertainty of control action as practice proceeded. In the second half of each trial there were few control actions, and here the decrease in sampling rate over trials probably reflects growing certainty that the system is not subject to spontaneous fluctuations.

The initially long duration of each observation and the large reduction of duration with practice were related to subjects' attempts to estimate the rate of change of temperature by direct observation. This is a relatively inefficient policy, since with such a slow system the difference between successive readings at a known interval gives more rate information than direct viewing, though

Table 1. Sampling intervals and practice in water bath temperature control (Experiment I)

Trial	15-minute period	Interval between inspection periods			Duration of inspections			Proportion of time spent looking at the thermometer	
		Mean (seconds)	s.d.	n	Mean (seconds)	s.d.	n	%	%
1	First	8.0	4.1	143	29.2	31.7	143	78.5	
	Second	10.4	4.9	146	25.2	24.5	145	71.0	74.7
2	First	10.9	6.5	159	23.5	19.9	158	68.2	
	Second	15.9	9.8	168	16.4	14.9	167	50.8	59.5
3	First	12.7	8.2	182	16.2	11.2	182	56.1	
	Second	19.1	14.1	164	14.0	10.4	163	42.2	49.2

Means for 6 subjects.

at greater cost in memory load and calculation. Subjects probably learned to adopt the latter more efficient policy with practice. However, even at the end of three trials they were taking nearly three times as long to read the thermometer (14 seconds) than to note the control setting (5 seconds). The precise reasons for adopting a particular sample duration need further study.

The reader may note that the minimum rate of about 1/3 sample per minute found in the earlier study was much lower than that of about two per minute found here. The difference can almost certainly be attributed to the fact that the subjective cost of sampling was higher in the former case when subjects were invited to read in their spare time during the experiment, than in the latter, when they had no alternative activity. Thus it seems desirable to exercise positive control over sampling 'cost' in future experiments.

In this study we found little evidence that any extra sampling was caused by forgetfulness, though in another study with the same system subjects have been found to forget system states within periods of the order of a minute (Cooke 1964a).

6.2. Sampling Interval and System State (Experiment I)

According to the uncertainty analysis, sampling intervals should be greater when the operator is more certain that the system will not drift outside permitted limits after he has withdrawn his attention. The occasions of opening the thermometer flap in the above experiment were therefore classified according to which of six possible states the system had been in at the time the flap was last closed and the corresponding intervals allotted to one of three groups (see Table 2).

Table 2. Sampling interval and system state in water bath temperature control (Experiment I)

Temperature rate of change	Middle half of permitted range (85·00 ± 0·25°C) Sampling intervals			Outer quarters of permitted range (84·50–84·74 and 85·26–85·50°C) Sampling intervals		
	Long %	Medium %	Short %	Long %	Medium %	Short %
Stationary (<0·1°/minute)	58	(38) (n=109)	4	33	(44) (n=43)	23
Slowly moving (0·6–2·9°/5 minute)	31	(56) (n=68)	13	22	(48) (n=54)	30
Quickly moving (>2·9°/5 minute)	9	(27) (n=22)	64	4	(11) (n=27)	85

Figures given are percentages of occasions on which the interval between the end of one observation and the beginning of the next was less than 9 seconds ('short'), 10–15 seconds ('medium') or more than 15 seconds ('long'), when the temperature at the beginning of the interval was in the condition stated in the margin.

For any given rate of change of temperature the subsequent sampling interval was found to be less, that is the sampling rate was increased, when the temperature was near either tolerance limit; and whether or not it was near the boundary, sampling rate decreased uniformly with rate of change of temperature. Both these findings are in line with the uncertainty analysis, whereas the sampling theorem does not predict any change in sampling rate with system state.

6.3. Control Performance under Restricted Sampling (Experiment II)

An experiment by Senders (1955a) on fast manual tracking showed that mean error increased when the percentage of time for which a display can be seen is reduced. This effect is predicted both by the sampling theorem and by the uncertainty analysis, and a further experiment was performed to confirm that it appears in slow process control as well as in fast tracking. Sixteen subjects were trained to a given performance criterion with unrestricted sampling, then divided randomly into four groups which performed two trials each with observation of the thermometer restricted to the periods shown in Table 3. Time-on-target was scored over successive periods of 5 minutes, and the averaged results are given in Table 3 and Figure 8.

Table 3. Control performance with restricted sampling in water bath temperature control (Experiment II)

Condition	Restriction		Time-on-Target	
	Interval between observations (seconds)	Duration of observation (seconds)	First 15 minutes %	Second 15 minutes %
A	Free*	Free	72·4	98·5
B	50	10	57·0	94·5
C	140	10	29·6	63·1
D	290	10	11·5	49·7

Figures given are mean times-on-target ($85 \pm \frac{1}{2}°C$) for 4 subjects, 2 trials each, expressed as percentages of the maximum possible time during the trial.

* Recorded mean interval = 15 seconds.

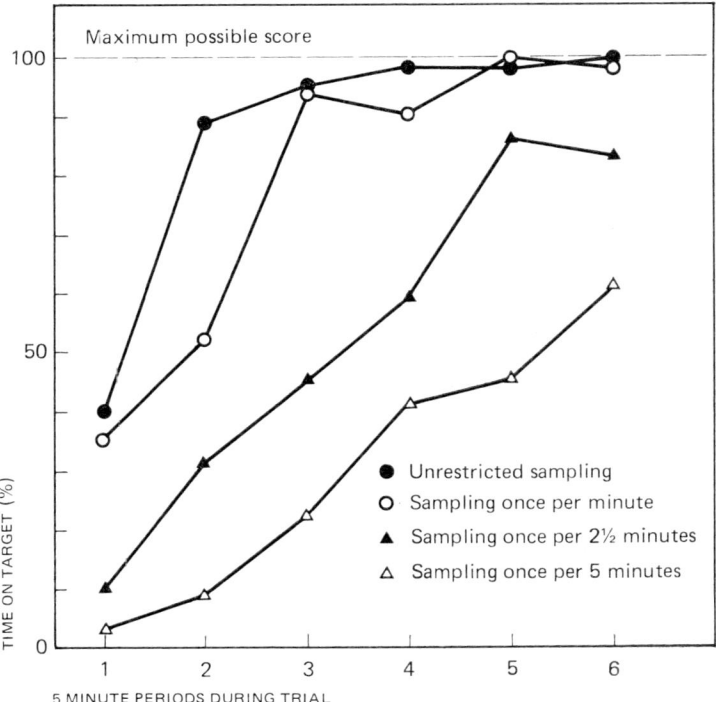

Figure 8. Water bath experiment II. Control performance under restricted sampling (see also Table 3).

Analysis of variance revealed statistically significant differences (at the 5% level or greater) between conditions and between first and second halves of each trial. As expected mean time-on-target increased through each trial and decreased with restricted sampling. Since the 50-second interval gave nearly, but not quite, as good results as the much shorter mean interval (15 seconds) chosen by subjects in free sampling, it would seem that a sample interval of slightly less than 50 seconds is optimum for the period of initial stepwise adjustment in this task. This rate agrees well with that predicted by the sampling theorem from the response lag of the system treated as a first-order control task, which was about 0·8 minute. Another way to restrict sampling rate would be by increasing its cost, and one might predict that the mean rate would be about one sample per minute during the first few minutes of each trial.

The half-hour duration of trials was too short for performance to reach the steady state in which very long sampling intervals would be expected, but by extrapolating the curves shown in Figure 8, it seems that 100% score might be reached after some 70–100 minutes. Once in a steady state, the results of industrial studies (see Section 5) suggest that mean sampling rate would be determined by the bandwidth of whatever random disturbance has amplitude sufficient to exceed the tolerance of $\pm 0.5°C$. Neither draughts nor changes in ambient air temperature nor supply voltage fluctuations were large enough for this and the only possible one seems to be the loss of water by evaporation, which caused a steady drift of some 0·40°C per minute. One might thus expect that a sampling rate as low as 5 per hour would be adequate, and the lowest enforced rate of 12 per hour in Experiment II should be more than adequate for 100% performance. Here again, further experiments extending over a much longer time are required to estimate the true minimum sampling rate.

7. Conclusions from the Field and Laboratory Studies

(1) The operator's basic minimum rate of sampling in the two process control tasks studied was determined by system bandwidth as predicted by Senders' application of the Shannon–Wiener sampling theorem, provided that account is taken of the allowed error tolerance by calculating an 'effective bandwidth'.

(2) However, a much more detailed analysis of factors contributing to the operator's uncertainty, its rate of growth over time, and the cost attached to sampling is needed to give even moderately accurate estimates of sampling rate in the various circumstances encountered when they rose above minimum.

(3) The problem of sampling could not be divorced from the more general problem of control, which in turn raised questions of required accuracy, cost of error, operator's knowledge of system structure, degree, type and predictability of disturbance, and effects of response lag.

(4) While forgetting was not positively identified as a cause of increased sampling rates, the data were consistent with this possibility.

(5) The data suggest the following empirical generalizations about sampling behaviour which agree fairly well with predictions from the uncertainty analysis given above (see Section 4):

    (a) When a variable is at its desired value and the system is correctly adjusted so that there is no residual drift due to small errors of control setting, the 'background' sampling rate is determined by the highest frequency component of random disturbance that has an *amplitude great enough to cause excursions exceeding the allowed tolerance*. This is the 'effective bandwidth' which the system presents to input noise.

(b) When a variable is within the specified range but the system is not quite correctly adjusted so that it tends to drift off, sampling rate is determined by rate of drift, and rises *when the variable is near either of the limits of its tolerance range*.

(c) When a variable is outside its tolerance band and the operator is making large stepwise control changes in an attempt to correct it, *a sample is taken after each control change at a time when response is expected to have reached some* 80% *of its final value*; if this sample is not followed by a further control change, one or two further samples are taken at similar intervals. Control changes whose effect is expected to be less than enough to exceed the tolerance range are not subject to this rule, which only applies when the operator is uncertain of the precise effect of control changes.

(d) Sampling rate rises whenever general observation of the system or its surroundings shows that anything unusual may be happening, even though it is not known to be relevant to the particular variable sampled.

(e) Operators may estimate the rate of change of a variable either by prolonged observation during one sample, or by remembering its value at one sample and comparing it with the next. In general they do not attempt to estimate higher derivatives.

8. A Procedure for System and Display Design

The basic fact that has become evident from these studies and from more general observations of process operator behaviour is that operators never pay continuous attention to a single display, nor do they divide their attention between displays according to a fixed periodic schedule. Instead they sample each variable or system state intermittently at a repetition rate judged from moment to moment to yield the best payoff in terms of information gained for the time and effort expended in observing, and the resulting pattern of division of attention fluctuates in a complicated way wherever two or more variables are being controlled at once, exhibiting wide variations of mean sampling rate according to current conditions in the system. Since anything less than continuous observation of each variable leaves some margin of ignorance, there is always a risk that significant changes of system state are being missed and that losses of efficiency or breakdown may occur; but on the other hand excessively frequent sampling represents an inefficient use of operator man-hours and hence low productivity.

The system designer presumably has to ensure that a satisfactory balance is struck between the two conflicting objectives of reduced risk and reduced operator work load, by determining the proper pattern and rate of sampling. But the operator cannot be forced to conform to a desired pattern since there is no way of strictly controlling his attention over more than short periods, and a solution can only be reached by enlisting his voluntary co-operation.

In other words, that sampling pattern which the designer decides is objectively optimum from the overall system viewpoint must be made to seem optimum from the operator's point of view, in terms of information gain for effort expended. In general, an adequate control of sampling behaviour is difficult for the designer to achieve and entails a quite fundamental appraisal of how and why information should flow in either direction across the man–machine interface in an actual or proposed system. In this paper we cannot enter on an extended discussion of the problem, but we will suggest a procedure for ensuring that the sampling problem is properly considered, first at the level of overall system design and second at that of detailed display design. In the first case the objective is to minimize the required sampling rate for each separate variable and to ensure that time-sharing is feasible between subtasks; and in the second, to minimize the ' cost ' to the operator of getting information about each variable or system state, to reduce his memory load, and to enforce a basic minimum sampling rate where this is deemed essential.

8.1. *System Design for Minimum Sampling*

Starting from the draft outline of a proposed man–machine system, the designer should first draw up a list of variables which together comprise a complete description of the current state of the system or process including all outputs and internal variables that the operator is ever likely to be interested in. Then each variable should be studied in turn, estimating and if possible reducing the frequency with which the operator will want to know its value in the various phases of operation by considering the determinants of sampling rate listed in Section 7. The analyst should note that not only quantities expressed in numerical form are variables but also factors assessed subjectively such as the state of a firebed or the turbulence of a liquid. The following five factors normally govern the sampling rate for a given variable:

(1) Its (true) *bandwidth*—roughly speaking the speed with which the system can permit the variable to change. This should be kept to the minimum needed to satisfy system performance requirements.

(2) The amplitude of any random disturbance or *noise* which may affect it. This again should be minimized as far as possible.

(3) Its *tolerance*—the latitude for variation about a desired value which is permissible without incurring a penalty for poor system performance. This will only be specified explicitly for the system outputs and perhaps for one or two major internal variables, but every variable has some tolerance range within which its variations can be disregarded. These should be ascertained, and where discretion exists assigned the maximum possible value.

Factors (1) to (3) together determine the effective bandwidth and hence the basic minimum sampling rate for the variable in question. If the tolerance exceeds the amplitude of random variation the required minimum sampling rate is zero, in which case the variable need not be displayed at all in normal operation; in other cases its operating salience during steady-running conditions can be gauged from the figure obtained, irrespective of the actual function or importance of the quantity in system operation. Two further factors may alter sampling rate under less general conditions.

(4) *Predictability* may further reduce the required rate during steady running. Operators can often forecast future system state changes from known patterns

of behaviour or from auxiliary information and where this occurs sampling can be less frequent. The designer's objective here should be to build in as much predictability as possible, by providing facilities such as graphic records for detecting patterns and in general he should take steps to ensure that the operator knows concretely what will happen next as much of the time as possible.

(5) *Control calibration*—sampling rate is increased whenever the operator makes control adjustments, because a variable's response to changes of a relevant control setting is imperfectly predictable (though the response must of course be predictable to some extent if the setting is to serve as a control). Calibrated controls minimize the extra sampling by reducing uncertainty and incidentally improve control efficiency so that calibration should be provided wherever possible. However, the accuracy of calibration need be no better than that required to bring the variable within tolerance. Since there is always a time lag in response to control action, the calibration will usually refer to the asymptotic value resulting after some specified waiting period has elapsed, provided that no further changes are made meanwhile. More sophisticated forms of calibration, such as the display ' quickening ' advocated by Birmingham and Taylor (1954), incorporate means of computing the response to arbitrary patterns of control action and these are ideal where they can be economically justified but much more often a graph or table of figures giving the steady-state response to various possible control changes is all that is needed. Lack of control calibration is probably the biggest single cause of inefficiency in manual process control, and it can be a most difficult facility for the designer to provide.

Once the sampling rates have been minimized for all the system state variables taken separately by scrutinizing factors (1) to (5) above and the expected rates in various phases of operation have been estimated, the designer should assess the proportion of the operator's time required for sampling each with the proposed displays and hence calculate a total work load. If this exceeds 100%, either the observation times must be reduced by better display design or sampling rates must be reduced still further, or more than one operator will be required. The work load is likely to vary widely in different phases of operation and clearly the worst case should be considered first as this determines the number of operators required. At this stage the analysis of work load entailed in sampling merges into straightforward work measurement and standard techniques can be applied.

The possibility should also be examined that control action taken to adjust one variable may react on others and cause increased sampling requirements. This is a fruitful source of overload and it can be overcome either by securing independence of control actions or by calibrating the side effects of controls.

8.2. *An Illustrative Example*

An instance of a relatively new man–machine system which appears to violate some of the design principles given above is the flight director system proposed for certain modern aircraft. Here the multiple displays, such as visual contact with the ground and pointer instruments which the pilot normally uses to fly a self-determined course, are replaced by a single circular display in which a spot or circle—the ' target '—represents the demanded orientation of the aircraft in the pitch and yaw axes, and a larger fixed circle—the 'marker'—represents its actual orientation. The pilot's task is to keep the target in the centre of the marker by suitable control action and he thus acts in a purely error-actuated control mode, performing a 'compensatory' tracking task; it is claimed that this minimizes his work load and maximizes his control performance.

By applying the above design procedure to pitch and yaw considered as system state variables, it can be seen that this display-control arrangement requires a sampling rate which is greatly increased over that obtaining in normal 'contact' or instrument flying, because

(1) Tolerance is left unspecified and its effective value is almost certainly small since the pilot has no means of telling what a given deviation 'costs' in terms of loss of efficiency or other penalty.

(2) Predictability is reduced because the normal auxiliary information as to aircraft behaviour is completely lost; where rate aiding is used the position is even worse, because this confounds error and error rate information.

(3) Control is exercised through a high-order system and no calibration is provided. The pilot probably cannot learn the control-display relationship with sufficient accuracy and his uncertainty is thus increased whenever he takes control action. These considerations together suggest that sampling rate will be much higher than the effective bandwidth of the system as determined by noise, bandwidth and tolerance really requires. One would predict that pilots would find it difficult to detach their attention from a director display to attend to their other subtasks since when they did so they would experience immediate gross uncertainty. If the pilot had only the central tracking task to perform the system would be feasible, but since there are many other demands on his time the sampling analysis would dismiss the flight director as an essentially inefficient type of man–machine interface in this particular system.

8.3. *Display Design*

Once the required sampling rates and tolerances have been ascertained for all the system state variables, the designer must ensure that the displays provided permit the operator to attain them with minimum expenditure of time and effort. Ergonomics specialists are already familiar with the general principles of display design needed to achieve this and no further emphasis need be placed on this aspect of the sampling problem except to point out that getting to a display may be a major factor in the 'cost' of sampling. Certain less familiar means of improving sampling efficiency may also be worth considering in selected cases:

(1) *Memorability of displayed data.* Since extra sampling is entailed if the operator forgets the value of a variable before he would strictly need to check it again, some thought should be given to making the different display variables 'memorable'. This is best done by giving each a distinctively different format to minimize the chance of mental confusion between them. Qualitatively-assessed variables such as the state of a firebed are unlikely to be confused with numerical readings such as steam pressures, but it is common to find

several numerical variables expressed in the same range of numbers and hence subject to mutual confusion. Quite simple devices can be used to overcome this defect, such as scaling one quantity in tens and another in hundreds, or using meters of different shapes, under the guiding principle that no two system state variables should be displayed to the operator in the same units on the same type of instrument. The search for distinctiveness tends, it is true, to destroy the symmetry and uniformity of layout which is desirable on aesthetic grounds and some compromise may evidently be required to secure layouts which are visually attractive as well as operable.

(2) *Operator-controlled devices for maintaining desired sampling rates.* The duration of a given sampling interval is normally determined by the operator's own internal time sense, which is known to be influenced by a number of internal factors and may be confused by other activities; thus he may sample a variable sooner or later than he intends because he has misjudged the time since he last observed it. Where this could have serious effects it may be worth while to install a resetting clock coupled to an attention-getting device so that the operator can arrange, so to speak, to warn himself when the display next needs attention. The recall signal may be auditory, such as a buzzer, or visual, such as a light shining on the instrument, and it should remain on until the operator has observed the display and reset the clock. A basic minimum sampling rate can be ensured by setting an upper limit on the length of recall interval that the operator can select.

(3) *Rate estimation.* Sampling is frequently concerned with estimating the rate of change of a variable by means of observations repeated at a set interval, the rate being assessed by the change that has occurred in a given time. This imposes a direct memory load on the operator, who has to remember the first value accurately in order to compare it with a second one later; and if he forgets the first value he must start again. Some form of built-in memory device such as a resettable cursor, or a means of writing down values at the time of observation, will abolish the memory load. It is also desirable to provide a means of indicating time elapsed since the value was recorded. These requirements are automatically met by a graphic recorder, but careful thought should be given to paper speed and scale magnification so that the operator can easily obtain accurate estimates of rate of change. The operator should be able to select two or more chart speeds to cater for both transient and steady-running conditions.

(4) *Indications of tolerance range.* Sampling rate is markedly dependent on tolerance, and the operator should always be able to ascertain rapidly whether a given variable is anywhere near its tolerable limits. Since these limits themselves vary according to current running conditions, they should be displayed in the same format as the variable itself and be capable of adjustment, for instance by a movable marker or coloured bands, on a pointer instrument, which the operator can reset as conditions change. It is not usually possible for the designer to specify tolerances once for all, as they are conditional on current requirements.

9. Needs for Further Research on Sampling Behaviour

The above conclusions and the suggested design procedure have unavoidably been based on incomplete evidence, since very few laboratory or field studies of attention and sampling behaviour in the literature refer at all directly to situations of common occurrence in practical man–machine systems. We urgently need further field studies of patterns of attention and sampling in operational systems preferably with highly skilled operators. The pattern of attention to displays should be recorded over long periods in specified phases of system operation, and wherever possible the observed sampling rates should be analyzed in relation to the predictability and subjective uncertainty of the variables sampled. Further questions for field study are the amount and type of forgetting to which operators are subject and the extent to which confusion between system state variables tends to cause it; the accuracy of time estimation and its relation to bandwidth as it affects sampling; the effects of operator uncertainty of a systems response to control action; and the effects of increased or reduced sampling ' cost '.

At a laboratory level it should be possible to test the hypothesis that individual sampling intervals and mean sampling rate are governed by the rate of increase of uncertainty directly by obtaining judgments from subjects of the likelihood that a system is in each of a number of possible states, at a series of intervals after it has last been observed. The results could be analyzed to determine the time course of the growth of uncertainty after sampling, and its dependence on system bandwidth and ' noise '. This should lead directly to the elaboration of what may be termed an informational theory of attention, which could have applications in fields other than process control. It is also desirable to investigate the effect of ' cost ' on sampling rate in relation to expected penalty for error, and hence to test whether each act of sampling is really determined by a calculation of probable payoff, as the uncertainty analysis suggests.

The authors wish to thank the management of Wolvercote Paper Mill for providing the facilities for field study and also the operators who collaborated in the study; Professor R. C. Oldfield, Director of the Institute of Experimental Psychology, provided laboratory facilities; the research was financed by the Human Sciences Committee of the Department of Scientific and Industrial Research and by the British Iron and Steel Research Association.

Manual Control of Slow-Response Systems

By E. R. F. W. CROSSMAN and J. E. COOKE

Institute of Experimental Psychology, Oxford University

1. Introduction

Many recent studies arising out of a need to understand the human operator's characteristics, if he is to be effectively integrated into a man–machine system, have been concerned with the behaviour of the human operator as a controller of mechanical and electronic systems such as guns, aircraft and fast-acting machinery. The operator's task in this kind of situation, generically known as tracking, is to follow a target by the use of a manual control which actuates a controlled member giving an output. If the target can be seen moving, the task is known as *pursuit* tracking, whereas in *compensatory* tracking only the error, that is the discrepancy between desired and actual output, is displayed. The usual laboratory method of evaluating performance is by analysis of the output as a function error, both being expressed as continuous function of time, and attempts have been made to establish a 'human transfer function' (North 1952, Sheridan 1960). The statistical approach, regarding input, output and error as informational (stochastic) variables has been attempted (Crossman 1960c) and it is apparent from the results that performance cannot be adequately expressed in terms of any single transfer function, since the operator may respond in complicated ways using pattern perception and apparently predicting his own response characteristics (Poulton 1957). What is needed in order to set up a theoretical model seems to be a fairly detailed analysis of the response to particular types of input, such as impulse, step and ramp functions, but little has been done on these lines.

So far all the work on manual control has employed systems having response times from small fractions of a second to a few seconds at most, so that the operator is exercising a manual skill without conscious deliberation. But many control tasks in industry and elsewhere involve systems of much slower response; for instance, the operator in a papermill has to adjust the machine to produce paper of a specified thickness, keep it running to this specification in the face of variations of raw material and other working conditions and adjust it to a new desired thickness in between runs. His errors in making these adjustments are reflected in loss of product and of machine production time, which may be of substantial economic importance. The response of paper thickness to a change of a particular control setting, such as the rate of pulp flow, has a time constant of about three minutes and the time taken to receive information back as to the thickness of the finished paper is about two minutes. Chemical and metallurgical processes involving heat transfer may have time constants measured in hours and, at the other end of the scale, those of some heavy aircraft are measured in tens of seconds. In all these cases an operator can exercise adequate control after a period of learning, but there is some evidence to suggest that manual operation of these slower systems may be far from perfect (Sell, Crossman and Box 1962). The use of contemporary types of automatic controls is not a complete solution because there are many cases to which they cannot be applied and it is also clear that human operators can perform substantially better than automatic controls in certain cases.

It would be of interest to know how human beings learn to control slow-response systems, to enable the operator's performance to be improved by design of equipment and by suitable training and also possibly to reveal the basis on which future more sophisticated automatic control systems could be designed. The laboratory work described below arose out of observations on process operators in industry (Crossman 1960a) and the results are now being used for the purposes mentioned as well as to guide further field studies.

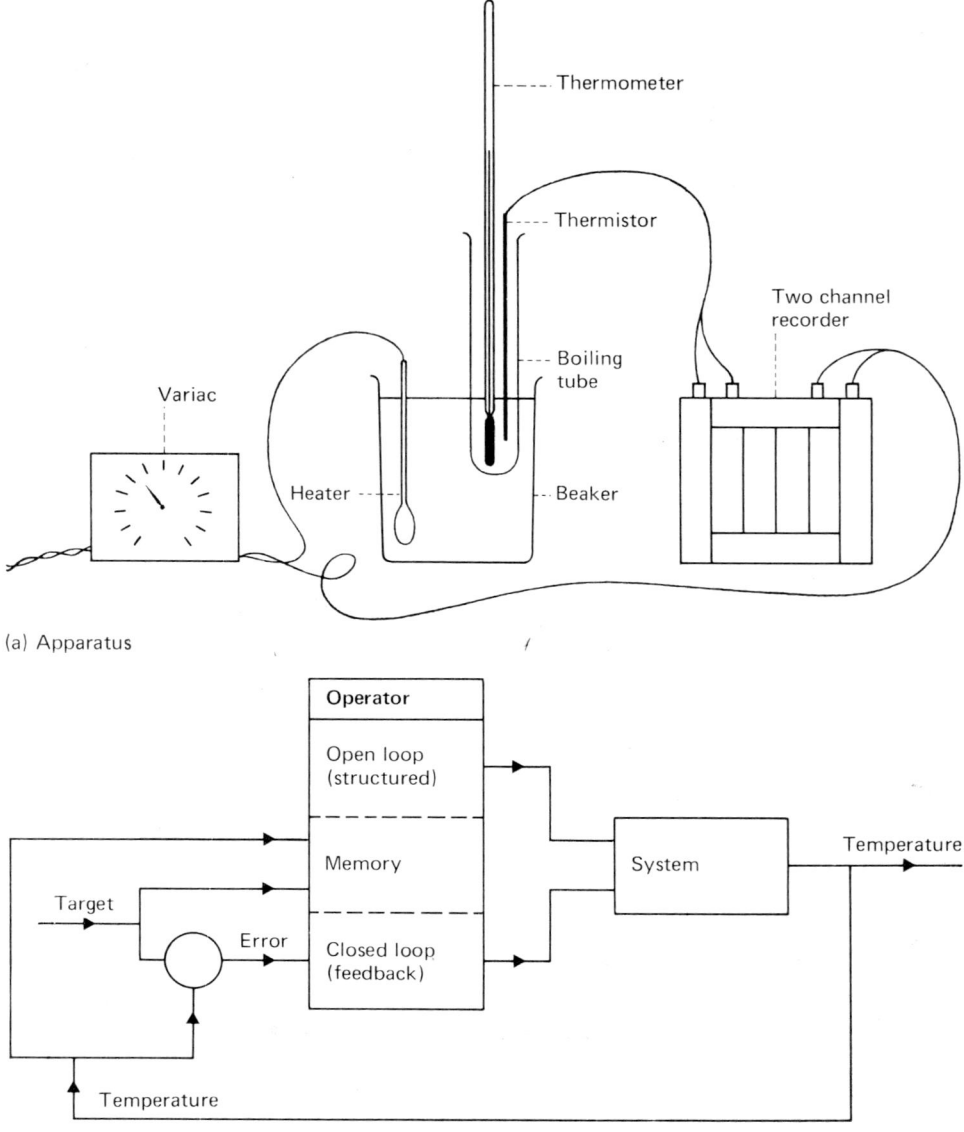

(a) Apparatus

(b) Block diagram of operator and system

Figure 1.

2. Experimental Method

We devised a laboratory task (Figure 1) having many of the features met with in the typical industrial process control situation. A beaker of water was supplied with an electric heating coil, connected to a variable transformer (0 to 200 volts) fed from the a.c. main supply; the temperature of the water was measured by an ordinary mercury thermometer with graduations of 1/10th degree and subjects were asked to bring the temperature up from a standard starting point (70°C) to a given target value (usually 85°C) and maintain it at this value for a given period (usually half-an-hour). They were allowed plus or minus half a degree tolerance and their errors were scored as r.m.s. deviation from the target value. Both temperature and voltage settings were recorded continuously on a pen-writer not visible to the subject. This was the standard (S) condition; in a more difficult version (the L condition) the thermometer bulb was surrounded by a boiling tube full of water, which gave a response time constant of about two minutes; in still another case (the DL condition) a test tube was placed inside the boiling tube to give a second smaller lag.

Subjects were introduced to the apparatus with a minimum of explanation and any comments they volunteered were recorded but no attempt was made to interrogate them while the experiment was in progress. At the end of their period of practice, all subjects answered a questionnaire designed to find out as much as possible about their understanding of the system in relation to their performance.

3. General Features of Control Performance

The normal adult subject can exercise adequate control almost from the beginning in the S condition (see Figure 2a). There is a certain amount of hunting up and down to find the right control setting but thereafter it may be left for periods up to 10 minutes. On successive trials, the period of initial hunting diminishes and a well-practised subject may make only three or four control changes in half-an-hour. The frequency of observation of the thermometer also falls rapidly both within the first trial and from trial to trial (see Figure 3).

In the L condition (see Figure 2b) subjects experienced more difficulty in achieving stability. Some managed to do so within the first trial (in 20 minutes or so) but others went on for five or six trials without managing to suppress the initial oscillation of temperature. During this initial period, the temperature typically swung two or three degrees above and below the target in a cycle with a period of five to ten minutes, and the control settings also varied in the same way but in opposite phase. With increasing experience, subjects reduced the amplitude of oscillation and also lengthened the period, finally achieving stability at about the same settings as were required in the S condition. Highly practised subjects in the L condition could also manage with very few control changes. The extra lag introduced by the small test tube in the DL condition increased the amount and duration of hunting.

Two factors determining performance were studied in more detail.

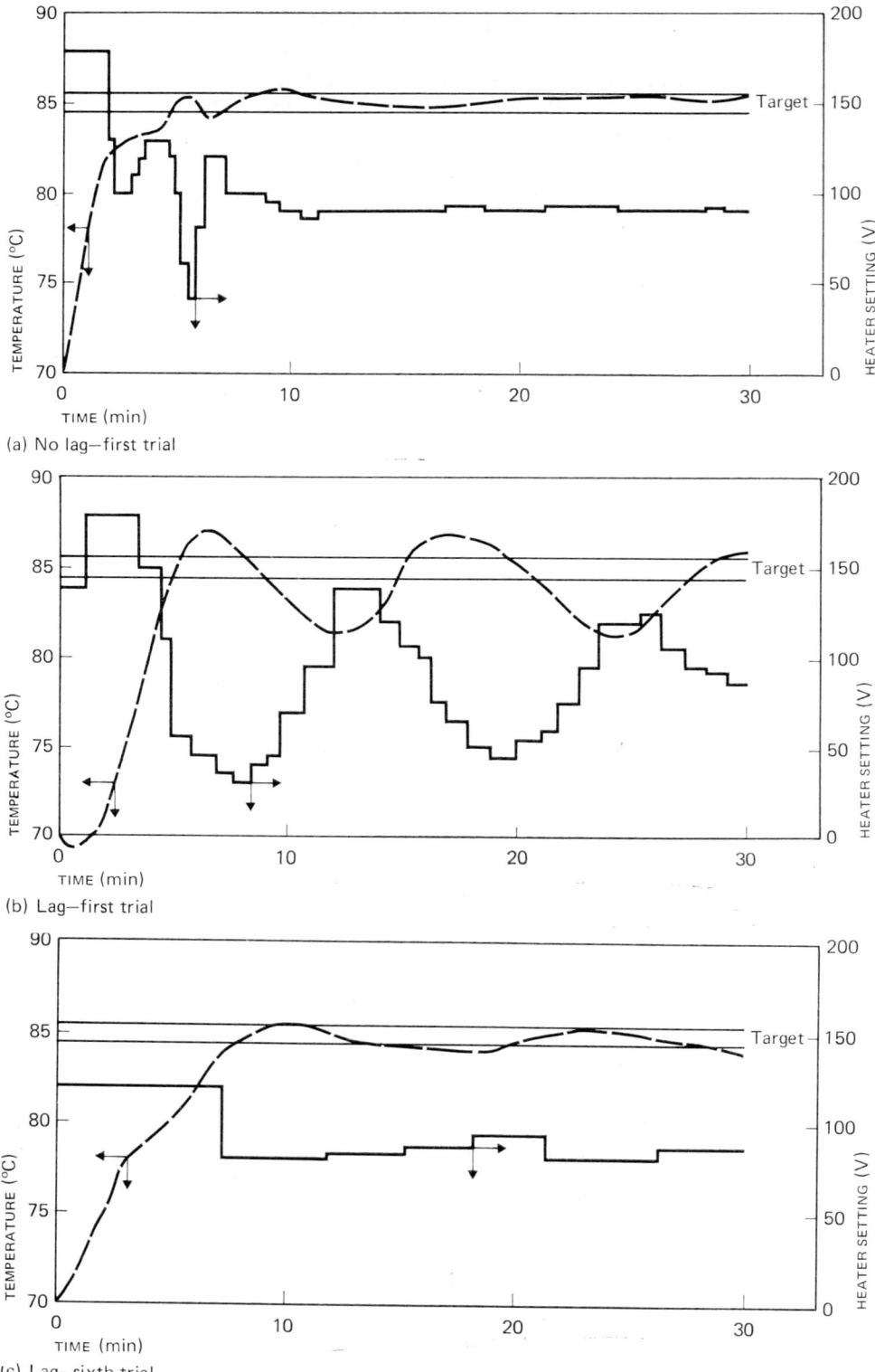

Figure 2.

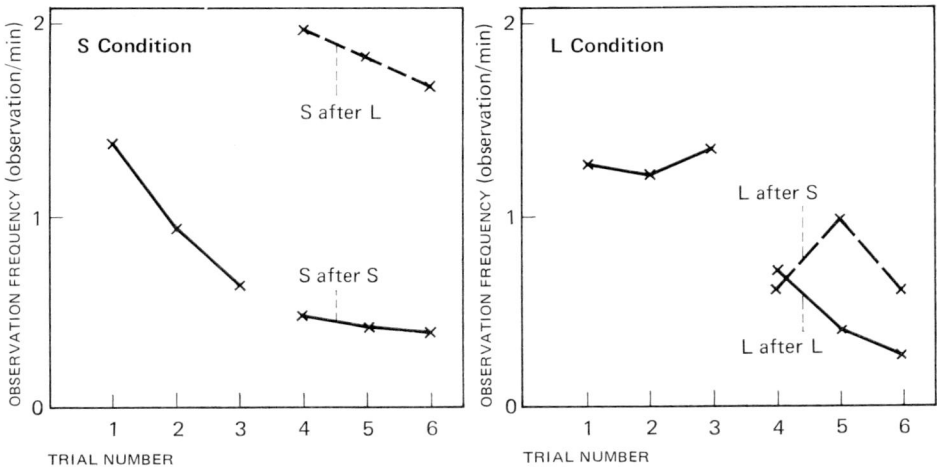

Figure 3. Mean frequency of observations.

3.1. *The Effect of Conditions of Practice*

To study the transfer of skill, *i.e.* the effect of having learned the difficult condition on performance in the easy one and *vice versa*, eight subjects carried out two sets of three half-hour trials each under conditions S, L; L, S; S, S; and L, L. The graph of r.m.s. error for the last 20 minutes of each trial (see Figure 4a) shows that initial performance was much worse in the L condition but improved to about the same level as in S and that transfer from S to L was moderate, from L to S very high. The number of control changes per minute (see Figure 4b) shows marked diminution in both conditions, but those who did L first used more control changes in the latter half of the experiment than those who did S first, which may be correlated with their relatively lower error score. The frequencies of observation (see Figure 3)

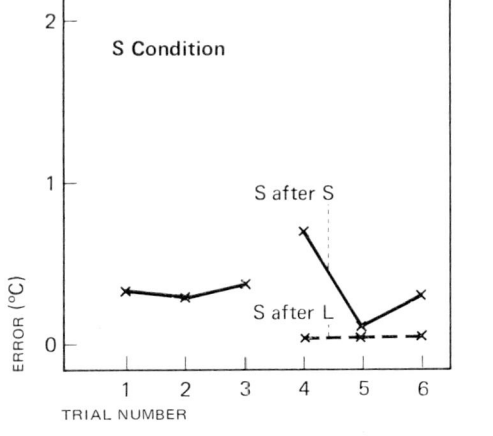
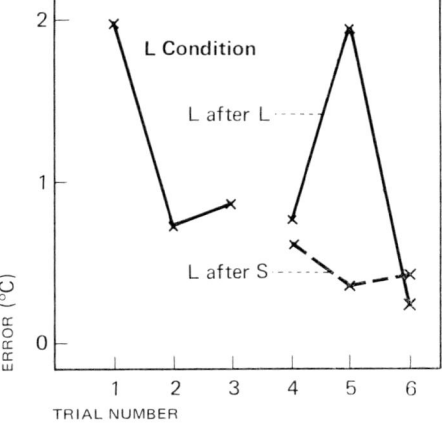

(a) Mean r.m.s. error

Figure 4a.

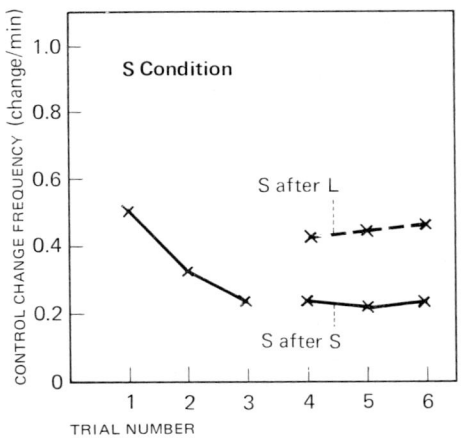 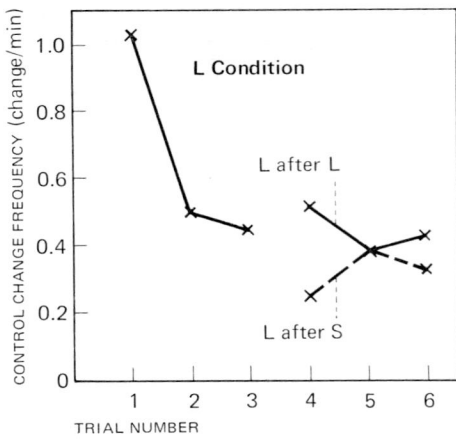

(b) Number of control changes

Figure 4b.

show a similar picture to that of control changes, but again those who did the L condition first made very markedly more observations than those who did S first. Thus it seems that transfer from a difficult control task to an easy one is likely to be better than *vice versa*. We can also conclude that where error is small, either frequency of control changes or frequency of observations can be used (inversely) to assess an operator's skill.

3.2. *The Effect of Instructions*

A further experiment was carried out to compare the value of different types of prior instruction on performance. A group given a scientific account of the manner in which heat was transferred from heating coil to water resulting in a change of temperature, performed markedly worse than one told simply what voltage settings were likely to produce what temperatures and roughly how much lag was to be expected. This result casts some doubt on the value of the widespread practice of instructing process plant operators in the elements of chemistry and physics.

4. Analysis of Control Behaviour

We were not able to extract much information from subjects' verbal accounts of their control behaviour or thought processes, except to show that there was very little conscious decision-making in connection with control changes. Most of the remarks were of the type " Yes, I think it's about time it should go up now " and " I seem to find 82 is quite a good setting ". One or two subjects initially expected to find a lag in the system but they were not at all clear about what caused it or how long it might be expected to be. Lacking direct information about the manner in which subjects make control decisions, therefore, we had to fall back on examining the detailed relationship between control behaviour and the current situation. The first question to be answered was to what extent control changes were influenced simply by the error and its rate of change.

Control setting could obviously not be treated as a straightforward continuous variable, since large changes were made at relatively long intervals, but when oscillations of large amplitude were taking place, as happened in early trials in the L condition, the successive settings could be smoothed into a nearly sinusoidal curve. A preliminary study (see Figure 5) of the error and its rate of change at instants when control actions were being made showed that

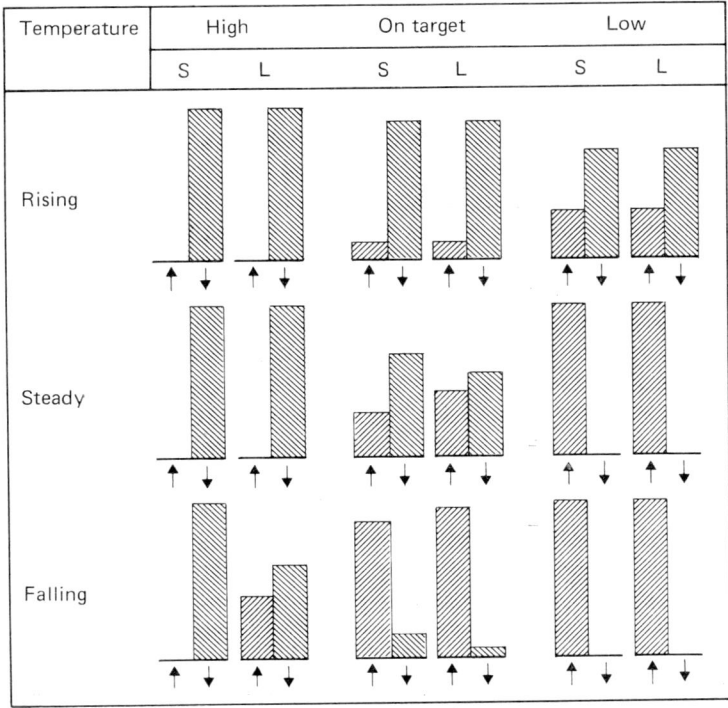

Figure 5. Histogram of percentage control changes up or down.

both of them entered into the determination of the direction and size of change; certain of the records were then subjected to multiple regression analysis, taking samples at half-minute intervals, with trials divided into 15-minute blocks (see Figure 6). At first there was a moderate negative correlation between control changes and temperature, tending to diminish, and a slightly higher one with rate of change of temperature, which also decreased. However, the highest multiple correlation of control setting on temperature and rate of change was only 0·77, so that there must have been some other partial determinant of control setting. The second derivative of temperature appeared to exert almost no effect on the decisions.

Thus one can approximately describe the performance of the human operator of a slow-response system such as this, at least in early trials on a fairly difficult task, by a transfer function with changing parameters; but on later trials, and from the beginning in easy tasks, the approximation becomes very poor and a different model is required. Examining the records of subjects asked to alternate between one temperature and another (see Figure 7a) it seemed that experienced subjects made large control changes according to a regular pattern with subsequent relatively small corrections, and from their subjective reports it was clear that they were making use of their knowledge of the absolute settings required to achieve different conditions. To check this point, subjects were asked to do the same task without being able to see the thermometer at all, that is, under 'open-loop' conditions (see Figure 7b). They were able to perform substantially better than chance and their sequence of control settings showed that they had a distinct idea of the size and timing of control changes required to effect the desired temperature changes. Comparison with the records from the 'closed-loop' condition (see Figure 7a) suggested that the

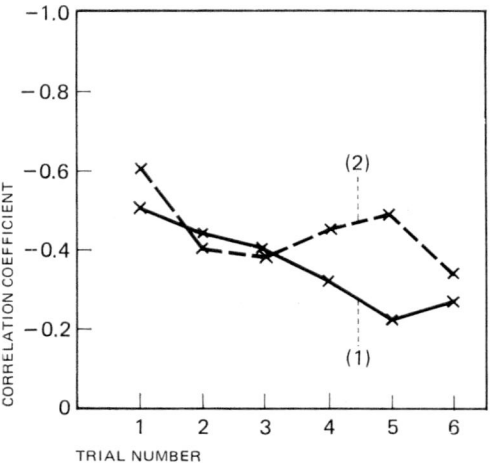

Figure 6. Correlation coefficient against trial numbers of (1) Control change with temperature and (2) Control change with rate of change of temperature.

latter could be seen as a combination of an open-loop 'structure' on to which had been superimposed small corrections for error. At an intermediate stage of practice before a fully structured pattern of action becomes possible, subjects seem to insert small elements of 'open-loop' behaviour into an otherwise 'closed-loop' performance. For instance, when they wish to correct a small steady error, they may use a short burst of maximum (or zero) control setting, which produces a drift in the desired direction.

The use of (non-random) open-loop behaviour implies that the subject must possess information, derived either from his previous experience of similar situations, which seems usually to be minimal, or from memories of the behaviour of the system in earlier trials. An important question arises how exactly does the subject reduce the large amount of detailed observation, which in principle he could store, process, and use later, to proportions manageable with his actual limited memory capacity? Further study of recorded behaviour seemed unlikely to answer this question directly, and we resorted to the more powerful but circuitous method of computer simulation.

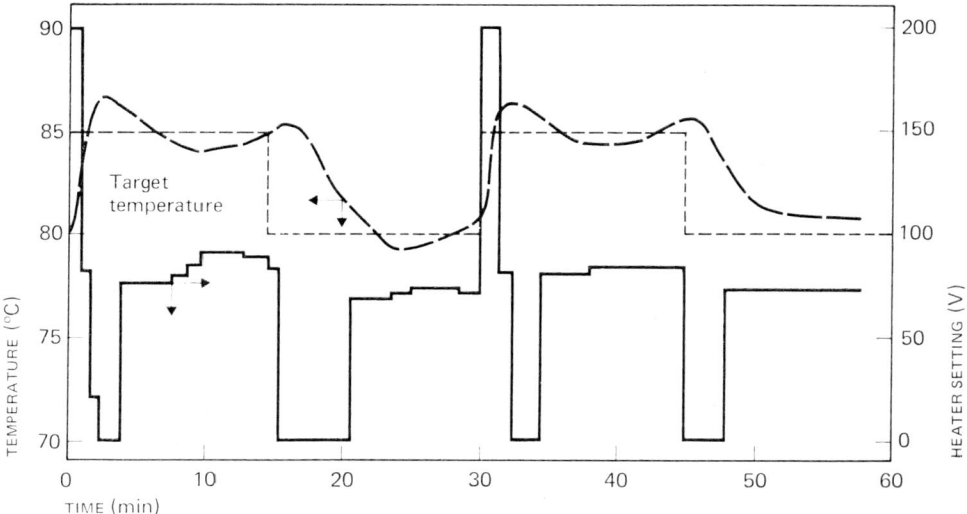
(a) Square wave with closed loop

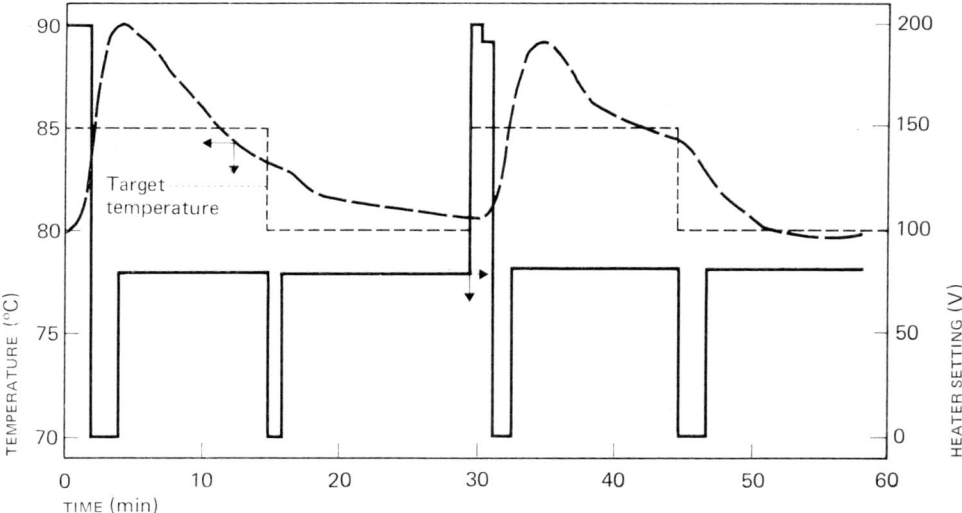
(b) Square wave with open loop

Figure 7.

5. Approaches to Computer Simulation Studies

The pioneer work of Newell, Shaw and Simon (1958) has shown that a synthetic approach to the study of thought processes gives more insight than direct analysis. Being unable to find out exactly how a subject solves a particular problem by asking him, one can instead attempt to construct a mechanism, usually a program for a digital computer, to solve the same problem from the same starting point and within the same limitations, for example of storage capacity and input discrimination, as the human subject. According to Turing's criterion, if a human judge is unable to distinguish between the performance of the machine, and the performance of a human subject, the machine may be regarded to a first order of approximation as a valid representation of the human behaviour.

It is first necessary to define the problem that the subject is trying to solve in precise terms, and then construct a program to solve it. Newell, Shaw and Simon (1958), Kochen (1961), Feigenbaum (1961), and others have done this for verbal and symbolic problems, but we do not know of any comparable approach to non-symbolic problems or ones requiring active output on the part of the subject. In our case, the problem is external, but to avoid connecting the computer directly to the apparatus, the system transfer function is incorporated as a subroutine in the main program, and one cycle, representing 20 seconds of real time, comprises a decision routine resulting in a new voltage setting, followed by a calculation of the temperature. The system subroutine uses empirical tables of heat input rate against voltage and heat loss against temperature for the main vessel, and of the response of the boiling tube and thermometer to a unit heat impulse at various temperatures. Voltage settings and temperatures are printed out at selected intervals, usually one minute.

We have not yet tested any true learning programs, and have been studying the effect of linear feedback applied to make control changes at discrete time intervals in ways characteristic of the naive normal adult. It has become apparent that no amount of manipulation of the parameters in a linear feedback system can duplicate the performance of a normal adult subject, but the results do bear a striking resemblance to the performance of some medium-grade mental defectives tested in a local institution. The following types of feedback transfer function have been tried, using always the lag condition.

5.1. *Control Changes Proportional to Error*

$$(V_n - V_{n-1}) = A(T_n - T_g) \qquad (1)$$

where

V_n = Voltage setting for the nth cycle

T_n = Temperature at beginning of the nth cycle

T_g = Target temperature.

The loop transfer function for this feedback has effectively three derivative terms in tandem, and should produce sustained oscillation if A exceeds a certain value. The output showed the expected behaviour (see Figure 8a) and the records from selected mental defectives are shown for comparison (see Figure 8b). The amplitude of oscillation is limited by boiling and the off position.

5.2. *Control Changes Proportional to Error plus Rate of Change of Error*

$$(V_n - V_{n-1}) = A'(T_n - T_g) + B(T_n - T_{n-1}) \qquad (2)$$

The derivative term could, as theoretically expected, be used to stabilize the system, producing exponential approach or decaying oscillation (see Figures 9a and 9b); some defectives gave similar records.

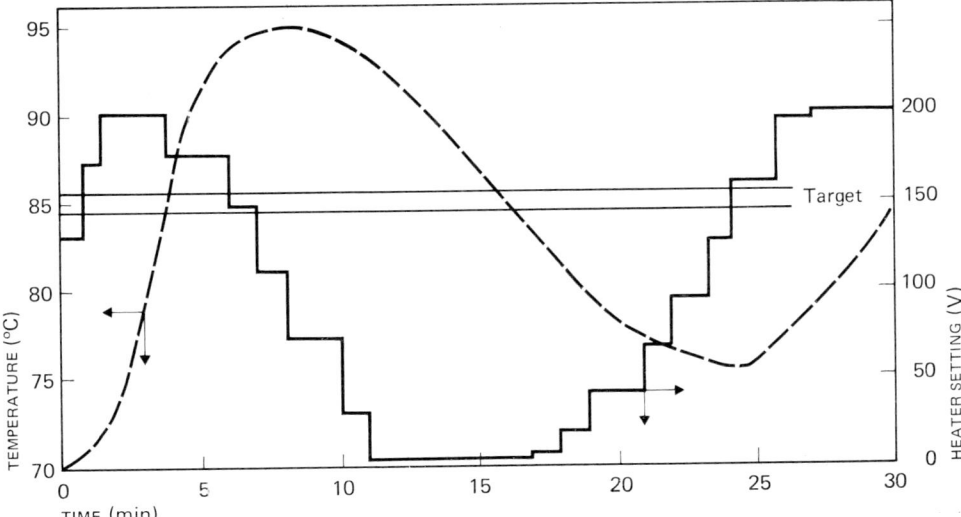
(a) Computer simulation. Proportional feedback only

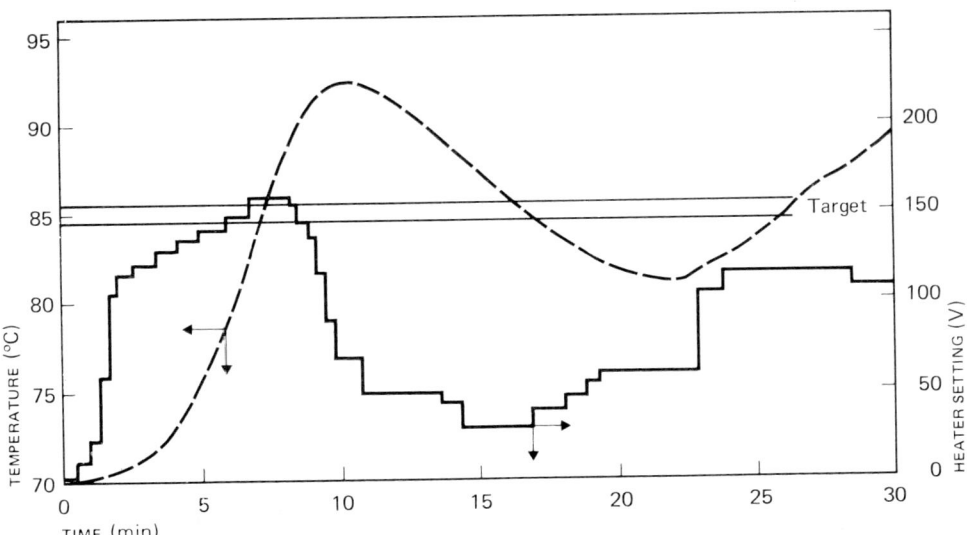
(b) Performance by medium-grade mental defective

Figure 8.

5.3. *As in 5.2. with Exponentially Decreasing Gain*

$$(V_n - V_{n-1}) = [A''(T_n - T_g) + B'(T_n - T_{n-1})] \exp(-Cn). \tag{3}$$

This feedback can give results like those of a slightly underdamped system but without need for critical adjustment of parameters. Figure 10 shows a simulation record compared with that of a normal adult on his first attempt. While the records look alike, the machine becomes insensitive to error, nor does it improve further on later attempts, so the simulation is only successful to a limited extent.

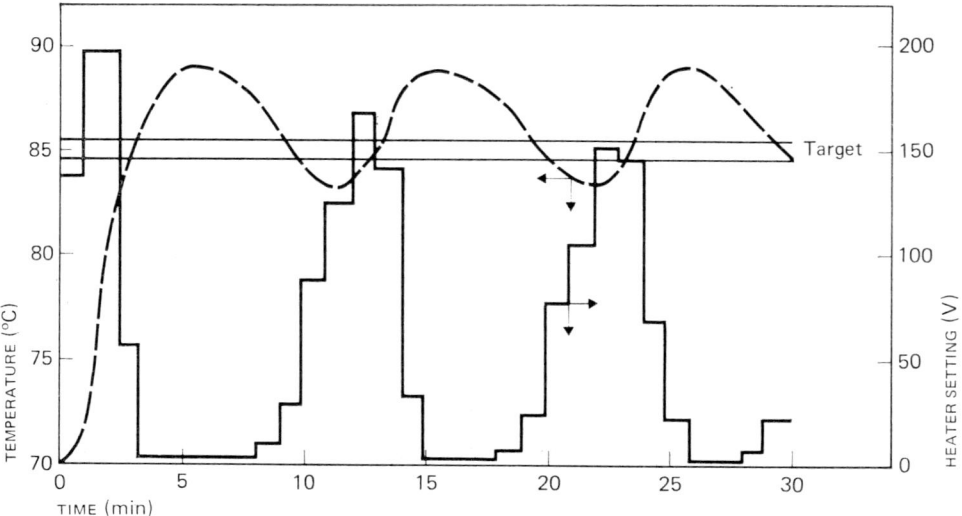

(a) Computer simulation. Proportional plus derivative feedback

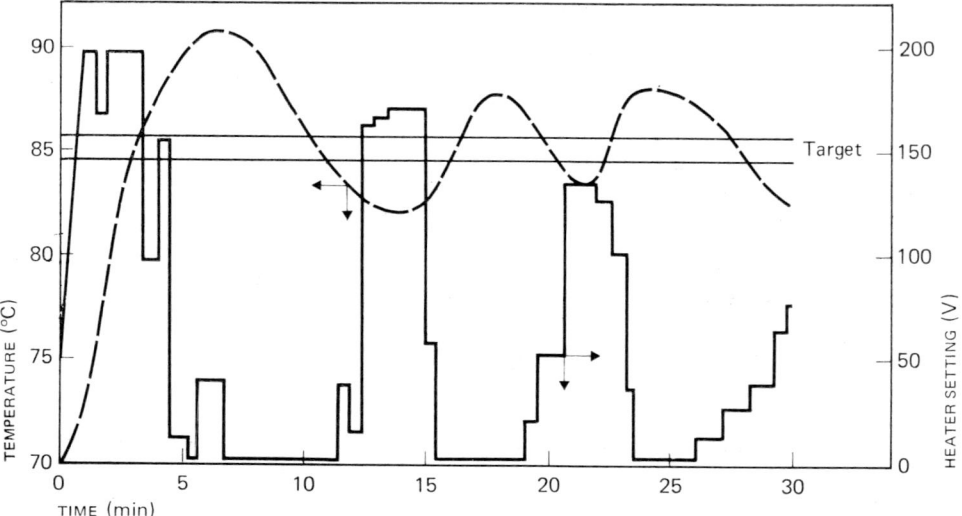

(b) Performance by high-grade mental defective

Figure 9.

From the simulation studies so far it seems that however the parameters are chosen, a linear feedback system cannot show behaviour like that of the practised adult subject, though it may be comparable to a new beginner or a subject of low intelligence. Beginners show only a brief phase of ' simple ' closed-loop behaviour, followed rapidly by something different which cannot be described in these terms. In the long run behaviour is always actuated by error, but the simple feedback model ceases to be appropriate, and one must consider how open-loop control could be exercised.

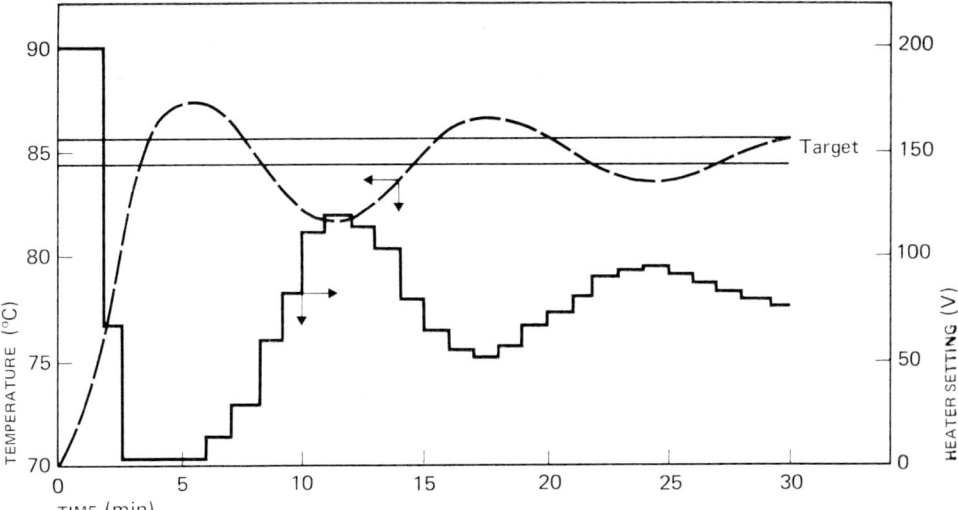

(a) Computer simulation. Proportional and derivative feedback with exponentially decreasing gain

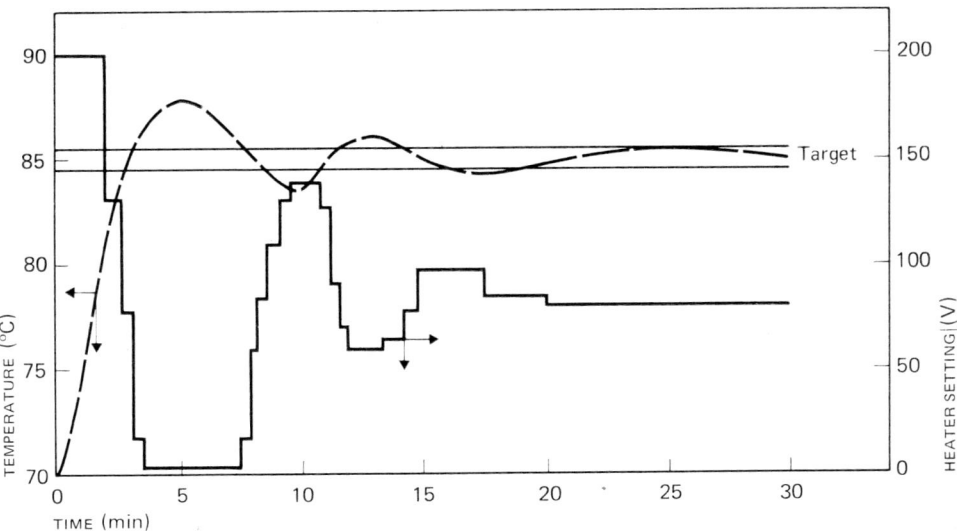

(b) Performance on first trial by good normal subject

Figure 10.

6. Open-Loop Control Strategies

It is difficult and not particularly useful to define precisely the difference between closed- and open-loop control (see Figure 1). The distinction lies in the relative weight given to contemporary information from the system in determining a control setting. In closed-loop it is used exclusively and in the pure open-loop mode it would be ignored in favour of historical data, but actual human operators consider the present state and past behaviour of the system (and of other similar systems) together, in some fairly complex way. For the present purpose we may say that action based on information from a time more remote than the longest system time constant, is open-loop control, for the data used are then independent of the present situation. We will now consider how historical information about the system's behaviour can be economically retained and used.

6.1. *Simple Scale Setting*

We have observed that the most useful single piece of information about the system (the thing most often stated in response to questions about the task) was the scale setting needed to maintain a desired temperature, and in experiments with changing goal temperatures the appropriate settings for each were also learnt. A simple form of open-loop behaviour consists then in simply re-setting the control to the value known to lead ultimately to the required temperature. This is inefficient because the time taken to reach the correct temperature is very long and only one or two subjects ever actually attempted this method. The required setting can be found in several ways, by the initial use of a decreasing gain approach, as described above, or by trying a series of settings in some sort of organized scan pattern, both of which involve initial closed-loop behaviour, or by interpolation from known values, which implies earlier experience.

6.2. *Known Settings with Optimized Approach Pattern*

A new goal can be reached more quickly by putting the control fully on for a given time, then off for another given time (or *vice versa*), and finally leaving it on the setting appropriate for the goal temperature. The times have presumably to be learnt by experience of the system. In trials with periodic changes of target but no access to the thermometer, practised subjects achieved surprisingly good results (see Figures 7a and 7b). It would seem that they construct a pattern of action for themselves progressively by matching the goal which they wish to reach against the probable effects of the control actions open to them. Error feedback is employed by the practised subject to tidy up the fine details of performance rather than to set the overall pattern.

7. Possibilities for a Heuristic Decision Program

The problem facing a naive subject (or program) has several aspects to it: he does not know what effect the control will have, or how much time lag there is, or what degree of random fluctuation there will be. A heuristic program should ideally be able to start from the beginning and manipulate the system in such a way as to gain the necessary information without at the same time losing control of the system. To some extent the strategy needed to gain information, and hence to improve future control, is in conflict with that needed to achieve good control at the present. For instance, observing the results of a single change over a longish period, say two minutes, would provide useful information for the future but might involve too much error.

The heuristic program must have an overall goal but also a number of sub-goals which it can attempt as stages on the road. At the start, for example, the sub-goal might be to make the temperature go up. Several actions are possible and a completely uninformed beginner must try these at random. As soon as some experience of the system has accumulated it can be used to predict the effects of each possible control action and select that which is most likely to arrive at the current sub-goal. The program could therefore have a recursive loop which would successively change the setting (or a dummy value) either at random or according to a scan pattern, predict each outcome and stop when one is found compatible with the current sub-goal.

A principle is also needed to determine how long to leave the control alone and this would presumably be to wait until the prediction on which the control setting had been based was shown to be either right or wrong. The time between control changes would then vary according to the correctness of the prediction; for example, the result of an early bad setting would soon be apparent, and the error resulting from a relatively good one, made after much practice, might only be seen after several minutes. The program need only observe the state of the system when there is uncertainty as to the result of a setting: in other words, well-grounded predictions could be trusted to be right for quite some time, and ' attention ' could be withdrawn.

In order to make predictions at all in situations which had not previously been experienced, the program would need a principle of generalization for minor variants of old situations and this raises the problem of how the results of past experience should be stored. It is clearly out of the question to remember *all* the past behaviour of the system; one possible approach using a limited storage capacity would be to divide the ' signal space ' of the memory up into very coarse regions (for instance, high, medium, and low temperatures rising, steady, or falling, gives nine ' cells ') and then to retain only the sequence of changes from one to another of these. Increasing appreciation of the task would then be represented by a further subdivision of the signal space and a longer sequence of succeeding states remembered. This finer subdivision and changed weight given different parts of the scale of each variable, would correspond to a change of ' adaptation level ' (Helson 1947), which could account for a significant part of the learning process.

There will necessarily be a fairly large random element in the early stages of such a decision-making process, diminishing to leave only predictable behaviour after long practice; subjects do indeed show such a change.

A difficulty is encountered at the beginning of this type of simulation study, since the adult human subject brings a large but unrealized stock of relevant experience to any new task. The subnormal presumably brings less which is one reason why the study of such subjects is valuable, but it is likely that a true learning program would have to go through an early stage of performance much worse than even a subnormal would show. The alternative would be to feed arbitrary information about systems in general into the program before starting it on the particular task.

8. Application of Results

There are two general ways in which the results from this kind of study can be applied, first to the analysis and improvement of manual control on new or existing systems, and second to the design of automatic control mechanisms.

It is clear from our industrial field studies that operators usually achieve much less than optimum performance in controlling slow processes, probably because they acquire less than the necessary information about the behaviour of the system, and thus make only moderately accurate decisions when acting in the open-loop mode. The inaccuracy and consequent error are accepted by most managers without comment and they seem to feel that error is inevitable with human operators. Following the line of thought outlined above, however, decisions could be made more accurate by collecting and using the necessary data, something which could be done without recourse to any extra equipment except paper and pencil. The approach also has obvious implications for the training of process operators, suggesting that they need to be taught not the physics and chemistry of the plant, but its precise control characteristics and how to use them to secure the best results.

Most equipment at present used for automatic control of process plant, appears to be based on the 'three-term controller', which is a standard unit for combining proportional, derivative and integral terms into a single control signal fed back directly to a control point. The operator is relieved of his closed-loop control work but he still needs to adjust the setpoint and possibly trim the settings from time to time. A development, known as adaptive control, provides means of altering the parameters of the system in accordance with higher-order feedback of a separate measure of 'goodness' of the overall results; there are several possible ways of doing this but most of them depend on some form of correlation technique. To our knowledge, there are no automatic control systems which can approach the flexibility of the human operator, derived from his ability to use the open-loop mode where appropriate. The progressive use of experience to enable efficient open-loop (pre-programmed) performance to be organized, is the human operator's speciality but there seems to be no reason why it should not be incorporated in an automatic control system. Such a system would necessarily have a heuristic element and would not be completely predictable. To some extent it would be capable of failure, but in compensation it could undoubtedly handle very much more complicated systems than the present equipment can, because of its facility to take a useful action without detailed feedback information. The machine version would no doubt overcome many of the limitations inherent in the human operator's learning and performance facilities, notably his shortness and inaccuracy of memory, and would to that extent be capable of much better performance. Such a 'heuristic controller' would probably need initial instruction from someone familiar with the general features of the particular control problem, as it would be too expensive to let it learn by trial and error from the very beginning. The procedure would be somewhat analogous to that of teaching a new operator his job.

The authors wish to express their thanks to Professors M. D. Vernon (Reading University) and R. C. Oldfield (Oxford University) in whose departments the research was carried out. The work forms part of a research project financed by the Human Sciences Committee of the Department of Scientific and Industrial Research.

An Investigation of Process Control Skill

By J. Spencer

Unit for Research on Human Performance in Industry, Department of Psychology,
University of Bristol

1. Introduction

For the past fifty years or so, industry has employed men variously called process men, process hands, or process operators. Until recently they have been in the minority and confined chiefly to the petroleum and chemical industries, but today men employed on process work are found in nearly all major industries; and it appears very likely that they will represent a rising proportion of the future industrial labour force. This makes it important to study the types of skill that are involved in process work, because, as Welford (1960) and Crossman (1960a) point out in their discussions of automation, there seems little doubt that process skills are not clearly related to any of the well-known and traditional craft skills. One obvious difference is that both in the display of information and in the execution of process decisions the process man is dealing only indirectly with his raw material.

Very little published experimental evidence exists on the subject of process operator skills although Hiscock described the development of selection tasks for chemical process operators as long ago as 1938. Unfortunately, the validation of the test battery adopted was not complete when the paper was written so that we do not know which of the ingenious series of tests were most predictive of process efficiency.

The investigation to be described is one phase of a study of process skills and is an attempt to study a simple example of this type of skill in the field. In particular, this investigation aimed to discover the extent of individual differences in control behaviour on a simple plant in an oil refinery. If differences exist and if they could be related to control efficiency in a meaningful way, then comparisons between good and poor operators ought to reveal the critical features of this particular process skill—whether, for example, the source of difference is in the perceptual, cognitive, or executive aspects of performance. On the other hand, if no differences exist, then it is important to try to discover if this is due to the task either being one which is too simple or closely prescribed in its operating procedures for difference to occur or being so difficult that natural selection among operators has occurred in the past history of the plant's operation resulting in a uniformly high degree of possession of skill by those studied.

2. Description of the Plant Investigated

The plant consists of a brick building housing a battery of centrifugal pumps and electrical switch gear. Outside this building are the large settling tanks, and nearby is a small office used by the operator for telephoning and paper work.

The plant operates in the following way. The feed to the unit is a light fraction of crude oil obtained from the distillation benches. The feed contains impurities which are removed by the plant in a two-treatment process. The first treatment consists of mixing the feed with a wash fluid which removes the impurities but introduces side effects which are corrected by the second treatment. In this the partly-treated feed is mixed with a neutralizing fluid after which the purified feed is pumped to the tank farm.

The wash treatment is completed in two stages. The impure feed is first mixed with wash fluid by a pump which delivers the mixture to a settling vessel, which is a large tank. In this vessel the two liquids slowly separate into two layers due to their different specific gravities. The separated and partly-washed feed is drawn off by the mixing pump of the second wash stage, which latter is a repetition of that just described. Similarly, the neutralizing treatment is composed of two successive stages identical in design to the wash stages.

Automatic controls are provided which stabilize the level of the separation surface in the settling vessels and proportion the amount of chemical recycle. Chemical recycle means that instead of the chemicals going straight through their respective vessels to waste, a fraction of the spent chemical is returned back to the pump which originally delivered it to the settling vessel.

The plant possesses considerable lag in response to changes either in the impure feed or in wash flow. It is approximately 2 to 3 hours under normal running conditions. And, in the opinion of one operator, if the levels in the settling vessels become seriously disturbed, it may take up to two or three days for the unit to settle down.

3. The Operator's Job

The unit runs continuously, each day being divided into three eight-hour shifts. During a shift one operator is in control. His work can be classified broadly into four aspects:

3.1. *Recording, Maintenance and Technical Liaison*

Three of the four activities which comprise the operators' job are (i) the recording of plant behaviour, (ii) simple maintenance and (iii) technical liaison. None of these is very demanding on this plant because it is physically small and technically simple.

Recording is limited to keeping a plant log of pump running times, flow changes made and so on. Inspection of the plant for recording purposes requires little time and effort because the plant is all at ground level.

Maintenance is very slight because fitters are employed to look after the automatic controls and electricians are responsible for pump motor repairs. The official requirements demand little more than cleaning sight-glasses on flowmeters, keeping the pump-house floor clear of oil or fluids and periodically freeing hand-wheel valves.

Technical liaison is occasionally necessary with one or more of five other departments or officials in the refinery. However, the rate of communication along any of the five channels is low, and generally consists of perhaps two or three brief checks with each of them during a shift.

3.2. Process Monitoring

The fourth aspect of the job can be called process monitoring, and basically this requires the operator to reduce a varying high proportion of impurity in feed to the unit to a constant very low proportion in the output. As an example of a control task this would represent a very simple form but for the fact that there is no direct measure of the proportion of impurity in the feed to the unit. With this constraint the operator achieves a degree of control only by reference to a measure of impurity obtained after the first stage of wash treatment. This takes the form of a qualitative test (referred to hereafter as the Q-test). A small sample of the mixture fed to the second settling vessel is tapped into a test-tube. A simple reagent is added and by noting the presence or absence of a colour change in the reagent the operator decides whether or not a sufficient wash is being given to the impure feed. Officially a test should be carried out every thirty minutes, but operators vary according to the state of the unit, making more frequent tests when the plant is disturbed.

If a colour change occurs the test result is positive which means that insufficient washing is being given to the feed. The operator corrects this condition by increasing the flow rate of wash fluid. A second test then shows whether the correction was sufficient or not. The actual chemical effectiveness of the wash treatment is affected by the rate of flow of feed to the unit, the rate of flow of wash fluid and by the ambient temperature of the plant. Consequently precise adjustment of wash fluid to give correct treatment and minimum waste of wash chemical is by no means simple.

The flow of neutralizing fluid is not critically related to the flow of wash fluid and normally the operator merely adjusts the hand-wheel valve occasionally in order to maintain the rate specified by the Process Laboratory. Only if he has to make a very large alteration to wash flow is he permitted to alter the neutralizing fluid flow and he must inform the laboratory when he does so.

4. Information Collected

For the purposes of this study, during every shift hourly records were made of feed, wash and neutralizing flow rates in the unit, and the results of Q-tests made at the same time as the recording of flow rates. In addition, the proportion of impurity in the feed to the unit was measured once per shift by the Process Laboratory and recorded. The type of crude oil (*i.e.* its geographical source) from which the feed to the unit was distilled was recorded together with any mishaps or other events not covered by the hourly recording of conditions.

Recording commenced on 4 May, 1959, and continued until 26 October, 1959. Engineering apprentices were kindly made available by the company to perform observation and recording duties.

The aim was to obtain for each operator a sample of 21 shifts equally divided into day, afternoon and night shifts. Various operational exigencies made it impossible to obtain this ideal sampling within a reasonable period and the distribution of samples actually obtained is shown in Table 1:

Table 1. Shift samples for operators and shift type

Shift	Operator					Totals
	A*	B	C	D	E	
Morning	9	7	6	9	8	39
Afternoon	7	8	6	6	6	33
Night	3	6	10	6	8	33
Totals	19	21	22	21	22	105

* Operator A was a spare man and did not therefore work on a regular schedule on the plant.

5. Results

The description of the process and its control that has been given makes it clear that, in spite of the apparently simple nature of the process, the exact quantitive formulation of the correct relationship between feed input and wash flow is extremely difficult. And in the absence of continuous measurement of the absolute flow of impurity into the unit it is impossible to determine directly the efficiency of control. In order to study operator differences under these conditions, certain assumptions have to be made.

The first assumption is that the average of the eight hourly readings for feed flow, wash flow and neutralizer flow represents the best estimate of the operators' choice of desirable running conditions for the shift.

The second assumption is that the impurity content of the feed stayed constant during the shift. Then, by multiplying the impurity concentration by the average feed flow, one obtains a measure of the average flow rate of impurity into the plant for the shift.

The question of the most likely relationship between impurity flow and wash flow was discussed with the technical staff and in their view the assumption of a linear law was a reasonable one to adopt. Accordingly, the third assumption is that, other things being equal, the best operator will show the most direct relationship between impurity flow and wash flow over his sample of shifts, *i.e.* as nearly as possible a one-to-one relationship between wash flow and impurity flow.

5.1. Shift Differences

In order to assess differences in control behaviour as between morning, afternoon and night shifts records for all operators were combined for each type of shift and three best-fitting straight line relations were calculated. For all three samples the line slopes were significantly greater than zero, but not different from one another. Hence there were no systematic shift differences. Such differences would not, of course, be expected on technical grounds. However, the relationship did not show a one-to-one correspondence between flows.

5.2. Operator Differences

When a similar analysis was made for operators large differences were found, indicating that some operators used more wash per amount of impurity than others. Comparisons between operators showed that only between operators C and D were the relationships significantly different, the remaining operators giving slopes intermediate to those of operators C and D. The difference between these two may be illustrated by indicating the percentage increase in wash flow that each would adopt for an increase in impurity flow of 300%. For operator C, wash flow would be increased by 20% and for operator D, by an increase of 200%. Obviously operator D approaches a one-to-one relation.

However, it might be argued that the sampled conditions for different operators were not the same, and that if the actual relationship between impurity flow and wash flow were not linear, then different operators might necessarily differ, because they were operating on a different part of the relationship curve. To check this point the average flows of wash and impurity were calculated for each operator sample. When the averages for impurity flow are compared as between operators, it was found that operator A experienced significantly higher impurity flows than operators B, D and E (t = 2·58, 2·36, 3·55 respectively, giving $p < 0.02 > 0.01$, $< 0.05 > 0.02$, $< 0.01 > 0.001$ respectively, when n = 38, 38 and 39). No other differences were significant. Hence we might expect A to show a control relationship distinctly different from that shown by the other operators, but in fact he showed a relationship lying between the extremes. So it may be concluded that, with the exception of A, all operators were operating over a similar range of impurity flows but showed different operating laws over this range; and the operating law characteristic of A is within the range of laws shown by his colleagues. The differences found are perhaps suggestive rather than conclusive, because only between operators C and D are slope differences significant. On the other hand, examination of the flows of wash and impurity for each operator sample (see Table 2) indicates that the small differences in impurity flow are accurately reflected in wash flow differences. This is in spite of the rather gross assumptions involved in the comparison.

Table 2. Average impurity and wash flows for each operator

	Operator				
	A	B	C	D	E
Average impurity x^1	640·57	498·83	560·51	537·93	471·28
σ ,,	161·8	175·4	194·8	148·9	471·28
Average wash x^2	629·77	557·31	570·85	576·63	515·43
σ ,,	129·9	136·6	101·7	143·6	131·5
Number of observations	19	21	22	21	22

x^1 In units of flow per hour. x^2 In gallons per hour.

5.3. Recording Periods

Due to the intervention of the holiday period the records were divided into two main batches. 81 shifts were recorded during the months of May and June; 31 shifts were recorded during October. (The total is even greater than shown in Table 1 because records which were not sufficiently complete for the analysis described previously could be used for the present analysis.) A marked difference was apparent between the two batches. During the second period, all operators showed a consistent tendency to select wash flows which were exactly one tenth of the feed flow into the unit. No such consistency was to be seen in the first period. The extent of this difference is indicated in Table 3:

Table 3. Percentage of shifts in each period classified according to the ratio: feed input (G.P.H.) to wash (G.P.H.)

Period of record collection	Ratio < 10:1	10:1	> 10:1	varied*	Total
May–June	53.0	2.5	1.25	43.2	99.9
October	16.1	64.8	3.2	16.1	100.2

* More than two wash flow changes during the shift, without any feed input flow change.

The raw figures on which the table is based were examined by χ^2 on a null hypothesis that the distribution of ratios was similar for the two periods. The result showed that there was a very significant difference between the two periods due to the high frequency with which a 10 : 1 ratio was chosen during the second period.

$$(\chi^2 = 55.82, \text{ 2 degrees of freedom, } p < 0.001)$$

This confirms that a marked change in operating behaviour had occurred between June and October. The technical staff explained this on the grounds that during the first period the distillation bench supplying the unit had been behaving very erratically due to complex chemical disturbances. During the period between the two batches of records these disturbances had died away to give the 'more normal' operating conditions of the second period.

It is clear that operator differences during the second period were very much reduced, in which case the differences described under Operator Differences underestimate the full extent of the operator differences because those results were based on the total sample of shifts. On the other hand, it is equally clear that differences between operators only became apparent when the process control conditions became abnormal.

5.4. Frequency of Flow Changes made during Shifts

An examination of the frequency with which operators altered feed and chemical flows during shifts revealed that, for the total sample of shifts, the average number of changes per shift were as follows: (i) 0.32 feed changes, (ii) 1.34 wash changes and (iii) 0.32 neutralizer changes.

Feed and neutralizer changes are made only on instructions from outside the unit, as already described, or when the operator was faced with a plant emergency. Wash changes would be expected to be more frequent in occurrence since they are under the operator's direct control. Even so, it can be seen that such changes occurred only about four times in every three shifts. The average incidence of changes per operator per shift was as follows— operator A, 2.00; operator B, 0.91; operator C, 1.13; operator D, 1.95; operator E, 0.74.

An examination of these averages to see whether the differences were statistically significant showed that operators A and D were significantly higher than B, C and E in the frequency with which they altered wash flow, but were not significantly different from each other.

For three operators sufficient samples of shifts were available from each of the two record periods to make possible an assessment of the differences between these three operators for each period separately. The results show that, during the first period, operators differed in the frequency with which they adjusted wash flows. During the second period, there were no significant differences. The results are given below:

	First Period			
Operator	C	D	E	Total
Number of wash changes	22	37	11	70
Number of shifts	13	16	14	43

	Second Period			
Operator	C	D	E	Total
Number of wash changes	7	8	5	20
Number of shifts	11	7	9	27

$\chi^2 = 10.79$, 2 degrees freedom (first period), $p < 0.01 > 0.001$
$\chi^2 = 2.12$, 2 degrees freedom (second period), $p < 0.5 > 0.1$

These results supplement those obtained from the examination of flow ratios. Operators differ under difficult conditions but not under easy conditions, and this difference applies both to the control position selected and to the frequency of control adjustment.

5.5. Correction Threshold

In the type of process control studied, the discrete nature of the error signals (*i.e.* positive Q-tests results) and of the control responses lend themselves to an examination of what may be called the correction threshold. This threshold is defined as the magnitude of a corrective control adjustment in response to an error signal, expressed as a percentage of the previous control setting. It is assumed that the lowest correction threshold will represent the most capable operator providing that he produces a satisfactory correction as a result of his control adjustment.

The method used was to study every record for the occurrence of a positive Q-test result and record both the magnitude of the corrective wash flow changes and the level of wash flow before the change. The correction was then divided by the previous wash flow and expressed as a percentage. The median of all the values so obtained for each operator was then recorded as his correction threshold and was as follows:

Operator	A	B	C	D	E
Correction threshold	9.6%	7.0%	10.8%	5.7%	6.3%

It is possible that correction thresholds merely reflect different methods of control by different operators, such that, for example, some operators prefer to make several small corrections, whilst others prefer to make a single large correction. If this is the case, a low correction threshold would not necessarily indicate a sensitive operator (*i.e.* the man who could judge to a nicety the minimum adjustment needed to correct his process), and therefore would mean very little in terms of skill level.

In the present case this possibility was checked by ranking operators for correction threshold and for incidence per shift of positive Q-test results and correlating the rankings obtained. The correlation was small, positive and non-significant. Hence it seems possible that the threshold is in fact one measure of control sensitivity. A correlation on five pairs of data is however no more than suggestive.

5.6. *General Control Behaviour*

On examination several shift records showed a temporal pattern of control which suggested that operators were attempting to minimize wash flow as distinct from just maintaining a *status quo* from the previous shift. Four typical examples of this suggested behaviour are illustrated in Figures 1a, 1b, 1c and 1d. In each figure the height of the black line represents the wash flow level. The small + or − signs show the results of Q-tests applied at a time corresponding to their position along the abscissa. With the exception of Figure 1d there was no way of proving that the interpretations of the behaviour are in fact correct. On the other hand, if they are not, why should operators have behaved as they did without receiving instructions to do so? (The records contained any instructions received during the shift and in the cases illustrated none was reported. Neither were there any feed flow changes which would of course necessitate corresponding adjustments to wash flow.)

6. Operator Interviews

Some months after the collection of records had been completed, four of the operators were separately interviewed about their work. The interviews were carried out on the plant and were of an informal nature in that a series of questions was put to the operator during the course of a general discussion about the plant. The operator was told that any comments about the plant or his job were welcome and could be made in strict confidence.

The interview material was studied to see how many specific items about his job each operator offered. The items mentioned were divided into two categories of information: 'control' and 'technical'. Control information refers to symptoms noticed by the operator and used by him to assess the state of the plant. It thus reflects the 'wrinkles' that he had learnt whilst actually controlling the plant. Technical information is any item which relates to a physical characteristic, the process variables or plant component but which is not directly relevant to the control procedure. Such information, for example, as might be found in a descriptive handbook of the unit, so that technical information reflects the operators' general understanding of the process and the plant. The number of points raised by each operator in each of the categories is indicated in Table 4:

Table 4. Number of items mentioned at interview classified by item content

Operator	B	C	D	E
Number of technical details mentioned	2	2	2	9
Number of control details mentioned	5	4	7	2
Total mentioned	7	6	9	11

It can be seen that E was much superior to the other operators in technical knowledge about the plant but made fewest references to control details. The other three operators were similar in the quantity and type of information

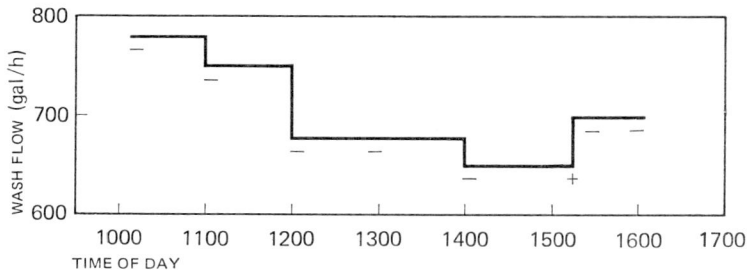

Minimising with small overshoot

(a) OPERATOR C, Shift 9

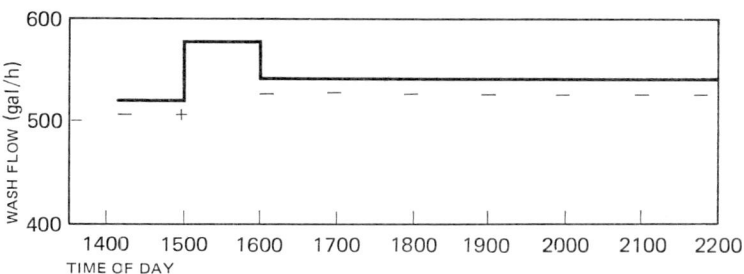

Correction of drift in level of impurity flow

(b) OPERATOR B, Shift 97

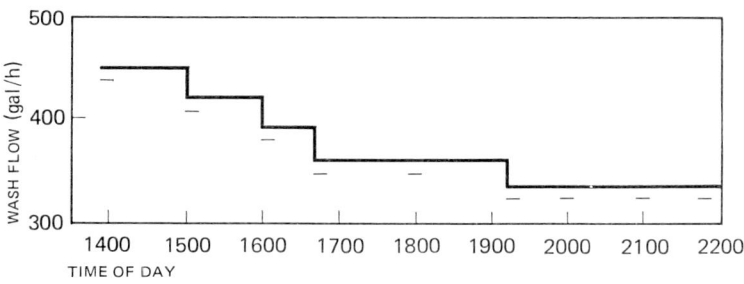

Minimising without overshoot

(c) OPERATOR D, Shift 130

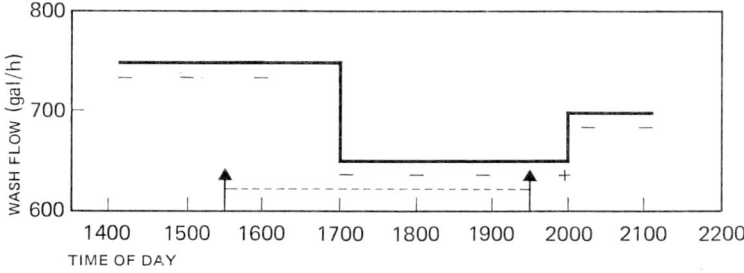

Anticipatory overshoot. Arrows mark the period of change-over from one variety of feed input to another. The new variety contains a lower impurity percentage.

Change in crude sources leading to anticipatory overshoot

(d) OPERATOR E, Shift 36

Figure 1. Examples of process control behaviour.

given. Interestingly, E was the only operator who considered that not enough technical information was provided about the unit, and he rather resented any suggestion that he was merely an operator and therefore did not need to know much about the technical minutiae of his plant. It is tempting to suggest that these results reflect two approaches to process control. On the one hand, there is the operator who is very knowledgeable about the technical aspects of his plant and because of this knowledge does not have to look for odd symptoms in order to control it; his schema of the plant is a rational one. On the other hand, there is the operator who has only a vague technical knowledge of his plant and must therefore resort to a laborious process of correlating various incidental phenomena of the plant (e.g. ' rattling ' in glass pipes, ' sweating ' on outside walls of vessels and visible gassing in flow lines) with each other and with his supposed control activity. His schema is empirical and will include several ' dodges ' and ' knacks ' relating to control of the process, some of which will be technically sound and some of which will be technically irrelevant. The ' technical ' type of process operator will tend not to report knacks of control because he cannot rationalize them in technical terms, although he may nevertheless employ them. The ' empirical ' type of process operator will report knacks because they are all he possesses by way of understanding the plant, and he will rationalize them in ways which are frequently quite incomprehensible to a technically-minded questioner.

7. Discussion

It was stated in the introduction that the major objective of this study would be the demonstration of individual differences between operators performing the same control task. Such differences were found but occurred only under plant running conditions which the refinery staff regarded as abnormal. Under normal running conditions there were no statistically significant differences between operators in their control behaviour.

Had operators differed from one another under normal running conditions it would have been feasible to continue the investigation in order to relate control behaviour to the degree of success achieved. After this it would have been possible to try to discover why one pattern of control behaviour was better than another and hence to discover the critical features of this particular example of process control skill.

The fact that differences occur only under abnormal conditions leaves the significance of such differences open to considerable doubt. Two possible explanations for these differences exist. The first is that they reflect different degrees of skill in controlling the plant and that they become more pronounced under the more difficult operating conditions caused by abnormalities in the feed to the unit. The second possible explanation is based on the existence of the two- to three-hour plant lag. This lag means that if a sudden change occurs in the feed to the plant it will be two to three hours before the output of the plant reaches a new steady output state. Consequently, if unusually large and frequent input changes are occurring, operators may be unable to achieve a steady condition. In the attempt to achieve this they alter their normal responses and so probably increase the unsteadiness by their efforts. To make matters worse, even if one operator were adopting a good strategy to deal with the abnormal conditions he is unlikely to achieve success in an eight-hour shift, after which the plant is taken over by the next operator who uses a different strategy. This explanation disposes of any attempt to relate the control behaviour observed with the degree of success that it achieves. Finally, it is clear that even if the first explanation were correct the abnormal input conditions together with the fact that plant lag is a large fraction of the duration of one working shift makes it unlikely that a particular sample of control behaviour could be related to its final outcome with reasonable precision.

The inability to interpret the results in a reliable way is very disappointing but as a whole the study is extremely useful because it clarifies the minimum requirements that must be guaranteed for a successful field study and it suggests better methods of solving the problem of process control skill.

The method of field study is time-consuming and basically unreliable because firstly, only a small sample of operators is available on any one plant. Secondly, it takes a long period to collect a reasonable sample of shifts for each operator, which is unsatisfactory because conditions may change during the sampling period as was found in the present study and because there is an increasing tendency to use evolutionary operation. This is an operating procedure in which different plant variables are systematically varied over small ranges with the aim of maximizing output by a series of successive approximations. The very fact that this recently introduced technique is being adopted emphasizes the technical difficulties of predicting the best relationship between plant variables.

Even if the difficulties just described are overcome, a worthwhile field study of process control skill requires the following minimum of information:

(a) Continuous recordings of the principal plant variables, which must include all control settings;
(b) The number and characters of all lags in the plant must be known with sufficient accuracy to allow the efforts of an operator to be related with the output due to these efforts;
(c) An adequate criterion of performance must be available. It must be such that for a given input condition of the independent variables and the desired output condition it is possible to calculate the required control positions of the dependent variables.

If these requirements can be satisfied, it will still require advanced techniques of mathematical analysis unless studies are restricted to very simple plants. Consequently, the psychological analysis of process control skills will almost certainly proceed more rapidly if other approaches are tried. Two of these can be suggested in the light of the above remarks and of experience gained during the study.

For a direct study of control skills the experimental simulation in the laboratory of plants selected from industry seems to be easily the most suitable approach. The benefits of such a method are obvious. An indirect advantage is that the learning process can be studied as well as the control behaviour of the fully trained operator. A difficulty involved will be the ease with which suitable subjects can be found who are prepared to spend sufficient time on the experiments. A possible solution to this would be to run the experiments as a full- or part-time job for the subjects. People obtained in this way are more likely to be representative of the process operator population than university students for example.

A valuable field study suggested by visits to several plants would be an examination of the relationship between operating instructions and type of plant. The extent to which process control work is skilful depends very largely on two factors, which are firstly, the scope and precision with which operating procedures are defined in operating manuals and secondly, the complexity of the plant controlled which includes both the number of variables together with their interactions and the number of process stages under the operators' control. Both factors are found to vary over a wide range in practice and it would be extremely interesting to discover whether, for example, the simpler plants tend to be those with the most specific operating instructions? The effect of this would be to stratify process jobs into two principal levels of difficulty, either very simple or very complex. This situation leads to considerable difficulties because if the difference in level is sufficiently large then it is difficult to fit men of varying capacities into jobs which are neither too simple nor too demanding. The implication of this situation might be studied by comparisons between related plants for variables such as sickness absence and job turnover. Information of this type is badly needed if future process work is going to be designed to suit the type of labour available. It would help to answer the following question for example. Does the very close specification of operating instructions rob a process job of both skill and responsibility and hence also of appeal? Or is it the reverse condition that leads to greater turnover—considerable operational freedom plus heavy responsibility?

8. Conclusions

It is concluded that a reliable interpretation cannot be made of the individual differences found in the investigation. This type of field study of process skill is considered to be too time-consuming in view of the uncertainty of the outcome, which is dependent on many factors other than those under immediate investigation. Consequently, alternative methods of tackling the problem of process skill are suggested. These may be summarized as being of two types. The first consists of experimental investigations of the acquisition and final performance of process skills on laboratory simulations of tasks existing in industry. The second consists of field studies to relate the complexity of plant under an operator's control to the degrees of precision and comprehensiveness of the operating instructions provided for the operator. Combined with sickness absence and job turnover data, such information might make it possible to design operating instructions in such a way that they form an efficient link between the demands of plant and the capacities of potential operators.

I am very grateful to Dr. E. R. F. W. Crossman and Miss Christine Smith for helpful discussion and assistance in the course of this work. I would also like to acknowledge with thanks the generous and untiring assistance of many members of the B.P. Refinery, Llandarcy, in particular Mr. M. Page, Mr. T. L. Williams and Mr. R. Blackwell. The research was financed by a grant from the Department of Scientific and Industrial Research.

An Analysis and Simulation of an Operator's Behaviour in Controlling Continuous Baking Ovens

By R. J. BEISHON

University of Bristol

1. Introduction

The concept of the man–machine system has proved valuable in providing a basis for the analysis of complex situations where men and machines work in close interaction with each other. In many cases these systems can be analyzed without difficulty and a number of suitable analytical techniques are available; see, for example, Gagné (1963). However, numerous man–machine complexes are developing in which men have to use a high level of *mental skill* with little or no manual component. These skills usually take many years to acquire and there is relatively little understanding of their fundamental psychological nature. Only a small amount of research has been done on the cognitive activity involved in these real-life tasks and most of the published work for example refers to game-playing tasks undertaken in the laboratory.

Industrial skills appear to be a promising field for research in this area for various reasons. Apart from the practical value of gaining a better knowledge of skilled behaviour for training and design purposes, industrial tasks are well suited for analysis. They usually have clearly defined goals and the machine part of the system to a large extent conveniently constrains the man's activity. Further, the situations which arise in industry are sufficiently complex to be non-trivial, but not so complex that a very high degree of mental sophistication is needed by the operator. The behaviour of people in industrial settings is also 'realistic' and genuine positive and negative rewards operate so that the motivational aspects of the situation are usually under reasonable control or at least known. For these reasons a typical industrial skill was selected for study as part of a general study of cognitive processes and the present paper describes an investigation of a cake-baking production unit controlled by one operator. The study aimed principally at analyzing the man–machine system in detail and at gaining an understanding of the underlying cognitive processes involved in the skill. The process and the ovenman's job are described first, followed by an analysis of the operating system. The development of a model to simulate the ovenman and his control behaviour is then described.

2. The Baking of Cakes

In modern bakeries of the kind studied here, cakes are produced on a semi-continuous batch basis; prepared mixes for each variety of cake are formed into appropriate shapes on specialized machines and delivered on baking trays to ovens. The trays are entered into the ovens by the ovenman who places them onto continuously-running endless belts which carry the trays through the hot zones of the oven. After leaving the oven the cakes are cooled, inspected and packed for sale. The complete production process is illustrated diagrammatically in Figure 1.

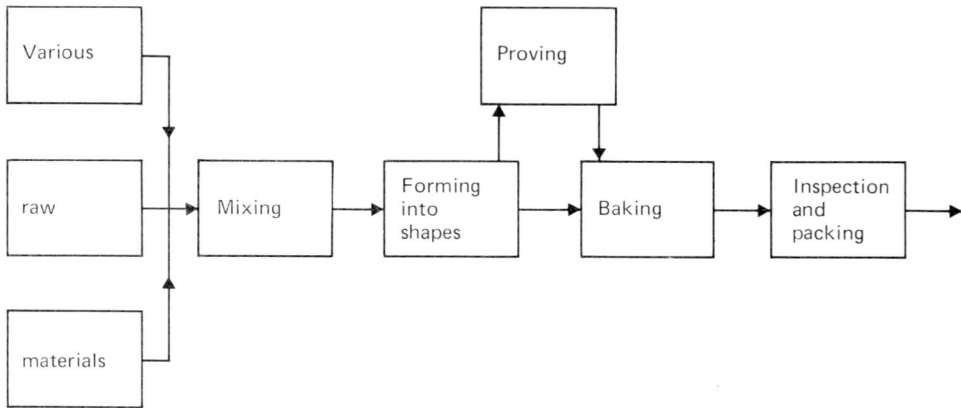

Figure 1. Block diagram of cake production process.

In the plant studied there are three continuous tunnel ovens in one piece of plant, two upper ovens and one larger lower oven; the diagram in Figure 2 shows the general arrangement. Each oven, which is about 13 metres long, has a layer of transverse gas burners above and below the conveyor belt so that the cakes are carried between them. Each gas burner can be switched on or off independently and the profile of temperature experienced by the cakes can be varied by altering the disposition of the lighted gas burners along the oven. Oven temperatures are indicated at two points about one-third and two-thirds along the length of each oven, see Figure 2; the range of temperatures available

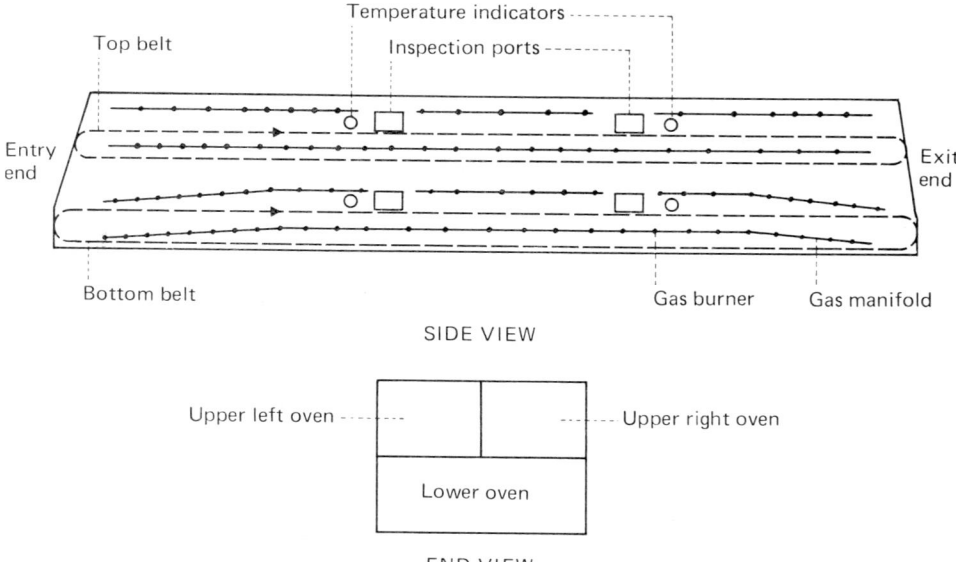

Figure 2. Diagram of oven system studied.

is roughly between 200°F and 550°F. The other major control variable is the *baking time* which is determined by the conveyor belt speed; this can be varied from 2 to 5 minutes. Each oven has two inspection ports, sited as shown in Figure 2; at these places the ovenman can see into the oven and inspect the partially cooked cakes.

3. The Ovenman's Job

The ovenman's main task is to arrange for the raw cakes to be converted into finished cooked articles. He has four principal aims:

(1) To ensure that the correct chemical transformations occur in the cakes.
(2) To achieve acceptable top and bottom colouration of the cakes.
(3) To obtain an acceptable degree of ' rise ' for each type of cake.
(4) To produce cakes in batches which are uniform with respect to the above characteristics within a batch.

To some extent the above aims, or output variables for the system, are independent of each other since each can be influenced separately by altering the burner dispositions and baking times. All four of the variables have to be assessed subjectively by the ovenman who attempts to match them to a ' standard ' of acceptable cakes. It should be noted that these four aims are the principal ones laid down by the management but that there are a number of subsidiary aims which have to be considered.

The system has a number of relatively independent *inputs* which can be listed as follows:

(1) Type of cake. (This includes the kind of cake mix, and the size and shape of the articles.)
(2) Size of the batch.
(3) Time the batch arrives for baking.
(4) Variations in the cake mix.

The ovenman has no control over these inputs and he must take account of any variations in them by adjusting the baking conditions accordingly.

It was necessary in the first instance to record in detail exactly what happened to the system in the course of a number of typical working shifts. Observations were made using a portable tape recorder which was kept running continuously to provide a convenient time base for subsequent transcription. Observers reported on the movements and actions of the ovenman, read out temperatures and burner conditions at approximately 5-minute intervals, and also recorded question and answer conversations with the ovenman. A radio-microphone technique was also used for the ovenman so that his conversations with other personnel could be picked up on a second recording channel. The data were transcribed onto *activity charts* in which the concurrent events in the various parts of the system are plotted on a suitable time base so that the behaviour of the ovenman and oven system can be followed graphically. An example of a typical day is shown in Figure 3.

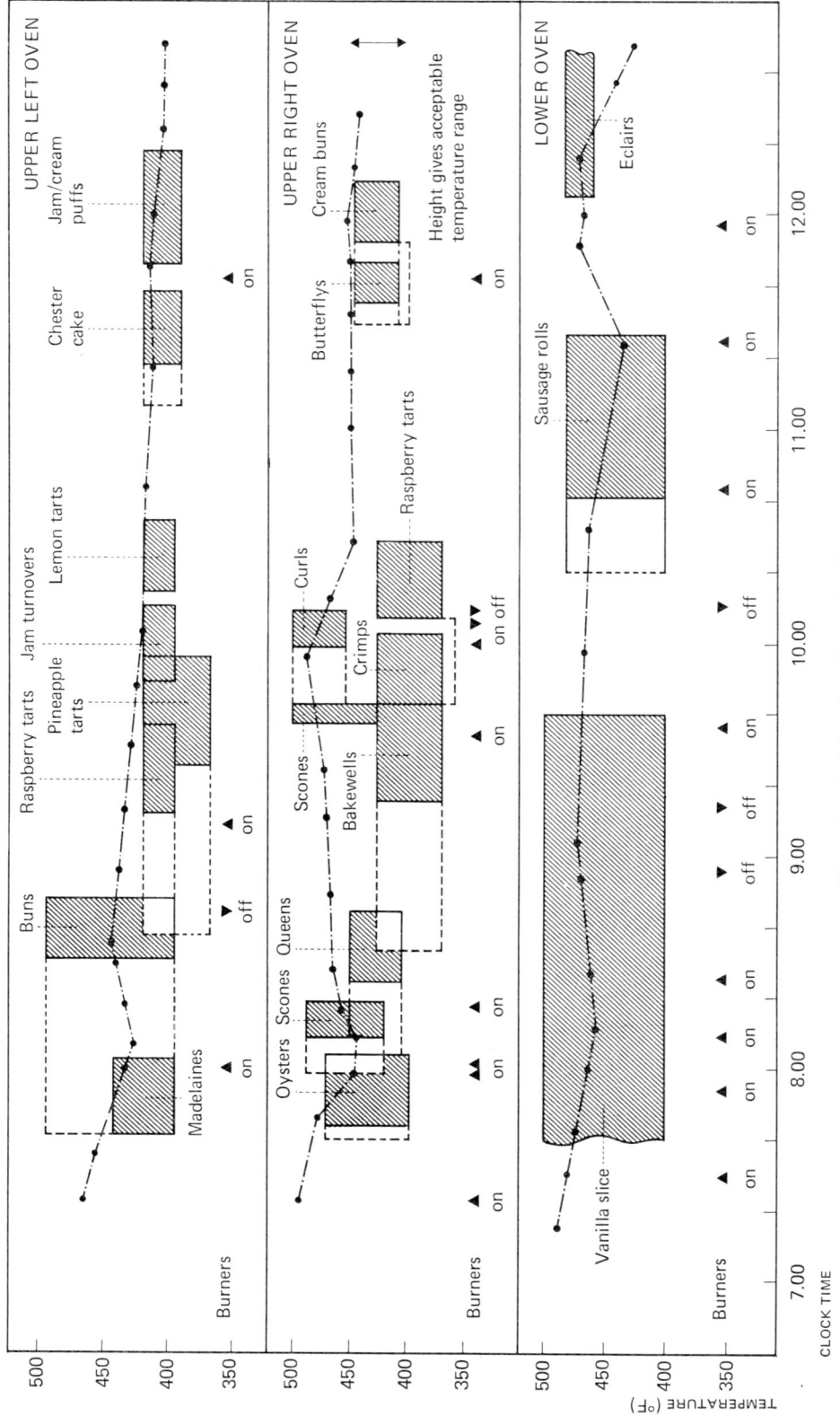

Figure 3. Activity chart for typical day.

4. Analysis of Observations

The overt behaviour of the ovenman could be broken down into a number of simple categories as set out in Table 1 below:

Table 1. Breakdown of ovenman's activity for a typical shift

Activity	% Time spent in shift
Loading oven	24
Moving racks	7
Control adjustments	8
Waiting	8
Inspections	3
Subsidiary work on another baking system (mainly manual work)	35
Miscellaneous (including meals)	16

(Figures rounded off)

It can be seen from the table that the percentage of time spent on control and inspection activity is only 11% of the total time spent at the plant. However, it is clear from the nature of the actions and comments of the man that a large part of the time spent on manual activity is also used to think about control of the process.

It became clear that there was a *standard baking procedure* which consisted of a number of phases normally followed through in sequence. At a general level this procedure describes the job and the way of doing it, but it does not make explicit any of the decision rules nor could the actual task, which involves many different cakes and three ovens working simultaneously, be done by simply following this procedure. When a more detailed decision analysis is carried out it becomes clear that there are a number of fairly distinct *routines* for dealing with the different phases of the task. The routines which can readily be identified are listed below:

(1) *Recognition:* cakes are recognized i.e. identified as a cake-type, and are also inspected and classified as to normality.
(2) *Oven allocation:* an oven is selected for the cake-type waiting or expected.
(3) *Oven adjustment:* control actions are made to bring the selected oven to a suitable state for baking the current cakes.
(4) *Entry:* cakes are entered into a selected oven when conditions are appropriate.
(5) *Check or Sample:* some items are checked at the inspection ports or exit end of the oven.
(6) *Feedback/Adjustment:* if inspection (see (5) above) shows faults in cakes, adjustments are made to oven conditions.
(7) *New item:* new cake-types are baked according to a trial-and-error procedure.
(8) *Abnormal items:* If the pre-baking inspection shows any abnormality in cakes, altered baking conditions may be needed.

A detailed examination of these routines shows that in most cases a body of facts associated with each routine is needed to enable the decisions in that routine to be made. For example, for each cake-type there is a preferred baking time and temperature profile; for a specific profile there is a suitable pattern of burners which will give the desired temperatures down the oven. With the preferred baking conditions known and the current state of the ovens known, a decision can be made as to which is the most suitable oven to use for baking that batch. Similarly, the decision to enter cakes will be made when the *preferred* conditions match the *current* oven conditions.

The existence of baking time and burner pattern information, and the way in which the ovenman can produce it when asked, suggests that he has a number of look-up tables in memory stores to which he has ready access. Further study of these has been made and the following tables appear to be present:

(1) Facts about the preferred times and temperatures for all the usual cake-types.
(2) Facts about the degree of tolerance each cake-type has for departures from the preferred baking conditions. (This will give information about the need for sampling when the cakes have travelled some way down the oven.)
(3) Facts about the burner patterns which will achieve the temperature profiles obtained from (1) above.
(4) Methods or procedures for getting the oven to change from one temperature state to another; this includes information about the times taken for the various changes.
(5) Expectancies concerning the kinds of cakes which will arrive for baking and also the time of day when they are likely to come.
(6) Methods or procedures for adjusting baking conditions to correct specific fault conditions which are detected on inspection of the partially, or completely, baked items.

This set of tables would provide most of the basic factual information needed to do the routines assuming that a procedure for the routine itself was available.

For several reasons the two components discussed so far, routines and look-up tables, are not sufficient to account for all the behaviour of the ovenman. In a system containing time lags such as the baking system, a single routine cannot always be followed through continuously to completion and often a new routine has to be started before the current one has finished and the two then alternated. There are also external stimulus events which can interrupt a current routine and which have to be dealt with before the original routine can be resumed. This suggests that there must be a directing program or *executive routine* (E.R.) which controls the sequential stream of behaviour in response to external and internal stimuli. In addition to an executive routine, there must also be *perceptual mechanisms* for dealing with the recognition of cake-types and for judging the quality of the output variables.

5. A Model for the Ovenman's Behaviour

The aim of this part of the project was to construct a model which would behave in the same way as the ovenman does, but having available only the same information as the man is known, or inferred, to have. The basis of the model is a central program-type procedure called the *main procedure* which links together the routines discussed in the previous sections. A flow chart for this main procedure is given in Figure 4. This sets out the way in which the different phases of the task might be linked and shows how one routine would follow on from another. Progress through the main procedure depends to a large extent on events taking place in the external system and must be controlled by the E.R. Flow charts for individual routines have been worked out and an example of one is shown in Figure 5.

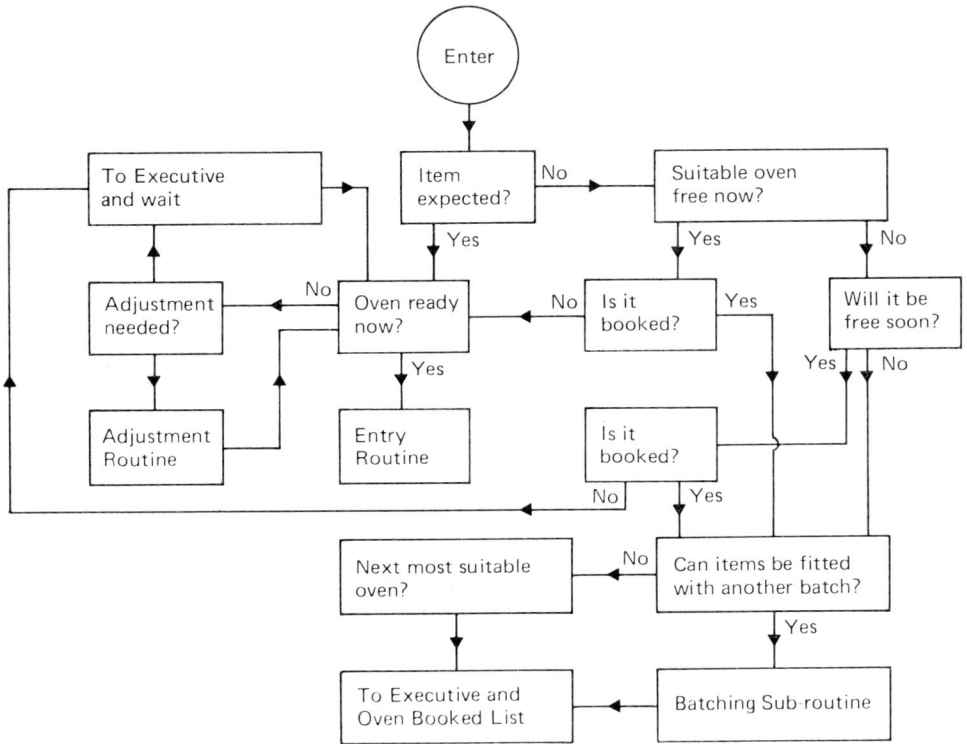

Figure 4. Flow chart for main procedure.

A major difficulty in constructing a simulation for a human operator's behaviour is in accounting for the sequence of events which occur in the ongoing stream of behaviour. A study of the records from the observations on the ovenman reveals fairly distinct sections which are clearly purposive and directed to a particular goal or end state. In general, these correspond to the routines described above but frequently a routine is not carried through to completion without interruption; also when a routine is completed the ovenman will often proceed to a new routine which appears to be selected arbitrarily. So although parts of the behaviour are understood, in the sense that rules for the steps in the sequence can be identified, the total stream appears disconnected and subject to random jumps from one routine or activity to another. When these cases are examined in detail, however, a pattern begins to emerge. *Interrupts*, which occur when some on-going stream of activity changes suddenly, appear to arise from two causes: *external* triggers or signals, and *internal* triggers. The external triggers are events which occur in the system and which

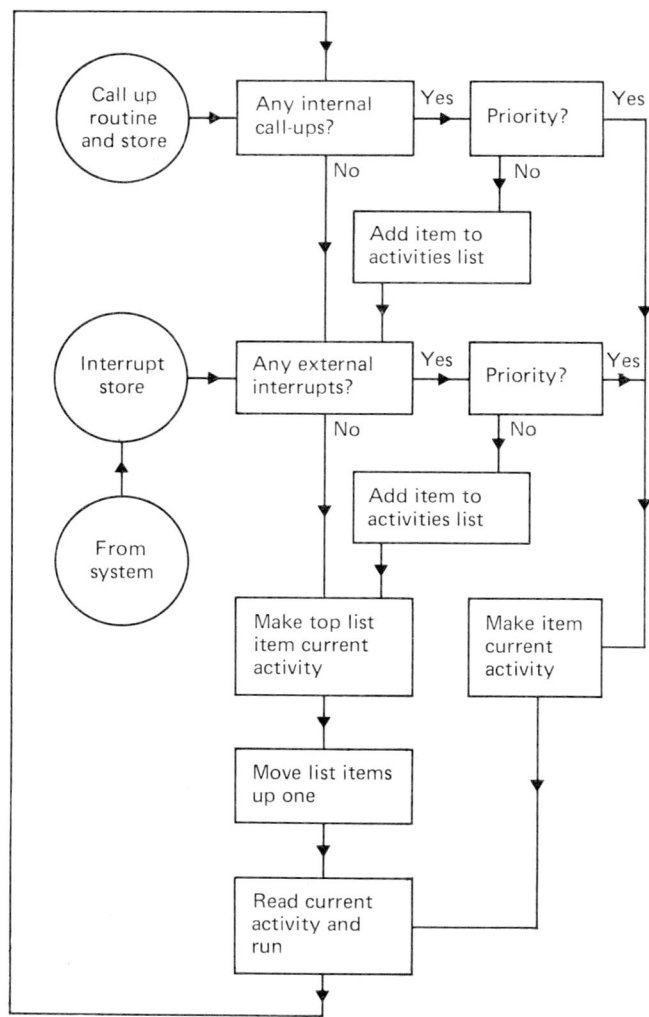

Figure 5. A procedure or routine to control selection of oven.

either attract the attention of the ovenman *directly*, such as a comment from another worker bringing up a rack of cakes, or *indirectly*, as when he notices that a new rack has appeared as he happens to pass the entry end of the oven. These external events will usually break into the current routine and the ovenman will attend to the new event for a time before returning to his original activity. Internally-initiated interrupts are observed when, for example, the ovenman stops while loading the oven and goes to look through the inspection port at a specific batch of cakes. This latter action implies that there is some *internal call-up* system which is set to alert the ovenman at some appropriate time in the future.

The jumps from a completed routine to the next one are less easy to account for; in some cases the progression is virtually dictated by the process, as when a batch of cakes arrives which the man has been expecting. He will identify these, check that conditions are in fact suitable and go on to enter them into the oven. In other cases the choice of the next activity is less clear and the ovenman himself may be unable to give a clearcut reason for it. In practice the choices appear to be made in relation to an *advance planning* routine which is concerned with organizing his activity over the next half-hour or hour period. This work is done in *anticipation* of events and hence much of the activity is done for reasons which may not be apparent *before* the events occur. The fact that the sequence of routines is not entirely dictated by external events suggests that the executive routine is concerned with handling and resolving the often conflicting demands placed upon the operator by the requirements of the production process.

The Executive Routine (E.R.)

The responsibilities of E.R. can be set out as follows:
    (1) Entering and retrieving call-ups for future entry to specific routine.
    (2) Handling externally-initiated interrupts.
    (3) Searching through future expectancies for anticipatory activities.
    (4) Keeping and up-dating a *list of activities* to be done next.

The main responsibility of the E.R. is centred on (4) above. This ' activities list ' will be composed of routines from the main procedure and activities associated with interrupts and anticipations. The items in the list will be positioned according to the current state of the oven system and will be made up of items from the main procedure for each of the cake batches currently being processed. The E.R. extracts the top activity on the list and carries this out, automatically moving the remaining items on the list up one place. The activities list probably covers a time span of between half to one hour ahead since the ovenman plans for this period in practice. Interrupts can either be placed at the top of the list, in which case they are dealt with immediately the current activity is finished, or they can be placed further down the list, depending on the result of conditional tests which would be applied.

To fit items into the list, and to keep track of events, the E.R. must follow some kind of cyclic scan procedure which looks at the internal call-ups and external information sources on a regular basis. This could be done by a clock pulse trigger system giving a priority scan, but it seems more likely that the scan is itself a list item which is put into, say, every third or fourth slot in the list. This means that the search for current items to add to the list, or updating of the list, can itself be delayed by series of priority external call-ups which are added to the top of the list. Behaviour of this kind is observed when the ovenman appears to ' forget ' a sampling or scanning action for a while when he has to deal with a number of external interrupts. Important scans or interrupts already in the list cannot, however, be kept down indefinitely and there is probably a mechanism which adds a ' tag ' to these list items each time they are kept down by the insertion of an item above them; accumulation of such tags eventually enables the suppressed item to operate as a priority interrupt itself.

An outline of a flow chart for E.R. is shown in Figure 6. Clearly a great deal more data would be needed before the priority orderings for the various interrupts and components of the routines could be established.

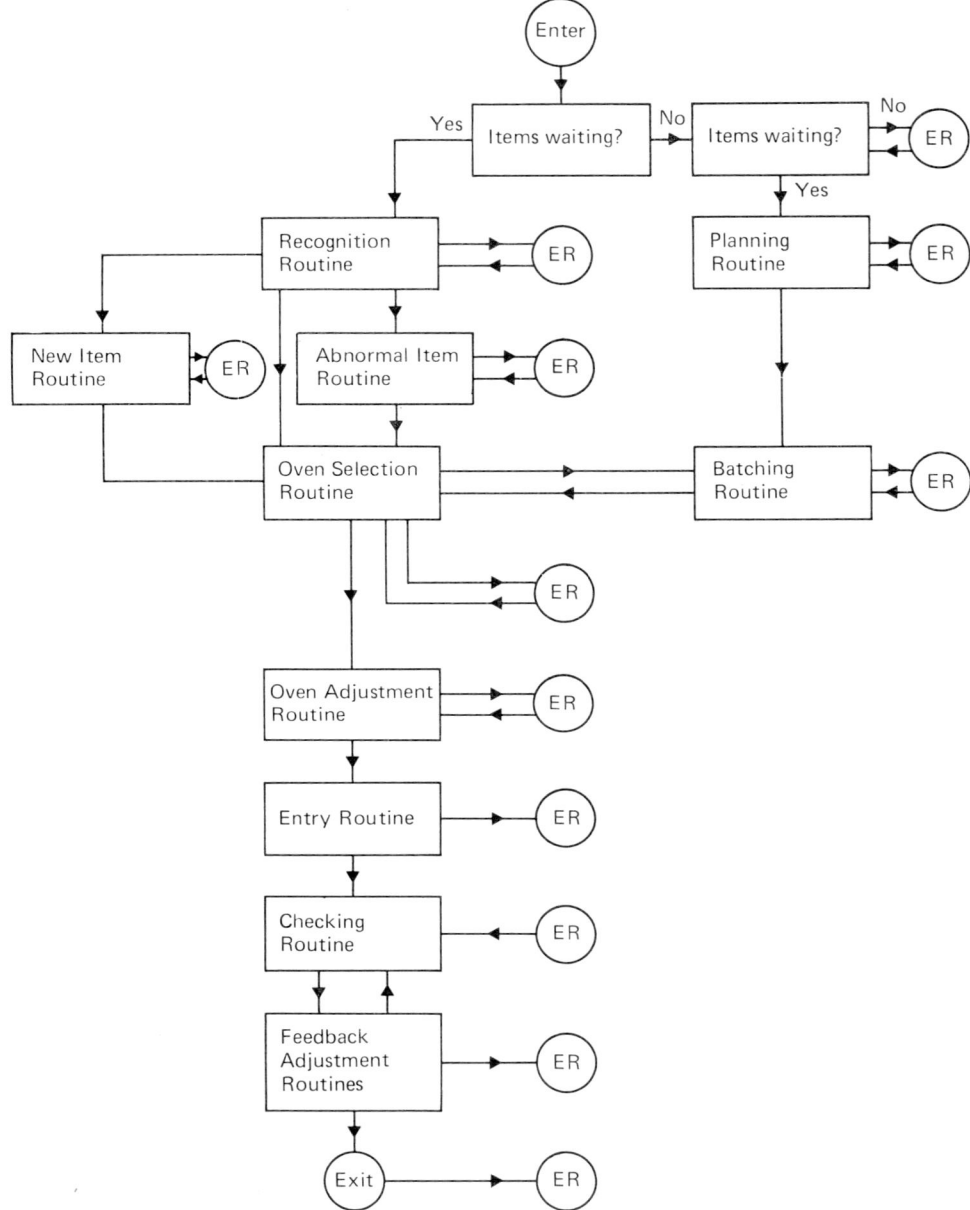

Figure 6. A structure for the Executive Routine.

The Rule Book concept

The usual way to test an information processing model is to program it on a digital computer and to simulate the physical system on the same computer so that the model's control performance can be studied. There are objections to this method in the present case: for example, the perceptual judgments required in many of the routines could not be incorporated into a computer program at present.

A possible alternative test procedure is to use a method which can be called '*the control game*', which is similar in some respects to the Turing 'Imitation Game'. This involves presenting a novice with the task and giving him the model to follow to see whether he will achieve a similar performance to that of an experienced man. The model would have to be set out in a special program form containing the look-up tables, routines and various executive scans so that it could be followed by a human subject. Essentially, this would be a *book of rules* for action in all the circumstances which arise on the plant and it would have to have a clock system to generate the sampling acts. The *rule book* would in fact be the model program, but presented in the form of a book with a linking page reference system which would take the game-player through the routines like a branching programmed textbook. The perceptual judgment problem could be overcome by giving the game-player, on request, perceptual classifications made by an experienced man who is standing by but taking no other part in the test. This test procedure has the merit that it takes place in the real situation and observations of the way the novice performs would immediately disclose any deficiencies in the rule book if the subject could not take a particular decision at any time.

A key concept underlying this rule book system is the assumption that human operators categorize continuous, and to some extent discontinuous, variables into a limited number of categories. For example, speeds of moving objects will normally be put into 5 or 7 perceptual categories.

If all the variables in a system are categorized in this way, the *state of the system* at one point in time can be described in terms of a bounded space in a multi-dimensional *system space*. For example, if a system had only two variables, say temperature and humidity, and these were each categorized into three classes, the system as seen by the observer would be in one of nine possible system states which form a two-dimensional matrix or array. It should be noted that humans do not necessarily categorize variables into equal intervals and some categories will expand in range as the absolute value of the variable increases. This means that the system states will not always be of the same 'volume' in a multi-dimensional space. It is clear from observation of the ovenman that he categorizes the variables in the oven system and it is possible to construct a multi-dimensional space which represents his view of the oven system. The variables put into the system space will be temperature, baking times, rates of change of temperature and the like. This concept of the system space with its separate states is important because without it the ovenman is faced with an infinite, or almost infinite, number of conditions or states in which the oven system could be. It is unlikely that the ovenman will carry an actual multi-dimensional system space for the complete system in his head, more likely there will be a large number of two- or three-dimensional subsystem spaces available. The position is probably even more complicated since the categorizations used by humans are not fixed in time and immediate past experience can change the category structure as adaptation level studies show.

There will be rules for transforming one system state to another, or rather, for moving from one state to another. These rules will be actions or patterns of actions which operate on the system to change it in a desired direction. So for each system state there will be a set of actions or *action states*, which if applied will take the system to a pre-determined new state. Where the system states represent a system which has an operating goal there will be an action state for each system which will move the system towards the goal. It is suggested that for a skill of the kind described here, the ovenman builds up a system state model together with a matching action state matrix which incorporates the decision rules necessary to achieve control. Further exploration of the system state/action state concepts can be found in Cooke (1965) and Beishon (1966).

6. Concluding Remarks

This attempt to analyze the skill of the ovenman illustrates the previously mentioned finding that what appear to be simple skills in fact involve much greater complexities than may be expected. The attempt to build a model at least produces a structure which, although far from perfect, is productive in suggesting concepts and specific mechanisms which can be tested against the data or by further experiment. It also suggests reasons why the skill might be difficult for a novice to perform and from this methods for aiding or training new operators can be devised. Improvements to the present set-up can be put forward: for example, much of the memory load taken up in tracking batches of cakes down the oven could be removed by using simple tag devices or mimic models geared to the conveyor speed.

The author would like to express his thanks to the management of the bakery and to the ovenman for his patient cooperation. Thanks are also due to Mr. J. E. Crawley, Mr. E. Foster and Miss N. Petty for assistance in collecting data. The project was supported by a grant from the Social Science Research Council.

A Study of Real-Time Human Decision-Making using a Plant Simulator

By L. Bainbridge, J. Beishon, J. H. Hemming and M. Splaine

1. Introduction

With the spread of automation and the increasing use of large, complex production systems, there has been a decline in the demand for manual control skills and a consequent increase in the use of what can be called *mental* skills. These skills involve decision-making processes and other intellectual activities which are as yet little understood. The lack of knowledge about mental skills is reflected in the dearth of training schemes for process workers. Often jobs are learnt by working under an experienced man, which is at best an inefficient training procedure and can lead to the perpetuation of poor working strategies. Attempts to replace human operators by control systems have also been hindered by this lack of knowledge, because many industrial processes are too complex and 'noisy' to be controlled by straightforward mathematical equation-based programs. An alternative is to replace the man by simulating him on a control computer, which has the advantage that it can work accurately without fatigue for indefinite periods. Before this can be done, however, it is necessary to know how the man does the task.

One practical problem of considerable importance which arises from the employment of mental skills is the need to know how hard a man is working when he is doing mental work. At present the allocation of men to tasks in large systems has to be done on an arbitrary basis, because it is not possible to predict accurately how much work a man can do in any given time on a new job. A method which would enable system designers to predict the load imposed by particular tasks would be invaluable for manpower planning and for man–machine interface design. The approach adopted by the writers starts from the assumption that a task will require a certain basic amount of information processing to achieve the desired performance goals. This idea means that an understanding of the underlying mental processes of skills is needed before a measurement system can be developed.

Mental skills are difficult to investigate in the laboratory because it is not usually possible to reproduce the complexity of plant conditions and the length of background experience common in industry. For this reason most studies have been carried out in the field, but it is not always feasible to interfere with production schedules and there are often limitations to the amount and extent of observing and recording which can be done. The availability of computer simulations of production plant does, however, offer a chance to experiment under something approaching realistic conditions. The process variables or parameters can be changed at will, all the data can be stored for future analysis and the pacing of the process operations can be varied from the real-time values. This latter feature offers great scope for mental load studies, since the speed at which the decision-making is done by operators is an important factor which is thought to determine the mental load level.

The present paper describes the use of an advanced digital computer simulation of an electric steel-melting shop for a study of decision-making and mental skill in operators. The task involves controlling the power supplied to five electric furnaces where there are important constraints governing the use of electricity. The task is one which is normally undertaken in large electric melting shops and the control actions available to the operator are realistic ones. For the purposes of this study the primary objective of control is to keep the half-hour energy consumption below a stated maximum. Secondly, restriction of the power input during certain states (*i.e.* oxidizing and refining) should be kept to a minimum. Thirdly, given the above two restraints, power input should be as high as possible in order to maximize steel output.

2. General Description of Plant Simulated

The plant simulated consisted of a projected melting shop with five electric arc furnaces. The furnaces are of 2×60, 1×90 and 2×135 ton capacity and have variable process times roughly in the range of 4 to 7 hr. In fact the cycle time depends on the quality of steel being made, carbon steels taking a shorter time, and high-quality stainless steels taking a considerably longer time.

The furnace cycle

The furnace cycle can be divided into the following states:
  (1) Charging (scrap charged to the furnace by overhead crane).
  (2) Melting (where the scrap is melted until a certain amount of kWh/ton have been consumed).
  (3) Further charging (more scrap).
  (4) Melting (as above).
  (5) Oxidizing (carbon removed to a specified level, dependent on quality).
  (6) Refining (furnace bath analysis adjusted, *e.g.* chrome added).
  (7) Tapping (steel poured into ladle held by tapping crane).
  (8) Fettling (furnace bath repaired and electrodes adjusted or changed).

The demand for power by furnaces

The amount of power the furnaces require during steel-making is state-dependent. The power requirements are

High power-requiring states—melting (12 MW for smallest, 25 MW for largest).

Medium power-requiring states—oxidizing + refining (4 MW, 10 MW).

States not requiring power—tapping, fettling and charging.

The simulation model

The model, written in GSP Mk II, represents the working of the melting shop in two ways.

The cranes that exist in the shop are represented, both for charging the furnace with scrap and for tapping and teeming the finished steel. A vacuum degassing plant, which is required for certain qualities of steel, is also represented. The furnaces are each sent through their cycles, process times being sampled stochastically, and certain phases only being entered when specific conditions are satisfied—*e.g.* tapping cranes being available before the furnace can tap, *etc.*

Power demand is also simulated. Each furnace state and furnace size has a mean power level allotted to it. The program samples randomly for each state using the mean and standard deviation to obtain a power level for the furnace state.

In large arc furnace melting shops a certain amount of power surging is experienced and this has been reproduced in the simulation to make judgment of power levels from the meter dials a little more uncertain.

Validation of the model

In a large sophisticated model of this nature, it is always a problem to validate the model results. In this case an added problem was that the melting shop did not exist. There was a melting shop containing two of the furnaces, and another with two small furnaces. The model was adapted to this size and run for a simulated month. The actual half-hourly power demand histogram was obtained and compared with the one produced by the model. This led to some changes being made to the power levels demanded in the intermediate power consumption states and it was then considered by both simulators and melting shop management to be acceptable.

3. The Simulation System

The interface system

The computer system used for this work has one of its output channels connected to an electronic decoding device which can read a string of output characters and activate relevant relays in a matrix of 16×12. This matrix of relays can be used to control the settings of meters, lamps, digital displays, *etc.*, on a display board. With this equipment, a ' plant ' instrument panel or mimic diagram can be operated by the computer according to the behaviour of a simulation of the plant. The computer simulation is normally speeded up to, say, twice or four times the speed of operation of the real plant.

The information system

Information has to be supplied to the operator about the current state of the plant. The information available to the operator is of two kinds: *automatically* displayed and *optionally* available.

Automatically displayed information is available on the display panel and on a teleprinter. On the panel the following information is given for each furnace: the current power consumption rate, the furnace state, the time this state started, the power level being used, and the number of baskets charged and remaining. For the whole shop, the total current power consumption rate, the amount of power consumed so far this half-hour and a ' discrepancy ' measure are displayed. The latter shows what amount of load needs to be shed, or what amount of capacity can be added, from the current point in time until the end of the half-hour in order to reach the maximum demand ceiling. It makes the basic assumption that furnaces will remain in their current states until the end of the half-hour. A digital clock driven by the computer and showing simulated time (to the nearest minute) is also provided. The layout of the panel is illustrated in Figure 1.

The teleprinter provides both a history of the operator's control actions and general information about the progress of the simulation. At the start of the simulation and each successive steel-making cycle, the operator is given the quality of steel each furnace is making. Information is also given as to the weight of scrap charged in each basket at the time the basket is charged. When a furnace starts a new steel-making state, an estimate of the end of state time (assuming that full power is maintained) is automatically given.

In addition to automatically provided information, the operator can ask the computer at any time to give him estimated finishing times for each current furnace state.

Figure 1. The display panel, showing the instruments for each furnace and the ring of coloured lights indicating the current furnace states.

The control system

To take control actions the operator must be able to intervene in the running of the simulation. He is provided with an *input* panel on which he can set control actions to alter power consumption levels. The operator interrupts the computer by using a manual interrupt facility. The computer is then made to read and store the control actions required, and its ' run ' condition is then restored, causing it to carry out the specified control actions. For a fuller description of this facility see Tocher (1965).

The operator can alter the power supply to the melting shop in three ways:

  (1) By altering the amount of power supplied to each and any furnace (at levels of none, 50, 75 and 100% of the amount of power required for the relevant state).

conveniently be set out on an information tree which runs parallel to the action tree. An example of the two trees is given in Figure 4, which deals with a hypothetical task of travelling from home to a new job:

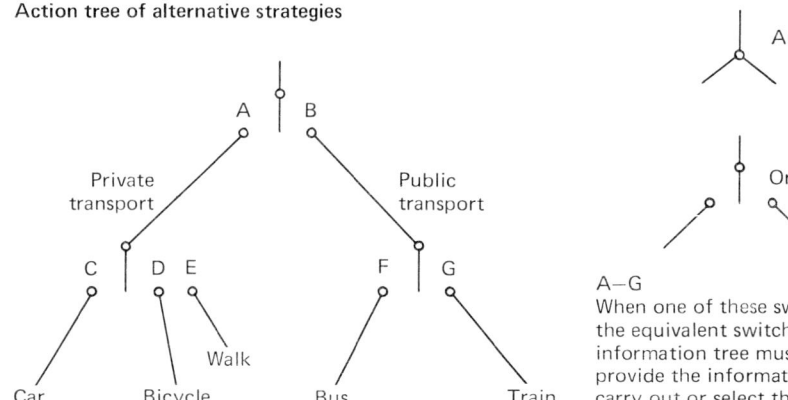

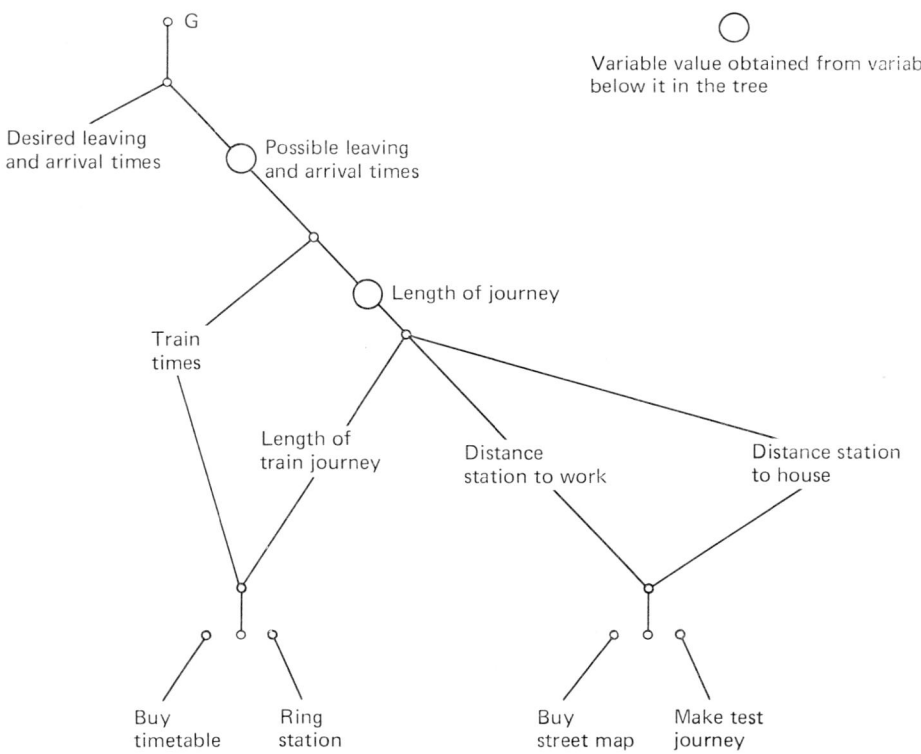

Figure 4. Action/information tree for hypothetical task of travelling from home to new job.

When this action tree structure is drawn out for the melting-shop task it has seven levels to cover the three main control aims. The information tree has fourteen levels which include all the sources of information available to the operator. This structure shows that to make certain decisions the operator has to proceed much further down the information tree than for others, and these will therefore take much longer to process and be more critical when there is a time stress. It is, however, obvious from verbal protocols that subjects do not follow continuous paths down the tree structures in the course of their thinking. Furthermore, the tree structure does not in its present form give the rules for linking information with action at the nodes or a procedure for entering and working through the tree.

Program models

The next step was a study of the possible decision rules and routines which might be used by subjects when doing the task. A decision routine for part of the information tree example given in the previous section, see Figure 4, is set out in Figure 5. From the verbal protocols many such routines for parts of the furnace control task could be identified. Routines of this kind deal with component parts of the overall task and they usually have to be entered at specific times or intervals. The selection of a routine at a particular time must depend on some higher-level initiating system or executive program, and it is at this point that the building of a program-type model becomes complicated. The limitations of the program approach are also evident when the verbal protocols are compared with the routines. The subjects do use these but may

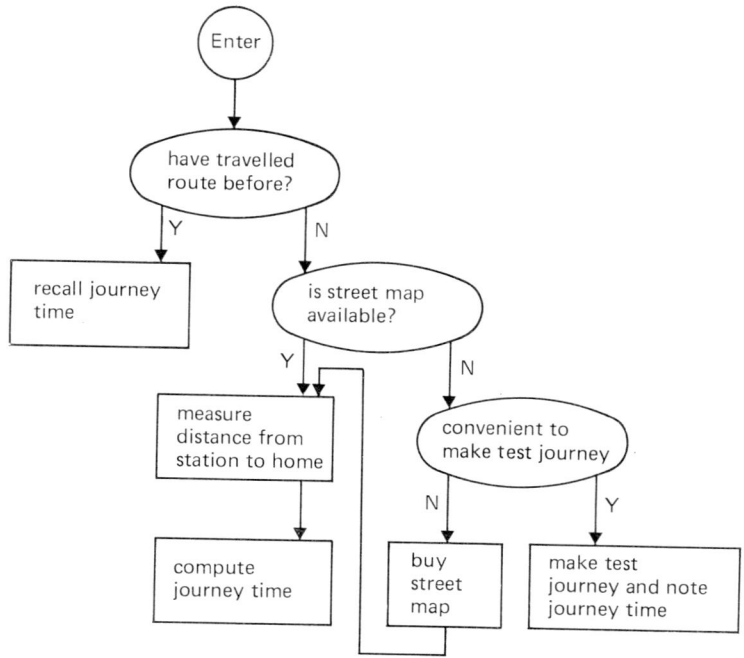

Figure 5. Decision routine for part of information tree given in Figure 4.

vary the way they use them from time to time. For example, a routine for the consideration of *furnace states* is used in the portion of a protocol shown in Figure 6. A program which would simulate all the different sequences of routines which appear in the protocols of even one subject would need a very large number of conditional entry statements. There is no evidence from the protocols that there is a long decision time related to the different choice of routes nor that conditional statements of any particular kind are used. Any attempt to write these in would be purely speculative.

C is on oxidation, now that's something you can make an estimate for, it's a quality so I must leave it alone ... oxidation, average length is 1 hr 30 min for C and started at time zero, no it didn't, it started at time 33 min, how confusing of it, so it's got nearly $1\frac{1}{2}$ hr to run .... I'd better check that. Oxidation for C 1 hr 30 min, started 50 min ago so it's got 37 min to go. D is now on oxidizing, D is going to go into reduce ... it's now using 4 MWs and that's not much ... at when? I had an estimate for D quite recently, now this estimate here, is this absolute time or time from now? (time on that clock) time on that clock, right, that's handy, so D leaves oxidizing for reducing ... I wonder why they oxidise them then reduce them? at 1 . 20....

Figure 6. Typical sample of protocol from inexperienced subject. (Note: This sample of text is analyzed in Figure 7. Experimenter comment is in brackets and ... represents a pause.)

Thought stream analysis

The course of thinking, as reported by subjects doing the task, does not follow either of the above model structures, and there is apparently some 'internal program' which controls the sequence of thoughts. At first sight, the verbal reports appear to be an almost random collection of terms unrelated to each other except that they deal with aspects of the current control task, but when the material is looked at in more detail a structure begins to emerge. The most obvious feature of the protocols is that they are composed of separate sequences of thoughts or *thought streams*, each of which follows a path of fairly closely linked items. The protocols can be rewritten to show the structure, as in Figure 7, which illustrates the portion of protocol given previously in Figure 6.

Once started, the thought streams follow a coherent route, although the course of a particular stream in an individual will be highly idiosyncratic. This is probably related to the associative nature of human recall systems and to the individual way in which each person learns how to deal with a particular aspect of the task. The pattern which emerges is that thought streams are initiated and the subject follows through a piece of connected thinking about this aspect of the task. At the end point, which may be the taking of some action, the subject jumps to a new stream which may not be directly connected to the previous one. The initiation of a thought stream may be internal, for example when a subject follows a sampling pattern looking at each furnace in turn. There is evidence from other studies on process control skills that this self-initiated sampling behaviour is a particularly important part of the skill.

When the protocols are tackled using this method, it is possible to show that the reset points where new thought streams start follow a logical pattern in time. This is partly shown by the small portion of the protocol given in Figure 7, which deals with a consideration of furnace states, going from furnace

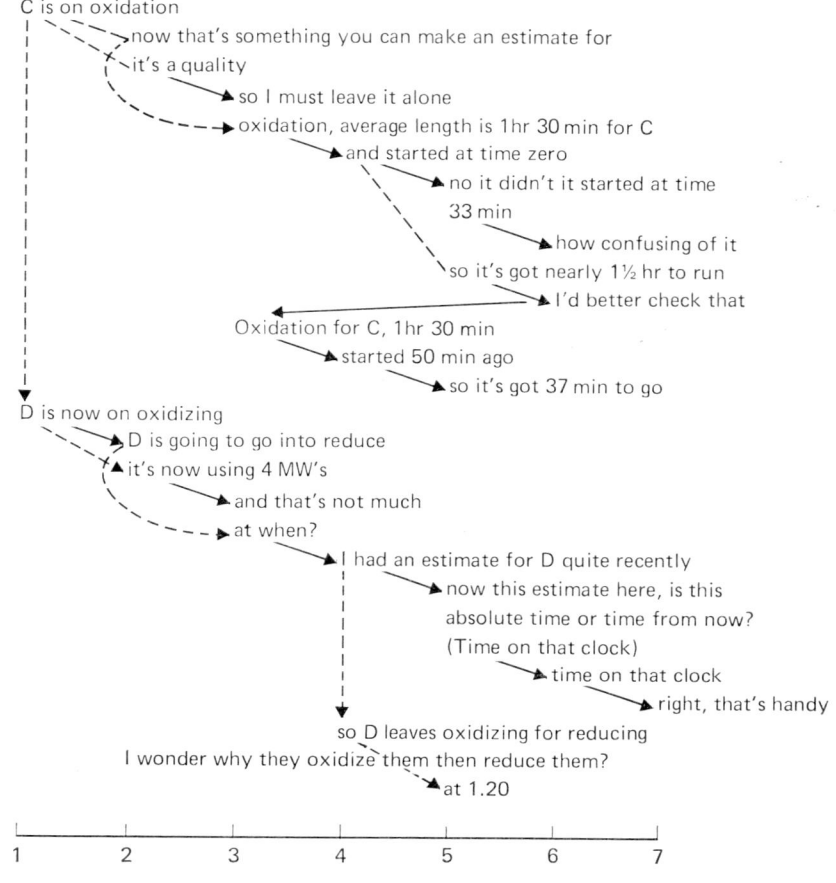

Notes:
(1) Time runs from top of page downwards.
(2) Items to left of page subsume those on right.
(3) Full arrows indicate that statement is related to immediately antecedent statement.
(4) Broken arrows indicate a relation to some earlier statement.
(5) No arrows indicate that no obvious relation exists.

Figure 7. Thought stream analysis for protocol given in Figure 6.

C to D. Analysis of the protocols by this technique cannot be done completely formally as yet, and the decision on the part of the analyst to classify an item as the start of a new stream is still in many cases intuitive. It is hoped that further analysis of this material will lead to some understanding of the program which controls the initiation and resetting of thought streams. One feature of interest which is shown up by the thought stream analysis is the existence of an *interrupt* system which appears to be similar to that used in data processing and on-line process control computers. The human subject will often jump out of a current thought stream and consider a new item(s) for a while then return to the original stream. An example of this is shown in Figure 8:

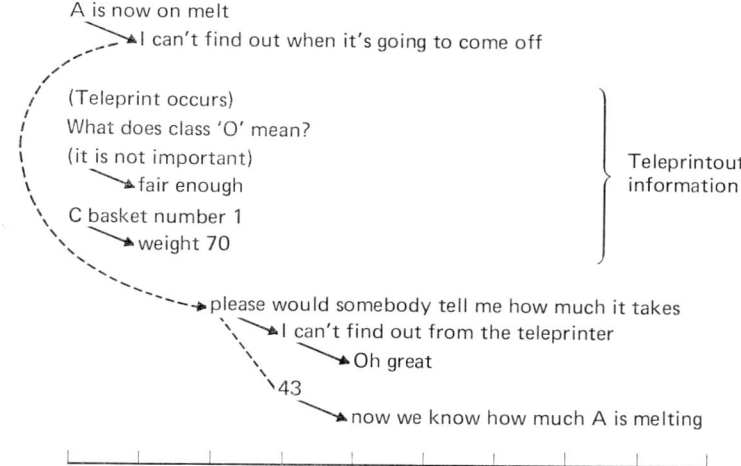

Figure 8. Sample of protocol from inexperienced subject showing the effect of an 'interrupt' occurring (in this example the interrupt is an unexpected signal from the teleprinter). (Notes as for Figure 7.)

6. Implications for Information Transfer Systems

Some general ideas concerning the design of information transfer systems arise from the work described in this paper. It is clear that operators use a variety of strategies in doing jobs involving mental skills and there is not likely to be any one optimal display or information system which will suit every person. When the operating procedure can be formally stated, and men can be instructed to follow an explicit set of rules, it is possible to decide from a study of the required decision rules what information they will need. The design of the information system in this case can proceed along the lines laid down by ergonomists and other specialists concerned with efficient transfer of data across a man–machine interface.

Attempts have been made to apply these principles to tasks where a high degree of mental skill on the part of the operator is required. It is common, however, to find well-designed control rooms, or information distribution systems, which supply men with information they do not use.

One consequence of this situation has been a growing awareness of the need to study the way in which these tasks are done, especially where time is critical or high accuracy needed. This has led to the provision of information which is designed to save computing time for the man, or to aid his accuracy in arriving at a value for a variable which is not normally displayed.

It is not possible to design an information system from first principles unless detailed operating strategies are known beforehand, and the best that can be done in these circumstances is to provide as many sources as is reasonable and to let operators select those they find valuable. This cannot normally be done without overloading display panels; one solution, however, which is becoming increasingly available is to use an on-line control computer to provide values from a wide range of variables on a cathode ray tube.

Although the action/information tree and program models did not describe the observed behaviour in the experiments reported, they are useful as techniques for making explicit efficient operating strategies which can be followed.

The information sources which are required to enable those strategies to be employed can also be obtained from the models, which considerably assists in the design of interfaces.

Study of verbal protocol material from experiments carried out on the simulator suggests that there may be certain dangers in providing the operators with too much ' useful ' information. This arises because people appear to work from an internal ' model ' of the system they are controlling. Very little is known about the form of this internal model, but studies on the subjects' running memory for variables in the system show that they keep mental track of important variables, even though these may be displayed in front of them. It appears that the model can only be kept in mind and updated regularly if the operator is more or less continuously involved with on-going control activity. This is supported by the observation that men have certain difficulty in taking over control of continuously-operating plant when coming on shift. This also applies to managerial personnel returning from holiday. There are, in addition, problems associated with motivational factors and arousal when men have too little to do.

7. Concluding Remarks

The study reported in this paper illustrates that a real-time digital simulation of an industrial process can be a valuable tool for the analysis of human decision-making. A computer-driven simulation makes it particularly easy for an investigator to reconstruct the sequence of events which occurred during an experimental session and also allows many experimental variables to be altered at will. Most of these variables could not be changed on the real plant at all.

With data from the simulation run and also from the introspective verbal report of subjects, models of the human decision-making process can be tested. The present study showed that two models of thinking which might have been used by subjects in this experimental situation do not apply directly. Analysis of the actual thought streams followed by people, however, suggests that there is an executive program underlying thinking which directs thought along specific lines. The program structure is obscured apparently because of the way humans use associative memory and thought sequences based on associations which come from their individual experiences and habitual thought patterns.

If the nature of the executive program could be made clearer, it seems likely that considerable improvements could be made in the information supplied to decision-makers as well as in the way information is provided. For example, it would probably be desirable that all personnel concerned with a particular plant or process should follow the same thought sequences in controlling the system so that optimal decision rules would be followed.

This work was supported by a grant from the British Iron and Steel Research Association for the study of mental load, and our thanks are due to them for their help. Thanks are also due to Dr. O. J. W. Gilbert, of Samuel Fox & Co. Ltd., for help in providing subjects and for assisting in the planning of the experiments. We would also like to acknowledge the help of Professor H. Kay, of the Psychology Department, Sheffield University, in providing undergraduate subjects. The authors thank the United Steel Companies Ltd. for permission to publish this paper.

Mental Loading of Process Operators: An Attempt to Devise a Method of Analysis and Assessment

By J. B. Kitchin[*] and A. Graham[*]

Imperial Chemical Industries Ltd., London

1. Introduction

Much attention has been paid in recent years to the problems associated with the current industrial trend towards production methods which make demands on the operator of a mental, rather than a physical, nature. However, laboratory studies on matters such as perception, vigilance and mental fatigue, have of necessity been conducted on narrow fronts. Since the scope of the whole problem is very great, the results of separate laboratory studies have not yet been integrated to provide industry with generally applicable and workable techniques which can be used in plant design and in the control of operator effectiveness. Further, much of the research work has been concerned with operators working under extreme conditions of load. While extreme loads (mental or physical) certainly exist in industry, they no longer exist to the extent which might be inferred from the emphasis given to them by research workers.

The industrial problem differs from the normal laboratory problem in three major respects:

(1) The mental load on the industrial operator is often the integrated effect of a complex set of independent or interacting factors, whereas the mental load on the laboratory subject is usually the effect of a small number of closely controlled factors.

(2) In industry, the operator's task lasts for 8 or 9 hours a day, five days a week, whereas the laboratory subject is loaded for relatively short periods.

(3) Peak loads in industry occur relatively infrequently and are of short duration, but in the laboratory peak loads are artificially produced over relatively long periods.

The work summarized in this paper was an attempt by Imperial Chemical Industries Limited to see if it were possible to develop a practical technique for assessing the mental load on process operators, against a background of the limited relevance of laboratory findings to complete industrial jobs.

Since the 'laboratory' for these trials was the manufacturing plants of the Company, the test conditions were of necessity much less closely controlled than the conditions of a properly conducted scientific experiment. Also, because of the lack of time and research facilities, a certain amount of subjective judgment was a necessary feature of the exercise. It should be emphasized at the outset, therefore, that these trials were not in any sense scientific experiments, but an attempt to develop an empirical system for practical use.

---

[*] J. B. Kitchin is Personnel Director of the Plastics Division of I.C.I. Ltd. At the time when the work reported here was carried out, he was Deputy Head of the Central Work Study Department of I.C.I. Ltd. in which department A. Graham is currently Head of Pre-Production Section.

Nevertheless, the authors believe that the 'works experimental' approach and the findings of the trials should be of interest to people on both sides of the gulf which sometimes appears to separate the biological research worker from the industrial manager.

2. Objectives of the Trials

For many years and for many purposes I.C.I. has made considerable use of the techniques of work study. As part of this activity, work measurement techniques have been used widely to assist management decisions on several types of problem, including plant manning and the devising of direct financial incentive schemes. In these two fields the work measurement techniques are eminently satisfactory provided that the work done by the operator is predominantly physical in nature. They have only a very limited usefulness, however, in studying activities which are predominantly non-physical.

In view of the trend towards more complex and highly instrumented plants, it was felt that an attempt should be made to devise some parallel technique which would provide information on that part of the process operator's contribution which cannot be expressed by work measurement. Such a technique would, it was believed, be of value in several types of industrial problem wherein it is important to know an operator's total contribution to the achievement of objectives specified by management.

The trials were initiated, therefore, with the intention of trying to develop a procedure for assessing, to an acceptable degree of consistency, the mental activities involved in some typical jobs in the Company. It was regarded as essential that the technique of assessment should be of practical value to management; a crude but workable tool was preferable to an 'accurate' but unwieldy one. Further, the technique had to take into account the established value of work measurement techniques in the area of physical work, and had to provide a sensible complement thereto.

The authors stress the importance of these practical considerations. It was not regarded as appropriate to try and measure mental work, in the sense of expenditure of 'mental energy'. Such an approach was best left to the research workers outside industry. Whether, indeed, such an approach is possible, is outside the authors' competence to say. However, in the present state of knowledge, it would in their opinion be exceedingly difficult to develop such an objective measurement technique which could be used economically in industry, bearing in mind the extent to which individual human characteristics and abilities influence the amount of 'mental energy' which the particular individual must expend in carrying out a specific mental activity.

3. The Scope of Work Measurement

In attempting to analyze the non-physical component of an operator's contribution, it became necessary to define carefully the extent to which conventional work measurement techniques could properly be used, in order to avoid any overlap. Clearly no work is purely physical, since mental work of some sort is an integral part of every purposeful human activity.

As a result of much study, it was shown that work measurement techniques, applied intensively, could give a satisfactory quantitative expression of three types of mental activity on a time basis:

(1) Mental activity involved in directing and co-ordinating muscular activity, *i.e.* during all defined physical movements of the body, including highly manipulative work.

(2) Mental activity in perception (taken to mean the actual receipt of information by any of the senses).

(3) Mental activity of the senses in searching for a random stimulus; in particular, alertness to pick up a random (but likely) signal demanding instant action.

Summarizing, work measurement, although predominantly a technique for measuring work which can be observed as being carried out physically, satisfactorily recognizes for practical purposes those mental activities which are an integral part of some physical activity and which are defined by the physical activity which they accompany in time.

4. A Basis for Assessment

It was desired to determine what other active contribution, if any, an operator made, which could not be determined quantitatively by work measurement. In view of the success achieved in the use of work measurement to determine the physical work of the operator, the possibility of using an analogous technique to assess the effort not covered by work measurement was considered. Work measurement expresses physical effort on a time and intensity basis and expresses the work content of the task in terms of the time the task will take to perform at a specified level of performance. The intensity of effort is recognized in two ways. Firstly, the operator's rate of working is rated against an accepted standard. Secondly, an allowance is made for time to recover from the effects of fatigue. This recognition of intensity of physical effort is based on the conception of the average operator, suitably skilled and trained for his task, and on judgment, based on experience, as to what proportion of an operator's physical capabilities it is reasonable to expect him to expend during the average working period. Although these concepts are, of course, empirical in origin and practice, a great deal of industrial experience has shown that this time-and-intensity approach is satisfactory for physical work measurement.

However, when consideration was given to the purely mental activities carried out by the industrial operator, it was evident that there was little data about the types of such activity, and even less about times necessary to perform them. Such evidence as there was, suggested that these times were extremely small and difficult to isolate. Furthermore, the intensity of mental effort caused by a particular demand depended on the abilities and skills of the operators concerned and probably also upon the type of mental activity called for, to a much greater extent than in the case of physical activities. It was thought that, as so little was known about the mental capacities of operators, the assessment of intensity of mental effort could only be a subjective judgment of doubtful validity.*

It was therefore decided to reject the time-and-intensity approach to mental effort, and try instead to develop a method of assessment which did not have a short-term time base.

The approach which appeared to hold out the greatest chance of sound development, was one which considered the type and complexity of the mental activity on each occasion when it was *demanded by the job*, if it were to be done at a particular level of efficiency specified by management. By combining the assessment of complexity of each mental activity with a measure of the number of occasions upon which it was exercised during a broad time period, it was thought that an assessment of the mental load imposed by the job might be made. Thus the concept of 'mental effort' was replaced by one of 'mental load'. The mental load was concerned with the demands made by the job, and did not attempt to take into account the ability of operators to deal with such demands. It did, however, involve consideration of the ways in which operators reacted to, and thought about, their jobs.

5. Types of Mental Activity

In the range of general worker jobs with which the investigation was concerned, it was thought that there would be a number of differing mental activities which formed part of the operator's total contribution after the physical and associated mental activities properly assessable by work measurement had been recognized. It was decided that any attempt to assess the mental load imposed by such activities should be based on a detailed analysis of the task rather than on any attempt at overall measurement or assessment. Such an analysis, to be of value, had to be able to differentiate between various kinds of mental activity.

At the beginning of the trials, but after consideration of a number of tasks carried out by a range of operators, it was thought that the following classes of activity might be found to impose, to a greater or less degree, a mental load on general workers in a process industry:

(1) Control operations
(2) The recognition of an achieved state
(3) Monitoring
(4) Inspection
(5) Memory
(6) Planning
(7) Mental arithmetic
(8) Alertness or Vigilance.

---

* The authors believe that these observations about lack of knowledge in this field are fair comment, judged in the context of I.C.I.'s investigation. However, it should not be inferred that the authors did not recognize the importance, in other fields of application, of the pure and applied research into mental activities being done by many other people. Indeed, the initial thinking of the I.C.I. investigators was influenced by discussions with several of these research workers. The authors wish to record their appreciation of the encouragement given, in the early days of the investigation, by Dr. E. R. F. W. Crossman of Reading University and Dr. N. H. Mackworth and his then colleagues at the Medical Research Council's Applied Psychology Research Unit.

In order to use these classes as the basis for the detailed analysis of tasks in the field it was necessary to define them with reasonable precision.

Control operations

This class covered the control of certain continuous variables or situations, in which the operator was required to examine and judge fluctuations within and outside the acceptable limits and decide on the corrective action to be taken, if any. The action took the form of adjustment to operating conditions, the sense and magnitude being determined by the operator. An example would be controlling steam pressure from a boiler plant under conditions of varying steam demand by adjusting the output of one boiler.

Recognition of an achieved state

This class was restricted to the operations where the progression of a variable or the development of a situation was (*a*) independent of the operator and (*b*) unidirectional, and where it was known to the operator that a predetermined condition would be arrived at which then left him with only a single predetermined course of action. This would occur, for example, in an exothermic chemical reaction, if the operator is required to take a specific action once a particular temperature has been reached.

Monitoring

This class dealt with the case where a variable was allowed to move within specified limits, and where action defined in nature and extent had to be taken if the limits were exceeded. The class was restricted to the monitoring of variables which were independent of the operator, and took into account the importance of anticipation by studying trends. This differed from the previous class in that the direction of movement of the variable was itself variable and there was no inevitability about the ultimate end point it would reach. For example, an operator on an instrumented plant might be required to watch the trend of the air pressure which actuates his instruments. If an undesirable trend develops he can take no direct corrective action, but can only report the matter to some other authority.

Inspection

This class contained inspection operations in which judgment between acceptance or rejection was required because the distinction between acceptance and rejection standards was not precisely defined. This might occur in the inspection of a product for colour, where fine distinction between shades is necessary.

Memory

This class covered the short-term memorizing of items of current information about a situation or process. It took into account the various items of information which an operator had to pick up at the beginning of each spell of work and retain in his memory during that spell. For example, he might have to remember what material was being processed in a particular batch reactor, and its state and progress. Or he might have to remember the number of compressors available for a particular duty during the shift.

Planning

This class was concerned with operations where an operator had to plan his work ahead so that a number of tasks could be fitted together into a programme, or where action had to be taken when a predicted state of affairs was reached. Examples would be planning the sequence of operations on a multiproduct batch process plant, and planning the optimum utilization of railway wagons of different types for despatching orders of varying sizes.

Mental arithmetic

During the preliminary considerations it was thought necessary to introduce a means of dealing with operations involving simple arithmetical calculations, and a tentative procedure was devised. This class was later deleted, because after close study it was felt that such arithmetic as was done by process operators was below the threshold of mental activities which the experiment sought to assess.

Alertness

It was initially considered that one type of mental activity had to be assessed on a time base. This activity was termed Alertness, and the term Vigilance might equally well have been chosen. Alertness was said to exist in operations in which the state of a process or situation was liable to change rapidly in a manner which required decisive and predetermined action to be taken promptly. The operator had to be in a state of readiness to detect critical stimuli, the occurrence of which was known to be likely but which could not be predicted accurately in time.

Towards the end of the experiment it was decided that, although Alertness in this sense did exist in some of the jobs studied, it could be adequately and appropriately recognized by conventional work measurement techniques, because the Alertness was almost always an integral part of some physical activity. This class was therefore deleted, and instead there was included the third type of mental activity already reported in Section 3 as being within the scope of work measurement.

Having defined, at any rate in a preliminary manner, the various classes of mental activity which one might expect to find in the range of tasks under consideration, it became necessary to devise field trials to determine the practicability of (*a*) recognizing the occurrence of these classes of mental activity and (*b*) setting up a system of quantitative assessment of such activities.

6. Organization of Experimental Trials

The preliminary work detailed above had been carried out by a small directing group consisting of experienced representatives of line management and specialists in labour management and work study. The authors were members of this group, which also guided the field trials. These were carried out by a number of similarly constituted teams consisting of 5–8 members operating in several of the Company's manufacturing Divisions. In all, about 40 senior people were engaged full time on the experiment for about four months. A range of jobs was selected in each Division and each team was briefed in detail as to the analytical methods to be used in examining the various jobs.

Between 50 and 60 complete jobs were studied, ranging from those demanding a high degree of skill and responsibility to those involving little or none. Thus the investigation covered a cross-section of all types of general worker jobs done in the Company, and was not restricted to those wherein the worker's non-physical contribution was clearly significant. Where it was possible, similar jobs were selected on two or more manufacturing sites in order to provide a cross check as to the validity of the techniques when used by independent teams.

Each of the operating teams examined in considerable detail the selected jobs in its own Division, calling into consultation as necessary the line management, supervision, and workers concerned. Much use was made of existing information derived from earlier work study and job evaluation investigations. From time to time during the course of the field trials discussions were held with the directing group to ensure that each field team was proceeding consistently. As might be expected, it was found as the investigation progressed that the original definitions and ideas required some modification in the light of experience. Any such modifications were agreed by the directing group before being adopted by the field teams. The descriptions of mental activities given in Section 5 are based on the definitions which were finally agreed upon.

7. Initial System of Scoring

The method of analysis so far described was, of course, only qualitative, whereas it was desired to find some quantitative expression of mental load. Since the approach was quite different from that of work measurement, or that used by any other investigators known to the I.C.I. team, it was clearly necessary to devise an original method of quantification. A quite arbitrary and tentative procedure of points scoring was decided upon, and different classes of mental load were treated in different ways, as follows:

Control operations. Points were awarded on a ' per occasion ' basis according to (a) the number of items of information which had to be taken into account by the operator, and (b) the number of possible courses of action open to him in making his decision about the action to be taken (or not to be taken). For the first attempt it was decided to give one point for each item of information which required to be taken into account in the analysis of the situation, and one point for each possible course of action open to him. The two sets of markings were then added together to give a points score per occasion.

Whether the linear and additive treatment was justified appeared doubtful at the outset, but the possibility of using non-linear scales was left open for future development.

Recognition of an achieved state. One point was awarded for each factor concerned in the definition of the state to be achieved. One point was added if there was a specially urgent relationship in time between the recognition of the achieved state and the action to be taken.

Monitoring operations. One point was awarded each time the variable was examined.

Inspection operations. One point was awarded each time an inspection resulted in the rejection of the item inspected. An additional point per occasion was awarded if the judgment was concerned with a balance between two or more factors. It was realized that this treatment excluded any credit for judgment followed by acceptance of the item. In the general case, however, it was felt that this was counterbalanced by the unwarranted credit given for rejects which had been so obviously outside specification as to demand no real judgment.

Memory. This was tentatively scored at a flat rate of ten points per item per working shift.

Planning. The scoring method was the same as that for *Control operations*.

Alertness. Assessment of this class of mental activity was quite subjective. The experimenters related the Alertness in each task to a 5-step linear scale related to the amount of Alertness judged to exist in driving a commercial road vehicle in certain specified conditions. This gave the ' Degree of Alertness ', which was multiplied by the minutes of duration to give a points score. This was exceptional in that it had a time base. As has already been noted, this class was eventually deleted.

Since the points scale under each class of mental activity was quite arbitrary, it was realized at the outset that if the described method of assessment were to be followed to a useful conclusion, it would ultimately be necessary to arrive at weighting factors for each class. Thus a total weighted score per shift, covering all mental activity not recognized by work measurement, could be calculated for each job. For reasons which will become evident, these weighting factors were never in fact finalized.

7.1. *Load over Working Period*

With the exception of the *Memory* class, the points scoring scales were on a ' per occasion ' basis: that is, the score indicated the relative mental load imposed by that activity when done once only. Although time measurement was not involved in deriving any of these scores, it became necessary to reduce them to a common time base to allow comparisons between jobs. It was decided to adopt the normal working period of a day or shift as the common time base; scores ' per occasion ' had, therefore ,to be adjusted according to the frequency of the particular activity, so as to give a score which represented that activity's contribution towards the total mental load imposed by the job over a whole day or shift.

Initially, frequency of occurrence was taken to have a straight multiplying effect on the mental load per occasion. That is, if a particular *Control operation* scored five points per occasion, and occurred 12 times per shift, then the *Control operation* load for this particular task in the job was represented by 60 points. Apart from the doubtful validity of the original assumption, which is discussed later, the problem arose as to the interpretation of frequency of occurrence. An instrument might have been examined 16 times per shift, yet only four occasions called for real judgment and only two called for remedial action. Thus the total mental load per shift imposed by this instrument could have three expressions, depending on whether the frequency was based on examination, judgment or action. It was felt that the judgment frequency was the most important, and the most appropriate in the context of the investigation, but was very difficult to determine. Action frequency, readily determinable, was accepted as the most practical basis for assessment.

8. Interim Results of the Experiment

The results took two forms. Firstly, for each of 50 whole jobs in the Company, there were figures purporting to represent the mental load per shift resulting from several types of mental activity. Secondly, a tremendous amount of new information about jobs, and understanding of the mental processes involved therein, had been acquired by a large number of experienced managers, engineers, labour officers, and work study officers.

It was a formidable task to collate the arithmetical results and to interpret them in the light of the often divergent views of the investigators. Each of the operational teams spent two days discussing with the directing group their own team's results, their interpretation of these results, and their views on the technique of assessment. During this period of recapitulation, the main questions to be answered were as follows: Did the method of analysis and the scoring procedure (assuming proper weighting of points in different classes could be agreed) provide a consistent, valid, and workable technique (or the beginnings of one) for assessing mental load in process jobs? If not, why not? Experimental teams were by no means unanimous in their replies to these questions, and individual views of some aspects of the technique ranged from cautious acceptance to forthright rejection. A good deal of constructive criticism was made, however, which enabled the directing group to revise its approach.

Consistency

Inadequate definition of classes of mental activity proved to be an obstacle to the attainment of consistency. Although considerable attention was paid by all teams to problems of definition, inconsistency arose between teams—and even between jobs studied by the same team—because of the practical impossibility of defining the classifications well enough for them to be comprehensive yet unambiguous. Difficulties also arose from inability to specify clearly at the outset the threshold level of mental activity below which an activity was decreed to be insignificant and therefore outside the scope of the technique.

Validity

Validity was difficult to deal with. Normal procedure for validating the results of scientific experiment could clearly not be used. There were in fact no absolute criteria by which the results could be judged. The best that could have been hoped for was that the total weighted scores inter-related the jobs in a way which seemed to make sense to the experimental teams; that is, that the technique gave an inter-relation which lined up reasonably well with one arrived at by making an overall, subjective, but informed and sophisticated judgment about the relative amounts of mental load in these jobs. In acknowledging the limitations of such a means of validation, the authors would stress that in the confusing complex of uncontrollable factors which affect human problems in the real industrial situation, such a subjective approach is often not merely the *only* procedure, but a quite satisfactory one.

In the event, the procedural defects of the experimental method made it inappropriate to attempt such a validation. It was more appropriate, and more profitable, to consider validation much more qualitatively, by discussing the experimenters' theoretical views on the nature of the mental work being assessed, and on their practical experiences of the embryo technique. Considerable divergence of opinion was found, as was perhaps to be expected. Some teams felt that the technique could be readily improved and adapted to give a valid means of expressing the kind of mental load they sought to recognize. Others disagreed, for a number of reasons. The main criticism was directed at the arbitrary system of points scoring, which did not make sufficient distinction between mental activities of varying complexity. Further, it was felt that the threshold had been set too low, and that the mental load attributed to many simple activities had been unrealistically high. Again, the straight multiplier approach to the frequency effect gave a distorted picture of mental load.

Several teams expressed the opinion that there was another type of mental load which existed in some jobs—notably in the control of highly instrumented plants—which the technique did not recognize. This was the background mental load continuously imposed on an operator by virtue of his having to bear in mind the state and significance of a number of concurrent variables relevant to the process being controlled.

Workability

When workability of the technique was considered, a greater degree of unanimity was apparent. The technique was extremely complicated and difficult to apply. Certainly a great deal of information had been thrown up which would be valuable in other respects; but, considering the technique merely as an assessment procedure, most people thought it was cumbersome and quite uneconomic as a practical tool in industry. It was generally felt that a simplified approach could and should be developed.

9. Simplified Technique

The directing group set themselves the task of developing an improved and simplified technique which took into account the constructive criticisms which had been made, and which was based on a new and clearer understanding of the nature of the problem and its possible solution. After much theoretical consideration, and a further limited amount of experiment, it was concluded by the central team that mental load could be satisfactorily expressed in two parts. These were the decision-taking load and the background mental load.

Decision-taking load

Considering the classes of mental activity in use at the end of the experiment it was evident that, with the exception of *Memory*, they all had a common element of decision-taking. The central idea of decision-taking was therefore chosen as a basis for a one-class assessment technique.

A decision-taking situation was said to exist when an operator's course of action was determined by consideration of the current factors in the situation. That is, when there had been no precise specification as to

                    WHAT had to be done
                    HOW MUCH had to be done, and
                    WHEN it had to be done

Thus a decision was involved if the operator had any discretion in the nature, extent, and timing of an action. It was accepted that a decision taken by a particular operator might call for pure reasoning, the application of memory patterns, or any combination of the two. Looked at in terms of the job, however, the nature of the operator's mental effort was not of real importance. For this reason, and because in fact it would have been impossible to establish the ratio of reasoning to memory in each situation, it was concluded that decisions should be analyzed on the assumption that only reasoning was involved.

Decisions were analyzed under five headings, and another arbitrary (but, it was thought, more realistic) points scoring method was devised, as follows:

(a) *The number of factors in the situation.* The score was obtained by subtracting one from the number of factors (items of information) relevant to the decision. The subtraction eliminated many simple situations wherein no real judgment was necessary in order to reach a conclusion regarding the course of action.

(b) *Complexity of comprehension of each factor.* Points from 0 to 4 were awarded by subjectively comparing each factor with a set of fixes. For example, no points were awarded for simple factors such as instrument readings and observation of simple physical facts and conditions such as a level in a sight glass. Four points were awarded for a factor which could be comprehended only by making an overall assessment of many interacting elements which constituted the factor, such as the state of a boiler fire-bed.

(c) *Memory.* One point was awarded for each factor brought to the decision-taking situation from the short-term memory.

(d) *Interdependency of factors.* One point was awarded for each pair of factors in the decision which were interdependent insofar as the desired value of one factor was dependent on the actual value of the other.

(e) *Delay characteristics of situation.* Mental load in a decision was increased if there was in the process an inherent delay in the feedback of the effects of any action the operator might take. One point was awarded if the delay was greater than one minute, and an additional point if the system had non-averaging characteristics.

For each decision, a points score per occasion was obtained by adding up the points awarded to that decision under each of the five headings above.

The original approach had been criticized because of its complication, and the revised one-class procedure went a long way towards meeting this criticism. The earlier feeling that the datum had been set too low, was met by the simple device of deducting one from the score attributable to the number of factors. This eliminated a great many very simple ' decisions ', indeed almost all single-factor ' decisions ' where the factor was in itself simple to comprehend. Further, the inclusion of a scale of comparative fixes for complexity was an attempt to remedy a criticized defect in the original treatment.

The last major criticism had been concerned with the effect of frequency.

Effect of frequency

It was decided to continue to base the assessment of mental load arising from a decision-taking situation on the number of times this situation led to positive action in the average shift.

The straight multiplying effect of frequency used in the experiment, however, was thought to be unrealistic. If a particular decision merited x points for one occurrence, and resulted in action 10 times per shift, then the total load per shift was not necessarily represented by $10x$. Repetition naturally meant greater familiarity with the situation, so that each repetition of a decision in a particular situation incurred a smaller amount of reasoning than before. The situation tended, in the extreme, to demand little more than automatic or reflex action. It was not possible, or indeed appropriate, to be very theoretical about devising a new scale of frequency multipliers. Rather, a scale was sought which not only looked reasonably sensible but gave sensible results when applied to the 'per occasion' scores. The following table of multipliers was ultimately drawn up:

Frequency of the particular decision	Multiplier
Not less frequently than once per 20 working periods, but less than once per working period	1
Once or twice per working period	2
3 to 8 times per working period	3
9 to 32 times per working period	4
33 or more times per working period	5

This scale was very much 'flatter' than the original one. Although much more experimental work was thought to be necessary, it was felt that any departure from this new scale should be in the direction of even more 'flatness'. In the extreme, it was thought possible that all multipliers might be unity. That is, that the effect of frequency might be ignored altogether, the total shift load of a decision being represented by the points score per occasion.

10. Subjective Validation

The revised one-class assessment was applied to 43 of the original jobs. Because the results of the original experiment on a 6-class basis had been fully documented, it was possible to apply the revised procedure without further field trials. After a certain amount of necessary consultation with the Division teams, the directing group was able to re-classify and re-score the mental activities originally recorded, as an office exercise.

It was possible, therefore, to produce for each job a number of points which represented the total decision-taking load in that job, being the sum of shift scores for each decision in the job. Each Division team had made a subjective judgment of the relative amounts of mental load in the jobs they had examined, without regard to any points scores derived during the first part of the experiment, and this was used as a yardstick by which to make a rough test of the validity of the analytical technique. The result of this test was reasonably satisfactory. By and large, the analytical technique ranked the jobs in the same order as the subjective judgment of the highly-experienced experimenters. There were some notable exceptions, but there were usually special features in these jobs which explained the discrepancy.

However, although the order of ranking was fairly satisfactory, the absolute values of the decision-taking loads were of unknown validity. In other words, the technique had placed the jobs fairly sensibly on the rungs of a decision-taking ladder, but little was known about the correctness of the spacing between the rungs, or about the length of the ladder and its position relative to the ground.

Background mental load

The above validation was done without considering the background mental load which was believed to exist in some jobs. This omission was made deliberately for two reasons. (1) The concept of a background load was formulated too late in the experiment to allow any development. (2) It was believed that, in terms of the relative effect on the operator, background mental load was much less significant than decision-taking load. Therefore, for this experiment, decision-taking load was regarded as a satisfactory expression of total mental load. Background mental load offered a useful field for further experiment, and it was tentatively proposed that this load might be roughly expressed by merely counting the number of concurrent sources of information in the process.

11. Conclusion

(1) The method of analyzing decision-taking situations showed promise as a step towards the development of a largely objective and practical means of ranking process jobs in terms of the mental load imposed on the operators. The step was perhaps a faltering one, but it was undoubtedly in the right direction.

(2) There was scope for further research on the problems of decision-complexity, frequency effect, and background mental load. However, the tentative decisions on these matters, made during the trials, seemed to be reasonably acceptable in the context of the immediate uses to which the results of the technique were likely to be put.

(3) The technique was complementary to the techniques of work measurement, inasmuch as it gave information on a part of the operator's contribution not expressed by work measurement. It was not complementary to work measurement in the sense of giving an expression of mental effort based on time and intensity which could be added directly to the time necessary for the physical work at a specified level of performance. However, in the authors' view, mental effort expressed as a rate of working is at this time a concept of little practical value in their industry.

(4) Many indirect benefits resulted from the trials, principally connected with the increased understanding of process-controlled situations which was gained by management. The authors believe that the knowledge which can be derived from such an analysis of mental loading can be of value to management in the following areas:

    (i) Plant design; in particular the design and layout of instruments and controls

    (ii) The study of existing process operating methods with a view to improvement

(iii) Operator specification and selection
(iv) The drawing up of plant operating instructions
(v) Operator training
(vi) The planning of operator deployment in advance of plant construction.

12. Some Final Observations

In these days of advanced techniques of manufacture, complex processes, automation and so on, many industries are facing problems concerned with the balance of physical and mental abilities demanded of their operators. It is frequently said that a new breed of industrial operator is becoming necessary, an operator of higher intelligence and with a greater understanding of modern technology. This is a very big subject, and outside the scope of the present paper. In comment, the authors would merely concede that technological change inevitably demands a re-appraisal of ideas on operator selection, training, and supervision. However, there has grown out of this general thought a popular, although in the authors' opinion ill-founded, belief that in modern industry an operator can be assumed to be thinking about his process if he is not seen to be working on it. It would be unfair to suggest that either management or men would necessarily phrase this belief in such unequivocal terms, but there does seem to be a tendency for this industrial mythology to colour many people's views on the subject.

The work reported in this paper did a great deal to get the picture into perspective in I.C.I. There is no doubt that significant decision-taking loads are imposed on certain operators, but by and large the experiment indicated that the mental activities of process operators are much less than is popularly believed. This is not to say, of course, that no thinking is done! To run a chemical plant with operators who are incapable of taking any but the simplest decisions is inconceivable. But in practice, in a stable manufacturing process, the mental load of reasoning and taking decisions often falls on the supervisor rather than the operator. It seemed, in fact, that once a certain degree of plant instrumentation and automatic control had been reached, the mental load on the operator was often much lower than the load imposed by less elegant processes which required the operator to exercise direct control.

So it appeared that, in some types of process and in some supervisory situations, a quantitative expression of mental load on the operator was of little importance. It was clear, on the other hand, that mental load and physical work load do not give a complete picture of the total contribution which operators are expected to make towards the achievement of objectives specified by management. That is, the experiment's attempts to *quantify* non-physical components of total contribution had underlined the importance of the *quality* of these components. Although an operator may be required only infrequently to make a major decision, his potential contribution is largely influenced by his ability and willingness to take appropriate thought and action during unsteady operating conditions and in cases of emergency. He must therefore have the proper attributes of character, intelligence, and skill, to enable him to recognise the infrequent need for a decision and to reach a sound one. And, of course, he must be in an organizational situation which motivates him to do so. This attempt to quantify the mental contribution required of process operators, therefore, indicated another very important area for further field research; that is, the area of character requirements without which the operator's physical and mental abilities are of little value to industry.

The authors are indebted to the many people in I.C.I. Ltd., whose hard work made this paper possible. In particular they wish to mention Mr. W. B. Stead, Work Study Manager of the Alkali Division of I.C.I. Ltd., whose diligence and patience as operational leader of the trials directing group was an inspiration to all his colleagues.

Copyright is reserved by I.C.I. Ltd.

The Interaction between Human and Automatic Control

By D. Attwood

Bowaters United Kingdom Paper Co. Ltd., Northfleet, Kent

1. Introduction

A papermachine is a complex man-machine system and presents many ergonomics problems. The problems can be divided into three groups concerned with

(1) Control of processes and materials (for example, furnish, consistency, moisture, basis weight).
(2) Remote handling of materials (for example, transport of pulp to Hydrapulpers, reels to supercalender and winder).
(3) Semi-repetitive maintenance (for example, grinding of press and calender rolls, wire changing).

In this paper, only the ergonomics aspects of the first group will be considered and basis weight alone has been selected for detailed study. This is because the problems of basis weight control are so well known and automatic control of basis weight is at last becoming commonplace. The study to be outlined here has been selected to illustrate the ergonomics analysis of an existing production system using direct observation and interview and owes a lot to the technique used by Sell, Crossman and Box (1962), although the actual results were obtained by (*a*) direct observation and (*b*) interviewing machine operators at three mills identified as A and B (newsprint mills) and C (a coating mill).

2. The Ergonomics Analysis

System goals. The ultimate goal of the papermaking operation is to convert wood into paper of dimensions and printing properties specified by orders received, using the least possible labour and materials and making the most economical use of capital equipment. Within this, the sub-goal of the papermill is to convert pulp into reels of paper and within this again the sub-goal of the papermachine is to convert thick stock into a specified sheet of paper 50–100 g/m², preserving at the same time a surface that will take a good print. Loss of paper due to breaks must be avoided.

The process. A, B and C are all Fourdrinier papermachines and C is equipped with a Massey coating system. In all three cases, the basis weight is adjusted by means of a stuffgate and basis weight is determined at each reel change by weighing five samples. Machine C has a single-position beta-gauge.

Man's role in the system. All the physical motive power is provided mechanically and man's role is to control its application. No automatic controls were used on the machines studied, so that all the control is exercised by human beings.

There are several kinds of control function involved:
(1) Primary adjustment, following a prearranged programme
(2) Secondary adjustment, needed to iron out any side effects of the primary adjustments or of other disturbances
(3) Timing control to synchronize weight changes with reel change, *etc.*

Each of these control functions may be carried out in either (a) an open-loop or (b) a closed-loop manner, depending on whether the operator has current knowledge of the results.

3. Detailed Consideration of Human Tasks

Primary Adjustment—Basis Weight

Since the system sub-goal is to produce paper of the basis weight required for a series of orders set out in a programme, weight changing is a primary adjustment. This is the responsibility of the machineman.

Open-loop adjustments. When the schedule calls for a change in nominal basis weight, the machineman decides what change in stuffgate setting is likely to produce it, indicates his intention to the reelerman and, when the time comes, he makes the appropriate alteration to the stuffgate. He is then acting as an open-loop controller.

An open-loop control system must be calibrated and, in this case, the machineman carries in his head a rough table of the stuffgate changes required for different basis weights based on his past experience.

When machinemen were interviewed, it was found that they all knew the stuffgate changes needed for various changes in basis weight, but their figures and the allowances suggested differed materially between individuals.

The permitted tolerance on basis weight is about $\pm 5\%$, but direct study of the effects of a basis weight change showed that several reels were out of tolerance after a major change and it seems therefore that the decision process could be improved.

Unaided human memory is used to gather the experience on which major stuffgate changes are based; but human memory for quantitative data such as these is poor. It is common practice to make a stuffgate change at the end of a reel so as to be on target for the next order. Unfortunately, the machineman does not always allow sufficient time for his change to have had full effect and often his sample (taken, say, 3 or 4 minutes after his adjustment) shows only half the required basis weight change and he makes a further entirely unnecessary adjustment, which he subsequently has to remove.

Machine C is equipped with a beta-gauge that monitors the base material before coating. This gives an immediate knowledge of results and should help the machineman to make corrective stuffgate changes much more rapidly. It was observed on machine C, however, that little or no use was made of the gauge. This could be because no one is particularly interested in the base weight. It is the machineman's job to keep the total weight (base plus coating) constant and the coaterman's job to keep the coating weight constant. Although this implies a constant base weight, it is not in fact a direct goal. If only one beta-gauge is to be installed on the machine, it would be far better on the finished sheet to give an indication of final substance, the machineman's goal. Ideally, of course, two are required, so that the coating weight can be obtained as well.

Since the actual weight fluctuates 2 or 3% over periods of 2–3 minutes and the beta-gauge displays only the value integrated over 5 seconds, the operator must visually 'integrate' or 'average' its readings over several minutes to decide whether an apparent departure from correct basis weight is steady or merely transient. Some form of storage could well be incorporated in the display both to enable a judgment to be made without prolonged inspection and to retain information when the machineman is elsewhere.

Closed-loop adjustments. The order usually calls for a run of several reels to be made to the same nominal basis weight and quality. As the order proceeds, the machineman can take corrective action to bring the basis weight into line with the nominal, using knowledge of the results of his first stuffgate settings and acting as a closed-loop controller. The error-feedback information comes through a human link, since the basis weight is determined at the dry end by the use of a balance. The results are written down and reported to the machineman. Since the samples can be obtained only at reel changes, the cycle *trial-error-feedback-fresh trial* takes some time to operate and, when an inaccurate initial change has been made, several reels are made outside tolerance.

There seem to be no set instructions for making corrections. For instance, on machine B, the machinemen could not immediately say how far the weight should deviate before they took corrective action. Eventually, it was said that on a making of 14 lb demy they would take action at 13·8 to increase the weight and at 14·4 to decrease the weight, but obviously these figures are not laid down and again the machineman is carrying in his head a rather diffuse table of corrections. All the machinemen on this machine stated that half a revolution of the stuffgate was about $\frac{1}{2}$ lb demy, but it was difficult to find out what magnitude of corrective changes were made. It seems that in this case the *goal* is not very well defined; although the target is said to be 14 lb demy, in fact the machineman finds it preferable to run heavy rather than light. An improvement in precision might be obtained here by giving the machineman a new goal (in this case, 14·1 lb demy) and saying that corrective action must be taken at, say, 14·4 and 13·8, although of course, if 14 lb demy is required, then the goal should remain 14 lb. The correction should also be indicated and, in this case, an instruction to change the stuffgate setting by $\frac{1}{4}$ revolution in the appropriate direction whenever these limits are reached should be given.

Some confusion exists, because in fact the machineman is never presented with an average weight, but with the weights of five samples across the machine. He averages these ' by eye ', but any action he might take is governed by the highest and lowest values. Thus, if five weights 14·7, 14·4, 13·9, 14·4 and 14·8 are given, then he would not lower the value because of the 13·9 reading.

It is not so easy to find out what governs slice settings. It is certainly not basis weight, the sole criterion appears to be a good hard reel. If complaints come back from the reelerman about the reel, then the slice will be adjusted and the dry line used as a yardstick for levelness.

Making Stuffgate Changes

On machine C, the machineman is provided with a valve labelled 0–16 in order to control the basis weight. At the time of the interviews, the valve was set at 4 for a base sheet weight of 20 lb DC. The machineman changed the setting by tapping the handle with a short piece of steel. The first machineman questioned estimated that $\frac{1}{4}$ inch movement would give a change of weight of 5 lb. The second could not say, but said that the setting was 6 for a base sheet of 30 lb. These two estimates agree moderately well.

This is a system with obvious ergonomics drawbacks. Even though this particular stuffgate may not have ideal flow characteristics, it could be provided with a simple gear reducer so that the machineman could carry out the small changes required with much greater precision. The stuffgate is placed at the backside of the machine, remote from the beta-gauge and from the machineman's normal position. On the other hand, the control of coating weight on this machine seemed to be far superior. The control wheel for regulating the weight was labelled 0–60 and the operator stated that 8 divisions was about $1\frac{1}{2}$ lb. Thus, the handwheel needed to be rotated 48° for $1\frac{1}{2}$ lb and, since the tolerance on weight is about ± 1 lb, it is obviously possible to make sufficiently fine adjustments.

On machine B, the adjustment seems fine enough, a half turn is equal to $\frac{1}{2}$ lb, which is probably remembered because of the roundness of the figures. Even if these were in error by 10%, since the stuffgate is used to make corrections, then no great problem should arise. The valve suffers, however, from backlash and, although the machineman takes this out by feel, he does not always achieve the correct setting. In one experiment in which a machineman was asked to raise the substance by $\frac{1}{2}$ lb, he made his appropriate movements to the handwheel, but there was no change in weight and it was found that the valve stem had not in fact moved. The machineman on this occasion had not overcome the backlash.

In general, machinemen during interview did not appear to understand the behaviour of backlash and an aura of mystery seems to surround the stuffgate.

This is because it is not ergonomically sound. Either the flow of thick stock to the machine should be recorded or the position of the valve spade itself recorded. If they are recorded, a suppressed zero will be required so that the small adjustments can be seen. Again, on machine B, the stuffgate is remote from the machineman's normal position where he receives information about basis weight.

Timing Control

All machinemen were aware of the time delay that occurs after a stuffgate change has been made, but none was aware of the real nature of this delay.

We have observed on machine A that very often the machineman obtains a sample at, say, time T and, even though he has in fact made the perfect adjustment, he makes a further change, because he thinks his adjustment is in error.

This is a tricky problem to resolve with existing equipment, although instruction might help. This time lag could be overcome with a specially-built stuffgate (that is, one that overcorrected, then moved back to the desired position).

4. Summary of Proposals

In short, then, the ergonomics analysis singles out the following points of weakness in the present system:

(1) Inadequate long-term storage and processing of data relevant to stuffgate decisions.
(2) Beta-gauge requires short-term storage and better display.

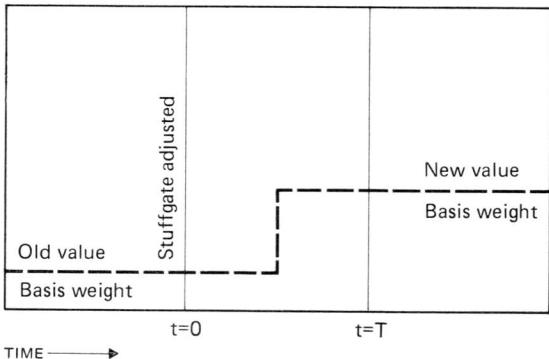

Figure 1. What the machineman thinks happens.

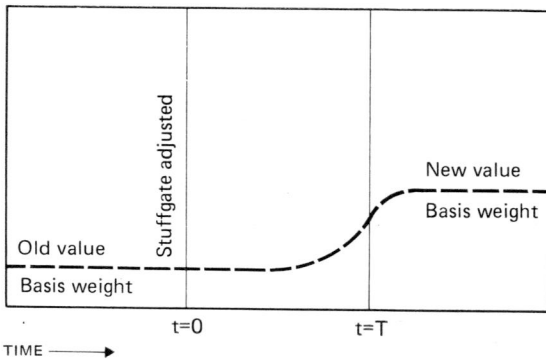

Figure 2. What really happens.

(3) Stuffgate control needs to be centralized.
(4) A display of the stuffgate setting required.
(5) A preselector mechanism to carry out stuffgate changes would be valuable.

5. Conclusions of the Ergonomics Analysis

The analysis described is only an outline. Several important aspects of mill operation have been ignored, nor have the detailed design considerations governing the proposed changes been given. Enough should have been said, however, to show how the ergonomics approach can be applied.

An ergonomics analysis involves technical and management considerations, as well as the human sciences, and a particular design problem can be dealt with only in the context of the whole system of which it forms a part. Undoubtedly, the changes proposed here could have been suggested without the analysis, but there would then be insufficient grounds for expecting useful results. There are many other changes that could be made, but it is believed that the analysis pinpoints those that could contribute most to operating effectiveness.

Most studies aimed at understanding the human operator's characteristics as part of a man-machine system are concerned with the behaviour of the human operator as a controller of mechanical and electronic systems such as guns, aircraft and fast-acting machinery. Attempts have been made to establish a human transfer function (North 1952, Sheridan 1960), but it is apparent from the results that performance cannot be adequately expressed in terms of any single transfer function.

Most work on manual control has employed systems having response times from small fractions of a second to a few seconds at most, so that the operator is exercising a manual skill without conscious deliberation. One of the more fruitful fields of study in the literature related to processes with slow responses is in connection with the control of atomic submarines. In physical terms, a submarine behaves in a similar way to an aeroplane, the only essential difference being the time scale, yet it is apparently true that human beings find it easier to control an aeroplane than a submarine. Chemical and metallurgical processes involving heat transfer may have time constants measured in hours and the response of basis weight to a change in setting of the stuffgate could typically have a distance-velocity lag of about 3 minutes, followed by a time constant of about 20 minutes. In all these cases, an operator can exercise adequate control after a period of learning, but (as the first part of this paper indicates) there is evidence to show that manual control of these slower systems is far from perfect. To revert to the submarine problem, apparently a quite difficult task is to place the submarine on the sea bed (the effect of overshoot can be imagined) and, of the simpler aids now employed, a predictor giving a graphic display of where the submarine will be in the next 7 minutes is one of the most useful for the submarine. From what was said earlier, it will be appreciated that, if a predictor were available on a papermachine to show what the basis weight was likely to be over the next 7 minutes, the operators would be able to effect a considerable increase in their control of basis weight.

The use of automatic controls is not a complete solution, because there are many cases to which they cannot be applied and it is also clear that human operators can perform substantially better than automatic controls in certain cases.

Crossman (Crossman and Cooke 1962) has studied the manual control of slow-response systems, but seems not to have appreciated the difference between distance-velocity (d.v.) lag and exponential lag of processes. He created a laboratory task having many features met in a typical process control situation, the most significant of which was that it had an exponential time constant of 2 minutes. He showed that manual operators very easily got the system into an unstable oscillatory condition with a time constant of about 10 minutes. When I published a paper (Attwood 1961) on the use of a beta-gauge to control basis weight, I included some studies on manual control that showed how papermachine operators managed to put the basis weight system into slow oscillation with a time constant of about 2 hours. Crossman was interested in these results and, after a discussion, I decided to construct a laboratory task based on Crossman's original, but including a distance-velocity lag. All the time constants were chosen to be as close as possible to the papermachine for which I had a number of results. Before describing the laboratory task, it is worthwhile to analyze the way in which papermachine A was controlled manually. This is shown in Figure 3 and can be explained as follows.

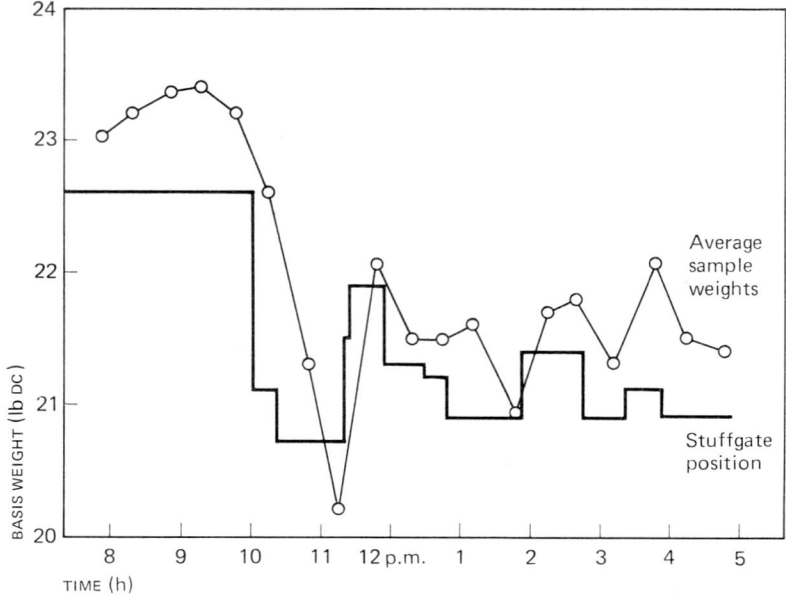

Figure 3. Basis weight change on a papermachine (from 22·9 lb to 21·3 lb double crown).

The programme called for a change in basis weight at 22.20 hours and it was to be decreased from a target of 22·9 to 21·3 lb DC. From 19.00 hours until 22.00 hours, average sample weights were being produced that apparently satisfied the machineman, although it was consistently 0·3 lb heavy. The recorder on the stuffgate showed that it was not touched during this period. At 22.00 hours there was a shift change and immediately (that is, 22.05 hours) the stuffgate was closed by a considerable amount.

A reel was thrown out at 22.20 hours and gave a basis weight of 22·6 lb, so the stuffgate was closed by a further amount. The next reel at 22.50 hours was spot on at 21·3 lb DC and so no correction was made. The next reel, however, was light at 20·2 lb and so the stuffgate was opened in two steps. The next result was too high at 22·1 lb and the stuffgate then closed. The system was now hunting viciously and, if the graph is followed, it will be seen that each adjustment is made based only on the immediate test result. The stuffgate under the machineman's control oscillates nicely from 22.00 hours until 4.00 hours, giving almost a classical trace.

Perhaps the most interesting feature is that the final position of the stuffgate is exactly where the machineman first put it. If he had left it alone, the oscillation would never have taken place and the basis weight would have been on target within $\frac{1}{2}$ hour.

Undoubtedly, systems such as these are difficult to control and controllability has been defined as the product of process dead time and disturbance bandwidth. If the system has a sampled-data control system, then empirically the sample period must be at least half the period of the highest frequency to which the system must respond. Thus, if we rely on data every half-hour, then frequencies higher than 1 hour cannot be affected by any control system whatever. The effect of dead time is more than twice as large as that of sampling

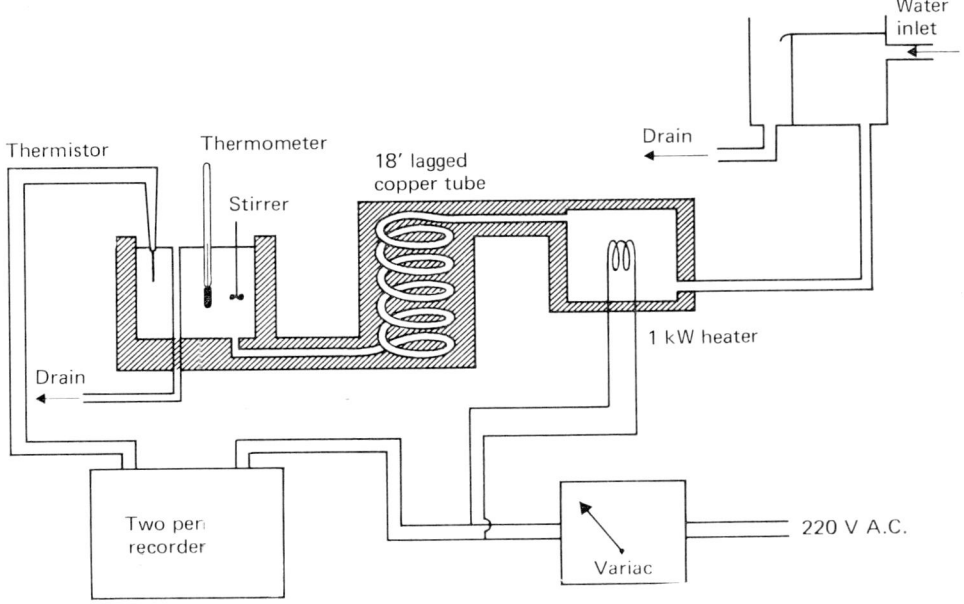

Figure 4. Laboratory control task.

period, but, if a process is such that the dead time cannot be altered, then the only way in which an improvement can be achieved is to raise the measuring rate—that is, by installing a continuous monitor such as a beta-gauge.

Figure 4 shows schematically the artificial task in which a controlled supply of tap water was fed to a kettle connected to a variable transformer (0–220 V) fed from the ac main supply. The heated water then flowed down 18 ft of lagged copper tubing to provide a distance-velocity lag into an agitated vessel filled with overflow and a mercury-in-glass thermometer. A thermistor was connected to the thermometer and a two-channel recorder used to record both variable transformer setting and the reading of the temperature.

Figure 5 shows the response of this process to a step change in the setting of the variable transformer from 120 V to 175 V. The response, of course, shows the typical response of a certain delay and a slow increase to the final temperature. The d.v. lag is about $2\frac{1}{2}$ minutes and the exponential lag has a time constant of about 10 minutes.

In the first set of trials, subjects were chosen from the laboratory and asked to change the temperature of the water from a value such as 40°C to 55°C. In the first set of trials, the operator was able to see only the thermometer and to adjust only the variable transformer, the recorder being hidden at this time. Figure 6 shows the result of the first three trials of a particular subject and three facts emerge:

(1) He very easily forces the system into oscillation.
(2) He learns about the process, as exemplified by the fact that he improves each time.
(3) There is a marked similarity between these results and Figure 3.

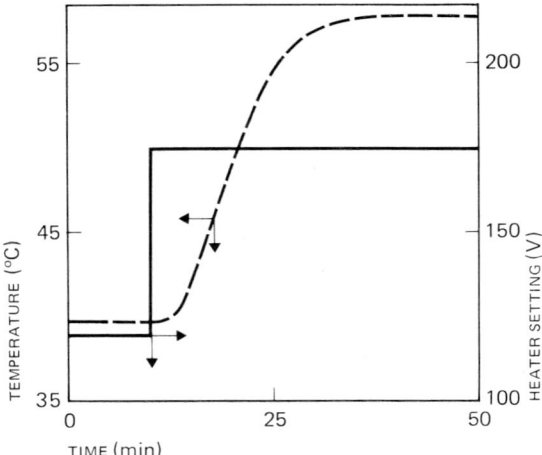

Figure 5. Process reaction curve.

To examine the charts in detail, it can be seen that the ' process ' is never brought under control in the first trial and the subject indulged in wild adjustments of the control.

In the second trial, the subject achieves a better performance and is starting to appreciate the system and eventually gets the process under control after 70 minutes.

On the third trial, there is less overshoot, nevertheless the process is never really in control.

This set of results has been selected as being representative of a typical *good* subject. Systems engineers tended to do slightly better, many using the first trial to perturb the system and therefore gain some idea of the system.

In studying the way in which most subjects set off to control the process, it was noted that many made far too many adjustments and of too large an amplitude and so a second set of experiments was arranged in which adjustments were permitted only at 5-minute intervals. The results of an average subject are shown in Figure 7. (These were a fresh batch of subjects who had not participated in the first set of experiments.)

In the first trial, there was the typical overshoot, but most subjects even on a first trial brought the ' process ' under control. By the third trial, most subjects were curbing the overshoot and, although not meeting the specification, were considerably better than the subjects who were allowed an indefinite number of adjustments.

In the third set of experiments, the mercury-in-glass thermometer was removed and the subject allowed to use the recorder. The results are shown in Figure 8.

The first trial using a recorder is a remarkable improvement over any of the other trials. There are no *typical* second trials, but a good proportion of subjects moved the setting of the variable transformer to the correct setting for the desired new temperature and waited. This may have been because most tests were scheduled to last the hour and, since control was often achieved

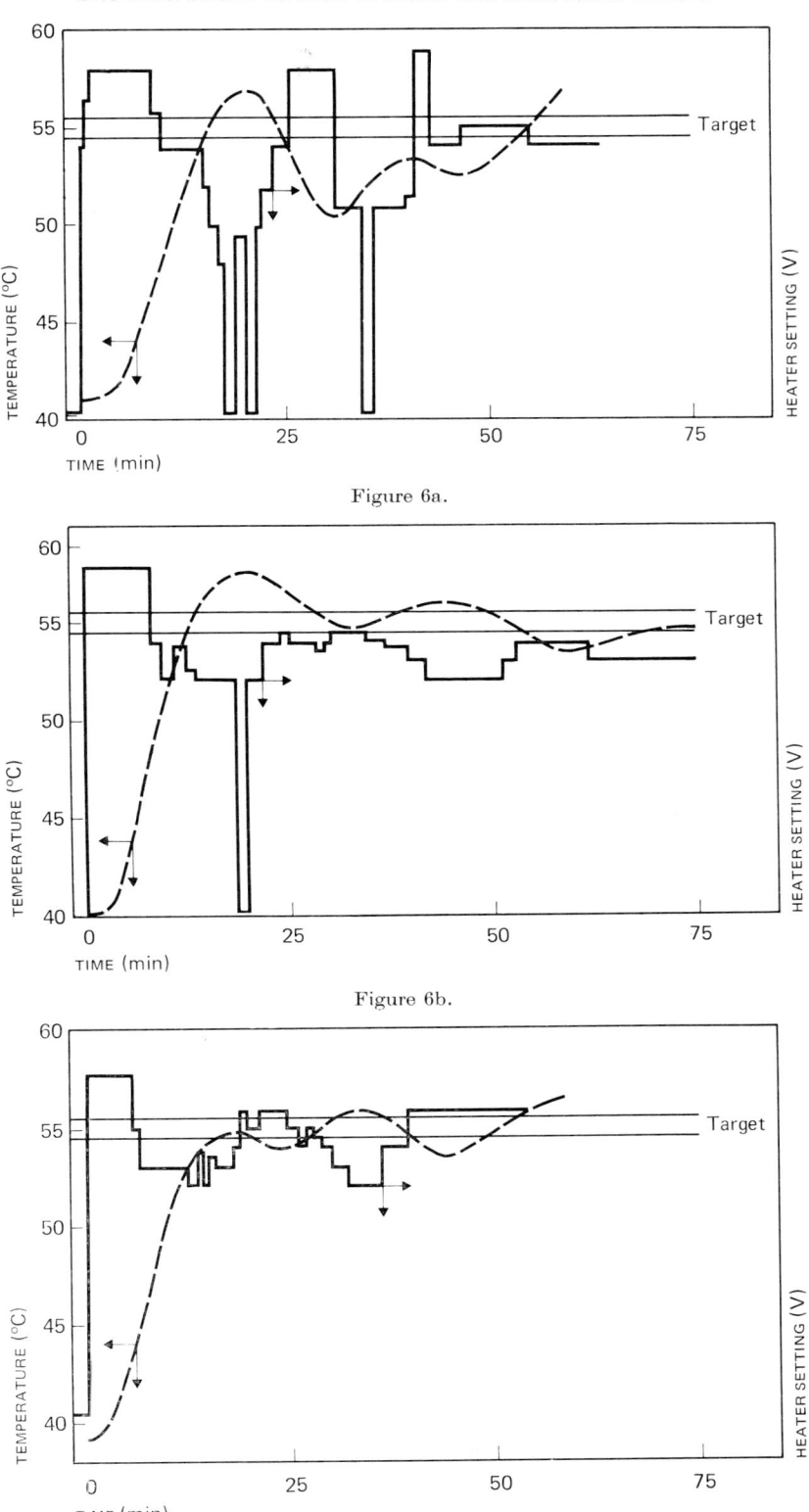

Figure 6a.

Figure 6b.

Figure 6c.

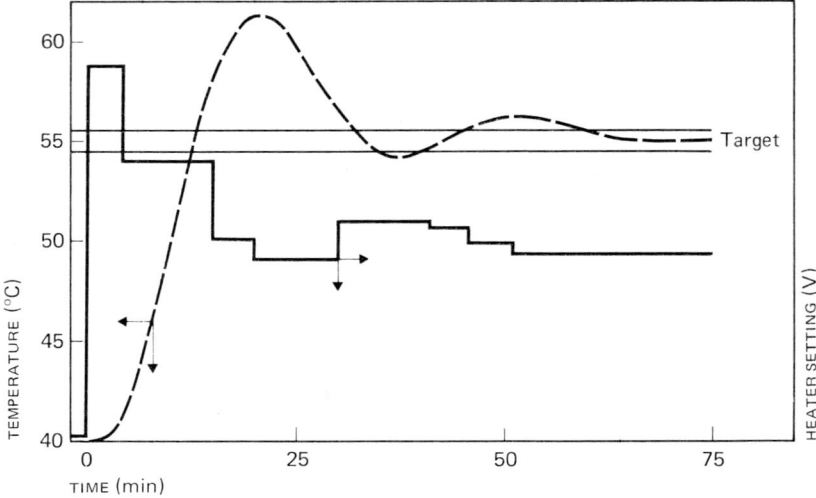

Figure 7a.

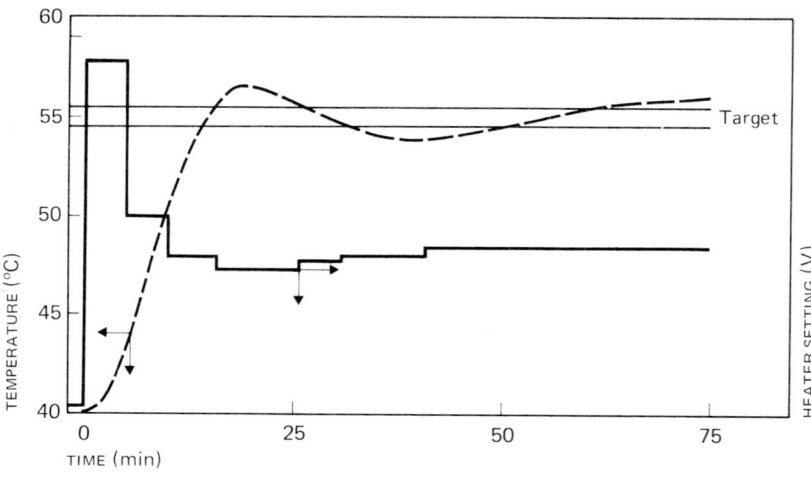

Figure 7b.

in half-an-hour, subjects had a further 30 minutes to observe that the setting they had determined was the correct one.

This set of trials, then, demonstrates the values of trend recording and the beneficial effect to be obtained by not making too rapid changes. A final run was arranged in which the optimum control setting was worked out, then applied (in a feedforward rather than a feedback manner) and Figure 9 is the result.

The most useful aspect of all this work was to be able to discuss it with machine operators and to use the facts as a basis for training. An understanding of the system is the first requirement in controlling it and lectures based on these experiments helped to minimize occurrences such as those epitomized in Figure 3.

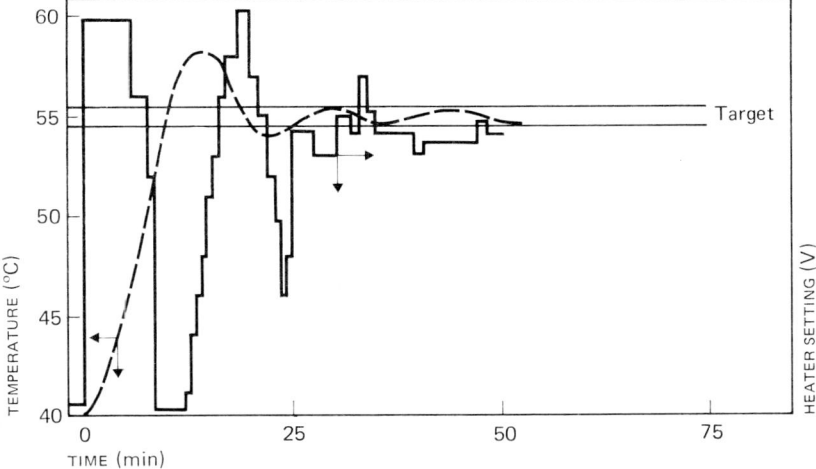

Figure 8.

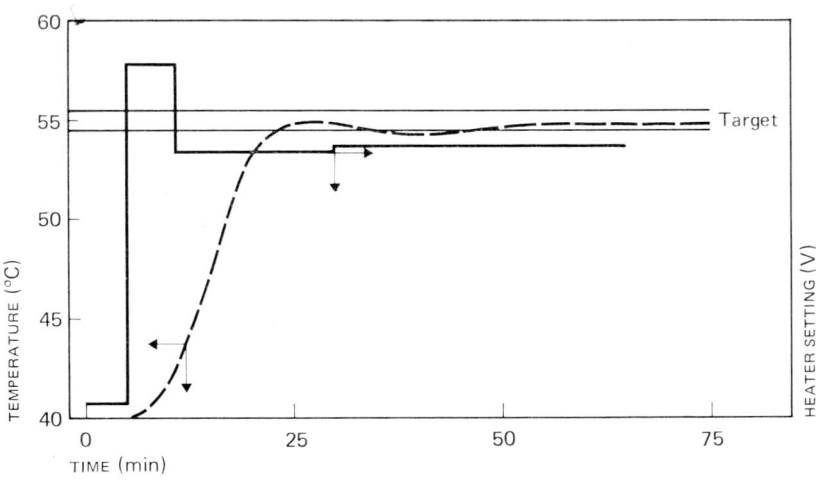

Figure 9.

With the introduction of computer control, quite different forms of presentation and control are used and it was decided to model the same process digitally, since more information was available on the laboratory task than on the papermachine to be fitted with digital control.

If X(*t*) is the value of the temperature at time *t* and X(*t*−1) is the value at time (*t*−1), *etc.*, and U(*t*) is an input at time *t*, *etc.*, then an equation of the form

$$X(t) = 0\cdot 01\ U(t-4) + 1\cdot 95\ X(t-1) - 1\cdot 06\ X(t-2) + 0\cdot 1\ X(t-3)$$

best describes the process. For example, if we consider a change of U from 0 to 1 at time *t* = 0, we have the values in Table 1:

Table 1

t	$U(t)$	$0 \cdot 01 U(t-4)$	$1 \cdot 95 X(t-1)$	$1 \cdot 06 X(t-2)$	$0 \cdot 1 X(t-3)$	$X(t)$
−1	0	0	0	0	0	0
0	1	0	0	0	0	0
1	1	0	0	0	0	0
2	1	0	0	0	0	0
3	1	0	0	0	0	0
4	1	0·01	0	0	0	0·01
5	1	0·01	0·0195	0	0	0·0295
6	1	0·01	0·057	0·0106	0	0·057
7	1	0·01	0·111	0·03127	0·001	0·091
8	1	0·01	0·177	0·0603	0·003	0·129

This response has been normalized to correspond to the response to step change in the laboratory task and gives almost the same shape when plotted as that shown in Figure 5.

A computer program was then written to operate in real time, which used this equation as the process model. In this case, subjects knew that they could select any value between 0 and 100 as the setting of the valve. At half-minute intervals, the computer would type out the latest temperature and say what the valve setting was and ask for a new setting. A typical print-out is shown in Figure 10.

Exactly the same procedure was then adopted as previously and the subjects were asked to control the 'process'. In this case, however, they sat at a teletyper and had to input a number between 0 and 100. The results of the first three trials of a good average subject are shown in Figure 11.

Typical print-outs of a whole run are too long to include in this paper, but they illustrate the type of error that can be made in inputting information via a typewriter and the wisdom of writing protective programs to allow only numbers between 0 and 100 to be used in the calculations was well demonstrated.

With Figure 11, the same sort of pattern emerges as was shown in the analogue case. Because the 'valve' can be adjusted only each half-minute, there was some restraint on the number of changes made, but it was noticed that subjects were in general more prone to make rapid changes in 'valve' setting than when they physically had to grasp a wheel and turn it.

This model could be extended indefinitely. It would have been instructive, for example, to have introduced some noise into the readings, also perhaps to have fed in a disturbance and this is work that might be done in the future.

6. Conclusions

Crossman listed six factors that make the control of a process difficult:

(1) When several display and control variables depend on one another.
(2) When the process has a long 'time constant'—that is, takes a relatively long time (minutes, hours or even days) to settle down after a disturbance or alteration of control settings.
(3) When important variables have to be estimated by the operator rather than measured by an instrument.
(4) When the readings of instruments at widely separated points have to be collated and the operator has to remember one while going to another ('short-term memory').

(5) When the operator gets imperfect knowledge of the results of his performance or when the knowledge arrives late (this is a very common condition).
(6) When the basic process is either difficult to visualize—for example, chemical reactions—or contradicts 'commonsense' assumptions or is too complicated to be held in mind at one time.

```
THE DIAL SETTING IS 0
WHAT NEW DIAL SETTING DO YOU REQUIRE? 0
THE TEMPERATURE IS 54·0882
THE DIAL SETTING IS 0
WHAT NEW DIAL SETTING DO YOU REQUIRE? 0
THE TEMPERATURE IS 55·5618
THE DIAL SETTING IS 0
WHAT NEW DIAL SETTING DO YOU REQUIRE? 0
THE TEMPERATURE IS 56·4003
THE DIAL SETTING IS 0
WHAT NEW DIAL SETTING DO YOU REQUIRE? 0
THE TEMPERATURE IS 56·6938
THE DIAL SETTING IS 0
WHAT NEW DIAL SETTING DO YOU REQUIRE? 35
THE TEMPERATURE IS 56·5249
THE DIAL SETTING IS 35
WHAT NEW DIAL SETTING DO YOU REQUIRE? 40
THE TEMPERATURE IS 55·968
THE DIAL SETTING IS 40
WHAT NEW DIAL SETTING DO YOU REQUIRE? 40

    INPUT DATA NOT IN CORRECT FORMAT. RETYPE IT
?40
THE TEMPERATURE IS 55·0907
THE DIAL SETTING IS 40
WHAT NEW DIAL SETTING DO YOU REQUIRE? 40
THE TEMPERATURE IS 53·9532
THE DIAL SETTING IS 40
WHAT NEW DIAL SETTING DO YOU REQUIRE? 40
THE TEMPERATURE IS 52·8895
THE DIAL SETTING IS 40
WHAT NEW DIAL SETTING DO YOU REQUIRE? 40
THE TEMPERATURE IS 51·9731
THE DIAL SETTING IS 40
WHAT NEW DIAL SETTING DO YOU REQUIRE? 40
THE TEMPERATURE IS 51·2001
THE DIAL SETTING IS 40
WHAT NEW DIAL SETTING DO YOU REQUIRE? 37·5
THE TEMPERATURE IS 50·5576
THE DIAL SETTING IS 37·5
WHAT NEW DIAL SETTING DO YOU REQUIRE? 37·5
THE TEMPERATURE IS 50·0325
THE DIAL SETTING IS 37·5
WHAT NEW DIAL SETTING DO YOU REQUIRE? 37·5
THE TEMPERATURE IS 49·6123
THE DIAL SETTING IS 37·5
WHAT NEW DIAL SETTING DO YOU REQUIRE? 37·5
THE TEMPERATURE IS 49·2854
THE DIAL SETTING IS 37·5
WHAT NEW DIAL SETTING DO YOU REQUIRE? 37·5
THE TEMPERATURE IS 49·0207
THE DIAL SETTING IS 37·5
```

Figure 10.

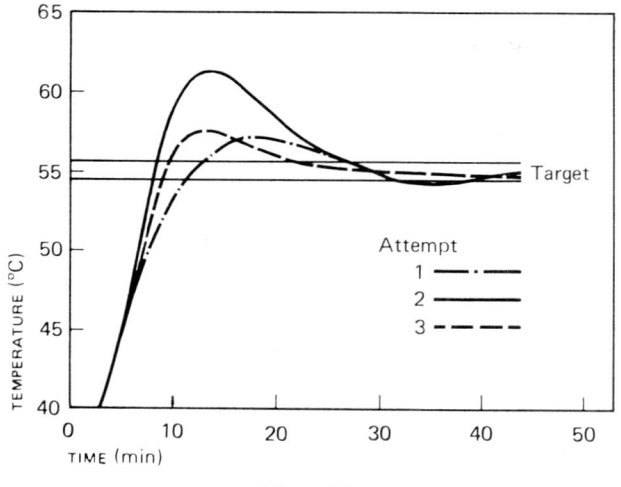

Figure 11.

Examples of nearly all these facets can be found in papermaking and this paper has sought to explore nearly all of these as they relate to basis weight control, particularly the effect of time constants.

One fact has been demonstrated that, if operatives are taught about the system and shown what plant responses are like, they can improve their performance. The value of trend logging has been demonstrated, also the value of allowing only minor changes in process variables to take place.

A great many of the proposals made in the earlier ergonomics study have now been implemented and basis weight control on machines without computers or beta-gauges is now much improved.

Mental Skills in Process Control

By H. Kragt and J. A. Landeweerd

Department of Industrial Engineering, Eindhoven University of Technology,
The Netherlands

1. Introduction

As technology changes, the functions performed by man are also changing. In order to construct man–machine systems with an increasing degree of complexity and of automation, it is necessary to investigate human capacities and limitations in performing the necessary system functions. This becomes increasingly important as the role of man becomes increasingly crucial.

In which direction do the required skills change? In all tasks which are performed by man, receptor, central and effector processes play a part. However, in industries which have a rather high degree of automation we see a reduction in tasks which impose a physical load on man. Instead, tasks in which mental skills predominate become increasingly important (*e.g.* Crossman 1960a, Beishon 1969, Welford 1968 and Bainbridge 1969). Information processing and decision-making assume a greater significance.

Thus, for example, Bainbridge (1969) writes: " More important aspects (than motor aspects) of process control are the mental skills of organizing serial attention to several parallel continuous variables and integrating this information in making control decisions."

The process operator in the central control room of a chemical plant exemplifies the type of task which we are talking about.

In order to describe the operator's job we have to define two concepts:

(1) *Disturbance*. This is a slow unwanted change in one or more process variables. This change can be a consequence of external circumstances, *e.g.* variation in the quality of raw material, but it can also be caused internally, *e.g.* deterioration of catalyst.

(2) *Breakdown*. This is a circumstance that abruptly interrupts the continuous flow of the process, *e.g.* a fault in a pump.

The operator's job—supervising and controlling the process—can be described as follows:

(1) Supervising the process and when necessary, in the case of a disturbance, adjusting the process.
(2) Minimizing the effects of breakdowns.
(3) Starting up and shutting down the process.

The individual operators do not all perform their job in the same way. In an identical process situation they clearly perform different control actions (Kragt 1971). We infer that they have an idea, a mental ' model ' of the invisible process which they control, and that this model does influence their actions. Bainbridge (1969), for example, writes: " One can suggest that the human controller has available some sort of simulation language for thinking about the process ". She calls this " the controller's internal model of the process ".

A number of problems arise:
  (1) Is it possible to demonstrate the existence of mental models?
  (2) Because it would be an internal model, we do not have methods of direct observation. How can we investigate mental models?
  (3) Because processes are not stationary it can be assumed that updating of the model is necessary. How does such a mental model come into being and how does it change with time?
  (4) Does the operator use more than one mental model?

Before investigating all these problems a first requirement is that we get insight in the way in which the operator actually performs. We did two experiments, an interview in the field (Kragt 1971) and a laboratory training experiment (Landeweerd 1968).

2. Experiment 1: The Interview in the Field

How does the operator actually set about his task, what does he do and what is he thinking?

These questions were studied by an interview carried out in the field.

2.1. Method

Operators on a process plant were interviewed. The interview had an open-ended form. This was possible because the number of subjects (operators) in the situation we investigated was small ($n = 12$). Because of the open-ended form the interview could best be tape-recorded and, since the subjects made no objections, a tape recorder was used. We started from the assumption that an interview is of greater value if the investigator first acquaints himself with the process to be investigated. To this end he was given an on-the-job training. As already mentioned, the object of the interview was to obtain more information about the operator-process situation.

During the interview the following items came up for discussion:
  (1) *Process description.* "Please could you tell me in your own words how the process works?" (With this question we wanted to make explicit his mental model.)
  (2) *'Make-believe' situation.* "Suppose you are completely responsible for the process. In view of your other duties you cannot be present in the control room all the time. Nevertheless, the process must be controlled. For this reason a number of men are at your disposal, *e.g.* trainees. But they do not have any knowledge about the process. You have some time to instruct them and you can choose as many of them as you think you need for controlling the process. What would you tell these people so that they will be able to control the process during your absence?" (With this question we wanted to investigate the relative importance of the different aspects of his task.)
  (3) *Critical incidents.* "You have been telling me about the process. Can you now tell me something about the difficult situations which have occurred in the last few years when you have been controlling the process or at least have been responsible for it?" (With this

question we wanted to obtain information about disturbances and breakdowns as seen by the operator.)

The investigation started with a pilot interview with one of the operators. The interview was then evaluated with that operator. As a result each of the above-mentioned points was divided into a number of questions. In this way we obtained a checklist which was used in the interviewing of the other 11 operators.

In addition we tried by means of the method of paired comparisons to rank 10 of the instrument dials in order of importance for control of the process. It was found that the 'importance' of a dial was a difficult concept for the operator. In his opinion the importance of a dial is determined by the condition of the process. Under different process conditions, different dials are important to him. Thus an ordering of the importance of these information sources can be obtained only by defining the process condition which is considered.

Before describing the results the following concepts need to be defined:

> STATE   The overall state of the process.
>
> State   The state of an aspect of the process, which in the present case is the control of product quality. (State is a subset of STATE).
>
> Breakdown   A circumstance which *abruptly* interrupts the continuous process.
>
> Subroutine   A standard sequence of mental activities followed by a standard sequence of manual activities, c.f. SR as defined by Bainbridge (1969).

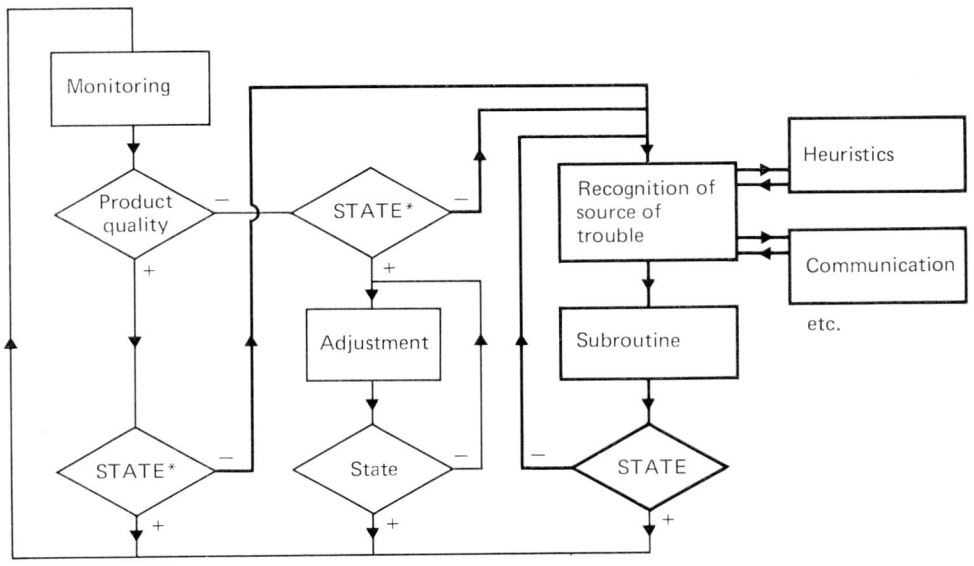

STATE*—'STATE' with exception of product quality

Figure 1. Decision scheme of the operator.

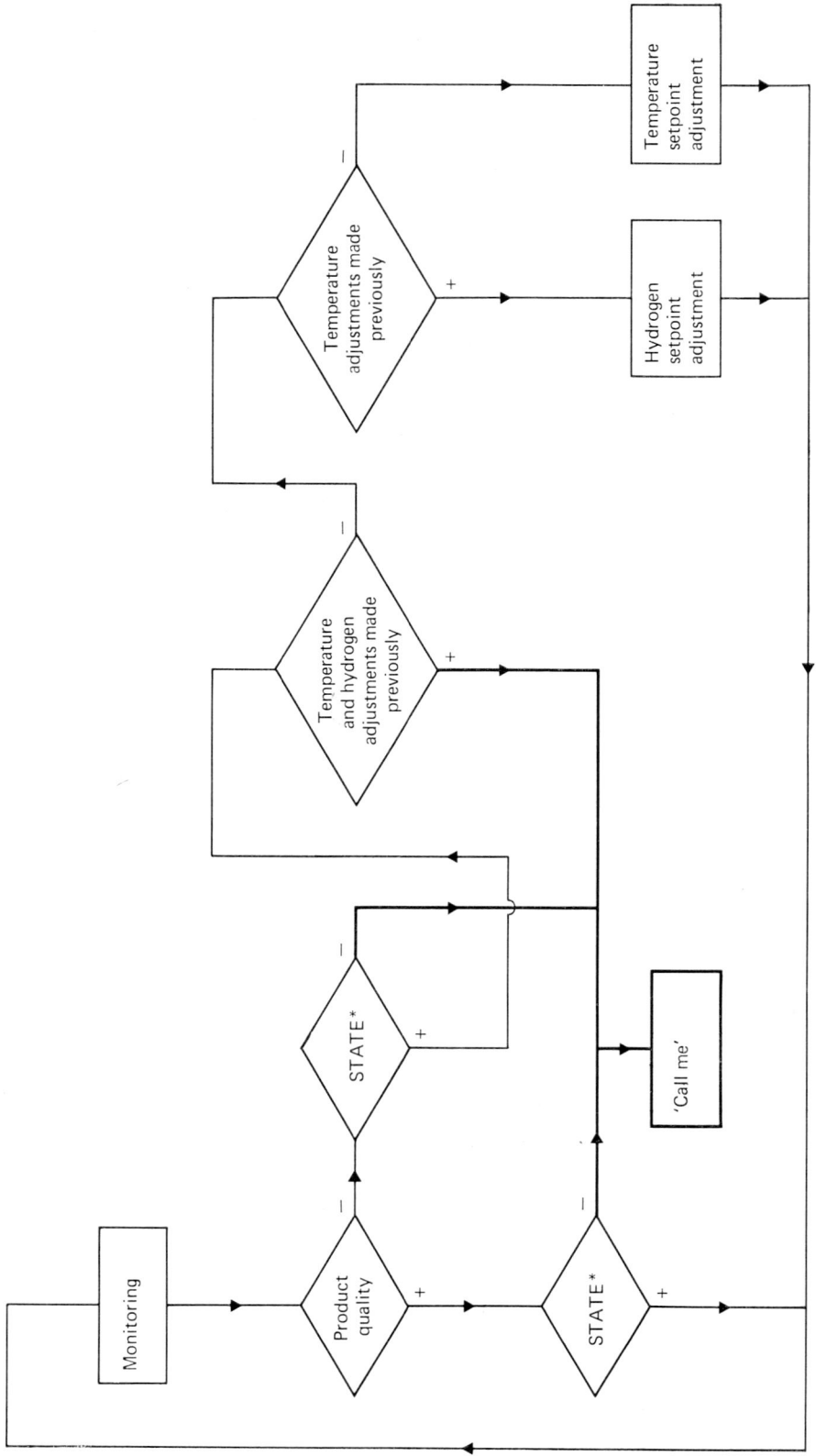

Figure 2. Decision scheme for the layman.

STATE*–'STATE' with exception of product quality

2.2. Results

The results are given in Figures 1 and 2. Figure 1 represents a decision scheme of the operator and Figure 2 one for the 'layman'. The thin and thick lines in these figures relate to the comparison of the figures given in Section 2.2.4.

We describe first four activities which are essential constituents of the job of the operator:

(1) Monitoring
(2) Adjusting
(3) Minimizing the effects of breakdowns
(4) Handing over process control responsibilities.

2.2.1. Monitoring

Inside the control room monitoring has a clear meaning for the operator: a regular watch must be kept to ensure that the process variables remain inside limits which are acceptable (to the operator). Outside the control room he inspects the plant system two or three times per shift for a possible leakage, blockage, *etc.* These activities the operator performs on his own initiative. In addition, the values of the process variables have to be filled in on a log once per hour. When the operator does not need to intervene in the process he is collecting information about it. In this case Bainbridge (1969) speaks of " stored information ", *i.e.* information which the operator will use later on if he has to intervene, often in preference to the readings then available.

2.2.2. Adjusting

As already stated, after a disturbance the operator adjusts the process. We make a distinction between

(1) A disturbance in product quality
(2) A disturbance in the STATE of the process.

A disturbance in product quality can be reduced by altering the setpoints of appropriate variables. Having done that, the operator will either continue to make adjustments or wait for his initial adjustment to affect the product quality.

The time lag of the process, *i.e.* the time for a control adjustment to affect product quality, was about 20 minutes.

In the case of a disturbance in the STATE of the process the operator tries to find out the cause(s). If he recognizes the disturbance from experience, his activities (standard sequence of manual activities) will be aimed at removing the cause.

If the cause lies outside the process, and thus outside his area of control, his activities will be confined to minimizing its effects.

2.2.3. Minimizing the effects of breakdowns

The behaviour of the operator when monitoring and adjusting the process is very different from his behaviour when a breakdown occurs. In this latter case he tries first of all to prevent the process from becoming unsafe (if the automatic safety systems have not already done this). After that he tries to remove the cause(s) of the breakdown and/or to minimize its effects. If the operator does not recognize the breakdown, because such an event has not occurred before or at least not to him, he will exhibit heuristic behaviour and may make use of the know-how of his shift colleagues (see Figure 1). It is especially in this situation that the shift manifests itself as a functional unity.

2.2.4. *Handing over process control responsibilities*

The continuous nature of the process is characteristic of the operator-process situation. At the end of a shift the operator has to hand over his task to a colleague on another shift. Possible difficulties are communicated in written form or verbally. Quite soon after the shift change the incoming operator will himself monitor the entire system both inside and outside the control room.

The question arises whether he will always be able to obtain from the previous shift all the relevant information concerning the process. Change of shift resulting in the loss of relevant information—of 'stored information' in Bainbridge's terminology—could mean an interruption in control of the process. Turning over control to people who do not know the process was an item in the make-believe situation of point 2 of the interview. It was noteworthy that operators wanted to limit the activities of the laymen to monitoring and to making adjustments necessary to counter a disturbance in product quality.

It is also noteworthy that the operator wanted to limit the number of laymen to one person who had control of the process. More people would interfere with each other, because the effect of a change of one process variable on the other process variables is not immediately visible on account of time lag. It is important to note that the operator wanted to be called as soon as problems of STATE other than product quality occurred (compare the thin and thick lines in Figures 1 and 2).

The operators suggested that one must have some experience in process control before being able to solve these other problems. In the operators' opinion this experience is necessary if one is to feel at ease in his job. Plant management often organizes a formal training programme to speed up this learning process. The problem then arises of the amount and content of the teaching material which is to be provided. For example, there is the question of how much information should be given about the physical and chemical features of the process. This somewhat theoretical training often causes a great deal of trouble to operators. Crossman and Cooke (1962) also mention this problem. The experiment which follows aims to shed more light on this.

3. Experiment 2: The Training Situation in the Laboratory

Is it necessary that an operator receive detailed information about the physical and chemical features of the process for which he is responsible or is it possible for him to perform adequately with information about relations between process variables?

This question was studied by an investigation carried out in the laboratory.

3.1. Method

We divided the subjects into two groups and gave them a control task. This task was to bring the temperature of the mixed air stream in the air mixer apparatus shown in Figure 3 from 90°C to 120°C and to hold it there. As already mentioned, chemical processes exhibit time lags. We therefore built such lags into our experimental equipment. In addition to the short process lag a pure time delay of about three minutes was introduced between the control knob and valve.

The subjects were students from a technical school. One group ($n=16$) received a full explanation of the process and the equipment with the aid of process and control diagrams and of inspection of the parts of the equipment and of their relationships. We call this group the I-group (informed group). The other group ($n=15$) received only an instruction stating that the objective was to control the temperature of the air stream and that this could be done by turning the knob. We call this group the NI-group (not-informed group). With the aid of a questionnaire we checked whether we had succeeded in differentiating the two groups in terms of process and equipment knowledge.

The experiment consisted of three trials, conducted one after the other and each lasting 10 minutes. We recorded the values of the temperature and the control actions of the subjects.

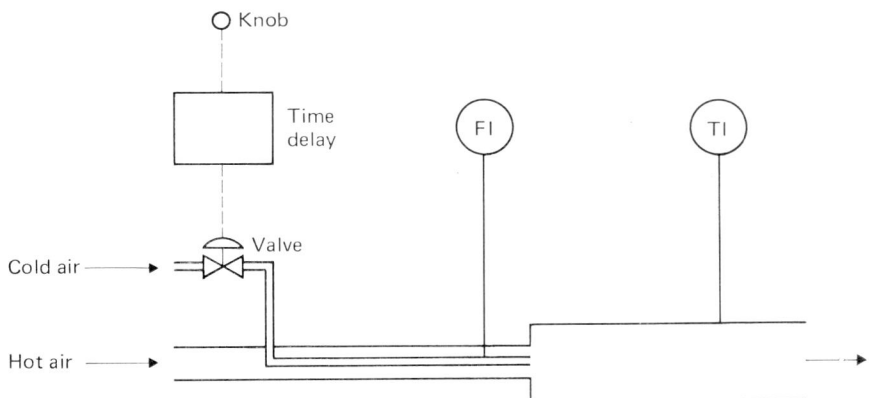

FI—cold air flow indicator
TI—mixed air temperature indicator

Figure 3. The air mixer apparatus.

The independent variable under investigation was the amount of process information furnished to the subjects. The dependent variable was the control performance of the subjects, which we defined as the mean absolute deviation (M.A.D.) of the actual controlled temperature from the desired value of 120°C, *i.e.*

$$\text{M.A.D.} = \int_0^{10} |e_t| \mathrm{d}t$$

This value is an error score, *i.e.* the higher the value the worse the control performance. Thus Figure 4a shows a performance which is worse than that shown in Figure 4b.

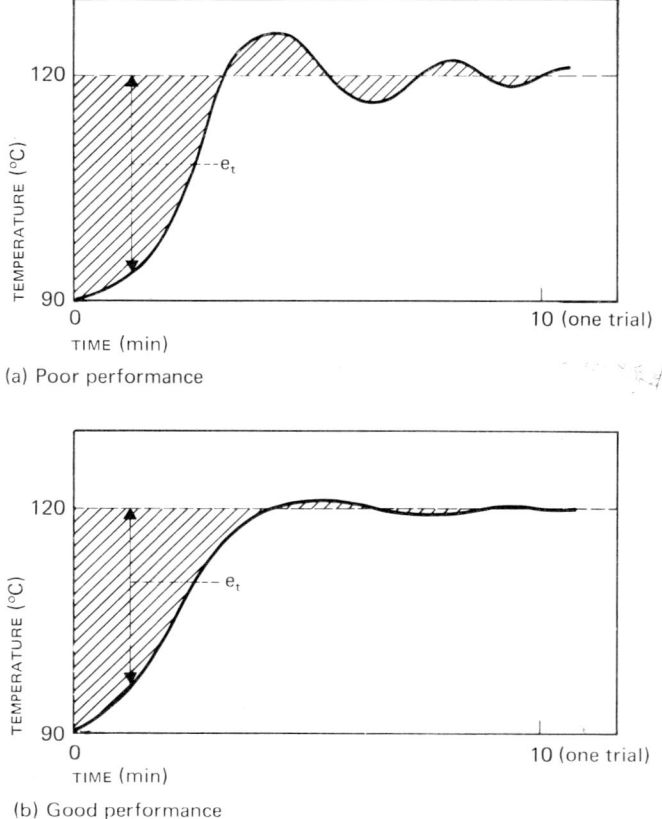

Figure 4. Operator control of temperature in air mixer experiment.

3.2. Results

3.2.1. Control performance

The more important results are shown in Table 1 and Figure 5. The difference between the two groups is not statistically significant, but there is a tendency for the NI-group to perform somewhat better and this persisted throughout the three trials.

3.2.2. Learning effects and additional findings

The results just given, in Table 1 and Figure 5, show that the groups improved their performance in the course of the experiment. We also recorded the manipulative activities of the subjects on the control knob. One of the

Table 1. Error scores in air mixer experiment

	Trial 1		Trial 2		Trial 3		Total	
			M.A.D.					
I-group	125.20	n.s.	69.20	n.s.	57.13	n.s.	83.84	n.s.
NI-group	107.63		51.31		51.19		74.71	

results obtained was that the number of control actions, shown in Table 2, decreased as the experiment progressed.

Normally the subject begins the run by reducing the amount of cold air with the knob that controls the cold air valve. After a lag the mixed gas temperature rises. The subject does not know exactly when to start adjusting the amount of cold air again, so that usually the temperature shows first an overshoot and then an undershoot. The subject is " hunting the temperature ", an effect which Crossman and Cooke (1962) called " hunting up and down ". Performance improved during the experimental sessions. During the initial " hunting up and down " the subject follows the temperature readings closely.

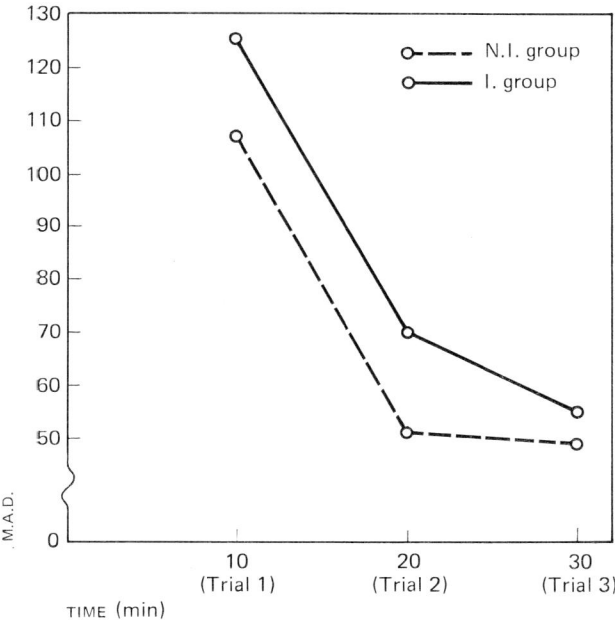

Figure 5. Error scores in air mixer experiment.

Table 2. Control actions in air mixer experiment
Number of control actions

	Trial 1	Trial 2	Trial 3
I-group	53·6	39·0	35·2
NI-group	60·1	54·2	51·7

This is a manifestation of ' closed-loop ' behaviour with control actions determined by feedback of information about the measured variable. Later on one observes more ' open-loop ', often ' bang-bang ', behaviour in which subjects close the valve, wait some time, open it fully, again wait some time and then make the final slight corrections. This confirms the findings of Sell, Crossman and Box (1962). Figure 6 gives examples of both ' closed-loop ' and ' open-loop ' behaviour.

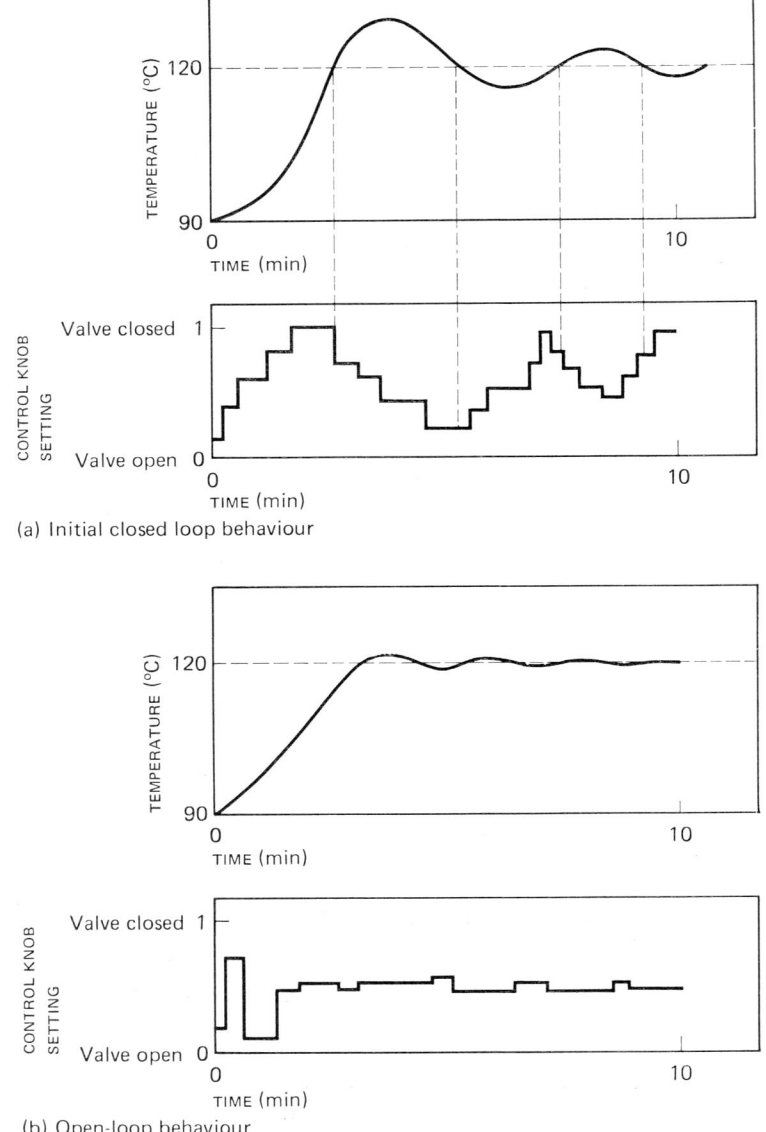

Figure 6. Control behaviour in air mixer experiment.

4. Discussion

Study of the tape-recorded interview results appears to support the conclusion that a distinction can be made between two types of mental model which the operator possesses:

(1) A ' routine ' model
(2) A ' non-routine ' model.

The operator appears to use the *routine model* when controlling the process after a disturbance in control quality. He might be prepared to hand over this activity to people who do not possess any knowledge of the process (the ' laymen ' in the make-believe situation of the interview). It appears that in such a situation a very limited knowledge of the process is sufficient. More information about the process would not be relevant to this activity, and would increase the time needed for instruction. Moreover, it could inhibit performance of the task. The results of the training experiment give an indication of this. These show that the group with process information does not control any better than the group without process information. This last group can be compared with the laymen in the make-believe situation. The information which was given to the I-group may have been too detailed for the task which they had to perform, resulting initially in mistakes and inferior performance.

The hypothesis that it was the irrelevant process information which inhibited the performance of the task is confirmed by our findings that the I-subjects in their verbal comments—which we explicitly obtained from them—talked initially, for example, about the valve that was opened and closed and about the amount of cold air that was supplied, but later on about the pointers that moved up and down. Therefore it is reasonable to assume that during the experiment the I-group learnt to control in terms of a less complex mental model than that which was originally offered to them.

The operator uses a *non-routine model* in situations in which a breakdown occurs. He then performs activities which he will not entrust to laymen and for which a specific knowledge of the process seems to be necessary. The formation and updating of the non-routine model (necessary for those aspects of the task which require it) takes place at the moment only by means of the experience which the operator acquires in the course of time as he interacts with the system. This acquisition process could be improved by directing the training of new operators towards this area. We believe that the non-routine aspects of the task should be listed and that an assessment should be made whether training may be carried out more effectively by simulation and by introduction of breakdowns on the real process.

From time to time even the more experienced operators will have to refresh or update their non-routine model. With increasing automation this has important implications. Sometimes the operator will be required to take over the task from the automatic equipment. Will he be able to do this if it is precisely this automatic equipment which prevents him from interacting regularly with the automatic control system, so that formation and updating of an adequate non-routine model is inhibited? More research is necessary to gain further insight into the way in which a mental model develops and to treat the problem of the model's development over the course of time. Research also needs to be done to answer questions such as: Who is fitted for the operator's job (selection)? How should the operator be trained (training)? How should the operator be evaluated (employee evaluation)? How should information about the process be presented to the operator (panel design)? How can one best use the operator's knowledge by a mutual interaction between plant management and operators?

Analysis of Verbal Protocols from a Process Control Task[*]

By Lisanne Bainbridge

Department of Psychology, University of Reading

1. Introduction

Most studies of human control performance are concerned with the tasks of the pilot and car driver, and investigate them using laboratory simulation. In these studies the controller has to make continuous movements at a speed such that the dynamic limitations of the human motor system are a major determinant of performance and this is the part of the human system component which is usually modelled.

Human control of industrial processes has received less attention (see Cooke 1965, Beishon 1966, 1967, 1969, Bainbridge et al. 1968, Bainbridge 1971, 1972). An industrial process is usually complex, with many input and controlled variables whose interactions and response characteristics may be little understood; also alternative control strategies may be available. Control may be needed simply to keep the process running at a steady state to produce a particular product by compensating for fluctuations in the input materials, or the process may go through a sequence of different phases in each of which the correct conditions must be attained and maintained, in some cases the process may have to be changed to make a product of different specifications. Events which require control responses are usually rare, for instance in the task discussed here 9–10 control actions were made per hour on average. Obviously, motor dynamics are not a factor limiting performance and this aspect of these tasks is trivial.

More important aspects of process control are the mental skills of organizing serial attention to several parallel continuous variables and integrating this information in making control decisions. The sampling aspect of fast tracking tasks has been widely studied, but the results cannot necessarily be extrapolated to industrial tasks in which there are long system response times or periods between actions. In a papermill studied by Beishon (1966, 1967) changes made to the first stages of paper-making appeared in the finished product 4 minutes later and 50 yards away. One might expect that the operator will have problems in correlating input and output changes together, and so learning about the process dynamics, when these changes occur widely separated in time, and also that he may not follow an optimum sampling strategy when there are physical and time costs on sampling some of the process variables.

As many complex industrial processes are now controlled by analogue controllers or digital computers one might say that human process control is rapidly disappearing, and becoming a craft skill of only academic interest. In these automated plants, however, human operators may still be retained to monitor control performance and for their flexibility in unprogrammed situations. At the moment we do not know enough about how men do these

---

[*] A revised version of " The Nature of the Mental Model in Process Control ", paper presented at the International Symposium on Man–Machine Systems, Cambridge, England, September, 1969.

tasks to be able to design optimum interfaces and task allocation, or selection and training programmes, or to know in what situations manual performance would be adequate.

This paper describes part of a study of operators controlling the distribution of electricity to a group of steel-melting furnaces. The task existed because the electricity board only allowed the steel works to use a certain amount of electricity in each half-hour period. While there were severe financial penalties for using more than this, the most steel would be made by using all the power available and by distributing it to the furnaces in a way which disturbed the steel-making process as little as possible.

2. The Control Task

The power controller has to direct power to five furnaces, each of which goes through a sequence of steel-making stages in a total cycle taking about 5 hours. (Another operator controls these furnace stages.) At any one time each furnace will probably be at a different stage of the cycle. The power controller's task has a shorter cycle of half-hourly periods in each of which the furnaces must not use more than 50 MW of power.

He has two displays related to present power usage which can be used for compensatory tracking; if these could be maintained at a given value the total power used in the half-hour would be correct. There are several problems in doing this. One is that each stage requires a different amount of power; some stages use a large amount, others $\frac{1}{6}-\frac{1}{3}$ of this, and some use none. Consequently the power required at one time may be greater than the average amount which can be used throughout the half-hour. If, however, a furnace changes later in the half-hour from using a large amount of power to using none and this change compensates for earlier over-usage, a cut-back of power in response to the earlier over-usage is unnecessary. Optimum control therefore consists of balancing current power usage against possible future events in the half-hour. Only if this predicted effect is unacceptable need the controller change the power supplied to the furnaces. The task of predicting the timing and effect of changes is complicated by differences in the timing and power usage of stages on the different furnaces, which differ in capacity and design; also the timing of some stages is more predictable than others. In addition, the power supplied to a furnace can only be set at discrete values (0, 50, 75, 100%) of the amount required at that stage, and the quality of steel made is affected by reducing the power supply to some stages but not others.

3. Method of Analysis

A preliminary report of the experiment and data collected appears in Bainbridge *et al.* (*op. cit.*). Both experienced operators and university students controlled a digital simulation of a melting-shop. (The computer also logged present display and control values once a minute.) Measures of subjects' control behaviour showed little difference between the two groups and, as so few control actions are made, attempts to correlate display variables with control actions do not provide much information about the way in which the subjects made their control decisions. To obtain more data on this the subjects were asked to 'think aloud' while doing the task; these verbal protocols were tape-recorded and the recordings transcribed. This study concentrates on the protocol data. More detailed reports are available in Bainbridge (1968, 1971, 1972).

While a protocol does not give complete, or necessarily reliable, data on the operator's thoughts, it is a source of much interesting information which could not be obtained in other ways. It is necessary to assume that there is some non-distorting mapping from the underlying thought processes to the verbal protocols.

The protocol is divided into a sequence of phrases, each phrase can for convenience be identified as a statement about one of the following:

(1) Present rate of power usage (P)
(2) MW used so far and time in half-hours
(3) Power usage prediction
(4) Comment on power usage and whether action required
(5) Choice of action
(6) Making action
(7) Furnace name and its current state
(8) Furnace state parameter
(9) Furnace state prediction, *i.e.* future state
(10) Furnace state parameter prediction
(11) General comment.

The phrases can be grouped into blocks, in which all the phrases have a common referent. The sequences of items in these blocks can be represented by algorithmic flow diagrams, as used for the description of computer programs. Figure 1a shows a section of protocol divided into phrases. Figure 1b shows the development of a flow diagram to describe phrases 5–14; upper case letters indicate items which appear in the protocol, lower case describe operations which the operator must have carried out. Figure 1c describes the same behaviour in a different notation which makes explicit the working storage, the result of each routine is 'stored' in a 'box' at its head. This can describe the way in which routines are not repeated unnecessarily, since if a box already contains a result this can simply be noted, if the box is empty or its contents are unreliable the routine can be carried out. Flexible behaviour can arise if there are alternative methods, *e.g.* analogue judgments or digital calculations, for obtaining the same data item. Where these diagrams are similar for several blocks of phrases these blocks are assumed to be different instances of the same behaviour, and the flow diagrams to be somewhat similar to the 'subroutines' of computer programs, as the sequence of operations described may deal with different furnaces and stage parameters on different occasions.

Having identified these routines, it is then necessary to account for the sequence in which these routines, *i.e.* the blocks of protocol phrases, occur. The protocols contain very few phrases describing the operator's strategy. Analyzing what determines the sequence of different types of behaviour cannot therefore be based on explicit evidence in the protocol phrases, as is done in analyzing the routines. Instead, one takes all the transitions from one type of behaviour to another, and identifies by trial and error a minimum number of variables which could define the contexts necessary to account for these transitions.

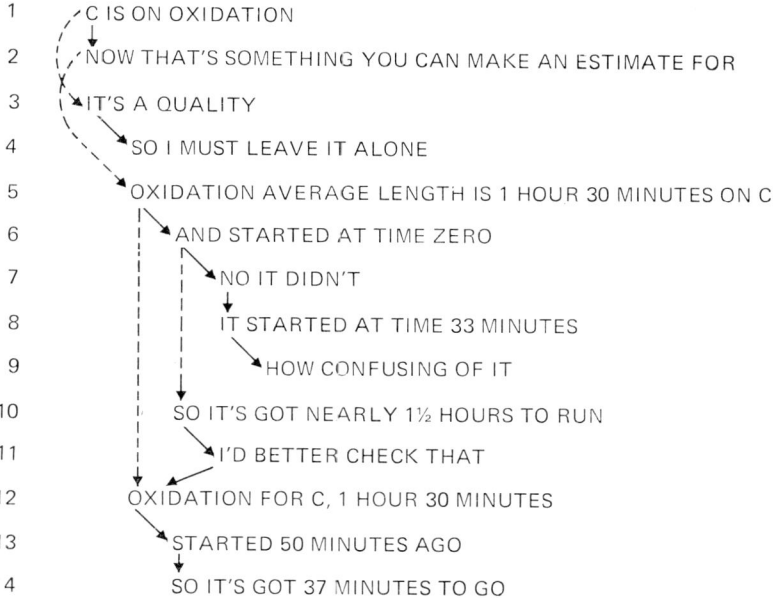

Figure 1a. Section of protocol divided into phrases. (Dotted lines indicate connections between phrases.)

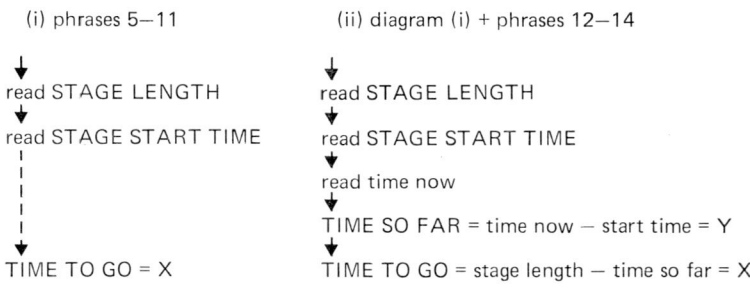

UPPER CASE: ITEM STATED IN PROTOCOL
lower case: OPERATION WHICH MUST HAVE BEEN DONE AS BASIS FOR EXPLICIT STATEMENTS

Figure 1b. Development of routines by combining evidence from several examples of the same behaviour.

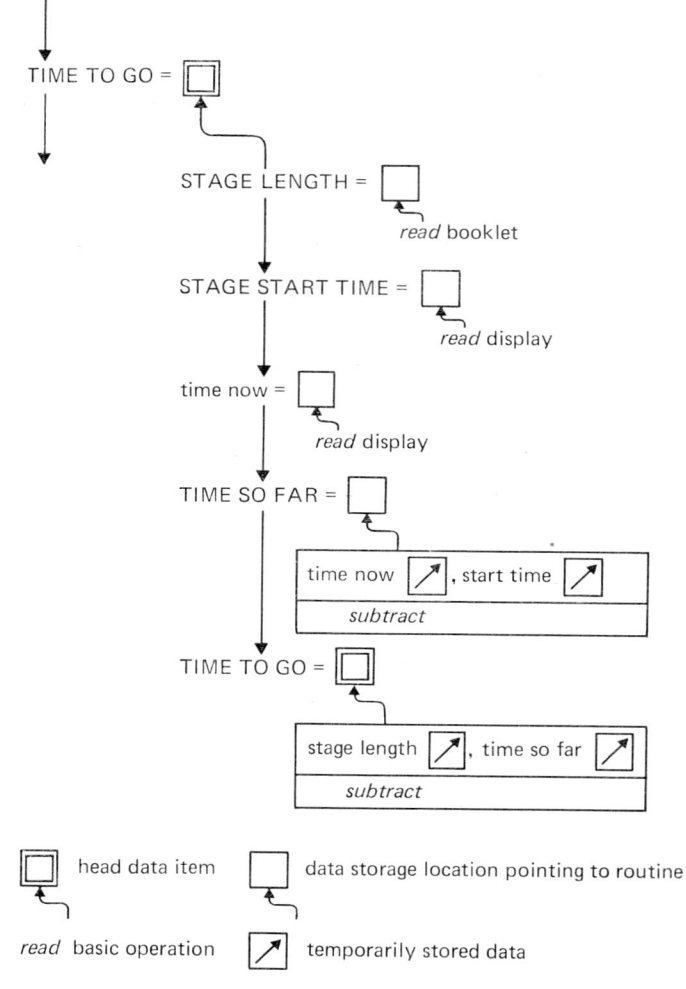

Figure 1c. The same routine described in 'box' notation.

4. Summary of Findings from Protocol Analysis

A summary flow diagram describing the sequence of activity in the protocol of S22, a melting-shop manager, is given in Figure 2. About a dozen routines were developed to account for the majority of phrases in the protocol. These routines obtained the data items listed in Table 1(A). The variables which determined the sequences of behaviour are listed in Table 1(B). The following major points can be made about the way in which this task is carried out, based on this type of evidence.

4.1. *Continuity of Control*

In controlling this type of slowly changing system the human operator makes control actions intermittently rather than continuously. Monitoring the control variables is also intermittent. Control variable phrases (types 1–4 in

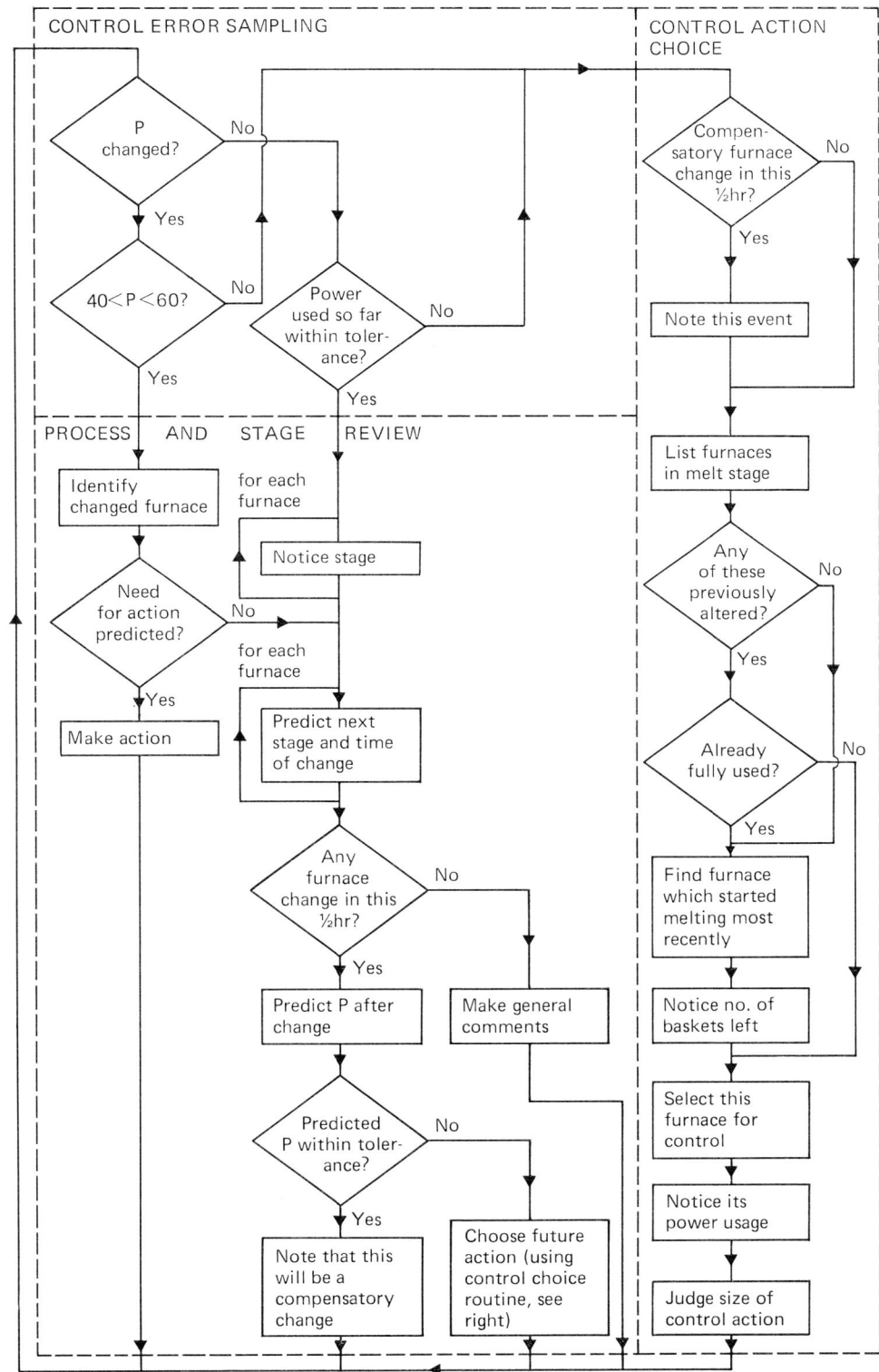

P: total present power

Figure 2. Simplified flow diagram underlying sequences of activity in protocol from S22.

Table 1. Data items found by main routines (A) and determining sequence of behaviour (B)

	(A) Basic routines find:	(B) Sequencing decisions use data about:
Action availability	(a) list of furnaces with power supply cut (b) furnace chosen for action (c) size of action to be made	(a) list of furnaces with power supply cut (b) furnace chosen for action (c) size of action to be made (d) furnaces previously altered
Stage lists	stages furnaces are in now, listed by type	furnace stages now
Predictions	(a) for each furnace: (1) next stage (2) time of change to next stage (3) power usage change at that time (b) control state after next power-changing event (c) action to be made after next power-changing event	(a) predicted events causing: (1) power usage change: up/down (2) control state change (b) future events in this half-hour (c) whether next event due soon (d) control state after next event (e) action to be made after next event

above list) alternate with blocks of other phrase types, in which the operator reviews the current states of the furnaces (types 7–11) or selects a control action (types 4–6). This is a true alternation, he evidently does not 'keep an eye on' the control variables while mentioning other parts of the task, as there are occasions when a significant change in a control variable occurs during a block of other phrases and is not mentioned until the other part of the task has been completed, and then in terms which suggest he has just noticed the value rather than delayed consideration of it.

4.2. Basic Sequences of Activity

The operator shows two major types of activity; which of these occurs at a particular time depends on whether or not the process is within acceptable limits.

When the control variable values are within his tolerance limits the operator reviews the general state of the system. He notes, for each furnace, its present stage, some of its parameters, and the stage it will go to next. If this stage change will involve a significant change in the furnace's power usage, he predicts the effect on overall power usage. If this future power usage will be unacceptable, he chooses a control action to be made when the stage change occurs. In this way he apparently maintains a 'mental picture' of the present and future stages of the furnaces. There is evidence that he often makes use of these stored data rather than reading values from the display panel each time they are needed.

Once this review is complete he makes general comments, chatting with the experimenter. During this time he apparently monitors the control variables, as he immediately returns to the task when there is a significant change. This is the only context in which he appears to monitor the control state continuously, rather than sampling it at particular points in his sequence of activity. When the control variables are not within tolerance limits control action choice

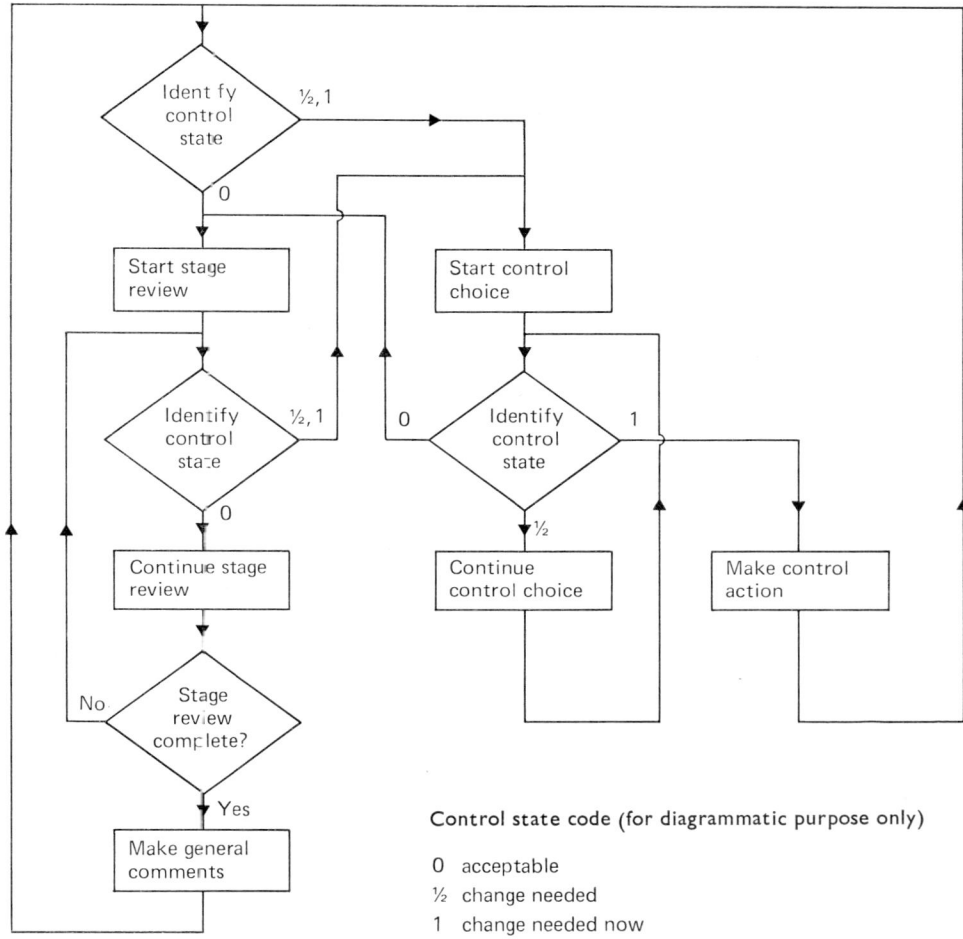

Figure 3. Direction of activity according to control state: sequences of activity in protocol from S22.

occurs. The operator first checks whether a change in furnace stage will occur which involves a change in power usage which will compensate for the present error. This may involve recursive use of the control action choice routine; if the next predicted change will lead to an unacceptable control state, the operator may consider what will be the best action to make when the change occurs. If there is no such event, he selects a furnace on which to change the power supply, on the basis of priority rules. If a furnace has changed stage since the last state review, this new stage is used in control choice, but the ' present stage picture ' is not updated. When all priority rules have been considered he continues to reiterate his control choice.

4.3. *Flexibility of Sequences*

The operator's behaviour can be described in general as in Figure 2, though it is actually more flexible. Although a wide variety of different sequences of activity appears in the protocol, it is possible to suggest a fairly simple method by which they might be generated. During each of the main behaviours described above, the operator checks the values of the control error variables at the end of each of its sections. It would have been confusing to show this in Figure 2. If this control check shows the same value as before, he continues with the main routine from the point at which he made the control check. If the control check shows a change in control state, he changes his activity appropriately, as shown in Figure 3.

Each of the two basic behaviours continues by investigating further parameters of the stages, or of the control choices, in order of priority. The result of such a strategy is that even if only the first part of one of the basic behaviours has been used an overview of the situation is available. This can be compared with a less efficient strategy in which each furnace would be fully investigated in turn.

4.4. Prediction of Future Events and Actions

A large part of both behaviours is concerned with predicting. The operator appears to maintain two main types of prediction: of the next event which will occur which involves a significant change in power usage, and of the action to make when a control action is next needed. Although these predictions are not maintained perfectly this strategy means that identification of a new system state, or choosing a control action, is often not made from scratch at the time, but by drawing on anticipations made earlier. Beishon (1969) also presents evidence from a continuous baking oven study, in which the operator had several concurrent tasks, that the operator maintains a list of events and activities covering a time span of $\frac{1}{2}$–1 hour ahead and that this list is updated by a special scanning procedure.

In the furnace control task these two types of prediction seem to be independent as they are related to the two main routines in different ways. The next event prediction is made during stage reviewing, and these data are used by the control choice routine; the prediction is not made during control choice if the data are not available. The control choice prediction is made during control choice behaviour, it seems to draw minimally on data obtained during stage reviewing and does not update the stage review. Control choice is concerned with stage parameters such as the time the stage started, and how much power it is using now, while stage reviewing notes mainly when this stage will end, and how much power it will use after that time.

4.5. Interrupts

It seems that external interruptions which are irrelevant to the task, such as drinking a cup of tea, or saying how many spoonfuls of sugar he takes, and digressions, such as to ask for explanations of an imperfectly understood display or part of the task, do not have a disruptive effect. After the interrupt, or digression, the operator returns to the point he was at previously. This is in contrast to the changes in direction of activity as shown in Figure 3. Here the changes in direction occur only at particular points in the sequence, as determined by the operator himself, rather than at any time as with external influences, and the new routine is followed without any reference to the previous one. The effect of interrupts is also discussed in Beishon (1969) and Bainbridge et al. (op. cit.).

4.6. Limitations of the Flexible Sequencing Strategy

This strategy for dealing with a changing control state by using the routine with highest control priority is an efficient mechanism, but can also be a source of error. For instance, when a significant change in overall power usage occurs, the operator immediately considers control action. He only investigates the cause of the change later if control was not urgent, so the 'next event' prediction may not be up-to-date when he chooses his control action. As another example, he may have predicted that when a certain stage change occurs he needs to make a given control action. Another stage change occurring after making the prediction and before the event may make a control change unnecessary, but if he has not repeated the prediction and changed his assessment he may continue to make the change. (The protocols can be the only source of explanations for apparently inappropriate actions such as these.)

4.7. Summary of Effects of Experience and Individual Differences

Studies of protocols from inexperienced operators doing this task suggest that inexperienced controllers also show the two main types of behaviour, choosing control actions or sampling the general furnace states; however, at first they use feedback rather than predictive control, and organize their data search less efficiently. For instance, they react to errors in power usage by making control actions, and only slowly learn to take future events into account in making control decisions. Similarly, at first they review the stages of the furnace in alphabetical order of furnace names, rather than grouping together furnaces which are in the same stage, as the experienced operators do.

Efficiency at updating stored information and passing data between main routines seems to be one of the main areas in which the effects of individual differences and experience with the task appear. Inexperienced subjects seem to be more limited in their ability to use data obtained by one routine in another routine, it seems that data remain local to one routine unless a 'common' store is explicitly established. One type of poor performance from experienced subjects is given by operators who are poor at updating their predictions and remembered state information as discussed above.

Another type of poor performance, independent of ability to think about the task, is shown by the subjects who can choose the action to make, considering more and more refined dimensions of this choice, but have difficulty in committing themselves to making it.

One major area of individual differences and experience lies in the length of the two main routines, e.g. in the number of parameters which may be considered, or in the complexity and accuracy of any assessments which may be made. For instance, inexperienced subjects work entirely by feedback at first, making no predictions about future events or actions and having little knowledge of the available control strategies, while the more sophisticated of the experienced operators may calculate exactly in kWh what the effect on power consumption of a given future stage change or control action will be.

It can be suggested that this 'depth of consideration' is related to the amount of processing time available, as well as to the knowledge of the task. As mentioned in Section 4.3, each behaviour starts with a global assessment, and continues to greater refinement. If the amount of time available for the routine is limited, then an inexperienced subject who is establishing his strategies, or an operator who is 'slow-witted', will not get to such depth in the routine as an experienced or quick operator.

4.8. *Possible Sources of Mental Load*

The same notions can be applied speculatively to the problem of the 'mental load' imposed by a task. Under the type of increasingly refined strategy outlined above, in any task where there are time limitations on performance, routines will only be used to a certain depth, so that this type of task will show a tradeoff between speed and accuracy, as has been shown to occur in the control of rapid movements.

Also, when the task loading is such as to cause stress reactions, this might impair the flexibility of the processes involved in transferring and updating data, as has been shown in studies of the effects of stress on memory.

5. Models of Human Process Control

Models of human control behaviour are usually concerned with describing the input-output relationships in control of a single-variable system with time lags of a few seconds. In the task analyzed here this 'control error–size of control action' decision is a small part of the operator's total activity; he is otherwise concerned to keep up to date with the state of a multivariable system. It is relevant to consider whether different models are appropriate to these two parts of his task.

5.1. *Size of Control Actions*

In this study the protocol phrases are mostly concerned with qualitative decisions, with identifying various aspects of the system, and these decisions are described in some detail. When quantitative decisions occur, such as identifying the present need for control or choosing the size of control change to make, the results are stated but reasons are rarely given. Cooke (*op. cit.*) and Beishon (1966) have found the same phenomenon in protocols from subjects controlling other processes with slow dynamics. This might suggest that the models used for fast dynamic tasks are appropriate, either of the transfer function type (see *e.g.* review by McRuer and Jex 1967), or of the finite-state machine (FSM) type (see *e.g.* Angel and Bekey 1968). In these models the solution is obtained either by plugging values into an equation or by entering a matrix. Beishon (1969) presents evidence that the operator uses a number of permanently stored look-up tables of control information. Both Cooke and Beishon (*op. cit.*) suggest FSM models for control of slow-response systems, and call this 'system state/action state' control.

On some occasions the control is described in detail in the protocol. In these cases the controller calculates the effect of a given size of control action on power usage, and chooses one with the required effect. This is a form of predictive control. Sheridan (1966), Kelley (1967) and Smallwood (1967) have presented control models which include an equation representation of the 'controlled element', this is used in fast time to make predictions of future behaviour on which control is based. Fogel et al. (1966) have discussed FSM controllers which include internal models of the external environment. Bainbridge's (1967) model contains templates for system behaviour which are used for prediction. Craik suggested in 1943 that human beings form some kind of internal representation of the environment. Unfortunately, the power controller's task is proportional so the data do not give evidence on the existence or nature of a mental model in the control of systems with more complex dynamics. Cooke (op. cit.) gives protocol evidence that subjects use a mental model to predict future behaviour when controlling a slow-response system.

Using protocols to obtain evidence of this type is partly confused by the way in which human decisions which have been made frequently in similar circumstances become habitual, so would not be given in a conscious report. It might be suggested that the method of control changes as it becomes habitual. Andrew's (1967) finding that, for simple control tasks at least, operation with or without an explicit model of the controlled process may be mathematically equivalent is relevant in this context.

5.2. Other Aspects of the Process Control Task

From the data presented here it would appear that an equation or FSM is not the most appropriate type of model for the controller's activities during control of slowly changing systems in which there are several interacting variables. Instead one might use an 'information processing' approach. From the findings summarized in Section 4 it appears that

(1) An operator uses flexible sub-routines when thinking about the task.
(2) At least some of these can be used recursively.
(3) Identifying the present and predicting the future system states and choosing a control action are carried out by separate routines which are inter-related by common data.
(4) On-going data about present and future system states and control actions are stored, but updating and transfer of these data between routines is not completely reliable.
(5) Non-task external interrupts do not disturb the sequence of activity; this implies a mechanism for 'keeping one's place' while doing something else.

Discussion of program models for complex cognitive activity, e.g. Reitman (1965), Baker (1967) and Beishon (1969), usually includes an 'executive' which organizes the overall sequence of activity. Figures 2 and 3 show how, in this task, alternative sequences of activity could be determined at decision points built into the routines rather than by some overseer of the task activities. However, although the alternative behaviours are consistent, and permanently available in that sense, the actual overall sequence is more flexible than the simplifications presented in the figures suggest, and further analysis of this point is needed.

5.3. The Controller's 'Mental Model' and 'Mental Picture' of the Process

In equation and FSM models the controller's internal representation of the system is an independent entity to which it refers, to predict future events. This could represent the controller's knowledge of the process dynamics. The protocol evidence suggests that this is insufficient to describe the whole of the operator's knowledge; this also includes the routines he uses to do the task, which describe the operations of the process and the operations which he can carry out on it.

Statically the whole structure of the routines used for doing the task would represent the operator's knowledge of the system, dynamically his control activity consists of processing through this structure in sequence.

Comparison of Tables 1(A) and 1(B) shows that the variables determining the sequence of behaviour are the same as those items which are stored in the head boxes of the main routines. This suggests that any decision about the best next behaviour is determined by the data in the head boxes. These stored data items could therefore be considered as the operator's on-going 'mental picture' of the current state of the process, providing the context in which he works.

6. Conclusions

Data from this study of proportional control of one variable in a slowly changing process, many of whose parameters have to be taken into account in making control decisions, corroborate and expand some aspects in earlier studies by Cooke and Beishon of more complex systems with slow-response dynamics and several concurrent control tasks. The information processing type of model used to structure the data stems from work on computer simulation of human problem-solving (see *e.g.* Reitman *op.cit.*). Some new concepts are needed in extending these ideas to the description of mental activities in process control. This task involves working within a fairly well-defined set of aims, priorities and available strategies rather than generating creative solutions to problems, 'solutions' for control state errors are known after sufficient learning. Instead, the difficulties of this task lie in working with a complex independent dynamic system which changes in real time.

The experiment described in this paper, and the initial data analysis, was supported by a grant from the British Iron and Steel Research Association. Professor R. J. Beishon, now at the Open University, obtained the grant, organized the experiment and suggested the collection and analysis of verbal protocols. Mr. M. Splaine and Mr. J. H. Hemming and Dr. K. D. Tocher of the Operational Research Department, The United Steel Co. Ltd., Sheffield, made available and helped with use of the digital simulation. The author would like to thank all those involved with this study.

Analysis of Operator's Work at Various Levels of Automated Production

By J. Daniel, F. Puffler and M. Stríženec

Institute of Experimental Psychology, Slovak Academy of Sciences, Bratislava, Czechoslovakia

At a national seminar on psychological analysis of work and professiography it was underlined (Daniel 1970b) that any intervention into a process, or any effort to influence it, unconditionally requires a thorough knowledge of its momentary state. This applies to every activity without exception. This stage cannot be omitted either by the technician or the physician, biologist or psychologist. While this logical claim has been implemented in numerous types of activity, it has not been sufficiently respected in the psychologist's practice. If, however, the psychologist is to enter into the essence of the problems he has to solve, then he too must be acquainted with the work specification and the conditions prevailing at the workplace.

Generally speaking, these analytical approaches may be said to have attained only the margin of psychological research due both to a lack of appropriate professional training (preparedness) of psychologists for such a research and an inadequate methodology.

The importance of analytical approaches towards the work of an operator has been emphasized particularly by Zarakovsky (1966), who has also proposed the system of grid diagrams enabling to record repeated operations in a graphic manner.

Difficulties adequately to analyze operator mental activity in information processing are pointed out by Hladký et al. (1970); quoting Kitchin and Graham (1961) they state that the field technique of measuring work may provide a satisfactory quantitative expression of only these three types of mental activity: (1) mental activity involved in controlling and coordinating muscular activity, i.e. body movements during work of a manipulative character; (2) mental activity in perception, i.e. actual information intake by one of the sense modalities; (3) mental activity of sense modalities in retrieving a random stimulus, mainly promptness in locating a random but probable signal. To analyze an operator's work Hladký et al. chose the algorithmic method; however, at the close of their study they state that an appraisal of the professional claim will also require that the time criterion of the course of the activity be also investigated. From the psychological aspect the time characteristic describes better the nature of the principal work mainly as regards the activating processes of the organism (attention, motivation, will), and agents inducing stress and emotional tension. A rôle is here played by, for example, the quantity of the activity performed in a unit of time, i.e. how often must the operator intervene during a working shift. When analyzing operator activity in a chemical concern, Itelson (1961) remarked that sensory and intellectual functions are here associated (analysis of the situation and of the ways to deal with it). The time analysis showed that an operator's main task consists in scanning and checking the instruments (63%), then comes servicing the instruments, directing the squad (26%), and controlling (11%).

The relation between operator activity and various types of automation was described by Crossman (1960a). He differentiated between nonstop production, programmed machines and centralized remote control. In nonstop production —which is the object of the present study—he lists the following types: a large concern with manual control, a large concern with automated control, conveyor belts, small machines. In an automated control process stabilization is assured by control recorders, while the operator sets the required value and checks the operation of automatic controllers. Setting lays claims on thinking (taking into account the effect of controllers and characteristics of the process), and thus an operator contributes significantly to the effectiveness of production. Generally a high degree of vigilance is not required. In manual control, an operator's skill can best be assessed on the basis of the speed and smoothness of change to altered operational conditions. This skill embodies perception, prediction, acquaintance with the control system and decision-making. The degree of difficulty of control depends on the mutual correlation between displays and controls, the time constant of the process, necessity of estimating parameters, incompleteness of data and difficulty of forming a mental picture of the process. In practice, these services are assured by a team of operators with specific assignments, and a chief operator.

1. Problem and Method

In view of the importance of analysis of operator work discussed above, the preliminary stages of our study included a technical description of four production departments at various levels of automation, and took into account also a different degree of claims on the operator. The next stage included time studies of the successive steps of various operations. Such studies are made as smooth time-measuring investigations of noncyclic operations which, in individual cycles, contain components of either an irregular series, or a nonuniform content, or of both an irregular series and nonuniform content. The procedure we adopted was close to the method of instantaneous observation, by which is meant a time study designed to ascertain the frequency of occurrence of various partial working activities. It enables to estimate, on the basis of probability, the frequency of recurrence of the activities observed after definite time intervals (according to Šedivý 1966). In addition, judgments by experts and operators' estimates were also made use of.

A technological and organizational description of the departments under study was given elsewhere (Daniel et al. 1971). Here attention was focused on operator activity at the master panel of the following departments:

(a) Atmospheric distillation

(b) Pyrolysis of benzene and gases

(c) Separation of pyrolytic gases

(d) Polyethylene production.

2. Results of Time Studies and Estimates

Table 1 was constructed on the basis of time studies in all the working shifts. It includes the percentage frequency of individual groups of activities (i.e. the mean value obtained through observation of several operators) in four departments of a chemical concern.

To obtain a more complete picture of the recurrence of individual types of activities, we asked some operators from each department independently to estimate the percentage of the frequency of various types of activities. By averaging these data we obtained Table 2 (the numbers express percentages).

Table 1

Type of activity	Departments			
	Atmospheric distillation	Pyrolysis	Separation	Polyethylene
Scanning of displays (on panel and console)	28	30	51	19
Panel control	5	6	5	5
Communication, consultation	15	21	19	8
Written agenda	17	4	3	12
Outdoor work at installation (control)	20	30	15	18
Rest pauses, meals	12	8	5	28
Others	3	1	2	11

Table 2

Type of activity	Departments			
	Atmospheric distillation	Pyrolysis	Separation	Polyethylene
Scanning of displays (on panel and console)	25	30	45	43
Panel control	14	9	17	17
Communication, consultation	19	28	13	11
Written agenda	5	3	4	16
Outdoor work at installation (control)	19	10	3	3
Rest pauses, meals	4	5	5	6
Others	14	15	13	4

In view of the considerable claims on thinking in the departments under study, particular attention was devoted to this mental activity, our aim being to compare the difficulty of operations from this aspect.

Four leading workers thoroughly familiar with the running of the departments under study were interviewed with a view to setting up the characteristics of various work operations (see Table 3). In addition, they were asked to rate the claims on thinking on a points scale (as a frame of reference we chose the department of pyrolyzed gases, where these claims for a normal operational run were rated as 10 points). The means of points by the 4 raters are shown in Table 4 (a higher number of points indicates a higher claim on thinking).

3. Comparison of the Departments under Study

The objective data and subjective estimates from the preceding sections made it possible to compare the departments in terms of claims laid on the operator's mental processes (see Table 3).

Because of the technological complexity and the consequent demands on control, the department of pyrolyzed gas separation may be considered as the most exacting from the viewpoint of overall mental activity. However, the measuring technique in this department is of a very good standard both on the

Table 3. Brief characteristics of operations as regards claims on operator thinking

	Starting of operations	Normal operations	Operations under partial breakdowns	Total breakdowns
Separation of pyrolytic gases (DPP)	Numerous parameters are to be followed. A knowledge of technological interrelations is required.	Highly complicated technology, complex mutual connections among instruments. Strict requirements on quality. Parameters (pressure, temperature) moderately exacting.	Breakdown of one of the sections causes interruption (breakdown) in others of the series.	Stoppage requires to adhere to a complex procedure to assure correct restarting of operations.
Pyrolysis of benzene and PB-PP gases	Starting operations are exacting indeed, are carried out fairly regularly and thus are familiar.	Technology not too complex (simple production lines). Parameters, especially as regards temperature (800–1000°C), exacting. Performance dependent mainly on correct temperature.	Economics of ethylene unit depends chiefly on adherence to pyrolysis parameters, hence emphasis is laid on speedy repairs.	Total breakdown if pyrolytic furnace has to be laid off. This requires considerable flexibility and knowhow.
Polyethylene	Carried out separately for every production line and fairly frequently. Is routine in operator training.	Not too complicated as regards technology (5 production lines). Exacting as regards pressure (1500 atm.). Numerous regimens required for various qualities of PE.	Breakdown requires prompt intervention, for it affects quality. Is under remote control.	Breakdown dangerous, but lay-off insured with safety valves. Manual layoff simple (press buttons at control desk).
Atmospheric distillation	Responsibility lies mainly with foreman.	Standard technology. Average parameters.	Breakdowns (except in furnaces) are not violent in character. May be remote-controlled from control desk or by manual control of armatures.	Stoppage of production is fairly simple.

technical side and also as regards the requirements of engineering psychology. As a result, the operator is away from the control panel for a minimum of time and thus can devote his attention to the display panels (see Table 1).

An unsatisfactory arrangement of display instruments on the panel and an unreliable measuring technique concur to put pyrolysis in second place, although the technology here is not so very exacting. The difficulty derives also from unsatisfactory means of intercommunication with auxiliary operators and adjacent departments. The low standard of measuring and controlling technique requires frequent activities directly at the installation which takes an operator away from his main tasks.

Of an approximately even degree are claims in the polyethylene department where the technological process is somewhat more exacting, but which requires a smaller number of interrelated parameters to be followed (usually three independent production lines). In addition, the measuring and control technique is on a satisfactory level. Breakdowns in this department, however, have far-reaching consequences (this is a source of high mental load), hence, there are at least two operators present all the time in the control room (as a result, there is here usually a relatively high percentage of rest time). As the easiest we may consider work in the department of atmospheric distillation IV, and this is because the relevant technology does not require such complex mental models of the controlled process. On the other hand, work here is rather exacting physically, especially in winter, for the operator is often called upon to intervene out-of-doors (not only to set operations running or stop them, but also for controlling normal production) or to control the activity of his subordinates (see Table 4).

Table 4. Rating of claims on operator thinking

	Starting of production	Normal production	Partial breakdowns	Total breakdowns
Atmospheric distillation	9.6	6.7	9.3	13.4
Pyrolysis of benzene and PB–PP gases	11.3	8.3	13	20
Polyethylene	10	8.3	12	17
Separation of pyrolytic gases (DPP)	16.6	10	15	23.3

After this comparison in the plane of overall claims on mental activity, we shall set down also the specific claims on perception and thinking.

As regards perception, the greatest difficulties arise in connection with unsuitable physical characteristics of displays (*e.g.* weak differentiatedness of various elements, glare off the instruments cover) and their unsuitable arrangement in relation to the controlled process, as, for example, in the case of pyrolysis. A further factor adversely affecting information reception from the panel is the large number of superfluous instruments or of such as are obsolete and unused for a long time. An example of such a state is the panel in the atmospheric distillation IV. In these two departments the principle of placing the most important display instruments in the centre of the panel has likewise not been respected.

As regards thinking, it may generally be said that the most exacting activity is that of starting production (following stoppage due to a breakdown or general overhaul). Here, the various parameters of the technological process must be synchronized to harmonize with a gradual step-up of production. Then come breakdowns (here the sequence of interventions is the normal operational running).

The statements by the leading workers on this point differ somewhat from this classification—they consider total breakdowns, then follow launching (starting) of distillation and separation—breakdowns in these last two operations—in the second place, partial breakdowns and starting of production in the third place, and normal operations in the fourth place. This divergence may be explained by the fact that these workers consider mental load under breakdowns as a component of the thinking activity.

The effectiveness of an operator's intervention depends on his experience, knowledge of technology and his mental model of the controlled process. The adequacy of this model or its application is affected in particular by the content and structure of the information displayed on the panel. From this point of view pyrolysis, even though technologically a relatively simple process, is the most difficult. This is because of the unsuitable panel arrangement and the necessity of ' on-the-spot controls ' and interventions out at the installations. In view of the adequate information presentation, but because of great demand on control, we may place gas pyrolysis in second place (the senior operator, besides following the process, must also coordinate and control the activity of his subordinates). A relatively smaller demand on operator thinking appears to be in polyethylene polymerization where the panel is suitably arranged, small claims are laid on team cooperation, although, on the other hand, the operator here works under a great mental load (possible breakdowns with far-reaching consequences to human lives and installations).

The least demanding is atmospheric distillation, though here too, complex problems of thinking may arise (because of a long-term time constant, prediction is difficult, analyses from laboratories come in at great intervals; the starting operation requires a great number of dynamic processes to be taken into consideration).

4. Conclusion

The lack of a methodological treatment of the subject of work analysis, particularly where mental activity predominates, makes it necessary for several approaches to be combined. In an analysis of operator work in automated production, use was made of objective (study of operational material, time studies) and subjective methods (interviews, estimates of time course by operators, rating of the degree of difficulty of the thinking processes). It was shown that the results from the objective and the subjective procedures are complementary and permit a faithful characterization of operator work to be worked out.

Translated from Slovak by P. Tkáč.

On Research into Operator's Thinking and Decision-Making

By Michal Strížene c

Institute of Experimental Psychology, Slovak Academy of Sciences, Bratislava, Czechoslovakia

Among the themes embodied in engineering psychology, those of thinking and decision-making have so far received the least attention. The first papers specially oriented to this subject have appeared only recently (John and Rimoldi 1955, Pushkin 1959, Kitchin and Graham 1961, Suvorova *et al.* 1961, Chebysheva 1963, Matyushkin 1964, Cooke 1964b, Cristian and Zbăganu 1964, Zinchenko *et al.* 1964, Galaktionov 1965b, Shaffer 1965, Rouanet and Gateau 1964). These papers are, however, concerned for the most part with some special method of research, or again, present a broadly drafted analysis of the operator's activity, with little space being devoted to thinking.

Taking this situation as our starting point we shall endeavour to present an analysis, from a methodological aspect, of the contemporary state of research on operator's thinking and decision-making. We wish in the first place to underline the enhanced claims put on mental processes by modern production; then we shall analyze the possibilities of applying the approaches of general psychology to thinking and shall concentrate particularly on the novel approaches to thinking and decision-making which have received, at least in part, an incentive from cybernetics, or refer more particularly to the operator's activity.

(1)

Automation in production brings about changes in the demands on the mental processes of the workers. This is especially noticeable in semi-automated production, but is likewise apparent at the first level of automation, where no automatic regulation intervenes as yet and man has to direct and control the course of the technological process. Man is here in contact with production through an intermediary (by means of signal and control devices), demands on perception thus being altered and, in addition, the role of special skills is lessened and claims on thinking and decision-making come to the forefront. The basic trait of these involvements is processing and a logical interpretation of the information obtained as well as selection of the optimum solution for a given situation. The operator represents the typical function of man in modern production, directing the latter through its information model and, in particular, maintaining the installation normally in operation. His activity depends on the type and level of automation of the production in question (perceptive performance still predominates at the lower levels). Different demands are imposed especially by non-stop production operations and by central remote control (Crossman 1960a).

Non-stop operations production requires from the operator, in particular, stabilization and optimization of the production process. In addition to perception, prediction and decision-making are here also involved. In decision-making, concepts from past analogous situations are utilized, but a more effective way is the creation of an internal ' mental model ' of the situation. This model enables the operator to choose the most suitable variant of intervention, the solution here being often intuitive (non-formalized aspects). Conceptualization of this model is necessarily affected also by the physical model employed (signal and control systems). A thorough logical processing of the information thus acquired may sometimes be impossible owing to the complexity of the process under operation, the mutual interdependence of many of the parameters and the necessity of certain data having to be estimated.

A centralized remote control represents a load for the operator's—despatcher's—mental activity, because the operations being directed (means of conveyance, power-houses) are inaccessible to him. His main task is to evaluate coded information and to decide between the alternatives determined.

The mental processes in both the types of activity are negatively affected by breakdowns in individual signal systems, or by stress from the great responsibility incumbent upon the operator (expensive equipment, great amount of raw materials and products). Further demands on the thinking activity arise from the necessity of coordinating and directing the activity of auxiliary operators.

Chebysheva (1963) distinguishes two basic types of mental tasks in work activity: diagnostic and prognostic. In the former, the cause must be determined on the basis of a complex of symptoms (all the essential conditions must be taken into consideration) and in the latter, the optimum response has to be selected in relation to the given group of conditions (estimating possible consequences of individual variants). A characteristic trait of thinking in the working process is the immediate connection between thinking and activity.

In directing the production process, the operator must take into account the complex, direct and feedback effects and therefore must consider also a number of possible causes. Processing of the obtained information and therefore directing of the production process may, according to Itelson (1961), be realized on the basis of universal technological principles, or with the aid of standard, stereotyped procedures, eventually according to momentary urgency (breakdowns), or with a view to feedback signals.

This multi-feature operator's activity must be subjected to a detailed analysis in order that the basic operational groups may be ascertained. Zinchenko and Majzel (1964) differentiate between information retrieval and servicing. According to them, the first group includes, besides perception, a sorting out of the problem situation and the second embodies task-solving, decision-making and the realization of intervention. Tichomirov (1965) raises justified objections to such a division, for the solution itself of the task is an active search activity on the part of the operator. The thinking process becomes involved already in perception of data from signals (information, selectivity, decoding) and sometimes is required in the very intervention of the operator into the production system (particularly if the controlling devices are not arranged in an optimal manner).

When studying the operator as the processor of information, Taylor (1963) differentiates between two tasks: discrete decision-making and continuous data processing. An important aspect of decision-making is that of the capacity of information processing and the solution of probabilistic situations.

This concise review of the demands made on the operator's mental activity shows that the simpler thinking processes come into action already at the stage of data perception from the control panel (demands on thinking are related to optimization of arrangement of signal devices), their task rises in determining problem situations, in creating 'model' solutions and in verifying individual variants of intervention into the production process. The total mental load depends on the type of production, exactness and reliability of the automatic equipment involved, feedback information, accepted tolerance in products, *etc.* A whole scale of thinking and decision-making processes may here be involved, beginning with simple situations of the type of disjunctive reaction time, up to complex intellectual performance in optimizing numerous parameters.

(2)

Investigation on thinking within the framework of general psychology pointed to a series of weighty characteristics and conditions affecting this mental process. Nonetheless, numerous questions still remain unsolved. At first, logical investigations were considered as the only approach to thinking, but it was only *Gestalt* psychology which helped the problem situation to be recognized and singled out as a basic experimental situation and method. According to the opinion generally accepted today, thinking becomes manifest in problem-solving (Taylor and McNemer 1955). Duncan (1959) defines thinking as an integration and organization of past experience, and problem-solving as the discovery of correct response. Kaminski (1964), in his turn, lays stress on cognitive structures and processes, analyzing their individual types, the process of their formation and the method of their determination.

According to Bergius (1964a), the object of research is understood biologico-functionalistically (behaviourism—thinking is considered as a system of simpler mechanisms), or phenomenologico-structuralistically (cognitive approach). Among questions of methods, the problem of their subjectivity or objectivity comes to the forefront. The essence of thinking—as shown by Anderson (1965)—is explained in very different ways (adaptive quality of behaviour; non-verbal phenomena in the organism; verbal behaviour; intervening variable; identification of thinking with consciousness).

Soviet psychology puts the problem situation into the context with notions and subjective conditions of the individual and embodies them into the conditions of theoretical or practical human activity (Matyushkin 1965). The basis is here given, in particular, by Rubinstein's concept (1960) that external causes act through internal conditions (principle of determinism). The principal link in thinking is analyzed through the intermediary of synthesis (the object is always ranged into new connections). Kostyuk (1959) in his review of Soviet work in the field of thinking analyzes questions relative to the essence of thinking (the process of reflection of reality), understanding (cognition of objects new to the experimental person), formation of concepts (generalization of cognition of objects, passage from perception to understanding) and problem-solving (analytico-synthetical activity, directed to the discovery of essential relations). He also takes note of phylogenesis and ontogenesis of thinking and the relationship between language and thinking.

The approaches of Soviet engineering psychology to questions of thinking were analyzed in our review article (Stríženec 1966c).

A phenomenological analysis does not permit a generalization of notions and, therefore, it is necessary to introduce theoretical constructions. The best known among them is the conception of productive thinking, the actual state of which has been described in detail by Bergius (1964b). A difficulty—the problem—arises when the motivated person cannot attain the goal immediately. In laboratory tasks either a systematic procedure is required (for instance, a labyrinth) or an original idea (for example, to connect 9 points in 4 strokes). Research to date shows that the processes of problem-solving depend on a situation analysis (what is required?), a material analysis (what is given?) and a conflict analysis (why does it not succeed?). Productivity of thinking resides in the knowledge that the task, as given, may have other forms too, and also in a new look at the original situation (figural and functional re-structuralization). In connection with problem-solving, questions of adjustment, motivation, expectation, the effect of experience, transfer, fixation, affects, social interaction, *etc.*, are studied.

The beginnings of the conception of problem-solving may be seen in Duncker's work (1945). He recorded the S's responses ('thinking aloud') during problem-solving. The author described the structure and the dynamics of the processes involved in problem-solving. Thinking is induced when the passage from the given to the required state cannot be realized without mediated activity. The solving process resides in the problem being unfolded (formation of functional significance of solution and its concretization). A series of intervening phases occurs, each being a solution in relation to the preceding, and a problem in relation to the succeeding phases. The author was conscious of the protocol being an incomplete recording of the process. Of course, on the basis of a larger number of protocols, it is possible to set up a 'genealogy' of process-solving (logical sequence of basic stages with data on the number of their incidence). The author interprets orientation as an organizing problem. In every solution, the overall psychological structure of the situation changes (stressing certain elements; appearance of new entities).

A factorial approach to thinking finds application in Guilford's work (1956). Here he distinguishes cognitive factors (becoming conscious of mental constructions), productive factors (achievement of a definite final result) and evaluating factors (judging of the correctness, effectiveness of the results of thinking). In convergent thinking, this is guided in the sense of one conclusion, and in divergent thinking investigation is effected in several directions. More recent research often neglects, according to Duncan (1959), an analysis of the thinking processes and gives only the number of problems solved by the subject. Research is centred on finding out the effect of transfer (instruction, training), method of presentation of the problem, comparison of problem-solving by individuals and groups (generally there is no difference here). In view of the use of different tasks non-dimensionality of variables, no integration of concepts has as yet taken place in the field of thinking.

The advocate of the phenomenological approach, Van der Geer (Van der Geer and Jaspars 1966), analyzes the latest concepts in the field of cognitive functions and, along with 'traditional' themes (transfer, group solution), points also to results obtained through simulation of thinking by means of computers.

Bartlett (1958) is of the opinion that thinking is a high level skill and consists of filling in a gap in a series of phenomena (by means of interpolation and a novel look). The sequence or the series of mutually connected steps can always be determined in thinking. The author differentiates four types of thinking: in a closed system, experimentally, everyday and artistic thinking.

Piaget (1966) has worked out an independent conception of thinking and he and his numerous pupils still develop this conception further experimentally. This author understands the act of thinking as a grouping together of operations according to certain, exactly defined, structures. He follows the development of thinking from the sensorimotor form of activity up to abstract thinking. The author takes a critical stand towards the behaviouristic theory and reproaches *Gestaltism* the introspective method (which does not permit the course of thinking to be followed) and does not recognize genetical development of forms.

If we compare the need of elucidation of the operator's thinking processes with the contemporary state of research on thinking within the framework of general psychology, we find that the high specificity of the complex man–machine systems does not allow the direct application of the findings relative to the simple static and exactly formalized problems (geometric, mechanic, verbal-logical tasks). Similarly, from the methodological point of view, a research on the operator's thinking is much more exacting.

(3)

New approaches to an investigation of thinking and decision-making were substantially affected by cybernetics. (Concerning Information Theory, see Herrmann (1964)). In the first place, it is the possibility of modelling certain aspects of the thinking processes by means of heuristic programming that stands out. Newell *et al.* (1958, 1961, 1963) interpret the processes of thinking in the subject as a process of symbol manipulation and presume the subject's behaviour to be guided by a program. If a computer program that imitates with sufficient accuracy a subject's behaviour in a large number of situations is worked out, then the program may be considered as a theory of behaviour. The authors refer to the *Gestalt* principles and in working out their programs (LT, GPS), they proceeded by comparing problem-solving from symbolic logic by the subject (who ' thought aloud ') with the computer performance. The heuristic approach (process based on the analogy, disintegration to simpler processes, estimates, *etc.*) proved to be an adequate means for overcoming the limits set to automata, by the use of algorithms.

The possibility of quantifying the degree of difficulty of the problem by means of information theory was exploited by John (1957) in his apparatus ' PSI ' (Problem-Solving and Information). He criticizes the paper-form approaches that had been used until then as unrealistic and stresses the need of recording qualitatively differing stages in the solution and passages among them, as also determination of difficulty of the task. The method is suitable for problems where it is necessary first to elucidate the final and calculable complex of relations among the elements and then so to manipulate as to obtain a single determined result. ' PSI ' consists of electromechanical elements inserted into Boole's computer. The display panel carries 9 pairs of keys and bulbs in a circular arrangement (inputs) and a 10th bulb in the centre representing the required output. Arrows indicate the existence and direction of the relationships among individual elements; however, the essence of the relation is not indicated (this is to be deduced by the S on the basis of logical experiments). The subject's task is to light the bulb by means of three indicated inputs. In manipulating the elements, the subject acquires the necessary information; nevertheless, instructions require a minimum number of steps and delay for completing the test. A marked number of different behavioural characteristics in the subject can thus be followed.

A detailed analysis of task uncertainty for the PSI apparatus was made by Rapoport (1958).

This PSI apparatus was also used by Rouanet and Gateau (1964) in connection with the selection of computer programmers. Certain methodical changes were introduced here. They evaluated problem difficulty on the basis of the number of elements in the solution branch and also of the number of branches entering the combination. By an analysis of the process the authors found two types of strategy. The influence of memory as well as of recordings of successively-obtained information proved to be without significance.

Of significant contribution to the research on thinking was the book by Bruner et al. (1956). The authors deal with the state of strategy of thinking and this in connection with the creation of new concepts. The known experiment with cards (picked out by the subject) pointed to four basic strategies: simultaneous survey (maximum gain of information at every step); successive survey (one hypothesis being verified at a time); conservative concentration (only one parameter being altered at a time); risky concentration (several parameters being changed at once). The strategies differ by the demands they impose on thinking and the speed of advance toward the goal. When the cards were shown by the experimenter and the subject had to express an optimum estimate, two principal strategies came out: total traits of the first card serve for an elaboration of the estimate and elementary (only certain traits go in to form the estimate). The selection of the optimum strategy depends on the type of the task, the time limit, the manner of obtaining information, etc.

In categorization by means of probabilistic cues, a difference must be drawn between decision-making on one single phenomenon and that on a series of phenomena. As a cue to both these types we may use frequency of events or a combination of partly valid cues. In case of conflict between the cues, the subjective preference for one cue is often seen to be employed. If the possibility of cue validation is lowered (lack of feedback information), the activity in problem-solving declines, or the effort at error reduction decreases. The subjective estimate of probability in categorization is greatly affected by the consequences arising from an erroneous categorization, as well as by the degree of confidence on the part of the subject in the given cue.

More recently, Stachowiak (1965) gives a detailed analysis in his book of the cybernetic model of productive thinking. Information—a psychological analysis of operative thinking—is a condition of technical modelling of thinking.

The author takes here as his starting point the concepts from neurocybernetics (optimization of perception, hierarchical arrangement of structural schemas, technical models) and analyzes in detail also the question of thinking machines. An analysis of the possibilities of a cybernetical approach to thinking processes in the scientist (for example, theory formation) embraces both, the comparison of four groups of scientific disciplines, and various ways of consideration (induction, deduction). This is, to a large measure, a continuation of Carnap's conception.

A review of the application of cybernetical approaches to human thinking may also be found in our monograph (Stríženec 1966a).

In his activity, man is called upon to solve multiple tasks and hence he must have an adequate command of the general methods of thinking, the general methods of approaching any arbitrary task. One such general method is the use of algorithm—an exact description of the sequence of elementary operations for the solution of arbitrary tasks belonging to a definite class (type). In his book, Landa (1966) deals in detail with learning by means of algorithmic instructions in solving geometrical and grammatical tasks at school. These instructions possess the essential traits of algorithms in a mathematical sense (determinateness, massiveness, resultativeness); nevertheless, they fulfil only approximately certain conditions (explicit recognizability of objects, final groups of objects). Similarly, the definition of the elementary operations in psychology and pedagogy must be made experimentally.

The author's work not only represents a contribution to didacticism, but it also elucidates here many basic aspects of algorithms of thinking activity. Non-algorithmic procedures determine activity in an ambiguous manner (uncertainty found in them leads to different activities in different persons in the same situation). An independent selection of activities whose highest degree is creative activity, is here required. The degree of uncertainty in the ways of solution may differ in different situations (similarly also, determinateness of individual steps). If the prescription states the number of operations out of which selection must be made, then the choice is easier than when this number of operations is not given. The use of non-algorithmic methods arises from the fact that in many situations the complete system of conditions and such factors as the sequence of operations, *etc.*, are not determined. In the course of solution, however, essential conditions become clarified, their coherence is determined, and thus algorithmic methods may be set up on the basis of non-algorithmic ones. Many examples may be found in scientific branches over the past years of algorithmization of previously non-formalizable procedures (as in, for example, diagnosis).

Fogel (1961) analyzed the logical complexity in decision-making and differentiated between deductive, abductive, inductive and prognostic decisions.

Deductive decisions are characterized by complete certainty—algorithmic processes are involved. Deduction may further be divided into moronic (primitive—conditioned reflexes), optimizing (criterion enables input signals to be distinguished) and adaptive (internal signal modifies moronic transformation). At a higher level of logical complexity noise, too, may possess a useful function—may help in creating new alternatives which are then judged.

Abductive decision-making involves a search for the causative factor according to the consequence and the directing rule. It consists of a series of deductive part-solutions. A marked degree of uncertainty is involved here, for the directing rule need not exhaust all the directive-causative relationships (this refers also to heuristic procedures).

Inductive decision is implied when a series of events requires a guiding rule to be found. Speed and reliability of the inductive transformation depends on the number of signals and their classes, appropriateness of the criteria differentiating the classes, *etc.*

Prognostic decisions are frequent with the operator (information is delayed). Extrapolation of the situation is effected in several stages: induction (transformation of the perceived information to hypothesis); deduction (creation of a solution model); and abduction (picturing the future situation).

These forms of thinking processes are also introduced by Zinchenko *et al.* (1964) with the proviso that information processing has a multi-level structure and definite types of information models must correspond to every class of tasks. According to the transformation of the information content we recognize three classes (types) of tasks: ' message-message ' (operator selects from among the input signals only those that belong to a definite class); ' message-order ' (on the basis of perceived information he determines the type of intervention into the object); ' order-order ' (he coordinates his own activity with that of other operators).

If the starting conditions can be recorded exactly, Neumann's metric criterion (1965) enables human thinking to be assessed (individual stages of problem-solving). On the example of the game with the ' Hanoi tower ' (transfer of discs of various sizes), he showed the possibility of constructing an algorithm of the task by means of Markov's chains and its subdivision during the course of thinking into comparable sectors. The matrix of passages from the initial to the final state enables the speed of execution of the problem to be evaluated.

Miollan (1966) made use of the same game to determine the degree of the subject's conviction about the correctness of part steps.

Posner (1965) considers problem-solving as a transformation of information. The effectiveness of thinking depends largely on the way information is presented (the greater the need for the transformation in information reduction, the less effective is the performance).

An experimental study of problem-solving in stochastic processes was made by Shaffer (1965). In correcting computer solutions, the operator lowered the optimal and improved the non-optimal solutions.

Cooke (1964b) followed the way in which an operator learns to classify important variables and to formulate gradually simple rules for decision-making.

The thinking process was analyzed by Rimoldi (1955), who determined the number, type and sequence of the subject's questions. He based his work on the assumption that the same solution may be the result of various mental processes. His technique may be utilized in diagnosis and kindred problems.

In connection with mental, conceptual models in the operator, Welford (1962) states that although this process is not exact, it nevertheless replaces a number of discrete estimates. It is necessary to find out which parameters tend to be abstracted into the model. The more complex the model, the more difficult it becomes to formulate it and the less it yields in results. An optimum model need not inevitably be the most exact and complete. If a simple conceptual model can be employed, the choice of operators need not be unduly strict.

Decision-making enables also the mental load to be expressed. Kitchin and Graham (1961) analyzed decision-making on the basis of the number of factors in the situation, their complexity, mutual dependence, participation of memory and delay of feedback.

An operator's work requires not only judgment analysis of the working situation (according to exactly set-down rules), but in view of the complexity and the uncertain character of the further development in the directed processes, also a priority selection of one variant of intervention over another, on the basis of judgment of both probability of achievement and value of the expected goal.

The theory of strategic games and statistical decision-making contributed to the creation of abstract models of conflict situations. An operator is involved in such situations when he has to choose one from among various alternatives, each of which has its advantages and its drawbacks.

Edwards (1961) has made a review of studies on human decision-making to the present date. A static situation implies a simple selection in an exactly-defined number of possible ways of activity. Here, we may differentiate situations without any risky selection (certainty about the outcome of every activity), situations entailing a risk selection (probabilities are known) and selection under uncertainty. The author takes for granted the fact that probability and utility may be given by a single number and he who is to make the decision chooses the alternative in which this number is the greatest. Edwards' model of a subjectively expected utility (SEU) is the most appropriate to decision-making; nevertheless, difficulties are met with in the setting up of utility and subjective probability scales.

However, in the course of the operator's activity there ensues a sequence of decision-making, the directed processes being changed as a result of these decisions—but also independently of them. Hence, changing situations imply a dynamic decision-making. Edwards differentiates here six different types of tasks.

Perfecting of decision-making processes is made possible by a confrontation of the initial data with achieved results, and a gradual acquisition of information (evaluation of this information processing is made possible by Bayesian statistics). Essential conditions of decision-making are the utility scale of goal and the subjective probability of its achievement. In probability evaluation by the operator, account must be taken of the difference between objective and subjective probability. A tendency towards overestimation of low and underestimation of high probabilities has been noted. Utility is based on preference of one alternative over another and this in turn is affected by a detailed knowledge of the directing process itself. Models so far fail to provide adequate explanation for the complex mental processes in decision-making; nevertheless, they at least make possible an experimental and a quantitative approach to some of the aspects of human decision-making.

Let us now consider some of the research studies more directly concerned with the operator's activity.

A practical application of algorithms in thinking activity has been described by Pushkin (1959, 1960) on the example of a railway despatcher. Algorithms may be utilized in modelling processes of control under laboratory conditions. Zavalishina and Pushkin (1964) analyzed in detail individual types of a despatcher's mental activity and on an abstract model (a variant of the 'game of 15'—shifting numbered cubes) they investigated the mechanisms of operative thinking.

Under operative thinking they understand the process of practical problem-solving on the basis of an internal model of the proposed activity (Pushkin 1965, Lomov 1966). Chess games as a model of operative thinking were used by Pushkin (1964) and Tichomirov (1966), who found heuristic processes in the choice of field of search, information transfer from one situation to another and from the process itself to a verbal plane. A comparison of heuristics in man and machine helps to clarify the existing structural differences. Similarly, Reitman (1966) has shown that heuristics—however expedient it may be for improving performance—does not represent as yet a theory of human thinking.

The operator often receives inaccurate and unreliable information and hence probabilistic situations must be investigated. Kozielecki (1966) has verified the existence of a mechanism leading to a self-confirmation of the hypothesis (information confirming the hypothesis is taken as true).

Oshanin (1966) points to man's ability to change the parameters of his behaviour in accordance with the conditions of his activity. This is made possible by the creation of an operative picture of the directed object which then appropriately processes the information obtained. In laboratory research the operator is left to direct by remote control the activity of the technical model of the object, which allows structural and dynamic characteristics of the operative picture to be ascertained. Taking these characteristics of the operative picture as his basis, the author designed experimental graphic representations which proved to be a more effective aid for the operator at a power station than technological schemas.

An experimental study of information processing was also made by Klix and Sydow (1966). This involved a sequence of binary decisions and the authors investigated the use of strategy and heuristic procedures. All the possible ways of operations solving were simulated on a computer. This enabled the general characteristics of information processing by man to be ascertained (invariants of cognitive structures).

Leplat and Bisseret (1965) studied information processing in an airport control tower despatcher (the object was to prevent possible conflicts between incoming airplanes). In the categorization of ' no conflict—possible conflict ', six variables had to be considered (speed, direction, altitude, *etc.*). To elucidate the essence, value and order of processing the variables, they made use of the operator's ' thinking aloud ' method. The authors realize, however, that the method is attended by marked drawbacks (effect of verbalization, consciousness of the activity and so on); yet the results obtained enabled an organogramme (a topological schema of operations organization) to be drawn up. It is presumed that the problem being solved becomes all the more difficult, the further it is located on the branch of a ' genealogical tree '. In view of the fact that experimenting in a real situation is difficult (various activities are included along with the reception and sending out of information), the authors set up a static experimental situation (display panel with signs enabling the required function to be measured, all the subjects being faced with an identical situation). Major interindividual differences and influence of the operator's skill—as regards duration of task-solving—were found. According to the choice of the first variable, two types of strategy may ensue, together with a different time structure of the process. In general, a combination of the static model with the organogramme proved to be a useful method. At the same time, the fact became clear that a study of the manner of presenting information must go hand in hand with that of information processing.

Galaktionov (1965a, 1965b) points to the possibility of the information processed by the operator being quantitatively evaluated. In complex tasks, the event is determined by a combination of several parameters, connected by causative bonds. A simple application of information theory formulae is not possible here, for events contain a different number of determining signs and the operator selects only from a definite part of the events. The author, therefore, suggests to take as the starting point the causative-resultant connections between events and their symptoms (to express them in the form of 'pedigree-charts'). Structural schemas represent algorithms of operator's work and enable a quantitative evaluation (on the basis of unconditioned probabilities, agreement between subjective and objective probability, *etc.*). The calculation differs for an equal and a different probability of incidence of events and also according to whether the operator's judgment is based on the probability of events or of symptoms.

Cristian and Zbăganu (1964, 1966) made an experimental study of the operator's activity at the control panel. In spite of different working conditions, situations exist which are typical for the given work and which are solved by typical procedures (and engender typical errors in their solution). Research on thinking has so far proceeded along two lines: general psychology and work psychology. An operator's activity embodies key operations which are indispensable for problem-solving. They create a sort of shortened algorithm in problem-solving. In the course of laboratory research, various problems were presented to the operator (chemical production) with adequate information. The subject tackled the problem by selecting some of the operations on the panel (pressbuttons) but in an optimal order. On a special display panel they followed the proceedings and, in case of need, could annul his previous interventions and make new ones. The solution by each subject was graphically compared with the ready-made programme (set down by the technician-specialist). A chart showed the course of the solution, the number and order of operations, annulments and erroneous interventions. When synthetic curves were plotted, key operations could be determined and also individual solutions could be compared with a group mean. Besides the graphic analysis, a quantitative analysis (number of operations and duration of the solution) and a qualitative analysis (realization of the operation and its time factor) were also carried out. The results showed that subjects skip certain operations and do not follow their expected order. The following types or relations were found in the operations: sequence, equivalence, incongruence. The time analysis underscored critical points. The solution is centred around key points (these are determined by means of synthetic curves at points of intersection with logical series). In the course of the solution, objective and subjective difficulties are encountered.

Certain partial concepts from our own research on operator's thinking processes in the chemical industry were embodied in our study (Striženec 1967a). In the first place we pointed to the different conditions in continuous production and in central remote control and then we clarified conditions which affect the course of an operator's mental process in production situations. We now endeavour to model certain aspects of an operator's thinking under laboratory conditions by means of the 'PSI' apparatus.

(4)

Automation in production, centralized remote control of energy systems, communications and the like, lead to the creation of new professions—operator, despatcher. These direct the respective processes by means of mediated control and generally at remote sites. Specific demands are thus made on their mental activity, information processing and decision-making. In view of the complexity of the situation, exact procedures set down beforehand (algorithms) are not adequate, for it is often necessary to process incomplete information, foresee the course of the processes, make a decision under uncertainty.

Classical psychology of thinking has brought in a number of concepts on man's thinking and analysis of problem-solving: it has, in particular, clarified the individual stages of this process—mental operations used, favourable and adverse conditions, effect of orienting and transfer, *etc*.

Nevertheless, this analysis has relied on relatively simple verbal, geometrical or constructive problems. At the same time, the starting conditions were uniformly determined and the progress of operations solving could be algorithmized, while the operator comes into contact with a probabilistically structured task. It is evident that the derived concepts on the rôle of various factors affecting thinking may also be applied in characterization of an operator's thinking. However, the basic question here is that of an objective analysis of the thinking process and decision-making in a complex production situation and comparison of this course with its optimum model. This then may lead to proposals for improving the manner of presenting information, facilitating conditions for creating a mental model of the situation, as well as an appropriate training of the operators for estimating probabilities, utilization of heuristic procedures in problem-solving, judging various components in decision-making, and so on.

New and important concepts, both in the field of algorithms and heuristics, have been brought in by cybernetics, or its application to mental processes. General questions of systems operations, evaluation of a great amount of information, models of conflict situations, represent not only an informational, but especially a methodological contribution to the research on thinking and decision-making by operators.

Some of the new approaches to the study of thinking and decision-making in general (Bruner, John, Edwards) represent also an enrichment of engineering psychology.

From among practical studies on operator's thinking, those directed to operative thinking are the ones that elucidate explicitly or by means of models the basic stages (operations) in the thinking process and this in the context of concrete operator's activity.

A quantitative and at the same time dynamic recording of the mental process is made possible by the graphic method (Cristian, Leplat, Galaktionov) which, in our view, deserves to be further developed, both theoretically and in its application to various types of the operator activity.

This field offers possibilities for developing cooperation with other disciplines, such, for instance, as operations research. In fact, an interdisciplinary approach to a research of the man–machine system (we have pointed out some of these problems in our study (Stríženec 1966b)) presents a fertile platform for resolving many of the questions involved.

Similarly as in other functions of man in the man–machine system, so also in processes of thinking and decision-making we must take as our starting point the systems approach and take into consideration the entire complexity of the mutual relationships in the technical and the human component of the directed system.

However, in the application of mathematical, cybernetical approaches, we should not omit the specific characteristics of the mental process—the creation of an internal conceptual model—which must be clarified by psychological methods and embodied into the context of psychological theory.

Translated from Slovak by P. Tkáč.

A Model for Describing Process Operator Performance

By D. R. Towill

Department of Engineering Production,
University of Wales Institute of Science and Technology (UWIST), Cardiff

1. Introduction

It is well known and accepted in industry that human operator performance is not constant, but varies with experience, training, and other factors (Dudley 1955, Seymour 1966, Barrow and Cawley 1971). Such improvement is not restricted to speed skill tasks such as assembly of switches and similar products, but applies equally well to activities involving mental skills and those involving the co-ordination of groups of operators, as will be illustrated later in the paper. A knowledge of expected performance is required for many reasons, including target setting, manpower planning, production scheduling, operator selection, training scheme evaluation, delivery date forecasting, and costing. Despite this interest, estimation of performance remains a difficult problem.

We may summarize the difficulties met in estimating human operator performance in industry as follows:

(1) On a day-to-day basis, there are random fluctuations in performance which can be a significant percentage of the moving average (Hitchings 1972).

(2) On a long-term basis, there is a trend towards increased performance, so that any model used must be capable of accounting for the transient nature of performance level (J. R. de Jong 1964).

(3) Deterministic effects, such as false ceilings on performance (Glover 1966), and periodic variations (Bevis, Finniear and Towill 1969), observable in the performance data, and which are often thought to be due to assignable (though at that point in time unknown) causes, are evident in many case studies.

(4) Considerable variations between operators in the performance of the same task, even for comparable experience, are to be found (Bevis 1970).

(5) Environmental, psychological, and physiological conditions in the practical situation can rarely be matched in laboratory trials, so that extrapolation of laboratory results is not always a realistic guide to human operator performance. For the real world, there is consequently a dearth of usable data, and a suggestion that more attention should be focused on industrial studies which at least would establish performance in that specific situation (Jones 1967).

(6) Although an intuitive theory of human operator performance improvement exists (Crossman 1959), it is extremely tentative, and is inadequate as a general predictor (Sriyananda and Towill 1973).

This contrasts strongly with the usual problems met by engineers in which the laws of physics may be used to understand the behaviour of hardware devices (see *e.g.* Towill 1970, Shearer, Murphy and Richardson 1967, Chestnut and Mayer 1959).

Many different professions influence the task and environment of the process operator, including engineers, work study practitioners, ergonomists, behavioural scientists and managers, hopefully all contributing to knowledge of the human operator, to increased productivity and to increased job satisfaction. There are inevitable difficulties in finding adequate common ground in such a multi-disciplinary activity. It is suggested that a model describing process operator performance adequately enough for the industrial situation, yet simple enough to visualize, will help establish this commonality quite apart from assisting in target setting, manpower planning, production scheduling, *etc.* This paper will define a suitable model, and describe the application to a world-wide selection of process industry case studies.

2. What is a Model?

When the output of a process operator, or group of operators, is observed and expressed as a suitable performance index, such as items checked/day, it may be plotted as a function of time as shown in Figure 1. In general, there will be, on average, an increasing trend, plus scatter about the trend. The equation describing the trend is the ' model ' which we are fitting to the data.

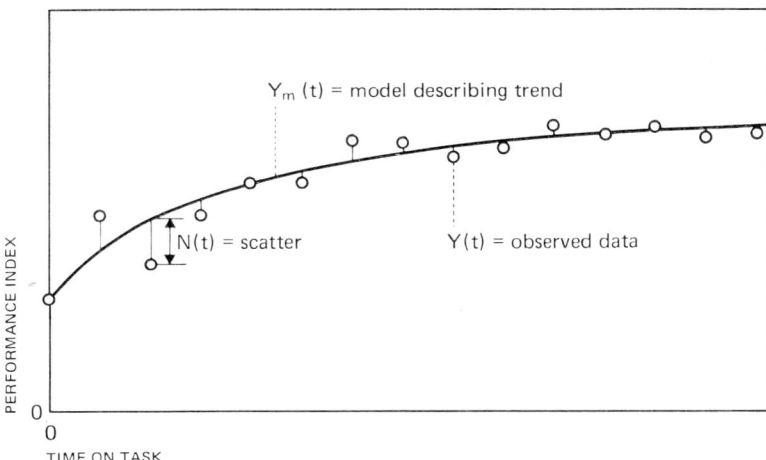

Figure 1. Variation of human operator performance with experience.

At any data point at time t, where t is the cumulative time spent performing the task, the basic relationship is defined by

$$Y(t) = Y_m(t) + N(t) \qquad (1)$$

where $Y(t)$ is the observed performance index, $Y_m(t)$ is the model estimate of the performance index appropriate to time t, and $N(t)$ takes account of all variations from the model, including modelling errors (Bevis, Finniear and Towill 1969). Because there is little in the way of theoretical guidance in the choice of the model, many empirical equations have appeared in the literature (J. R. de Jong 1964, Glover 1966, Cochrane 1968, Baloff 1970, Levy 1965).

Having chosen the equation, the parameters (*i.e.* the unknown constants relating $Y(t)$ to t) must be estimated. In some cases this involves curve fitting by eye, but a standard method is to formulate a sum of error squared function, and then, using a digital computer, to find the parameters which minimize this function. Our 'goodness of fit' is then defined by the least sum of error squared obtainable using the given form of equation. Using the definition of Equation (1), the function to be minimized in this way is simply

$$\sum_{i=1}^{i=n} E^2_i = \sum_{i=1}^{i=n} [N(t)]^2 \tag{2}$$

for n observation points.

3. Why Use a Model?

At this stage the general reader may well ask: "Why bother to devise a model to fit the data? Why not just use the data?" If we are only interested in history, and in one set of results, this would be reasonable. If, on the other hand, we wish to forecast future performance from past data, not only is a model (however crude) essential for describing the trend, but in some effective predictive methods such as the Kalman filter (Kalman 1960), we must mathematically model the scatter as well. In other instances we may wish to compare historically the performance of different operators, different groups of operators, different shifts, even similar functions under the control of different managers. Under these circumstances, a model is the most compact way of describing the trend. Vast quantities of data may thus be compressed into lists of parameters which may be easily interpreted. Where the scatter varies statistically from case to case, statistical properties such as variance may also be used to advantage to compress the data.

4. The Time Constant Model

As mentioned previously, there are many models proposed in the literature to describe human operator performance improvement. In this paper, consideration is restricted to the time constant model defined by

$$Y_m(t) = Y_c + Y_f(1 - e^{-t/\tau}) \tag{3}$$

Y_c is the initial performance, $(Y_c + Y_f)$ is the final performance, which is approached asymptotically, and τ is the learning time constant. To indicate the improvement in performance possible with experience, it is sufficient to say that it is common for Y_f to be greater than Y_c. As shown in Figure 2, at time $t = \tau$, the performance predicted by the model is $(Y_c + 0.63 Y_f)$, and at time $t = 3\tau$, predicted performance is $(Y_c + 0.95\ Y_f)$. τ varies considerably from task to task, and may be days, weeks, or months. It should be noted that for mathematical convenience, the first data point must correspond to $t = 0$. Hence, if data are sampled at weekly intervals and $\tau = 6$ weeks, the performance is $(Y_c + 0.63\ Y_f)$ at week 7.

The parameters Y_c, Y_f, and τ are fundamental properties of the task for the conditions under which it is currently performed. If conditions are changed, then the change in performance can be quantified by estimating the new parameter values.

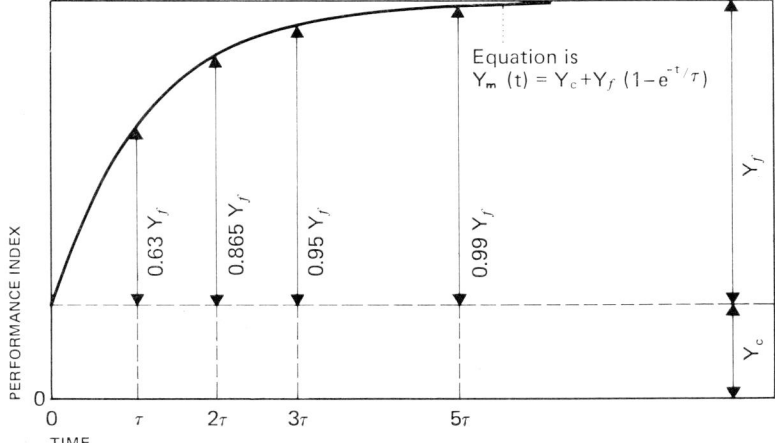

Figure 2. Curve of the time constant model.

Simple though the time constant model is, it has been tested and found to be an adequate description of performance index increase in a wide variety of applications. As a general principle, it is advantageous to use observed data to estimate a few model parameters with confidence, rather than to estimate the parameters of a more complex model with less confidence since it is frequently found that the simpler model is a better fit to the data (Taylor 1970), so that we should seek the simplest acceptable model. The time constant model has only three parameters, Y_c, Y_f, and τ. Furthermore, the interaction between these parameters is self-evident from Figure 2. Some typical results of applying the model to industrial processes are tabulated in Table 1. The first four cases have been obtained from the literature as referenced in the table

Table 1. Time constant model parameters for various industrial tasks

Industry	Task	Data source	Y_c	$(Y_c + Y_f)/Y_c$	τ
Pharmaceuticals	Product packaging	Kadota (1968)	100 products packed/day	1·60	24 weeks
Steel	Startup of rolling mill	Baloff (1970)	4·6 equivalent weight rolled per shift	2·26	20 weeks
Printing	Introduction of new 2-colour press	Levy (1965)	1950 pressings/hour	1·23	7 weeks
Chemical	Sampling and adjustment of product mix	Barrow and Cawley (1971)	1·17 blends achieved per shift	1·71	14 weeks
Electronic	Assembly	Bevis, Finniear and Towill (1969)	12·00 boards/day	6·5	3 weeks
Cigar	Material selection and processing	Bevis, Finniear and Towill (1969)	17·00 boxes/day	2·35	3 weeks

and not in association with UWIST. Consequently some assumptions are necessary to recast the data in the appropriate form, so that the parameters are very approximate, but are thought to be representative. It is reasonable to suppose that the data quoted are for a minimum standard of product, *i.e.* there is no suggestion that improvement in performance is obtained at the expense of quality. For the case studies quoted, the physical significance of the performance index varies widely, as attested by the units of Y_c. Some instances refer to individual operators, and other cases refer to groups of operators.

5. Comparison of Crews Running Printing Presses

In the work of Levy (1965) the introduction of new two-colour printing presses was described in detail. Each crew consisted of a press man in charge plus two helpers. Two shifts were operated per day and each of the three crews worked these shifts at various times. During some shifts the crew simply ran the press using material 'made ready' by the previous shift, whilst on other shifts the crew had additionally to prepare their own material. The investigator was able to break down the output into the different shifts, different crews, and different operating conditions. For each of the three crews, the extreme model parameters only have been evaluated and tabulated in Table 2. Initial debugging effects are discounted since production records were maintained only after major teething troubles were overcome.

Table 2. Time constant model parameters estimated for two-colour offset printing press

	Crew number								
	1			2			3		
	Y_c	Y_f	τ	Y_c	Y_f	τ	Y_c	Y_f	τ
Shift No. 1			hrs			hrs			hrs
(with made-ready available)	2300	1400	184	2400	400	196	2900	700	127
Shift No. 2			hrs			hrs			hrs
(without made-ready available)	1800	500	151	1950	550	232	2400	500	147

Considerable differences are observed between the model parameters describing the performance improvement of the three crews. Quite apart from the effect of 'made ready', leaving the crew free to concentrate on running the press, the shifts are significantly different. This is attributed to the direct supervision of shift 1 in which the press man seemed to feel less responsible for the quality of his output compared with shift 2, in which the press man seemed to feel a great sense of responsibility possibly leading to over-enthusiasm to correct minor defects. This example illustrates the use of the model as a compact description of crew performance improvement compared with viewing several hundred overlapping data points.

6. Using the Scatter Properties to Advantage

In addition to studying the model parameters Y_c, Y_f, and τ, a knowledge of $N(t)$, the model residuals, can also be used to advantage. $N(t)$ may be random, periodic, or indicate a false ceiling by virtue of a plateau effect shown in Figure 3. As a general guide, the standard deviation of $N(t)$, $\sigma_{N(t)}$, has been

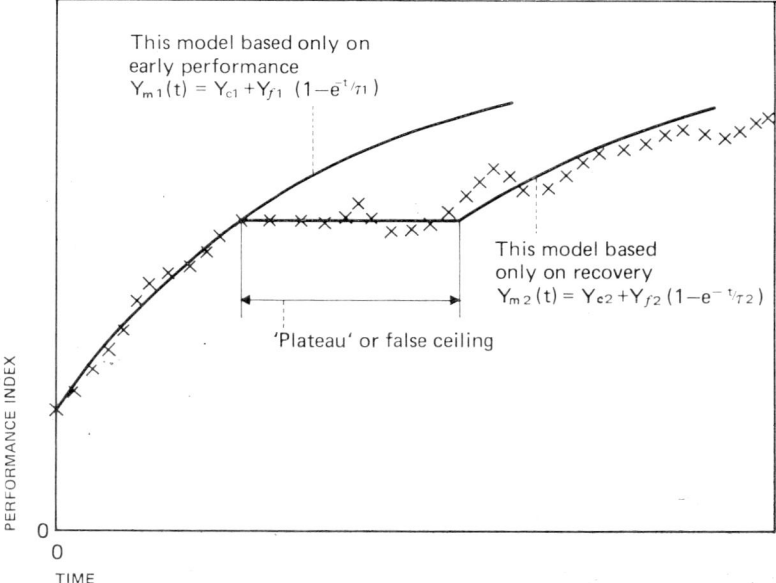

Figure 3. Plateau effect and subsequent recovery in performance.

established as of the order of 4% Y_f for a well controlled task, and 10% Y_f for a poorly controlled task (Hitchings 1972). There is some correlation between successive residuals even in the well controlled cases, suggesting that $N(t)$ cannot be completely modelled by the assumption of white noise. $N(t)$ controls the range between which future performance is expected to lie. There is some evidence to suggest that good training schemes, and good management practice, reduce scatter and hence the standard deviation of $N(t)$ in addition to resulting in a higher average value of the performance index during training. A formula for plateau detection has been derived and applied to an industrial case study (Sriyananda and Towill 1973), which reference also showed that corrective action resulted in a subsequent performance recovery also adequately fitted by the time constant model as shown in Figure 3. Sinusoidal scatter does pose problems for certain period ranges, but may sometimes be alleviated by suitable filtering of the parameter estimates (Bevis, Finniear and Towill 1969).

7. Historical Determination of Model Parameters

Where the time constant model is used for historical comparison, as in Section 5, a number of simple techniques exist to estimate the model parameters provided that data are available for several multiples of τ. If we estimate Y_c and Y_f by inspection of the data, then Equation (3) may be rewritten, with $Y(t)$ substituted for $Y_m(t)$, as follows (Towill 1972):

$$\frac{t}{\tau} \cdot \log_{10} e = -\log_{10}\left[1 - \frac{Y - Y_c}{Y_f}\right] \tag{4}$$

By plotting $\left[1 - \dfrac{Y - Y_c}{Y_f}\right]$ on a log scale versus time on a linear scale, τ may be simply estimated from the slope of the graph, as shown in Figure 4. Of course, since the curve fitting is done by eye, the value of τ depends on the

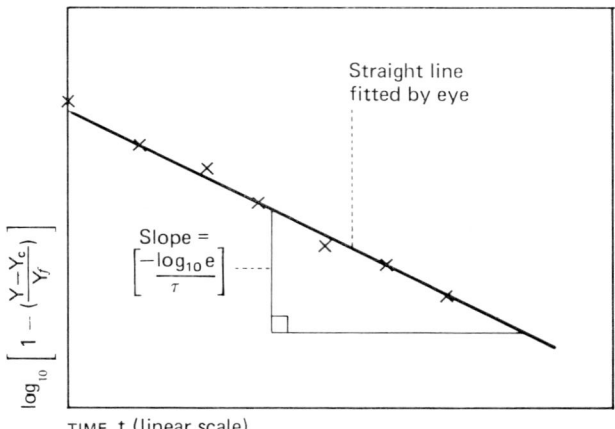

Figure 4. Determination of model time constant graphically when all data $(t \to \infty)$ available.

analyst. A further method for estimating τ historically is to difference successive values of $Y(t)$, to form a new sequence

$$(Y_{i+1} - Y_i) = (Y_1 - Y_0), (Y_2 - Y_1), (Y_3 - Y_2), etc. \qquad (5)$$

Each of these numbers is then multiplied by $\Delta T\{i + \tfrac{1}{2}\}$, where ΔT is the time between data samples; τ is then given by (Towill 1973b)

$$\tau = \left[\frac{\Delta T}{Y_f} \sum_{i=0}^{i=n-1} (Y_{i+1} - Y_i)(i + \tfrac{1}{2}) \right] \qquad (6)$$

This simple method does not require curve fitting to estimate τ. The method is sensitive to fluctuations in the observed data, and if the fluctuations are severe, some smoothing of the raw data is advantageous.

8. More Sophisticated Parameter Estimation Techniques

In many cases it is highly desirable to update model parameters as observed data become available rather than wait until the steady-state value of $(Y_c + Y_f)$ is approached; corrective action can then be taken as appropriate. One advantage of describing the performance improvement phenomenon by the time constant model has been the immediate recognition of the parameter estimation problem as the identification of a dynamic system with first-order lag and gain terms from the early part of the step response when the observations are masked by considerable scatter. Figure 5 shows how the estimates of Y_f and τ may change as measurements are made. The use of the models to forecast future performance is also shown. Three methods already developed successfully are

(1) Least squares error fit (Bevis, Finniear and Towill 1969)

(2) Kalman filter formulation (Sriyananda and Towill 1973)

(3) Impulse moment updating (Towill 1973a).

Of these, the Kalman filter and the impulse moment updating method require far less computational effort than the least squares error fit. The impulse moment updating method works well even with scanty, noisy data, but requires two smoothing constants to be chosen. On the one hand, this is a disadvantage since the smoothing constants fundamentally control the trade-off between rapid estimation and noise rejection, but on the other hand, if the simple computations are repeated for several combinations of smoothing constants, then the expected range of future performance is also estimated (Bevis 1970). To date, the Kalman filter and impulse moment updating methods rely on a suitable estimate of Y_c being available, as did the initial least squares error algorithm, which has recently been updated as a three-parameter curve fit procedure (Hitchings and Towill 1973).

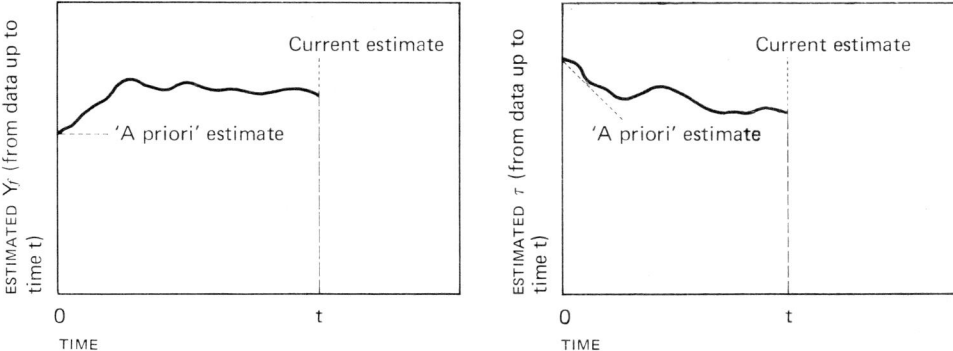

(a) Variation of parameter estimates as extra data become available

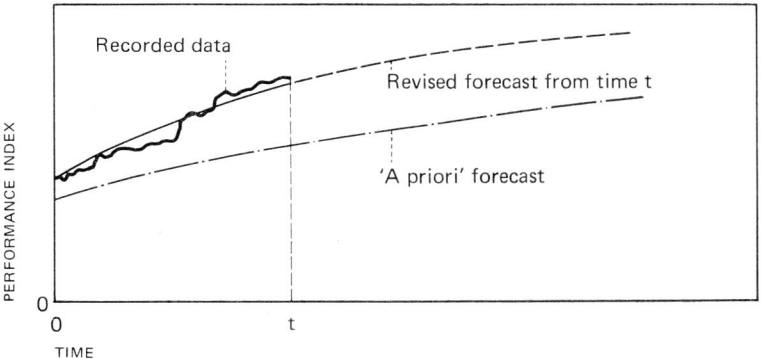

(b) Updating forecasts

Figure 5. Using updated model parameters to revise forecasts.

9. Conclusions

The paper has introduced the concept of using the time constant model to describe human operator performance improvement. Model parameters vary enormously from process to process and even between operators or groups of operators performing the same task. Using the model greatly simplifies the solution of many problems met in industry, including forecasting, costing, and manpower planning. It is also possible that the model may assist in providing a common focal point for the many professional disciplines influencing the process operator task and working environment.

Outlook for Computer Process Control

By DEPARTMENT OF LABOR, WASHINGTON, D.C.

[*The following is an extract, consisting of Chapter 7 and Table 23 of the report, which describes the impact of the process computer on the job of the process operator. Some photographs of processes given in the original are omitted.*]

Although installation of process control computers resulted in practically no change in employment or displacement of individual workers, significant changes in job duties of operators, technicians, and other employees were reported at survey plants.

Changes in Employment

The installation of process computers had little immediate effect on employment in survey plants. Over the period that computers were installed, changes in general economic conditions, product demand, and the introduction of other forms of technology were the major factors that influenced the level of total plant employment. Except for one plant where all major processes are under computer control, workers in units using process computers made up a relatively small proportion of total plant employment, ranging from 0·1 percent in a steel mill to about 6 percent in a chemical plant (see Table 9). The employment changes in survey plants varied greatly. At 6 of the 11 survey plants that provided data on employment, total plant employment increased over the period one year prior to the first computer installation to one year after the most recent installation; at the five other plants, employment declined.

Total employment in production units over the same period also was relatively unaffected by the introduction of process computers. Employment in 7 of the 12 computerized production units for which data were provided remained unchanged; employment increased at three other units, and declined at the remaining two units.

Displacement

According to management and union officials interviewed, no layoffs and little displacement took place in units with operations placed under computer control. Since labor costs made up a small proportion of total costs in most processes studied, the objectives for introducing computer control frequently were to increase or optimize production rather than to reduce manpower. Another reason for the relatively small displacement was that operating crews in the highly instrumented control rooms generally were at a minimum consistent with efficient operations prior to the introduction of the computer. Moreover, even though the computer eliminated some duties of these employees, the same size crew generally was retained to cope with any emergency arising from the malfunction of the computer or process equipment. In some cases, for example, operators were required to perform manual operations which duplicated automatic computer operations to retain skills needed for emergency manual control. In other instances, such as the computerized hot strip mill, operations normally shifted between manual and computer control, and, therefore, crews of the same size were needed and retained for both operations.

A few instances of displacement and reassignment to other plant units were reported. At a large chemical plant, for example, the jobs of 7 out of a total of 57 laboratory analysts were eliminated when a process computer system was introduced in a control laboratory to perform much of the computational, analytical, and data-logging operations formerly done manually by the analysts. The computer system automatically provides quick and accurate chemical analysis of a large volume of samples and produces finished laboratory reports. Of the seven laboratory analysts displaced, five were transferred and upgraded to higher-paying technician jobs elsewhere within the plant, one analyst died, and the other analyst went on military leave.

Table 9. Employment in computerized units as a percent of total employment in survey plants[1]

Plant	Total plant employment	Unit employment Total	Percent of total plant employment
Papermill	740	35	4.7
Chemical facility	8 004	42	0.5
		16	0.2
Chemical facility	727	[2]	[2]
Chemical facility	470	26[3]	5.5
Petroleum refinery	2 775	17	0.6
		21	0.8
Cement plant	359	17	4.7
Steel mill	18 945	386	2.0
Steel mill	12 375	214	1.7
Steel mill	13 973	19	0.1
		23	0.2
		27	0.2

[1] Most recent year available was used for those units for which employment data were provided. Comparable employment data not available at three survey plants.
[2] Since all major production units at this plant are computer controlled workers in these units constitute a high but unspecified proportion of total employment.
[3] Total for two units.

In another example of displacement, the jobs of three employees per shift at a petroleum refinery, a stillman and two stillman helpers, were eliminated as a result of the advanced forms of instrumentation installed as part of two computer control systems. A total of 13 employees in the two units were reassigned to jobs elsewhere in the plant.

One technique for measuring the displacement effect of computer process control is to compare manpower requirements of new plants designed for computer control with manpower requirements of plants of the same type and capacity using conventional control. Officials at a large survey chemical plant built with computer control estimated that about 20 employees more than the current complement of 300 production workers probably would be needed if the plant were not computer controlled. Fifteen of these employees would have been operators needed to log information and perform some control tasks; the other five would have been accounting clerks required to prepare summaries of operating data and other reports for management.

Table 10. Distribution of modified jobs at survey plants

Category	Total number	Percent of total	Modified jobs In affected production units	Modified jobs In other units	Example of job titles used at survey plants
Total, all categories	352	100·0	249	103	
Managing or supervising	27	7·7	11	16	Production superintendent, general foreman, performance supervisor, shift foreman.
Systems engineering and related work	25	7·1	9	16	Plant test engineer, control engineer, results engineer, research engineer, instrument engineer.
Process operation	216	61·4	216	0	Machine tender, head operator, cracker operator, kiln burner, BOF operator, annealing line operator, boiler-turbine operator, clerk.
Laboratory analysis and related work	55	15·6	0	55	Laboratory technician, laboratory analyst.
Instrument maintenance and related work	29	8·2	13	16	Instrument technician, electronics repairman, electrician.

Source: Data from 11 survey plants.

Changes in Job Duties and Skills

The single most important effect on employees in production units was the change in job duties. As indicated in Table 10, process operator positions made up the majority of modified positions. The changes in their duties generally were caused by the shift from manual to automatic computer adjustment of instruments and related devices. The survey plants reported that the computer generates information not previously available on process conditions which the operator can use to 'fine tune' the process and performs many calculations which were formerly done manually. Moreover, improved alarm systems incorporated in computer systems installed in survey plants in some instances greatly assisted the operator to perform monitoring duties. Some examples of changes in duties resulting from computer control are presented in Table 11.

The installation of process computers, in addition to resulting in a modification of existing jobs, required a number of new positions as discussed in Chapter 8.

How jobs are modified in a unit where computer control is installed is illustrated by the experiences at an 80-inch hot strip mill in a steel plant. This mill was operating approximately 75 percent of scheduled production runs under computer control when visited by BLS staff, and conventional control the remaining 25 percent of the time. Computer control will be extended, however, when programs are written to handle certain types of steel which presently are processed under conventional control.

The most distinguishing advantage of the computer-run 80-inch mill is its greater speed in producing uniform products within specifications. Under conventional control, operators make settings from reference tables based on standard width and rolling resistance specifications of various steel grades.

Operators need about 2 minutes under normal conditions to reset a mill for processing a slab order that varies from the preceding slab rolled; the computer resetting time is only 6–8 seconds for the entire mill. During rolling operations under manual control, operators make adjustments to the standard settings, but the speed of the mill is limited by the ability of the operators to react to changing mill conditions. In comparison, the computer reacts almost instantaneously.

Of 33 existing occupations in the hot strip mill, duties of only 9 were modified by computer control while the remaining 24 were unaffected. Forty employees, or 19 percent of the total mill work force, were employed in these nine occupa-

Table 11. Changes in major job duties of selected unit employees caused by computer process control

Job title	Unit	Description of major duties	
		Before computer control	After computer control
Machine tender	Paper machine in papermill	Responsible for paper machine crew, and all paper made on machine. Checks paper-making equipment and customer order. Set flows, temperatures, pressures and speeds at own discretion. Manually adjusts basis weight and moisture controls. Prints samples and checks paper for defects.	Computer sets flows, temperatures, pressures, and speeds and monitors these operations. Computer controls basis weight by changing stock flow, and controls moisture by changing steam flow. Machine tender performs some control and monitor duties as before and is available in case of emergency.
Clerk	Styrene unit in chemical plant	Calculates operating ratios, manually logs gage readings, and prepares weekly plant reports.	Operates computer console and input / output equipment, translates information to and from machine language, feeds data into computer, operates off-line program to perform calculations, and interprets computer output. Compiles reports on a daily basis and calculates more operating ratios than before because computer makes more information available.
Head operator	Ethanolamine unit in chemical plant	Controls unit by operating 40-foot control panel on plant floor with 40 to 60 different controls and gages. Manually adjusts analog controllers, reads and logs data, and performs simple chemical analysis.	Computer monitors, records, alarms, and manipulates process control mechanisms automatically. Operator sits in a miniaturized control panel in air conditioned room and makes only a few manual adjustments to process variables, performs chemical analysis, and manually logs some data, though the latter are not needed except to keep alert and abreast of process conditions.

Table 11.—Continued

Description of major duties

Job title	Unit	Before computer control	After computer control
Lab analyst	Control laboratory in chemical plant	Performs numerous calculations for interpreting chromatograph charts to obtain chemical composition of process samples. Manually logs data and prepares reports.	Puts samples into chromatograph and adjusts setting on computer console while system automatically carries out analysis. Computer provides quick, accurate chemical analysis of sample data and finished reports for management use. The system eliminates human errors in calculation, and relieves lab analyst of monitoring functions. Lab analyst is free to perform nonroutine analysis.
Senior operator	Ammonia chemical plant	Makes adjustments to process setpoints using manually adjusted automatic controllers. Adjustments consist of minor changes in instrument settings to keep temperatures and gas composition within predetermined limits, and major changes to compensate for uncontrolled variables such as changes in weather.	Computer now makes most adjustments automatically; however, if major upset occurs, computer alarms operator and automatically shifts to manual control. Operator still performs many manual operations such as startup and shutdown of plant, and still writes out logging reports, though computer automatically logs most important variables.
Operator	Polymerization unit in petroleum refinery	Manually adjusts setpoints and controls unit using automatic controllers. Logs data manually, filling out data sheets by hand every 2 hours. Not able to log all data needed to run process at best levels.	Computer controls key temperatures, pressures, rates of flow, and catalytic process. However, it cannot cope with emergencies. Operator determines extent of problems, although computer assists by alarming, and takes each loop or whole process off computer control if necessary. He performs numerous manual control operations.
Operator	Fluid catalytic cracking unit in petroleum refinery	Manually adjusts automatic analog controllers at control console. Monitors automatic data logging equipment.	The computer controls a large part of process, although the operator still performs much manual control. The operator can take any part or the whole process off computer control in case of emergencies. The computer does most logging.
Kiln burner	Kiln department in cement plant	Monitors and adjusts instruments manually or by adjusting set points on automatic analog controller to control variables such as kiln temperature, speed, raw material feed rate, etc., relying mainly upon experience as guide. Maintains records manually.	Computer scans process and automatically makes adjustments of key variables, including kiln speed. Computer monitors numerous other variables, reads instruments, compares and analyzes data, and prints out reports. Kiln burner uses these reports to make changes manually or to adjust set points on controllers.

Outlook for Computer Process Control

Table 11.—Continued

Job title	Unit	Description of major duties — Before computer control	Description of major duties — After computer control
BOF operator	Basic oxygen furnace in steel mill	When computer not operating:[1] Operates and monitors numerous levers, dials, and other devices in controlling the furnace. Refers to set of charts to derive proper quantities of scrap, hot metal, lime, and oxygen to use for specific heat.	When computer operating:[1] Operates computer which calculates and transmits instructions on amount of scrap, molten iron, lime, and oxygen to use in preparing specific heat. Adjusts control devices so that predetermined additives will be fed into furnace. Prepares production reports using computer-supplied data. Has option of making adjustments to the computer-generated instructions and occasionally verifies computer instructions by manually making computations based on data in sets of charts.
Plater operator	Tinning line in steel mill	Checks and makes corrections in process to maintain strip quality. Selects group of plating cells to be used for specific order, uses efficiency formula to determine amount of current to be sent through plating cells for specific line speed and coating weight, and manually adjusts plating current accordingly. Responsible for production equipment; establishes plating, current, and line speed practices; and all required records.	Selects plating cells to be used in the same manner as before, but computer automatically adjusts current for specific line speed and coating weight based on incoming order data and an efficiency formula which are manually dialed into the computer memory. Still monitors instruments and, if necessary, overrides system and adjusts current flow manually. Relieved of some monitoring duties because computer monitors and alarms in case of trouble.
Annealing line operator	Continuous annealing line in steel mill	When computer not operating:[1] Manually sets dial to desired temperature for each of eight furnace zones based on formula which considers strip thickness, line speed, and temperature. Sets production schedules, maintains line speed, furnace temperature, and related variables, and monitors control panels.	When computer operating:[1] Computer monitors and operates some controls. Operator oversees computer output equipment and modifies computer program to improve control of annealing line. Other duties same as before.
Boiler-turbine control operator	Electric generating station	When computer not operating:[1] Operates boiler and turbine control panels to maintain proper steam temperature and pressure, fuel supply, and efficient combustion conditions. Starts up and shuts down turbine-generator unit, synchronizes generators, and regulates load voltage and frequency. Performs switching operations by remote control to maintain continuity of service and keeps extensive manual data logs.	When computer operating[1]: Operator performs many of the same duties as before, since computer operates primarily as a data logger. With the aid of the computer, operator controls boiler and turbine operations through dials and gages located on central control console and decides what pressures, temperatures, speeds, etc., should be changed and to what degree. Keeps only small log sheet since computer does most logging. Previously teletyped information to load dispatching, but now computer sends data automatically.

Table 11.—Continued

Job title	Unit	Description of major duties	
		Before computer control	After computer control
Results engineer	Electric generating station	When computer not operating:[1] Responsible for overall operation and performance of controls and instruments. Makes performance calculations, insures water purity, checks coal quality, etc. Studies long-term trend data and uses it to reduce losses and improve equipment, raw material and fuel use, and other operating efficiencies.	When computer operating:[1] Uses computer to aid in making performance calculations more frequently and more accurately. Computer, though not fully operational, reduces time spent on calculations and allows more time for analyzing data and making recommendations for better plant performance.

[1] Unit built with computer control.

tions at the time of visit. The extent to which the computer modifies each of the nine pre-existing positions is shown in Table 12.

Job duties of the three positions affected most by computer control—recorder, assistant roller, and coiler operator—are shown in Appendix B-3. This information, taken from company job descriptions, shows that the duties performed automatically by the computer are crucial to the operation of the mill. Consequently, in many computer installations, operators continue to log data and adjust variables even after the computer assumes these functions. If the computer should fail or prove inadequate to cope with certain situations,

Table 12. Extent of job modifications in hot strip mill

Occupation title	Total number of major duties	Major duties automated by computer[1]	
		Number	Percent
Total	84	26	31.0
Recorder	10	5	50.0
Assistant roller	12	5	41.7
Coiler operator	8	3	37.5
No. 1 rougher operator	13	4	30.8
No. 2 rougher operator	12	3	25.0
Speed operator	8	2	25.0
Crop shearman	9	2	22.2
Roll hand	6	1	16.7
Assistant speed operator	6	1	16.7

[1] Performed automatically when mill is under computer control.

Source: Company records.

the operator is called on to perform these duties. Therefore, he must retain his proficiency at controlling the process.

A list of the 26 major job duties performed automatically under computer control, by functions, is provided in Table 13.

A number of employees outside of units using process computers also experienced changes in job duties and skills in survey plants, as indicated in Table 11.

At a petroleum refinery, for example, nine instrument men were given training in computer and instrument maintenance and were assigned to perform normal maintenance and repairs on the computers and related instrumentation installed in two units. These workers required greater skill and ability than instrument men working on conventional equipment. These men were selected from employees who had received additional electronics training previously; however, their job classifications and wages were not changed.

Changes in Grade Status

Most of the production workers in the affected units did not experience a change in grade status due to computer process control. Although some jobs were modified, these changes, for the most part, encompassed only a portion of the total duties of these positions and were not sufficient to result in a higher wage classification. In at least one instance, changes in job duties which may have resulted in upgrading were offset by substantially improved working conditions, a factor also considered in wage determination. Moreover, job descriptions were general in content, allowing considerable changes in jobs without reclassification.

In a few instances, however, employees were upgraded because of the change. The installation of a process computer at a large chemical plant, for example, resulted in the upgrading of four operators by one rate step. A formal job evaluation study indicated that these operators had assumed additional responsibilities. In the new system, operators had to interpret a significant amount of data provided by the computer and, as a result, were expected to run the plant closer to operating limits. However, physical working conditions, a factor in the job evaluation system, remained essential the same.

Table 13. Type of job duties performed by computer in hot strip mill

Function	Number of major job duties involving this function performed automatically under computer control	
	Number	Percent of total[1]
Total	26	100.0
Operate or set controls	14	53.8
Record data	5	19.2
Receive and/or communicate information	5	19.2
Operate equipment	2	7.7

[1] Because of rounding, the sums of individual items may not equal 100.

[The following table is taken from Chapter 11.]

Table 23. Outlook for further occupational changes at selected survey plants because of computer process control

Survey plant	Outlook
Papermill	As paper machines come increasingly under computer control, the duties presently performed by crews will be reduced. Possibly within 10 years, a single crew, perhaps larger than a current single crew today, will be able to operate two paper machines. Within 10 years, less labor probably will be required in the operations of threading the machine, changing paper grades, and cleaning the machines than at present. The quality control capability of the computer probably will eliminate the present occupations involved with testing and inspection. Also, instrument maintenance will become much more systematic and demand a higher level of technical skill.

Survey plant	Table 23.—Continued
	Outlook
Chemical plant	Labor costs as a percentage of total costs in large chemical plants are very low. Emphasis, therefore, is on improving control and reducing raw material costs rather than reducing manpower requirements. In analytical laboratories, labor costs are the largest expense. Consequently, use of computers is expected to have a great impact on manpower in laboratories. Computers in the analytical control labs will affect both supervisors and technicians. Through the use of computer systems which include data transmission lines and remote chromatograph stations, laboratories may be able to double present loads. Although this chemical plant does not yet have a permanent computer control group for systems design and programing, it probably will have one in the future, because applications are growing so rapidly that the company cannot afford the loss of programing skills and computer knowledge which occurs when computer project groups break up.
Chemical plant	The size of the computer systems engineering group is expected to increase from 3 to between 6 and 9 workers, including systems engineers, programers, and technicians. Computer systems, however, are not expected to have much impact on the employment of operating personnel, since operators will be employed to assure operation of the plant during emergencies with which the computer cannot cope. Training of programers and technicians will become more important, since the adverse effects of lack of training in computer technology only are beginning to be felt. The shortage of trained process computer personnel is likely to retard more widespread use of computer process control in the petrochemical industry.
Petroleum refinery	Most units at this refinery have been utilizing automatic controllers for some time; therefore, the operating staff is small and not much change is anticipated. Maintenance employment, which has been declining due to a continuing consolidation of small units into larger and more efficient ones, is expected to continue to decline slightly because of the utilization of computers, which allows equipment to operate for longer periods between shutdowns for maintenance. The computer applications group is not expected to grow much larger. If more technical manpower is needed, the companies' policy will continue to be to borrow personnel from other parts of the corporation to work on specific projects. Lack of qualified technical manpower for new key positions is a fairly universal problem. For the industry as a whole, more process engineers with chemical engineering backgrounds and computer knowledge will be needed. Standardized process computer programs, however, could reduce the need for programers.
Petroleum refinery	The company can foresee complete automatic control in the future. Such installations would have a computer in complete control of all process operations. The operator would remain only as a monitor. If this plant is to increase utilization of process computers, however, it needs more skilled programers and instrument men who are trained in electronics.
Steel mill	Engineers and maintenance workers will need to acquire some knowledge of computer control systems and the capabilities and methods to maintain them. More maintenance workers and systems engineers will be needed. Additional programing skills also may be required.
Steel mill	Further use of process control computers is not expected to lead to any notable labor displacement. Operators will continue to be needed at least as backup men to run production processes manually in the event of computer system failure. More maintenance personnel may be required, and maintenance job skills will have to be extended and upgraded.

Table 23.—*Continued*

Survey plant	Outlook
Electric power plant	The amount of time spent calculating performance requirements and testing is expected to be reduced because of computer control.
Electric power plant	Nuclear power plants may tend to decrease the number of plant personnel due to increased automation, including computer process control, less maintenance, and elimination of coal handling. Skill levels in nuclear plants probably will be higher.

Source: Based on interviews with officials at nine survey plants.

The Human Operator in the Computer-Controlled Refinery

By J. J. DE JONG

Koninklijke/Shell-Laboratorium, Shell Research N.V., Amsterdam, The Netherlands,

and E. P. KÖSTER

Psychological Laboratory, Utrecht University, The Netherlands

1. Introduction

In the fifties and early sixties a number of papers were published (Baker and McIlheran 1962 and Knight 1954) describing the oncoming ' no-man's plant ', in which the unattended operation was pictured and the impression was given that this type of automation was the one which would soon become the rule in the process industry rather than the exception.

Not only has this prophecy not come true—with the exception of pipeline pumping stations, gas and oil well clusters and a few relatively simple treating plants all refineries still have operators—but we can make the prediction that in the next few years newly constructed plants for supervisory purposes will continue to rely on the human operator. An analysis of the characteristics of human beings, as compared with those of instruments and computers, will make it clear that man as one of the components in the tripartite arrangement operator/control equipment/plant has powerful capabilities.

There have been cases where the rules governing human behaviour, particularly in communication, have not been observed sufficiently, which has sometimes led to operational difficulties. This should be a warning to take human beings very seriously.

In Table 1 a comparison is made between a human being and control equipment.

Table 1. Comparison between qualities of a human being and those of control equipment

	Favourable	Unfavourable
Human being	Can improvise; has imagination; can observe non-quantified phenomena; is self-correcting; has a fringe area of consciousness; can easily adapt himself to circumstances.	Not always reliable; potentially emotional; has to work in shifts; not capable of constant performance.
Control equipment	Reliable under almost all circumstances; large combinatorial power; active 24 hours a day; capable of constant performance.	Requires maintenance; requires considerable preparatory work; costly.

From this we can see that a human being possesses a number of qualities which are indispensable in the supervision of plant operation and for which an equivalent is hardly to be found in equipment. On the other hand, instruments and computers are superior in respect of the execution of certain other tasks. Therefore the problem of how to design a plant control and supervisory system is a synthesis problem which can be formulated as follows:

" When designing the control system for a process plant optimal use should be made of the individual characteristics of each of the three components: the operator, the control equipment and the plant. If necessary—and if possible—these characteristics should be adapted."

It should be noted that the plant is a fairly rigid system; possibilities for adaptation are limited. Human beings also are relatively rigid in their behaviour. Consequently, scope for adaptation is mainly in the control equipment.

Of the three components in the system it is the operator about whom very little is known. Here we will make an attempt at investigating his behaviour and at the same time at outlining those areas which have to be studied in more detail.

It is as well to start our analysis by making a distinction between two sets of operational circumstances:

(A) The operator thinks that the plant is running properly.

(B) The operator has become aware of some abnormality and tries to correct for this.

Of course, there are a few more sets of circumstances: starting up, shutting down, switching. Since these are almost always characterized by an increase in attention from Operations, they will not be discussed here.

What is meant by ' running properly ' is a matter of discretion. In order to avoid any misunderstanding, in this paper this situation will be defined as a set of operational conditions at which the plant produces products of the desired quality, from the given feedstock, at the appropriate rate, in the right yield and against acceptable—not necessarily minimum—cost. We shall refer to this situation by saying that the plant is in the ' productive domain '.

Further, we assume that the plant is controlled by some combination of instruments and computers (called control equipment) which takes care of automatic control, announces off-normal conditions and provides for the necessary displays.

The questions now to be answered are, firstly, what tasks should be performed by the control equipment under the two sets of circumstances (A) and (B) and, secondly, what information and manipulation means should be given to the operator to enable him to carry out his share of the task adequately. Once the first question has been answered, the second problem can be solved much more easily.

2. Analysis

A. *The Operator Thinks that the Plant is Running Properly*

Even under these circumstances the operator is, in fact, in a mental state of uncertainty. Two ways are open to him to reduce this uncertainty and thus to improve his confidence: a carefully designed automatic alarm system which, when necessary, attracts his attention by audible and visual stimuli, and the routine, more or less regular, checking rounds of his control panel.

Studies made by us in a few modern refineries have demonstrated that, even for a good operator, the alarm system alone is not sufficient. The absence of a signal announcing off-normal conditions is just not identical with the presence of a signal of normal conditions. Obviously, the operator has his doubts about the effectiveness with which alarm systems warn him of off-normal operating conditions and he therefore continues to make his checking rounds.

Unless alarm systems reach an extraordinarily high level of resolution and reliability this situation is likely to remain. Evidently, the usual equipment lacks the foresight which is typical of man and enables him to anticipate events. Even if such an anticipating faculty were incorporated in the equipment, the absence of an alarm might still not be as reassuring to him as the presence of a positive signal about the—present or future—state of the plant.

Complementary to the alarm system is the checking round which almost every operator makes at more or less regular intervals. By means of this he checks a number of measuring points or trends, by sampling them, thereby satisfying himself that everything is in proper order and, at the same time, acquiring information from which he tries to derive future events.

It is very interesting to know in what order of preference and at what frequency the operator checks his various sources of information.

We have assumed that his behaviour is governed by three different control principles.

In the first place, he tries to detect any direct violation of a constraint, such as quality specifications, given yield figures, firing and loading rates, *etc*. In order to avoid such violations he tries to operate against those constraints by maintaining safety margins, often set by himself (feedback constraint control).

In the second place, he tries to anticipate such future violations by trying to deduce from the various displays data which, if properly extrapolated, might give him an early warning of imminent trouble (anticipatory constraint control).

Thirdly, he will try to optimize certain operating conditions (optimizing control). This, as we shall see, should be regarded with some reserve. Here the operator is confronted with future situations which are not only complex but often stated rather vaguely, particularly in their side effects. We should not forget that a human being, in mentally processing information, can only handle a very limited number of variables at once. Because of the considerable degree of interaction in petroleum refining, process optimization is often characterized by the simultaneous manipulation of a great number of process variables. Taking into account that, moreover, all these process variables are in the dynamic state, one can see that the problem is very complex, and perhaps, beyond human capacity.

Evidently the operator applies these principles simultaneously. However, there are marked differences between the three and these will be reflected in his attitude.

Once the operator has detected that a constraint has been violated (feedback constraint control), he will try to rectify the situation and thus will be in the situation described hereafter under heading (B).

Anticipatory constraint control is not so simple. Figure 1 is a three-dimensional sketch, describing the case of a single-sided (maximum) constraint control variable.

At time zero the operator checks his record and makes certain that the signal is lower than a *limit value*, set by himself, which in turn is somewhat lower than the *constraint* value. The operator is in the 'green' operating zone. He now turns away from his record and one can imagine that he starts a mental process of extrapolation, trying to estimate the chance of the signal becoming equal to the limit value, which would mean that he would enter the 'yellow' operating zone. Of course, his uncertainty about the value of the signal grows with increasing time: immediately after the time zero the distribution curve is somewhat steep and narrow, but it widens with increasing time. The operator assumes (of course not explicitly) a probability level for the event of the signal becoming equal to the limit value. In the course of time he thus constructs a 'phenomenal limit curve', in Figure 1 represented by the dot-dash line, which typifies the signal value which will be exceeded only in a small, but acceptable, fraction of all cases. The moment when the phenomenal limit signal value reaches the limit value the operator goes for a check, updates himself and thus starts a new series of mental extrapolations.

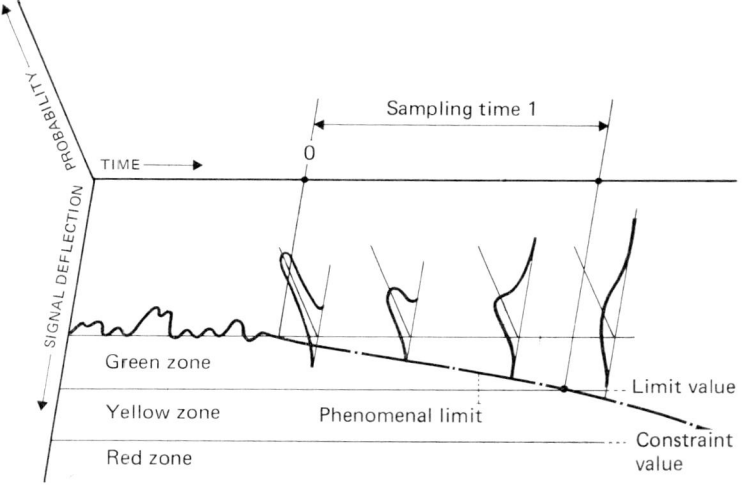

Figure 1. Phenomenal limit curve.

We may therefore suppose that the shape of the phenomenal limit curve, which reflects the operator's uncertainty about the process variable, and the limit value, which is the behavioural constraint set by the operator himself, determine the frequency of checking a particular process variable. Of course, both the shape of the phenomenal limit curve and the magnitude of the limit value are dependent upon a number of external and psychological factors. It seems worthwhile to analyze these factors in some more detail.

The shape of the operator's phenomenal limit curve for a particular process variable will be influenced by the following factors:

(1) The characteristics of the record (Smallwood 1966, 1967, Sheridan 1969, Senders 1964, Rasmussen 1968c) under normal operating conditions. It is thought that in particular those lower-frequency components which have an amplitude of the order of the width of the green operating zone play an important rôle in this respect. These lower frequencies constitute the true signal for the operator, and his experience of their normal fluctuations is the keystone on which he bases his estimate of the Gaussian distributions representing the possible spread of the signal value at given moments after his last check of the

record (see Figure 1). Although not as important, the faster components (*e.g.* noise) are also relevant, since they may obscure the value of the lower-frequency components. At certain critical signal-to-noise ratios it may become virtually impossible for the operator to filter out the signal. The resulting increase in uncertainty may influence the shape of the phenomenal limit curve, but is more likely to have an effect on the magnitude of the limit value.

(2) The occurrence of sudden upsets of a non-Gaussian nature. Sudden upsets are in principle infrequent phenomena. They are usually due to equipment failure. Much of their importance for the operator depends upon external factors such as availability of spare equipment and direct cost in terms of damage to equipment or loss of production. The operator's experience of sudden upsets will have some influence on his phenomenal limit curve. After one has happened the probability of infrequent occurrences tends to be overrated for quite some time.

(3) Motivation. The motivation of the operator plays a multiple rôle in determining the phenomenal limit curve. As pointed out earlier, the phenomenal limit curve typifies the signal value which will be exceeded only in a small, but acceptable, fraction of all cases. The motivation of the operator directly influences his choice of the acceptable fraction. The more highly motivated he is, the smaller will be the fraction he considers acceptable.

Apart from having a direct influence on the shape of the phenomenal limit curve, motivation is also of indirect consequence. The probability estimates which form the basis for the Gaussian distribution curves in Figure 1 are themselves subject to change by motivational factors. The probability of an event may easily be overrated if the operator is highly motivated to prevent that event from occurring. Since the shape of the phenomenal limit curve depends to some extent on the shape of the extrapolated distribution curves, it may vary with the motives of the operator, even when the operator keeps his risk-taking behaviour constant by leaving his choice of the acceptable fraction unaltered.

So far we have discussed the factors having an effect on the phenomenal limit curve. The limit value is influenced by the following factors:

(1) Motivation. While motivation has an important but secondary influence on the shape of the phenomenal limit curve, it is the primary factor in determining the magnitude of the limit value. The stronger the operator is motivated, the narrower will he make his own behavioural area by setting low limit values.

(2) Characteristics of the record under normal operating conditions. The noise level of the record will have a direct influence on the setting of the limit value if the signal can hardly be detected any more. If, on the other hand, the signal can easily be filtered out of the noise, the fast components are sometimes completely neglected in setting the limit value. The operator who neglects alarms coming from a noisy signal is a good example. In this behaviour motivation again plays an important rôle.

(3) Experience of the rate of change of the process variable in the limit value region of the record. Normally the value of the process variable is in the green operating region and only infrequently will it come close to the limit value.

Therefore, the operator has relatively little information about the rate of change of the process variable in that zone of the record. The consequent uncertainty keeps his limit value low and this in turn results in less information being provided about the behaviour of the process variable beyond that limit.

(4) *The number of other variables that the operator has to supervise.* One should not forget that an operator supervises a number of process variables at once. The mere number of these variables interacts with his setting the limit value. If he is extremely busy because he has to supervise a very large number of variables or because one of the variables is off-normal, he will work with larger limit values. Here again, motivation plays a rôle.

From the foregoing it will be clear that motivation, although certainly not the only factor determining the sampling behaviour, is a factor of considerable influence.

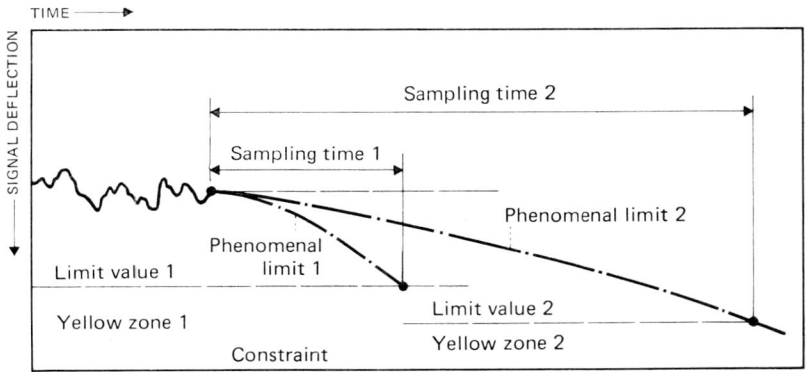

Figure 2. Sampling time at two motivation levels.

Table 2. List of motives of the operator

Category	Code	Description
		The wish to avoid:
Safety	S–1	Situations which would endanger his own health or even life.
	S–2	Situations which would endanger the health or life of his fellow workers.
	S–3	Situations which would result in physical damage to his plant.
Production	P–1	Spoiling the earlier-produced contents of a run-down tank.
	P–2	Jeopardizing product quality.
	P–3	Jeopardizing product yield.
	P–4	Lowering the plant throughput.
Economy	E–1	Unnecessarily high fuel consumption.
	E–2	Excessive other operating cost.
Personal	L–1	Situations in which much work has to be handled.
	L–2	Situations in which very little work has to be done.
	L–3	Situations which would bring him in conflict with his supervisor or his fellow-members of the crew.

Note: This list is not exhaustive.

As shown in Figure 2, strong motivation will result in a short sampling time since the (more sharply bent) phenomenal limit curve will reach the (lower) limit value level earlier. Because of this double effect of the motivation on the sampling frequency it may be expected that we can use the sampling frequency to study motivation in a more quantifying way.

Of course, actually the situation is more complicated, since the operator has to check a great many process parameters during his round. For reasons of economy he will combine various parameter checks, but it is thought that the stronger he is motivated the less will he be prepared to deviate from the pattern outlined above.

Before proceeding further it is necessary to examine Table 2, where the motives of the operator which may play a rôle in the operation of a plant are listed.

It is thought—but this opinion is open to criticism—that the study of the order of priority in which operators rank these motives may form the key to the solution of the problem formulated in the beginning of this article. Various methods can be followed: the study of the sampling frequency being one, protocol-taking when observing operators being another.

As a first approximation, we may assume that jobs for which the operator is strongly motivated should be done by him unless it has been proved that control equipment can do the job better. On the other hand, jobs for which the operator is little motivated should be left to the control equipment unless it has been proved that the operator can do the job better. We shall meet with this principle again in discussing situation (B).

B. *The Operator has Become Aware of Some Abnormality and Tries to Correct for This*

In analyzing situation (A) we have seen how the sampling behaviour of the operator is governed by motivation, control principles and plant dynamics. The question to be answered now is: how does an operator arrive at his decisions when he wants to remedy an undesired situation?

Firstly, there are simple rules-of-thumb. For instance, when the flash point of the gas oil is too low, increase the flow of stripping steam; or, when the stack becomes too smoky, increase the air flow to the furnace.

A rule-of-thumb is almost always based on a one–one relationship between two process variables. It should be noted, however, that owing to the present tendency to increase the automation level the number of one–one relationships is becoming somewhat small. Consequently, the basis for rules-of-thumb disappears. Nevertheless the rule-of-thumb forms the basic element of the lowest level of the operator's hierarchy in his dynamic, conceptual model.

Interesting work has been carried out by Crossman, Cooke and Beishon (1964) to establish the nature of such models. Much, however, is still unknown; the field is hardly explored and further research is urgently needed.

When the number of process variables that interact when the operator takes remedial action increases, the situation becomes really complex and it is here, we think, that human decision-taking becomes somewhat subjective. It is well known that even with skilled operators each has his own method for remedying trouble! This is not surprising. The operator is confronted with a 'problem-solving' job in which there are many parallel but different solutions. He is more or less on his own; he must rely on imaginative power rather than on experience. Rules-of-thumb hardly apply, since the problem is multi-dimensional and dynamic effects play a rôle.

Although both for a human being and for control equipment, in this case a computer, the job will be a very difficult one under these conditions, man is likely to be superior in his performance. A strong appeal will be made to the favourable characteristics of a human being as listed in Table 1. Also, the game aspects of the job may be attractive to man.

The computer would have an almost impossible job: its plant model first would have to be updated for the upset which has aroused the attention of the operator and incited him to action. In particular, the proper computer action in the case of an upset of a structural character, such as failure of a pump or of the power supply, would require considerable prior model development work. This may be justified in the control of space flights but not in industrial applications.

A (simplified) example is given in Figure 3, representing a plant having two degrees of freedom (f_1 and f_2).

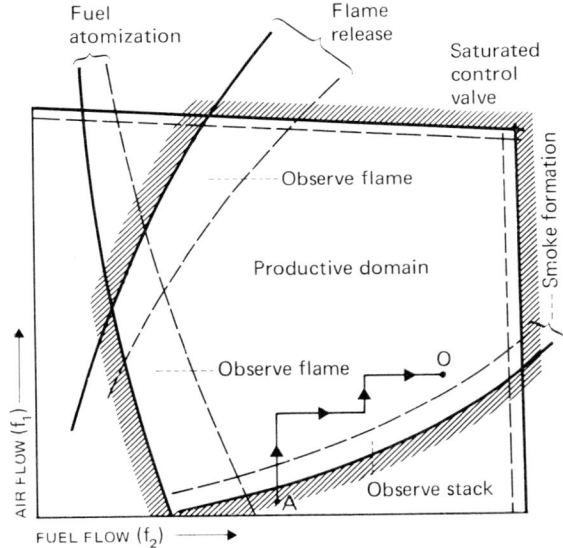

Figure 3. System with two degrees of freedom.

A furnace is such an example, the air flow to the burners being f_1 and the fuel flow to the burners being f_2. In the drawing various constraints have been given: one for flame release, one for smoke formation, one for proper atomization and two for flow. The operator maintains ' yellow ' operating zones, as mentioned before, for each of the constraints. Their margins differ, however. Also indicated in the figure is the operating point O.

Now let us suppose that by some stimulus the operator is warned that the furnace is in the alarm position A. The operator will consider it his primary task to bring the plant back to the productive domain. He will check the various sources of information and will come to the conclusion that an air blower has tripped. As the furnace is equipped with air/fuel ratio control the fuel flow is taken to the minimum value. The operator will give orders to start an emergency (spare) blower and, this being done, will bring the plant back to normal operation, often via manual control in two or three steps. Having achieved this, further refinements of, for instance, minimum fuel conditions could be his next target.

This is a simple case; in a more complex one, with more than two degrees of freedom showing considerable interaction, the route back from the alarm position to the productive domain is rather erratic, built up from a sequence of individual small steps in the various process variables.

As said before, this is the sphere of the operator. Nevertheless, it is thought that much better means and methods should be developed for him in the next few years. Particularly, well directed training schemes and aids and, perhaps, more or less accurate process simulators, although rather costly, might be considered as a first attempt.

3. Review

Reviewing the position, the results can be presented in the form of a block diagram (Figure 4) constructed from the various elements we have met.

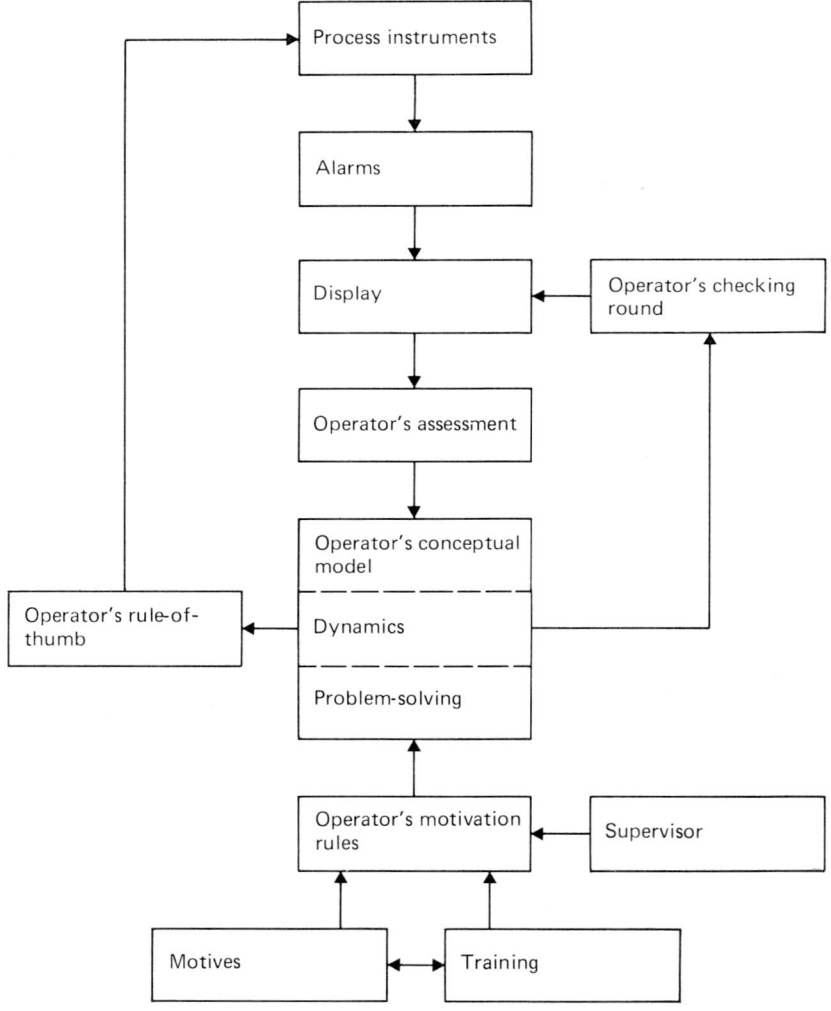

Figure 4. Block diagram of operator's activity.

4. Conclusions

Although much of the material presented here has to be checked further, and many statements made are open to criticism, the following conclusions can be drawn:

(1) Man has strong capacities for the control and supervision of processing plant.

(2) Alarm systems and checking rounds are complementary means. There is considerable room for improvement of the former.

(3) Motivation plays a rôle in the operator's behaviour. A study of the ranking of motives might lead to a proper apportioning of work between the operator and the control equipment.

(4) To get an insight into the motivation ranking the sampling frequency during the checking round should be studied.

(5) After an upset which calls for more than trivial operator action it should be the primary task of the operator to bring the plant back to the productive domain. Better means should be developed to enable him to do this difficult job properly.

(6) Attempts to demand from an operator that he should optimize process operation have to be regarded with reserve.

5. Final Remark

It is the main purpose of this paper to foster further discussion and research on this difficult but intriguing subject. Ultimately this might prove rewarding.

Operator Interaction with a Computer-Controlled Distillation Column

By B. West[*] and J. A. Clark[†]

Department of Chemical Engineering, University of Manchester
Institute of Science and Technology (UMIST)

1. Introduction

The process operator is a sophisticated technician who is expected to have a considerable skill in the control of the system for which he is responsible. His rôle has changed as plants and control systems have become more complex, but it is only recently that the functions and needs of the operator have received much attention.

The recent work on man and computer in process control by Edwards and Lees (1973) gives a review of the studies which have been done on the process operator. In fact very little in the way of formal studies of the process operator has been done on computer-controlled plants. This is perhaps to be expected since computer control systems are still relatively new. However, it is known that a number of such systems have not produced their expected performance and part of the reason could be due to the lack of understanding of how the operator reacts to a computer system.

This paper describes a series of preliminary experiments conducted by Clark (1972) in order to give some insight into the problems of operators who are using a computer control system. These tests were carried out on a computer-controlled pilot plant with experienced operators supervising the system.

2. Objectives

The aims of the project were
(1) To investigate the effects of different display types on an operator's ability to control a plant under partial manual control. Specifically, the experiments would expose a number of operators to a control task, give them time to learn how to perform the task and then expose them to different environments whilst performing progressively more difficult tasks. Their performance would be continuously monitored.
(2) To investigate the effects of different display types on an operator who is supervising the operation of a plant under complete computer control. This would involve the input of deliberate faults and the monitoring of the operator's reactions to the upset conditions.
(3) To develop general test procedures which could be used to take operators with a wide range of experience and background through similar tests.

---

[*] Now with Imperial Oil Enterprises Ltd., Sarnia, Ontario, Canada.
[†] Now with Roche Chemicals, United Kingdom.

3. Plant and Control System

The system used for the experiments is part of the pilot plant in the Department of Chemical Engineering at the University of Manchester Institute of Science and Technology (UMIST) (Stainthorp 1970). The plant is a continuous fractionating column separating a mixture of methanol and iso-propanol into about 98% pure products.

The column is mild steel, 9 inches in diameter, 40 feet long and packed with $\frac{1}{2}$-inch ceramic Raschig rings to a total height of 30 feet. The reboiler is heated by steam at 70 p.s.i.g. and the condenser is cooled by water. Figure 1a shows the column and control system in schematic form.

The plant can be controlled either by a conventional instrument panel or by the digital computer system which has a control panel and a logging teleprinter. A schematic arrangement of the control room equipment is shown in Figure 1b.

3.1. Conventional Control Panel

The conventional control panel, shown in Figure 2, contains two- and three-term controllers with manual and automatic control stations and displays of the 'quick-scan' type. The distillation column can be completely controlled manually or automatically from this panel. Records of the performance of most variables are kept on chart recorders which display about three hours' history which is visible 'at a glance'.

3.2. Computer Control Panel

The computer system can provide a complete control system for the column, independently of the conventional panel (Stainthorp and Searson 1967). The computer control panel is shown in Figure 3. The digital windows display the setpoints and the measured values of the variables which are selected on the rotary switches. In addition, requests and changes can be inserted by the operator using the rotary and toggle switches in various combinations.

Under normal circumstances, the plant operators use the whole system, both the conventional and the computer panels, to control the plant in the way best suited to their needs. For example, they use the conventional panel for obtaining a quick review of how the plant is operating, while they use the digital display and the log-out to obtain accurate information about the process. This situation is somewhat artificial because of the duplication of the control systems. Therefore in the tests it was necessary to cover up some of the displays in order to examine the effects on the control behaviour of the operators.

4. Experimental Work

Two main types of test were carried out. One is a test of manual control which requires that the operator control the plant during an operating point change. The other is a test of surveillance of the overall operation of the plant while it is being controlled by a computer. The tests were carried out with either full or partial displays and with either partial conventional panel control or partial computer control. The test series for each operator was arranged so that the more difficult tests, i.e. those lacking in displays, were carried out later in that series.

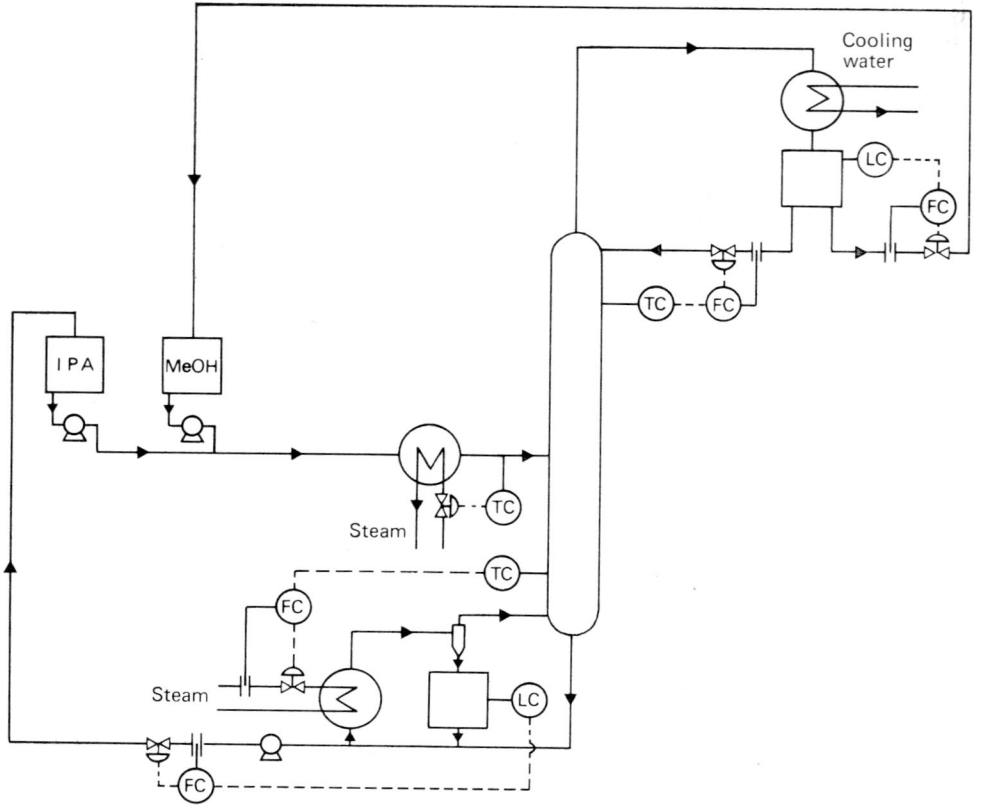

(a) Distillation column

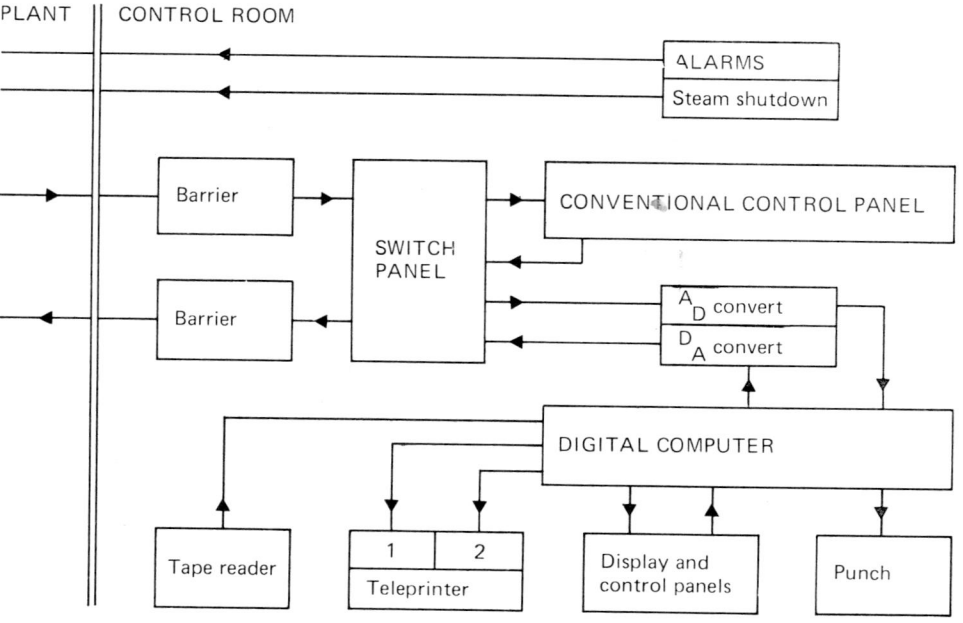

(b) Control system

Figure 1. Computer-controlled pilot plant.

Figure 2. Conventional control panel.

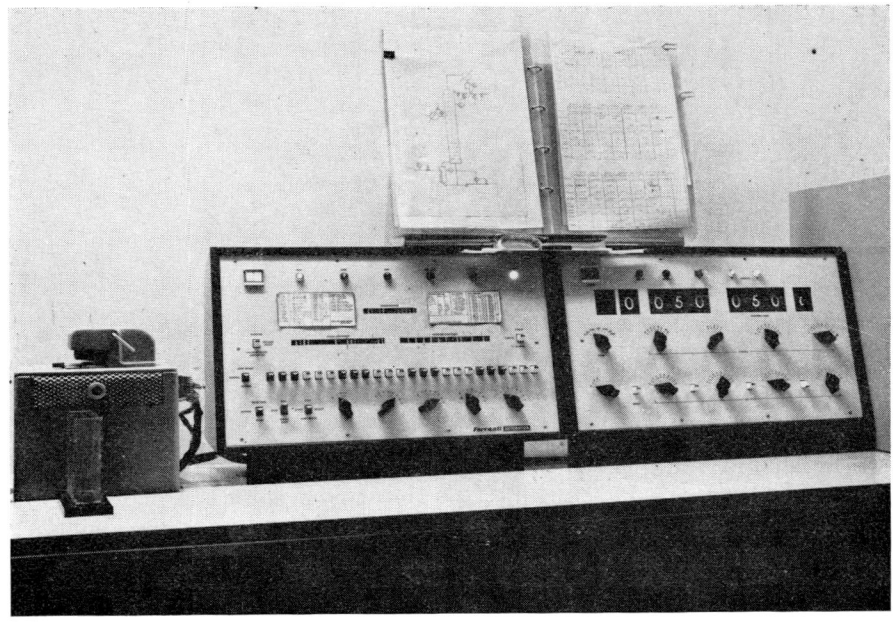

Figure 3. Computer panel.

4.1. Manual Control Tests

The series of manual control tests were carried out by most of the operators. Although the column can be fully controlled automatically, the operator was required to perform the control of the product purity. This is a multivariable problem analogous to more complex problems which operators encounter in industrial situations.

The distillation column was allowed to run to a stable operating condition and the operator was asked to change the operating point, namely to increase the purity of both the top and bottom products. This was to be achieved by decreasing the top control plate temperature and increasing the lower control plate temperature by manipulating the reflux and steam flow rates.

The operators were given precise instructions as to what they had to do and what displays and controls would be at their disposal. They were left to devise their own control strategies. Effectively, the control problem splits into two parts, the movement of the column operation to the region of the new operating point and then the fine control to get operation exactly at the new target values.

The tests were carried out by the various operators using different combinations of displays and control actions. A series of tests of increasing difficulty with the various display and control situations was carried out. The order of the tests which each operator undertook allowed him time for familiarization with the control problem. The testing was done round the clock because the pilot plant was in 24-hour operation.

The displays available were the conventional panel, the computer panel and the logging teleprinter, which was used to give a standard block log and also to produce a printout of one variable at any time on demand. These displays were used in various combinations, as shown in Table 1.

Table 1. Display and control configurations used in tests

Controls
    (1) Panel—manual control from conventional panel
    (2) Computer—manual control from computer panel

Displays
    (1) Full conventional panel and computer panel
    (2) Conventional panel only
    (3) Computer panel only
    (4) Portions of both panels
    (5) All displays covered

Teletype
    (1) Block log of plant variables at frequency requested by operator
    (2) Block log at fixed 2-minute interval
    (3) Block log at fixed 4-minute interval
    (4) Single-variable log on demand

The actions of the operators during their control task were monitored by the computer system which scanned all the variables on the plant, including those which the operator was manipulating. A special program calculated the integral of the modulus of the error of each of the two variables which the operator had to keep at a target value. This error integral was the main measure of the success or otherwise of the operators' actions.

A detailed log of the conditions on the plant was punched onto paper tape at one-minute intervals. Because it was on tape, it was not available to the operator as a display. In addition to this monitoring, the operator was asked to give a running commentary or ' protocol ' (Bainbridge 1971) of the actions which he was taking and the reasons for them.

All these data were then used to analyze the effect of the various types of problem on the operators' performance during the tests.

4.2. Surveillance Tests

A short series of tests was carried out using three operators and with the plant under complete computer control. Full and partial display systems were used and a variety of failures were created or simulated. Table 2 shows the disturbances and the operators were told that they might occur at any time during the two-hour test period.

The performance of the operators in identifying the failure and correcting for it was monitored in the same way as for the control tests.

Table 2. Disturbances injected in surveillance tests

(1) Simulated control valve and measured value signal failure (reflux and steam)
(2) Fuse blown in chart recorder
(3) Feed pump failure
(4) Product pump failure
(5) Top product control valve failure
(6) Air failure to top product and reflux control valves; reflux control valve jams open

5. Experimental Results

Some of the results of the two series of tests are presented and discussed in this section. It must be borne in mind that the objective was partly to gain experience in setting up and running such tests and, therefore, the information has not been completely analyzed; this is for later work in the research programme. It was also rather difficult to present the results of the tests in a concise way and consequently much more detail is contained in the thesis by Clark (*op. cit.*). One of the objectives of future work must be the development of methods of reducing the data into an easily-handled yet meaningful form.

5.1. Test Results

The complete details of the series of tests which amounted to about 100 are far too extensive to present here.

The displays varied from full panel display to a very limited display of digital information on the teletype. The different display options used are shown in Table 1. The two methods of control were panel control, meaning manual control using the conventional panel equipment, and computer control, meaning manual control via the computer panel, resetting DDC flow loop setpoints. Various combinations of display and control were tested.

The basic test series for each operator is shown in Figure 4. The upper part shows the operator's behaviour in the first part of the test run when the operating point was being changed. The lower part shows his behaviour in the fine control part of the test. The vertical axis for each graph is the strategy adopted, as defined in Tables 3 and 4. The series of tests by different operators were not identical but were of similar levels of difficulty.

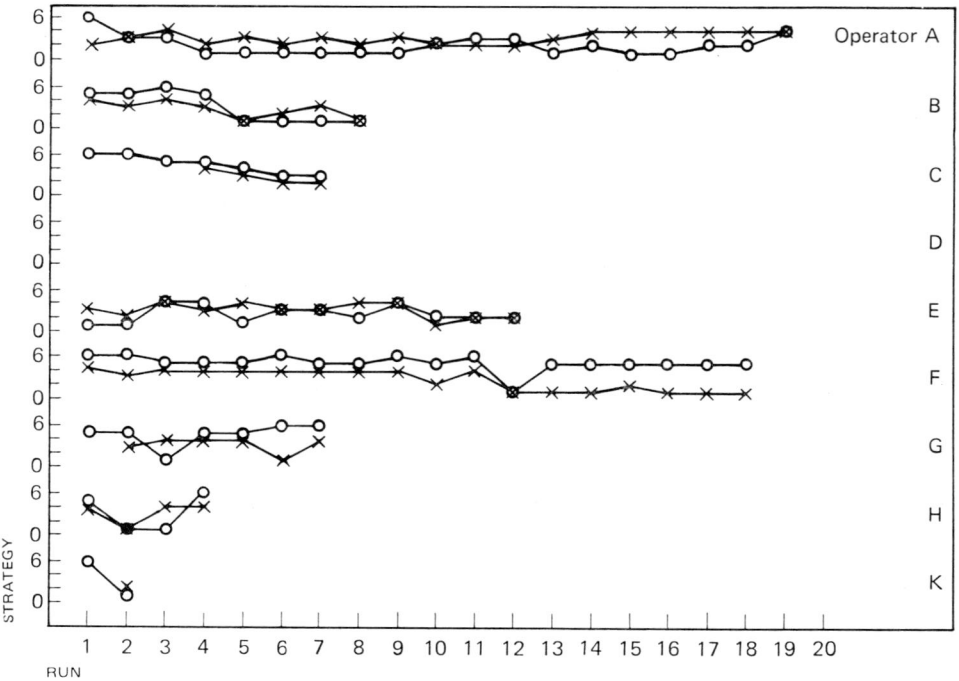

(a) First half of tests

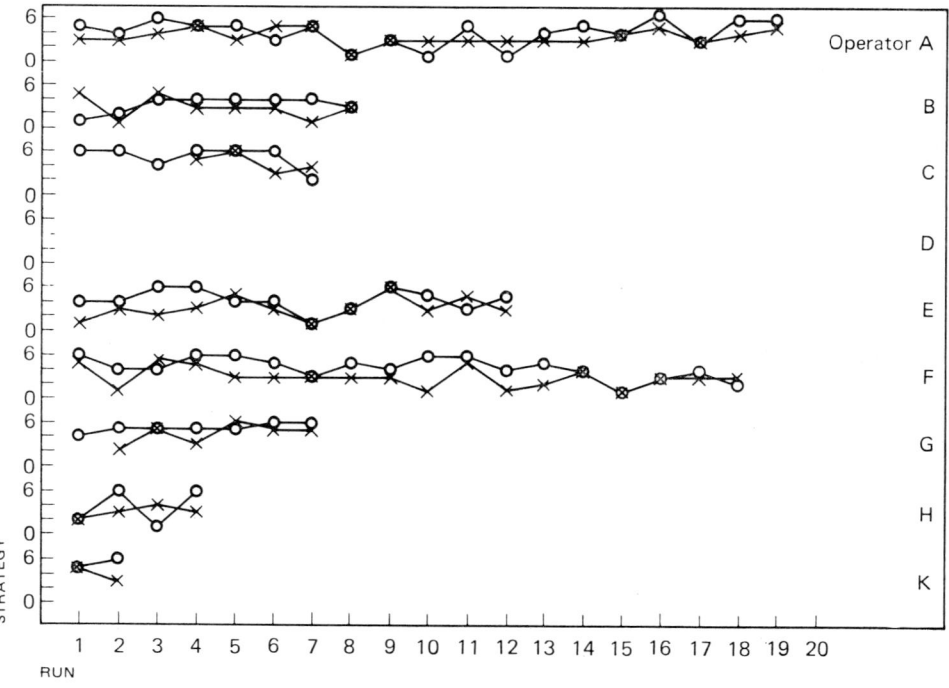

(b) Second half of tests

Figure 4. Strategies of operators in manual control tests.

Table 3. Strategies in first half of manual control tests (0–20 minutes of test)

Steam
- A1 Immediate overshoot increase
- A2 Full increase ⎫
- A3 Rapid increase ⎬ First increase occurring within 10 minutes of start
- A4 Slow increase ⎭

Reflux
- B1 Slight immediate increase, followed by rapid increase
- B2 50–100% full immediate increase, then constant flow until 20 minutes
- B3 Constant flow initially, then rapid increase
- B4 Constant flow initially, then slow increase
- B5 Initial decrease, then rapid increase
- B6 Initial decrease, then slow increase

Full	Up to maximum desired flow
Overshoot	Over maximum desired flow
Rapid	Reaching full flow within 20 minutes from start
Slow	Not reaching full flow within 20 minutes from start
Constant	Flow not altering for 10 minutes
Immediate	Within 5 minutes of start

Table 4. Strategies in second half of manual control tests (20–90 minutes of test)

Control
- C1 Usually anticipates overshoot and makes anticipatory change
- C2 Usually awaits overshoot and makes corrective change

Steam

Number and average size of changes (kg/h)
- D1 Few, $<\tfrac{1}{2}$
- D2 Many, $<\tfrac{1}{2}$
- D3 Few, $\tfrac{1}{2}$—$1\tfrac{1}{2}$
- D4 Many, $\tfrac{1}{2}$—$1\tfrac{1}{2}$
- D5 Few, $>1\tfrac{1}{2}$
- D6 Many, $>1\tfrac{1}{2}$

Many .. $\geqslant 8$ changes
Few .. <8 changes

Reflux

Number and average size of changes (kg/h)
- E1 Few, <1
- E2 Many, <1
- E3 Few, 1—2
- E4 Many, 1—2
- E5 Few, >2
- E6 Many, >2

Many .. $\geqslant 12$ changes
Few .. <12 changes

The control performances of the operators are shown in Figures 5–7. Each test run was monitored and an error integral was produced to measure the success of the strategy. These values are shown for the control of both the upper and the lower temperatures. The results are grouped to show the effects of full and partial displays and of panel and computer control. The run numbers correspond to those in Figure 4. The plain numbers are runs with full display or panel control, the bracketed numbers runs with partial display or computer control. Operators C and G ran a more limited series of tests while operator E ran extra tests to compare a standard fixed-interval block log against a single-variable demand log.

5.2. Operator Behaviour

The response to the different types of control problem and to the different displays and controls available varied considerably between operators. However, there were some common trends.

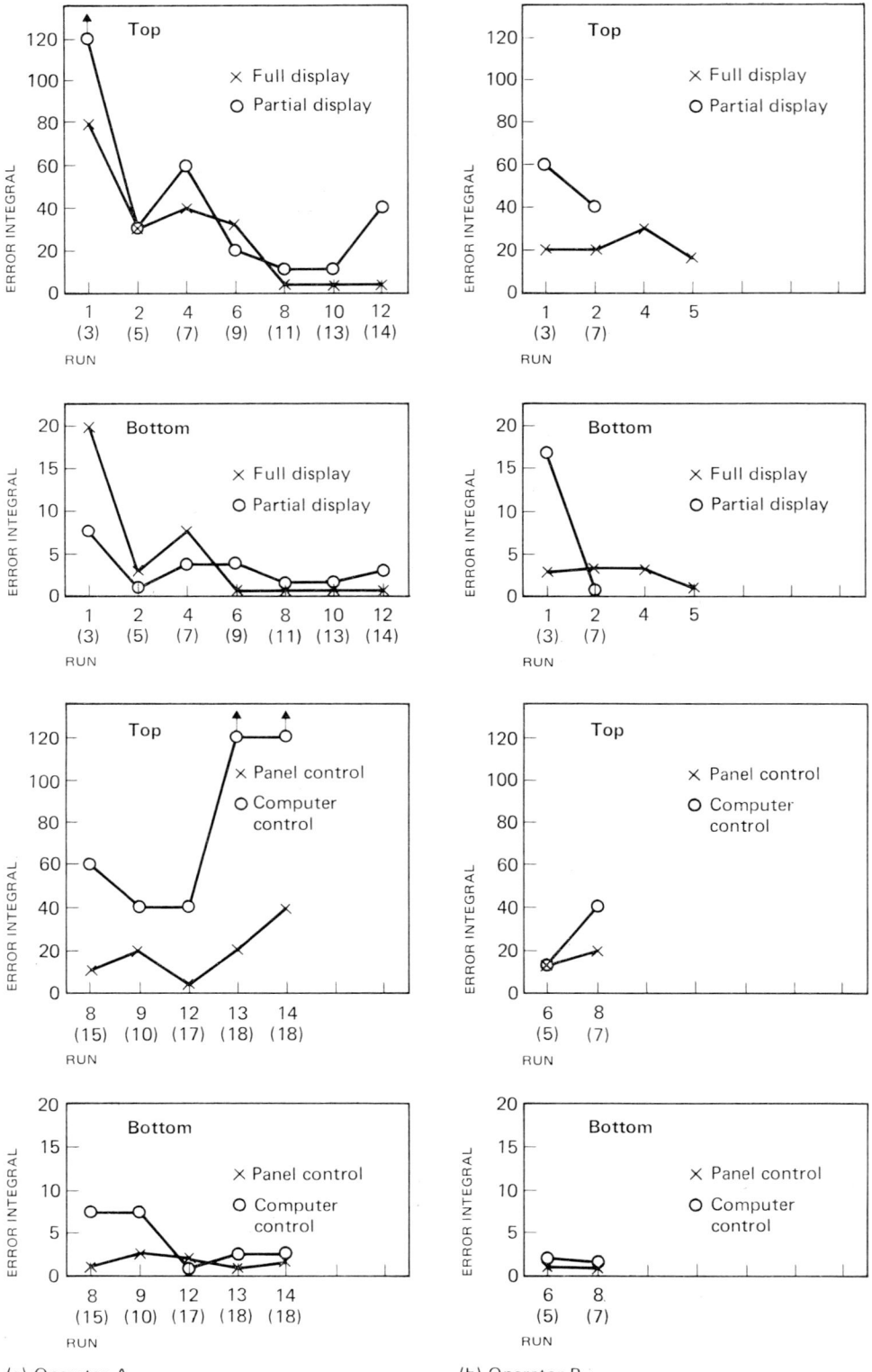

Figure 5. Learning curves of operators in manual control tests.

5.2.1. Control strategies of operators

The control problem was the changing of the operating point of the distillation column. The operator has the choice of how that change might be made, within the constraints of the display available and the method of imposing the control action. The control problem was not straightforward, because it was necessary for him to realize that there was a considerable interaction between the top and bottom of the distillation column.

The strategies chosen by the operators varied considerably. A list for the first stage of control is given in Table 3, showing how the reflux and steam flow rates might be changed in order to move to the region of the new operating point. They are arranged in order of desirability, the lower-numbered ones corresponding to strategies which give good control performance and low error integrals. The higher numbers represent worse strategies which give higher error integrals. The second part of the control problem was to hold the column at its new operating point. This stage is referred to as fine control and the operators' strategies were classified as shown in Table 4.

The learning curves for each operator performing his series of tests are shown in Figures 5–7. It is obvious that nearly all the operators improve their control performance as they gain more practice and experience in the control problems and become familiar with the display and control system which they have to use. The variations in the strategies adopted by the operators are shown in Figure 4 and generally the strategies adopted tend to remain the same or return to the original after an experimental excursion. This seems to indicate that the individual operator has a strategy developed from his past experience and that the type of system does not, in the short term, affect this strategy. Operators B and C are exceptions to this, since they developed better strategies and retained them; they were also two of the more experienced operators.

The method of implementation of the strategy was obviously dependent upon the method of control available. Thus some operators who had no direct feedback of information on the steam flow control loop developed a predictive control procedure based on the number of turns of the steam controller manual output knob. Another factor which emerged with some operators, was that their control performance was better when they were given information at a logging interval of two minutes than at one of one minute. The timing of information flow has an effect on the timing of the operator's control action, prompting him to make changes even though the plant cannot have responded to previous control actions. With the distillation column, the effect of a change would not be seen at all after one minute but would be beginning to have a noticeable effect after two minutes.

The operator's control strategy might be determined by his experience and training. In the short term, he would be capable of modifying his method of applying the strategy in order to give the best results. In the long term, it is quite possible that the operator's whole view of the process might be modified by the type of display and control system. An interesting comparison would be between operators who had developed strategies solely in the conventional type of control panel and those who had been exposed only to computer systems.

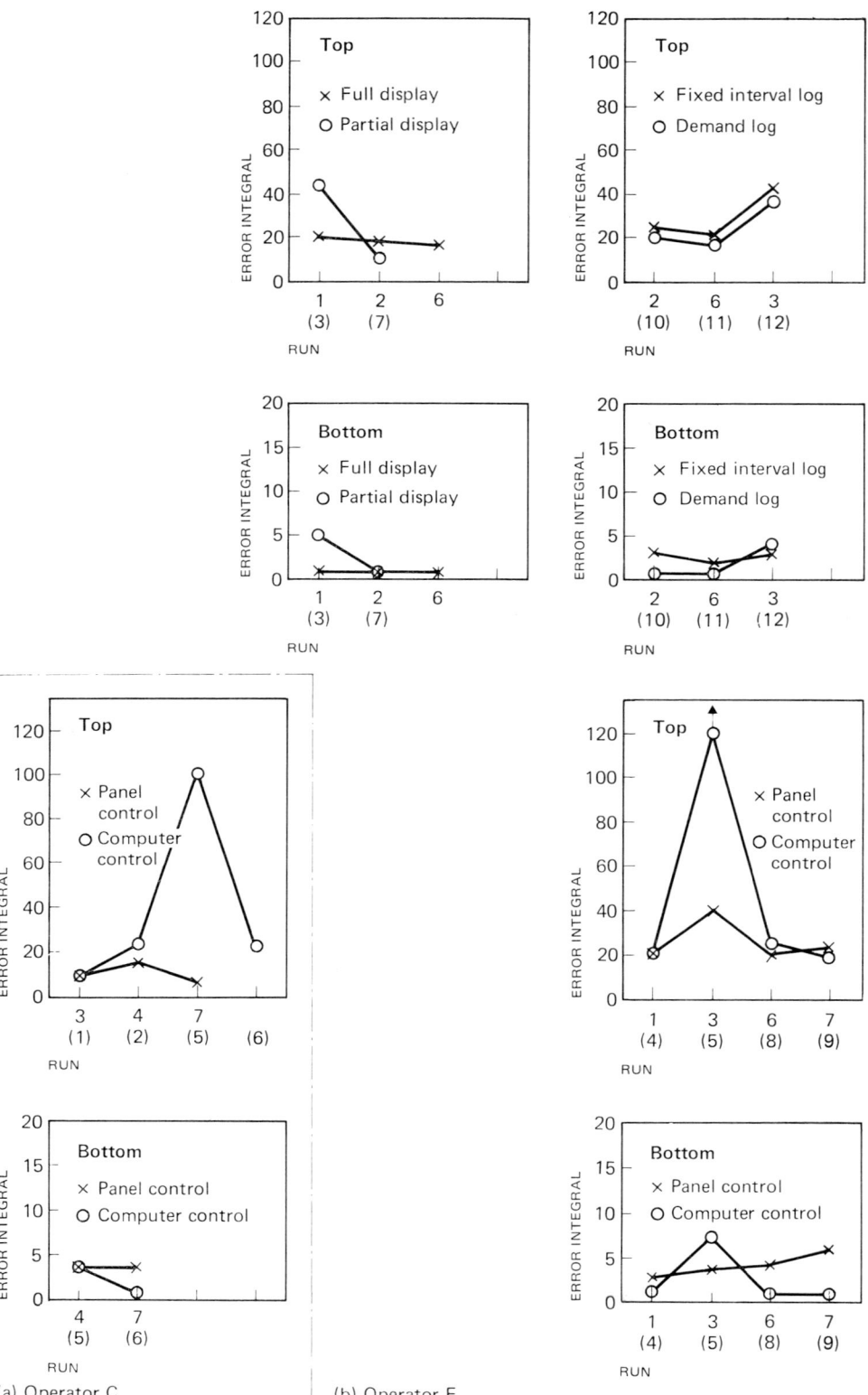

Figure 6. Learning curves of operators in manual control tests.

5.2.2. Operators' response to breakdown

A short series of surveillance tests was carried out with three of the operators, using both full and partial displays. A number of points emerged from these tests concerning the operators' reactions to unpredictable upsets.

The operators tended to concentrate on the upset conditions to the exclusion of the rest of the plant and this led to neglect of the problems in other areas. The tests showed the operators' reliance on the display of adequate information, and in particular the usefulness of what would normally be redundant displays.

The presence of a gradual disturbance was difficult to distinguish from the slow drifting which can sometimes occur. This indicates the need for a special sort of display which the operator could use specifically for his surveillance task. The use of digital displays should be considered very carefully. The printed digital displays were used in the tests but on several occasions were misread, mainly because of the manner in which the variables were coded. The analogue chart displays were found to be much more useful and less inclined to give the wrong impression about the plant operation. This contrasts with the manual control tests, where in the second half of the test the chart displays were less useful than the digital displays.

The surveillance test runs were to some extent artificial in that the operator was alert to the fact that an upset might occur within a limited time period. In practice, a plant might run for days or weeks without a major unexpected upset and so the operator's frame of mind would be much less prepared for trouble. The implications of the operator's performance in the tests suggest that for these types of disturbance the display system can have a significant effect on the way he goes about finding and correcting the fault.

There is a case for the development of displays which can be easily and cheaply implemented by computer systems and which provide operators with an information flow similar to that coming from a conventional panel. This display problem has been discussed by several workers (Rasmussen 1968a, Edwards and Lees 1973).

The need for a display for the surveillance of plant states has been emphasized by Dallimonti (1972) and a display which aims to meet this need, the status array, has been proposed by West (West 1972, Stainthorp and West 1973). In this, the status of the plant is displayed as a pattern which indicates the condition of several of the most important plant variables. Thus the operator can see the state of the plant at a glance. The array also has important applications in the development of computer-generated operating decisions.

5.2.3. Learning behaviour of operators

The rate at which the control task is learned can be shown by the reduction in the error integral for the variables under the control of the operators. All the operators learned to perform better as the series of tests proceeded. There were isolated cases where performance was much worse, but these were related to specific problems such as the operator's trying out a new strategy or simply making a mistake. The rate at which operators learned how to achieve the best control performance varied widely.

An interesting fact which is shown in the learning curves is that in the initial learning period it made little difference which display system was used. This tends to support the argument that the operator has a fixed idea of how

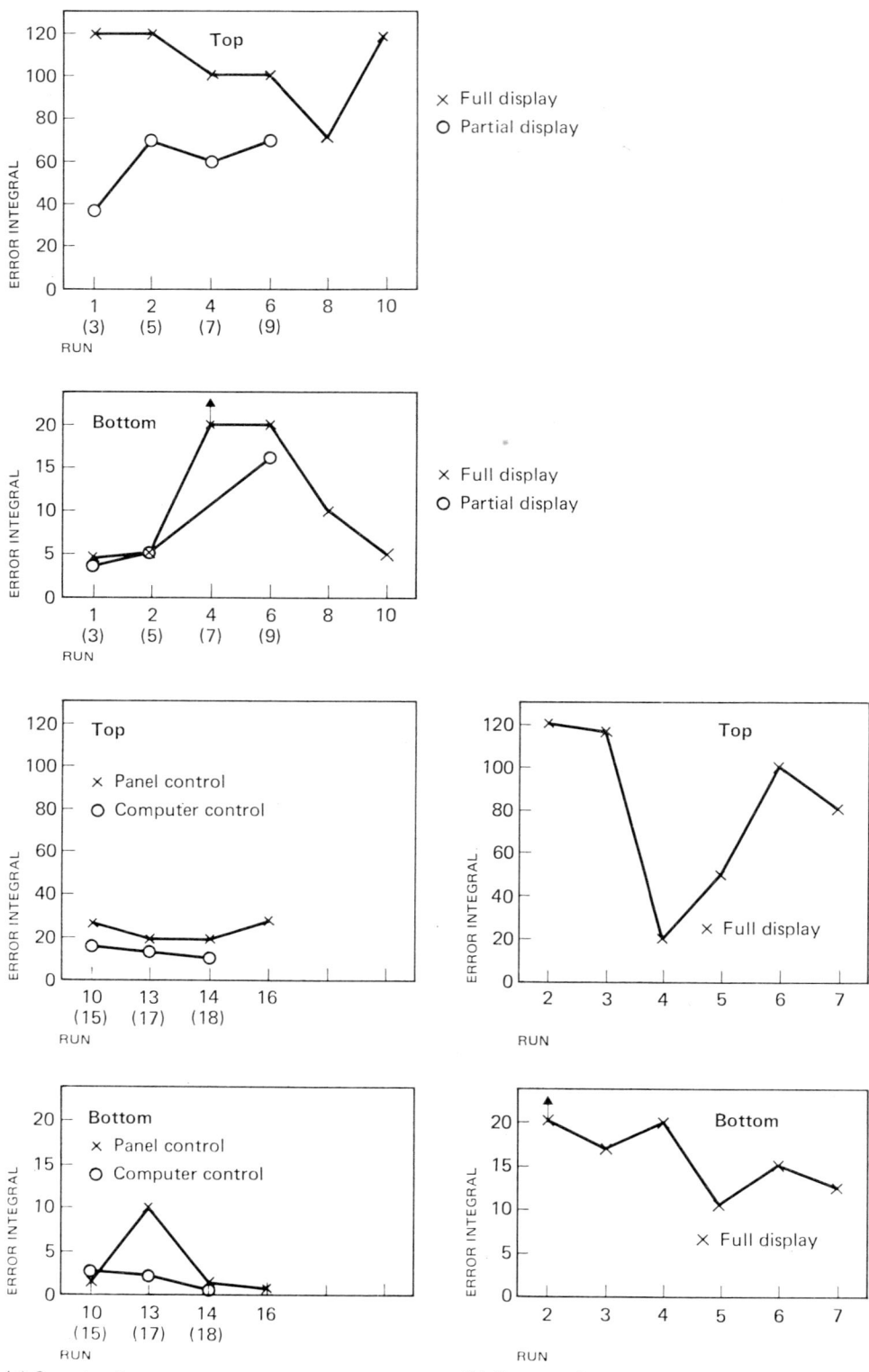

Figure 7. Learning curves of operators in manual control tests.

to handle a situation but that he has to adapt his method of implementation to the system which is available.

Comparisons between the absolute performance of different operators is not possible because there were no directly comparable sets of tests. In addition, it would be necessary to take much more account of the secondary effects, such as the time of day when the tests were performed, the state of operation of the other plants and the operator's state of mind.

An example of the ability of some of the operators to learn to exploit the system at their disposal was shown by the two who used the special digital demand printout in a systematic fashion. The display logged on demand digital values of variables to a teleprinter. This was in addition to, or instead of, a standard printout. The two operators assembled a list of variables which they regarded as important and logged them out in a data block of their own design at regular intervals. Their objective was to enable them to pick out easily any variations in the values of the variables. They found the printout particularly useful in the surveillance tests when the conventional panel had been obscured. Other operators, although aware of their colleagues' action, did not attempt to duplicate it and used the demand display as a means of getting spot values of variables when they needed them.

The operators in this series of tests all had a minimum of five years' experience with the pilot plant facility, on top of their varied industrial experience. It would be of interest in future tests to examine the effects of the different display and control systems on the ability and learning rate of inexperienced operators. The use of specific types of system to reinforce good strategy development during training might also be examined.

5.3. *Effect of Display Systems*

The effect of three different types of display system was examined. The full conventional panel display contained all the instruments including chart recorders. The computer display consisted of the digital panel displays and the standard teleprinter log. An additional printout was available on demand on the teleprinter. Various combinations of these displays were used in the tests.

The learning curves show how the different displays affect the performance of each operator. The loss of analogue chart recorders did not have as big an effect as might be expected and this was probably partly due to the fact that these displays were not a great deal of use in the second half of the manual control tests when the operator was trying to control the plant accurately at its new target value. The most useful aspects of the chart recorders were during the first part of these tests when the operator was changing to a new operating point and in the surveillance tests where he obtained from them a very good and rapid impression of how the plant was responding.

Various rates of display of information on the teleprinter were tried and it was found that there was little difference between a four-minute and a two-minute log but that control performance deteriorated at faster rates. This would suggest that with such logs it would be important to match the rate to the dynamics of the plant from which the information is flowing.

Digital displays were found to be subject to errors in reading, which in several tests led to small upsets which produced high error integrals.

The operators were in general suspicious of new types of display, such as the demand digital printout. They were much more inclined to take over complete manual control if upsets occurred when new displays or restricted displays were in operation.

Most operators were familiar with the performance of control actions through both the conventional and the computer system. Nevertheless, it was observed that fewer control actions were taken when the computer system was being used.

The main points about displays may be summarized as follows:
    (1) It was clear that analogue chart displays are valuable as trend records and that if such displays are limited an adequate alarm or status display system may be needed.
    (2) The display of information in digital form only can lead to a lack of adequate 'feel' for an upset situation and, even in use for accurate control, values can be misread.
    (3) The rate at which digital information is presented to operators can also influence their control actions.

5.4. Operator Variability

The variation between operators was quite wide. Each operator had had a different amount of industrial experience but an equal amount of contact with the pilot plant (see Table 5). This means that they would have well-formed ideas about plant performance.

Table 5. Industrial experience of operators

Operator	Experience in chemical industry	Experience of distillation columns in industry	Industry (years)	UMIST (years)
A	Yes	Some	3	5
B	Yes	Little	8	5
C	Yes	Much	7	5
D	Yes	None	4	5
E	Yes	Some	4	5
F	Yes	None	8	5
G	No	None	0	5
H	Yes	None	5	5
K	Yes	Little	4	5

(Length of experience)

The strategy diagram, Figure 4, indicates that with the exception of two operators, B and C, the strategies were not generally improved, although there was some fluctuation between strategies which could have been caused by the operators' wish to perform their own tests.

The improvement in control as measured by the error integral is again very varied. Some operators improved very quickly, others only very slowly. The variability of results within a given operator's series is due to the many outside influences which can have a very serious effect on performance and which must be considered in the design of any display system.

6. Conclusions

The series of tests were intended to give some general indications of the effects of display and control systems on operators. In addition, they were meant to assist in the development of a more extensive test series involving operators from industry with varying levels of experience.

The most gratifying result is that the operators tended to adapt to their environment without too much difficulty. It appears that with experienced operators each has his own concept of how the process responds and, presumably, of how various kinds of upset occur and how they should be corrected. The type and quantity of information display does not in the short term affect this. It does affect the way in which the operator implements his strategy and this in turn affects the quality of control. An example of this is the effect of a very rapid logging rate, which encourages some operators to take action when it is not appropriate.

A problem which is virtually impossible to remove from the experimental situation is that of the introduction by the operator of his own experimentation. This is probably responsible for some of the strategy changes and 'bad' results recorded by some operators.

The rate at which operators learned to carry out their tasks varied widely, as might be expected. Some operators were able to devise extensions to the system made available, others just accepted things as they were.

These factors highlight the need for flexible systems of display which are adaptable to the needs of individual operators and can be changed with plant operating state. Also, the operators need to have adequate training in how the system works and in how they might best utilize it for their own individual display needs.

Obviously, more work needs to be done in the area of computer-driven displays for process operators. A more detailed analysis of these experiments is needed in order to develop better ways of categorizing the large amount of information. The long-term effects of even more automation need investigation in order to provide the supervisory operator with a satisfactory role in such a system.

The authors would like to thank the process operators of the UMIST pilot plant for their assistance in this work and one of us (Mr. Clark) would like to thank the Science Research Council for financial support.

On the Communication between Operators and Instrumentation in Automatic Process Plants

By J. Rasmussen

Electronics Department, Research Establishment, Danish Atomic Energy Commission, Risö, Denmark

1. Introduction

Industrial process plants are normally supervised by a complicated instrumentation system which, in co-operation with one or more human operators, controls the process under general routine conditions, such as normal operation and start–stop operations, and monitors the operation in such a way as to allow abnormal conditions to be detected and counteracted by suitable, *i.e.* safe and economic, measures. The allocation of tasks to operators and instrumentation depends upon the degree of automation, and the requirement of narrow operation tolerances and operation close to the tolerable limits for plant components has to a great extent led to automation of the normal operation, while abnormal operation and fault conditions still require highly qualified actions by the operators.

The situation is then that several tasks connected with the normal operation are taken out of the hands of the operator, who thus loses touch with the plant, at the same time as the steadily increasing complexity of the plants during abnormal conditions places on the operators the demand of still more knowledge of the functions and reactions of the plants.

Even in plants having a very high degree of automation of normal and abnormal operation, situations will occur in which the human operator has to control the operations, for example the initial operation following the installation of new major parts or major repairs, and the longer the periods are between such demands on the operator, the more efficient the means of communication between the plant and the operator have to be.

The digital computer is now finding its way into the control system of automatic plants. Up to now it has been used especially for information processing in connection with automatic control and monitoring of plants, but not to any great extent for improvement of the communication between plant and operators.

In the present report the tasks of an operator at an automated plant are discussed with a view to formulating the basis for an appraisal of the possibilities of using the digital computer to improve this communication.

2. Co-operation between Operator and Instrumentation

The tasks in which the operator and the instrumentation system co-operate may be classified into several different functions. The *measuring function*, which is the conversion of representative variables in the process into signals suitable for further data processing, is at present carried out almost entirely by transducers in the instrumentation system, although in certain types of plants the capability of operators for detecting small changes in the operation by otherwise undefined changes in the odour or noise conditions is still utilized.

The *control action*, which conversely transforms the signals from the instruments into changes in the parameters of the process by means of actuators, can to a great extent be mechanized, but the function is often carried out by operators in cases where the frequency of control actions is so low that mechanization is uneconomic. Besides, manual control may be an important standby for normally automatic actions. The *data processing* ties measuring and control together and is the function requiring the most complicated co-operation between operators and instrumentation. In complex process plants this co-operation places great demands on the information display function, which by means of sound and light signals, meter indications and graphic recordings converts the information present in the signals of the instruments into a form that can be further processed by the operators.

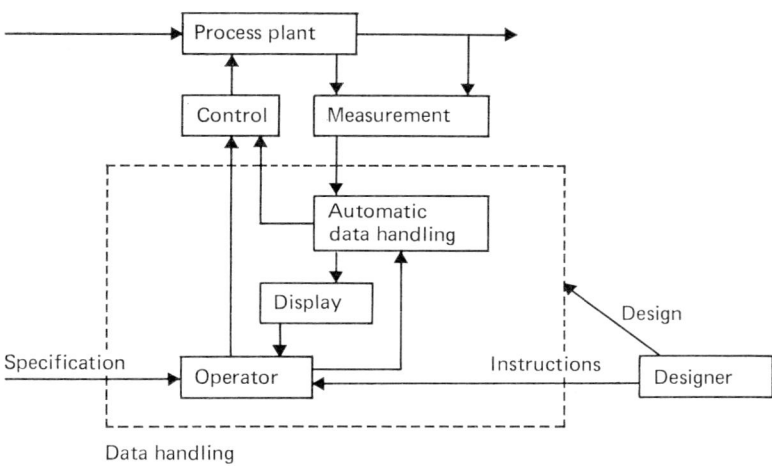

Tasks for Control System; Operator and/or Instrumentation

Normal operation: Optimizing of operation
Sequence control (*e.g.* start–stop)
Recording of operational information

Abnormal operation: Detection of abnormal states
Identification, evaluation of consequences
Decision, choice of appropriate counter-measures
Action, control of correcting sequence

Figure 1. Schematic diagram of control system.

It is a condition for the development of automation that the necessary data processing can to an increasing degree be carried out in the instrumentation system without any action on the part of the operator; this in turn means that the equipment required for advanced data processing must be accurate, economical and reliable.

An electronic system, to be economical and reliable, must be based on units, produced in numbers, and the development of the practical possibilities of automating process plants has been characterized by the mass-produced electronic process controller, which is so flexible that the same type of unit can be adjusted to a wide variety of processes.

During recent years the development has been highly influenced by the digital computer, which is a mass-produced, and thus reliable and economical, unit that can be fitted by programming to meet highly advanced and specialized needs for information processing in process automation.

This feature, together with the high operating speed of the computer, which makes it possible to share its time among many functions and thus perform these with a reasonable amount of equipment, makes it attractive to utilize the digital computer in process instrumentation even though its highly centralized structure is not very attractive for instrumentation purposes from a reliability point of view.

The high degree of interconnection between the different functions of the digital computer may lead to serious consequences of faults in the instrumentation; besides it makes it more difficult for the operating personnel to maintain a general understanding of the functioning of the system.

The rapid development of the prices of integrated circuits and subsystems and thus of digital computing elements will presumably in the future contribute towards a continuation of the decentralized structure that characterizes conventional instrumentation systems, since it will be attractive from a reliability (decentralization) as well as an economic (simpler programming) point of view to use control systems comprising several computing elements.

The introduction of the digital computer in process instrumentation should thus not be looked upon as a revolution, but as an evolution of the technological and economic possibilities of further utilization of automatic data processing in the instrumentation, and it is still important to base the layout of instrumentation systems and their adaptation to the process and the operator on the vast experience gathered from the operation of conventional systems.

Especially in its relation to the operators in industrial processes the digital computer has been encumbered with the tradition established by its users in the administrative and scientific fields; communication facilities such as typewriters and line printers have been transferred directly from these fields to the industrial scene, where in most cases they will be inappropriate.

In order to formulate the demands for a suitable form of communication between operator and plant it is necessary to define the functions of the operator in more detail. In the following discussion his tasks are classified in a simple way into groups covering: tasks during normal operation, during changes in operating conditions such as start-stop procedures, and during monitoring, e.g. detection and identification of failures.

3. The Operator's Task during Normal Operation

During periods of normal operation the operator and the instrumentation in co-operation have to ensure that the process plant as a whole is in an economically optimal condition.

Regardless of the level of automation, the operator for this task needs accurate information on the main data of the plant, presented in a way that allows him to compare directly with the primary operational specification given to him.

These principal plant data are normally presented to the operator by big, clear indicators located in a central position which allows them to be read by the operator even if he is carrying out other tasks. In conventional systems meters of great size or indicators/recorders are often used. The main data should be compared with the primary specification to a good accuracy; they are not to be compared mutually, and therefore presentation in digital form with indication of measurement units should be preferable to analogue presentation.

In plants with a moderate level of automation the control of the normal operating conditions is often carried out by a number of rather simple feedback controllers, which control the individual plant parameters in correspondence with secondary references adjusted by the operator to satisfy the primary specifications.

For this function the operator needs more secondary information about the conditions in the different feedback loops to be able to supervise the result of his adjustments. In this respect there are no special demands on the layout of the display equipment. The operator will be able, without hurry, to act on the basis of his daily experience, and his task will normally be well-defined and limited. His intervention in the operation of the plant, based on his evaluation of the operating conditions and specifications, will be of an experimental nature, he can use a trial-and-error technique in a reversible way and correct his actions if they prove wrong. In this situation, the operator's working conditions are favourable, provided that the interdependence between the primary operational specifications and the secondary control reference values is not too complicated.

To make the operator responsible for the adjustment of the control loop references—setpoints—may be advantageous to his other tasks. Different operators may have different ideas of the optimal operating conditions and therefore may have a tendency to check the adjustment of the setpoints at shift take-over and during operation to make sure that conditions are optimal. This frequent experimentation with the process will contribute to the operator's understanding of the behaviour of the plant and thus increase his ability to perform a monitoring function. This may be of importance for plants without frequent manual start-stop operations.

At higher levels of automation the different setpoints in the control loops will be calculated by the control system itself and automatically brought into correspondence with the primary operation specifications, and the rôle of the operator during normal operation will be purely supervisory.

4. The Supervisory Task

This task, to which both the operator and the instrument system contribute, may be divided into three parts: *failure detection*, i.e. the discovery of a departure from the normal, specified operating conditions; *identification*, i.e. the determination of the nature, location and cause of the abnormal condition; and finally the *corrective action* upon the process, which is based on an *evaluation* of the consequences for the plant of the different possible modes of continued operation and a *decision* regarding the optimal action.

Detection of failures is usually not possible solely on the basis of the information utilized by the operator during normal operational optimization, since a large group of abnormal situations and failures will not appear in this information or will be recognizable here at too late a stage. The operator should therefore have at his disposal detailed information on the state of operation in the different subsystems of the plant.

A great deal of this information is not needed by the operator for his optimization of the normal operation; he only has to check that the data remain within the range of normal operation. Most of these secondary data have no immediate correspondence with the primary specifications for the plant operation, and it is therefore important to lay out the display function in such a way as to increase his awareness and his memory of the normal ranges.

Normally this is done so that the instrument system compares fixed limits with measured data representative of abnormal situations demanding immediate action by the operator, and gives a warning signal when the limits are exceeded, while failures that have only minor consequences for the operation of the plant are covered by the measurement data merely being presented to the operator.

This presentation has to be such that the operator only has to run an eye over the instrument panel to ascertain whether the operation is normal. The layout of the control console can facilitate this task to a high degree even in conventional systems: related measurement data are grouped together, normal operating conditions are indicated clearly, for example by edgewise meters arranged so that the pointers are normally in line or meters that can be rotated so that the pointers normally point in the same direction. Meters have to be grouped so as to indicate clearly the different subsystems.

The essential thing in this connection is to obtain an overall view of the process by intercomparison of data rather than a high-accuracy reading of individual data.

The great data handling capacity of the digital computer can be utilized to relieve the operator of the failure detection task in a very efficient way. The monitoring of the measurement data can be highly effective, a great number of data can be included in an automatic alarm scanning, and the alarm limits may be made dependent on the operating conditions of the plant; for instance they can be changed during startup. Furthermore, the digital computer is able to monitor the relation between data by making simple comparisons or more complicated calculations such as heat or mass balances, and in this way the instrumentation can be made more efficient and alert than the human operator. It may be considered a drawback that one takes from the operator a task that keeps him in touch with the process, which is essential for his correct action in failure situations. For the operator to be effective, it is therefore necessary that he has the possibility of obtaining and maintaining a general view of the conditions of the plant.

When an abnormal state of the plant has been detected, the *failure has to be identified* with good certainty and its cause and the consequences upon the continued operation must be evaluated. To the operator this is quite a different task from the normal optimization of the operation. In the case of more serious failures the allowable response time may be short; the task will not be to solve a well-defined problem, but rather to formulate the problem corresponding to the pattern of data presented. The situation will be characterized by a set of abnormal data, each of which may occur rather frequently during the daily work (*e.g.* instrument failures), but which in just the combination in question may have been caused by a serious or dangerous failure that would have been considered very improbable in advance. This means that the operator is not allowed to trust his daily operating experience, but has to base his decisions on detailed knowledge of the functioning of the plant and its response to the different types of failures. He should be imaginative enough to postulate a comprehensive set of possible causes of the failure situation on the basis of the immediately available information and then, after processing of more detailed information, to make a well founded decision.

The great difficulty is usually to ensure—by training, layout of control console and plant, *etc.*—that the correct and in many cases very improbable cause of a failure is among the possibilities that occur to the operator. Experience shows that an incident is not seldom allowed to expand, not because the instrumentation fails at the critical instant, but because the explanation of the abnormal situation that first comes to the operator's mind by virtue of his experience corresponds to more trivial routine failures, whereas less probable failures have much more serious consequences for the plant and should therefore have absolute priority in his mind.

If one chooses to define the cause of such an incident as a human failure, it is very reasonable to discuss whether the blame should go to the operator or to the designer, who chose the information environment of the operator. In quite a few cases such failures may be classified as ' technical failures ', since the development of the incident may be due to a rather high frequency of unimportant failures that have contributed to the experience of the operator and thus influence his reaction in the case in question.

In his task of identifying the failure and evaluating its possible consequence for the plant, the operator must therefore be supported by the designer of the system. The information directly available in the form of measurement data and alarm data has to be displayed in a suitable way, and the operator's need for knowledge of the reactions of the plant to failure conditions must be supported as much as possible by incorporating the designer's knowledge into the instrumentation in the form of automatic evaluation procedures that analyze the alarm and measurement data patterns.

In modern plants the task of the operator in an abnormal situation is initiated by the fact that an alarm system detects that one or more measurement data have exceeded the range of normal operation. In small plants it is possible for the operator to get a sufficient overall view of the situation on the basis of a simple indication of the individual alarms, but an alarm system does not have to be of very great size to necessitate special means of supporting the operator. In conventional systems, this is done by indication of the latest alarms in a way that separates them from earlier ones by a different character of light, by special indication of the first alarm in a sequence, *etc.*

Where it is decided to use an extensive alarm system in a larger plant, *e.g.* by installation of data loggers or digital computers, so that a great number of variables are monitored, perhaps even with alarm limits depending upon the operating conditions of the plant, the operator will lose his general view if the output information is presented to him unsorted. The more detailed monitoring will result in long sequences of secondary alarms, and it may be of significant assistance to the operator that the designer incorporates in the instrumentation, as an automatic sorting procedure, the result of an evaluation of the reactions of the plant in such a way that the operator is presented with information on the primary and essential alarms only to an extent sufficient for the preliminary identification of the failure. It is not appropriate to record the alarm information in tabular form with typewriters or line printers. A clearer presentation is obtained with plain text incorporating parameter identification and data in conventional alarm status displays or computer-controlled picture displays (CRT), which might also be utilized for the presentation of results from the more comprehensive analyses mentioned below.

The information from the alarm system will normally only be able to serve as a rather coarse guide in the identification of a failure and to locate the failure to one of the subsystems of the plant. The operator must supplement this information with a survey of the conditions in the plant as a whole and in the subsystem in question.

Such a survey comprises sets of related data characterizing the actual operating conditions. Experience shows us that a human operator is able to accept a large amount of information directly when it is presented to him in analogue form as a situation or a picture, while information in alphabetic or digital form requires conscious acquisition by detailed reading, a slow and very selective procedure.

Analogue presentation of measured data by means of meters and recorders, as normally used in conventional systems, can give the operator a good overall view of the operation if properly laid out, since he need not go into detail in reading the meters, but can perceive the meter deflections as a pattern. In his preliminary failure identification he has no need for accurately measured individual data, but only for comparison and classification of data in sets.

In the case where a digital computer is used in the instrumentation, there are further possibilities of supporting the operator in his survey of the operating conditions. Related measured data can be coded by the designer into series of graphic pictures representative of the plant as a whole and of subsystems, which may supply the operator with a very efficient means of comparing data.

By thus elaborating a number of graphs giving surveys of the conditions in representative systems, functions and situations, the designer may ensure that the operator is presented with all relevant data in close relation as a supplement to the alarm information.

Already at the formulation of his first hypothesis about the cause of the failure the operator will thus have all relevant information available in a clear form. This will increase his possibility of finding a correct explanation as the first one, and he may avoid the hesitation and fidget in which he may find himself if he has to change his working hypothesis several times because important new information turns up when he evaluates the detailed data to confirm his findings.

An efficient coding of the information in sets as graphic patterns will also counteract the tendency of a human operator to limit his attention to very few parameters in a critical situation and to let the hypothesis he has already made influence his interpretation of the supplementary information he is seeking.

The most important feature of these graphic patterns or pictures is that they give the operator that overall view which in conventional systems he can get by running an eye over the instruments in the control console. He should, however, have the possibility of supplementing this with accurate, detailed data as easily as he can read the meters and recorders in conventional systems.

This detailed information should be easily obtainable, preferably in digital form, with a clear indication of the name of the parameter and the engineering units, or as graphic curves showing the evolution of the parameter in time; for instance the operator may call the information from his graphic patterns by means of a ' light pen '. If the system is arranged so that it is only possible for the operator to call detailed information from a survey pattern, it is possible to avoid the situation where he uses detailed information without considering its relation to the general conditions in the system.

Examples of a possible layout of such displays are shown at the end of the report. This type of display is today used especially in aviation systems; its application in computer-aided design is developing rapidly, and the same tendency is to be expected with respect to its use in process control systems.

The advantage of these displays is not so much that they can be used to give ' mimic ' diagrams, as known in conventional plants, but rather the possibility of coding the information effectively in a symbolic form which the operator can perceive as patterns or pictures.

In the discussion given above the possibility for the designer of analyzing in advance the reactions of the complete plant to the different types of failures and the corresponding data and alarm patterns is only utilized to provide a basis for selection of the parameters of the plant that are to be monitored by the alarm system, for the design of a simple alarm reduction function and for the classification of data into appropriate sets for the graphic displays.

The capacity of the computer makes it attractive to support the operator further with the results of the designer's previous analyses of the plant. This can be done by incorporating an automatic procedure in the instrumentation, which, initiated by an alarm, analyzes the alarm and data patterns and directly localizes the primary fault. It may be extremely difficult, if not impossible, for the designer of a large plant to carry through an analysis that takes into account not only all failures in the plant itself and the instrumentation, but also the combination of failures, which may cause serious disturbances.

How far it pays to go in this direction in an actual plant depends upon which situation is the more dangerous: that the operator in a given situation does not have sufficient knowledge about the nature and functioning of the plant, or that the designer has not foreseen the situation during the design phase and has therefore not included it in the automatic analysis. One has to realize that direct automatic identification of the primary fault based on a not completely comprehensive analysis, which assumes that an operator critically evaluates the result of the analysis, involves a great risk of further decreasing the probability that the operator takes into consideration very improbable, but hazardous failures not dealt with in the simplified analysis of the designer and thus of the instrumentation.

If one utilizes a simplified analysis of failure conditions in this way, one may therefore be in the paradoxical situation that it is as risky for the operator to trust the analysis too much when it indicates a probable cause of the failure as to incline towards distrusting the analysis when it indicates an *a priori* improbable cause.

A better result will presumably be attained if the automatic analysis is allowed to follow principles that the operator will immediately accept. The analysis should then, as the operator will be inclined to do, deal first with the simple and most probable causes and currently keep the operator informed of the result.

In the case of more frequent and routine failures one then obtains an automatic identification of the failures, while in the case of more complicated and rare failures the analysis will rapidly exclude the simple and trivial causes. This will save the operator's time so that he may concentrate on the more rare and serious situations on the basis of a limitation of the possibilities; thus the situation can be avoided where the operator forms a sequence of preliminary hypotheses which he may not be willing to reject.

In this way, the operator may acquire more faith in the analysis, and it will suffice, when a new plant is put into operation, to incorporate a simple automatic analysis, since it can be gradually expanded according to the operational experience gained; further, the display function may be based immediately on the conventional tradition.

When a failure has been identified in this way, *a decision must be taken* concerning the appropriate corrective action. This decision has to be based upon detailed knowledge about the trend of the operational conditions resulting from the failure and the influence of the possible corrective actions on the abnormal plant. Knowledge of this category will not be kept up by the operator to any great extent during normal operation, and besides he has to make his decision under mental pressure; thus a decision based upon common knowledge and understanding of the principles underlying the plant may not be reliable.

Like the automatic failure identification, an automatic decision function must be based upon a thoroughly comprehensive *a priori* analysis of the plant under abnormal conditions, and in many failure situations the decision will therefore rest with the operator. Automatic safety action will be necessary against failure situations that are too dangerous for the plant and demand very rapid counteraction.

Automatic safety actions have to be based on simple criteria that can be automated with highly reliable equipment and may be proved comprehensive in all circumstances by an analysis. Therefore they must be simple but drastic actions, capable in all circumstances of bringing the plant into a safe state, for instance by emergency shutdown. The operator will furnish a back-up for this safety system and moreover will prevent less important failures from developing to such an extent as to initiate the safety system action and thus interfere drastically with the operation.

The decisions of the operator in situations foreseen and evaluated by the designer can be supported by instructions learned by the operator, but in order to be reflex-like and reliable such knowledge must be kept up by exercises. It may be appropriate to incorporate in the instrumentation such information as may support the operator's memory, for instance by making it possible for him, after the identification of the failure, to call comments in clear text in an alphanumeric display. In more definite situations the operator may be supported by a computational function that gives him, on a fast time scale, the result of a simulation of the trend of the operational state of the plant and the effect of his intended corrective actions. This may be required for his evaluation of necessary corrections in case of Xenon poisoning in a nuclear reactor or ' cold plugs ' in a once-through boiler.

5. Changes of the Operational State of the Plant

The problems of the operator in case of corrective intervention in the operation of a failing plant are in some ways the same as those connected with normal start–stop procedures, which may also be very infrequent in automatic plants. In both cases, the operator has to choose the correct procedure and to carry it through without mistakes. The task of the instrumentation is in both cases to assist him in memorizing the procedure, avoid mistakes in his manipulations and give him the possibility of judging their influence on the plant.

Changes of the operational state, *e.g.* startup, are in large plants characterized by a complicated sequence of operations following a fixed procedure; the sequence and the duration of the individual operations may further depend upon the state of the plant. The operator thus has to carry through a complicated and often lengthy procedure, in some plants even at rather long time intervals.

The operator should only carry out the individual manipulations after checking that the necessary plant conditions are fulfilled, and he should have sufficient means for a check of the effect of the manipulations upon the plant. The choice of the sequence of manipulations and the check of the necessary conditions may be based on a learned or written procedure, which may be present in the form of more or less detailed instructions. The operator's memory may be supported if the procedure is partly incorporated in the control system as an interlock system. This is to some extent the case in conventional systems, and the great data handling capacity offered by digital computers makes it attractive to increase this automatic interlock or let the instrumentation directly control the sequence of operations.

The interlock function is today often preferred to the automatic control of the sequence because it may be impossible or very difficult to carry through an analysis sufficiently detailed in all circumstances of the sequence and the necessary conditions for each step and the operator's evaluation of the different situations may therefore be needed as a supplement to the function of the instrumentation. In both cases the operator has a monitoring task, and he therefore needs information that gives him a survey of the conditions in the plant and its subsystems by means of displays with the same characteristics as those mentioned in the discussion of his identification of a failure, supplemented by information describing the state of the interlock system, for instance textual information presented by means of a light tableau or cathode ray tubes.

If the operator is responsible for the control action, the display system must give him feedback of information about the effect of the control actions upon the plant. To make sure that an operator having correct intentions chooses the proper control knob, one attempts in conventional systems to give the knobs and the corresponding meter indications characteristic forms and to group them clearly according to their functions in such a way that the operator sees the control console clearly divided into subsystems and functions and may thus immediately pick the right knob.

In large, modern plants like power stations, the control console is often very extensive. The designer tries to avoid this by centralizing the functions to some degree in such a way that manipulations and monitoring of their effect are carried out by a smaller number of devices whose functions are selected by the operator with switches. This is not in accordance with the need for a clear layout of the console, and it may be necessary to enable the operator to check whether the instrumentation has accepted his order correctly before he asks the system to carry it out.

This centralized layout is natural in particular if the presentation of information to the operator is concentrated by the use of a digital computer; it will be an obvious solution to use the varied display possibilities of the digital computer to provide an effective control of the choice of orders. A survey display of the conditions in different parts and subsystems of the plant may, for instance, serve to indicate what control actions and orders the operator can use in the situation concerned. He may choose the appropriate order by means of e.g. a light pen, and the display may indicate how the order has been accepted by the system before he executes the order by means of a general 'Go' knob.

In complicated plants, rapid and closely controlled start and stop procedures may be decisive for the economy and safety of the plant, and the procedures may be so complicated that manual operation is too risky. The trend is therefore towards a more extended use of automatic start and stop operations, and the present development of the different types of digital data processors seems to indicate that they will be used in future because of their low price compared with that of tailored hardware systems. The task of the operator will therefore develop towards effective action in abnormal situations, and maintenance, but the demands on the instrumentation with respect to furnishing the operator with information in an effective form will not decrease, even in highly automated plants.

The thorough analysis of the function of the plant necessary for the automation of startup and shutdown procedures will contribute to the basis for the evaluation that is a condition for the automation of the choice of proper corrective action in case of failures in the plant. An effective automatic control system, able to control the operation within a wide range of conditions, is also a necessary condition for the application of automatic intervention in case of failures and for a differentiation of these actions beyond the choice between normal operation and complete shutdown.

6. Operation of the Control System

The highly concentrated layout of the control system and the display and operational devices natural for computer-based systems require an expedient layout of the operation of the control system itself. It is important that the operator is able to call a survey display with the same ease with which, in conventional systems, he surveys the console, and it must be as simple for him to get accurate data as to read a meter.

The electric typewriter, normally used with digital computers, is not an appropriate tool for the operator in the tasks discussed above; in the long run there is no weighty reason why the operator and the plant should communicate by writing letters, especially since electromechanical devices have proved to be wanting in reliability. Information from the system should only be recorded if it has to be stored for later use, and if so, it should be stored in a form suitable for automatic processing (magnetic or punched tape). For the operation of the instrumentation it is not appropriate either to employ general keyboards on which alphabetic or numeric codes can be used; also for digital systems properly grouped and clearly texted keys with individual functions will be preferable. Where the operator is a part of a reversible control function, e.g. when he controls the references in a control loop, it is still expedient to let him operate analogue knobs, e.g. rotary knobs with scales. The display system may be appropriately arranged so that with individual keys the operator can choose all the graphic surveys to be shown on the screens, while the search for detailed data is carried out in close contact with the overall situation as shown by the graphics, e.g. by means of a light pen.

The electric typewriter may rather be compared to the soldering iron of the repairman of the conventional systems; it may thus serve as a means of control of programs and for changes of programs, and hence for changes in the functioning of the system.

7. Recording and Storage of Data

As mentioned above, recording of data is only appropriate as storage for later use in connection with operational and economic evaluations and with evaluation of special historical relations, e.g. failures.

At regular intervals, e.g. every hour, a complete recording of all measured data should be made on punched or magnetic tape; in abnormal situations all

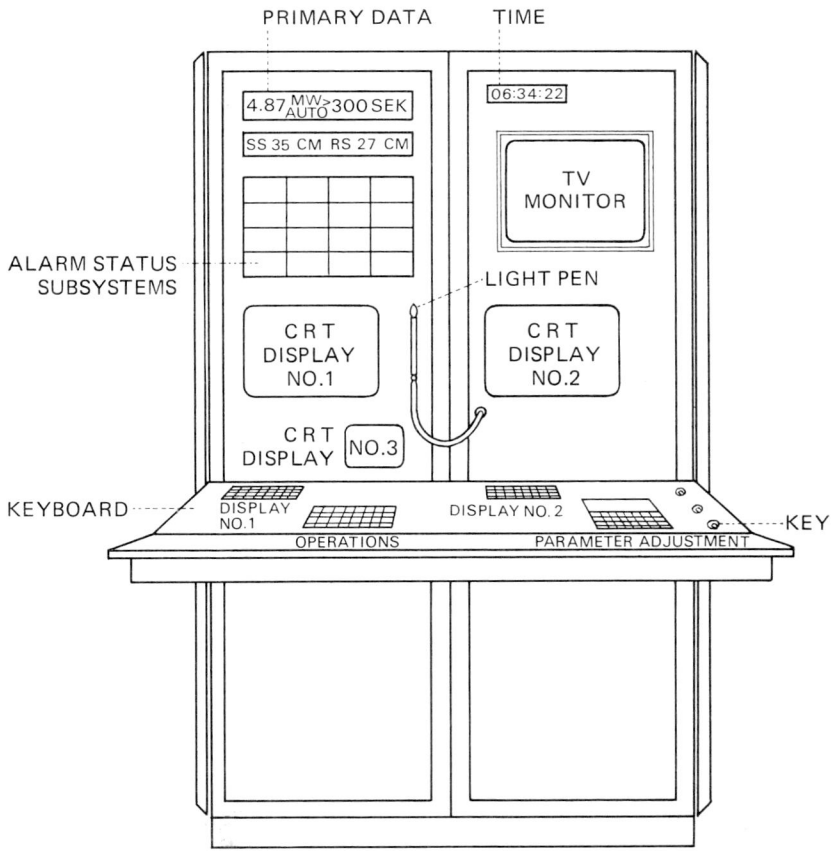

Figure 2. Preliminary layout of experimental control console of the DR2 reactor, a 5 MW pool-type research reactor.

alarm information together with measured data for a suitable time period before the fault should be recorded; likewise it may be convenient to record all the operations of the staff with indication of time. The operator may from time to time have comments to make on the operation and plant condition, for instance at shift take-over, and these comments should be included in the recorded material.

All this operational information may be sorted and processed off line.

8. Conclusion

A discussion of the tasks of the operator in automatic process plants seems to indicate that his need for information characterizing the operational state of the plant may conveniently be classified into three groups. In the task of optimizing the normal operation, he needs an accurate and clear presentation of rather few primary operational data which may be easily compared with the main specifications of the operation. For normal monitoring of the operation and for evaluation of the conditions of the plant in case of failures, it is essential for him to have a large amount of data presented in a way that makes it easy and convenient for him to compare data representative of the operational

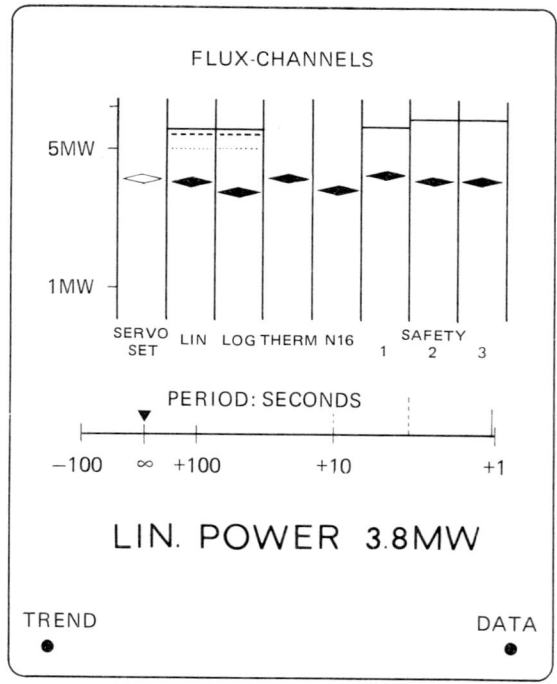

The thermal power is computed from measurements of coolant flow and temperature difference.
———— indicates the automatic shutdown limit,
– – – – the automatic power set-back and
· · · · · · the alarm limit.

Below are shown the orders, to be chosen by light pen, for indication of accurate digital data or trend. The measured value from the linear flux channel has been chosen here.

Figure 3. Survey display to be called by the operator for monitoring of the power measuring equipment.

conditions in different systems, functions and situations, and thus to establish an efficient survey. Finally, he must have convenient access to accurate measured data and their trends in support of more detailed evaluations of failure states.

Furthermore, there will normally be a need to support the operator in his identification and decision function under abnormal operational conditions. This may be done by supporting his general knowledge of the plant and its reaction by incorporating automatic analyses in the instrumentation, based upon the analyses made by the system designer.

The data handling capacity of a control system utilizing a process computer may be used with advantage both to code and reduce the information presented to the operator and to carry out efficient analyses of abnormal operational conditions.

It is very difficult to judge beforehand the importance of the different aspects discussed here and their influence on the reliability of the human operator. The main reason for this is the adaptability of the operator, which enables him to compensate to a very large extent for less appropriate layout of the instrumentation. Difficulties will only appear in process plants or in situations in which the mental load on the operator is very heavy.

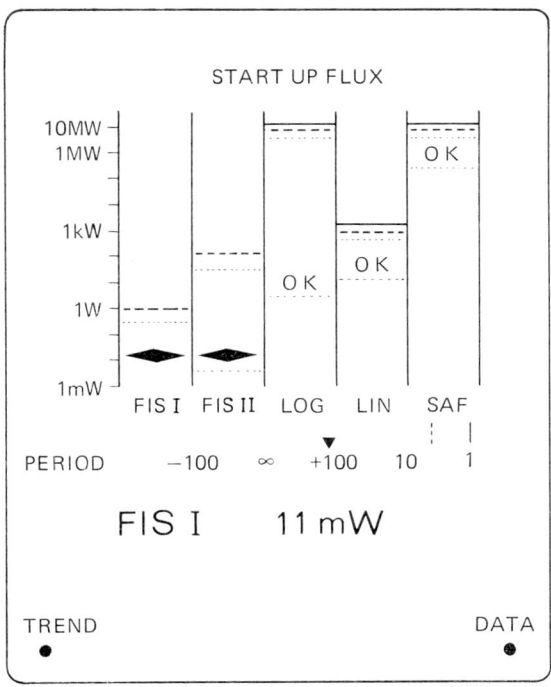

Interlock and alarm limits are indicated by · · · · ·, power set-back by – – – – and automatic shutdown by ———. Channels that are 'alive', but have too high a measuring range, show 'OK': this signature is replaced by ◂▸ when the flux reaches the measuring range. In the data field the data from Fission Chamber Channel 1 have been chosen by the light pen.

Figure 4. Survey display allowing the operator to compare measurements of neutron flux in all startup channels.

Explicitly formulated knowledge of the qualities of the human operator as a part of a system is very limited; in particular, it does not cover all his functions. The utilization of a new technology in the communication between operator and plant should therefore be based on the experience from conventional systems and the traditions of the operator of such systems, supplemented by information from realistic experiments with the new technology.

As an example of a possible layout of a display system utilizing a digital computer Figures 2–6 show a series of display formats which are parts of an experiment at the Risö reactor DR2. Here communication and traffic problems between operator and plant will be studied particularly, together with reliability problems and their dependence upon structure of the system, *e.g.* upon different degrees of centralized structure.

The report gives the following references:
Jordan (1963); Davis (1958); Williams *et. al.* (1967); Rasmussen (1968b).

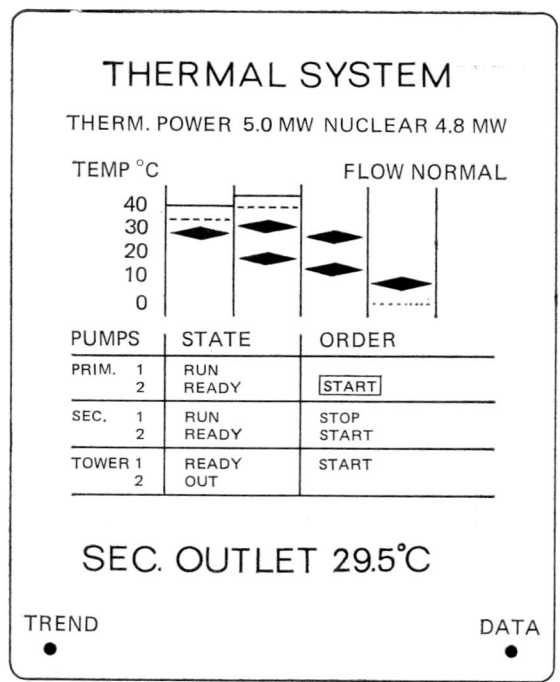

Inlet and outlet temperatures of the primary and secondary cooling systems are shown together with pool and cooling tower temperatures. For the cooling pumps and tower fans are shown the operational conditions together with the orders allowed by the interlock system. Orders not allowed are not shown, *e.g.* stop orders are only shown for the primary pump when both pumps are running. Orders are selected by means of a light pen, and acceptance is indicated by computer. Here is shown acceptance of start order for Primary 2 pump. The order is carried out by the operator by means of a general action key.

Figure 5. Survey display for the thermal system.

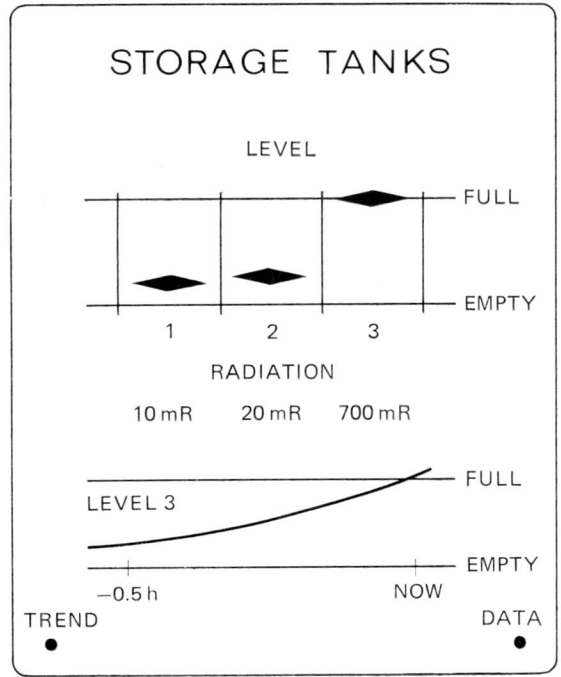

An alarm has indicated Tank 3 full. The operator has then called the display by means of a keyboard and has ordered the indication of the trend in the data field by the light pen. The display combines the information necessary for the operation of the tanks. The radiation levels are shown in digital form as they should not be compared, but related to the instructions.

Figure 6. Survey display for active storage tanks.

This discussion is based upon impressions from incidents and accidents in automatic plants, traffic systems, *etc.*, reported in the literature, supplemented by discussions with the operational staffs at Danish power stations and on the reactors at Risö. I want to thank the members of these staffs and Mr. P. Timmermann of the Electronics Department of Risö for illuminating discussions and Mr. F. Steenbuch for his review of the translation of the report.

Detection of Instrument Malfunction by the Process Operator

By S. N. Anyakora[*] and F. P. Lees

Department of Chemical Engineering, Loughborough University of Technology

1. Introduction

A major function of the process operator on a modern chemical plant is the maintenance of the integrity of the measurement and control system. On plants which have computer control or are otherwise highly automated this monitoring function of the operator becomes an increasingly large proportion of his job.

An important part of the monitoring task is the detection of malfunction in the measuring instruments and regulating elements. Other aspects include such things as the adjustment of control loops which have become unstable or otherwise unsatisfactory and the maintenance of potential correction on loops.

Improvement of the reliability of operation in chemical plants is of great importance for loss prevention and detection of malfunction is a crucial aspect of reliability. Since the human operator is the component most frequently used by the designer to detect malfunction, it is of some interest to consider how he does it.

It should be emphasized that the prime concern here is not with high integrity protective systems but with the whole range of measurement and control instrumentation on the plant.

2. Definition of Instrument Malfunction

Any discussion of malfunction should strictly be preceded by some definition of what is meant by the term. Broadly speaking, malfunction of a measuring instrument occurs if the instrument gives an output signal which represents an incorrect value of the measured variable and malfunction of a control valve occurs if the valve gives an incorrect relationship between the input signal, the pressure drop, and the flow. Since complete freedom from error is not possible, it is necessary to define some limits within which error is acceptable. Usually it is the steady-state error which matters, but unsteady-state error due to sluggishness may be important.

If detection of malfunction is to be carried out by a process computer, then it is necessary for the control engineer to define malfunction precisely in advance. The function of the computer is then limited to making comparisons which indicate malfunction when it occurs. The process operator, however, does not appear to make such a clear separation between definition and comparison. His decision-making process seems to include both. He recognizes a pattern of behaviour which is in some way unusual and decides whether to define this behaviour as faulty. Thus with an operator the two processes of definition

---

[*] Now with Dunlop Rubber Co. Ltd., Fort Dunlop, Birmingham.

and comparison probably do not occur in two separate, sequential stages as they do with a computer.

The malfunctions which are of primary interest are those which seriously affect the quality of control, whether automatic or manual. The permissible error therefore depends on the function of the instrument and varies greatly. The definition of such errors in advance by a control engineer is likely to involve considerable calculation and simulation. Their definition by the operator requires, correspondingly, judgment and experience.

There is, therefore, no simple definition of failure which the operator uses, but this is perhaps not too serious a difficulty since he is concerned mainly with relatively gross errors.

3. Malfunction Detection by Operator

In general, malfunction in an equipment may be discovered on checking either its condition or its performance. Detection from condition is illustrated by observation on the plant of a leak on the impulse line to a differential pressure transducer or of stickiness on a control valve. Detection from performance can be made by observation in the control room of an excessively noise-free signal from the transducer or of an inconsistency between position of valve stem and measured flow for the valve. Most checks on instrument condition require that the operator visits the equipment and uses one of his senses to detect the fault. Most performance checks can be made from the control room by using instrument displays and are based on information redundancy.

Some of the ways in which the operator detects malfunction in instruments can be illustrated by considering the way in which he makes use of one of his principal detection aids, the chart recorder, for this purpose. Some typical chart records are sketched in Figure 1.

The operator detects error in such signals by utilizing some form of redundant information and making a comparison. Some types of redundant information are

(1) *A priori* expectations
(2) Past signals of instrument
(3) Duplicate instruments
(4) Other instruments
(5) Control valve position.

Thus it may be expected *a priori* that an instrument reading will not go ' hardover ' to zero or full scale, that it will give a ' live ' rather than a ' dead ' zero reading, that it will exhibit a certain noise level, that its rate of change will not exceed a certain value and that it is free to move within the full scale of the instrument. On the basis of such expectations the operator might diagnose malfunction in the signals of Figures 1b to 1f.

The firmness of such expectations may vary, however, with the plant operating conditions. For example, during startup, zero readings on some instruments may be correct. Some variations of the expectations or some confirmatory checks may be necessary.

It may not be possible to decide *a priori* what constitutes a reasonable expectation. The level of noise, for example, tends to vary with the individual

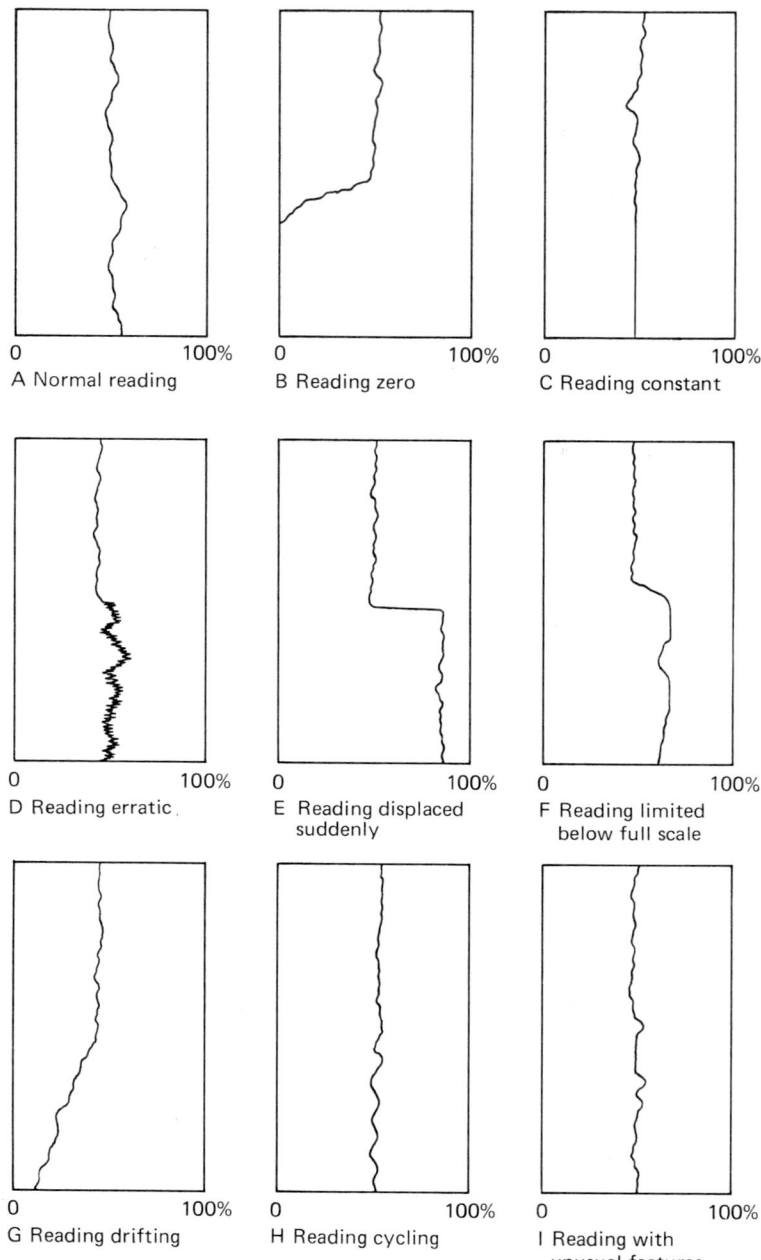

Figure 1. Typical chart recorder displays of measurement signals.

measurement. In this case the operator must use his knowledge of the range of variation of the noise on a particular instrument in the past. Thus Figures 1c and 1d might or might not indicate malfunction.

If there is a duplicate measurement, then detection of the fact that one of the instruments is wrong is straightforward, although it may not be possible to say which. However, duplication is not usual in the normal instrument systems which are of primary concern here. On the other hand, near-duplication is quite common. For example, the flow of a reactant leaving a vaporizer and entering two parallel reactors may be measured at the exit of both the vaporizer and the reactors and the two flow measurement systems provide a check on each other.

What constitutes a reasonable signal may depend on the signals given by other instruments. Thus, although a signal which exhibits drift, such as that of Figure 1g, may appear incorrect, a check on other instruments may show that it is not.

Some types of variation in a signal, such as change in the noise level, appear easy to detect automatically. Others, such as that shown in Figure 1i, are probably more difficult, especially if their form is not known in advance. Here the human operator with his well-developed ability to recognize visual patterns has the advantage.

There are a large number of ways in which the readings of other instruments can serve as a check. Some of these are

(1) Near-duplication
(2) Mass and heat balances
(3) Flow-pressure drop relations
(4) Consistent states.

This last check is based on the fact that certain variables are related to each other and at a given state of operation must lie within certain ranges of values.

The position of control valves also provides a means of checking measurements. This is most obvious for flow measurement but is by no means limited to this.

Many of the checks described do not show unambiguously that a particular instrument is not working properly. Often they indicate only that there is an inconsistency which needs to be further explored. However, this information is very important.

It is clear that in building up a store of information which can be used to provide the redundancy required for malfunction detection the operator is involved in a complex learning process.

4. Malfunction Detection by Computer

The scanning of process measurements for alarm conditions is a standard function of a process computer (Jagt 1968). The most common alarms are absolute and deviation alarms. The alarm limits are expressed in the first as absolute values of the variable and in the second as deviations of the variable from its setpoint. Rate-of-change alarms are also used sometimes.

These alarms are intended to detect real and undesirable changes in the process variables. In addition, however, some simple tests are sometimes used to check whether the measuring instruments are functioning correctly. These are normally 'hardover' checks on whether the signal is within the nominal input voltage range. Other less-used checks are on 'dead' zero and excessive rate of change.

Some checks on instrument condition may be also used. Open-circuit detection on thermocouples is probably the most common.

Other methods of instrument malfunction detection used include those based on multiple measuring instruments and on simple models or relations. These methods have been reviewed elsewhere (Anyakora 1971).

A major difficulty with all such checks, both those on process variables and those on instruments, is that there is a tendency for too many false alarms to be generated. The design of alarm systems, however, is beyond the scope of this paper.

5. Industrial Examples of Malfunction Detection by Operator

Some data from a survey on the failure rates of instruments in the chemical plant environment have been given previously (Anyakora, Engel and Lees 1971). The failure rates of some of the principal instruments, abstracted from that survey, are shown in Table 1.

Table 1. Reliability data for some common instruments in the chemical plant environment

Instrument	Number at risk	Number of faults	Failure rate (faults/year)
Impulse lines	1099	416	0·77
Flow measurement			
Differential pressure transducer	636	559	1·73
Transmitting variable area meter	100	48	1·01
Level measurement			
Differential pressure transducer	130	106	1·71
Float-type level transducer	158	124	1·64
Capacitance-type level transducer	28	3	0·22
Pressure measurement			
Differential and absolute pressure transducer	233	124	1·41
Temperature measurement			
Thermocouple	772	191	0·52
Resistance thermometer	479	92	0·41
Mercury-in-steel thermometer	1001	13	0·027
Control valve	1531	447	0·60
Valve positioner	334	69	0·44
Controller	1192	164	0·29

The way in which the operator diagnoses malfunction is illustrated by the comments which he makes. These comments, which were made about the same instruments, are given in Table 2. They were obtained by examination of the job tickets sent in by the operators to the instrument maintenance workshops. They have been slightly altered where necessary so that most of them assume a standard form but the essential meaning is preserved. The comments selected for inclusion are in general those which are most explicit. In a large proportion of cases little was noted except that the instrument was, in some undefined sense, faulty.

The actual fault found by the maintenance fitter is also given for those cases where it was noted on the ticket and where it is not already obvious from the operator's comments. The items are classified according to the instrument which was actually faulty, regardless of whether the operator attributed the fault to that instrument, to another instrument or to the control loop as a whole. Many of the entries represent several cases similar both with respect to the comments made and to the fault found. The code numbers in the table are explained below.

Table 2. Diagnosis of malfunction in particular instruments by the process operator

Instrument	Operator's comment	Fault	Classification
Impulse lines	Reading zero	Line blocked Line frozen Line leaking	M1.1
	Reading full scale	Line blocked	M1.2
	Reading constant	Line blocked Line frozen	M2.1
	Reading erratic	Line blocked Line leaking	M2.2
	Reading sluggish	Line blocked	M2.3
	Reading falling	Line frozen	M5.1
	Reading inconsistent with mass balance	Line partially blocked	M8.1
	Reading low	Line blocked Line frozen	M9.3
	Reading high	Line blocked	M9.4
	Reading faulty	Line blocked Line frozen Line leaking	M13
	Control erratic	Line leaking	C1.1
	Control sluggish	Line blocked	C1.2
	Control faulty	Line blocked	C2
	Control valve stays closed	Line blocked	V3.1
	Control valve action apparently reversed	Line frozen	V5.3
Flow measurement: Orifice and differential pressure transducer	Reading zero	Orifice blocked Restrictor blocked	M1.1
	Reading full scale	Bellows distorted	M1.2
	Reading erratic	Flapper-nozzle badly fitted	M2.2
	Reading fell suddenly		M3.1
	Reading limited to value below full scale		M4.2
	Reading inconsistent with local flow measurement		M6
	Reading inconsistent with level measurement		M7.2
	Reading low	Flapper-nozzle damaged	M9.3
	Reading not zero with control valve closed		M10.2
	Reading inconsistent with control valve position		M10.3
	Reading faulty	Equalizing valve not fully closed	M13
Transmitting variable area flowmeter	Reading erratic	Float sticking	M2.2

Table 2.—*Continued*

Instrument	Operator's comment	Fault	Classification
Level measurement: Differential pressure transducer	Reading constant		M2.1
	Reading limited to value below full scale		M4.2
	Reading inconsistent with manual measurement (dip stick)		M6
	Reading not zero but level known to be zero		M9.2
	Control erratic		C1.1
	Control valve not responding to low level		C1.5 or V7
Pressure measurement: Differential or absolute pressure transducer	Reading inconsistent with local pressure measurement		M6
	Reading high (alarm did not activate when pressure fell)		M9.4
	Intermittent fault (alarm activated intermittently)		M12
	Control sluggish		C1.2
Temperature measurement: Thermocouple	Reading zero		M.1.1
	Reading erratic and low		M2.2 and M9.3
	Reading sluggish	Looose connection in head	M2.3
	Reading inconsistent with another temperature measurement		M7.1
	Reading low		M9.3
	Reading high		M9.4
	Reading faulty	Loose connection in head	M13
		Insulation broken	
		Water in head	
Control valve	Valve position inconsistent with controller output		V1
	Valve passing fluid when closed	Plug and seat faulty	V2.1
	Valve not passing fluid when open	Body blocked	V2.2
	Valve stays closed		V3.1
	Valve not moving	Shackle pin loose	V3.3
		Stem seized and bent	
		Seat blocked	
		Sticking	
	Valve not closing fully	Body blocked	V4.1
	Valve not opening fully	Trim bent	V4.2
	Valve movement erratic (on auto)	Sticking	V5.1
	Valve movement erratic (at low flow)		
	Valve sticking		
	Valve hunting		V6
	Valve stem twisted		V9
	Control erratic		C1.1
Valve positioner	Valve not moving	Arm corroded and loose	V3.3
	Valve not closing fully	Several faults	V4.1
	Valve not opening fully	Positioner misaligned	V4.2
	Valve movement erratic	Positioner misaligned	V5.1
		Arm rubbing on trim	
	Valve movement sluggish	Positioner misaligned	V5.2
	Valve hunting		V6
	Flow measurement reading erratic	Positioner faulty	M2.2
	Control faulty	Flapper bent, restrictor blocked	C1.6

Table 3. General classification of instrument malfunction diagnoses by the process operator

Measuring instruments
- M1 Measurement reading zero or full scale
  - M1.1 Reading zero
  - M1.2 Reading full scale
- M2 Measurement reading noise or dynamic response faulty
  - M2.1 Reading constant
  - M2.2 Reading erratic
  - M2.3 Reading sluggish
- M3 Measurement reading displaced suddenly
  - M3.1 Reading fell suddenly
  - M3.2 Reading rose suddenly
- M4 Measurement reading limited within full scale
  - M4.1 Reading limited above zero
  - M4.2 Reading limited below full scale
- M5 Measurement reading drifting
  - M5.1 Reading falling
  - M5.2 Reading rising
- M6 Measurement reading inconsistent with duplicate measurement
- M7 Measurement reading inconsistent with one other measurement
  - M7.1 Reading inconsistent with near-duplicate measurement
  - M7.2 Reading inconsistent with level-flow integration
  - M7.3 Reading otherwise inconsistent
- M8 Measurement reading inconsistent with simple model
  - M8.1 Reading inconsistent with mass balance
  - M8.2 Reading inconsistent with heat balance
  - M8.3 Reading inconsistent with flow-pressure drop relations
  - M8.4 Reading otherwise inconsistent
- M9 Measurement reading inconsistent with plant operating state
  - M9.1 Reading zero but variable not zero
  - M9.2 Reading not zero but variable zero
  - M9.3 Reading low
  - M9.4 Reading high
  - M9.5 Reading otherwise inconsistent
- M10 Measurement reading inconsistent with control valve position
  - M10.1 Reading (flow) zero with valve open
  - M10.2 Reading (flow) not zero with valve closed
  - M10.3 Reading otherwise inconsistent
- M11 Measurement reading periodic or cycling
- M12 Measurement reading showing intermittent fault
- M13 Measurement reading faulty
- M14 Measurement instrument tested by active tests
- M15 Measuring instrument condition faulty

Control action and controllers
- C1 Control action faulty
  - C1.1 Control erratic
  - C1.2 Control sluggish
  - C1.3 Control cycling
  - C1.4 Control unstable
  - C1.5 Control error excessive
  - C1.6 Control otherwise faulty
- C2 Controller performance faulty
- C3 Controller tested by active tests
- C4 Controller condition faulty

Control valves and valve positioners
- V1 Valve position inconsistent with signal to valve (this requires independent measurement of position)
- V2 Valve position inconsistent with flow (but not necessarily flow measurement)
  - V2.1 Valve passing fluid when closed
  - V2.2 Valve not passing fluid when open
  - V2.3 Valve position otherwise inconsistent with flow measurement
  - V2.4 Valve position inconsistent with one other measurement
  - V2.5 Valve position inconsistent with simple model
- V3 Valve not moving
  - V3.1 Valve stays closed
  - V3.2 Valve stays open
  - V3.3 Valve stays part open
- V4 Valve movement less than full travel
  - V4.1 Valve not closing fully
  - V4.2 Valve not opening fully
  - V4.3 Valve travel otherwise limited
- V5 Valve movement faulty
  - V5.1 Valve movement erratic
  - V5.2 Valve movement sluggish
  - V5.3 Valve movement otherwise faulty
- V6 Valve movement cycling
- V7 Valve or positioner performance faulty
- V8 Valve or positioner tested by active tests
- V9 Valve or positioner condition faulty

6. General Classification of Malfunction Detection by Operator

It is clear from Table 2 that there are many recurring themes in the comments made. For example, the types of behaviour which are indicative of malfunction in measuring instruments are very similar regardless of whether the variable measured is flow, level, pressure, or temperature. An attempt has, therefore, been made to classify the methods used by the operator to detect malfunction. This general classification is given in Table 3.

The main instrument categories used in Table 3 are measuring instruments, controllers, and control valves and valve positioners. Control action and loop behaviour are considered together with controllers. The principal methods of detection are listed for each of these categories. The last items in each category cover other faults in performance or condition. The application of the classification is illustrated in Table 2 where the code numbers used are those given in Table 3.

A distinction is drawn between the use of a simple model and of plant operating states to check a measurement. The essential difference is that whereas in the first case the operator's test resembles a set of equations, in the second it resembles tables giving sets of values consistent with each other and with the operating conditions.

The modes of behaviour listed do not in general show unambiguously that an instrument has failed but they do usually indicate a more or less strong presumption of malfunction. Moreover, because some methods involve a comparison with one other instrument, such methods only show that one of these instruments is faulty without indicating which. Thus a zero or full-scale reading or a drifting reading would normally need to be tested using one of the other checks before deciding that the instrument is faulty, while a discrepancy between a flow measurement and a control valve position only indicates that a fault exists in one of these.

Some further guidance is available, however, from knowledge of the probabilities of failure of different instruments. On any particular plant the operator does usually know which instruments are likely to be troublesome.

7. Computer-Aided Malfunction Detection by Operator

The approach adopted in the most advanced computer control systems is to try to choose that allocation of function between man and machine which gives the best system performance rather than to attempt to achieve complete automation for its own sake (Fitts 1962). Frequently, of course, the best solution does involve a very high degree of automation. Moreover, the right allocation of function changes as the technology advances and new techniques are developed. However, there remains at present a very large number of functions for which man is usually found to be the most appropriate component available to the system designer. These considerations are applicable to the particular function, instrument malfunction detection, which is considered here.

The problem of automation of instrument malfunction detection is illustrated by Bowen's (1967) description of the checkout facility for the *Apollo* programme:

" Historically this was planned as a more-or-less completely automated facility, but this concept quickly ran into difficulties. Difficulties arose from the fact that the system is continuously changing. Experience in the *Mercury* and *Gemini* programmes has indicated that a large number (perhaps 100) of design or procedural changes occur from one shoot to the next. An automated check-out system would have to have extraordinary flexibility to accommodate all these changes in short enough time and with sufficient reliability to maintain its identity as an *automated* system."

The account given earlier of the detection methods used by the operator shows how rich and varied these are. Although some of these techniques have been automated and used in computers, they are limited in number and in power.

It may be assumed that automatic methods will continue to be extended and refined. It is indeed a prime objective of this paper to provide background material for such work. As long as such techniques, however, are not completely adequate the importance of the operator should be recognized and his needs catered for.

The point has been well put by Crawley (1968): he criticizes any approach which involves automation of functions if " the men were to be effectively designed out of systems before the achievement of automation performance superior to that achieved by a carefully designed integrated man-computer system."

Some of the tasks involved in malfunction detection are more readily done by a computer and some by the operator. Thus, for example, as J. J. de Jong (1964) has pointed out, scanning is a natural task for the computer and diagnosis for the operator. In the specific context of instrument malfunction detection, the strength of the computer is that it can store a large number of definitions of malfunction, in the form of comparison algorithms and algorithm parameters, and can execute these comparisons quickly, accurately, and reliably on many instruments. The strength of the operator by contrast is in carrying out complex, subtle and unforeseen definitions and comparisons, in recognizing visual and event patterns, in devising and conducting confirmatory checks, in utilizing his senses to investigate equipment conditions and in applying his ability to learn to all these aspects.

The diagnosis of malfunction in instruments has been studied by Rasmussen (1971). Although his experiments were conducted on men maintaining electronic equipment rather than on process operators, they were done with the latter in mind. The work illustrates the fact that in such diagnostic tasks men do not rely on a complete functional understanding of the equipment or on a fully systematic fault tracing scheme, but use experience and rules-of-thumb and take short cuts.

If it is accepted that the operator has an important part to play in the detection of instrument malfunction, the emphasis in design should be on an operator-controlled, computer-aided malfunction detection system. This subject, however, is beyond the scope of this paper.

8. Displays for Malfunction Detection by Operator

Perhaps the most important aids to malfunction detection which the operator has are his displays. In a conventional control system this means primarily the recorders. As described earlier, the operator uses a wide range of detection techniques based on chart records. If he is provided instead with a control computer in which his displays are limited to digital indication, and that only on demand, then he suffers a severe degradation in the facilities available to him for malfunction detection. This loss may or may not be compensated by the incorporation in the computer program of some automatic detection methods. It may, therefore, be advisable, at least from the point of view of instrument malfunction detection, to provide the operator with displays by retaining some chart recorders.

Alternatively, some form of computer graphics may be used. In principle, computer-driven c.r.t. displays offer a much more powerful facility for malfunction detection. These displays are beginning to be used in process control for other purposes and thus to become available for this purpose also.

One use of the c.r.t. display is to show trend records and thus displace chart recorders. However, some care is required in the design of the display if it is to be a facility which is truly equivalent to the recorder with respect to malfunction detection. For example, the operator learns much from the noise on a chart record and this may undergo modification on a c.r.t.

The use of other c.r.t. displays for malfunction detection is not well-developed. Bowen (1967) has illustrated how much better malfunction of an engine gimbal is shown by a phase-plane plot than by a trend record. Wolff (1970) has developed a polar plot of system state, which has been further developed by Coekin (1969) and which might be applied to malfunction detection. Displays of the power spectrum of measuring instruments and displays of actual measured value and of measured value calculated from valve position have been suggested by Anyakora (1971). Whatever their particular merits, these ideas indicate the sort of ways in which process c.r.t.s. might be used for malfunction detection.

9. Conclusion

The detection of error or incorrect operation in the system is an essential function which a process control system must perform. Usually this function is assigned to the process operator. The object of this paper has been to analyze how he performs this function.

This analysis provides useful background whether this function is to be assigned to man or to a machine.

It has only been possible to touch very briefly on certain related problems, such as automatic methods of detection, computer-aided operator detection, and computer-driven detection displays. Other related subjects which have not been discussed at all include the identification of critical instruments, the duplication of instruments and computer alarm analysis. All these aspects, however, are relevant to the creation of systems with high reliability.

The Present and Future Contribution of the Human Operator to the Control of LD Steelmaking

By J. E. CRAWLEY

BISRA—The Corporate Laboratories, British Steel Corporation, London

1. Introduction

All LD plants at present in production throughout the world employ operators with process control responsibilities whether or not the plant uses a computer. It seems highly likely that this situation will remain essentially unchanging for some time, *i.e.* in ten years from now all plants will still have operators with control responsibilities. What seems equally certain, however, is the fact that the present nature of the steelmaker's job in existing plants using manual control methods is very different from the jobs which the operators of the future will be performing in the newest LD shops in ten years' time.

This is the generally accepted view consequent on the development of automation in its broadest sense and in its application to LD operation in particular. The purpose of this paper, therefore, is to discuss how the human operator fits into this scheme of an advancing technology, how his contribution to process control will depend on the control system chosen for LD operation by a particular management, and how the steelmaking crew will share their skills (both traditional and those more recently acquired) with the computers that are destined to play an ever-increasing role in steelmaking, as in every other major process.

One important point needs to be stressed before going into details. It is that, for the foreseeable future, control systems for LD operation should be conceived as integrated systems rather than as manual systems with computer ' advice ', or computer systems with human monitors. The emphasis is going to shift slowly and surely towards computer techniques, but overall efficiency as judged by the economics of precise operation is going to rely on operator skills of one sort or another for some time to come; this contention is fundamental to the arguments to be developed in this paper.

2. Components and Variables in LD Operation

If the inputs and outputs of LD conversion are reduced to a simple equation, this can be illustrated by

$$\text{Charge} + \text{Oxygen} + \text{Time} = \text{Steel} + \text{Slag} + \text{Waste Gas}$$

The individual variables associated with each component are tabled in Figure 1, in which it will be seen that as well as all the dependent variables on the output side, there are a number on the input side which are also dependent, such things as hot metal composition and temperature. This serves to illustrate the point that the variability of the output from the blast furnaces is in itself a demand for a flexible control scheme in the BOS plant. The fact that information regarding hot metal parameters can be fed forward to the steel plant is not sufficient to guarantee control if the variance on these parameters is excessive. The development of dynamic models for control purposes

COMPONENTS					
Charge	Oxygen	Time	Steel	Slag	Waste gas
VARIABLES					
Weight hot metal	Volume	Charging time	Weight	Weight	Volume
Temperature of hot metal	Lance height	Standing time	Temperature	Temperature	Temperature
Hot metal composition	Nozzle type	Tapping time	Composition	Composition	Composition
Weight scrap	Pressure	Blowing time			
Scrap composition					
Weight limestone					
Weight spar					
Weight other flux					
Weight coolant					

Figure 1. Variables in the LD process.

is therefore a natural consequence of the partial inability to control the LD process on inputs, because of the limited accuracy of the static models and the considerable noise which enters the control system. These considerations are as valid for manual control as for more sophisticated methods based on computerization, since operators have a rudimentary dynamic model themselves as a basis for their control actions.

3. The Present State of Manual Control

3.1. Scope

To define an average manual control system is an unrealistic exercise, since it involves blurring essential differences in practice necessitated by specific production requirements. In addition, the type of plant will certainly place constraints on the methods of control used by the operators. What does seem to be justified, however, is an analysis of the improvements achieved in certain aspects of manual control. All these, as will be explained, have been brought about by improvements in instrumentation or information handling techniques. Having listed the variables in the system, it is now necessary to break these down into a form which takes account of the sequence of control actions and the priority these have in relation to

(1) The requirements of process control

(2) Safety of plant and personnel

(3) Economy of operation.

This tabulation is shown in Figure 2. As will be seen, those factors listed under 'Pre-blowing' include variables such as nozzle type, which is a variable with influence on many heats, although most variables in this category, including all those under 'Variables influencing process control', involve a certain amount of decision-making for each individual heat. This latter group forms the basis of the static control of the process, and it is these variables, incidentally, which form the nucleus of any computer control scheme incorporating a static model of the process.

	Pre-blowing	In-blow	Post-blowing
Variables influencing process control	Weight of hot metal Weight of scrap Charging time and duration Weight of fluxes.......... Type of fluxes.............	Lance height Oxygen blowing rate Blowing duration Weight of coolant Time of flux additions	Weight and type of ladle additions Standing time Tapping time and duration
Variables influencing safety of plant and personnel		Hood pressure Oxygen content of waste gas	
Variables influencing economy of operation	Nozzle type Percentage scrap Sequence of operation, etc.	Oxygen volume Blowing time	Waiting time

Figure 2. Variables in the LD process under operator control.

3.2. Static Control

If we examine these particular input variables, it will be noticed that a good number involve information concerning weighing operations some of which are directly under the control of the operators themselves, *e.g.* vessel additions. The weighing of hot metal and scrap, however, takes place remote from the vessel and this necessitates a two-way flow of information concerning weight data. The operators' ability to maintain good static control of the process is therefore determined by

(1) The accuracy of the weighing operations themselves
(2) The availability of accurate information concerning the hot metal temperature and composition (which enables changes in scrap weight to be made)
(3) Rapid communication with the hot metal and scrap stations (to take advantage of the above information)
(4) The limitations of the crude model (nomograms, *etc.*) used for charge calculations.

The importance of most of these factors has long since been recognized, and almost all plants have taken advantage of developments in weighing practice and the use of charge calculations for control purposes. The fact, however, that hot metal temperature information is not considered important enough to warrant inclusion in charge calculations in some plants is indication enough that further improvements can be made. It must be remembered that this represents a loss of inherent controllability before blowing is even commenced.

3.3. Dynamic Control

When the variables influencing process control during blowing are considered, we move to questions of feedback control and the kinds of information which constitute useful information for control purposes during refining.

At this stage reference is made to Figure 3, which illustrates the information and control flows associated with manual control of LD operation. The control loops concerned with the static information already referred to are shown on the input side. The block diagram also depicts the dynamic control actions

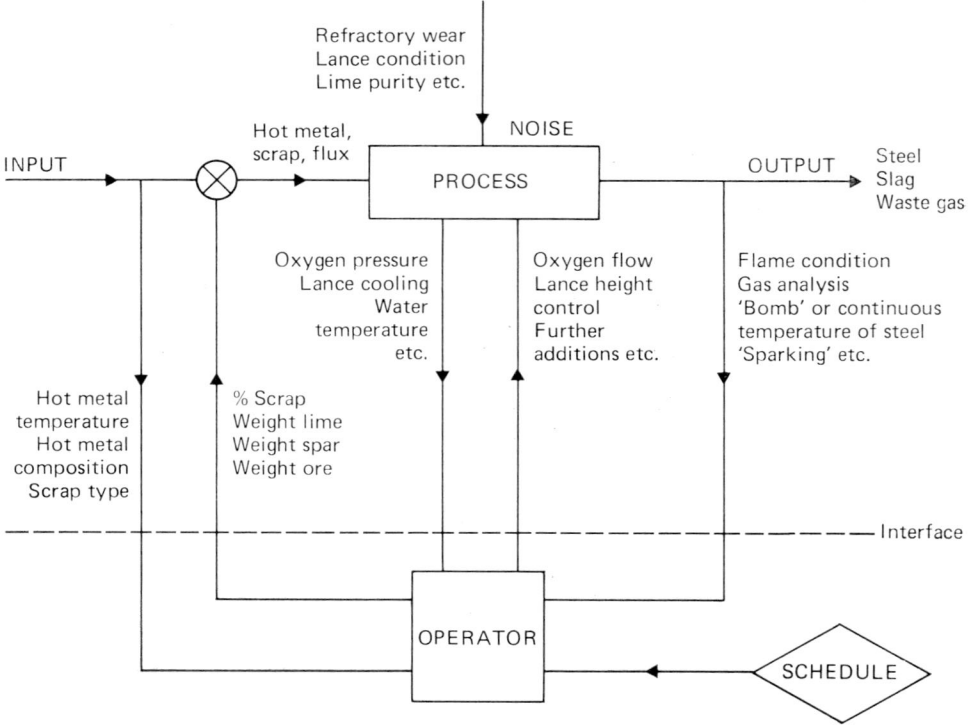

Figure 3. Manual control of LD steelmaking.

available to the operator during blowing of the converter. The actual variables under his control are

(1) Lance height
(2) Oxygen blowing rate
(3) Vessel additions
(4) Blowing time.

To a certain extent the first three can be controlled in an open-loop mode, *e.g.* lance height can be preset according to time of blowing, and vessel additions can also be made by the clock. If any flexibility of control is to be exercised by the operator, however, this will necessitate making decisions on the basis of feedback information from the process. The information which the operator can have from the vessel during blowing at the present stage of development is as follows:

(1) Flame condition
(2) Nature of ejections from the vessel
(3) Gas analyses data
(4) Lance cooling water temperature
(5) Running time of blow
(6) The form of 'sparks' breaking on the vessel shell
(7) Bomb thermocouple measurements.

On turndown at the end of blowing further information is available:
  (1) Dip thermocouple measurements of steel temperature
  (2) Rapid carbon determination by techniques such as the Leco or liquidus arrest method
  (3) Quantovac analysis of steel samples
  (4) FeO content of slag by rapid X-ray fluorescence methods
  (5) Oxygen content of steel by electrolytic cell or other methods.

This information, some inherent in the process, some achieved as the result of considerable instrumentation research and development, represents virtually all that is presently feasible. How is it used by the operators for control purposes during blowing?

Let us first examine the requirements of control; these are more easily listed than achieved in LD operations. They are realistically, it is hoped, seen to be as follows:
  (1) The very high probability of achieving the specification requirements on *first* turndown—these requirements being for composition and temperature
  (2) The certainty of achieving specification after reblowing, if re-scheduling is not possible
  (3) The maximization of yield
  (4) The minimization of tap-to-tap time
  (5) The maximization of the tonnage of finished steel per ton of oxygen blown
  (6) The minimization of ancillary costs arising from refractory consumption and lance life, *etc.*

It will be noted that the time span of these requirements shows considerable variation; although most of them are sought in each individual heat, others are of long-term interest.

If we produce a ranking of these requirements, it is self-evident that first and foremost will be the achievement of the specified composition and temperature for a particular grade. The major problem facing the operator, therefore, is the control of his four principal variables, acting on information from some or perhaps all of the factors listed as providing feedback information. This effort is directed at the selection of an endpoint in blowing time at which the carbon content and the other elements of the charge and its temperature are satisfactory for the grade being produced.

The incidence of reblowing is the best indicator of the effectiveness of an individual control scheme, although the differences in grades produced make for easier control in some cases, *e.g.* low carbon steels are easier to control for carbon than the medium range. In the early days of LD steelmaking the incidence of reblowing to achieve specification was considerably higher than at present, and considerable use was made of the hard feedback of dip temperatures and Quantovac analysis to hit target after a short corrective reblow.

The great efforts made during the past few years to obtain information concerning carbon content and temperature during blowing have advanced control of this process to a point where full closed-loop computer control is becoming viable. This is not to say—and it is a point to be emphasized—that the standards of manual control could not be improved by providing the operators with the same information upon which the computer depends for control. It would be interesting, indeed, to know the potential of operators in LD control who had this undoubted advantage over some of their colleagues whose principal source of information is still flame condition over the converter.

4. The Rôle of the Computer in LD Control

It is no purpose of mine to evaluate the pure economics of computer control of LD operations in this paper. I will simply content myself with saying that the case for static model control is now, in my opinion, unanswerable. The further advantages of dynamic control—subject to instrumentation requirements and an enlightened approach to control philosophy—are available also for those who are prepared to spend the worthwhile time and money on implementation.

In considering how computers can be used to control this process, it is soon apparent that, as already indicated, two levels of control can be attempted, both completely analogous to manual methods of operation.

4.1. *Static Models of the Process*

The possibility and limitations of controlling the process on inputs have already been considered. The degree of control it is possible to exercise obviously depends on the accuracy of the model of the process used for charge and additions computations. As has been widely reported, the basic definition of the process in terms of a static mathematical model involves the solution of four equations:

(1) A mass balance

(2) A heat balance

(3) An oxygen prediction

(4) A lime prediction.

Each equation is a function of at least six variables and in some cases up to ten. It is apparent, therefore, that the complexity of obtaining a substantially better control of inputs and additions involves fast computations and direct data entry to the computer. This is the practice now employed by the most advanced manufacturers with on-line control. These static models usually have the following outputs:

(1) A recommended make-up of the initial charge in terms of tonnages of hot metal and scrap

(2) The tonnages of converter additions required for fluxing and coolant (if required)

(3) A prediction of the oxygen requirement to complete the blow.

The actual values of oxygen blowing rate and lance height are not usually included in the model outputs, but for consistency in model performance, a prerequisite is consistency in the regulation of these two variables in blowing practice.

4.2. *Dynamic Models of the Process*

These are basically mathematical representations of the physical chemistry of the process, which are updated by feedback from process parameters. The object of the exercise is to control lance height, oxygen blowing rate, and vessel additions in order to achieve measured and predicted carbon removal rates, and acceptable steel temperatures at the end of blowing.

I think it is true to say that the limited application of these techniques at present is solely due to the inadequate nature of the feedback information from the process in terms of its accuracy, reliability, and expense. This is basically a problem for the instrumentation engineers, and with confidence in their ability to provide the necessary information, it is very probable that dynamic control of LD operation will be the rule rather than the exception in five years' time.

5. Allocation of Function between Process Computers and Operators

5.1. *Integrated Control*

The diagrammatic representation of an integrated man-computer control scheme is illustrated in Figure 4. In addition to the man-machine interface shown in the previous figure, two more interfaces have appeared; one is between the computer and the process and the other is between the operator and the computer. In this last category comes the teleprinter terminal in the Lysaght's Normanby works as described by Mr. A. Woodhead. This man-computer link can also have the form of a series of digital or analogue displays with keyboard input facilities or, in probably its most sophisticated form, a cathode ray tube display with either a keyboard input facility or ' touchwire ' entry on the face of the tube itself.

The diagram illustrates the possibility of placing particular loops under manual or computer control—from an extreme condition on the one hand of complete manual control with computer logging to the situation of closed-loop computer operation with manual monitoring across the operator-computer interface. In this latter situation, overall decisions regarding the mode of control would remain with the man who would thus be effectively delegating all control decisions to the computer.

5.2. *Allocation of Function*

How do we allocate functions between men and computers? The facile reply is that an individual decision should be passed to whichever of your two information processors is better able to produce a satisfactory answer. In some respects these sorts of decisions can be classified according to a system where the particular abilities of men and computers are taken into account; for example, men are usually better at pattern recognition than computers in their present stage of development. A relevant example in steelmaking is that of determining the true temperature from the e.m.f. output of a bomb thermocouple; a noisy trace would present severe difficulties to a program, whereas an operator can extract the necessary information and enter it into the system.

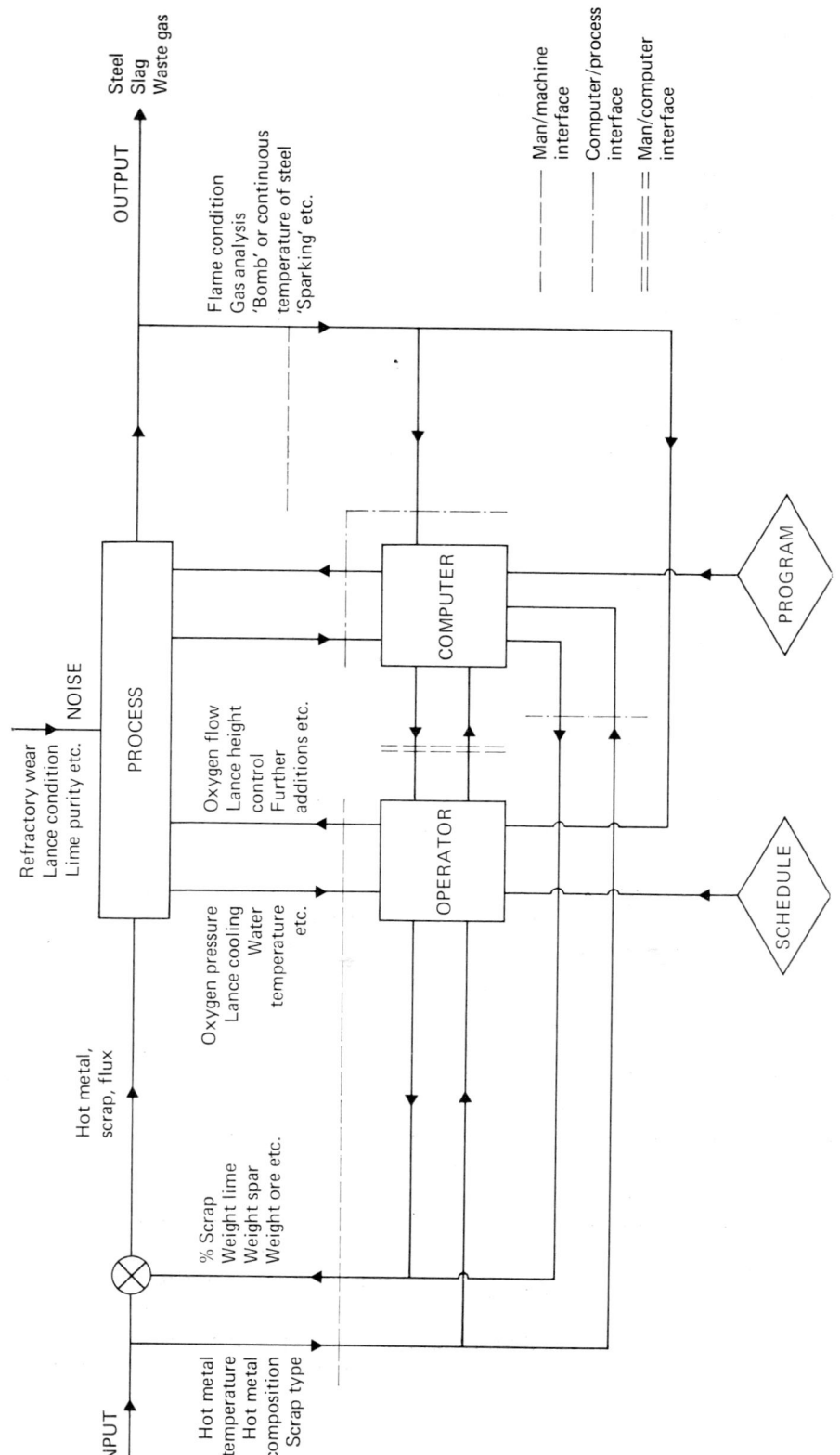

Figure 4. Integrated control of LD steelmaking.

The goal of such an analysis of information processing requirements is the best possible system performance. An important point which is assuming greater significance here is that although computer performance is in a sense independent of load, poor performance from the operators can result from too low a loading as well as too high. In a system where more and more decision-making is passed to computer software, it is desirable that the human being should be left with a minimum job content to sustain arousal, interest and consequently performance.

One important point remains. In any situation the peripheral processing only obliquely relevant to the control problem, which is unique to human controllers, is an advantage they will hold for some time to come. This is why it is essential to develop the communications between men and computers so that there may be a dialogue where both are making a genuine contribution to overall control.

6. The Future Contribution of the Operators in LD Control

6.1. *The Short Term*

What the immediate future holds is probably best considered from an examination of the plans and likely developments of plants currently at the design stage. The integrated control approach is being implemented in the new Port Talbot plant of the South Wales Group, and hence is a reasonable example to use for discussion.

The system places high priority on a communication system linking the plant, the computer and the operators. While it is possible to consider this plant operating under closed-loop computer control in two years' time, perhaps less, it is equally possible that best system performance will be achieved by leaving the men in the system to the extent that they will be comprehensibly informing the operator of the precise state of control, and the man will therefore

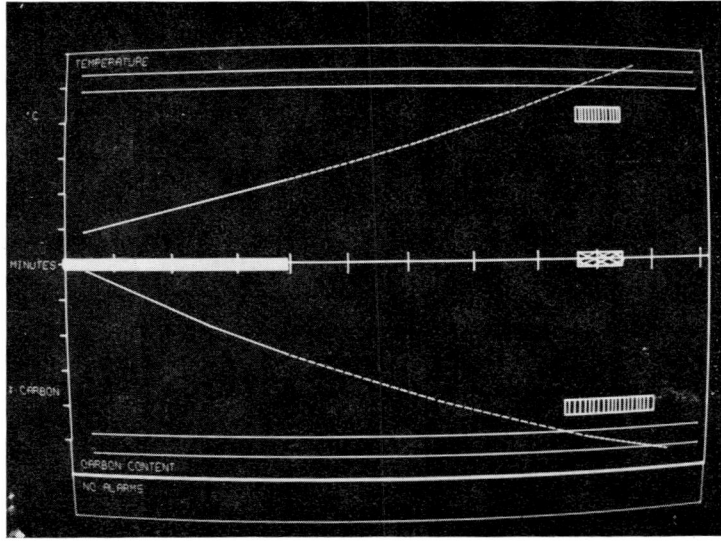

Figure 5. Display of steel carbon content and temperature in LD process.

be able to make small refinements by way of 'instant programming' not feasible in the computer software.

[To illustrate this point, Mr. Crawley showed a short film.]

Figure 5, a still from the film, demonstrates the way in which the computer displays to the operator a simple prediction as to the existence of a satisfactory end-point to the process, thus enabling the man to allow the computer to proceed with a satisfactory strategy or alternatively to attempt to improve performance by a control strategy of his own. We feel that by using display systems of this sort a much greater understanding of the computer system can be achieved by the operators with a consequent partnership between the two.

As a further illustration of the use of these display systems in steelmaking, Figure 6 shows a display of advised decarburization and actual decarburization as an aid to first-stage control.

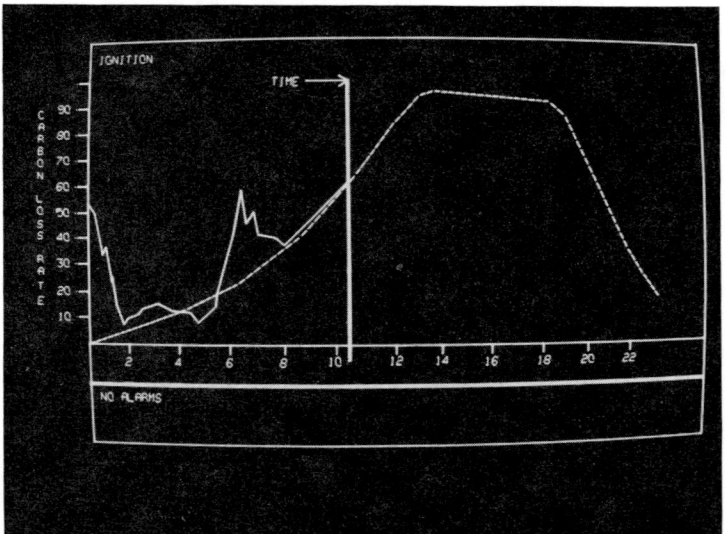

Figure 6. Display of steel carbon loss rate in LD process.

6.2. *The Long Term*

How are things likely to develop in the period five to ten years ahead? I think there is little doubt that moves will be made to reduce responsibility on the operator's part while building up the responsibilities of the computer system. As already mentioned, this could be a somewhat short-sighted policy if the men were to be effectively designed out of systems before the achievement of automation performance superior to that achieved by a carefully designed integrated man-computer system.

A likely development is a type of game-playing situation in which men can interrogate process models and add the instant programming facility already mentioned. The appeal of this type of approach is the stronger because it retains the interest and motivation of the men, which should lead to both job satisfaction and the best possible partnership in performance.

7. Conclusions

What I have attempted in this talk is

(1) To make a survey of the skills required of operators who are manually controlling the whole of the steelmaking operation, and how these might be augmented by better information in terms of both quality and quantity.

(2) To analyze the requirements of steelmaking control from the point of view of allocating decisions to human beings and to computer software, *i.e.* to that information processor best suited.

(3) To point out the need for an approach to LD control, thoroughly integrated, until the day when the only men in the control room will be maintenance men: the operators will be both standby controllers and the monitors who have responsibility for making the ultimate decision whether they or the computer should exercise control. This requirement, so easily dismissed in a few words, is what will occupy and tax all those who design control systems where computers and men should, and indeed will, work together as a single unit of which the efficiency is something none of us can ignore.

(4) Finally, the film has demonstrated one possible treatment of part of this essential man-computer dialogue in a process the economics of which will have an important bearing on the future trading position of the Corporation. We surely cannot afford at this time to allow others to show us the way forward. What I know of the ideas and the plans in Great Britain suggests that British LD practice can lead the world in five years' time. Let us make every effort to see we do.

A Simulation Study of Computer-Aided Soaking Pit Scheduling*

By P. J. A. KETTERINGHAM and D. D. O'BRIEN

BISRA—The Corporate Laboratories, British Steel Corporation, London

1. Background to the Research

In common with other large process industries, the steel industry is moving rapidly towards more automatic control of its major manufacturing processes. The advantage of this move is obviously linked to economy of control, and the estimated financial benefits of automatic systems are so attractive that there is a tendency to introduce them without sufficient evaluation. There have been instances in the past where the transition from manual to fully automatic control has taken place so quickly that difficulty has been experienced in obtaining the stated potential benefits. Too often, total control of a process is given to automatic systems with little or no reference having been made to the vast amount of control experience gained by the operators of the manual system. It is considered that, in some circumstances, an intermediate stage of control by the integration of men and computers can offer a superior level of performance than present manual systems and may be easier to implement than fully automatic systems.

Many problems can, however, still arise when the control of complex processes is shared between man and computer. Even with relatively simple information handling systems, where no direct plant control function is exercised, the predicted cost benefits of the new system will not be realized unless careful consideration is given to the interface between man and the computer. The cost penalties associated with such poor systems design could be high and are liable to lead to considerable delays in implementation. It is not possible to foresee all the problems that are likely to arise with the introduction of untried computer-based systems, but it is felt that the chances of successful implementation can be greatly enhanced by the use of simulation and validation exercises.

The simulation exercise can be used for system debugging and, most important, the interaction between the man and the computer can be studied and optimized. Alternative levels of interaction between man and the computer and the allocation of responsibilities to each can also be evaluated.

The important activities can take place in a controlled environment representative of the production line, but without the inconvenience associated with on-line experimentation. The simulation also allows selection and training programmes to be formulated. This benefit may enable management to judge the likely response of the operators to such systems and perhaps minimize possible adverse reaction.

The main disadvantages of this approach are clearly the cost and time involved in conducting such trials. However, with sophisticated production control systems, the financial penalties associated with poor design may be high and

---

* A revised and expanded version of " A Computer-Based Interactive Display System to Aid Steel Plant Scheduling ", paper presented at the Conference on Man–Computer Interaction, Teddington, September, 1970.

so justify this commitment. It is essential that the cost of such trials be accurately forecast and balanced against the savings in systems implementation costs, before commitment is made.

2. Introduction

The objective of the work described here is to develop optimum methods of bringing about an effective integration of man and computer. It is hoped that the findings of this series of trials would result in recommendations that could be used throughout the British Steel Corporation.

Three steel industry manufacturing areas, steelmaking, blast furnace control, and soaking pit scheduling are among those likely to benefit from the introduction of joint man–computer control. Fully automatic control would be highly desirable on economic grounds, but this is not likely to occur in the near future. The integrated approach is likely to offer significant cost benefits over existing manual systems and, moreover, be a useful transition between existing and fully automated systems. The control systems required for any of these areas will be complex and thus evaluation by simulation is considered essential.

This paper describes the work carried out to evaluate by simulation a computer-based interactive display system that could be used to improve the scheduling of ingots through soaking pits.

3. The Soaking Pit Scheduling Problem

In order to understand fully the soaking pit scheduling problem, it is necessary to explain briefly the main features of the manufacturing processes before and after the pit area.

Hot metal arrives at the steelmaking plant and is charged to the vessel. Steel is then made to a particular quality which ultimately depends on the order book requirements and the metallurgical makeup of the constituents. The material flow from the melting shop is irregular due to operational reasons mainly concerned with the need to satisfy rigid quality and temperature regulations. The cast is then teemed into moulds and left to solidify. The length of time taken to solidify depends mainly on the cast quality and thus, as there is a large number of different qualities, the tracking of casts through the system is complex. When the ingots have reached the solidification temperature, the moulds are stripped from them and the ingots are then transported to the soaking pit area.

The main function of the soaking pits is to heat ingots as economically and efficiently as possible to a uniform temperature suitable for rolling, but the problem does not end here, as the rolling mill requires ingots to be supplied at a steady rate so that it may operate efficiently. This means that the decisions made in the soaking pit area are critical to the smooth operation of the rolling mill.

The major decisions are concerned with the allocation of incoming casts to available pits. To satisfy the short-term objective, *i.e.* to reduce heating costs, casts must be charged to pits as rapidly as possible. To satisfy the longer-term objective, *i.e.* maintaining a steady flow of ingots to the mills, the scheduler must know the time history of the cast and the efficiency and characteristics of each soaking pit in order to predict the likely ready-to-roll times.

Although the majority of this information is theoretically available, there is clearly too much for any scheduler to handle if efficient predictions are to be made. Attempts have been made in the past (Johnson 1968) to present most of the process information in a visual or analogue form, but certain difficulties arise in the operation of such systems. Often, so much time and effort is required manually to update such systems that they fall into disuse and reversion to the original system is common. Clearly this is a situation well-suited to the use of a digital computer (Guest and Tocher 1963, Fiddy and Johnson 1967).

The computer can take over the routine information handling and calculating activities so that the scheduler is left in a purely decision-making rôle. Such a computer-based system can be used to aid both short- and long-term decision-making as follows:

(1) The efficient handling of the information concerning the progress of casts through the manufacturing processes will enable the scheduler to be in a position to plan for the arrival of casts. He will also be able to highlight potentially critical situations and plan accordingly by re-scheduling or re-routing.

(2) The ability of the computer to perform complicated calculations quickly will enable the scheduler to examine the possible outcome of a number of projected courses of action so that he can choose the action best suited to his requirements.

The main problem associated with the use of such a system is that if it is difficult to use, then it will not be used efficiently as with the manual systems. Thus every consideration should be given to developing optimal links between the operators in the system and the computer. Information must be entered easily and unambiguously from the shop floor and the scheduler should have rapid easy access to the facilities provided by the computer. It is pointless developing sophisticated routines within the computer if the entered information is unreliable, or communication is so complicated that the operators see no benefit in using the system provided.

4. The Proposed Solution

The main purpose of the proposed system is to

(1) Provide accurate information on the progress of casts through the manufacturing system.

(2) Provide good estimates of the time of arrival of casts at the soaking pits.

(3) Provide meaningful predictions of the likely ready-to-roll time of any combination of ingots and soaking pits.

The basis of the scheduling model is that each cast will have a minimum standard track time dependent on its quality. The progress of each cast is followed through the manufacturing system and, as data are entered into the computer, the estimated arrival times of the casts are updated. In this way the scheduler has a clear indication of the existing state of the processes before the soaking pits.

The other main feature of this decision aid is the prediction facility. Here the heating characteristics of each soaking pit are stored within the computer and used, along with the track time of the cast being used in the trial, to give an estimate of pit ready-to-roll time.

The display, input and communication systems that would be necessary to provide the above facilities are shown in Figure 1. As shown, there are two types of information associated with the tracking of the material in the manufacturing system. Formal information, inputted via the data entry points, is best handled by the computer, e.g. cast numbers, qualities, delays, stickers, *etc*. This information can be checked, sorted and stored automatically and presented to the scheduler when he requires it. Informal information enables the scheduler to keep in touch with the current situation by using the normal intercom and telephone links.

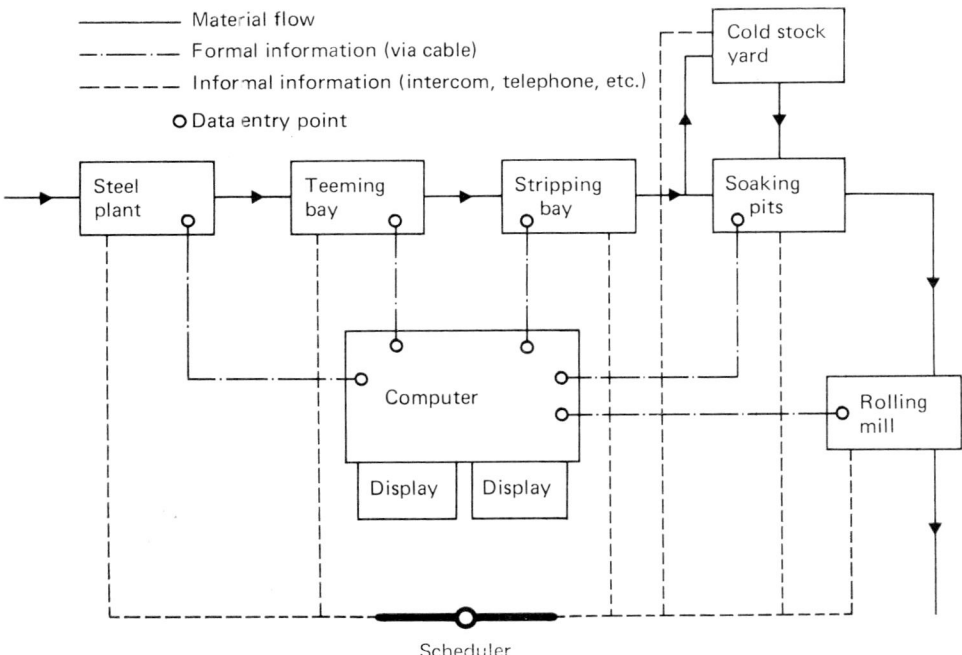

Figure 1. Computer-aided soaking pit scheduling system.

The allocation of information to either of these two categories requires detailed understanding of the scheduler's rôle and his relationship with the other manufacturing areas.

In the proposed system formal information is presented to the scheduler via two CRT display units. Such devices are available commercially and have already been used in industrial applications (Donoghue 1967) and have been the subject of much research (Gould 1968, Cropper and Evans 1968). The method of communication between the man and the computer was selected after an extensive survey of the devices available (Hersh and Shackel 1968). It appeared that the touchwire display offered the greatest potential in this particular application. The touchwire display was developed at the Royal

Radar Establishment (R.R.E.), Malvern (Johnson 1967), and has only recently been applied to the steel industry's problems (Meredith, Flint and Feinstein 1970). The method has a number of economic advantages over other available methods, and these are listed.

Basically, the device consists of a perspex mask into which are embedded a number of wires. As the operator touches a wire the capacitance of his finger is sufficient to initiate an electrical impulse which is sent to the associated computer. When a wire has been touched the computer records this fact and causes the next display in the control sequence to be shown on the screen. By carefully designed software the scheduler can be led through the required control sequence, with checks being made to prevent inadmissible touches.

The main advantage of this system from the human factors point of view is that only information relevant to an immediate decision is presented to the operator. All redundant and distracting information is excluded, thus easing the load on the scheduler and reducing the possibility of an incorrect decision being made.

The two displays recommended for use in the scheduling situation are shown in Figure 2:

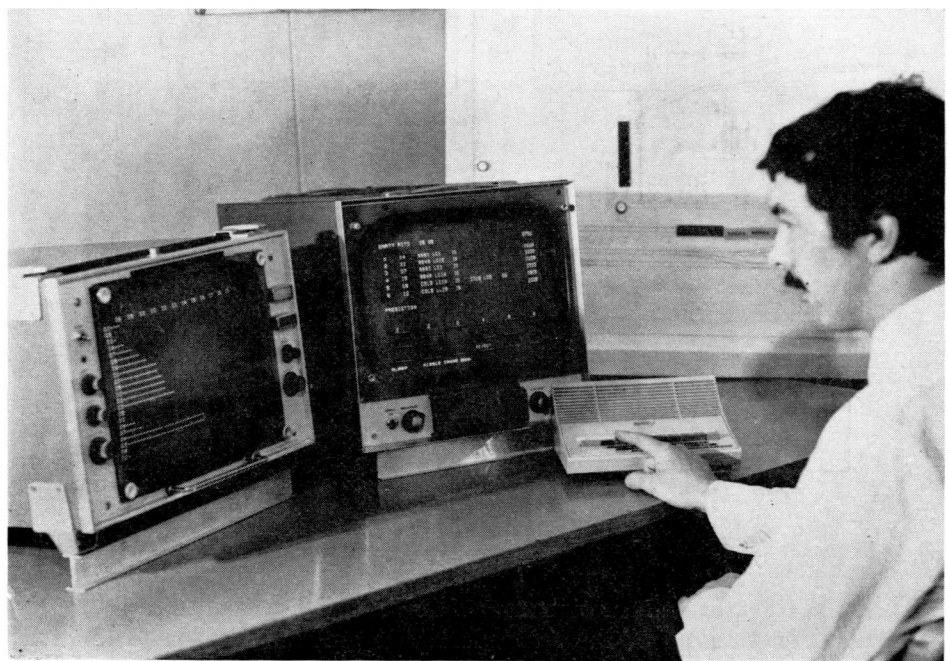

Figure 2. Scheduler's two CRT displays.

The display on the left (Figure 3) is a simple electronic data display (EDD), which presents a permanent analogue picture of the state of readiness of the soaking pits. The pits are arranged in ready-to-roll order and the length of line indicates the time left to soak before rolling. The analogue display was chosen as it presented all the information relevant to the scheduler's forward planning requirements.

A Simulation Study of Computer-Aided Soaking Pit Scheduling

Figure 3. CRT showing permanent display of state of readiness of soaking pits.

A twelve-hour timescale is displayed along the top of the screen and the information shown on the screen is updated every 15 minutes. The other special features provided are shown in Figure 4:

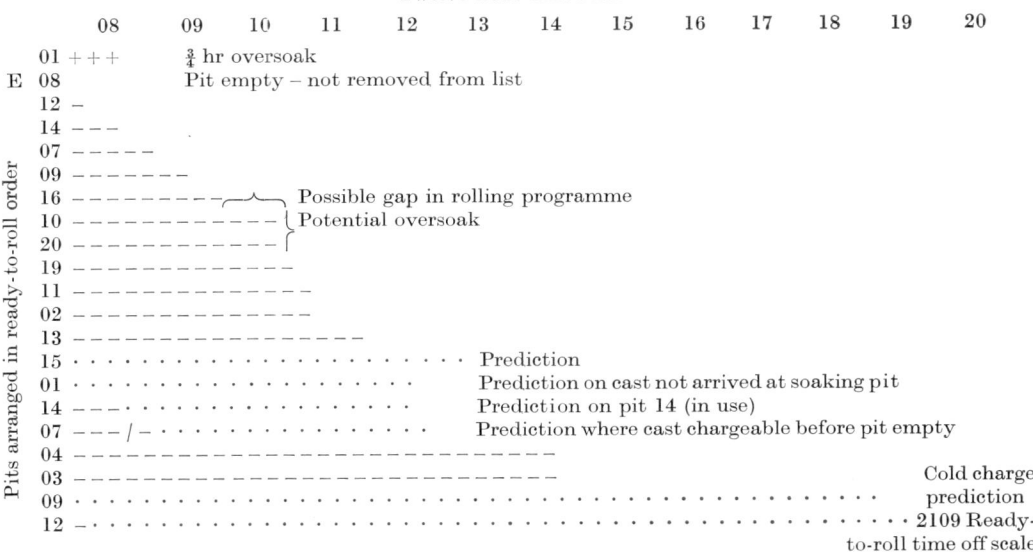

Figure 4. Special features of display shown in Figure 3.

The other display is an interactive display through which the scheduler can communicate with the computer.

The format shown in Figure 5 is the one from which all other formats are generated. The scheduler can at any time return directly to this start or rest picture by touching the REJECT wire provided on all subsequent formats.

Figure 5. Interactive touchwire CRT.

The actual time is continuously displayed in the top right corner of the screen and a list of empty soaking pits, in 'hottest first' order, in the top left. The bottom line of the screen is reserved for alarm states to be displayed and the rest of the format is occupied by the touchwire and data lines.

The following facilities are provided on touching each of the labelled wires of the rest picture:

PIT NO. On initiation of this sequence the scheduler is able to call down stored data concerning the contents and estimated ready-to-roll time of any pit. One touch will also display a list of the first six pits arranged in ready-to-roll order. A facility is also provided for cancelling information on any pit should that pit be emptied.

CASTS. This sequence gives the scheduler all information on the casts already in the manufacturing system. A typical example of this information is shown below:

9848	LC1A	24	24	09.00	L
cast identification number	quality	total number of ingots in the cast	number left to allocate to pits	estimated arrival time at pit	loaded out at the stripping bay

As the cast is injected into the system at the melting shop an estimated time of arrival at the soaking pits is calculated on the basis of a minimum standard track time for that quality. If any of the information requires changing, or if delays have occurred during the progress of the cast through the shops, this is entered using the relevant data entry point. As the cast gets nearer the pit area the estimates of arrival time become more accurate.

A letter ' T ', ' S ' or ' L ', as in the example shown, indicates the approximate position of that cast in the manufacturing system. T means that the cast has commenced teeming, S that it has started to be stripped and L, loaded on to transporters for shipment to the pit area. A facility was provided in the sequence for storing information about ingots that had been sent to cold stock, and this information was used in subsequent analysis. It must be remembered that supplementary information can still be obtained via the traditional communication channels.

TRIALS. This sequence of touches enables the scheduler to game-play with the computer. A typical sequence is illustrated:

(1) The scheduler selects TRIALS from the rest picture and a list of incoming casts is presented.

(2) He examines this list, the empty pits list and the EDD so that he can select a pit which is available about the time that the cast is estimated to arrive.

(3) After selecting the pit a hot cast from the cast list can be selected or, alternatively, the cold stock list can be called up. This selection removes all other irrelevant cast information from the screen.

(4) A number of ingots of this cast can now be selected, either the full pit capacity or the balance of the cast. In some instances it is desirable to amalgamate casts in a pit, and a facility is provided for this eventuality.

(5) On confirmation of these data, the computer calculates, on the basis of a stored heating model, the first estimate of ready-to-roll time. The details of this trial together with the estimated ready-to-roll time are displayed to the scheduler. He then visually compares this information with the EDD and decides whether to accept this particular trial or proceed with another. There is a facility to store six such trials on the touchwire display for comparison purposes.

(6) Having selected the trial or trials most suitable to his requirements he enters them as predictions. This automatically places a dotted line in the correct position on the EDD.

(7) The scheduler can then decide whether this arrangement of variables best suits the mill rolling programme. He can take into account other considerations such as meal breaks, maintenance requirements, equipment failures and roll changes before he decides on the final mill rolling order.

PREDS. This touchwire sequence allows the scheduler to call down all the data referring to the predictions displayed on the EDD which are formed as a result of a trial or game-playing activity. Here the computer is used simply as a memory store so that, when a cast arrives and requires charging, the scheduler refers to the prediction list and issues his instructions accordingly.

A sequence of touches here provides the scheduler with a means of repeating predictions if the cast concerned has been delayed in the manufacturing system and of cancelling a prediction if it is no longer required. A sequence is also provided to accept a prediction by changing a dotted line to a full line as soon as a pit has been loaded.

STOCK. A list of locally-held cold stock is displayed on touching this wire. This information could be entered in the planning department which, from the order book and steelmaking programme, usually decides cold charging priorities.

The facilities provided by this display system depend on a number of important factors, as follows:

(1) The information fed into the computer from the manufacturing units must be accurate. It is essential that the design of these data entry points be given full consideration in the earliest stages of the design of the system.

(2) The accuracy of any predictions given by the computer is a very important factor in determining the overall effectiveness of the system. If the initial prediction of ready-to-roll time is inaccurate, then the game-playing facility will not be used. It is necessary, therefore, that a good model of soaking pit performance be developed before a system of this type could be used on line. A number of soaking pit control schemes in the British Steel Corporation have been or are in the process of being developed. All these models under development are capable of ultimately providing the basis of a scheduling system similar to the one described.

The simple first estimate model used in this exercise relied essentially on the existence of a linear relationship between soaking time and track time for each pit. The slope of these lines varied according to the efficiency of each pit and could, in the real situation, be updated as the pit characteristics changed. In order to simulate the effects of the updating of these first estimates, a fixed alteration to the ready-to-roll time was introduced two hours after the pit had been charged. This update was also based on the operating efficiency of each pit.

5. The Simulation Trial

The objective of this trial was to test the feasibility of the proposed interactive display system as an aid to soaking pit scheduling. It was important to discover whether the novel facilities provided in this system would be used by real steelplant operators in the way intended. The results of the trial and the comments of the operators would be used to optimize the design of the interface which would, if the trial proved successful, form the basis of a validation exercise.

The simulation trial was carried out in two rooms, one serving the function of the scheduler's control cabin and the other the experimental control room (see Figure 6).

A Simulation Study of Computer-Aided Soaking Pit Scheduling

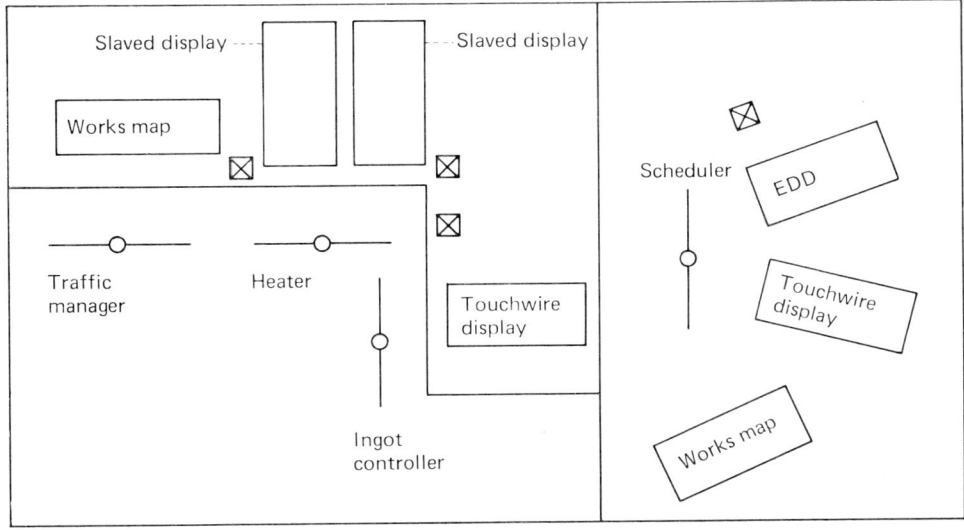

Figure 6. Room layout for simulation trials.

The scheduler's room (see Figure 2) was provided with the EDD and touchwire display previously described, a map of the soaking pit area, and an intercom unit. The map allowed the scheduler to plan the movement of trains, transporters and cranes in this area. A number of the experimental subjects (schedulers) were unfamiliar with the plant layout and the map proved very useful during the training runs. The intercom enabled the scheduler to speak to the simulation control room and *vice versa*.

The simulation control room (see Figure 7) was responsible for the complete monitoring of the trial.

Members of the control team were allocated duties as follows:

(1) One member was responsible for the injection of new casts into the system according to a prearranged schedule via a touchwire display (see Figure 8). This display was also used to introduce all delays due to mechanical, electrical and transportation failures.

(2) The second member acted as a soaking pit heater and was provided with two monitors slaved to the scheduler's display from which he recorded data by hand. He could feed back information to the scheduler concerning the progress of specific soaking pits and also control the rate of charging and drawing the pits.

(3) The final member of the team was responsible for all traffic movements and he ensured that the trains and cranes were used in a representative way.

A complete description of the hardware and software used in this exercise is shown in Appendix 3.

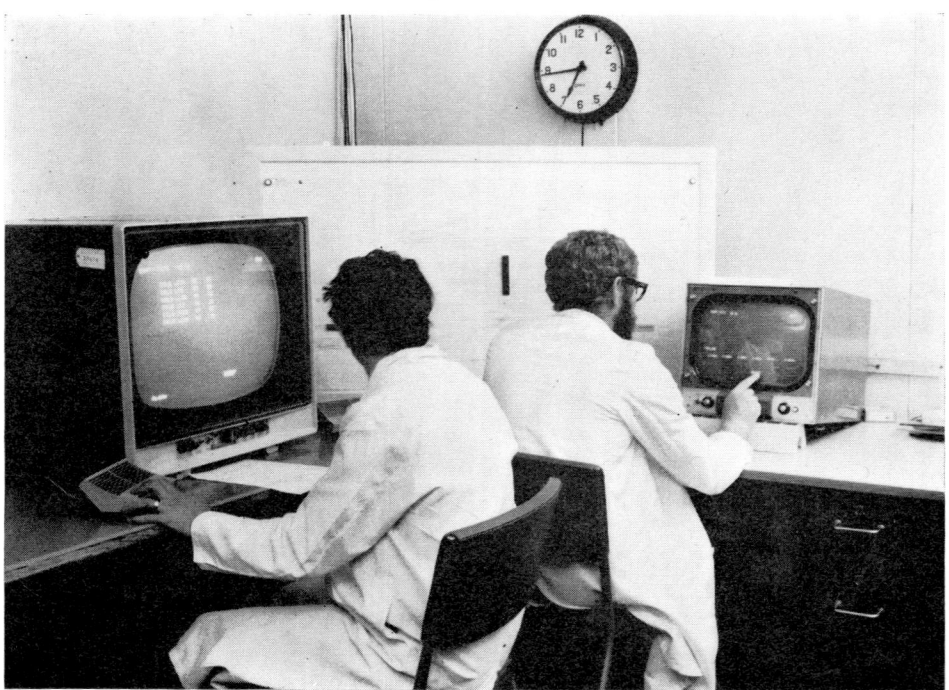

Figure 7. Simulation control room.

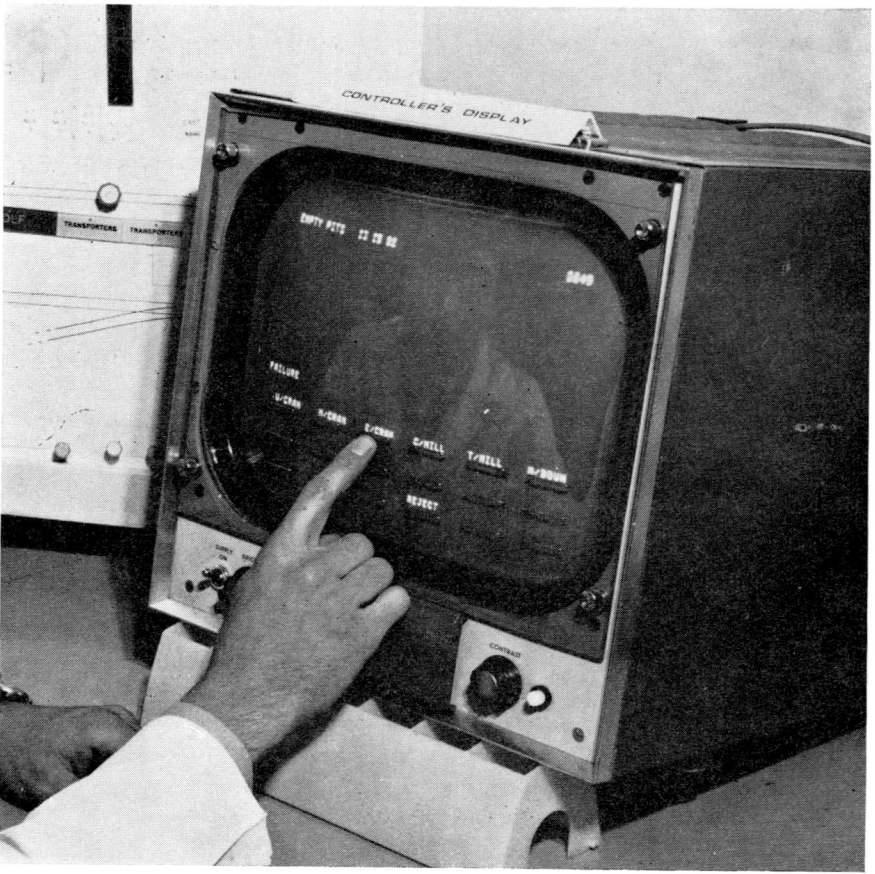

Figure 8. Experimenter injecting new casts or delays from additional touchwire CRT.

A Simulation Study of Computer-Aided Soaking Pit Scheduling

6. Experimental Design

Although it was hoped that generalized recommendations would result from the simulation trial, it was considered necessary to simulate a particular steelworks so that realism could be added to the trial. Consequently, a relatively modern works using typ'cal steelmaking practices was chosen.

Simulation data were therefore collected from the plant and time distributions of the more important operation cycles were constructed. Typical distributions of the following data were obtained:

(1) Tap-to-tap times of both the LD and open-hearth plants
(2) Quality distributions and hence the required minimum standing times
(3) Teeming time
(4) Stripping time
(5) Number of stickers
(6) Transportation times
(7) Delays in the melting shop, stripping bay, *etc.*
(8) Crane movement times
(9) Crane charging and drawing rates
(10) Ingot rolling rates
(11) Mill delays and failures
(12) Cold stock availability.

Each of these factors was introduced into the simulation in a way representative of the actual works situation. A typical schedule of operations, as used by the experimental controller, is shown below:

Time	Cast No.	Teeming T	Stripping S	Loading L
2.10	9870	*		
2.50	9871	*		
3.00	9868		*110	
3.40	9868			*5
3.45	9871		*	
3.50	If charging—charger down 10 min—mechanical			
4.00	9872	* charger OK		
4.10	9869		*75	
4.25	9871			*5
4.50	9869			*
4.50	9873	*		
4.55	9870		*75	
5.30	Ingot chariot—electrical 20 min			
5.40	9874	*		
5.45	9870			*
5.50	Ingot chariot OK			
6.40	9874		*	
6.50	9875	*		

7.10	85 foot transfer bed—15 min		
7.15	9874		*10 2STKS
7.20	9872	*	
7.25	Transfer bed OK		
8.05	D1883	*	
8.05	9876	*	
8.30	9875	*55	
8.30	9873	*	
8.35	9872		*
9.10	9873		*
9.25	If charging—cover crane down		
9.45	9876	*	
9.50	Cover crane OK		
10.05	9875		*

Note: All delays are in minutes.

Although the simulation was based on particular works' data, a reasonably wide cross-section of schedulers would be required to test the system effectively. Therefore two schedulers each were supplied from another two works of the BSC together with the two from the simulated plant. Prior to the trial each scheduler was given a detailed document listing the objectives of the trial, a description of the steelworks simulated and an introduction to the display system to be used.

Due to administrative reasons it was considered impractical to use a fully balanced experimental design and so each pair of schedulers attended for one week and carried out the following programme:

Day	a.m.	p.m.
1	Introduction	Equipment familiarization and training
2	Training	Run 1, Subject 1
3	Run 2, Subject 2	Run 3, Subject 1
4	Run 4, Subject 2	Debriefing

In this way the simulation was run continuously. Thus, as in the real situation, the conditions left by one scheduler acted as the starting conditions for the man on the next run.

As the time base of the simulation could be varied, it was possible in the early stages of training to slow down or halt the exercise to discuss the situation and any potential problems. In this way it was possible to describe the facilities provided without completely disrupting the simulation. It was also found useful when explanations of the simulation rules were required (see Appendix 1).

Each scheduler was given a full trial shift using all the facilities. The experimental runs were started only when schedulers were completely familiar with the system. These runs, which were scored, were started on a real time base, but the schedulers soon required the simulation to be speeded up. It has been discovered in preliminary experiments that a rate of $2\frac{1}{2}$ times real time did not impose any artificial time stress on the schedulers and so this was set as a maximum. In the real situation, periods of inactivity would be utilized for informal communication and social interaction.

During the 12 shifts the computer continuously recorded all the schedulers' game-playing and other activities. This was printed out at the end of each shift and a typical example of a trial sequence is shown in Appendix 2. A written record was also taken by the heater controller of all actions performed by the scheduler. These notes were later analyzed and used to improve the design of particular formats and modifications were made to the more ambiguous or complicated touch sequences.

The subjective opinions of the schedulers and their comments on the applicability of such a system in their work situation were also recorded.

7. Discussion of Results

It can be seen from Table 1 that, apart from the one particular exception, the number of ingots rolled on each shift was higher, in some instances significantly so, than the average production figure of 190 per shift. The average number of ingots rolled in the simulation was 210 per shift compared with 190 per shift for a similar period in real life. Although this increase of 10·5% is significant, it must be stressed that comparison with real-life figures can often be misleading. The major problem associated with this type of comparison is selecting representative production figures that are completely typical of actual steelworks operation. There rarely exists a period in a steelworks where all manufacturing units are acting normally at the same time so that comparison between simulation data and real life tends to be unrealistic. However, these comparisons are necessary, and so the period chosen for comparison in this exercise was the same period from which the simulation data were obtained.

Table 1. Results of simulation trials

Shift	Scheduler	Ingots rolled	Ingots charged	Cold ingots charged
1	1	171	206	31
2	2	204	206	42
3	1	211	199	26
4	2	221	222	16
5	3	191	168	32
6	4	209	246	64
7	3	220	192	20
8	4	193	215	32
9	5	222	247	32
10	6	236	212	39
11	5	224	214	42
12	6	216	232	41

An interesting point that is illustrated from Table 1 is the difference in performance between the subjects. Schedulers 1 and 2 rolled an average of 202 ingots per shift whilst 3 and 4 averaged 203 ingots per shift. The biggest improvement, however, came from schedulers 5 and 6 who sent an average of 224 ingots per shift to the rolling mill. This difference between schedulers was entirely expected as schedulers 5 and 6 were from the plant under simulation and were therefore very familiar with the geographical constraints of the system simulated, aware of the scheduling rules and had a very detailed knowledge of the operations in the soaking pit area. Consequently, their performance was well above that of the other schedulers, indicating the potential cost benefits associated with systems of this type involving experienced operators with sophisticated computer aiding.

Table 1 also shows the total number of ingots charged on each shift and the number of ingots charged from the cold stockpile. There was a noticeable overall increase in cold charging (nearly 8% up on real figures) and this indicates that an even larger increase in pit output could have been obtained had more hot steel been produced by the melting shop.

Table 2 shows the relationship between oversoak and mill delays and this illustrates the difference in strategies used by the different schedulers. Clearly, an optimum level of oversoaking and mill delay allows not only a continuous flow of ingots to the mill to be maintained but also provides sufficient flexibility to cope with varying mill and heating requirements.

Table 2. Relationship between oversoak and mill delays

Shift	Scheduler	Not hot delays (min)	Oversoak pit (min)
1	1	80	495
2	2	8	705
3	1	62	750
4	2	47	330
5	3	54	510
6	4	48	0
7	3	21	405
8	4	67	360
9	5	15	1080
10	6	3	780
11	5	10	720
12	6	3	1120

The three groups of schedulers placed emphasis on different aspects of the problem. Schedulers 1 to 4 attempted to minimize oversoaking and this policy on occasions led to periods where no hot steel was available to roll (called 'not hot' delays). Subjects 5 and 6, in contrast, tended to build up large oversoaks in order that the mill could be kept running when available to do so. There is obviously a time when the cost of the extra oversoaking (*i.e.* increased heating cost, loss of yield due to scaling and the cost of pit congestion) outweighs the saving associated with continuous mill operations. It is hoped that before a computer system of this type were to be introduced, a detailed study of the cost advantages of these different strategies would be undertaken.

The overall comparison between the not hot delays achieved in the simulation and real life showed an improvement of 34%. Clearly not all the not hot delays that are incurred in real life represent completely lost time, as routine maintenance is carried out in the mill during these periods. This improvement is large enough, however, to suggest that significant savings in mill running costs could be obtained using a system of this type. This fact, and the reduction of 22% in oversoak, suggest that whatever the input and output constraints, scheduling has been considerably improved.

During the trial a continuous record was taken of each scheduler's game-playing activities. A typical trial sequence and explanation is shown in Appendix 2. Table 3 is a summary of the game-playing activities which once again illustrates a considerable difference between schedulers.

Table 3. Game-playing activities of schedulers

Scheduler	Trials done, sum of two shifts	Trials accepted, sum of two shifts	Predictions accepted, sum of two shifts
1	135	52	30
2	63	46	34
3	115	32	25
4	116	50	33
5	55	44	35
6	58	48	32

Allowing for the fact that the number of alternatives available is dependent on the number of pits available and the number of casts in the system, the number of trials performed by each subject should be approximately the same. Clearly this is not so, as schedulers 1, 3 and 4 performed considerably more trials than the others. The explanation for this low number of trials for schedulers 5 and 6 is probably that they had the advantage of knowledge of the plant which aided their decision-making. They used this knowledge automatically to reject, before trial, most of the more unlikely arrangements of the parameters. They were also more inclined immediately to charge a pit with an incoming cast as soon as a pit became empty. This of course dramatically reduces the number of alternatives available and hence the number of trials required. This strategy is linked to the overall method of approach of these schedulers to tolerate a high level of oversoak in order that mill delays are drastically reduced. It remains to be seen which strategy is the most economically effective.

Table 3 also shows the number of trials that were carried out for each one accepted. On average, the ratio of trials performed to those accepted was around 1·95 but it varied from 1·25 to 3·60 due to the difference in schedulers' varying strategies. The final column, predictions accepted, gives an indication of the flexibility of the system. As circumstances in the plant change, so trials that have been formulated as acceptable may need to be revised. The difference between columns two and three indicates the number of times that the scheduler was required to change his plans. This type of in-built flexibility is essential if any system of this type is to work in a real environment.

Table 4 shows the total number of pit hours lost per shift and gives another good measure of scheduling performance. As has already been shown, schedulers 5 and 6 were inclined to charge pits as soon as they became available. They rarely fell into the trap of adjacent charging and drawing of the pits and would often alter the drawing sequence to optimize this factor. It is expected that only a short time will be required for the unfamiliar schedulers to reach the same level of performance as the ones with experience and knowledge of the plant. The average time lost was over 8 hours per shift across all the pits, indicating that there was plenty of spare capacity still available had it been required.

Table 4. Under-utilization of pits by schedulers

Shift	Pit hours lost
1	10.30
2	9.35
3	8.45
4	2.55
5	14.45
6	9.30
7	24.50
8	7.20
9	5.30
10	3.35
11	4.25
12	5.25

As has already been noted, the comments of the schedulers concerning certain difficult or ambiguous operations were recorded. These will be used to improve particular display formats and reduce the possibility of incorrect data being entered. The overall opinion of the schedulers was that the system they had used showed distinct advantages over existing manual or paper-work systems. They believed that this system would relieve them of a considerable information handling and manipulation load, so that they would be more free to concentrate on important decision-making.

Although these results must be viewed with all the usual reservations concerning simulation trials, they are encouraging enough to justify progression to the next stage of the research programme, the validation trial. Here the feasibility of the ideas generated in the simulation trial will be tested in a real plant to discover whether the stated economic benefits can be met. Only after this has been completed can one really be certain that the system proposed is likely to meet its estimated financial advantages.

8. Conclusions

The proposed system, when tested in the simulation environment, led to an improvement in performance over the existing scheduling methods. Mill delays and oversoaks were significantly reduced and as a consequence mill output was increased. The results are sufficiently encouraging to proceed to the next stage, the validation trial.

The simulation trial provided a suitable means whereby the scheduler–computer interface could be designed, tested and proved. It is felt that this type of exercise, followed by a validation trial, offers distinct advantages over the method of the direct on-line introduction of some sophisticated computer systems.

The touchwire system proved to be a very effective method of communication between scheduler and computer. The techniques involved in the operation were quickly and easily learnt by the schedulers. They were soon capable of efficiently entering and recalling data held in the computer. It can be noted here that the touchwire display has many advantages over more conventional methods of man–computer communication, not the least of which is to be found in the training area.

The simulation trial highlighted some important omissions in present soaking pit scheduling operations. It is necessary that accurate costing of the different strategies associated with oversoaking and mill stoppages be undertaken before the proposed system is introduced. Only then can the scheduler be in a position effectively to choose between alternatives.

The authors would like to thank the rolling mill managers of the three works for supplying the schedulers who took part in the exercise. Grateful thanks go to these schedulers, without whose help this trial could not have been run. Finally, the authors would like to thank the Ministry of Technology (now the Department of Trade and Industry) and the administrators of Building 123, RAF West Drayton, who allowed the carrying out of this simulation trial.

Appendix 1. Simulation Exercise

Rules and Guidelines

(1) Pits 13–16, 10 ingots maximum.

All other pits, 16 ingots maximum.

(2) Neighbouring pits must not be charged and drawn at the same time. With pits 1–4 and 13–20, two pits must be left between a pit being charged and one being drawn.

(3) When drawing any of pits 12–20, pit 12 to the pit being drawn cannot be charged, *e.g.* pit 17 being drawn, pits 12–17 cannot be charged.

(4) Three cranes may be used for charging or drawing purposes at any one time. Crane drivers to be specified by the scheduler.

(5) When west charger is down, pits 19 and 20 cannot be charged or drawn. Pit 18 may be drawn or charged if maintenance personnel are advised and agree. Give half an hour warning of intent.

(6) If the rolling programme necessitates a change of size in the continuous mill, advice must be sought from the mill as to the length of time required for the change.

(7) Mealtime must be taken between $2\frac{1}{2}$ and $5\frac{1}{2}$ hours after the start of the shift.

(8) Different qualities of ingots charged to a pit must be suitably grouped.

(9) Wherever possible, attempt to charge no more than two qualities to a pit.

(10) Inform the heater of the proposed drawing programme for his evaluation.

Appendix 2. Explanation of a Typical Trial Sequence

The following is a copy of the computer printout which shows a typical game-playing sequence recorded during the simulation trial:

SOAKING PIT SCHEDULING SIMULATION.   TRIALS ANALYSIS SHIFT 6.

	PIT	CAST	NO. INGS.	TIME END SOAK
TRIAL	02	9884	16	07.04
TRIAL	13	9884	10	07.20
ACCPT. TRIAL	13	9884	10	07.20
TRIAL	02	9884	12	07.28
TRIAL	09	9884	12	08.26
TRIAL	15	9884	10	07.26
ACCPT. TRIAL	09	9884	12	08.26
ACCPT. PRED	13	9884	10	08.24
TRIAL	15	9887	10	05.48
TRIAL	02	9887	16	06.07
TRIAL	11	9887	16	06.43
ACCPT. TRIAL	15	9887	10	05.48
ACCPT. TRIAL	11	9887	16	06.43
ACCPT. PRED	09	9884	12	08.40
TRIAL	02	COLD	13	
		COLD	03	12.47
ACCPT. TRIAL	02	COLD	13	
		COLD	03	12.47
ACCPT. PRED	02	COLD	13	
		COLD	03	13.14

The following is a description of its most important features:

(1) The scheduler is occupied with the allocation of incoming cast number 9884. He has pits 02 and 13 empty and so tries these first.

(2) The times are approximately the same, indicating similar pit characteristics, but he decides to select the prediction on pit 13 as this best suits his rolling programme. He then instructs the train and crane drivers accordingly.

(3) Having selected this trial, he is now concerned with the placing of the remaining 12 ingots of cast 9884. He tries the final empty pit and two pits that are due to be drawn in the near future.

(4) He accepts the trial on pit 09 and issues instructions to the train and crane drivers.

(5) After a time, which includes a delay due to a sticking pit cover, the crane driver informs the scheduler that pit 13 is charged. He accepts the prediction on this pit and the computer updates the ready-to-roll estimate based on the recorded track time. It can be seen that, because of the delay in charging, the first estimate of pit ready time is updated by 1 hour. If the delay had occurred before charging, the scheduler could have repeated the trial to obtain a more up-to-date prediction. He could then have decided if this arrangement still best suited his projected requirements.

(6) The next cast due to arrive is 9887 and, as this is a short track-time cast, he will be keen to charge the cast to pits as quickly as

possible. He repeats the procedure shown for the previous cast and allocates 10 ingots to pit 15 and 16 ingots to pit 11.

(7) He is then told that the remainder of cast 9884 has been charged to pit 09 and so he transforms the dotted line to a full line on the EDD by accepting the prediction.

(8) As no more casts are due to arrive in the near future and pit 02 is still available, he consults the cold stock list and charges two batches of cold ingots of different qualities to this pit.

Appendix 3. Simulation Software and Hardware System

By P. G. Cole

Software Systems Division, Plessey Electronics Group, West Drayton

The System

A diagram of that part of the Building 123 system used for this simulation is shown in Figure 9 and a description of the function of the hardware involved is given below.

(1) The simulation was based on two Plessey XL2 ($2K$) 36-bit word computers (1.1 and 1.2) interfacing with each other via a common store.

(1.1) The program contained in this computer performed the following tasks:
   (a) Drive for the scheduler's touchwire display.
   (b) Calculations of soaking times for pits based on stored pit characteristics.
   (c) Update of various information required by the scheduler.
   (d) Transfer of data to the common store for use by the other computer (1.2) in updating the EDD.
   (e) Storage of data necessary for off-line analysis of a simulation run.

(1.2) The second computer supplied the remaining features of the simulation as follows:
   (a) Using information formed and stored in the other computer (1.1) for generation of the analogue display of the EDD.
   (b) Transfer of data to the common store for use by 1.1. in providing information on pits, *etc.*
   (c) Drive for the controller's touchwire display.
   (d) Storage of data necessary for off-line analysis of the simulation runs.

(2) The simulation also utilized four separate $1K$ central stores which contained the following:

(2.1) Constants for generating the various frames in the touchwire sequences used by the scheduler's and controller's touchwire displays.

(2.2) Information built up during the simulation run by both computers and later used for off-line analysis.

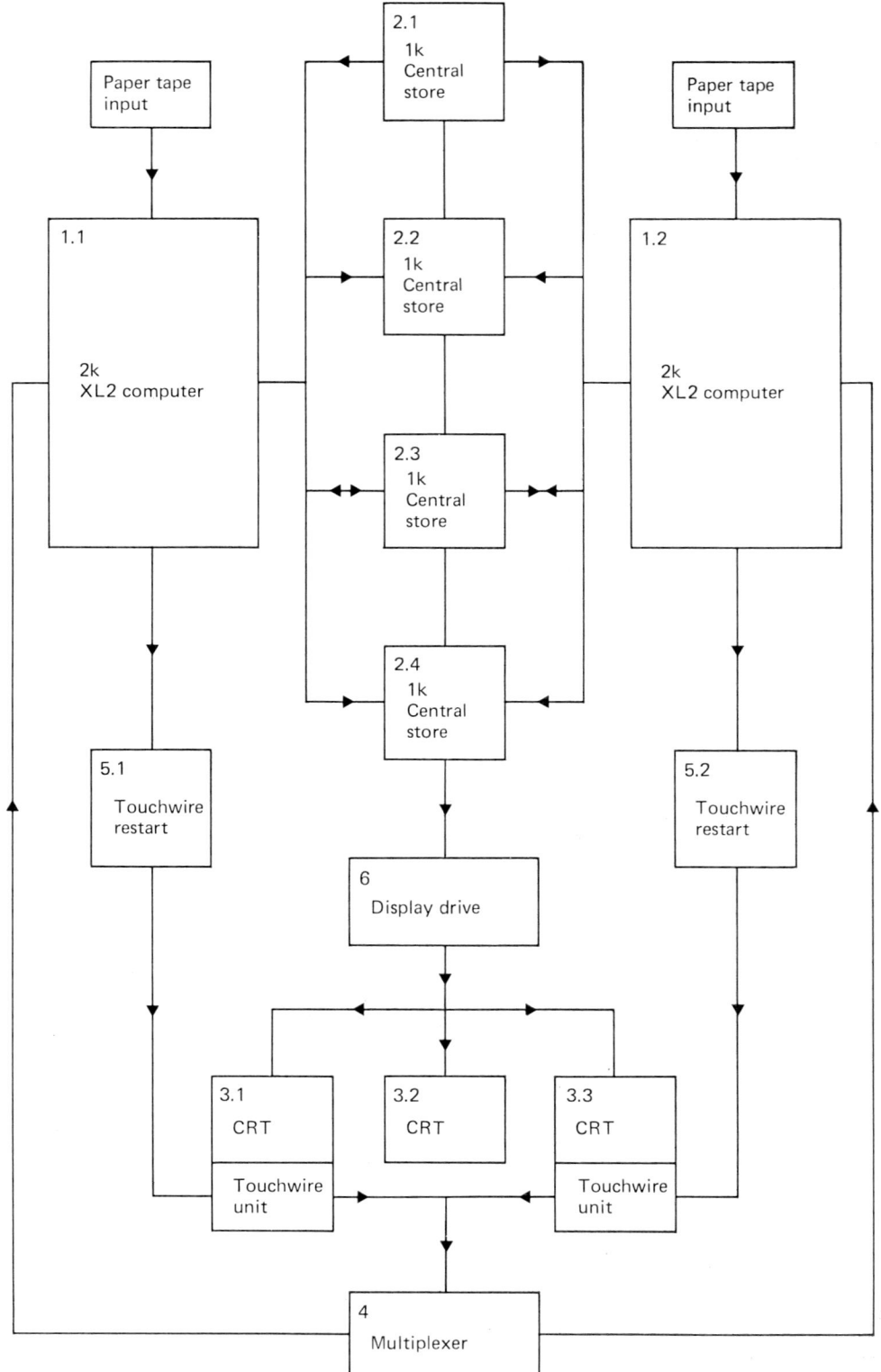

Figure 9. Computer system used in simulation trials.

(2.3) Data used by both computers for
  (a) Generating the information lists of the touchwire displays.
  (b) The analogue displays on the EDD.
  (c) The constants required for the heating model.
  (d) Information concerning all casts used throughout the simulation runs.

(2.4) Information currently displayed on the three displays. This store was updated by both computers and was used in conjunction with the display drive unit (6) to generate the required frames of the EDD and touchwire displays.

(3) The three displays used in the simulation were 625-line TV monitors. The tubes were of a reasonably long persistence giving a flicker-free display. The cycle time for the displays was $12\frac{1}{2}$ per second.

(3.1) The scheduler's touchwire display (see Figures 2 and 5) had three lines of six touchwires and a further 10 lines for information purposes only.

(3.2) The EDD presented a maximum of 23 lines of information concerning the contents of various pits and a further line giving the simulation time scale for up to 12 hours in advance.

(3.3) The controller's display (see Figure 8) was similar in layout to 3.1.

(4) The multiplexer was used to store a schedule bit and wire code for each of the touchwire displays. The schedule bit was set on release of the touchwire and the five-bit code, giving a maximum of 32 touchwire codes, was read whenever the schedule bit was recorded.

(5) The touchwire re-start which cancelled the schedule bit in 4, was initiated whenever a code was read and the appropriate programming action taken. Each touchwire unit had its own discrete re-start, *i.e.* 5.1 and 5.2.

(6) The display drive was capable of driving four separate displays and displaying on a TV raster with a maximum of 102 lines of 59 characters each, the maximum number of lines on each display being 25. The 64 different characters formed using a 7 by 5 matrix include alpha and numeric characters and selected symbols. In the simulation two displays of 19 lines each (the touchwire displays) and one of 24 lines (the EDD) were generated.

The Program

The computer program and the data required to generate the initial pictures were loaded in by paper tape. The simulation speed was selected using the keys provided on the computer console and could, at any time during the run, be varied.

The program can conveniently be divided into three parts as follows:

(1) The major part filled one XL2 computer and drove the scheduler's touchwire display. There were five sequences provided for the scheduler, giving the facilities listed in the main report. These sequences were all provided with a means of back-tracking to the previous frame in the sequence and rejecting the input completely if so desired.

On initiation of the executive (enter) touchwire the data input during the sequence was packed into two 36-bit words and transferred to the common store area from where it could be accessed for use in updating the analogue display. Checks were imposed on all sequences in order to guarantee the validity of the final input.

Various inputs needed for analysis were packed, as mentioned above, and sent to a central store. At the end of a simulation run a further program was loaded into one of the XL2 computers to decode this information and print out the sequences in the format shown in Appendix 2.

(2) The second part of the program generated the analogue display from data held in the common store. Regeneration of this display occurred whenever a change to the display format was necessary following a touchwire input or a time scale update. The following inputs necessitated a change in the display:

- (a) Accept trial—would display the information as a prediction, *i.e.* a dotted line, in order of ready-to-roll time.
- (b) Accept prediction—would convert the dotted line to a solid line and re-shuffle if necessary.
- (c) Cancel prediction—would cancel the appropriate dotted line prediction and re-shuffle the remaining lines.
- (d) Repeat prediction—would re-shuffle the display and if the difference in ready-to-roll time were sufficiently large, display the repeated prediction in a new position.
- (e) Empty pit—would remove the solid line or oversoaks associated with a pit when it had been emptied, and then re-shuffle the display.

The display updated every 15 minutes of simulation time, so reducing the lengths of both solid and dotted lines with the exception of delayed predictions. At the same time the time scale was shifted from right to left across the top of the display by one unit.

(3) The other major section of the program was responsible for driving the controller's touchwire display. There were three sequences provided for the controller giving the following facilities:

- (a) CASTS—provided the facility to input the next cast in the system, to inject delays of varying lengths onto any cast in the manufacturing process, and to reduce the total of ingots in a cast because of stickers in the stripping bay.
- (b) PIT NO.—gave the controller the facility to empty and fill pits on instruction from the heater.
- (c) FAILURE—allowed one or more of six failures to be displayed on the scheduler's alarm line, *e.g.* mill down.

Once again checks were imposed on all these sequences. At the end of each simulation run the common data held in the central store were dumped onto paper tape and re-loaded for the next run. This enabled the next shift to start with the conditions left at the end of the previous shift.

Analytical Techniques in Training Design*

By K. D. DUNCAN

Department of Psychology, University of Hull

1. Describing Human Performance

To begin at the beginning, consider how the performance of an industrial task may be described. In the pharmaceuticals industry the task of 'analgesic compounding' consists of operations such as weighing ingredients, tumble-mixing the ingredients, and granulation. (The familiar aspirin tablet is one of many produced in this way.) Taking just one of these operations, weighing ingredients, one could and, for training purposes, probably should redescribe it, in terms of the selection of a container, use of the weighing machine, selection of a scoop and one could even specify the approximate number of scoops of the various ingredients which would be necessary. In fact, this would not be simple because the ingredient powders change considerably in density. One could go further and specify hand movements such as pick up scoop, place in bin, transport to container drum, and so forth, although probably few training officers would go this far. They would implicitly or explicitly recognize that few, if any, novices need detailed explanations of how to handle a scoop.

Implicitly or explicitly the training officer would select a level of description which appears to be appropriate. Sometimes this may be a rather gross account of performance. For instance, describing the duties of a hall porter might entail no more detail than the statements that he must, for example, call taxis, take up and bring down luggage, arrange for early calls, provision of newspapers and tea or coffee in bedrooms. Similarly, the preparation of a simple dish may be adequately stated for training purposes at the recipe level, but in *cordon bleu* cooking, many of the steps in preparing the dish may require extensive redescription of the various sub-routines involved, for example use of a *bain-marie*—but not if the new recruit has been apprenticed to an Escoffier. *So the level of description which is appropriate depends in some way on the task and on the trainee who has to learn to perform it.*

Experimental psychology endorses the view that skilled performance may be observed at many levels of detail. Specifically, the acquisition of skill seems to consist of changes from smaller to larger units of performance. Classical studies of morse telegraphists and typists traced the progress of these skills from operating with single letters, to syllables, to words and eventually to phrases (Bryan and Harter 1899, Book 1908). Anyone who has learned to speak a foreign language will recall the, sometimes painful, progression from halting strings of words, to phrases and sentences. He will, if he listens to a skilled simultaneous translator, be amazed at the lag between the original speech and the translation. This expertise deals in units of three or four sentences, even short paragraphs.

A recent review of the experimental evidence defines the acquisition of skill as dealing with incoming data and outgoing actions in larger units; as the

---

* An expanded version of the paper presented to the N.A.T.O. Conference on The Measurement of Human Resources. Lisbon, 1973.

recognition of sequences of events and the establishing of performance routines. Commenting on the classical research, the author notes that these pioneers did not pursue in detail the central problem of *how* higher units are formed out of lower units (Welford 1968). Indeed, successive generations of pure and applied psychologists have only rarely gone beyond recognizing the problem and, as is the irritating way of central problems, it remains central.

There have been notable exceptions. Annett and Kay (1956) have persuasively argued that skill involves perceiving the redundancy in series of events which enables larger performance sequences to be organized. G. A. Miller, Galanter and Pribram (1960) proposed that a higher unit may drive one or more lower units, whilst testing for a mismatch between an actual and a model state of affairs. Depending on the mismatch there may be more or less *activity* by the lower units and, since the lower units are also model-matching devices, there may be more or less *variety* of observed behaviour until the controlling mismatch is removed.

Now variation of performance with a constant outcome, in other words, flexibility or adaptability, is a characteristic, some would say *the* characteristic, of skilled performance. So Miller, Galanter and Pribram's suggestion of how lower units are organized into higher units is an appealing one.

Everyday observation, laboratory studies, theories of skilled performance, all suggest that, if task analysis is to be a serious practical enterprise, it must deal with the level of description problem. An adequate method must also recognize the associated problem of how smaller units of performance are organized into larger and characteristically cohesive, purposive units of performance. In short, it should be no surprise if the classical molar-molecular controversy in psychology proved difficult to escape in the applied field.

That skilled performance may be described at several levels of detail is recognized by a number of writers on task analysis (King 1964, Folley 1964a, Smith 1964, Mager and Beach 1967). Some specify how many levels of description are to be employed. Thus Smith (1964) proposes *four* levels of description, namely *jobs*, e.g. motor mechanic, *duties*, e.g. tuning the motor, *tasks*, e.g. adjusting the carburettor, removing, cleaning, adjusting or replacing spark plugs, and *elements*, e.g. turning a screwdriver adjustment anticlockwise. Mager and Beach (1967) distinguish *three* levels of description which they name *vocations*, e.g. painter, X-ray technician, landscape gardener, *tasks*, e.g. preparing a surface, mixing paint and *steps in performing a task*, e.g. selecting appropriate paint, removing old finish. Again, Seymour (1966) is very explicit. One must choose a *single* level of analysis, " To prevent confusion a uniform level of breakdown must be maintained ". He cites three levels from which one can be chosen for most purposes (Crossman 1956d, Seymour 1954, 1959).

The T.W.I. (Training Within Industry) Job Breakdown, perhaps the most widely-used method in Britain, ignores the problem or leaves the level of description to the discretion of the analyst. The T.W.I. scheme assumes that supervisors can be trained to collect adequate data for industrial training by listing in a table the operations in a task and in a separate column commenting on any relevant difficulties which they encounter or anticipate that a novice will have to overcome.

If, then, the problem is recognized, there is no general agreement as to the terms for designating different levels of description, nor as to the number to be employed, although a *fixed* number is generally assumed. The several levels of description which have been proposed are at best exemplified rather than defined.

Between the most general statements of procedure and the language of physiology or anatomy there are *in principle* an indefinite number of levels of description which will clearly be difficult to limit or specify. It will later be argued that this should not be attempted, but rather that a method of analysis is needed which is flexible, which varies the level of description *in the same task* and which does so on some systematic basis. First, however, it is necessary briefly to discuss 'part-task training', to which advocates of task analysis are almost invariably committed in one way or another.

2. Part-Task Training

Parts and Wholes

Applied psychologists in Britain have used part-task training methods for a variety of reasons. Both King (1964) and Seymour (1966) advocate designing training programmes in which each part of the task can be practised from the outset at the operational speed. This is claimed to promote confidence as well as enhanced effort from realistic goal setting.

Other part-task training schemes have achieved substantial reductions in training time by reducing complex tasks to components which are manageable by the novice. Thus trainee shoe-machinists were first exercised in positioning, guiding and controlling the machine. These operations were then combined in stitching exercises without thread. Finally, stitching with thread on fibre components was practised until mastery of the whole machining task was achieved. In this way, a course in elementary machining was reduced from one year to eight weeks (Singleton 1959).

Whole-task training may be inefficient for another reason. Seymour (1966) has shown that in a variety of short-cycle, usually repetitive, tasks, certain components are more difficult than others and more importantly are more susceptible to training. The level of description employed is that of work study, for example, the speed and accuracy of the 'position' element in tasks like capstan lathe operation improve considerably with practice, whereas the 'move' element improves comparatively little. Thus, part-task training concentrating on those elements of the task which most improve with practice is more efficient than simply practising the whole task. Similarly, packers of wood screws can work more quickly if they can pick up a gross of screws at a time. By concentrating practice on judging the feel of a number of screws held in the hand, Seymour was able to reduce the training time from 26 to less than 10 weeks (Seymour 1959).

Some of the success of part-task training may be attributable to the reduction in errors which it makes possible. Errors, particularly early in training, may be difficult to eradicate, especially in the older trainee (Kay 1951, von Wright 1957), although some older trainees *prefer* to learn the whole, or at least, prefer longer periods of practice (Belbin *et al.* 1964). Error avoidance by reducing the task to more manageable components is a simple, but perhaps not the only, mechanism involved.

A favoured form of part-task training is the *cumulative part method*, one feature of which is that the parts receive differing amounts of practice. Welford

(1968), citing classical work, has pointed out that the extent to which an item has been learnt can serve as a distinguishing cue during recall. This effect might have reduced confusions in a Post Office sorting task, in which some 600 associations were mastered by cumulative part-training (Belbin *et al.* 1964). It might also have contributed to the procedure learning by fading of prompts which is discussed later in this paper. (Although derived from the operant conditioning paradigm, retrogressive chaining is nonetheless a cumulative part method and the inherent differential practice of items tends to be ignored by reinforcement interpretations (Duncan 1971a).)

Two *caveats* usually figure in the part-task training debate. The trainee may learn an ideal way to perform a part in isolation, which is far from ideal when it is performed in the whole task. This may happen in speed skills (Crossman 1959). Secondly, many tasks require difficult co-ordination of their components, such that the operator has to distribute his attention efficiently between them, or to perceive essential relations between them. Clearly these tasks must be practised as a whole to a large extent, but whether *any* degree of part-task training would be inefficient is debatable. It has been argued that the superiority of the whole method of training is a function of task complexity (Briggs and Naylor 1962, Naylor and Briggs 1963), but whether tasks in general can be ordered on a single dimension of 'complexity' seems doubtful.

Category-Specific Training

To the foregoing reasons for part-task training must be added another which has been a major subject of debate and controversy for over a decade. This is the appealing view that skilled performance is a 'many-splendoured thing', that the parts of tasks should be classified into psychologically different types or categories in order to identify appropriate training methods and conditions. Surely, task analysis *should* be a technique not simply for deciding what the task consists of, but also for determining, as directly as possible, what different *kinds* of training are required.

It does not seem likely that the best training methods for erecting scaffolding will be the same for the inspection routines of the quality control supervisor, or for the co-ordination of procedure and decision-making by the air traffic controller. On the other hand, it does seem plausible that the formal similarities between the skill of a doctor and a radio repairman—symptom interpretation, search, component adjustment, replacement and repair—should require essentially similar training techniques. Manifestly the *content* of training would differ, but it seems reasonable to expect instructional *method* which succeeds with electronic troubleshooting to be equally successful with medical diagnosis. It would be extremely helpful if one could add to statements of bare performance requirements the most effective training techniques for each of them. The *rationale* of task analysis should amount to more than the tautology that to learn a task entails practising its components.

Fortunately this view is well documented, *e.g.* Gagné (1965b), R. B. Miller (1963). What now follows, therefore, is only a comment on the general difficulties and promise of the taxonomic approach. In particular, the methods of 'micromotion study' and 'behavioural analysis' will be considered, since both have aroused the interest of British applied psychologists and both have been influential in their different ways.

Micromotion Study

Seymour's demonstration of the increased efficiency of part-task training used items in Gilbreth's list of movement elements which, *prima facie*, seems a convenient way of describing many sorts of performance. The therbligs of micromotion study with the associated techniques of observation, such as cine-photography with camera speeds in the order of a thousand frames per minute, constitute perhaps the first serious attempt at a taxonomy of naturally occurring human performance in real-life situations. Most science and technology must begin with some agreed methods of classifying and describing data, so it is important to be clear about our objections to Gilbreth's attempt. The therbligs seem to have been adumbrated in a rather *ad hoc* fashion, but, more seriously, they do not turn out to be the ultimate elements of performance which were intended. It is difficult to discern any *rationale* in a scheme which treats as elements such diverse categories as ' transport loaded ', ' rest ', ' use ' and perceptual elements like ' search ' or ' inspect ' which vary greatly in their complexity, not least in the training problems they pose.

Nevertheless, it is a pity that subsequent generations of work study practitioners have not pursued the line of Gilbreth but, as Conrad (1951) pointed out, in practice have mostly reverted to the Taylor tradition of time study, developing, for example, the various methods-time-measurement schemes, with their absurd assumptions about average man, average effort and combinations of sophisticated statistical procedures with subjective ' allowances ' as large as 30% of movement time in some schemes (*e.g.* for ' difficulty ' or ' rest '). All this takes no account of the planned, organized nature of skilled performance, a difficulty to which Gilbreth's scheme drew attention and again, unlike Gilbreth, either ignores perceptual activities or, as Conrad puts it, assumes that perception takes place at the speed of light.

It was to be expected that, with the movement away from short-cycle repetitive tasks in industry, Gilbreth's *techniques* would be abandoned, but his *approach* has been abandoned too. In consequence a profession, who *by their day to day experience*, are well placed to contribute to the development of a useful classification of human performance, are now unlikely to do so. How many psychologists, in the latter half of the twentieth century, are as close to man in his work place or in the instructional situation, that is as close to the natural phenomena which must be classified, as was the early eighteenth century Swedish naturalist Charles de Linné?

The problems to be overcome by a psychological Linnaeus are formidable. As in any science two systematic criteria should ideally be met, namely, that the categories should be *mutually exclusive* and *exhaustive*. It is questionable whether they have been met in the various attempts at a workable taxonomy. Cotterman (1959), E. E. Miller (1963), Stolurow (1964), and Gagné (1965a, 1965b) have all attempted to meet the criterion that categories should be mutually exclusive by careful formal definition. The second systematic criterion, exhaustiveness of the list of categories, has been dealt with in two main ways. An approach taken by Cotterman (1959) and Stolurow (1964) was to carry out massive surveys of the range of tasks in the learning and training research literature. Folley (1964b) and E. E. Miller (1963) adopted another, less effortful, expedient of including a catch-all category defined to to include any behaviour not otherwise classified.

Meeting the systematic criteria, it should be added, is desirable, rather than a *sine qua non*. A scheme which does not meet them can be extremely useful as an *aide-mémoire*, as a device for retrieving information from the experimental literature when confronted with a task which the analyst feels in his bones has features which have been previously researched. But the systematic criteria are desirable, because they should enable the good agreement between independent analysts specifying training for the same job which one would expect of an adequate taxonomy. Of the many advocates of task analysis, Stolurow (1964) was probably the first to attempt to assess the *reliability* of his scheme. Stolurow had eight psychologists, all distinguished in the training research field, independently analyze descriptions of tasks taken from the 'method' sections of journal articles. Their lack of agreement was impressive, especially when one considers the material they were asked to classify. More studies of this kind, using descriptions of real-life tasks, are badly needed, since no method, however valid on logical grounds or in the light of research, will be empirically valid unless it is reliable.

Clearly, the major criterion to be met by a satisfactory taxonomy is a set of categories which have demonstrably different optimum learning conditions. Among the first to attempt to define such categories were psychologists who applied 'behavioural analysis' to instructional problems.

Behavioural Analysis

The contribution to task analysis directly and indirectly by Skinner should never be ignored. A direct contribution has been Skinner's unrelenting insistence on the need to specify entry and terminal behaviour, the responses already 'in the repertoire' and the responses which will define mastery. This in turn directs attention to the problem of how the student progresses from the one to the other. For Skinner this is a matter of 'shaping', that is selectively reinforcing the variety of responses which are initially emitted (to use his language) and in this way shifting the pattern of responses by successive approximation towards the behaviour which constitutes mastery of the task.

Whether or not shaping is an appropriate or useful model for instruction and training of the human subject is controversial. It has been pointed out (notably by Lumsdaine 1962 and Cook 1963) that the programmer of instructional material is mostly preoccupied with how to *elicit* responses, rather than with reinforcing *emitted* responses, which seems to correspond less to Skinner's *operant* conditioning than to classical *respondent* conditioning. Nevertheless, an important indirect influence of Skinner has been the applications to training of 'behavioural analysis' (*e.g.* Gilbert 1962, Mechner 1965, 1967).

The behavioural analysts' prescriptions of training *régimes* distinguish sharply between different kinds of learning. This is well illustrated in their treatment of conceptual learning and serial learning, for which the learning conditions differ and indeed are specific to these categories. The starting point for conceptual learning is the familiar operational definition of generalization within a class and discrimination between classes. The specific learning conditions require a set of stimuli or exemplars to which the learner must make the same response, e.g. ' indicative mood ' or ' organic compound ', and also a set of stimuli which the novice may mistakenly take as exemplars and to which he must learn to make alternative responses, e.g. ' subjunctive mood ' or ' inorganic compound '. The approach is well illustrated by Mechner's (1965) analysis of the perceptual skill of interpreting electrocardiograph traces which requires the diagnostician to recognize and distinguish between, for instance, patterns of infarction and ischaemia.

Many people would take issue with this view of conceptual learning, namely, that the only conditions require the preparation of an inventory of exemplars and non-exemplars, the view, to quote Mechner and Cook (1964), that " a concept is defined in terms of its instances, members and manifestations ... Behavioural analysis of a concept lists appropriate instances and non-instances". It can obviously be argued that the learner might learn a rule which defines whether some given instance is or is not a member of a particular category, or in the case of complex concepts, that the learner must both distinguish relevant attributes and master a combination rule (Haygood and Bourne 1965). The point being made, however, is that precise, category-specific conditions for conceptual learning are postulated, not that they are necessarily correct.

Gilbert's (1962) well-known proposal that invariant series of responses, or in Skinnerian language ' chains ', are best learned retrogressively is important for the same reason. Again, category-specific learning conditions are postulated, with the result that, not only is the particular assertion subjected to empirical test, but also that other workers become interested in the question of how instruction of invariant series of responses is best managed. Gilbert's (1962) argument for retrogressive chaining is apparently that, at the beginning of an exercise, the last response in a chain is the one which will most readily be strengthened or reinforced since it is closest to the reinforcing influence of completing the chain. Once learned, performance of the last response itself becomes a reinforcing event, thus its immediate predecessor in the series is the response which may next be most readily reinforced. This response in turn becomes a reinforcing agent and so on.

The learning sequence for a chain of responses numbered 1 to 10 would first practise 10, then 9 and 10, then 8, 9 and 10, and so on. Retrogressive chaining is therefore a ' cumulative part ' method. However, it should be noted that the technique described by Gilbert (1962) and Mechner (1967) would initially prompt performance of the whole chain, or a substantial part of it, then gradually ' fade ' prompts retrogressively. Whatever the merits may be of the retrogressive chaining notion, the associated *technique* of prompting and fading of prompts during learning is in itself attractive, since it minimizes errors and, it might be argued, is for that reason rewarding for the learner.

The retrogressive chaining principle aroused considerable interest, indeed one text, addressed *inter alia* to student teachers, cites Gilbert's illustration of retrogressive chaining applied to the learning of long division as an example of how laboratory paradigms may be extended to complex human learning (Staats and Staats 1963). Empirical studies, however, have failed to support retrogressive chaining. A progressive learning sequence has been found as good or better for lists of consonants and numbers (Johnson and Senter 1965), for a missile preparation procedure (Cox and Boren 1965), for poetry (Hartley and Woods 1968) and for learning series of instructions for starting up a unit of chemical plant (see Table 1).

Table 1. Mean time, trials and errors under three fading techniques

Fading of prompts	n	Learning			n	Retention errors		
		Time (min)	Trials to criterion	Errors		First test	Second test	Overall
Progressive	14	16·76	14·40	3·68	9	6·11	2·78	4·44
Retrogressive	13	19·66	15·75	5·73	9	5·67	1·44	3·56
Middle-outwards	14	16·94	14·62	3·93	9	3·00	0·89	1·94
Error variance estimate		14·02	4·54	6·50		2·33	2·33	2·33

In this study it was argued that the earlier a response in a series is brought to mastery by fading its prompts, then the more it will be overlearned. In an efficiently-managed programme, the more difficult a response is to learn and retain, the earlier in the programme it should be mastered, that is, have its prompts faded. Other things equal, the nearer a response is to the beginning or the end of a series, the less difficult it should be (Hovland 1938). To maximize overlearning at the end of the series by retrogressive fading of prompts, or at the beginning by progressive fading of prompts, should both be inefficient compared to starting to fade prompts at or near the middle. It was found that the order of fading of prompts had little effect during learning, in terms of time, or trials to criterion, or errors. However, a delayed post-test which consisted of giving subjects the printed lists of instructions to learn for three minutes and then testing them on two occasions, showed significantly fewer relearning errors for fading of prompts from the middle of the list, compared with the retrogressive and progressive fading conditions (Duncan 1971a).

Whilst, then, the training propositions of the behavioural analysts have been challenged, it is important to recognize that their propositions are amenable to empirical test. This, taken with their attempt to formulate analysis in terms of identifying category-specific learning conditions may be attributed, at least in part, to Skinner's commitment to a rather direct extension of principles, developed by laboratory experiment, to the instructional situation and the analysis of human performance in general.

The development of defensible categories of learning and performance is a difficult, but potentially fruitful enterprise. Category-specific training methods, whatever their origin, are probably best regarded as *hypothetical*, as a useful basis for pilot training schemes. This strategy is adopted by the method of task analysis which will now be illustrated.

3. Task Analysis—An Illustration

Progressive Redescription

It will be clear that the method of task analysis which is now described makes many assumptions. To make the account as coherent as possible, discussion of the assumptions is postponed for the moment.

Recognizing that skilled performance can be described at many levels and that the problem is what to record, at what level of description and in what degree of detail, the task is analyzed by a method of progressive redescription. Analysis begins with the most general statement of the task, and determines what subordinate operations are entailed, then the operations they entail and so on. The first stages of the analysis of a continuous process control task are illustrated in Figure 1. This task is chosen as an illustration because its various subordinate operations comprise a range of skilled performance which includes tracking, procedure-following, discrimination, concept attainment and problem-solving. Other tasks which have been analyzed in this way present less variety of components, *e.g.* electrical maintenance of transfer lines, controlling a steel radiator production line, the operation of office printing machines and the legal procedures of ' conveyancing ' when houses are bought and sold—a high-grade clerical skill.

Information recorded is minimized by ceasing analysis whenever the probability, p, of inadequate performance or the costs, c, to the system of inadequate performance are together unacceptable. Alternatively, analysis ceases when the training required for adequate performance is clear.

Although Figure 1 only illustrates the first stages of analysis of this task, further description has already ceased in the case of four subordinate operations. These have been underlined. It is assumed that the trainee operator is probably able to push buttons (operation 139), make a telephone call (operation 169) and learn with acceptable errors to keep the log in his first week in the control room, *i.e.* p is appreciable but c is negligible (operation 8). Fourthly, the training for acceptable performance is clear in the case of operation 160, obtaining a sample at R2 Condenser Drain Valve. The nature of this training will be discussed later, since it is a major requirement for this task, which involves some 130 manually operated valves on open plant. Thus the degree of detail reached, at the point where analysis is broken off, can vary considerably *in the same task*.

Whether or not the rules for analysis which will now be presented are defensible, they are *explicit* and exclude collection of data *ad lib*. Data collection is not analysis. By incorporating p into the rule for analysis, it is recognized that the population of students or trainees is always to a degree ' sophisticated '. The practical problem is to decide which sub-routines they can already perform and which not. Cost, c, as used in the analysis rule, is broadly defined in terms of anything which the system values. It includes costs not only in the sense of financial losses accruing from wastage of material or damage to tools and equipment, but also considered are consequences of performances which might contribute to illness hazards, or which constitute a threat to safety in the workplace, or which affect the demands made on other people elsewhere in the plant. Training in safe practices and training of emergency procedures is not therefore the subject of a separate analysis. Such training should be an integral part of the whole training scheme and not something which is grafted on as an afterthought.

Figure 1 shows only the first stages of analysis. Other representative extracts are discussed later and are illustrated in Figures 3 and 4. The complete hierarchy of operations in this task is shown in Figure 2. The task presents a variety of training problems but, before discussing these, a distinction will be made between *operations* and *plans*.

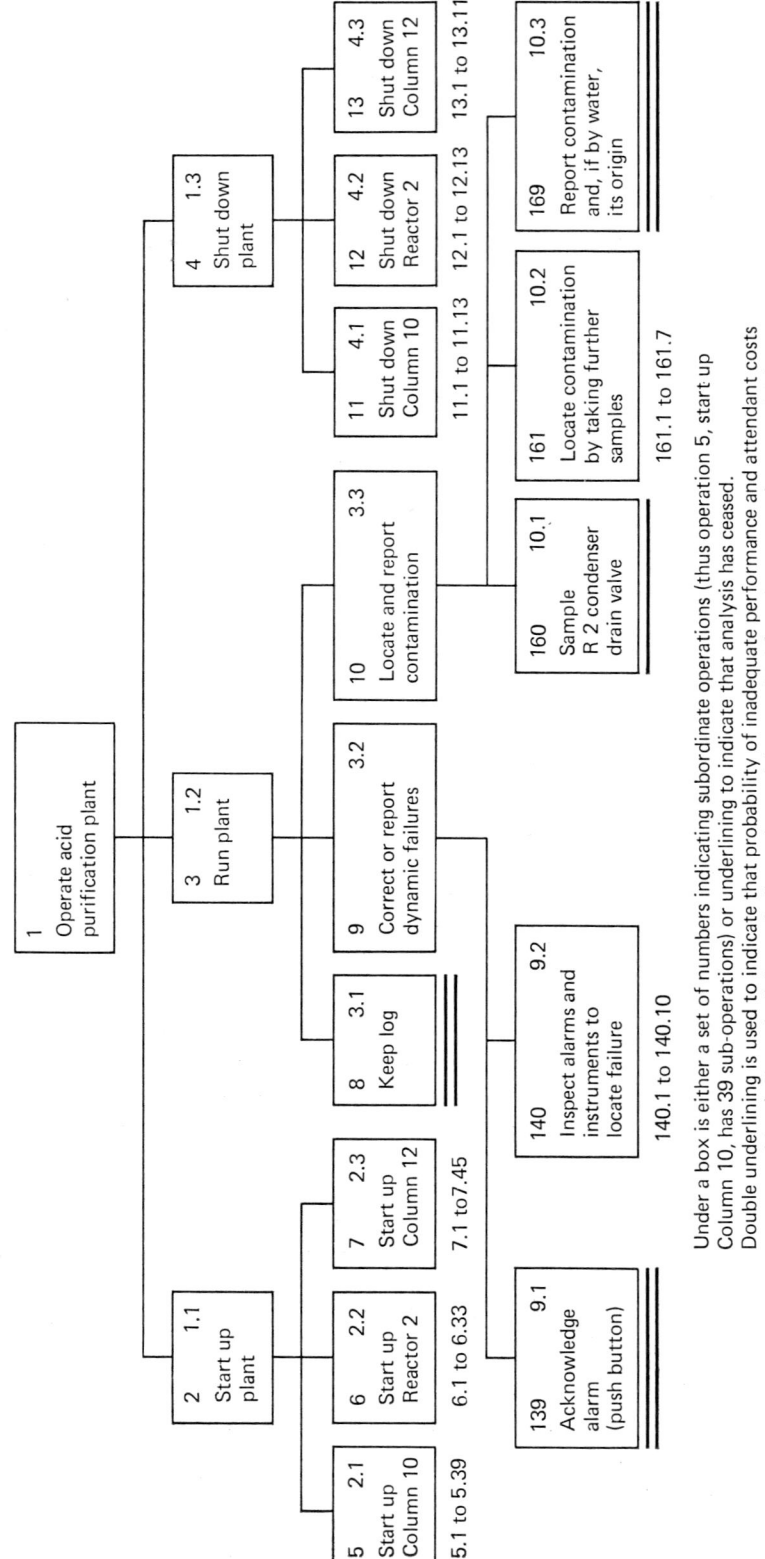

Figure 1. Main operations in the acid purification task.

Analytical Techniques in Training Design 293

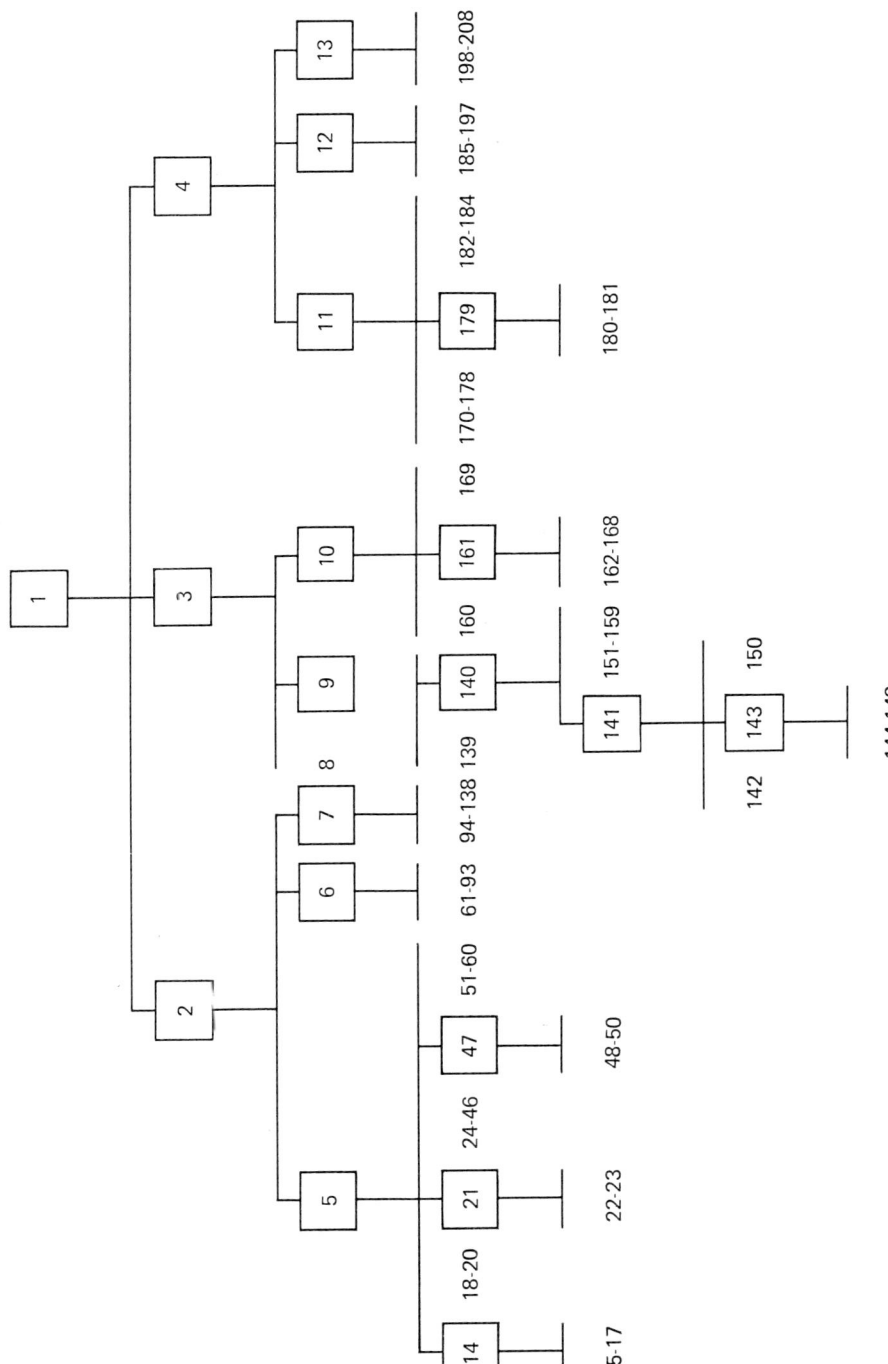

Figure 2. Box diagram indicating hierarchy of all operations recorded in the acid purification process control task.

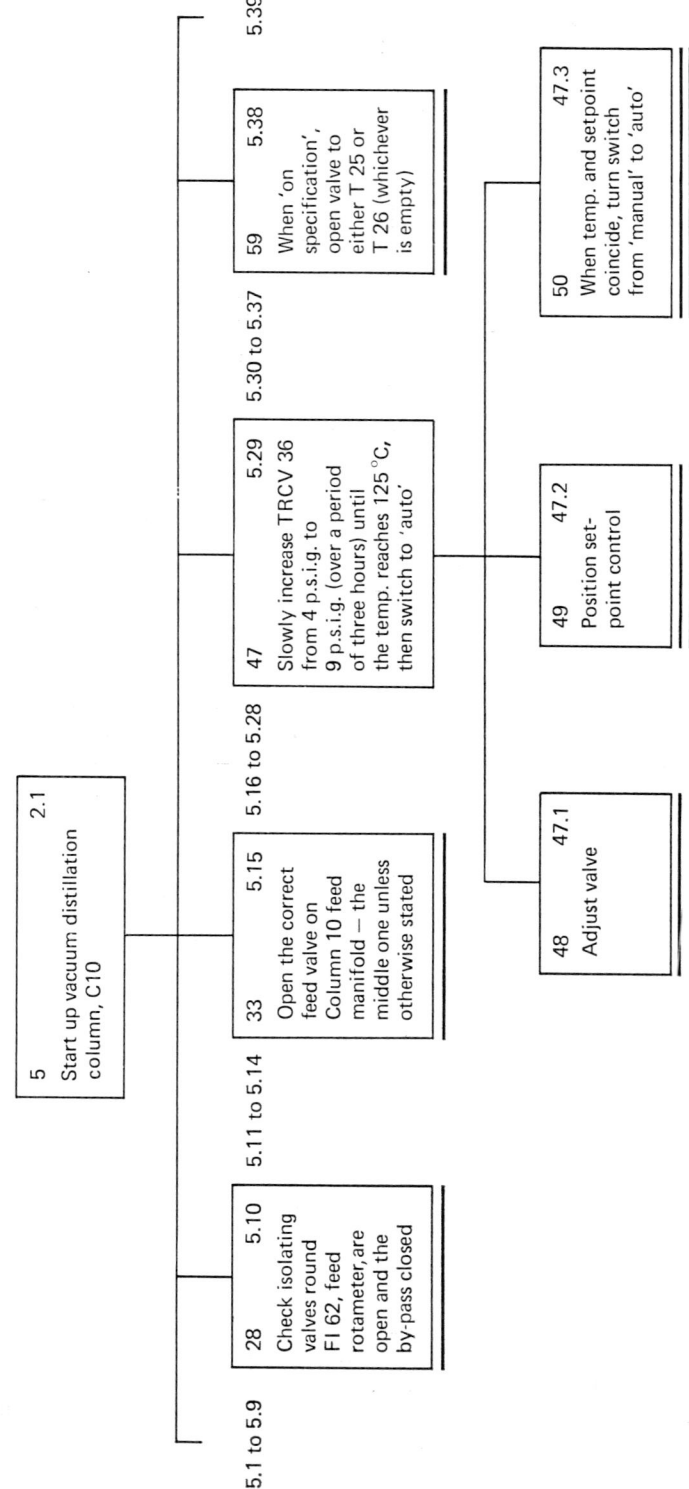

Figure 3. Representative subordinate operations in a startup procedure.

Operations and Plans

To redescribe an operation in terms of its subordinate operations implies a plan. Performance of the task requires that subordinate operations are appropriately *selected* and ordered in *sequences*. A plan is operationally defined in terms of the manner in which subordinate operations are selected and sequenced. A familiar plan is the invariant sequence or procedure. Thus 'starting up Column 10' (operation 5 in Figures 1 and 2) involves not only 39 subordinate operations but also a plan, namely, that these are carried out in a fixed sequence. Representative subordinate operations of this procedure are shown in Figure 3.

Locating contamination (operation 161 in Figures 1 and 2) involves seven subordinate operations, which may be carried out to obtain samples of the product at different points on the plant, and a plan which selects and sequences them. However, this plan will select a varying set of sampling operations and will vary the sequence in which they are carried out in order to locate the source of contamination. Thus if an operation obtains a contaminated sample the next operation would be one which samples further upstream; if the sample obtained were 'clean' one of the operations sampling downstream would follow. An efficient plan would clearly minimize the number of subordinate sampling operations to isolate the sources of contaminant. Representative sampling operations can be seen in Figure 4.

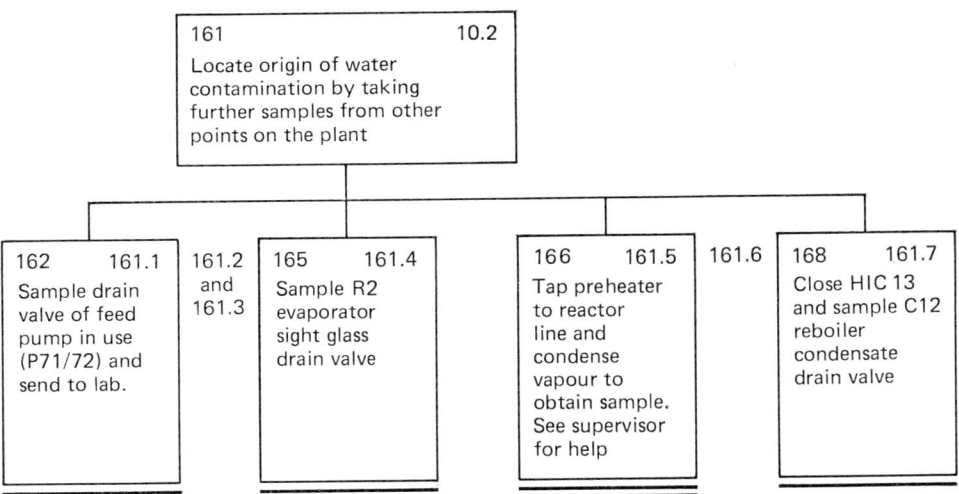

Figure 4. Representative subordinate operations in locating contaminant.

Operations—Plant Valve Discrimination

One difficulty of this task is discriminating the many hand-operated valves on the plant. There are 128 hand-operated valves on the open plant which are not labelled and which must be correctly identified during control of the process. These valves must be distinguished from an extremely cluttered background and from other valves in the vicinity (see Figure 5). The skilled operator apparently identifies a valve from cues in its immediate context such as the configuration of lines, vessels and other plant components. It was therefore decided to use outline drawings of plant, during training, which emphasized these cues for identifying valves (see Figure 6).

Eighty-two of the valves may be classified as 'inlet', 'outlet', 'drain', 'isolating', or 'by-pass' valves, the type or class of valve being defined by its situation

Figure 5. A slave valve and sensing device with by-pass and isolating configurations.
(*Photograph by courtesy of B.P. Chemicals (International) Ltd.*)

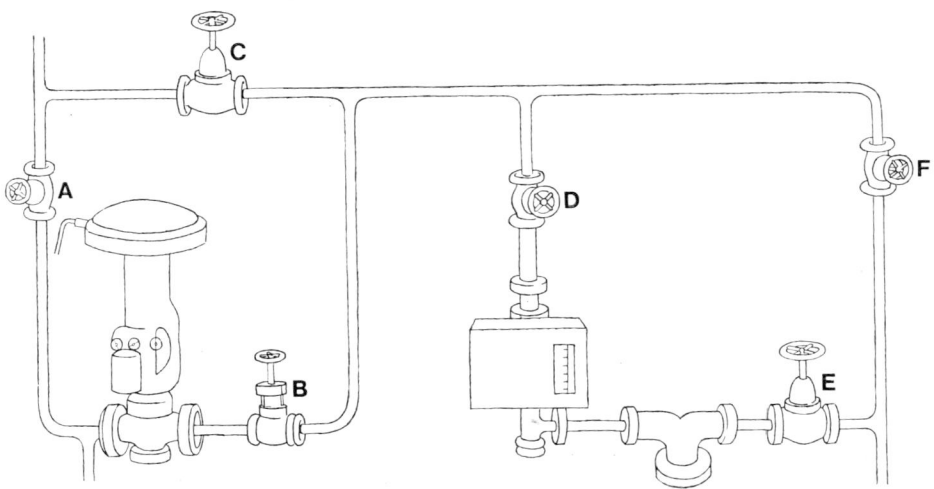

A and B are isolating, C by-pass, valves about the slave valve on the left. D and E are isolating, F by-pass, valves about the sensing device on the right.

Figure 6. Outline drawings of the by-pass and isolating configurations in Figure 5.

in the lines about pumps, automatic flow controllers, or sensing devices (see operation 28 in Figure 3 and operation 162 in Figure 4). Relevant context for these valves is largely determined if novices are trained to generalize within and discriminate between these types or categories. A pump inlet line enters the pump horizontally and the outlet or discharge line leaves it vertically. Application of this rule identifies the inlet valve and the outlet valve about any pump and also the drain valve which is on a branch of the outlet line.

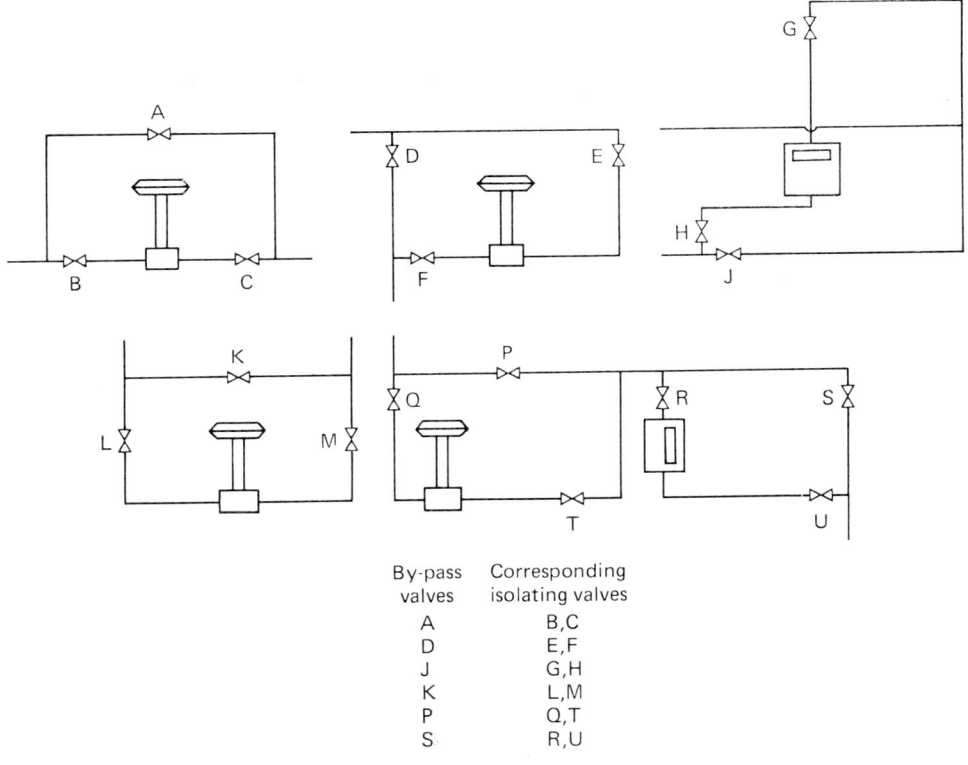

Figure 7. Some by-pass and isolating configurations.

Similarly, relevant context for identifying isolating and by-pass valves consists of plant lines, specifically the by-pass line and the line through the sensing device or flow controller. It is fairly clear in Figure 7 that to open valve A and to close valves B and C would by-pass and isolate the flow controller (which could then, for instance, be removed for servicing). However, training to distinguish between isolating and by-pass valves entails using more exemplars. It is not nearly so clear as to which valve is which in some of the variations of functionally equivalent plumbing which are encountered on the plant, a few of which are represented schematically in Figure 7.

There remain, however, 46 unlabelled hand-operated valves which cannot be classified, but which must nevertheless be correctly identified and, indeed, failure to do so would in some cases prove extremely expensive. It would be possible by operation of valves such as that in operation 59 (Figure 3) mistakenly to route unprocessed acid feed stock to intermediate storage or pure product tanks. It is not easy to recommend efficient training to prevent such errors. If the valves are not labelled, the only training expedient is to ensure overlearning and, in a few cases where this is possible, to draw the trainee's attention to distinctive plant features in the immediate vicinity, for example, the shapes of the reboiler and the evaporator for the sampling operations 165 and 168 (see Figure 4), the position of the feed lines to the distillation column for operation 33 (Figure 3), or, in the case first mentioned, the orientation of the condenser to the reactor (operation 160, Figure 1).

So the proposed training solution of the plant valve discrimination problem is to enable more effective use of intrinsic task information, either in the form of directing the trainee's attention to particular features of the plant or by providing him with conceptual frameworks.

Operations—Console Instrument Locations

Besides discriminating some 130 hand-operated valves on the open plant, the operator must also discriminate between some 50 controls and indicators on an instrument console in the control room. One of these instruments is the temperature recorder-controller, TRC 36, with its steam remote controller, setpoint control and automatic or manual switch (operations 48, 49 and 50 in Figure 3). These control room instruments are labelled, but it is essential for two reasons that the operator has mastered instrument *locations* and does not need to rely on scanning the labels to find one of them. On the one hand, when plant failures occur, he will have very limited time for diagnosis and should not have to waste any of this time searching for an indicator. On the other hand, he must be able to perform extremely quick sequences of console operations in the event of an emergency shutdown of a unit of plant such as a distillation column or a reactor. The costs of inadequate performance, to recall the analysis decision rule, are unacceptable.

Swift location of console instruments seems to be an instance of what, in some taxonomies (Gagné 1965a, 1965b, Gilbert 1962), is called 'multiple discrimination'. The basic requirement for this category of learning is to make the cues distinctive, so emphasis of the position cues was attempted by having trainees practise labelling outline drawings of the instrument console. It was also decided to try to apply a principle, which has been recommended for this kind of learning, namely, grouping potentially confusable cues. This was done by having trainees practise the locations and functions of all flow instruments together, and likewise by grouping practice of all temperature, pressure and level instruments. A comparison study found that practice in labelling outline drawings did indeed enhance learning of instrument locations, but that this application of the grouping principle had no significant effect (Duncan 1969).

Operations—Control Responses

The responses in this task are almost invariably easy, calling for little more than demonstration to a novice. Responses such as ' position setpoint control ' and ' switch from manual to auto ' (operations 49 and 50 in Figure 3) present little difficulty. Similarly, probability of inadequate performance is minute in the *handling* of the 130-odd valve wheels on the open plant—provided that the trainee is told that the valve is closed by turning the wheel clockwise and opened by turning it anticlockwise.

However, operation 48 (Figure 3) is an exception. It is one of two operations in which the response as such presents a training problem (a similar operation is entailed in the startup of Reactor 2, operation 6 in Figure 1). Both operations involve continuous adjustment of a steam valve to increase temperature at an optimum rate. Temperature is displayed by a pen recorder, thus the skill consists in compensatory tracking of an ' acceptable slope ' on the pen record. Limits within which such a slope is acceptable can be defined and demonstrated to the trainee, thus usefully augmenting the intrinsic task information. The main difficulty, however, is the learning of plant dynamics, specifically in learning to correlate valve movements with consequent changes in the temperature pen record. Systematic practice of these two tracking operations on the plant is out of the question and simulation of the display-control relationship could be expensive. However, these operations occur on predictable occasions, i.e. during startup, the course of which is known, and a more economic solution therefore seems to be to have novice operators learn these two operations under the observation and, if necessary, guidance, of an experienced still-man or plant supervisor.

Plans—Procedures

In considering training of the *operations* in this task, the analyst is on fairly familiar ground. This is not the case for some of the *plans*. The point has already been made that several of the plans, those for starting up and shutting down the three principal units of this plant, are the familiar *fixed* sequences or procedures. These plans do not ordinarily present difficult training problems, compared with plans which *vary* the selection and sequence of subordinate operations. Indeed the familiar procedural plan only presents a problem when, as in this task, it is a lengthy sequence. Since fixed sequences of as many as 45 subordinate operations were involved, it was decided to construct job aids for startup and shutdown procedures. The nature of the task is thereby changed, intrinsic task information has been drastically augmented. Information which the trainee might otherwise have to memorize has, as it were, been placed into an external store and a much more realistic training objective of correctly retrieving information from the store has been substituted. Or, at least, mastery of the procedural guides for startup and shutdown of plant is the short-term objective. In the long term it is intended that the trainee should master these long procedures without being dependent on the procedural guide. To this end, the subordinate operations which were seen by experienced operators to go together, were grouped under a relatively small number of headings, e.g. "start feed", "heat the still", "start reflux". It was in fact these functional headings which were learned by subjects in the fading of prompts experiment described earlier.

Plans for Fault Location

Sheer length of sequence aside, fixed-sequence plans will present few difficulties. Rather it is variability in the selection and sequencing of subordinate operations which makes learning a task difficult and which characterizes many sorts of skilled performance. Indeed, one reason for operationally defining the plan in terms of selection and sequencing of subordinate operations is to give the task analyst some practical purchase on a widely recognized feature of skill, namely, that performance can vary considerably whilst the end or the goal remains constant. Variation is of the essence in the difficult fault-finding plans. One fault location plan has already been briefly described. Periodically the operator sends samples of the pure product for laboratory quality control analysis. A common adverse laboratory report is of water contamination and an experienced operator must determine its origin by taking further samples of product at different points on his plant. He must decide in the light of successive laboratory reports an appropriate sequence of sampling operations with always the same end in view, to minimize sampling costs. As can be seen in Figure 4, the cost of sampling operations can vary considerably in terms of convenience, *e.g.* a sample might sometimes be quickly and conveniently obtained from a drain valve in liquid form. On the other hand, it may be necessary to take a sample at a point in the plant where the product is under vacuum in gaseous form, in which case it will be costly in terms of time, inconvenience or even hazard.

Initially, to enable the trainee to perform this plan two *régimes* were considered. Under one *régime*, the trainee was simply given the decision tree and practised using it in an exercise in which the instructor provided him with simulated laboratory reports for given faults. The faults occurred in random order and with frequencies corresponding to their specified probabilities. In the second training *régime*, the trainee had a flow diagram showing the differing fault probabilities and sampling costs and was simply instructed to minimize the latter. In other words, he had to try to work out an efficient plan of his own. Using two groups of the company's apprentices as subjects, the two *régimes* were compared in terms of excess sampling costs, that is in terms of the sampling costs entailed in locating the faults by the most efficient strategy. During initial practice the group who used the decision tree, not surprisingly had average excess sampling costs of zero and a variance of zero, whereas the group which had to work out a search plan on their own had excess sampling costs of 31%.

However, the company was not only interested in differences in *régimes*, but also in different criteria, namely retention and transfer. Deprived of the decision tree, the first group performed worse on both of these criteria. On the retention criterion the group who had initially found faults using the decision tree now had excess sampling costs of 47%, whereas the group that had had to work out a search plan on their own had significantly different average excess sampling costs of 26%. The two groups did not differ on the transfer criterion, *i.e.* a search task of the same form with differing fault probabilities and costs of sampling distributed differently, but again the difference favoured the group whose members had been left to work out their own search plan during initial practice (Duncan 1969).

The possibility of training only a limited number of apprentices in each of the two conditions on any one occasion raised the question of the contribution of different delays between training and testing to the retention and transfer effects. There was no significant decline in transfer as a function of training to testing interval and performance on the transfer task was superior to that of an untrained control group. On the other hand, in the retention data, there *was* significant evidence of forgetting but only in the group whose initial practice was with the decision tree. Apart from the theoretical interest of this finding, if it proved to be genuine, two important practical implications would follow. This plant, like many others in industry, presents unexpected, rarely occurring and therefore rarely practised contingencies or emergencies. The applied psychologist asked for advice on training for such contingencies, is haunted by the shape of the classical retention curve. He may suggest simulating emergencies as a solution, but this can be expensive, even dangerous if it is realistic, and if it is not, the familiar attitudes of fire practice and boat drill tend to develop. So the possibility of isolating and concentrating training on components of skill which do not deteriorate over time is attractive. Secondly, and of more general interest, is the possibility of training criteria which are stable over time, therefore as valid immediately after the trials of a technique or device as delayed retention testing with all its administrative and methodological problems.

The 'temporal course of transfer' has been largely neglected since a series of experiments in the late 1930's by Bunch and his associates. Working in the main with verbal tasks, Bunch found that transfer effects do not decline over time as do retention effects (Bunch 1936), at least not in situations where transfer depends on the subject learning to apply a general principle or method. The few subsequent studies, reviewed by Ellis (1965), confirm Bunch's findings and both Ellis and Bunch conclude that learning which is specific to the task is the relatively perishable component.

Returning to the contamination problem in the acid purification plant, the subjects who had learned the rather specific search plan specified by the decision tree may have done so at the expense of learning how to work out search plans or a more general search strategy. This in turn suggests that search strategy, once acquired, is rather stable over time, whereas the routines of a specific search plan are relatively poorly remembered. These are, however, *post hoc* interpretations of an experiment which was designed primarily to measure the effects of different training *régimes* on retention and transfer, rather than decrements over time. The number of subjects for each combination of time interval and training *régime* was rather small.

A second experiment therefore attempted a more adequate test of whether or not the difference between retention and transfer previously found in simpler tasks is also found after learning the complex search task. All subjects practised search problems with a decision tree (see Figure 8) and were encouraged to learn search strategy as well as the efficient search routines for the particular problem. They could therefore learn either search strategy or the specific routines embodied in the decision tree or both. Thus the amount of retention may be determined by the subject remembering the specific decision tree routines, or remembering search strategy, or possibly both. Any decline in retention over time should therefore be less marked to the extent that the subject is able to learn search strategy. This ability should largely determine the amount of transfer and, on the assumption that search strategy is well remembered, should do so regardless of the interval between training and transfer testing.

Figure 9 shows retention and transfer after three intervals between training and testing and also the performance of untrained control groups on each task,

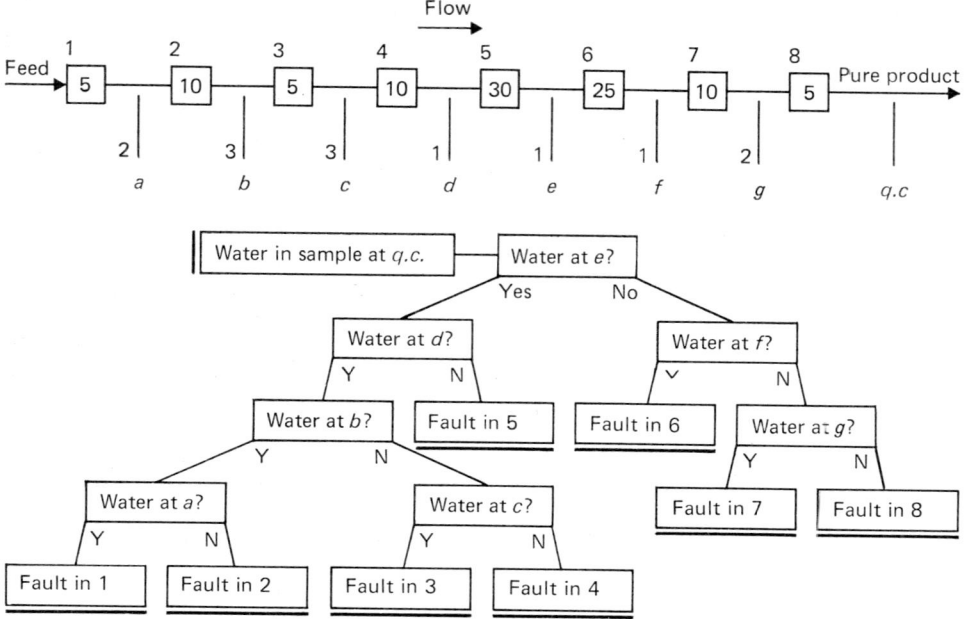

The diagram illustrates one feature of an industrial acid purification process. The acid passes through a series of heat exchangers, boxes 1–8, any one of which may leak. The consequent water contamination is initially detected at the quality control sampling point, q.c. A leaking heat exchanger is isolated by taking further samples at points a–g; thus a sample at d, for instance, which is not contaminated, eliminates boxes 1–4, leaving boxes 5–8 still suspect. Because cost of sampling varies in chemical plant, each sampling point has a corresponding cost index of 1, 2 or 3. The figure inside each box is the approximate failure probability. The decision tree minimizes sampling costs over a random series of faults occurring with frequencies corresponding to their specified probabilities.

Figure 8. The location of contaminant problem.

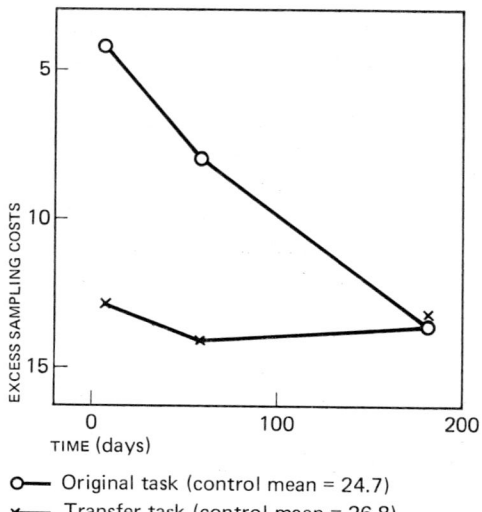

○— Original task (control mean = 24.7)
×— Transfer task (control mean = 26.8)

Figure 9. Scores on fault location tests.

all in terms of excess sampling costs in locating 20 faults. Whereas the differences between transfer on the three occasions are small and not significant there is a significant and substantial decline in retention.

As one might expect, there are highly significant differences in retention and transfer between subjects of high and subjects of low ability, ability, that is, to learn search strategy, measured for this purpose by initial unaided location of 10 faults. As Figure 10 shows, ability level is related to the amount of transfer regardless of the interval between training and testing, whereas in the retention data there is an interaction between ability and occasions. The retention of high-ability subjects does not differ significantly over the three occasions, but the retention of low-ability subjects does, 80% of the variance being attributable to highly significant regression on the retention intervals. This is consistent with the prediction that declining retention would result from subjects forgetting the specific decision tree routines and that this would be less marked in high-ability subjects because of their superior learning of search strategy (Duncan 1971b).

Evidently search strategy is well remembered and a specific search plan is more easily forgotten. In practice, a decision must be made whether or not to trade retention and generality of learning of search strategy for the excellent

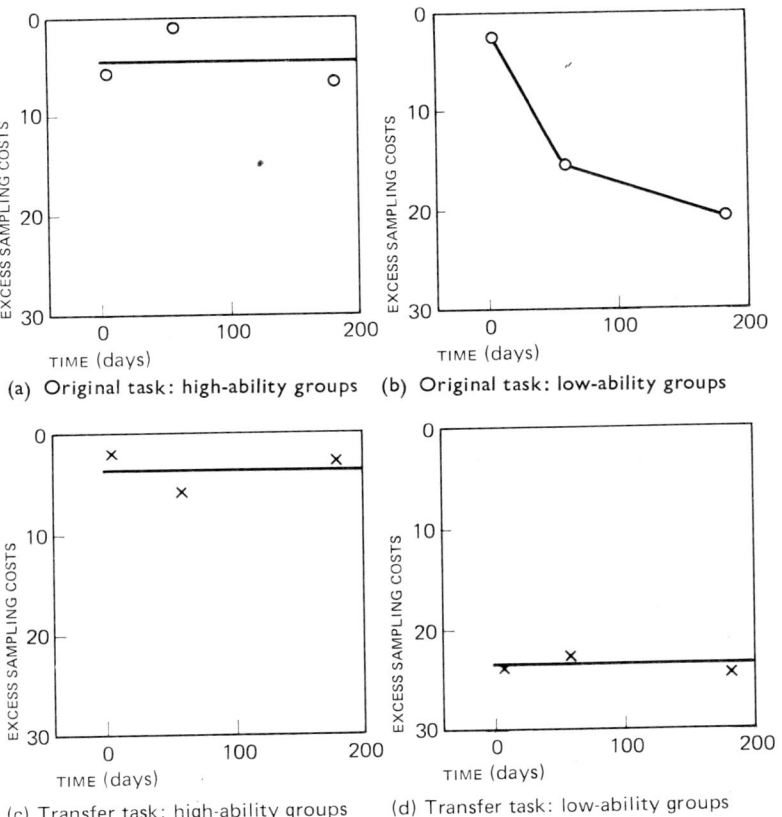

Figure 10. Scores on fault location tests of high and low 'Ability' groups—see text.

performance which is immediately obtained when the subject is simply provided with a decision tree, or whether to adopt some expedient which attempts to achieve both. Such a decision can only be made in terms of the objectives of the personnel subsystem and not by the task analyst who should rather draw attention to the training options and their consequences.

Plans for Control Room Fault Diagnosis

A similar decision is required for the plan which selects one of 10 subordinate operations when the control room alarms are set off by a plant failure, for example failure of a pump, or an empty feed tank, or failure of a steam supply. For some failures, the corresponding subordinate operation can restore normal conditions, *e.g.* by switching the flow from a defective pump to a standby pump. For other failures the appropriate subordinate operation consists of reporting the trouble. In both cases, the operator must act quickly, typically within about 3 minutes, otherwise the process will either run down or essential conditions such as temperature and flow will move so far out of tolerance that the purification process ceases. Clearly the costs of failing correctly to report and, where possible, remedy a failure which would otherwise cause a shutdown, are unacceptable. Also, in situations requiring a subordinate operation reporting what has failed and initiating repairs or adjustments by the plant's maintenance men, the operator must still select the appropriate subordinate operation quickly, otherwise the pattern of control room indications may rapidly be obscured by other failures which the primary failure has induced. The plan is difficult and selection of the appropriate subordinate operation must be done in conditions which are stressful because of the limited time available and the possibility that automatic safety devices may also fail.

Diagnosis, *i.e.* interpreting the instrument indications, is difficult because of considerable overlap between the indications of different failures. Take, for example, the kind of failure which can occur in one plant unit, the vacuum distillation column. If the steam supply heating the column fails, boiling ceases, the level of liquid in the base of the column will rise, the level of distilled liquid which is collected in a vessel called a reflux drum will fall and very soon the flow indicators on the lines leaving the reflux drum would fall to zero. However, these indicators would also fall to zero if the reflux pump, which pumps liquid out of the reflux drum, were to fail. Furthermore, all these indications would be produced by failure of the ejector, a steam-powered device which maintains the vacuum. Another complication is that rapid slowing of distillation due to rise in pressure can occur because the reflux pump has failed, in consequence the level of distilled liquid in the reflux drum has risen, blocked the vacuum lines and effectively produced all the symptoms of ejector failure. These three failures give some indication of the overlap of symptom patterns and, while distinguishing between these three alone might not be very difficult, the operator must distinguish between not three but 10 such failures.

Again, as in contaminant location, two expedients were considered to enable the operator to execute the difficult and at times stressful control panel diagnosis. One group of trainees practised diagnosing faults on a simulator (Figure 11) and achieved a high level of performance using the decision tree in Figure 12.

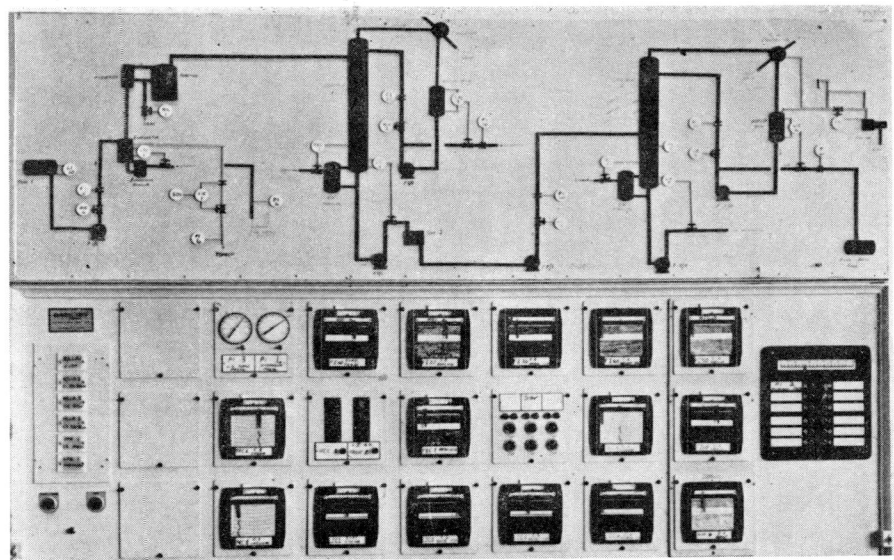

Figure 11. The Carmody 'Universal Process Trainer'.
(*Photograph by courtesy of B.P. Chemicals (International) Ltd.*)

A second group practised fault diagnosis on the simulator but without the decision tree. This group was given instructions which it was hoped would enable them to learn the relationships between plant failures and control room indications and, in this way, be enabled to work out the plan for fault diagnosis not just for this process but also for others. The instruction consisted of an account in simple terms of the flow of product through the plant and the various control loops. The flow diagram on the simulator in Figure 11 was used for this purpose. Subjects, who were trained in groups of 5 or 6, were then asked in turn what would happen if a particular failure occurred. This elicited patterns of symptoms which were built up on the simulator instrument console. Thus the symptom patterns for the 10 plant failures were demonstrated and the reasons for each of them discussed.

This instruction had some modest success in terms of correct diagnoses on a retention test. Performance on the same test of the other group, when deprived of the decision tree, was significantly but not markedly inferior. However, on a transfer test which required fault diagnosis on a plant simulation of comparable complexity, there were no significant differences in correct diagnoses either between the two groups or between them and an untrained control group. On both tests the number of incorrect diagnoses was unacceptable for plant operation (Duncan 1969). Evidently general strategies which support this kind of fault diagnostic plan are not easily trained.

With a view to developing better training schemes, it was decided to study fault diagnosis by a very experienced operator using simulations of a number of different plants. By persuading the operator to 'think aloud', a strategy was recorded and subsequently checked for consistency, by withholding control room instrument indications until the operator asked for them. In this way, the more general strategy for diagnosing faults represented in Figure 13 was developed. This strategy will support not merely fault diagnosis in this plant but in several other plants consisting of distillation and reactor units.

It should perhaps be emphasized that the general strategy presented in Figure 13, based as it is on observations of diagnoses of simulated faults and protocol analysis, is not seen as *necessarily* representing the psychological processes which occur in response to the alarms and indications of real faults in the control room. Rather the general strategy in Figure 13 is seen as specifying a training *régime* which should enable diagnostic plans to be executed in several situations. In particular, training sequences are envisaged in which the trainee's decisions are prompted, corrected or confirmed at each stage in the series of decisions leading to a diagnosis, rather than the kind of training sequence which presents an array of indications and merely informs the trainee, when he has made a diagnosis, as to whether or not it was correct, or perhaps what the diagnosis should have been. This is an analogous distinction to the

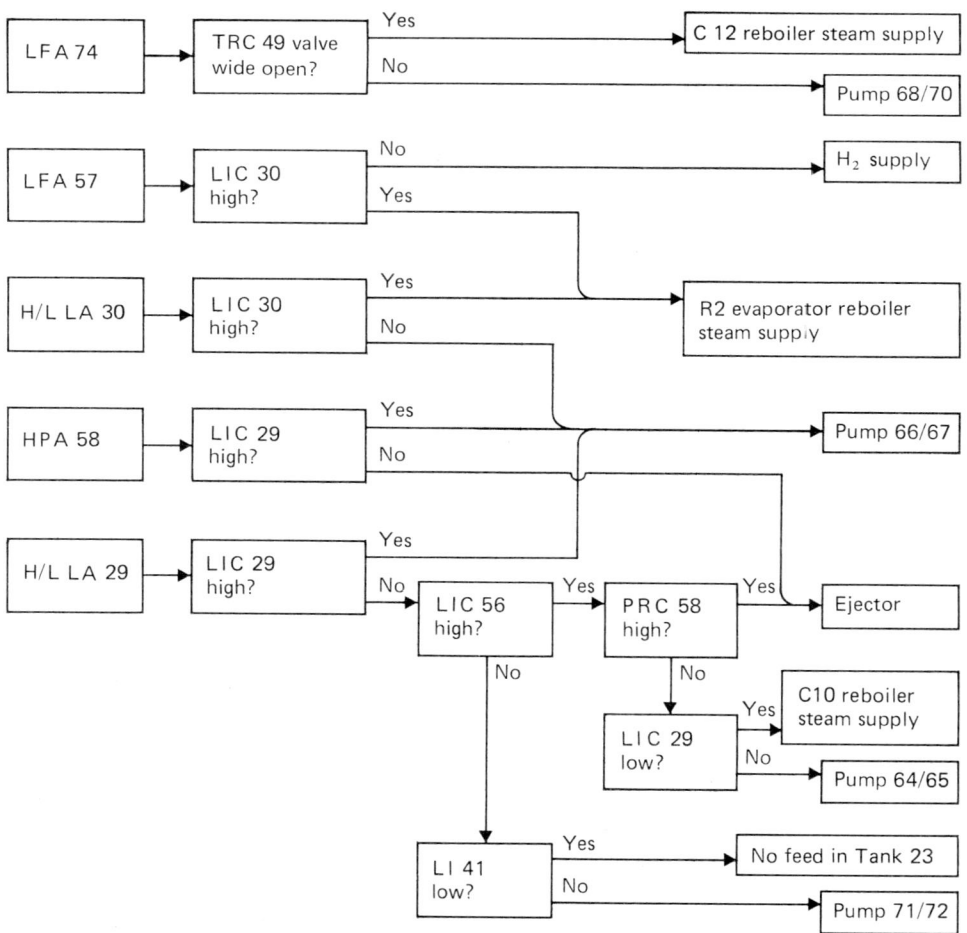

In the event of several alarms at once select the one which is highest in the above list

Figure 12. Decision tree for control room fault diagnosis—see text.

Analytical Techniques in Training Design 307

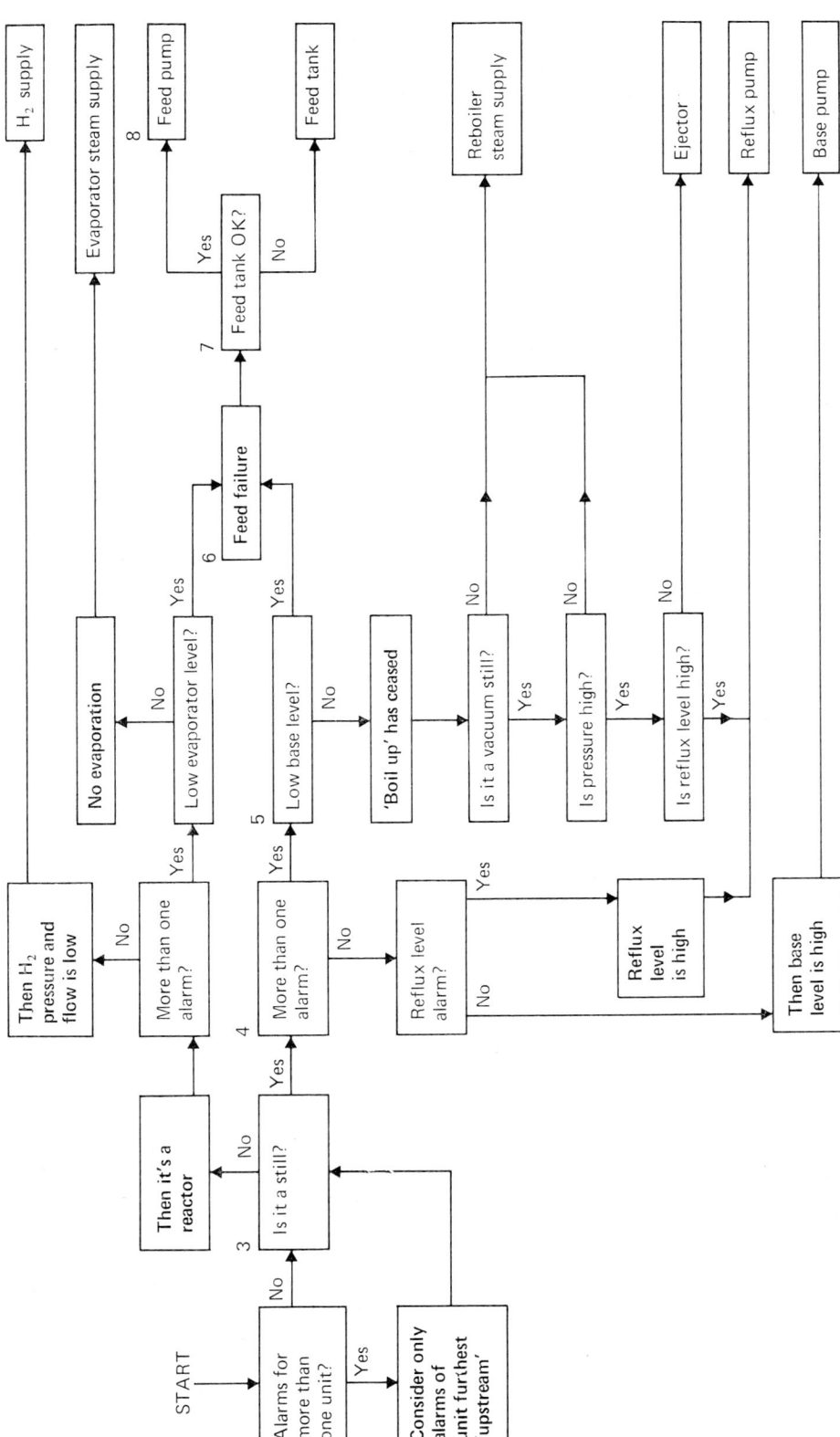

Figure 13. A general decision tree for diagnosing failures in a chemical factory involving distillation columns and hydrogenator reactors—see text.

distinction made in other skills between *concurrent* feedback of information and *terminal* feedback of information (Holding 1965).

No doubt there will be the usual problems of any augmented feedback or augmented KR, problems of weaning, problems of how to withdraw the extra help. On the other hand, it should be possible to avoid the situation early in training where an incorrect diagnosis has been made and the trainee does not know at what stage or in what way he went wrong. This is a familiar and, as far as one can tell, a frustrating experience for a trainee who attempts to apply some kind of logic or strategy when learning diagnostic skills. Figure 13 may or may not represent the general diagnostic strategy of an experienced operator who, for that matter, may be a pattern perceiver, a parallel rather than a serial processor. Nevertheless, any powerful training technique must specify how to augment intrinsic task information during the *intra-problem* interval, between problem presentation and problem solution. Thus far experimental training schemes have been encouraging, but not conclusive, in terms of the level of *general, i.e.* transferable, diagnostic attainment.

4. Training Design

The point has been made that task analysis is necessarily complemented by pilot training schemes. Its nature is hypothesis generating, to be complemented by appropriate hypothesis testing. But in one respect the analysis departs from completely neutral task description—it assumes that skilled performance is hierarchically organized. In this one respect therefore it *prescribes* training, it is prescriptive with regard to training sequences. This is not to say that analysis will specify a unique training sequence. In the acid purification control task, the order in which fault diagnosis, fault location, startup and shutdown procedures are trained is not specified, but, for each of these operations, the analysis *does* specify antecedent mastery of plant valve discrimination and control console instrument location. In other words, the task hierarchy *constrains* the sequence of training. Practice of a given operation should not begin before its subordinate operations have been learned.

In the process control task training course it was decided that practice in procedures should precede practice in fault location and fault diagnosis. So when these last operations were practised, the trainee had already learned, indeed to some degree overlearned, the necessary subordinate operations on the plant and in the control room. Therefore at this stage, the trainee could more easily concentrate on the difficult fault location and fault diagnostic plans, but this sequencing decision was an intuitive one, it is not prescribed by the analysis.

Mager's (1961) research into the sequences preferred by the trainee raises two points in connection with the method of analysis described here. Firstly, when the task hierarchy allows for more than one possible sequence at a particular stage in the programme, then one would do well to consider the sequence preferred by the trainee, since to do so apparently has powerful motivating effects. Also to be considered carefully, since this analysis generates learning sequences which progress from lower to higher order operations, is Mager's subjects' evident desire to see 'the big picture' at the beginning of training. This observation and the tendency of many training officers to start a training course with some kind of 'technical story' (Shriver *et al.* 1964) leads one to suspect that the student's interest is probably aroused in the early stages of training by a description of the structure of what he has to learn. It has been suggested that representations of the task such as those in Figures 1, 3 and 4 might help to serve this purpose, but the suggestion has thus far not been tested. It does, however, seem reasonable in view of the claims which have been made for the effectiveness of ' advance organizers ' (Ausubel 1968). It is interesting, if highly speculative, to link this argument with the requirement of programming languages like ALGOL for declarative statements at the beginning of the programme, *i.e.* the declaration of terms which are not primitives in the language concerned.

A shortcoming of this and other methods of analysis, which must be acknowledged, is that it tends to address the problem of training individuals, when increasingly the problem of how to train teams is being encountered in industry, not least in continuous process control tasks such as those found in petrochemical industries. It is known from studies of radar crews that the performance data of individual members does not reveal the extent to which they co-ordinate their activities (Alexander *et al.* 1962). Perhaps no single individual has the information which is necessary to learn to improve the co-ordination of his activities with those of his colleagues. In this case, the training problem is not different in principle from the individual training problems which have been discussed. The intrinsic task information is inadequate and must be augmented if the team is to learn to co-ordinate its activities. Or the problem may be that what behaviour on the part of individuals constitutes effective co-ordination with other members is either not clear or not agreed. A study of the effects of discussions between crew members suggests that this may be the case (Jensen *et al.* 1961).

Can it therefore be assumed in analysis and training design that the information necessary for individual learning and performance should be examined in the same way regardless of whether it comes from other people or from inanimate sources? Is it necessary to distinguish between performance of the individual alone and performance of the individual in the presence of others? An influential paper by the social psychologist Robert Zajonc (1965) suggests that such a distinction must be made. Reviewing the conflicting findings from studies of the effects on individual performance of the presence of others, Zajonc points out that decrements were found when the subject's task required substantial learning, whereas increments attributable to the presence of others were found when the task required well-established performance or little or no learning. Whatever the mechanism may be for this neat reconciliation of the findings of social facilitation experiments, the psychologist seriously interested in training should consider that, other things equal, trainees in the early stages of learning a task will probably work best alone, but that their performance may even be enhanced, if they work in the presence of others, as their scores approach an asymptote.

Training design, properly considered, raises questions which are not just training questions, questions which are best answered by other disciplines or in consultation with other disciplines such as social psychology. The analysis of the acid purification control task tried to show that there will often be more than one way of securing adequate performance, sometimes more than one training solution to a problem and some solutions which are not training solutions at all. Task analysis must recognize not only training problems but problems of equipment design, problems of personnel selection, placement and development and problems of education.

5. Communication with Other Professions

Equipment Design

The engineering of the hardware in any system necessarily sets limits on personnel strategies in selection and training. Two features of the acid purification plant will serve to illustrate this point. Instrumentation and associated alarm systems may either provide a large number of signals of specific failures, for example, "The feed pump to the evaporator has stopped", or a much smaller number of signals, typically that a parameter, for example a flow or a liquid level, is out of tolerance. The former instrumentation philosophy is, from the engineering point of view, expensive but it removes, or drastically reduces, training costs, whereas the latter instrumentation philosophy is relatively inexpensive from an engineering point of view but does present the difficult training problem of fault diagnostic skill. A rational solution would probably trade off the costs of equipment design and of training in this situation. The trade-off might also take account of personnel selection and placement strategies, which recruited more or less intelligent operators for this task.

In the same way it would be rational to consider trade-offs of this kind in the case of operating plant valves. Durable labelling in an open acid purification plant is costly. For this process alone there are 130 such valves. However, 90 of them are easily identified given mastery of four or five functional categories, *i.e.* for these, training is not so time-consuming and retention may be better. It is the remaining 40 valves which will be costly in terms of training and expensive mistakes due to forgetting, since there are no rules to support identification and each must be separately learned. The point in this trade-off is that the psychologist would distinguish, where engineers or accountants might not, between the cost of labelling all the hand-operated valves on the plant and the 30% or so which present disproportionately high training costs.

From human factors work on both sides of the Atlantic there is a growing understanding of how psychologists and design engineers may collaborate. The collaboration achieved so far may be modest but, at least in British industry, is probably under-utilized.

Personnel Selection, Placement and Development

Recruitment for the acid purification control task and others of comparable difficulty varies. The preferred policy is to promote operators of less complex plant or 'pump and line men', men who already have relevant experience, in short, a population who are already capable of many of the subordinate operations in the task. Specifically, such men will be able to distinguish between, for example, isolating and by-pass valves, or be familiar with instrument nomenclature and therefore will more rapidly master the location of instruments on the control room console. On occasions, men who are new to the company or indeed sometimes new to the process control industries, are appointed to perform this task. Invariably, the new operator, from whatever background, is confronted for the first time with an automatically-controlled process.

These processes are perceived by operators and management alike as extremely demanding. Conscientiousness and intelligence are seen as important in preventing shutdown and locating product contamination. There is talk of boredom, particularly on night shifts, which is perhaps to be expected when intelligence has been a criterion in appointment to the job. It is also recognized that boredom can impair performance and that the most able are not necessarily the most diligent.

The contradictory requirements of this task, and other personnel factors, present rather general problems in the way in which they interact with training design, or the use of job aids such as decision trees. Arguments favouring the use of decision trees were that performance supported by them should be less dependent on intelligence and that relaxation of the intelligence criterion would permit more freedom to appoint operators on other grounds such as conscientiousness. It was generally appreciated that employing intelligent men to do very little for long periods of time, but to perform intellectually difficult operations on rare occasions, was an unhappy situation. Given that, on occasions, fault location, for example, might have to be time-shared with emergency actions on another system, then one could add the further argument that, under these conditions, performance supported by decision trees should be less vulnerable to disruption. However, the dangers of trading retention and possibly transfer for efficient performance were also seen. The loss of transferable skill is, in the event, the more serious, since, as subsequent experiments showed, it is fairly stable over long periods of time.

Whenever an industrial task has a problem-solving component, like the fault diagnostic and fault location operations in the acid purification control task, it may be possible to use decision trees to support performance which, at least on short-term criteria, may be indistinguishable from that of a very skilled man. In the short term at least, the same behaviour can have very different bases. It will generally be very much easier to *program performance* to meet immediate short-term criteria than to *program learning* of the general principles which apparently support enduring problem-solving skills. Which of these courses of action is taken or whether some intermediate strategy is adopted, may be decided in the light of many personnel factors which will now be briefly discussed. All, however, hinge on the objectives of some system and in practice on the rationality of its management. Unfortunately, decision trees and other algorithmic techniques have been described in terms which are hardly conducive to rational evaluation. At one extreme, they have been described as devices for reducing man to an automaton and, on the other hand, have been somewhat sensationally defended as intelligence amplifiers.

In practice, one basis for choosing whether or not to use decision trees, is the nature of the trainee population. Less able groups may be expected to follow the procedures specified by a decision tree with more success than they would have from interpreting general principles. Indeed, less able trainees may be enabled to perform problem-solving tasks of which they would otherwise be incapable. On the other hand, for more able populations, extensive use of decision trees with little explanation might make a task intrinsically boring and would largely exclude any gains from the transfer of learning over different tasks involving the same principles. It would also fail to exploit transfer from previous learning to the current task. If mobility of operators from plant to plant within a factory, or within a company, is an objective of a personnel system, then training generalizable skill would clearly be preferred wherever possible.

The stability of the population to be trained will also be important. High labour turnover will tend to make the use of decision trees more economic since mastery of general principles will usually entail longer periods of instruction or more sophisticated instructional techniques. A danger to be considered, however, is that in situations of high labour turnover, the use of decision trees, and consequent boredom among the more able subjects, may in fact augment, or be a principal cause of, the labour turnover problem.

Education

The acid purification control task and the increasing number of tasks like it in industry raise problems which invite collaboration with education, or at least problems which *prima facie* fall within the province of education. Intellectual skills are increasingly a feature of the industrial scene. *What* principles taught in *what* way will support or facilitate carrying out the fault location and diagnostic plans which control of the acid purification process requires? It seems clear that at some stage the trainee must practice identification of failures consistent with a set of symptoms and must also practise locating the origin of water contamination from a series of laboratory reports. The problem is how to introduce him to the consequences of pumps stopping, of steam or cooling water supplies failing and of heat exchangers leaking steam or coolant into the product. A minimal technical story was tried but with only modest success.

It is possible that teaching more general principles which are relevant and which extend beyond the restricted context of this particular plant might well support mastery of these difficult fault location and diagnostic plans. But this mastery would be the training research psychologist's main or sole decision rule for what principles to teach. It might not be the educator's decision rule, which would most likely be syllabus-oriented, that is to say, the set of principles selected for teaching would be coherent and representative of some body of knowledge. An unfortunate feature of the dialogue between education and training has been a tendency either not to recognize that different decision rules are applied, or simply to assert that one set of rules is ' correct '. In consequence, neither the objectives of education nor training may be realized. The study by Williams and Whitmore (1959), which tested both maintenance men's knowledge of electronics theory and their ability at fault-finding in field equipment, showed that learning of the latter had hardly begun on leaving the school and only increased with length of service in the field. From a strictly training point of view, little had been achieved which was immediately useful and the sooner practice in operational situations began the better. From an educational point of view, the outcome is less than satisfactory, for although scores on tests of theory were initially high, they declined rather drastically with increasing periods of service in field units.

These are specific instances of a more general lack of accord between two professions which, in principle, would collaborate to their mutual benefit. The disagreement is well illustrated in the differing attitudes to the objectives of instruction. The "taxonomy of educational objectives" (Bloom 1956) is largely concerned to codify the extent and variety of existing objectives in education. Existing objectives in education are regarded as given and the major concern seems to be to indicate in what ways they differ and in what ways tests may be devised to see if these different objectives have been attained. Indeed, major uses of the taxonomy have been classifying test questions (Stanley and Bolton 1957) and in this way checking the validity of test content (Cox 1965). This contrasts sharply with the attitude of psychologists working in industrial and military training, who regard any instructional objectives as open to strict questioning in terms of eventual contribution to some systems objectives.

The *milieu* of education is one thing, that of training quite another. Training must meet stated objectives because the military or industrial systems which it serves must meet stated objectives and must meet them more or less efficiently. However, education is arguably serving the aims and aspirations of a social system, a system with ill-defined objectives. Consequently, the conscientious teacher is confronted very frequently with ill-defined objectives, such as fostering an appreciation of music and painting or encouraging a critical attitude which seeks out premises, identifies questionable ones and questions them. Now it might be possible to 'unpack' such complex objectives as these into operational definitions and to devise effective instructional techniques, but the psychologist will do well to recognize that this is a more

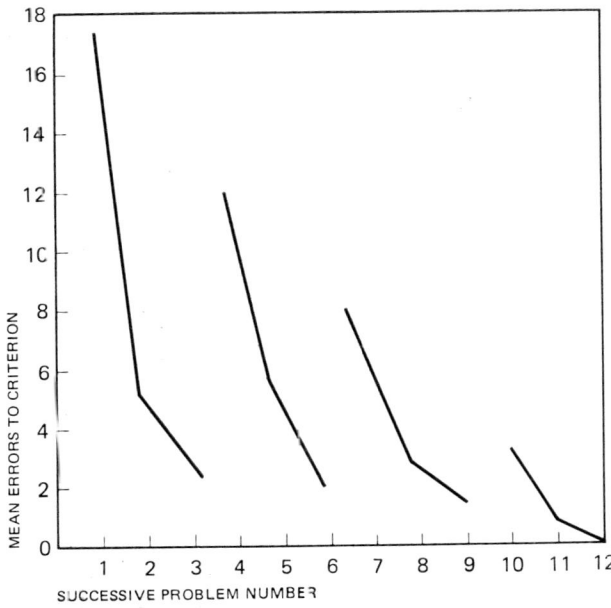

Figure 14. Performance on a series of rule learning problems. Each set of three successive problems is based on the same principle. All four primary concept types are represented with the order counterbalanced across subjects (after Bourne 1970).

difficult exercise than he is accustomed by his discipline to undertake. It should, nevertheless, be undertaken by someone.

Discriminating between functionally different categories of valves on process plant may seem a minor problem compared with the higher-order concepts which have to be mastered in schools and universities. Indeed, by confining his activities to learning tasks, which, in the current state of the art, he can demonstrably influence or control, the psychologist necessarily lays himself open to accusations of indulging in trivia. Nevertheless, the gap between what can be achieved by applied psychology and what must be attempted in educational practice is narrowing. A good example is in this very field of concept attainment, specifically in the recent work of Bourne (1970). The family of curves in Figure 14, each curve demonstrating the acquisition of a combination rule in concept learning, will be familiar to some readers. What is remarkable is the sharp descent of the *starting point* of each curve after the rule is changed. This higher-order learning, swift recognition that the rule has changed and rapid identification of the new rule, is indeed a skill to be conjured with. Of course, intellectual skills of this higher order of abstraction have long been known to exist and have long been the business of education. However, this elegant experiment provides psychologists with *one* way in which they can talk about higher mental processes without the familiar unpleasant feeling of not really knowing what is being talked about.

6. Task Analysis—Assumptions

Levels of Description

The method of task analysis just described makes a number of assumptions which must now be examined. The problem of levels of description is a natural starting point.

No attempt is made to define levels of description, nor to specify a list of performance elements. A workable list of performance elements would be one way of achieving a rigorous method of analysis—as Gilbreth saw. But in the current state of psychology such an approach to the problems of training does not seem to be realizable or even foreseeable.

In the absence of such a list, task analysis may achieve some rigour, first of all by proceeding from general to detailed statements and *by observing an explicit rule* as to when analysis must cease. The rule which is proposed, based on the probability, p, of inadequate performance and the cost, c, to the system of inadequate performance, besides being explicit, is hopefully exhaustive of the major considerations in any personnel problem, namely the existing capabilities and dispositions of people and the many different outcomes of their behaviour, which may be more or less costly to the objectives of the organization in which they exist. The formal definition of p recognizes that its value is determined and may be changed, not only by industrial training, but by other areas of expertise such as human engineering and equipment design, personnel selection and placement, personnel development policies, occupational guidance, education and manpower studies. The definition of c, on the other hand, recognizes that personnel problems can only be defined and solutions can only have meaning in terms of the *values* of some system.

The decision to redescribe an operation should, strictly speaking, depend on the product of p and c. The mundane operation of filling a bucket would not ordinarily require much redescription, nor would filling a vessel with water if the feed line is remotely controlled with considerable time lag for, although this would make the value of p rather higher, the value of c would be zero or near zero unless the system is suffering from a chronic water shortage. On the other hand, filling a beaker with radioactive isotope might well be redescribed in some detail because, although the probability of inadequate performance, p, is not very high, the consequences or costs of inadequate performance, c, would probably be unacceptable. All this is not to say that the analyst must always obtain accurate measures of p and c. Depending on how important or critical the training scheme is, p and c might be based on more or less extensive data collection, but, for the most part, it is envisaged that p and c will be estimated subjectively. The point at issue is not accuracy of measurement, rather that the multiplicative relationship is recognized—if if either p or c is zero, then the product is zero and no further redescription is required.

The point must be made that *some* rule specifying what information to include and what to exclude from the analysis of a task should be explicit *if the analysis is to be viable in practice.* This is a criticism of other methods of task analysis. Sometimes an arbitrary level of description is implicitly assumed to be appropriate which, if it is too fine, fails to reveal higher-order operations and how the task is organized, or, if it is too gross, fails to describe perceptual acuity and motor co-ordination when these are crucial for performance of the task. Sometimes the philosophy of analysis seems to be to record everything, on the assumption that the information required for training or anything else must be somewhere in the record. This leads to the generation of masses of paper and other records and the risk that analysis will be abandoned. It also means that the training officer gets a mass of information from which he must somehow extract the useful details for a training course and introduces another time-consuming stage into training design.

Having adopted a method of task analysis by progressive redescription, it seemed essential for practical purposes to attempt an operational definition of the relationship between superordinate and subordinate terms. A distinction is therefore made between *operations* and *plans*. The redescription of an operation includes (1) a set of subordinate operations, and (2) a plan which is any selection and sequencing of subordinate operations which completes the superordinate operation, *i.e.* which achieves its goal.

Use of 'Operation'

An operation is an action statement indicating how the action is completed or achieved. Since no psychological elements are assumed, an operation is a statement in natural language. It is an instruction to *do something*, which is intelligible to a competent operator, which is as plain and non-technical as possible, but which is not necessarily without some peculiar expressions if these are current usage. For instance, such terms as " crack the valve " or " kettle level " or other shop-floor jargon and dialect may be part of the statement of an operation. Indeed, such expressions are often a convenient shorthand for what would otherwise be complex and tortuous statements.

If an operation is *not* redescribed, more formally, if it is a *primitive*, the analyst has decided that the trainee, or a trainee population, can perform this operation with acceptable probability of success, or that, by various expedients, acceptable probability of success can be assured. It is useful to distinguish between two sorts of difficulty which may have to be overcome to achieve acceptable performance: difficulty in performing the action, or difficulty in processing the signals entailed by the operation. Thus, on the one hand, performing some of the operations in the acid purification control task entailed distinguishing different indicators in the control room and manually operated valves on the open plant. On the other hand, an operation was described in which the rate at which a steam control valve was opened constituted the difficulty. Difficulty in performing an operation is not necessarily overcome by training, but might be resolved, for example, by changes in equipment design, specifically by enhancing displays, or by changing display-control relationships.

Stating operations in the form of natural language instructions, keeping the analyst's notes about the nature of difficulties and possible training, *etc.*, quite separate, has the advantage that procedural guides and operating instructions can be rather directly extracted from the analysis and used as they stand. In the task analysis just described, the long procedural guides for starting up and shutting down units of plant could be extracted with a pair of scissors.

Use of 'Plan'

If an operation cannot be treated as a primitive, *i.e.* it is redescribed, then a plan must be stated. A plan is any selection and sequencing of subordinate operations which *completes* the superordinate operation or achieves its goal. It should be added that sequencing includes timing of subordinate operations. Mastery of the timing, or of the time-sharing involved in a task, can, of course, constitute a major difficulty.

A plan may be stated more or less precisely. The fixed sequence or procedure is a common and very precise plan. Sometimes plans for variant selection and sequences of operations can be precisely stated. An example in the acid purification control task is the plan which specifies that, at fixed intervals, the operator always performs one operation, sending a sample to the laboratory and then, depending on the laboratory report, he either does nothing, or reports a contaminant, or, when the contaminant is water, both reports and begins the operation of locating it. If it is possible to state a plan in the form of a precise rule, specifying the set of permissible sub-routines, then obviously this should be done. However, plans cannot always be stated with such precision. The plan for fault diagnosis requires the selection of a subordinate operation which will either correctly report a plant failure or remedy it. Just how this is to be done is, at this stage, not clear, nor is it clear how the plan shall be executed for locating the source of water contaminant, which simply states that costs of sampling should be minimized. But that these difficulties exist is necessarily made clear, because the method of analysis insists that when operations are redescribed a plan must be stated.

Plans may also be more or less efficient. When the operations of a skilled man are redescribed, the plans may not necessarily be consistent, rational, optimal or even explicit. But they should always be stated. It will sometimes be possible, before considering the difficulties in mastering the plan, to restate it more precisely, or substitute a more efficient plan on logical grounds. The latter will sometimes be the case when a plan has been derived from observing an experienced worker. As already noted the experienced worker's performance is only one source of data for the task analyst and the standard of his performance is not necessarily the objective of a training scheme. The location of water contaminant in the acid purification task exemplifies an insidious feature of a lot of searching activity. There are many possible sampling sequences, varying considerably in efficiency, but which will all find the fault. If the operator confuses his 'success' in finding the fault with successful strategy, then he may superstitiously cling to whatever strategy he adopts—especially since it always works. Simply practising may have this effect whenever intrinsic task information does not indicate improvements. *Practice is not instruction.* The general principle that intrinsic task information may have to be augmented, if performance is to improve, applies no less to plans—indeed, in the case of plans, it may present special difficulties.

Is it not possible that the reason why some social skills are so elusive, so subtle, is that whilst we recognize them when they occur, that is to say we recognize successful outcomes when we see them, we tend to observe the operations, which are probably not difficult and therefore not very informative. What we do *not* perceive is the nature of the *plan* which varies the operations in such a way as to guarantee the outcome. Such plans are likely very complex, in the sense that mastery of effective selection and sequencing rules is not easily achieved. But, as in Fiedler's 'contingency model', it is the selection and sequencing of operations in the social skill we call leadership which is of the essence and which ensures that the outcome, the leader's manifest influence, remains constant (Fiedler 1968).

Hierarchical Analysis

This specification of how operations and plans should be stated is an attempt at a logically consistent set of rules for describing the performance of a task. Statements of operations and plans are NOT statements about psychological processes. These statements may have to be made in language which has psychological connotations, but such connotations are incidental and best regarded as hypothetical. Statements of operations and plans must be regarded as psychologically 'celibate' for practical purposes, since, as has been demonstrated here and by other applied psychologists, the same performance may be supported by quite different psychological processes. Furthermore, the psychological processes which support some performance may be very obscure. Any method of task analysis which required human performance to be described by *categorical* statements about psychological processes would be unworkable, for it would assume that a complete and theoretically consistent psychology exists.

However, although seeking to avoid statements of operations and plans in psychological terms, the method of progressive redescription is based on the view that behaviour is hierarchically organized. In particular, it assumes a model of man like that put forward by Miller, Galanter and Pribram, although some psychologists might consider it an unwarranted liberty to borrow the word 'plan' and give it a special definition for task analysis. However, it does attempt, at the outset, to represent the flexible, adaptive character of skilled performance, the facility to achieve constant outcomes in a variety of ways.

This is one reason for a form of analysis based on the assumption that behaviour is hierarchically organized, much as a computer is controlled by executive or control programs with their sub-routines. Another reason for the formal representation of task data in this way, for wandering from what R. B. Miller (1963) called ' task description ', is that a complete and psychologically neutral account in terms of stimuli and responses does not seem feasible. Even if the effective stimuli for skilled responses in industrial situations can be specified, this involves *ad hoc* assumptions about what is a functional unit of behaviour, assumptions which become more numerous and arbitrary as tasks and the systems they are helping to control become increasingly complex, as new technologies develop and methods of production change.

Laboratory experiments in psychology usually *do* specify unambiguously what responses the subject is required to make to what stimuli. The experimenter may spend a considerable amount of time in so designing the situation and quite rightly. But this discipline is unlikely to encounter the problem of levels of description which plague the psychologist analyzing skilled performance in the control room, on the shop floor, or in the office. Psychologists working in the laboratory, as Robert Glaser (1968) has nicely put it, do not *analyze* tasks, they *invent* them.

Task Analysis and Training Design

When proposals are made for training, or any other measures to improve performance of either operations or plans, then, like others, this method of analysis appeals to psychology. But these proposals are hypothetical. Task analysis is a *hypothesis generating* activity. It is the business of training design to evaluate the various training proposals empirically, ideally in pilot training schemes, or other experimental training studies. Training design is a *hypothesis testing* activity.

Consider the limited power of task analysis to support decisions about training methods when a course is at the design stage. The analyst's propositions about training methods are likely to be, at best, ordinal statements. This would be no handicap in the situation where the only consideration is *which* of a set of possible training techniques will be most effective. More common, however, is the situation in which a training method identified as superior is also relatively costly in terms of training personnel, time, devices, *etc.* The decision will then rest on *how much* more effective the method is, compared with cheaper alternatives, in terms of performance, accuracy, speed, *etc., i.e.* quantitative information which will invariably have to be determined empirically. In still other situations the propositions of task analysis will be different, or even opposed, for different training criteria. This situation is exemplified in the fault location and fault diagnosis training methods proposed for the process control task. Such training propositions are not trivial, but it should perhaps be noted that the psychologist who points out conflicting considerations in a training problem, without the *quantitative* information to resolve it, will not always encounter unqualified enthusiasm. This underlines the complementary relationship between task analysis and training design based on pilot training schemes.

7. Conclusion

Besides addressing the topic of analytic techniques in training, this paper has attempted to identify points of contact, however few, with other disciplines, to recognize gaps which have to be bridged and explicitly to acknowledge disagreements in principle. Following task analysis, it will often be the case that there is more than one, or perhaps several, solutions to the sponsor's problem. Besides training, the solutions may involve equipment design, or selection, placement and personnel development schemes, or education. Better communication between disciplines is important, because the implications of solutions to personnel problems which are chosen in practice, are not all seriously considered by the sponsor. Or, if the implications are not ignored, the sponsor's stated objectives may be short-term and only optimize a system which is part of larger and largely unexplored systems. One frequently suspects that optimization within the larger context is rarely considered by anyone. The larger context may be an industry, a nation or a whole way of life.

The method of task analysis which has been described deliberately formalizes the study of a task in its context. It would be arrogant to assume and indeed it is not assumed that other analysts ignore system context. Rather, the method of analysis has been devised so that it cannot be performed at all without continually considering two major system constraints, namely the performance capabilities of a population and the objectives of the system in terms of which inadequate performance is costly. One of the reasons for this insistence on continuous reference to system constraints is to acknowledge that technologies and professions, in an important sense, *serve* a system. It is the system's values which determine a particular implementation of expertise—in training just as in any technology. For the application of task analysis, it does not matter whether the system's objectives are far-sighted and philanthropic, or short-sighted and misanthropic. It is only necessary that they are clear.

The author is grateful to Professor W. T. Singleton, at whose invitation the original paper was presented, and to the Department of Employment and the Chemical and Allied Products Industry Training Board for grants in aid of his research.

How to Use Simulation Techniques to Determine Optimum Manning Levels for Continuous Process Plants

By H. P. Munro, F. W. Martin and M. C. Roberts*

Industrial Engineering Department, Shell Haven Refinery, Shell U.K. Ltd., Stanford-le-Hope, Essex

1. Introduction

Whenever the sizes of shift crews for continuous process plants are being decided several questions arise:

(1) What level of plant operation should be allowed for?
(2) How many operators are required to provide this level?
(3) How much time will this number of operators have available for other work and how long will idle spells be?

This paper describes one method by which these questions can be answered. Initially, however, certain items of policy have to be decided:

(1) Level of plant operation. Four levels can occur: 'normal', 'minor upsets (or unsteady)', 'major upsets', and 'full emergency'.
(2) Occupancy. Having allowed for meal breaks and relaxation allowances, up to what level should occupancy be permitted? How often does an operator think about his job? It is doubtful if one can answer this last question accurately.
(3) At what rating should the manual component of jobs be evaluated? Likewise, what relaxation allowances will be given?
(4) What meal and other breaks are permitted?
(5) What average delay to delayable jobs is acceptable?

In the system described, the answers applied to the above items are:

(1) Restrict occupancy to 80% or below. Whether this is the correct limit is not known but it appears to work satisfactorily.
(2) Rate at 65 (0/100 scale) and apply a 12% relaxation allowance to all jobs.
(3) Allow for one 20-minute and two 10-minute breaks per man per shift.
(4) Delay length depends on the type of unit.
(5) An allowance is also made for minor plant upsets (*i.e.* the 'unsteady' state mentioned above). This can vary according to what type of unit is considered and in practice varies from five minutes per hour to a zero allowance.

It is considered from experience so far obtained that the above conditions will permit sufficient time for the crew to cover the 'major upsets' and 'full emergency' conditions.

No allowance is made to cover absence due to, say, holidays, sickness, or training; this depends on other factors outside the scope of this simulation.

---

* Now with Personnel Administration Ltd., London, S.W.1.

2. Establishing Input Data

A list of the operating jobs has to be produced. This can take a considerable time and it is essential that this list is as accurate as possible. All members of operating units can contribute to this. In addition, jobs should be subdivided into ' delayable ' and ' non-delayable ' categories if possible. Having obtained these data it is equally essential to question the reason for doing the job and particularly its frequency per shift. How often does one get an answer, " We always have done this X times per shift " ? The mere act of inquiring about frequencies may reduce them.

The methods of evaluating the duration of each job including travelling time to and from the job are orthodox industrial engineering techniques such as Method Time Measurement (MTM), standard data, and self-timing.

The work content of each job is evaluated in time units assuming the job will be carried out by an operator working at a rating of 65 on the BSI 0/100 scale. To this time, allowances are added for relaxation and this new time is the job time used in the simulation. Additionally, for each job we need to give the frequency of occurrence and the number of men required to do the job and allocate a priority from a choice of two. Priority ' One ' jobs are those which should not be delayed or if delay is inevitable it should be kept to a minimum. Priority ' Two ' jobs are those where delay is acceptable. Finally, the job is given a serial number, and all this information is put on punched cards—one card for each job.

3. Sorting of Data in the Computer

These cards, together with the necessary control cards, are fed into the computer and are initially sorted into a suitable form for simulation.

Priority ' One ' and priority ' Two ' job cards are handled separately but in exactly the same way. The jobs are sorted into order of duration and each job is represented with its frequency, duration, and manpower requirements. The computer has, in effect, established the frequency distribution of job durations, which is then split into 50 sections or quantiles (sections of equal probability mass). The mean duration for each quantile and the probability that two men will be required for any job in that quantile are calculated. (From experience on the type of plant considered to date it has been found that no job requires more than two men.)

At this stage the computer prints out the job list together with the results of the above calculations and additionally gives for all the jobs in each priority class the average job duration, the average interval between job occurrences and the overall probability of two men being required.

The computer has been programmed to assume that the inter-job interval distribution is a negative exponential, with mean equal to the mean interval between jobs.

4. Pseudo-Random Numbers

The distributions are sampled in the simulation program by generating random numbers uniformly distributed in the range 1–50 and relating these to the numbered quantiles. These are not true random numbers, but are numbers generated by a formula of this type :

$$R_{n+1} = KR_n \bmod (P)$$

where $K = 8192$ and $P = 67\,099\,547$.

The series gives pseudo-random numbers which will not repeat within a cycle somewhat in excess of 67 million.

Note : $2 = 10 \bmod (4)$
because 2 is the positive remainder when 10 is divided by 4.

5. Simulation within the Computer

The simulation model is completed by specifying that a crew strength of given size is available. The total crew is set idle at the start of the simulation and the distribution of intervals between jobs is sampled to find the time which elapses before a job arises. Idle time is then credited to the idle men until the job is due. The simulation 'clock' is then advanced to the time the job is due. Then its duration, and whether one or two men are required, is determined by sampling the relevant distributions. If enough men are available to do the job they are assigned to it and credited with a period of busy time equal to the job duration. If men are not available to do the job, the job is delayed until sufficient men have returned from previous jobs. The delay to the job is recorded within the computer.

The model is run in this way proceeding in intervals equal to the time that elapses before the occurrence of the next event. After eight hours of operations have been simulated (*i.e.* an eight-hour shift) the number of jobs that have been begun and the total delay to jobs is recorded within the computer and a new shift is inaugurated. The program assumes that men busy at shift-end are replaced by members of the new shift as they come on duty. The simulation proceeds in this manner for as long as has been requested by the control card. In practice usually two weeks are simulated because it has been found that the distributions and results of simulation are statistically stable after about ten days have been simulated.

6. Priority

To date the program has been developed to handle two categories of jobs, priority 'One' and priority 'Two'. Two principles of priority logic have been tested. The system used ensures that if any priority 'One' jobs are delayed, they are subsequently carried out as men become available before any further priority 'Two' jobs are initiated. Hence delays to priority 'One' jobs tend to be minimal.

The alternative logic scans ahead of time and tries to ensure that men are always available to carry out priority 'One' jobs and will hence delay priority 'Two' even though men are available by reserving these men for the priority 'One' job about to occur. It is preferred to use the former type of logic, because it is felt that the latter type will break down if the proportion of priority 'One' jobs is large in relation to the total.

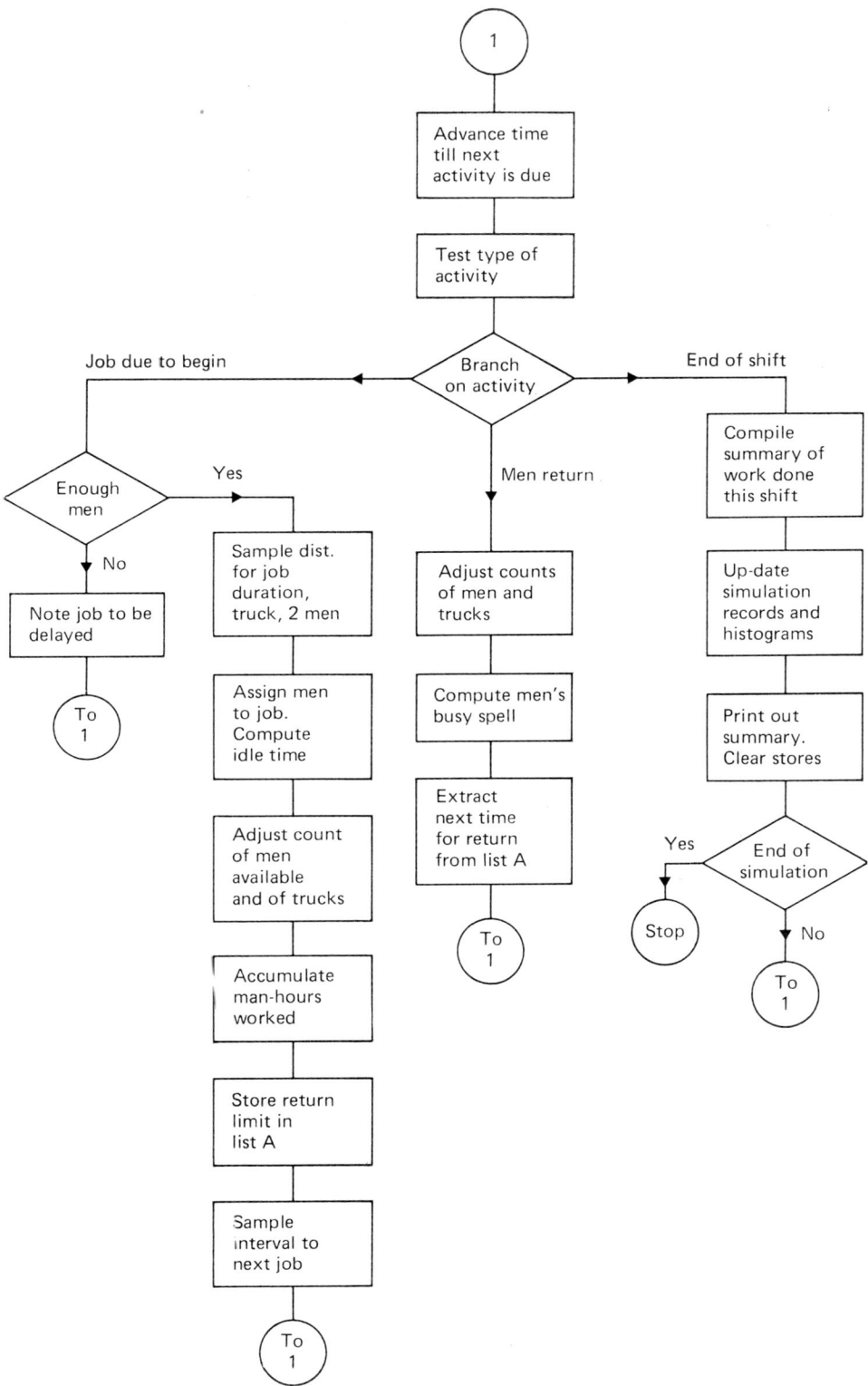

Figure 1. Flow scheme for a tank farm manning simulation program.

7. Flow Scheme

The flow scheme of the program for a Tank Farm manning simulation is shown in Figure 1. Here there was an additional factor in that some jobs required the use of a truck and hence for each quantile the probability of a truck being required was calculated and this distribution is held in the computer for sampling as required. This program also originally printed out results for every shift, which is no longer done, as the program has been altered so that the results are not printed out until the end of the simulation run.

8. Results of Computer Simulation

A sample of results is given in Table 1 for varying crew strengths of one unit and a comparison of selected results of three units is shown in Table 2. Figure 2 shows the distribution of the length of idle time periods for one unit.

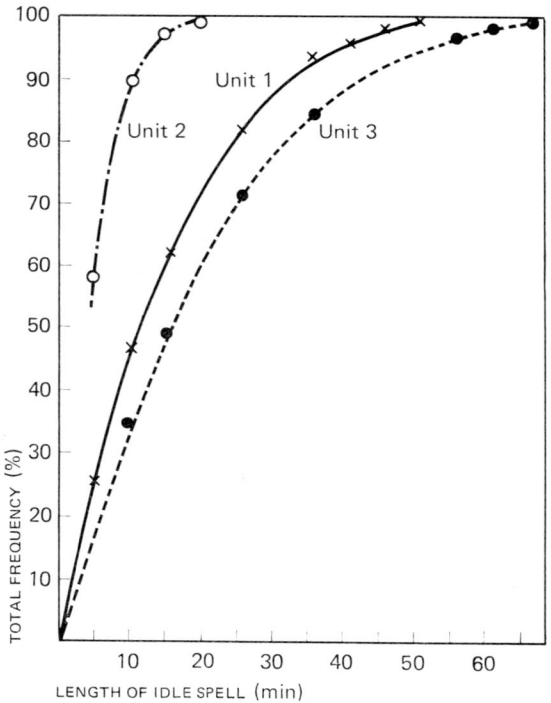

Figure 2. Cumulative distribution of idle spells.

In Table 1 the maximum permissible delay was prefixed at "desirable 10 minutes maximum 15 minutes". It will be seen that there is conflict between 'occupancy' and 'acceptable delay'. From experience to date it has been found that the acceptable delay is the more stringent requirement than occupancy. It is also more difficult to determine what is an acceptable level of delay.

Table 1. Sample of results for varying crew strengths of one unit

Parameter	Crew strength			
	4	5	6	8
Number of jobs simulated	2034	2462	2030	2034
Occupancy of crew (%)	57·0	46·6	37·5	28·4
Average man-hours/shift (h)	18·21	18·66	18·21	18·21
Average idle spell (min)	14	18	23	32
Average busy spell (min)	18	15	14	13
Average number of jobs done per shift	67·8	68·4	67·7	67·8
Probability of job being delayed	0·36	0·18	0·07	0·01
Average delay to jobs (delayed only) (min)	21	11	7	4
Average duration of jobs (min)	13	13	13	13
Average interval between jobs (min)	7	7	7	7
Average number of men idle	1·7	2·7	3·7	5·7
Probability of working more than one hour without break	0·07	0·04	0·04	0·03
Number of trucks needed	4	4	4	6
Probability that entire crew busy	0·26	0·12	0·04	0·01

It is interesting to see in Table 2 how the nature of the jobs affects results. Longer average durations produce longer average delays. This is, of course, to be expected from the scheduling problem involved.

Table 2. Comparison of results of three units

	Unit 1	Unit 2	Unit 3
Crew strength	3	7	5
Occupancy per man (%)	67 (2–93%)*	80·5	65 (4–74%)
Average idle spell (min)	14	3	19
Standard deviation of idle spell (min)†	12	3	15
Average delay to delayable jobs (min)	17	5	32 (4–62)*
Probability of such delay	0·51	0·47	0·36
Average duration of jobs (min)	14	12	29
Average number of men free at one instant	1	1	1

* Unacceptable result.
† If the standard deviation is S, then ±2S will cover 95% of all cases.

When comparing results of the three units in Figure 2 the following points apply if minor maintenance is to be done by operators:

(1) No minor maintenance has been included in the job list for simulation, so any minor maintenance has to be done during the simulation 'idle time'.

(2) It is generally recognized in this sort of situation (random arrival of jobs) that one should not schedule operators to over 80% occupancy—to cater for peaks and surges of jobs. Therefore total work load of operating and maintenance jobs must not exceed 80% of available man-hours.

(3) It is not considered that available spells of time less than 20 minutes long are of any use for scheduling any extra maintenance work.

For unit 1, with crew strength of 3, occupancy for operating jobs = 67%, *i.e.* 16 man-hours occupied per shift.

Maximum desirable occupancy $= 80\% = 19\cdot2$ man-hours per shift. Available for maintenance $= (19\cdot2-16) = 3\cdot2$ man-hours per shift.

The distribution of idle spells from the simulation tells us how much idle time is available in spells of 20 minutes or longer. This is 44%. (Note: although 25% of the idle spells are over 20 minutes the amount of time involved in these spells is 44%.) Therefore 44% of $3\cdot2 = 1\cdot8$ man-hours per shift is available in spells of $\geqslant 20$ min for minor maintenance.

9. Conclusions

Simulation is possibly the best method yet developed for determining the optimum size of shift crews for continuous process plants.

It is probably best to man for the level of plant operation described as 'minor upsets (or unsteady)'. There is in fact a large built-in safety margin because we have chosen a rating of 65 (0/100 scale) plus a 12% relaxation allowance when allowing time for any given job.

Under 'major upsets' and 'full emergency' conditions, the operators are naturally motivated by the occurrence to work at ratings in the region of 100 or more without relaxation until the emergency is over.

Acknowledgment is made to Shell U.K. Limited for permission to publish this paper; to the Computer Section, Stanlow Refinery, for their help in developing the Computer Simulation Program; and to all other past or present members of Industrial Engineering Department at Shell Haven.

Chemical Technician's Certificate of the City and Guilds Institute: Syllabus

CITY AND GUILDS INSTITUTE
London

[*The following is an extract. The sections of the syllabus for options other than Process Plant Techniques are omitted. The course also includes practical work and a project.*]

SYLLABUSES
086—CHEMICAL TECHNICIAN'S CERTIFICATE

Part I

1 Safety

NOTE: The following syllabus is intended to introduce the more common aspects of safety and safe practice, and it is intended that these topics shall be introduced as appropriate during the teaching of all parts of the course. Features of a more specialized nature are mentioned at the appropriate points in the technological syllabuses which follow. Matters relating to safety aspects may be expected to enter into examination questions in all parts of the scheme.

GENERAL

1. A general survey of the more important hazards likely to be encountered in the chemical industry, particularly in relation to chemical laboratories and plant, including fire, explosion, chemical, toxic, low and high pressure work, use of glass, radiation, electrical and mechanical hazards.
2. Safe disposal of waste and residues.
3. The need for a responsible and sensible attitude to practical work in the laboratory and on the plant. Good housekeeping, *e.g.* labelling, sealing and opening of containers. General neatness and tidyness, personal hygiene; removal of contaminants; dermatitis.
4. General safety precautions and safety legislation; protection of eyes, face, hands and body.
5. Simple first aid treatment of burns and scalds, attack by corrosive chemicals, poisoning cuts and electric shock.
6. Artificial respiration and resuscitation.

FIRE

7. Main fire hazards including volatile solvents. Flammability limits. Static electricity.
8. Use of flame-proof equipment and safe heating devices, *e.g.* sealed radiant heaters. Operation of fire extinguishers and their limitations.
9. Fire blankets and asbestos sheets.
10. Fire alarms and fire drills.

Explosion

11 Main explosive hazards including fuel gases; hydrogen gas, peroxide formation in ethers, explosive vapours, dusts. Explosive limits. Static electricity.
12 Danger of flying glass.
13 Use of purging techniques and safety screens.

Low and High Pressure Gases and Reactions

14 Main hazards associated with low pressure techniques: implosions. Vacuum cages and screens. Correct operation of vacuum pumps.
15 Main hazards associated with high pressure techniques: explosions.
16 Gas cylinders: colour coding and correct method of transport and use.
17 Safety precautions; lutes, bursting discs, relief valves.

Chemical and Toxic

18 Main chemical hazards including
   (a) corrosive chemicals: acids and bases
   (b) substances that react violently with air or water
   (c) toxic substances: solids, liquids, gases, and toxic vapours including mercury, benzene.
19 Protection against chemical hazards: protective clothing, eye baths, showers. Correct transfer of chemicals from containers.
20 Safety pipettes. Operation of fume cupboards and hoods.
21 Correct action to take in the event of spillage of dangerous chemicals.

Glassware

22 Care in the handling of glassware: carriage, storage and correct use of glassware and glass equipment. Removal of tight stoppers. Fitting of glass rods, tubes and thermometers into corks and bungs.
23 Correct assembly of glass apparatus: examination of glass apparatus for flaws, *e.g.* using NICOL prism, avoidance of strain.
24 Cleaning of glassware: hazards associated with cleaning agents.
25 Cutting glassware: precautions when cutting glass rod and tubing, removal of sharp edges.

Radiation

26 Hazards including those from X-rays, U.V., I.R., micro-wave, nuclear emission.

Electrical

27 Principal electrical hazards: mains supply and high voltage devices. Earthing and insulating.
28 Dangers arising from build-up of static charge. Methods of minimizing such dangers.

Mechanical

29 Hazards associated with machinery in motion. Hoists and lifting equipment. Safe handling of loads. Flexible connections.

Section A

| Laboratory Procedures and Industrial Practice | Basic Science and Calculations |

1. Note-taking and recording of results. Care, use, and adjustment of microscope as means of identification and for measurement, e.g. sizes and numbers of particles. Care, use, and cleaning of glass, porcelain, silica, nickel, platinum and polythene vessels. Elementary glass blowing, cutting, bending, jointing, including T joints on glass tubing up to 15 mm dia. bore of borosilicate glass. Use of glass fibre. Correct use of compressed gas cylinders and reducing valves. Pressure gauges. Use of gas burners. Use of compressed air.

Atomic nature of matter, atomic numbers, atomic masses and isotopes. Elementary treatment of periodic classification of elements. Co-valent and ionic bonds. Qualitative treatment of energy changes in physical and chemical processes. Symbols, formulae, atomic and formula weights. The mole concept. Avogadro's Hypothesis. Avogadro's Number. Equations and theoretical yields. Oxidation and reduction. Crystals as arrays of ions, atoms or molecules in lattice. Dissociation in solution. Electrolytes and non-electrolytes. Experimental demonstration of relationships between pressure temperature and volume of a fixed mass of gas.

2. Preparations and other experiments involving the measuring and weighing of solids and liquids including volatile substances. Determination of loss on drying. Care and use of balance and weights, including automatic balances.

Simple treatment of main properties of oxygen, sulphur, nitrogen, calcium, iron, copper, carbon, hydrogen, chlorine and sodium. Some common dangerous gases. Calculations of yields and efficiencies in the preparations opposite.

3. Use of temperature-measuring devices, e.g. mercury-in-glass thermometers, thermocouples, resistance thermometers, pyrometers.

Thermal expansion of solids and liquids, elementary electrical theory, parallax. Temperature scales and conversions. Heat units. Conversion of non-SI units to SI units. Heat capacity, specific heat and latent heat. Conduction, radiation, convection.

| Laboratory Procedures and Industrial Practice | Basic Science and Calculations |

4 Separation and purification of substances by re-crystallization, sublimation, distillation at atmospheric pressure and use of activated charcoal and ion exchange resins. Extraction of solids and liquids by solvents. Soxhlet apparatus, percolation, continuous extraction and elutriation. Dean and Stark method of moisture determination. Determination of freezing points, melting points, boiling points and boiling ranges as criteria of purity. Use of electrical heating.

Liquefaction, evaporation and sublimation in terms of kinetic theory. Simple adsorption. Solubility curves. Partition coefficients. Precipitation by ionic exchange. Vapour pressures, partial pressures. Saturated vapour pressure, principles of hygrometry.

5 Use of manometers (water, mercury). Measurement of gaseous volumes above and below atmospheric pressures. Transfer of gases from one vessel to another.

The gas laws and absolute temperature scale. Diffusion.

6 Determination of density and specific gravity of solids and liquids. Use of hydrometers, pyknometer. Measurement of viscosities by tube, falling ball and Redwood.

Specific gravity and density. Simple treatment of viscosity. Effects of temperature on physical properties.

7 Preparation and storage of standard solutions of acids and bases. Acid-base titrations to required accuracy. Choice of indicators. Mixed indicators. Use of pH meter, test paper, capillator. Kjeldahl determination.

Principles of volumetric analysis. Normality, molarity, ' factors '. Molality. Limits of accuracy. Proportions, percentages w/w, v/v, w/v. Use of logarithms, slide rule. Transposition of formulae. Significant figures and approximations, graphical representation of data. The pH scale.

| *Laboratory Procedures and Industrial Practice* | *Basic Science and Calculations* |

8 Fuses, voltage- and current-measuring devices. Use of shunts and resistances to extend instrument ranges. Multimeter. Simple experiments with potentiometer. Electro-deposition methods of analysis.

Conductors and insulators. Quantity of electricity. Ohm's law. Simple electric circuits. Principles of the potentiometer. Simple cell. Lead accumulator. Faraday's laws. Electrode potential, and electro-chemical series; electro-chemical corrosion, a.c. and d.c. electricity. Magnetic fields and forces on current-carrying conductor in a magnetic field.

9 Techniques for the preparation of inorganic and organic substances, using large- and small-scale laboratory equipment, to include:
   (a) heating with electrical, gas and liquid heating devices,
   (b) drying of solids, liquids and gases,
   (c) separating by filtration and centrifuging.

Introduction to organic chemistry and homologous series. Structural isomerism, including mention of stereo-isomerism, saturation and unsaturation addition and substitution reactions.

Section B

10 Introduction to distillation practice: fractional, steam, flash. Reflux ratio timers. Types of still heads and boilers. Distillation at reduced pressure. Solvent recovery and product collection. Vacuum controllers. Correct lubricants. Distillation practice at high vacuum. Vacuum pumps (mechanical and diffusion). Leak testing. Packed and plate columns. Micrometering pumps for continuous distillation. Methods of heat insulation.

Outline of distillation theory, including reduced pressure, steam distillation, fractionation and other azeotropic distillation.
Simple heat balance concepts.

Laboratory Procedures and Industrial Practice

11 Experiments to illustrate the importance of the initial inspection of all material. Sampling techniques of solids: Riffle, coning and quartering, grinding and sieving.
Experiments to show importance of correct sampling, taking and preparation of samples.
Sampling of suspensions and liquids.

12 Gravimetric analysis. Use of hot plates, oven, furnace, and radiant heaters. Methods of filtration under suction. Use of filter aids. Correct conditions for precipitation, drying, and ignition.

13 Volumetric analysis involving complexing reagents, precipitation titrations and non-aqueous systems.
Preparation and use of standard solutions of potassium permanganate, potassium dichromate, sodium thiosulphate, iodine, silver nitrate, ammonium thiocyanate, E.D.T.A., buffer solutions. Hardness of water determinations, and plant cooling water analysis. Fischer determination of moisture (manual method).

Basic Science and Calculations

Elementary statistics, mean, mode, standard deviation and applications in quality control. Pictorial representation of data. Histograms, nomographs, frequency curves. Use of desk calculating machines.

General study of the groups of the elements based on the extended Periodic Table. More detailed study (excluding manufacture) of the following elements and their compounds as examples of the group concerned: hydrogen; sodium; calcium; aluminium; carbon and either tin or lead; nitrogen; phosphorus; oxygen, sulphur; chlorine, iodine.
The concept of transition elements with particular reference to copper, iron and either chromium or manganese. Simple treatment of mass action effect. Chemical equilibrium and its disturbance by changes of temperature, pressure and concentration. Catalysts and their use in industry.

| *Laboratory Procedures and Industrial Practice* | *Basic Science and Calculations* |

14. Detection of nitrogen, sulphur, halogens, and phosphorus in organic compounds. Determination of molecular weights by boiling-point and freezing-point methods, using empirical constants. Preparation of organic compounds and assessment of purity. Use of glass-jointed apparatus, semimicro apparatus. Simple hydrogenation preparations. Some quantitative determinations of organic functional radicals, *e.g.* carbonyl, carboxylic acids, hydroxyl, peroxide. Saponification.

   Very brief description of main properties of functional groups as illustrated by alcohols, phenols, ketones, aldehydes, monocarboxylic acids, esters, ethers, amines, amides, alkenes, alkynes, alkyl and acyl halides. Elementary consideration of benzene and its properties. Diazonium compounds. Outline of industrial production of olefines, acetone, alcohols.

15. Gas sampling. Use of Orsat apparatus. Determination of calorific value of fuels. Determination of flash points and boiling ranges. Use of flowmeters, rotameters, rotary gas meters.

   Principles of calorimetry with particular reference to solid, gaseous and liquid fuels.

16. Chromatographic techniques; column, paper, thin layer, ion exchange. Gas–liquid chromatographic apparatus.

   Qualitative and experimental treatment of partition and adsorption, and RF values. Range of adsorbents available.

17. Use of Abbe refractometer. Introduction to spectrophotometric and spectrographic methods of analysis. Colour matching experiments with pigments to illustrate the general principles involved. Introduction to use of visible, infra-red, and ultra-violet instrumental methods of analysis. Demonstration of simple U.V. and I.R. sources. Measurement of typical wave lengths in line spectrum. Simple experiments with thin lenses and prisms. Nature and generation of visible infra-red, ultra-violet, and X-rays. Use of filters and monochromators.

   Brief outline of the principles of optical systems for instrumental analysis. The nature of colour and physiological perception. Brief treatment of the importance of type of illumination. Description and measurement of colour; additive and subtractive colour mixing. Appreciation of limitations and recognition of common faults. Rectilinear propagation of light, reflection, refraction and refractive indices; thin lenses and prisms. (Mirror and lens formulae not required.) Elementary treatment of wave nature of light, electromagnetic spectrum, diffraction. Qualitative description of absorption and emission spectra. Example of present-day applications of electrical discharge in gases at low pressures.

| Laboratory Procedures and Industrial Practice | Basic Science and Calculations |

18 Automatic gas–liquid chromatography. Conductimetric titration. Potentiometric titration. Moisture determination by Fischer—manual and automatic.

Brief outline of cathode ray tubes. Thermionic emission, valves and transistors; thermistors.

19 Visits to works to study industrial chemical processes as exemplified by selected industries. Use of a small-scale pilot equipment or plant for representative unit operation.

Short accounts of industrial unit operations and equipment used for
(a) separation and filtration (gases and solids)
(b) distillation
(c) evaporation
(d) mixing
(e) absorption
(f) grinding
(g) drying
(h) heat exchange
(i) combinations of these operations in a simple process
(j) construction of simple process flow sheets and drawings with appropriate B.S. symbols.

Part II

Basic Syllabus

It is assumed that students will receive instruction in all the topics listed in the Safety syllabus as an integral part of the course. Any matters relating to safety may be expected to enter into examination questions.

1 Methods of Synthesis

| *Suggested hours* | *Laboratory and Plant Procedures* | *Associated Theory* |

| | | METALS AND NON-METALS |

20 1 Preparation of simple inorganic salts especially those of transition metals. Assay of salts prepared, using the appropriate methods.

Revision of periodic table and general relationship of the elements. Special characteristics associated with transition elements; physical properties, variable valency, complex formation. The concept of electronegativity as a determinant of bond type.

Suggested hours	Laboratory and Plant Procedures	Associated Theory
16	2 Preparation of metal complexes, *e.g.*, potassium trisoxalatochromium (III) trihydrate, dipyridyl hexachlorplumbate. Analysis of complexes prepared by appropriate methods.	BONDING Pictorial and descriptive treatment of the shape of molecules and of complex ions. Hydrogen bonds.
8	3 Study of crystal form by microscopy. Study of crystal form by model making.	CRYSTAL STRUCTURE Simple and complex ions in crystals; giant molecules, metallic structures, interstitial compounds. General properties of pigments including crystal form, particle shape and size, refractive index and relationship to hue, strength, opacity and light absorption.
41	4 Preparative organic chemistry based on methods of introducing functional groups. Reactions of functional groups with particular reference to those mentioned in the Associated Theory column opposite. Diazotisation, azo dyes and pigments, *e.g.* azo-benzene-2-naphthol. Arylamide yellow. Infra-red spectra, chromatography. Hazards associated with carcinogenic materials, pyrophoric materials and explosive materials. Students' attention should also be drawn to the relevant sections of legislation dealing with such materials, *e.g.* Dangerous Drugs Act, Pharmacy and Poisons Act.	ORGANIC CHEMISTRY The concept of functionality. Bi- and poly-functional molecules including dibasic acids, amino-acids, hydroxy-acids, polyhydric alcohols, acetoacetic esters, butadiene and isoprene. Simple aromatic chemistry including reference to the directive effects of substituents. Naphthalene and anthracene as illustrative of polycyclic systems. Simple heterocyclic molecules illustrated by furan, thiophene, pyrrole, pyridine, piperidine, ethylene oxide. Simple treatment of optical and geometrical isomerism; steric hindrance. Introduction to carbohydrate chemistry. Brief treatment of relationship of colour to constitution; chromophore, chromogen. Petroleum and natural gas as raw materials for the chemical industry.

Suggested hours	Laboratory and Plant Procedures	Associated Theory
		POLYMERIZATION
29	5 Preparation of polymeric materials, *e.g.* polystyrene, nylon, glycol/phthalate and glycerol/phthalate resins. Characterization and determination of molecular weight of polymeric materials.	Introductory treatment of addition and condensation polymerization as exemplified by polyvinyl, polyester and epoxide resins; co-polymers. Solution and emulsion polymerization. Factors affecting reaction, methods of initiation, molecular structure and physical properties. Autoxidative polymerization. Determination of molecular weights of polymers. Reactivity of polymers; its modification by chemical and physical agents. Degradation; plasticisers and fillers.

2 Techniques of Isolation and Purification

Suggested hours	Laboratory and Plant Procedures	Associated Theory
		SOLVENTS
29	1 Examination of typical solvents for: flash point, evaporation rate, specific gravity, refractive index, colour, clarity and odour, solvent power, water content. Vapour toxicity. Solvent removal. Solvent extraction. Use of mixed solvents with or without complexing agents to control solubility. Revision of distillation at high, normal, and low pressure. Use of Vigreux, bubble cap and packed columns.	Consideration of solvents and diluents, evaporation phenomena, solvent power, solubility parameter, flash point.
		SURFACE CHEMISTRY
15	2 Use of ion exchange columns and slurries.	Adsorption from gases and solutions onto solids. Application in chromatography, surface area estimation, heterogeneous catalysis. Dispersion. Colloids; importance and preparation, electrical properties, electrodialysis. Surface active agents.

3 Assay and Estimation

Suggested hours	Laboratory and Plant Procedures	Associated Theory
15	1 Care and use of equipment for emission and absorption spectroscopy and spectrography, including flame photometers, photomultipliers, densitometers, filter photometers, spectrophotometers for visible, U.V. and I.R. ranges. Precautions in the use of sources.	SPECTROSCOPY Visible, ultra-violet and infra-red spectrophotometers; X-rays. Interaction of electromagnetic radiation with liquids and solutions; rotational, vibrational and electronic transitions. Beer–Lambert Law.
15	2 Electrometric methods of titration. Use of amperometric and polarographic equipment (manual and motor driven).	ELECTROCHEMISTRY Conductance: Faraday's Laws; transport numbers, ionic mobility, specific, molar and equivalent conductance. Variation of conductance with concentration of strong and weak electrolytes. Calomel electrodes, glass electrode. Extension of pH to include pNa and pCl and their use experimentally. Buffer solutions. Hydrolysis. Oxidation-reduction potential: polarization phenomena: depolarizers, polarography, dead stop end points, amperometric titrations.
8	CHROMATOGRAPHY 3 Chromatography (gas, liquid and vapour phase). Column chromatograms, use of fraction separator, inorganic and organic separations. Two-way paper chromatograms. Electrodialysis and desalting.	See 2.2.

Suggested hours	Laboratory and Plant Procedures	Associated Theory
	TITRIMETRIC ANALYSIS	
23	4 Use of potassium thiocyanate, ceric sulphate. Use of potassium iodate and bromate, titanous chloride. NOTE: Titrimetric and gravimetric methods of analysis and physical methods of characterization from the Part I Course syllabus should be applied in the analysis of products and raw materials involved in practical work.	See 1.1. Stability of reagents.
		ISOTOPES AND RADIOACTIVITY
16	5 Detection and measurement of radioactivity. Instruments in use in laboratories and on process plants. Precautions and uses of sealed sources. Legislation: ionizing radiation regulations.	α, β and γ emission. Use and safe handling of isotopes (radioactive and stable) in laboratory and industry.

4 Chemical Plant

Suggested hours	Laboratory and Plant Procedures	Associated Theory
		CHEMICAL PLANT
44	1 Use of pilot-scale apparatus to exhibit various dispersion methods in the formation of dispersions and emulsions. Operation of small-scale or pilot plant. Heat exchangers. Vacuum, pressure, and centrifugal filters. Driers, *e.g.* ovens; rotary, fluid bed, spray and freeze driers.	Main features of storage and distribution of solids, liquids and gases. Description of some common pumps and valves. Methods and machinery for mixing, milling and dispersion; pre-mixers, roll, ball, sand/bead, kinetic energy and attrition mills, high speed (cavitation) dispersers and heavy duty paste mixers. Operational principles and influence of mill-base composition on efficiency.

Suggested hours		Laboratory and Plant Procedures	Associated Theory

Suggested hours		Laboratory and Plant Procedures	Associated Theory
		Distillation and absorption columns. Reaction vessels and stirrers (agitators). Simple heat and mass balances. Legislation relating to chemical plant. Any appropriate regulations pertaining to local industry should also be included.	Appreciation of factors governing the design and assembly of process plant including the treatment of effluent. Principles of fluid flow. Principles of selection of materials of construction; ferrous and non-ferrous materials; glass, ceramics, plastics, rubbers. Principles of heat and mass balance.
12	2	Use of typical instrumentation rig, experience of feedback control, cascade control and proportional band operation. Correct use and care of instruments used to record and control pressure, temperature and flow.	INSTRUMENTATION The fundamentals of instrumentation. Requirements of instrument theory and design (but not details of electronic circuitry). The use of recorders and controllers of pressure, temperature, and flow as typical aids to plant control and efficiency. Significance of measurements; instrument errors and recognition of faults; effect of external disturbances.
5	3		SERVICES Use of steam, hot liquids, coolants and compressed air as reactor jacket services. Use of high and low pressure steam. Hazards associated with the use of high pressure steam, hot liquids, coolants, compressed air and gases under pressure. Economics of gas, oil, electricity, and solid fuel as heat sources.
4	4		DRAWINGS Interpretation and construction of simple drawings and flow diagrams. British Standard terminology for chemical plant (BS974).
4	5		CORROSION Mechanisms of metallic corrosion and its inhibition by the use of surface coatings, *e.g.* paints, platings, galvanizing, ceramics.

5 Protection of the Environment

Suggested hours	*Laboratory and Plant Procedures*	*Associated Theory*
6		Disposal of wastes: solids, liquids and gases. The responsibilities of the technician. Legislation relating to the protection of the environment, *e.g.* Clean Air Act. Economic factors involved in preventing pollution.

Elective Syllabus for Process Plant Techniques

Suggested hours	*Laboratory and Plant Procedures*	*Associated Theory*
	MOVEMENT AND CONTROL OF FLUIDS	
	GASES	
20	1 Determination of equipment efficiency and performance. Pressure drops through pipes, fittings and valves. Determination of Reynolds Number.	Simple interpretation of Bernouilli Theorem and Reynolds Numbers. Basic knowledge of fans, compressors and blowers; their operating pressures and principal applications in industry. Common types of seal. Streamline and turbulent flow. Compression ratios. Bursting discs.
	LIQUIDS	
26	2 Determination of pump efficiencies and characteristics. Pressure drops through pipes. Fluidised and fluid beds.	Introduction to non-Newtonian fluids. Types and applications of pumps in common and local use including centrifugal (single and multi-stage), gear, reciprocating and vacuum pumps, metering pumps. Introduction to pump characteristic curves. Pump seals and packings, including mechanical seals. Key points in starting up and shutting down pumps. Diagnosis of faults during pump running and remedial action. Glandless pump.

Suggested hours	Laboratory and Plant Procedures	Associated Theory
10	CONTROL OF MOVEMENT 3 Use of sectioned valves; where appropriate, stripping and re-assembling of valves.	Inertia of moving fluid systems. Main types of valves in common and local use, their limitations, advantages and disadvantages. Main features and operating conditions of plug, gate, globe, butterfly, diaphragm, relief, reducing and high pressure valves. Factors influencing selection of valves for a particular duty. Valve glands, slip-plates.
51	CONTROL 4 Calibration of venturi meters, notchmeters and orifice plates. Practical work involving use of temperature and pressure measuring instruments. Plant visits to illustrate control instruments.	Detecting elements for temperature control, thermocouples, resistance thermometers, bimetallic strips, pyrometers. Measurement of flow by pitot tubes, orifice plates, venturi tubes, rotameters and notchmeters. Hot wire anemometer, magnetic meter. Level determination by means of pneumercators, torque tubes, quantity meters. Concept of control loops. Outline of some typical automatic control valves. Brief description of the function of the following controllers: ratio, cascade, split range, over-ride, end point, time cycle and forward feed.
22	WATER FOR PROCESS USE 5 Hardness of water determinations. Costing of steam usage in evaporation and drying processes.	Sources of water and its quality. Temporary and permanent hardness; dissolved solids. Treatment of water for varying uses in industry by chemicals, resins, distillation, flocculation and deaeration. Possible desalination of sea water; reverse osmosis. Present and future water supply and demand in immediate locality. Boiler scaling. Properties and uses of steam in chemical processes. Some common steam traps. Use of steam tables.

Suggested hours	Laboratory and Plant Procedures	Associated Theory
	TRANSFER OF HEAT	
33	6 Determination of heat transfer coefficients. Measurement of thermal conductivities of insulating materials and optimal economy of use. Construction of heating and cooling curves for reactors.	Principles and applications of heat exchangers for gases and liquids. Fixed tube, floating head, 'U' tube or 'hair pin' and brazed fin heat exchangers. Materials of construction and thermal insulation. Outline of general mechanism of drying. Spray, drum, rotary, tray and freeze driers. Co-current and counter-current flow. Liquids as heat transfer media. Effect of streamline and turbulent flow on heat transfer. Water cooling towers.
	DISTILLATION	
21	7 Practical work to demonstrate the effect of operating variables on the performance of a column. Determination of product yields and composition. Material balances. Climbing film evaporators.	Continuous and batch distillation. Rectifying and stripping columns. Comparison of the use of bubble cap, sieve tray, valve cap, and packed distillation columns. Reflux ratios, constant reflux ratio and effect on efficiencies. Outline of calculation of theoretical plates. Causes, recognition and control of flooding and frothing. Instrumentation necessary for column control.
	EFFLUENT DISPOSAL	
17	8 Practical work to give an appreciation of physical problems involved in removal of mists and finely divided solids.	Problems associated with and avoidance of waste. Effects of pollution on visibility, health, vegetation and rivers. Inversion and plume patterns. Industrial methods of control and disposal of solid, liquid and gaseous effluents. Cyclones, electrostatic precipitators, scrubbers. Testing of liquid effluents. Alkali and Clean Air Acts. The function of River Authorities. Oil water separators. Radioactive wastes.

Part III
Full Technological Certificate
Qualifying Examination in Chemical Technology

1 Chemical Calculations

The purpose of this section is to give the student an understanding of the principles of mathematical operations used in his technology and to enable him to appreciate the principles of data presentation, data manipulation, and result evaluation and presentation.

It is intended that these topics shall be presented within the context of chemistry and it is envisaged that realistic situations will be used to illustrate their uses.

BASIC MATHEMATICAL OPERATIONS (15 hours)

1. Slope and area determinations, linear-logarithmic and logarithmic conversions and routine in both data interpretation and instrumental techniques.
2. Differentiation using either graphical or mathematical methods: Slopes of simple traces, maxima and minima; use of optical methods; use of electronic comparative techniques. Examples from instrumental techniques and simple physico-chemical evaluations.
3. Integration using either graphical or mathematical methods: The need to sum cumulative results to obtain a total quantity: use of Simpson's and similar rules, triangulations, planimeter, ball and disc and electronic integrators. Examples from calorimetry, gas-liquid chromatography, *etc.*
4. Logarithmic conversions: The need to linearize exponential and power equations; the use of linear-log and log-log graph paper. Examples from radiochemistry, spectroscopy, adsorption and washing problems.
5. Illustrations of the general fields of applications of such mathematical operations. The usefulness in analytical operations of derivative traces.

THE DISPLAY OF RESULTS (10 hours)

6. The common occurrence of more than two variables in a chemical process or system. The need to use triangle co-ordinates and nomographs as a means of presenting the information.
7. Graphical: sections of three-dimensional diagrams presented in a two-dimensional manner. (Two-component phase diagrams.)
8. Nomographical: the use of nomographs for the interpretation of simple linear expressions. (Boiling point, composition, pressure as variables.)
9. General: non-manual means of displaying data. Cathode-ray screen. Digital print-out. Use of x.y. plotters.

MEASUREMENT ERRORS (15 hours)

The handling of measurement and mathematical data requires an assessment of the reliability of the results and their presentation in a meaningful manner, especially in the evaluation of a plant process where it is necessary to seek the reasons for products being outside specifications.

Students should be encouraged to assess the errors on their own measured variables and to present the results correctly.

10 Errors
   (a) Random and systematic errors.
   (b) Accuracy and precision.
   (c) Representation of errors.
   (d) Scatter of results.
   (e) Mean and standard deviation.
   (f) Standard error of the mean.
   (g) Confidence limits and reliability.

11 A brief treatment of evaluative errors and result fitting.

MEASURED VARIABLES AND COSTING (10 hours)

12 General examples of chemical or plant processes to be examined, illustrating the necessity to select correctly the relevant chemical variable, detection system and manner of display.

13 Examples of simple costing showing the need to adhere to prescribed tolerance limits.

COMPUTERS AND CALCULATING MACHINES (10 hours)

14 Principles, construction and operation of manual and electronic calculating machines. Use and limitations.

15 Principles of operation of a digital computer, hardware, software, storage, time-sharing. The language of computers, writing a program (language to be determined by college facilities), chemical applications (laboratory and plant situation).

NOTE: It is suggested that half of the available time should be devoted to practical exercises involving calculators and computers.

2 Chemical Instrumentation

It is intended that the items in the syllabus shall be treated from the point of view of their usefulness in illustrating the design and use of instruments for chemical purposes.

SOURCES OF RADIATION (8 hours)

1 Black body radiation. I.R. sources; Nernst, Globar.

2 U.V/Visible sources; tungsten filament, quartz-mercury, hydrogen/deuterium.

3 Microwave sources; klystron; radio-frequency sources (N.M.R.)—(brief mention).

4 X-ray and X-ray sources.

5 Line sources: hollow cathode lamp.
6 Power sources (power packs). A.C., D.C., supply transformers.
7 Arc and spark sources, lasers, discharge, flame (brief mention).
8 Xenon arc.

Monochromators, Optics (8 hours)
9 Filters, interference filters; dispersion by prism and by reflectance grating (including basic theory); lenses, mirrors, construction of monochromators, rotating sectors. Single and double beam systems.

Detectors (14 hours)
10 Photographic: visible and non-visible (including basic theory of photography).
11 Photoelectric effects: vacuum phototube, photomultiplier, semi-conductor photocells, photo-emissive cells, photo transistors.
12 Geiger-Müller counter, scintillation counter, proportionality counters.
13 Thermal detectors: thermocouple, bolometer thermistor, resistance thermometer, thermoluminescent detector and pneumatic detector (brief mention).
14 G.L.C. detectors: thermal conductivity, electron capture, flame ionization, flame emission.
15 High impedance voltage and current detectors.
16 Vacuum measurement: discharge tube, pirani, thermocouple, penning, ionization gauge, McLeod gauge.
17 R.F. receivers.

Amplifiers and Circuits (10 hours)
18 A.C., D.C. amplification; high impedance amplifiers.
19 Diode, triode (tetrode, pentode: briefly); thyratron. Semi-conductors; crystal diodes, transistors.
20 Basic electronic circuits; half wave rectification, full wave rectification, voltage regulation, current regulation, transducers. Capacitors, emitter followers; cathode follower; valve voltmeters.
21 Reading and interpreting a circuit diagram.
22 Bridges: basic Wheatstone, conductance, potentiometers, polarography. Servo-mechanisms.

Results and Display Units (4 hours)
23 Voltmeters, ammeters, chart recorders, cathode ray oscilliscopes, digital meters, counters, scalers.
24 Automatic recorders; potentiometric recorders, deflection and null type. Impedance matching; matching of recorder circuits, use of shunts. Integrator and print-out.

INSTRUMENTAL TERMS AND SIGNIFICANCE (4 hours)
25 Gain, damping, noise, full scale deflection, sensitivity, *etc.*

FAULT RECOGNITION (6 hours)
26 Circuit comprehension, performance evaluation.
27 Use of meters (Avo, *etc.*).
28 Practice in construction of simple circuits and testing of equipment in *e.g.* Spectrometers, pH meters, conductivity bridges, polarographs.
29 G.L.C. Detector systems, *etc.*

AUTOMATED EQUIPMENT AND ON-LINE ANALYSIS (6 hours)
30 Automatic titrimeters, autoanalyzers, computer-controlled G.L.C.
31 Introduction to control of chemical plant; discussion of sampling devices, special sensor heads (*i.e.* high pressure pH electrodes), process analyzers, infra-red, G.L.C., transducers.

3 Introduction to Supervisory Studies

It is expected that case studies and rôle-playing exercises will form an important part of the course and students will be encouraged to develop their facility in both written and oral communication.

NOTE: No questions on Section 3 will appear in the examination question papers. This syllabus will be tested by means of the project.

THE CHEMICAL INDUSTRY (10 hours)
1 Historical development of the chemical manufacturing industry; the influence of technical developments, discoveries and inventions; developments in methods of manufacture and production.
2 A review of the main branches of the chemical industry: petrochemicals, agrochemicals, heavy organics, heavy inorganics, dyestuffs, pharmaceuticals, polymers, fine chemicals.
3 Major companies in the U.K., U.S.A. and Europe. Types of ownership of industrial organizations. Amalgamations which have influenced industry.
4 Geographical distribution of the chemical industry; major sites, reasons for situation.
5 Sources of raw materials, imported and indigenous.
6 Markets: major products, main customers.
7 Economy of the chemical industry: turnover, earnings, investment in major projects.
8 Future developments, *e.g.* proteins from petroleum, electro-chemical, microbiological, photochemical synthesis.

THE CHEMICAL FACTORY (10 hours)

In this section the organization and structure typical of the chemical factory are examined.

9 Research section: research objectives, organization and costing of research, function of the technician.

10 Development section: laboratory to plant scale-up, associated problems, semi-technical scale.

11 Production sections: production plant, raw materials, handling, the process, the product. Control, including on-line and off-line analytical control. Services, steam, water supplies, *etc.* Effluent disposal including pollution control. Maintenance. Function of managers and supervisors.

THE CHEMICAL SUPERVISOR (40 hours)

It is probable that at this stage in his career the Chemical Technician will have some responsibility for junior workers in a works laboratory or a section of plant, and therefore some supervisory skills are important. This section is particularly suited to a presentation involving supervisor games.

GENERAL

12 The qualities of leadership. Promotion of good working relations. Analysis and handling of workers' problems and prevention of interference with production. Union relations.

COMMUNICATIONS

13 Giving of clear instructions to workers concerning job content and job method. The technique of preparing and presenting information in a simple and deliberate manner. Verbal briefing of skilled workers. Instruction of learners in industry.

WORK STUDY

14 Improving of work methods and making the best use of available resources in machines, materials and manpower. Modern method study practice and co-operation between supervisors and work study and planning departments.

ACCIDENT PREVENTION

15 The supervisor's responsibility in industrial accident prevention. Recognition of potential dangers and their elimination. Safeguarding action against danger.

EDUCATION AND TRAINING

16 The rôle of the works' training department; on-the-job and off-the-job training. The function of the technical college and courses available.

Study of Operators Information Requirements at Trawsfynydd

By Operational Research Section and Nuclear Plant Design Branch, Central Electricity Generating Board

[*The following is an extract. The original numbering of sections and figures is retained. The report does not necessarily represent the final view of the Central Electricity Generating Board nor does it describe the present control room facilities.*]

1. Introduction

This report describes a study, initiated by Nuclear Plant Design Branch, of the functions of the operators, their information requirements and how these are satisfied during the startup of a nuclear power station.

The emphasis is on the central control aspects, since the main aim of this report is to present information on practical operation which can be used during the design of future power stations. These new stations will have a greater degree of centralized control than hitherto and hence even more attention must be paid to the design of the central control facilities. Functions which are at present carried out locally are only considered in relation to this future method of operation.

The report is based on a study made at Trawsfynydd. It includes

(1) A general description of the control room and the associated facilities.

(2) A description of the operator's information needs during each stage of the startup of a reactor unit, with comments on the way in which these are satisfied and recommendations for changes.

(3) A discussion of the implications of the study in relation to the design of future control rooms.

(4) The conclusions that, although much thought was given to ergonomics aspects in the general design of the instruments and the shape of the control desk, more study in future stations should be given to the functions of the operators, their information needs, communication, the layout of the desks and the design of the control room.

2. The Control Room

The principle of control adopted at Trawsfynydd is that of centralized control from the main control room of the reactor, gas circuits, and main plant parameters during normal running. The boilers and turbines are controlled from local panels during startup, shutdown and certain other operations.

The control room is manned by an Assistant Shift Charge Engineer, who is the Control Room Supervisor, two Assistant Engineers (Operations), each responsible for operating one of the units, and an instrument reader.

The control room staff work in close co-operation with the Assistant Engineer (Operations) in charge of the turbine house and the Assistant Charge Engineer in charge of each reactor. They also have contact with the other operating staff at certain times, *e.g.* when boilers are on manual control they have direct communication with the operators on the local panels and when the dump condensers are in operation there is a direct link with the operator controlling the valves.

The layout of the control room is shown in Figure 1. It is situated directly off the operating floor of the turbine hall with windows along the opposite side overlooking the cooling ponds and the surrounding hills. The reactor building is reached by leaving the Control Room, going to the ground floor by lift or stairs, and walking along a short covered path.

The layout of the control desk for one unit is shown in Figure 2. The sections of the desk for the other unit are a mirror image, but the layout of the controls and displays within each section is the same for each unit.

The control desk is supplemented by vertical panels providing more detailed information on the plant, alarm fascias and controls for the boiler and individual reactor rods. The general layout of these back panels is shown in Figure 1.

It is possible to carry out all normal control actions and to cancel the main audible alarms from the main desk. However, all alarms must be reset at the back panels and some indications and recorders needed during normal operation are also located on the back panels.

3. Operators Information Requirements at Trawsfynydd

3.1. *Plant to be Controlled*

The station at Trawsfynydd comprises two reactors each supplying heat to six boilers. The steam from each reactor is fed to a range which supplies the four turbines. The startup condition considered in this report is that one reactor is already running and is able to provide warming steam to the incoming plant.

The startup of a reactor and associated plant from the quiescent condition involves the following activities:

(1) Pre-start checks
(2) Approach to criticality
(3) Raising power to 1 MW
(4) Raising power to 1–15 MW
(5) Raising power to 15–150 MW
(6) Balance at 150 MW
(7) Bringing turbo-generator into service
(8) Float incoming reactor onto the range
(9) Bringing the reactor to full power.

The pre-start checks can take as little as $\frac{1}{2}$ hour after a trip or as long as 24–36 hours after a major shutdown. The approach to criticality (40 kW) occupies 6 hours, 40 kW–150 MW $1\frac{1}{2}$–2 hours with $1\frac{1}{2}$ hours balance at 15 MW for checks, balance at 150 MW takes 2 hours and from 150 MW to full power 1 hour. All the times are approximate and assume a trouble-free run-up. The detailed sequence of operations which has to be carried out is shown in Figure 3.

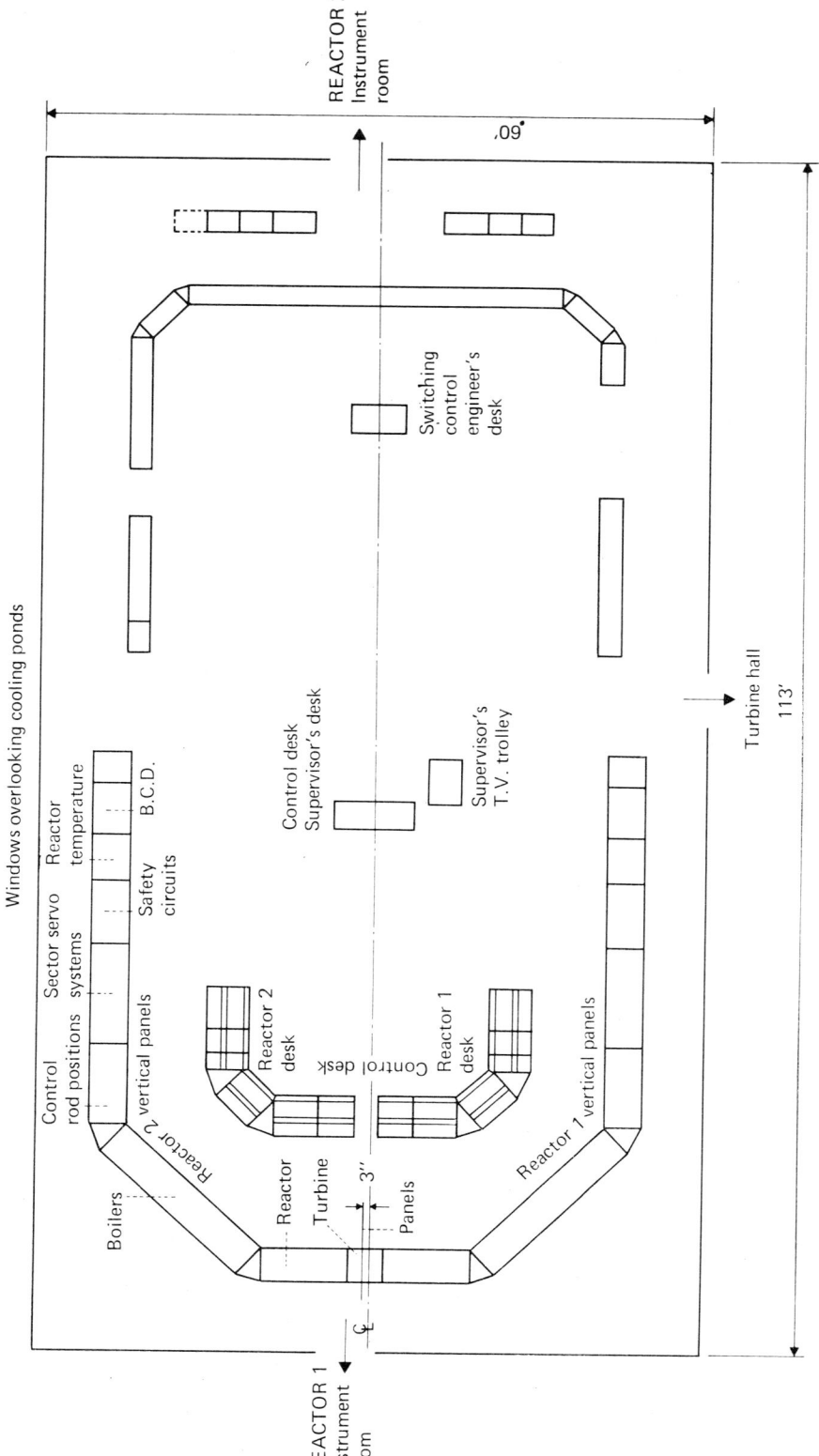

Figure 1. Layout of Trawsfynydd control room.

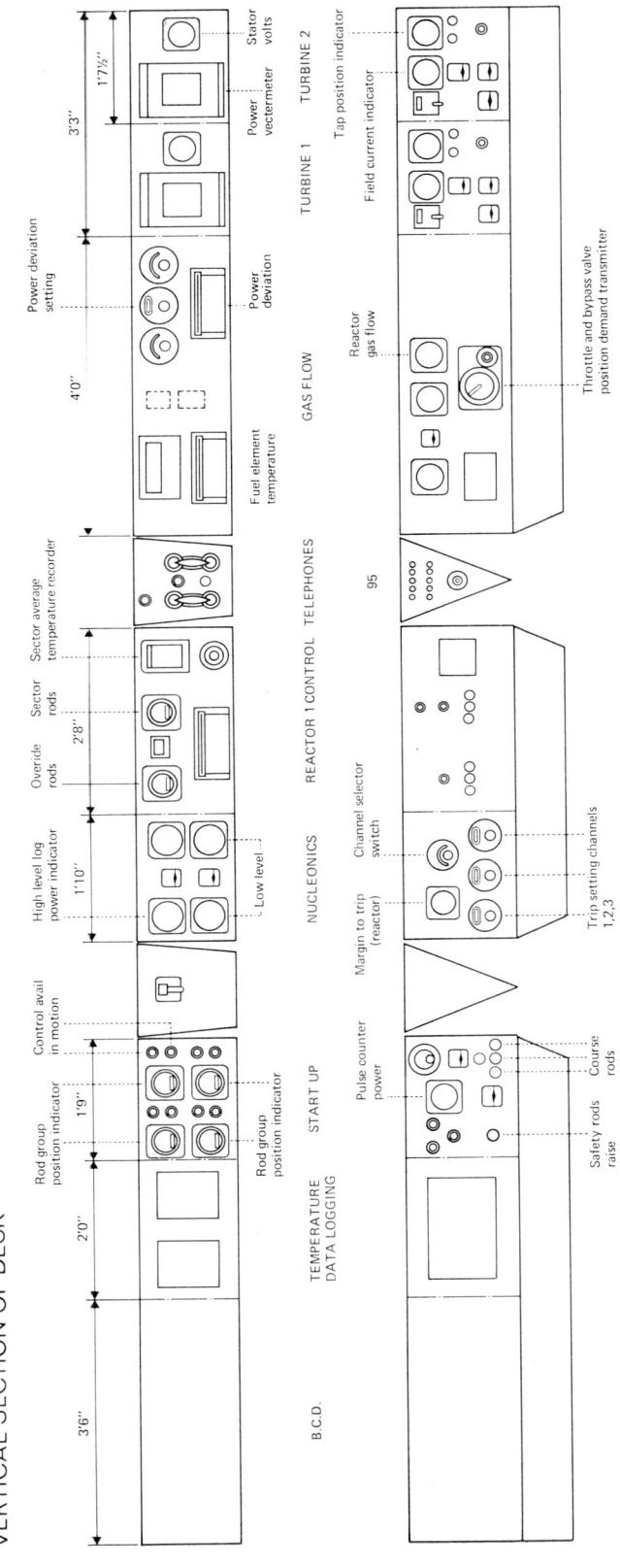

Figure 2. Layout of control desk at Trawsfynydd.

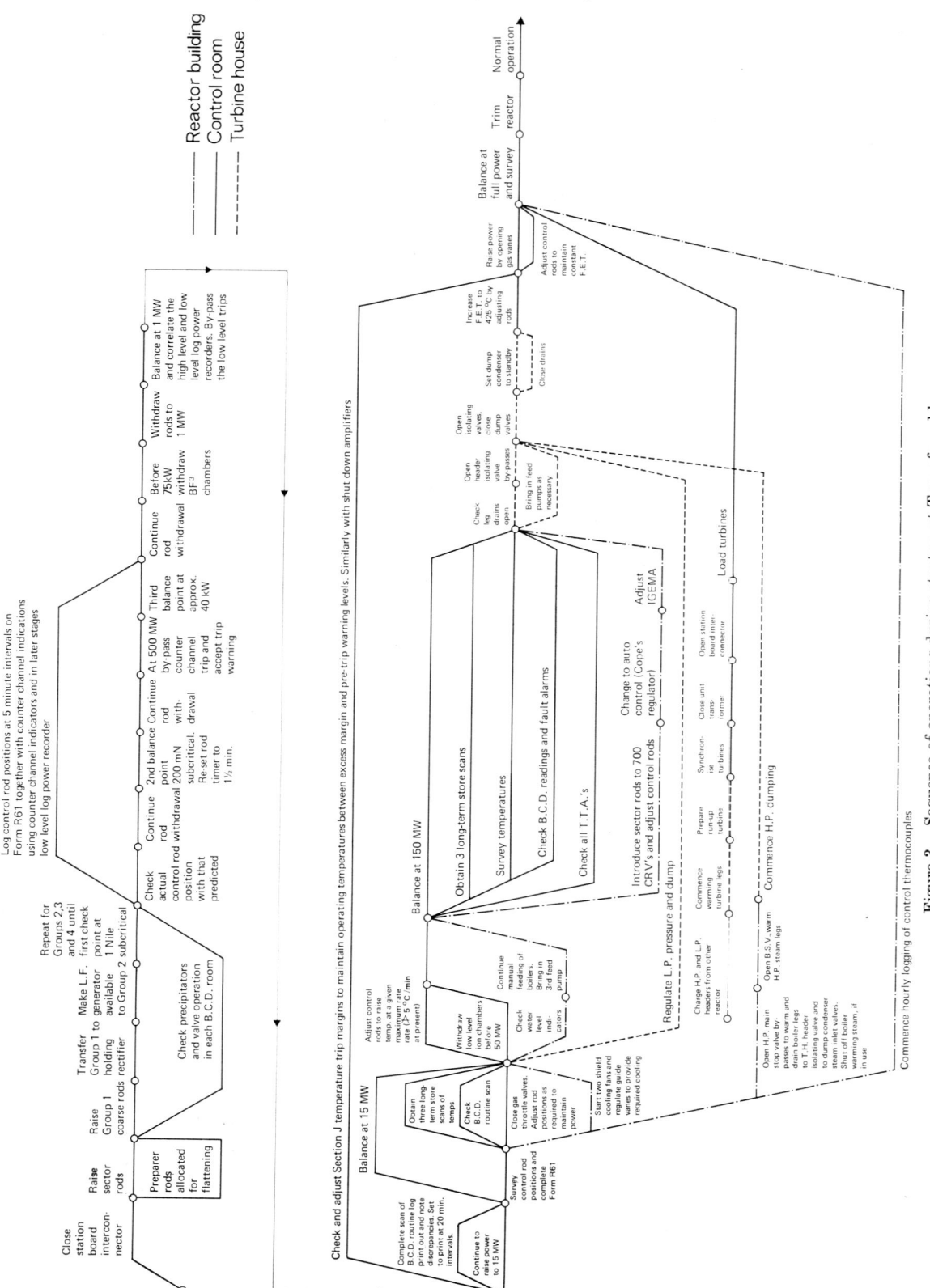

Figure 3. Sequence of operations during startup at Trawsfynydd.

3.2. Pre-Start Checks

These were not covered in detail by the study but Figure 4 gives the state of the plant before the startup as outlined in the station Startup Instructions.

State of Plant

Item	Operational State/Limits		
1. Station	One reactor in service and available for operation up to the full attainable power. Other reactor shut down. H.P. and L.P. steam ranges interconnected. Two turbine-generators in service at least, one other available.		
2. Reactor	Reactor shut down. All coarse group and sector rods inserted. L.F. supplies available. Safety rods withdrawn. Counter channels inserted and trip functions operational. Count rate not less than 75 c.p.s. Low level log ion channels inserted and trip functions operational. B.C.D. equipment either in normal service or on shutdown monitoring.		
3. Gas circuit	Gas circuit pressure 185 p.s.i.g. approximately (110 p.s.i. minimum pressure to clear control rod startup interlock). A minimum of four gas circuits in operation. Reactor gas inlet temperature of 190–200°C achieved and maintained by circulator power. Circulators on operational circuits running on main motor with throttle valve open. Non-operational circuits isolated by closure of at least the cold duct valve.		
4. Safety Circuit Setting	*Excess Margin Alarms*	*Pre-Trip Warning*	*Trip Alarm*
Counter channels	2 W (20 c.p.s.)	$\frac{1}{2}$ kW (5×10^3 c.p.s.)	50 kW (5×10^5 c.p.s.)
Low level log power	250 W (5×10^{-11} A)	2 MW (4×10^{-7} A)	10 MW (2×10^{-6} A)
Low level log period	—	—	20 seconds
High level log period	—	—	20 seconds
High level linear power	100 MW margin from trip level	40 MW margin from trip level	100 MW
Fuel element temperature in peripheral sectors	60°C margin from trip levels	10°C margin from trip level	30°C above normal full load operating level. (Set up to 470°C before startup.)
Fuel element temperature in Sector J	*Excess margin trip* at 60°C below upper trip level	10°C margin from upper trip level	Maintained 30°C above actual temperature, by continuous adjustment during changing power conditions.
Outlet duct gas term	60°C below trip level	15°C below trip level	25°C above full load operating level. (Set to 395°C before startup.)
5. Rate of fall of gas pressure	—	—	Trips at a change in gas pressure greater than 3 p.s.i./min. (D.M.I.T. characteristic.)
S.S.D. rod release mechanically	Fall in reactor gas pressure of 2 p.s.i./sec —no operation. Fall in reactor gas pressure of 4.5 p.s.i./sec—releases within 3 seconds. Fall in reactor gas pressure of 10 p.s.i./sec—releases within 1 second.		
Loss of one supply to 11 k.v. boards	Initiates pre-trip alarm on three guard lines.		
Loss of both supplies to 11 k.v. boards			Initiates reactor trip by opening three guard lines. Operates at all power levels.

State of Plant

Item	Operational States/Limits
6. B.C.D. operation prior to startup	Maintenance work affecting rotary valves, precipitators (above the available spares), or both computers, to be complete and checked prior to achieving criticality. Return all valves, precipitators, computer(s) to normal service. Weighting factors A, B, C to remain as set for previous operation or adjusted as advised by Operation Superintendent. (A—factor for all groups on the reactor. B—factor for all groups on one 40-way valve. C—factor for one group on a 40-way valve.) Routine log print-out to be set for a 'weighted' log, printing at 20-minute intervals on achieving criticality. Reset computer differential alarm program to compare the present reading with the one previous (I.M.D.).
7. Thermal shield system	One fan operational on each side of the reactor. Flow reduced (a) to maintain the minimum pressure vessel metal temperature above 75°C during the reactor shutdown period, (b) to maintain the concrete temperature at the underside of the pile cap less than 90°C. Vault dampers (four) closed in to achieve (a) but not exceed (b). Control thermocouples covering the pressure vessel, skirt and concrete are specified in an amendment to handbook 1.4.1. (Thermal shield system). Control thermocouples being logged at 12-hour intervals, during shutdown period (12.00 hours and 24.00 hours).
8. Fuelling machine	One fuelling machine and the following auxiliaries/services available for operation: Sliding joint. Fuel chute. Appropriate closure unit, from floating spares. Reeling trolley. Vent and vac system. Clean CO_2 for purging/pressurizing. Charge face crane. 415 V supplies. Discharge facilities to the pond; either to the acceptance bay or via I.F.D. route to pond corridor.
9. Feed system	Reserve feed tanks interconnected and at normal working level. Feed ranges interconnected on both suction and discharge. Feed pump operational as necessary for the running reactor.
10. Boilers	A minimum of four boilers in service. H.P. and L.P. drum water levels at half glass. Direct reading gauge glasses in service, Igemas available. One circulating pump for boiler section in service. Feed on hand control; hot feed available with half the station in operation. H.P. and L.P. boiler pressure at approximately 200 p.s.i.g. L.P. steam being fed to a dump condenser to control reactor gas inlet temperature at approximately 200°C. H.P. boiler stop valves closed.
11. Steam ranges and dump condensers	Two dump condensers available, with dump headers interconnected. Boiler leg/dump header isolating valves open on incoming reactor. Turbine house H.P. and L.P. main steam headers interconnected. Warming steam to the boilers of the shut-down reactor is provided through the header interconnection.
12. Turbine-generators	12.1 When one reactor is shut down, the other remaining in operation, the preferred arrangement of turbine-generators is that one set shall be in service on each side of the station (steam ranges interconnected). See amendment to Vol. 1 Handbooks, Section 1.2.3. 12.2 The remaining two turbines must be available for full power operation of the incoming reactors. Unless a lengthy period of low power operation is acceptable in light of circumstances prevailing, at least one of these turbines should be available for normal operation by the time reactor criticality is achieved.

Figure 4. Normal reactor startup procedure at Trawsfynydd.

3.3. Approach to Criticality

The object here is to bring the reactor from a quiescent state to criticality. This is done by raising the group rods (changing from one group to another when a group is fully withdrawn), until the counter channel indicator shows a reading equivalent to 40 kW.

The main controls which are used during this time are the group raise/stop/lower pushbuttons and the group selector switch. The raise pushbutton is left in operation until a timer (set at 12 minutes initially) requires it to be reset. The operator then resets it and checks the rod position indicators (group and individuals), the counter channel meter, and the period meter.

The main reason for looking at the individual rod position indicators is to ensure that they are all moving in step. When a new group is being raised, it is also necessary to check that the fully-in indicator lights go out. The transfer of control from one group to another is carried out by the Reactor Assistant Charge Engineer in the rod marshalling room.

As the flattening programme is behind schedule a number of rods are allocated by the Reactor Physicist as ' flattening rods ' to ensure a more even distribution of temperature across the reactor at later stages of startup. These rods are not withdrawn from the core as far as the others in their group. The connection and disconnection of the drive for these rods also has to be carried out in the rod marshalling room.

The operator is under no stress at the beginning of these stages and only has to monitor the period meter and counter channel indicators to see when they begin to show an indication. During the later stages of the approach to criticality the operator becomes more interested in his displays, in particular those showing low level log power, count rate and doubling time. He now starts to monitor more closely the recorders showing count rate and low level log power.

Doubling time at this stage must be kept larger than 80 seconds, but in fact is usually kept around 200 seconds, to give a margin of safety to avoid trips which may occur due to spurious signal pick-up.

During the approach to criticality the operator has a number of other things to do. He has to obtain a B.C.D. print-out to check that it is working correctly. From 1 nile subcritical onwards he also has to record at five-minute intervals the count rate and control rod position. The reciprocal of count rate $\times 10^3$ is calculated with the aid of a slide rule and a graph is drawn of this against control rod position. This should give a line which when extrapolated to cross the axis will indicate the estimated control rod position at criticality.

All three counter channel readings are plotted and greatest reliance is placed on the most consistent. The operator also has to check that the control rod positions are as predicted on the startup certificate at the count rates equivalent to 1 nile and 200 mN subcritical.

If during the whole startup period actual conditions deviate by a given amount from that predicted on the startup certificate, the Reactor Physicist must be notified and all operations are suspended until he has given further instructions.

From 200 mN subcritical the timer for control rod movement has to be reset to $1\frac{1}{2}$ minutes so that from this stage onwards the operator must stay near to his control desk.

The graph of the reciprocal of count rate $\times 10^3$ against rod position gives a prediction of the control rod position at criticality. The actual indication of criticality is given by the counter channel recorder. At Trawsfynydd power is held at the 40 kW power level (which is near to criticality) to allow the operator to cross-check the pulse counters and low level log power channel instruments.

Comments

With the geographical type of display of individual control rod positions in use at Trawsfynydd (see Figure 5) it is difficult to separate one group from another—a more satisfactory arrangement at the time of startup would be to display all rods in one group together, or in one line. This would also assist in checking that the correct rods have been allocated for ' flattening ' and that these move out when switched back to normal operation.

Figure 5. Arrangement of control rod position indicator at Trawsfynydd.

When the ' flattening rods ' have to be brought back into normal operation and when any group of rods is completely lifted out of the reactor, the reactor operator has to locate and communicate with the Assistant Charge Engineer in the reactor block so that he can change over the electrical supplies. (The changeover is carried out at the supply panels so that better interlocking can be provided.) This does not appear to cause any special problem, although errors could occur because the control rods are designated Groups 1, 2, 3, 4 in the main control room but 1A, 1B, 1C and 1D in the rod marshalling room. It would be desirable to have a common nomenclature at each location.

Recorders are generally necessary to indicate the rate at which changes are taking place and to help the operator balance the reactor and hold it at a given power level. When balancing, power is held at a steady level by manipulating the control rods to keep the recorder trace steady on one reading.

The operator, however, does not make much use of recorders during this stage, because those which are showing a reading (such as that for count rate) are situated on the back panel. These are not visible from the seated position at the main desk and it is not easy for the operator to read them when he is standing. Some early reactor trips at Trawsfynydd were ascribed to the operator not looking at these recorders. The station is proposing to install a startup trolley with the necessary recorders on it so that these can be brought to a convenient position when required.

3.4. *Raising Power to* 1 MW

During this stage power is quickly and evenly raised from 40 kW to 1 MW, within the limiting factors of a given rate of rise of fuel element temperatures (the maximum permitted is 10°C/minute but the normal rate at present in use is 1°–2°C/minute) and a doubling time of at least 80 seconds (in practice nearly 200 seconds at present).

The operator is again concerned with operating the control rod pushbuttons. He operates these whilst observing the low level log power meters and recorders showing the power levels, the fuel element temperature recorder and the doubling time meter. In addition, the operator has to remember to withdraw the pulse counters before the power level of 75 kW is reached.

At 1 MW the reactor is again balanced to allow the cross-checking of the high and low level log power meters, since the power level is now getting out of the low level range. All three channels are examined and the cross checks are made on whichever channel gives the best agreement. After this the low level log power and period trips must be bypassed to prevent the reactor being unnecessarily tripped.

Comments

No indication is given of the need to withdraw the pulse counters and it appears that at present the operators rely on using a copy of the startup instructions as an *aide memoire*. It is recommended that an alarm should be fitted to remind the operator that this action is necessary.

[*There here follow further Sections* 3.5–3.9 *on raising power from* 1 *to* 15 MW, *raising power to* 150 MW, *bringing turbine-generator into service and floating incoming reactor into service.*]

3.10. *Bringing the Reactor to Full Power*

This is the final stage of the startup and involves raising the power of the reactor to its maximum as quickly as possible, subject to the restrictions imposed by turbine considerations, *e.g.* a maximum rate of increase of H.P. cylinder temperature of 5°C/minute. Monitoring of the turbine parameters is carried out in the turbine house.

The reactor operator keeps under close observation the fuel element temperature recorder and other instruments used during the earlier stages of startup. He is particularly interested in the maximum fuel element temperature and when this reaches the desired setting (usually around 425°C), he progressively opens the gas throttle valves, maintaining the fuel element temperature by adjusting the control rods. The temperature trip alarms and shutdown amplifiers are still reset as necessary.

When the throttle valves are fully opened, the reactor is balanced and held at constant power to allow a fuel temperature assessment to be made and the temperature of the hottest fuel (Tsm) to be calculated. If this calculation indicates that this temperature is below the maximum allowed, the rods are raised further until the indicated fuel element temperature is increased by 5°C. This operation is repeated and fuel temperature assessments made until the correct temperatures are reached.

Temperature distribution calculations are now made by plotting temperature contours on a map of the reactor. If a more satisfactory distribution is likely to give more power output, the sector rods are adjusted to bring this about after xenon equilibrium has been reached.

At this stage a fourth feed pump is required. The turbine house Assistant Engineer (O) must remember, as before, to check and start this pump when necessary.

Comments

The importance of communication is again apparent during this stage because, although the power raising by the opening of the gas throttle valves is still controlled from the main control room, the information on which the rate must be based is only available in the turbine house.

More recorders would again be useful. In particular, a recorder in the Main Control Room showing the rate of rise of H.P. cylinder temperature would enable the rate of increase to be monitored more precisely. A steam pressure recorder would indicate the relationship between steam generated and consumed.

This is a difficult time because the controls for the rods and throttle valves are not close together. The operator must move between them, to operate controls and check indicators. However, when the sector servo control is commissioned this difficulty will not arise.

If information on temperature distributions across the reactor could be presented directly and continuously in a more suitable form, the process of achieving and maintaining optimum conditions would be accelerated. Some form of pictorial display is required to give an easily understandable and general overall picture. The commissioning of the sector servo system will also go some way towards this.

Nomograms are used to calculate the temperature of the hottest fuel element temperature (Tsm) from the hottest measured fuel element and channel gas outlet temperatures. According to information given during the visit, the Tsm is usually based on a measured channel gas outlet temperature. However, because the safety rules require that it is always a fuel element temperature which is patched to the recorder on the desk, the operator cannot continuously monitor the required channel gas outlet temperature. It might be that this rule should be re-assessed to see if it is still correct. Also, a finer scale on the temperature recorder is required and provision should be made for the indication to be backed off. The present indication requires to be read to 1° on a total scale length of 600°.

4. Implications of the Study for the Design of Control Rooms

4.1. *Introduction*

A number of points of more general application have arisen from this study which should be considered during the design of future control rooms, particularly since more emphasis is now being placed on centralized control. This section is not intended to be a detailed exposition on the design of control rooms but only brings together those aspects which this particular study has raised.

It must particularly be borne in mind that the men in the system both at Trawsfynydd and at future stations perform two main functions:

(1) One group, working as a team, are in charge of the operation of the stations and responsible for running as efficiently as possible. To do this they have displays provided to give them information on the state of the plant and the controls which influence this state.

(2) The second group must be able to take over manual control of the operation of certain subsystems in the event of a breakdown of the automatic or mechanical plant.

These men perform an essential duty and account must be taken of their capacities and limitations when the control room and other equipment is being designed.

One important question to which there is, as yet, no definite answer is " How much should we automate? " The problem particularly arises where complete automation for the normal control of the plant is economic but where maximum security under all conditions is required.

Two choices are available:

(1) The system is made completely automatic and the man is expected to monitor its performance and take over in an emergency.

The advantage of this system is that the plant is likely to run closer to optimum conditions, because the automatic controls can watch over the whole system.

(2) The operator is integrated into the system and full automation not introduced.

The advantage of this system is that if there is a failure, the operator is always well aware of the present operating conditions and will thus be better able to assume full manual control.

At Trawsfynydd at present the plant is running under the second condition, *e.g.* the operator is continuously adjusting the rod positions to take account of changes in power. When the sector servo system is fully operational, control will be more like that outlined in (1).

Human operators are most closely integrated into the control system during planned changes in power. They have enough time to get acquainted with the current plant conditions and are in close touch with the whole situation throughout the operation. They will immediately know if any of the main parameters start to go outside the desired values.

4.2. *Communication*

One aspect which must be given further thought is the communication system. With centralized control the man in the control room must be able to know what is going on in any part of the plant. One of the main reasons that a man is put in charge of the system is that he is flexible and can deal with unforeseen circumstances. Such a circumstance at Trawsfynydd is the continued failure of the control valve controlling the steam flow to the dump condenser; at future stations other difficulties will arise. The communication system should therefore be provided to enable the control room to communicate with roving operators. In noisy parts of the station ear defenders should be provided with receivers fitted inside them.

Control rooms should not be any larger than necessary because of the difficulty of speaking across them and of maintaining an integrated working team. This difficulty is particularly apparent at Trawsfynydd during synchronizing and when adjusting the Sector J temperature trip settings on Reactor 2. On the other hand, they must not be so compact that they become overcrowded when a small number of visitors enter the room.

Where two people must communicate with each other it is essential that they use a common nomenclature. The difference in the naming of the control rods between the main control room and the reactor building has already been mentioned. The B.C.D. compressors are similarly designated 1A–1D and 2A–2D in one place and numbered from 1–8 in another. This is very likely to cause errors.

4.3. *Design and Layout of Controls and Displays*

It is essential that the operator is presented with the information he requires to do his job in the most suitable form for him to decide what action to take. It should be provided in such a way that the risk of misreading the information is at a minimum.

Consideration must also be given to the amount of information which the operator requires to be able to run the plant. It was not possible at Trawsfynydd to design the control room so that the operator can see all the indications and reach all the controls without moving from one point. A particular illustration of this is the difficulty the operator has in reaching both the group rod controls and the gas throttle valve controls. However, as some items are only required during startup, it should be possible to provide a special startup desk, although this would involve duplication of some indicators and controls which are in continuous use. (This is now being actively considered for Trawsfynydd.)

With a view to saving space, controls are sometimes arranged so that they can be selected to operate different motions. The shutdown amplifiers at Trawsfynydd illustrate the kind of problem which this can raise. There is one dial to provide nine indications (*i.e.* three channels in three thermal columns) with a selector switch and three setting-in controls, one for each channel. It is thus possible for the operator to try to set one channel when the indicator is set to another.

With the development of more sophisticated data handling techniques it is possible for information to be presented on demand. One of the ways in which this is being considered is by the use of cathode ray tubes showing digitally the state of various parts of the plant. At Trawsfynydd, some reactor temperatures are printed out in digital form. It is difficult for the operator to understand the overall situation when presented with this mass of figures and so he spends some time putting them into a form he can appreciate, *i.e.* by drawing equal temperature contours across a map of the reactor.

Although there are times when the operator does require exact and precise information on plant parameters in digital form, it is not easy for him to appreciate an overall picture of the general situation from completely digital displays, particularly if they are changing. Pictorial displays (*e.g.* of the type now being developed for use in aircraft 'head-up' displays) can be designed to illustrate the overall situation and to show the operator those parts of the process on which he should obtain more detailed information. When digital information is used, special care must be taken to ensure that it shows the information in the clearest way and that large amounts are not presented at one time. The data processing system should, as far as possible, work out and display trends, *etc.*

When an operator has manually to change a variable at a given rate, he cannot do this effectively with the aid of an ordinary dial indicator. Due to the inadequacies of human short-term memory and difficulty in estimating time, he cannot always remember continuously the previous reading. Similarly, if he is looking for trends in a process, he cannot detect these easily with a moving pointer dial unless he can see the pointer moving. Although it is possible to detect trends from a digital print-out, this is not easy when the readings have other random fluctuations imposed on them. Most people when faced with the need to look for a trend from printed data, particularly when there is any 'noise', translate it into a graphical form. Thus it is essential to install recorders or provide similar displays on cathode ray tubes, to show trends and to give control information.

When a variable must follow a prescribed rate of change, the recorder face should be provided with facilities to indicate the desired rate of change (similar to a protractor). Alternatively, this can be drawn on the instrument face by means of a chinagraph pencil or on the chart itself with an ordinary pencil. Aids such as these simplify the comparison of desired with actual values. Recorders are also very useful for monitoring the performance of automatically-controlled items of plant, *e.g.* drum level and feed water rate.

Display systems should be designed so that information is presented in a hierarchical fashion. The operator should be able to assess the overall situation on one major display and decide from it those parts of the system on which he requires more detailed information. The sector servo system will be a display of this type.

An example of a failure at Trawsfynydd to present information in this way is that operators are expected to detect burst fuel cans from the B.C.D. print-outs. This is not a satisfactory way of asking the man to do the job. A more efficient procedure would be to use the recorder showing counts in the ducts as the initial indication. It is not easy to use the recorder for this purpose at present, because the normal setting is too coarse for any gradual trends to be easily detected. If reset to a finer scale the readings move off scale. Facilities for backing off the fine scale reading should be provided so that it can always be positioned on the recorder scale. If the random noise present is too great to allow a reasonable trace, then effort should be devoted to reducing this.

Another item of information mainly needed during startup is the present direction of flow of steam and water through the plant. This is not shown to the operator at present in an easily understandable form. A simple mimic diagram is desirable, either animated by the valves themselves, or else manually dressed by the operator as the valves are opened or closed. The first type of display could be presented on a cathode ray tube.

Operators always need some feedback information about their control actions. Two instances were observed during the study at Trawsfynydd where the operators were not getting this adequately. The reactor operators were seen to be pressing the rod movement stop button a number of times. This is not due to any experience of failure of this control (although some of the other stop buttons need to be pressed very hard to make them work), but to their not being able to see quickly that the movement had actually stopped. The provision of finer scale indicators or lamps which light up continuously when the rods are in motion would overcome this. (The light in use at present only comes on about once every 10 seconds.)

The other example is mentioned earlier and concerns the running up of the turbines to 500 r.p.m. The operators here either do not get adequate information from the standard dial or else do not have fine enough control on the initial entry of steam to the turbine. With centralized control it becomes important that these factors are considered.

It is axiomatic that the relationship between controls and displays should be realistic and standard throughout the control situation, since this will reduce the risk of human errors, particularly those due to an operator going to the wrong plant item. This requirement is not always met at Trawsfynydd. All the motorized valve controls (at least 192 in the control room and on the local boiler panels) are positioned incorrectly in relation to the indicators. The indicators show the valves closed with the needle on the left; the pushbutton to close it is on the right. Normally it is expected that the indicator will move towards the button which has been pressed. The power meters similarly bear the same relationship to the rod control pushbuttons. To raise power, *i.e.* move the indicator to the right, the left hand (raise rods) pushbutton must be pressed. The tap change control on the main control desk also has a similar reversal of the control-display relationship. The display moves clockwise, but the raise pushbutton is on the left and the lower pushbutton is on the right.

The control layouts for the two reactors at Trawsfynydd suffer from a major design deficiency as panel positions are mirror images of each other. This means an operator trained on one who has learnt a pattern of movements in response to certain stimuli, has to follow a reverse pattern when he moves to the other desk. The panels themselves, however, are not mirror images in that layout of the controls and displays on the individual panels for Reactor 1 are the same as for Reactor 2 except for the rod speed and sector control switches on the sector servo panels.

Attention should be given during design stages to ensuring that the right scale length is available at all stages of operation. Mention has already been made of the B.C.D. duct recorder and temperature recorder.

Controls which give ambiguous indications, *e.g.* because it is difficult to distinguish the handle from the pointer or in which the handle moves the opposite way to the pointer, should be avoided. Mistakes have been made at Trawsfynydd and at other stations due to controls of this type being moved the wrong way. Where pistol grip and similar switches are used, the handle should also act as the pointer.

A large number of instruments, especially those concerned with the boiler, were not working during the study, although this was carried out some six months after the station first generated. During a follow-up visit four months later a number were still not working or were inaccurate.

4.4. *Alarms*

Alarm systems should be designed so that indication is only given of conditions which are abnormal for the present power level. During startup at Trawsfynydd many alarms appear which indicate what is a normal state at that time. This is particularly evident on the boiler panel and should be avoided, since it makes the detection of genuine alarm situations more difficult.

The alarm lamp flashing rate at Trawsfynydd is such that it is possible to miss a new alarm when glancing around the room either because it is seen as a steady light or is not seen at all. A more rapid flashing rate would remedy this.

Indication should also be provided to remind operators to take actions such as removing the pulse counters. The only *aide memoire* at present is the startup instructions.

The existing alarm system at Trawsfynydd does not provide enough information when a second failure occurs on an item of plant already alarmed. This is due to be modified.

4.5. *Design of the Main Control Desk*

Control desks should be designed so that

(1) The operator can either sit or stand at will.
(2) He can reach all the controls and see all the displays which need to be used together at any one time without moving from one spot.
(3) There is ample room for documents, log sheets, *etc*.

Operators should be able to choose whether to stand or sit. It is not desirable to make an operator stand for long periods, but, on the other hand, he will probably wish to stand during periods of continuous activity such as startup.

An attempt has been made at Trawsfynydd to produce a desk which is ideal from an anthropometric point of view. The operators can, in theory, either stand or sit and still have the writing desk, controls and displays at the correct working height in relation to their heads and bodies. A profile of the desk is shown in Figure 6. This has been achieved by having a high desk with toe space at the bottom for use when standing and a raised foot rest which can be used in conjunction with a high seat when sitting.

However, the ideal aimed for has not been achieved in practice. The chairs are not strong enough to stand up to the continual use and there is a lot of play in their supporting column. The chairs are on castors which are on a large base. With this base it is not possible to get the seat itself close enough to the desk to achieve a comfortable position and the room allowed for the operator's knees and legs under the desk is not adequate.

Although a writing ledge has been placed all round the desk, this is only suitable for small pieces of paper and there is no provision for large log sheets. It is also difficult for the operator to see much of the back panel from the seated position. During startup and other complicated operations the operator must stand, because it is not possible to reach all the controls from one point.

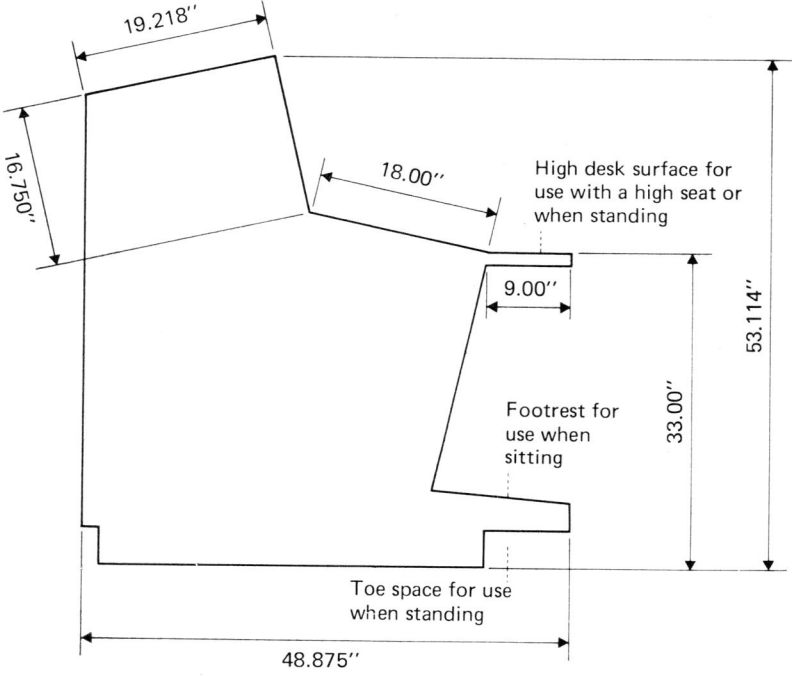

Figure 6. Profile of control desk at Trawsfynydd.

4.6. *Lighting*

Lighting of control rooms is not always given the attention it deserves. In particular, glare can cause trouble in two ways:

(1) Light from a light fitting or from a window can shine into the operator's eyes when he is looking at a panel or,

(2) Light can reflect off instrument faces and make reading of the dials very difficult.

The presence of windows in control rooms which are either in the direct view of or behind operators increases the risk of glare considerably. If the operator at Trawsfynydd looks at the vertical panels of No. 1 reactor, the daylight from the windows reflects off the glass of the instruments and obscures them. Also, if he looks towards the panels of No. 2 reactor, even when he is standing at the No. 2 control desk, he is looking towards the light and his attention is attracted towards it; this causes considerable discomfort.

Venetian blinds which would prevent the daylight from shining over the top of the control panels should be fitted.

5. Conclusions

The study has shown that much thought was given to ergonomics aspects of the controls layout for Trawsfynydd at the design stage. The station shows a marked improvement over the early nuclear stations in this respect. This is particularly apparent in the general design of the instruments and the shape of the control desk.

However, the study has shown that in future stations more consideration must be given to the following:

(1) *The functions of the men in the control system*

The extent to which operators should form part of the control system requires further investigation so that the maximum use can be made of man's advantages, such as his flexibility and the ability to deal with unexpected occurrences, and at the same time take account of his limitations.

(2) *The operator's information needs*

Information about the system being controlled should be presented in a hierarchical fashion, *i.e.* the operator should be able to get overall information on the system or subsystem to indicate those parameters on which more detailed information is required. This may require greater use of trend indicators than at present and the development of pictorial types of display. This kind of information is also necessary for those other members of the staff who only come into the control room for short periods.

Alarms should only indicate what is an abnormal condition for the current state of the plant.

(3) *Communication*

Although the importance of communication between the central control room and items of plant or roving operators has always been appreciated, the frequency of plant faults involving communication with operators in unexpected locations, some of which may be very noisy, has perhaps been underestimated. Extra expense on portable communication equipment to enable the control room to contact plant attendants wherever they are on the plant might be justified.

(4) *Design and layout of control desks*

It should be ensured at the mock-up and design stages that the operator can sit in comfort at the desk, can reach the controls, has adequate room for his knees when sitting, toes when standing, *etc.*

The controls and displays should be laid out in the same way on each unit and all mirror images should be avoided, as is present policy for new stations.

(5) Design of the control room

Controversy still rages as to whether control rooms should have windows giving a view outside the room. It is important, however, to ensure that where windows are installed venetian blinds or their equivalent should be provided to prevent glare and reflections.

(6) Importance of detailed design

It has become apparent in several places in this study that a number of apparently minor items have not been given the design attention which they deserve. Many of these phenomena only become apparent when items of equipment from different manufacturers first come together on the site and it would be desirable to make some arrangements to deal with such problems. Typical examples of these are the failure to have completely standard nomenclature, the lack of venetian blinds and the failure to have satisfactory seating. The cost of remedying these faults would be very small compared to the overall station cost and the difficulties they cause.

The assistance of the Station Superintendent and his staff at Trawsfynydd Power Station and the Headquarters Nuclear Operations Branch in the preparation of this report is gratefully acknowledged.

Socio-Technical Approach to Problems of Process Control

By P. H. ENGELSTAD

Work Research Institutes, Oslo, Norway

1. Introduction

This paper describes a concrete experiment conducted by a team of social scientists in the Hunsfos pulp and paper mill during 1964–67 under the supervision of the author. This is part of the research team's complete programme for which Professor Einar Thorsrud (Work Research Institutes, Oslo) and Professor Fred E. Emery (Human Resources Centre, Tavistock Institute of Human Relations, London) have been responsible. The study is one of the four experiments carried out in different industries under the so-called Industrial Democracy Project, an action research programme sponsored jointly by the Norwegian Federation of Employers (NAF) and the Trades Union Council of Norway (LO) (Thorsrud and Emery 1969).

The primary objective of this programme was, through a systematic redesign of jobs, to improve the conditions whereby men could exercise more discretion and have greater influence over their own work situation. To achieve these goals, however, neither party was willing to sacrifice the rising standard of living resulting from economic growth in industry.

Existing evidence indicated that one could reduce the feeling of alienation and release human resources in the company if jobs could be constructed either in accordance with the well-known principle of job enlargement or with the more promising model of partly autonomous work groups. The changes required were expected to be primarily related to the type of technology involved, taking for granted that the changes were in accordance with basic constraints imposed by the psychological needs of job-holders (see the next section and Appendix 1).

The research task was conceived of as twofold. Firstly, to give practical demonstrations of new principles of job design and, secondly, to encourage the diffusion of possible results that were found useful. In the following, we shall confine ourselves to the first task in general and to the experiment at Hunsfos in particular.* Consequently, it should be noted that, although this one field experiment might properly illustrate the socio-technical approach as such, a full evaluation of the results achieved by this research programme requires the four field experiments to be considered as a whole.

Even though the specific goals of this project have been different from what might be conceived of as of major concern by participants in this symposium, the author believes that there should be a convergence of interest over the problems of control in those complex systems, including technical as well as human components. Before describing our case material, we shall very briefly consider the problem as we see it and indicate some of the principles that have served as guidelines in the carrying out of our research.

---

* The other field experiments were carried out in a wiredrawing department at Christiania Spigerverk, Oslo, in a department for assembling electrical panels at Nobo, Trondheim, and in a fertiliser plant at Norsk Hydro, Porsgrunn.

2. The Socio-Technical Approach

Improved production control in industry has hitherto very much been looked upon as a question of finding the best technical solution to the problem, whereas organizational factors were not taken so much into consideration, particularly during the design phase. This takes for granted that people, within their physical capacities, will be able to cope with and adapt to whatever type of task structures and variances they are left with. This procedure has led to a compartmentalization of the organization. Hence, many of the artificial segregations of crafts advocated by the trades unions are also reflections of traditional management practices. To our mind, it appears evident that these procedures must have resulted in sub-optimum solutions for the socio-technical system as a whole, since the reliability of the total system in this case will be decided by its weakest link. It should be noted that, with the general development towards automation, the location and character of the socio-technical interface will change, though such an interface will always persist at some level of an enterprise. Furthermore, in a period when almost everyone in society receives an increasingly higher education, it appears to be a paradox that the jobs, in particular at the lower levels in industry, still tend to be rigidly delineated, offering little scope for variation, learning and joint problem-solving and decision-making.

The socio-technical approach is based on organizational thinking that, within the unavoidable constraints of the technology, encourages as far as possible local initiative and responsible autonomy.

In our terms of reference, enterprises and their subsystems are considered as open socio-technical systems. Hence, like other living systems, they are open to matter-energy-information exchanges with an environment. Without trying to go more deeply into any of the principles that are a consequence of the open-system characteristics of the enterprise, the following may be listed as being of particular relevance to the present project:*

(1) The primary task of a manager is to control the boundary conditions of his unit.

(2) The goals of an open system can be understood only as special forms of interdependence between the system and its environment.

(3) The goal state has the characteristics of a steady state, which requires (a) a constancy of direction and (b) a tolerable rate of progress.

(4) Steady state can be achieved only through leadership and commitment.

(5) The basic regulation of open systems is self-regulation.

(6) As individuals have open system properties, the enterprise must allow its members a sufficient measure of autonomy.

It is well known that motivations and attitudes of job-holders are not decided only by external rewards and sanctions, but also by certain intrinsic

---

* For a condensed presentation of the principles of system theory referred to, see Emery (1969) (Introduction).

characteristics of the tasks. Hence, empirical evidence suggests that workers prefer tasks (Emery 1959)

(1) Of a substantial degree of wholeness (that is, which show a strong *gestalt*)

(2) Where the individual has control over the materials and the processes involved.

These requirements have been further translated into a set of psychological job requirements (Appendix 1).

The co-existence of a social and a technical system involves a coupling of two part-systems, each independently governed by its own laws, towards a common goal. As the contributions of these systems are essentially complementary, special attention must be paid to the interdependencies between them.

The two systems are primarily coupled through the reciprocal allocation of tasks to work rôles, each of which is able to form systems of a higher order. Existing evidence shows that, when unit tasks were small, job enlargement has been a useful organizational model (Walker 1950 and Guest 1957). In the English coalmines, where a number of tasks exceed the one man/one shift unit, it appeared that technological requirement as well as human needs could be adequately met by an autonomous work group (Herbst 1962 and Trist *et al.* 1963). The same principles of job design have later been applied also in the textile industry (Rice 1958). In these cases, the problem of identifying naturally bounded areas (in the sense that they had a high potential for self-regulation) was relatively easy. This task is considerably more difficult in an integrated pulp and paper technology where

(1) The dependence relationships of process variables form a complex network along the process.

(2) The continuity of production, the level of throughput and the restricted buffer capacities in the process, to be effective, require that the disturbance control sequences be operated at appropriate speeds.

In order to identify units that would optimally meet these requirements, a method of analysis based on task structure has been developed. The so-called *matrix of variances*, which is based on the dependence relationship between state characteristics of the material, has been useful in identifying natural clusters of variances that are to be allocated within the same organizational unit (Appendix 2) (Engelstad 1969b).

Finally, conditions for self-regulation can be improved by various changes in the social and the technical systems. This is best illustrated by our case material.

3. Hunsfos Pulp and Paper Mill

This account is an abstracted and rewritten version of a much more detailed report on the Hunsfos experiment, 1964–65, written for another purpose (Engelstad 1969a). Further reference to this report will not be made in the following.

The Hunsfos mill is situated in a small community, about 10 miles north of the industrial seaport of Kristiansand, in the very south of Norway. The rural surroundings as well as the tidiness of the workplaces contribute to the general impression of a friendly atmosphere when one is visiting the site.

Since the end of the last century, the company has been the major employer in the community and, even in 1963, employed almost 50% of its adult male working population. About 80% of the Hunsfos labour force of 900–1 000 had close links with the community and the mill through their families, often employed by Hunsfos for three generations. The personal relationships at work are stable and closely linked to the religious, political and economic life of the community. The workers and foremen have been recruited mainly from the local district; the managers and most of the technical staff have moved in from other parts of the country. Hunsfos has a strongly professional management, respected both within the industry and within the plant, also a local union leadership with effective working relations with the central union headquarters in Oslo.

The company is one of five integrated papermills in Norway that offer the full range of the major technologies—mechanical pulping, chemical pulping and papermaking. Of the approximate total of 80 mills in the country, Hunsfos ranks fifth in terms of total sales. In 1964, the mill converted 200 000 m³ of timber to 20 000 tons of mechanical woodpulp and 34 000 tons of chemical pulp. This again resulted in a total output of 65 000 tons of paper. The production covers a wide range of qualities within the sectors of magazine, packaging and fine papers. Total sales, of which 85% were exported, came close to 80 m N.Cr.

The economic situation of the pulp and paper industries in Norway has been difficult for years and Hunsfos during the last ten years, in order to meet the challenge, has carried out two large reconstructions and investment programmes.

In 1959, the company, as the first one in Europe, introduced the magnesium bisulphite process in order economically to exploit the firs and hardwoods that combined are more prevalent than spruce in the south of Norway. Soon afterwards, fully-continuous running, based on a four-shift schedule, was introduced to maximize plant utilization. A number of technical improvements have been effected, including the reconstruction of some of the papermachines. This has allowed the company gradually to change its paper grades toward qualities of a higher converting value.

4. Selection of the Chemical Pulp Department for Experimenting

In September 1964, the management and the trades union at Hunsfos agreed to have the research team find a suitable area in the plant to introduce new principles of job design experimentally. From a research point of view, sites would be acceptable only in so far as they would have

(1) Process technology characteristics
(2) A high potential for diffusing possible results to the company as a whole.

Initially, this left us a choice among wood preparation, mechanical and chemical pulping, stock preparation and papermachines. Interviews with employees covering all levels of responsibility in these areas of production provided a detailed picture of the rôle system and how the technical interdependencies were coped with by rôle interrelations. The attitudes expressed by the employees were taken as clues to the fit or lack of fit of the social and technical systems.

A matrix of variances, based on the dependence relationships between state characteristics of the materials in different parts of the process, was constructed in close co-operation with some of the process technologists. Our focal concern, unlike that of the design engineer, however, was with those variances arising from the technical system that required responses from the organization of individuals if the production goals were to be achieved. The matrix helped us to identify where these variances arose in the technological process and where in the subsequent stages of production they could be identified, communicated or acted upon. The matrix was worked out in close co-operation with technologists in the company. Our analysis also entailed working over historical records of plant operations, estimating cost/benefit ratios for possible changes in different parts of the mill and collecting labour force statistics that would indicate social costs incurred by different departments.

It was agreed to start the experiment in the chemical pulp department. Taking into consideration such factors as the dependence structure of the variances in the materials, the spatio-temporal aspects of the process, potential input-output measurements and certain variables in the social system, this department appeared to be a naturally bounded socio-technical unit with a relatively high potential for self-regulation. It appeared also to be an optimum choice, because

(1) The department showed an opening for significant improvement in that some of the variances in the timber, if not coped with in the chemical pulping, could be met in the papermaking only by downgrading the quality (and economic value) of the paper. (To a much lesser extent, mechanical pulping had the same effect.)

(2) Located in between the wood preparation and the papermill, changes in the mode of chemical pulp operations would exert maximum leverage on these parts.

(3) Local leadership on the management as well as on the union side appeared to be sufficiently capable and willing. This we expected would offset the resistance to change that might be expected from the senior operators (10 out of 15 of whom were over 50 years of age) and from some of the men who were apt to stick to their viewpoints or to seek isolation.

5. Tasks Arising from the Technical System

The chemical pulp process. For readers familiar with pulp and paper technology, any detailed description of the manufacturing process and the technical equipment can obviously be dispensed with. I shall therefore describe only those aspects of the technology that were found to be of particular importance for this experiment. Only a schematic presentation of the equipment therefore has been reprinted from a company report (Figure 1).

The technical system of the chemical pulp department consists of five converting processes carried out in different, but adjacent areas—boiling, screening and bleaching, and the preparation of boiling acid and of bleaching liquids.

As the reader will know, chips of spruce, fir and hardwood are boiled separately in large digesters with acid magnesium bisulphite. (In the wood, the two major components of lignin and cellulose form a rigid three-dimensional structure.) Under the right conditions of acid concentration, temperature, pressure, time, *etc.*, the lignin is dissolved and the cellulose fibres are released. The fibres, together with other undissolved material, are washed and prepared for further separation in the screening section; the lignin and the used boiling liquid go to waste.

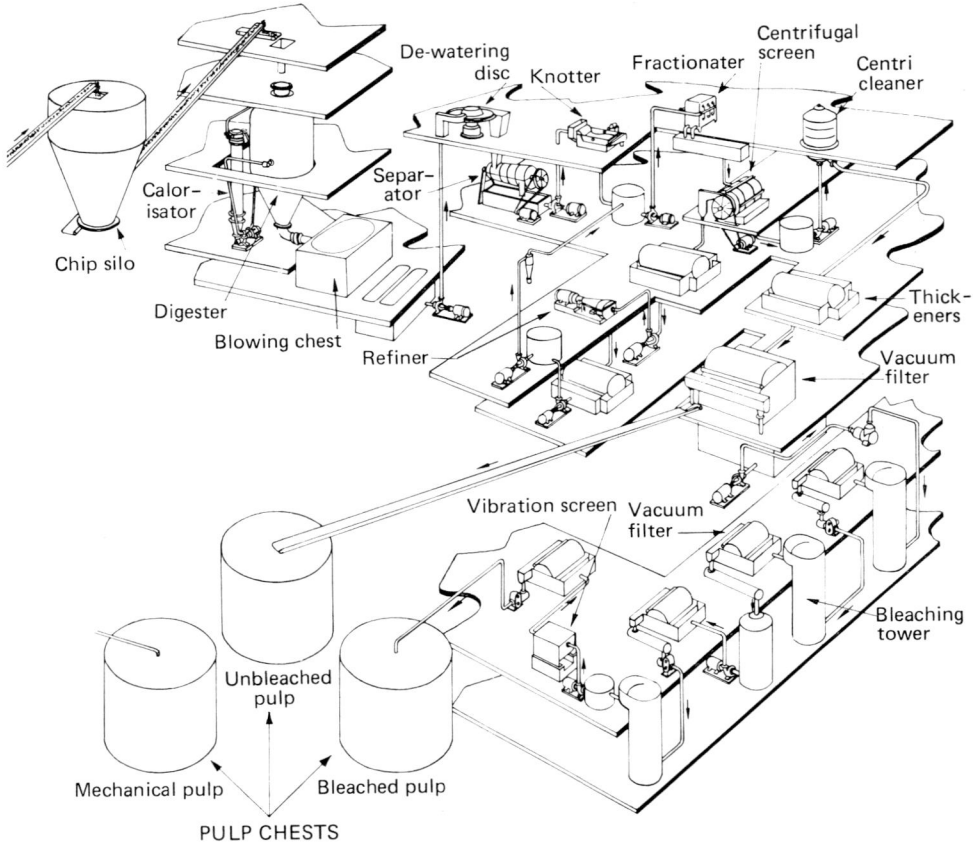

Figure 1. The chemical pulp department.

Fresh acid magnesium bisulphite is drawn from a buffer tank, to which acid is continuously fed after it has been prepared from magnesium oxide and sulphur dioxide in a separate section.

A complex system of screens raises the homogeneity and purity of the fibres by removing unboiled wood particles (knots, splinters, *etc.*), small fibre fragments (fines), as well as sand, bark, resin and other impurities. From the screening section, the spruce pulp goes to buffer storage as unbleached pulp, whereas the fir and hardwood are transferred to the bleaching floor.

The bleaching liquid, prepared from chlorine and sodium hydroxide in a separate section, is used mainly to dissolve residual lignin still attached to the fibres and colouring them. The three pulps together with the mechanical woodpulp constitute the major inputs to the papermill.

Variances in the technical system. The following groups of variances arising from the system's technology were of particular relevance to be controlled by the social system:

(1) The use of fir as one of the raw materials had led to serious pitch problems, which were only partly brought under control. Whenever sticky resin accumulated on the screens or in the bleaching equipment, extensive cleaning was required.

(2) Since the growing and storage conditions of the timber vary a great deal, some of these input variances would be transmitted along with the flow of materials and, if not controlled, would reduce the paper quality.

(3) The conversion of spruce, fir and hardwood batches in the same equipment induced additional variances, owing to pitch contamination one with the other and the mixing of fibres of different wood species.

(4) The variances resulting from mechanical breakdowns had been extreme during the period after the introduction of the bisulphite method, but, by 1965, they had been reduced to a near-normal level.

Key characteristics of operator tasks. These are

(1) The individual part-processes were by themselves relatively complex and demanding. Spatially separate from each other, the present level of their performance could be sustained with a limited number of contacts with other areas. Hence, they appeared to form a strong *gestalt* by themselves.

(2) In addition to the cluster of internal interdependencies, however, a number of important relationships still existed between the part-processes and across shifts. For example, the boiling and the bleaching operations were interdependent in terms of removing the lignin from the fibres and the 16-hour cycle between filling and emptying each of the four boilers required close co-operation and contact across shifts. Hence, the naturally bounded unit tasks clearly exceeded the traditional one man/one shift type of work rôle.

(3) Finally, it became evident in this case, as in others, that the requirements of the technology were not fully known and predictable. As previously indicated, the pitch problem was far from being fully understood and the variances in raw material made it impossible to predict what problems the operators at any time would have to tackle. Moreover, the properties of the technical equipment would change somewhat over a period. This implies that the designated process control standards were arbitrary ones based on current knowledge. Hence, they ought to be adjusted to the extent that the changing properties of the technical system caused a relocation of the optimum point for some of the process variables. For example, the evolutionary operation technique is based on this fact (Box 1957).

6. The Respond Resources in the Social System

Formal organization. The department organization included seven shift positions and four shift teams, plus one daytime worker preparing the bleaching agents. A senior operator was charged with the responsibility for each of the other four part-processes. These men belonged to the highest of two formally recognized status levels. There were also a boiler assistant, a screener assistant and a reserve on each shift who, together with the daily worker, made up the second grade of operators.

In supporting rôles outside the department were two laboratory technicians providing data for process control. In case of mechanical breakdowns or pitch troubles, the operators had to rely on maintenance men and cleaning people being called in from other areas by the foreman. Special contact man positions had been set up to facilitate communications between maintenance and operations.

Four shift foremen (plus one assistant foreman to cover absentees) were responsible for the chemical and mechanical pulping, even though the two processes were not technically interdependent. The levels above the shift foremen included the general foreman, the production engineer, the pulpmill manager and the general manager.

It should be noted that the number of operator positions is strictly prescribed in the central agreement between the employer and the trades union. This arrangement, having a long tradition in the Norwegian pulp and paper industry, is specific to this industry. This had undoubtedly added to the tendency of a strict delineation of work between individual job-holders, a well-known result of traditional job design in industry. Being of crucial importance to the problems of self-regulation and process control in this kind of technology, this point will be further explored in what follows.

Wages and bonus. The total wage of the operator includes hourly pay, shift allowances, regular overtime, additional hours and production bonus. Generally speaking, the complexity of this arrangement makes it difficult for the average man to see any direct connection between his efforts and his wage packet.

In accordance with this, the production bonus was based on the number of batches produced, even though the papermachines used to be the bottleneck in the production line. Thus, by leaving out the quality aspects of the pulp, which the operators could influence and by which alone *they* could facilitate the production of the papermachine, the production bonus, though paid out on a group basis, could not in fact function as a group goal. This is of particular significance, since management (at that time, extremely anxious to build up the quality reputation of the company in the market) could through a quality bonus have effectively translated such a quality-oriented policy into operational terms at the lower levels in the organization.

Of particular interest also are the additional hours, a form of extra pay earned by the men for odd jobs done in addition to their permanent tasks and within their regular working hours. This exemplifies one of the measures used by management in order to cope with the lack of flexibility on the shop floor, to be considered in the following section.

Segregation of operator jobs. Since 1961, the total manning had been gradually reduced through natural turnover, the major part of which used to occur in the spring. Recruitment was done mainly therefore through the annual intake of holiday reserves for the summer months. Operator training was, in keeping with the tradition in the industry, limited by the notion of one man/one job. Hence, when a man had been permanently selected for one department, further advancements would be confined to the more recognized jobs in the same area.

The segregation of jobs and lack of overlapping skills in the permanent shift teams had made the work organization increasingly unable to cope with the existing variances as the number of stand-ins in the general manpower pool was gradually reduced. In the chemical pulp department, for instance, one multi-skilled reserve had been introduced on each shift in order to stand in for absentees and otherwise to help out with odd jobs. Even if it had functioned, however, this arrangement would probably have proved inadequate to solve the flexibility problem on the shop floor. As it was, the lack of balance between the higher skill requirements for this key position in the shift groups and, on the other hand, the pay, security and working conditions offered, resulted in a disturbingly high turnover among the reserves.

Traditionally—and not only in the pulp and paper industry—management has seen apparent advantages in strict delineation and specification of individual jobs. The time needed for training is short and the supervisory control is strengthened through a clear definition of what each worker is accountable for. The workers for their part will tend to react to this system by interpreting the job specification as the maximum they owe rather than the minimum.

Beyond the first line of defence established by the union, the men make out of the job specification and customary practice a second line of defence against management. Moreover, within the welter of expectations about what is mine and what is yours, the men create a pecking order among themselves based on who gets the cosier jobs and who gets the less attractive ones.

Consequently, while the individual jobs may be lacking in intrinsic satisfaction, because of this rigid definition and segregation, they gain psychological significance because of what are merely relative advantages. As the men come to base their judgment of themselves and others on their ability to seize these relative advantages, they become stronger defenders of this system of job design than would be warranted by the built-in limitations for self-fulfilment.

As an example of this insidious trend, our *post hoc* analysis of the records revealed that one of the four digesters was a particularly good piece of equipment for pulping a certain wood. This we found was not public knowledge. In discussion, however, we found that one of the boilermen had already discovered this long ago and kept it to himself. This suggested to us at least that the lack of learning in the department was due not only to a *laissez-faire* attitude or feeling of uncertainty among the men, but that the system failed to encourage the men to share self-acquired knowledge, as they did not regard themselves as integrated members of a group.

Operator responses to task requirements. Our analysis of tasks and attitudes showed that, among the first three psychological requirements (Appendix 1), these jobs lacked mainly in the interest, excitement and self-enhancement that comes from being able to learn to do one's task better. Knowledge of results appeared adequate so long as learning was inhibited. The degree of variety and demand and the scope for personal control were higher than is usually found in industrial jobs and felt to be so by the operators.

This explained the relatively high level of job satisfaction expressed in interviews with senior operators and older workers, who had little reason to want to change in order to participate in a more comprehensive learning process that might disturb some of the privileges they had obtained. The more dependent nature of the assistant jobs and the particular situation of the reserves explain the lower level of satisfaction expressed by the second grade operators.

Interaction of operator rôles with foreman and management rôles. The position of the shift foreman in the chemical pulp department was introduced as a management response to increasing variances and planning problems arising after the changeover to the magnesium bisulphite method. This was in accordance with the traditional approach to organizational problems on the shop floor. These include such measures as specifying individual jobs in more detail, strengthening the hand of the supervisor, calling in specialists, introducing a new level in the organization, *etc.* In this case, a short-term solution was achieved at the cost of a more serious long-term problem.

Recruited from among the best operators, the foremen would only with extensive training succeed in forming a leadership and planning position clearly ranking above and essentially complementary to the operating group. Familiar with operator work and lacking the means and self-confidence to lift himself to a new level, the foreman tended to focus his attention primarily within the work group rather than on controlling its boundary conditions. Hence, the foreman had developed the practice of being constantly on the move as a troubleshooter within the department; he would then do most of the unpredictable tasks that the operators were reluctant to carry out without special compensations (see remarks on additional hours), perceiving such tasks as falling outside their own strictly defined jobs.

The behaviour of the foreman then became part of a vicious circle of job segregation by reducing the job content and thereby further limiting the learning and growth potentials of the operators. As the first level of management was in this way lowering itself in order to complete the tasks within its particular area of command, so each higher level was correspondingly pulled down to fill out what was then lacking in control and co-ordination. The adverse consequences of such work organization at the floor level will easily affect all levels of management, a fact typically found in large organizations. Even at Hunsfos, these tendencies were evident. By filling in for their subordinates, the managers and foremen were subtly redefining their own jobs in a way that reinforced the tendencies of the men on the shop floor not to show more initiative than was demanded by the traditional job design. Thus, the vicious circle was established.

7. Conditions for Optimum Control by Self-Regulation

When the goals and purposes of an enterprise are operationalized on different levels in the organization, it is not arbitrary which of the factors—throughput, quality, material, labour, *etc.*—are given the highest priority in the ongoing optimization processes on each level. According to the theory of open systems, the choice of priorities will depend on conditions outside as well as inside the enterprise. Hence, at Hunsfos, we felt that key problems of optimization on the two lowest levels of the socio-technical system were the following:

(1) *Process control* to achieve for each product a given set of quality specifications minimizing machine hours, cost of material, labour cost, *etc.* Among the cost factors, primary attention is usually paid to machine utilization.

(2) *Production planning* to achieve optimum allocation of products and orders for market requirements as well as production costs. Whereas the individual customer would vary in terms of quality demands, time of delivery, *etc.*, machine downtime would depend on the size of the orders, the production sequence of products, *etc.*

The two activities are obviously interdependent and complementary, yet the latter area potentially contains tasks for which a new type of supervision could develop.

For the process control function, this type of technology requires that it matches an extended interdependency network, as well as meeting the demands for immediate responses in the social system. This implies that the control sequences have to be explored in detail. Generally speaking, a self-regulating production system requires at least the following components:

(1) *A production unit* that converts a specific input material into a specific output.

(2) *An output standard* against which the output of the production unit can be judged at any time.

(3) *A measuring device* that can detect deviations from the target output standard and feed the information back to a ' brain ' unit.

(4) *A ' brain ' unit* that can translate the information received into a new set of operational instructions, appropriate to returning the production performance to the target, while also taking the momentary input characteristics into consideration.

(5) *An operation unit* capable of carrying out the operational instructions.

(6) *An input standard* (usually identical with the output standard of the preceding production unit) against which the input can be judged and a feedforward to the ' brain ' unit of information about momentary deviations.

Applied to man-machine systems, this classification implies that human elements to some extent will be part of the control sequence either by performing the component tasks or by transmitting information between the components. The effectiveness of the feedback loops will therefore depend on

(1) The properties of the components
(2) The transmission of information.

Firstly, considering the qualitative aspect of pulp production, we found that, among the output criteria most relevant to process control, only degree of digestion, brightness and tearing strength were measured systematically by the laboratory technicians. Cleanliness was judged subjectively from special test sheets, but factors such as pitch and homogeneity were too expensive or difficult for regular measuring. While there were no measurements on the quality of the input chips, information about pH value and percentage of sulphur dioxide in the acid was available. The use of standards and control limits were rarely based on statistical calculations. Because of the great variances observed in some of the quality measurements of individual batches, it was difficult to reveal long-term trends in the process control. The lack of feedback on this level reduced possibilities for continuous learning and control. With some improvements, we felt that these measurements might form the basis of a temporary bonus that would make potential group goals visible to the operators. Since the measurement requirements were insufficiently met for us to bring such aspects as throughput, yield, waste or material costs directly into the experiment, we shall only note in passing that the lack of measuring devices for dry weight and moisture content of the chips in the boilers restricted further learning among the boilermen.

Secondly, in order to keep the feedback loops as short as possible, we suggested that information and decisions be brought to the lowest organizational level for meeting the requirements for skill and responsibility, also that they be kept within the fewest work rôles that the constraints imposed by the technology and the means of communication would allow for. Hence, the well-known benefits of specialization and centralization, which tend to extend the information flows across special barriers (work rôles, skill differences, levels in the organization, *etc.*), must be weighed not only against the obvious costs, incurred by delays and misinterpretations of the information, but also against the loss of task motivation and job satisfaction that pertain to tasks of a substantial degree of wholeness (a strong *gestalt*) and allowing the men themselves a sufficient measure of control over the materials and processes (see Section 2).

As a consequence, the segregation of individual operator jobs and the division of labour among operator, laboratory technicians, cleaners, maintenance men and the supervisory levels were not necessarily optimum in terms of the total control requirements of the chemical pulp department.

A practical example of an inadequate feedback loop was test sheets showing the degree of cleanliness of the unbleached pulp, against which the screening performance was judged. These sheets were prepared by the laboratory workers about 1 hour after the screening of a new batch had begun. Instead of returning these sheets immediately to the screener, who could then correct the ongoing process according to the information given, the sheets were formerly sent to the foreman and some of the supervisors in other departments. Since the foreman was frequently away from his office, the feedbacks to the operators were often delayed. This is a very obvious case, because there was neither a question of the workers' ability to interpret the information embodied in the test sheets nor any doubts that the other departments would also benefit by a change in this feedback procedure. The critical factor was the speed of the feedback.

Considering the technical means of communication, it appeared that telephones were missing at some critical points and that the system of written information could be improved upon.

Finally, since it was evident that optimum conditions for control could be achieved only if the flow of information matched the technical interdependencies of the process, the actual communication network among operators was analyzed before and after the experiment (see Section 10).

8. Programme for Redesign of Jobs

Based on the previous analysis, it was assumed that an optimum socio-technical system in the chemical pulp department could be achieved only if

(1) The men as a group took greater responsibility for the operation of the department as a whole.

(2) They were enabled and initially encouraged to increase their understanding and control of the processes.

Consequently, increased autonomy for extended groups (across shifts) was a plausible name for the principle forming the basis of the experiment. The method of introducing change was to be step-by-step problem-solving by small groups consisting of a representative from the workers, supervisors and management. Among the prerequisites for the development of partly autonomous work groups were

(1) Specification of the group's boundaries in relation to the environment (adjacent units).

(2) Clarification and definition of what had to be measured in terms of quality and quantity of raw materials and services both received and delivered by the group as well as specification of quality control limits for the various criteria.

(3) A proper incentive, such as a bonus, which could stimulate the group to co-operate.

The following specific measures were to be introduced in order to support the group arrangement:

(1) Training the operators to make them as far as possible qualified for all tasks within the department.

(2) Allocation of a special repairman to the operator group to cope with smaller breakdowns requiring immediate attention.

(3) Setting up an information centre on the shop floor where measurements and other information were quickly available so that everyone would be aware of the current situation in the department. (If necessary, statistical methods would have to be employed.)

(4) Arranging suitable conditions for department employees to meet in smaller or larger groups when necessary.

(5) Installation of telephones in each department section.

(6) Electing a group representative on each shift to facilitate communications.

9. The Process of Change

The changes suggested in the programme were accepted by the management and by the majority of the workers in the department.

Gradually, but not without resistance on the part of some of the men concerned, the various measures were introduced with support from top management and from the union. In addition, operator training was linked to job rotation for the assistants, attempts were made to retrain the foremen and certain technical improvements were introduced in the bleaching. At the same time, the initiative in the socio-technical change process in the department was transferred from the research team to a project action committee (with one representative each for management, for the foremen and for the operators), then to the department management. Finally, by January 1966, with the introduction of a marginal group bonus paid on cleanliness, tearing strength, degree of digestion and brightness, the new basis for operator participation was established.

The subsequent years of 1966 and 1967 can (in terms of our dependent variable, the level of personal participation) be divided for analytical purposes into a search, a growth and a stagnation phase. Hence, abnormal variances in the timber inputs initiated a search among the men for new means of process control.

With a return to normal inputs before the summer 1966, the results of the above effects, combined with the effects of the change in job design, had made the men experience a situation that allowed them to exercise more discretion. In 1967, however, the project did not get the necessary attention from the management, which at that time had to concentrate their efforts on market problems and a technical reconstruction programme. As will be seen, pulp quality reached a peak in the growth phase and thereafter stabilized at a higher level than before the experiment. Space allows only for a brief summary of the key points in the analysis and the major conclusions.

10. Summary of Analyses and Results

The experiment was designed in such a way that pulp quality as measured by the bonus would be the best single index of operator performance. It is agreed within the company that a general improvement in pulp qualities has been achieved (Table 1). This applies to the bleached pulps in particular. In line with this, the number of extremely bad batches has also been reduced during the experiment. For the majority of the individual quality variables (for each pulp), there appears to be some correspondence between quality achieved and the changes in the conditions for operator participation.

Table 1. Average quality bonus per week and per batch across all types of timber related to half-year periods of the experiment

Period	Average/week %	Average/batch %
First half-year	100	100
Second half-year	145	140
Third half-year	124	137
Fourth half-year	124	123

This broad picture of the bonus trend is confirmed by the more detailed breakdown on pulp qualities.

Before inferring too much from these broad indices, we had to explore whether

(1) The improved quality was achieved at excessive costs.

(2) The improved quality was due to improved performance on the group level.

(3) There was some evidence that the men took a greater interest in their work.

(4) The improvement could have occurred without the men changing their approach to the job.

(5) The men themselves perceived the new situation as favourable.

Taking these points in turn:

(1) There is no evidence that quality has been achieved at the expense of an increased consumption of material resources. The major costs (fibre, yield, chemicals and machine utilization) that had shown decreasing trends before the experiment continued to fall during the experiment (Table 2). There is, in fact, some indication that the experiment may have contributed to an increase in yield. It was agreed that manpower should be kept constant during the experiment.

Table 2. Measures of cost of various materials before and during the experiment

Materials	Nine month period before experiment	Twelve month period during experiment	Percentage improvement
Magnesium oxide per ton of pulp	106·0	91·0	14·0
Chlorine per ton of pulp	87·3	73·5	15·8
Sulphur dioxide per ton of pulp	128·0	123·0	3·9
Pulp yield per m³ timber	100·0	103·8	3·8

(2) The improved control of pulp quality can to a large extent be ascribed to the men who as a group assumed greater responsibility.

(a) The quality development of the main product (fir pulp), which goes through all steps in the process, also the bleaching, shows a clear improvement in cleanliness and tearing strength (Table 3). At the same time, the changes in the kappa number show that the boilermen have changed their strategy from overcooking to undercooking, whereas the changes in brightness show that the bleachers have moved from underbleaching to overbleaching (Engelstad 1969a).

Table 3. Bonus as a percentage of the theoretical maximum for purity and tearing strength

Quality dimension	Type of wood	Search	Phase Growth	Stagnation
Cleanliness (spots)	Fir	42	61	60
	Hardwood	45	53	53
	Spruce	3	21	10
Tearing strength	Fir	63	90	71
	Hardwood	76	96	93

The terms underbleaching and overbleaching are to be understood as relative to the given standards for kappa number and brightness respectively. Nevertheless, these standards are arbitrary ones based on current knowledge and judgment about what would be required to achieve a given pulp quality with the available raw materials, technical equipment and labour force.

A detailed analysis of the situation revealed that the trends in pulp quality indicated could be explained only if the operators, on the basis of the new conditions established, had to some extent changed their attitudes towards the task and their way of working.

From previously seeking to optimize within their own delineated work area, therefore, it appeared to be a change in orientation towards optimizing on department level, which required an increasing awareness of the technical interdependencies between the part-processes (for example, the removal of lignin in cooking and bleaching respectively). In other words, the operators now tended to take responsibility as a group.

This conclusion was supported by measurable changes in the pattern of communications and the increased problem-solving activities in the work groups.

(b) Analysis of the communication data shows that the flows of information after the experiment match the technical interdependencies in the process more closely than before (Engelstad 1969a). At the same time, the men as a group have attained a higher level of autonomy. It also appears that the assistant operators have now become better integrated into the groups. Table 4 shows that the increased interaction in 1967 in all essentials refers to the substantial growth in inter-operator communication (+70%).

Table 4. Number of contacts per shift before and after the experiment

Contact	1965	1967	Difference %	1965 %	1967 %
Operator/operator	26·0	44·1	+70	25	34
Lab. technician/operator	37·7	37·7	0	36	30
Foreman/operator	34·6	39·4	+14	33	31
Foreman/lab. technician	7·6	6·7	+13	7	5
Total	105·9	127·9	+21	101	100

(c) Concrete examples of operator participation in problem-solving and decision-making within the department during the experiments also indicate that the men have increased their capability to operate as a team.

(3) The operators have, during the period of the experiment, contributed a number of suggestions for improvement of the technical equipment and the working conditions in general, demonstrating an interest in the job that they previously had not shown (Table 5). At the same time, the operators have become more interested in problems of process control, timber utilization and costs.

Table 5*. Number of suggestions advanced and accepted in the operator meetings

Date of meetings	Shifts	Acid	Boiling	Screening	Bleaching	Total
15th March 1966	3+4	5	5	11	3	24
25th March 1966 (additional)	1+2	1	9	3	3	16
August 1966	1+2+3+4	2	4	3	4	13
Total		8	18	17	10	53

*As a comparison, the company suggestion scheme had produced approximately one suggestion per year in the chemical pulp department for the period 1958–64.

(4) Obviously, factors other than those included in the experimental design may have contributed to these improvements. It is unlikely, however, that the improved performance gained in the department during the experiment can be assigned to unilateral management actions (regardless of operator response) either in terms of the technical improvements introduced or in terms of the directives given. Indications of this were the lack of pressure from the men before the experiment for improvements in equipment or instrumentation and the fact that, when management's major concern in the summer 1966 turned to input costs, this had no effect on the strategies being followed by the operators in the department. As far as our evidence goes, the improved control, the increase in operator suggestions and other changes in group activities were primarily due to the voluntary efforts of the men.

(5) No doubt the experiment as it developed in 1966 caused many operators to build up considerable expectations and the feelings of disappointment that were brought out in some of the interviews clearly refer back to the fact that the project was in 1967 only half-heartedly followed up in the department because of other priorities. Unfortunately, at this crucial point in the experiment, new measures necessary to sustain growth in the desired direction, that many had hoped for, were not introduced. In accordance with the logic of systems, it is unlikely that changes in a part will be sustained over an extended period if the changes are not reciprocated by sufficient adjustments in the total system (Angyal 1941). Within areas where permanent learning has taken place or new technological conditions have been established, however, the socio-technical system in the department appears to have reached a new level of functioning. This applies to pulp quality, operator skill and the degree of flexibility in the shift teams.

11. Further Developments in the Company

The preconditions for a work group or department to assume the increased responsibility conveyed by a higher level of group autonomy are that (1) critical variances in the process can be brought under control and (2) the change in job design and operator rôles is sufficiently supported by adjustments in tasks and rôles of the foreman and of the management. Changes in tasks and rôles on department level, however, in the long run require adjustments on company level as well. In practice, this implies that the new principles of job design must be integrated into the objectives, policy and style of management, to guide the activities at all levels in the organization. In principle, a part of a system influences other parts only through its effects on the total system.

Accordingly, during the autumn of 1966 and the spring of 1967, experiences from the chemical pulp department produced discussions of company policies among the top management. It was decided to follow up the project within the company with a new experiment in the papermill, where a team of operators would run two of the papermachines without shift foremen. The changes in job design that were introduced in 1968 have otherwise mainly corresponded to those in the chemical pulp department, but the initiative in the change process has consistently been carried by the parties concerned through a temporary project action committee. The first six months' agreement about experimentation was extended for another six months. Nine months after the jobs had been redesigned, one could ascertain definite growth in commitment to the new way of working among operators and management. The operating team had then showed that they were able to utilize their machinery in a very flexible way, even without shift supervision and the productivity trend proved very satisfactory.

Finally, by 1969, the company had decided on a three-year plan for redesigning the organization that will include

(1) Comprehensive operator training for multiple skills and increased technical insight.

(2) Doing away with shift supervision of the old type. (By 1964, it had been an explicit policy to strengthen the hand of the foreman.)

(3) The introduction of a management philosophy that encourages local problem-solving activities.

In particular, on the basis of what we have seen in the fourth field experiment at Norsk Hydro, we believe that this way of working will lead to a self-sustaining learning process that will improve the reliability of the human component in the process of control as a whole.

Appendix 1—Psychological Job Requirements

(1) The need for the content of a job to be reasonably demanding in terms other than sheer endurance, yet providing a minimum of variety (not necessarily novelty).

(2) The need for being able to learn on the job (which implies standards and knowledge of results) and go on learning. Again, it is a question of neither too much nor too little.

(3) The need for some minimum area of decision-making that the individual can call his own.

(4) The need for some minimum degree of social support and recognition in the work place.

(5) The need to be able to relate what one does and what one produces to one's social life.

(6) The need to feel that the job leads to some sort of desirable future.

Appendix 2—Matrix of Variances

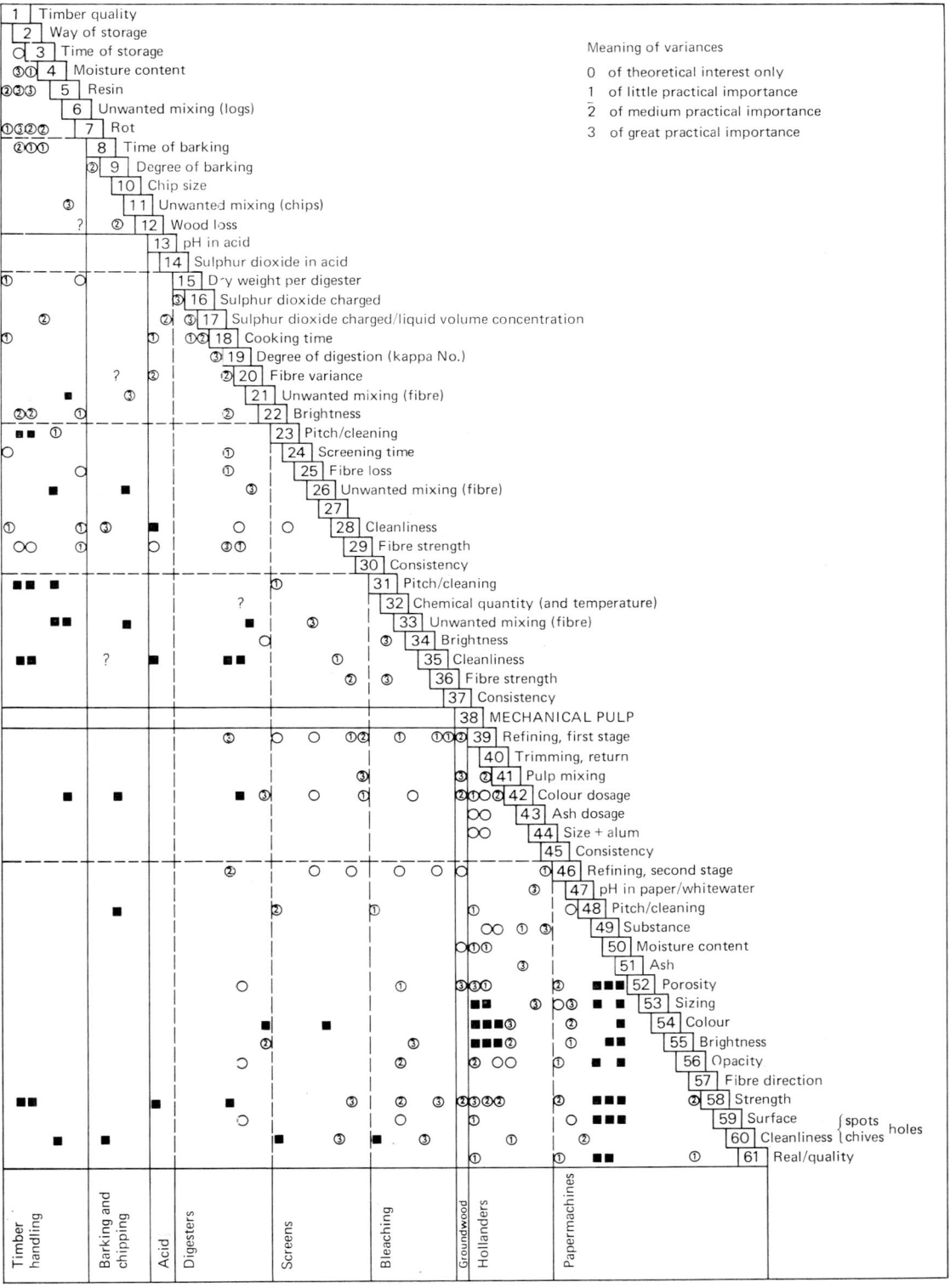

Research on the Process Operator

By F. P. Lees

Department of Chemical Engineering, Loughborough University of Technology

1. Human Factors and Systems Engineering

As the process of technological change has accelerated, it is no longer possible to rely on gradual evolution to achieve a satisfactory adaptation of man's tools and tasks. It has become necessary instead to try to foresee potential problems and to design to overcome them. The discipline which is concerned with this problem is ergonomics.

The development of ergonomics, and its transatlantic near-equivalent human factors, has been strongly influenced by the problems of the complex and large-scale man–machine systems used in the fields of defence, aerospace and computers. In these systems particularly it is important to try to get the design right first time. Thus much of the fundamental research work and of the applied design experience has been in these areas.

Inevitably, ergonomics has itself undergone some changes of direction. Of particular significance in the present context is the development alongside 'classical ergonomics' of what has been called 'systems ergonomics' (Singleton, Easterby and Whitfield 1967). Classical ergonomics is seen as concerned primarily with the compatibility of man and machine, although it has moved considerably beyond the 'knobs and dials' emphasis in the early work. Systems ergonomics deals essentially with the human factors aspects of achieving system objectives. This results in several changes of emphasis. There is a greater demand that experimental work should meet real-life criteria rather than those of the experimental psychology laboratory, or at least that there should be means of relating the latter to the former. The ergonomist interests himself more in all stages of the design process and in particular in the early stages where many of the most crucial decisions are made. And he becomes more involved himself in the actual design of industrial systems.

Human factors is now an established aspect of systems engineering. The role of human factors in systems design is illustrated in Figure 1. Two points may be emphasized. First, human factors should be introduced at all stages of the design. Decisions on aspects such as allocation of function have important ergonomics implications throughout the system. Human factors is too often abused by being assigned a cosmetic or rescue rôle. Second, the design process is a highly iterative one. For clarity only one iteration loop is shown, but in fact iteration occurs at all stages of the design process.

As an activity ergonomics has many similarities with engineering; it is in fact sometimes called human engineering. The engineer uses the work of the physical scientist, and the ergonomist that of the psychologist, as an aid to system design.

Two important emphases in human factors, therefore, are the systems criteria and the system design process. These are also fundamental for research work on the process operator.

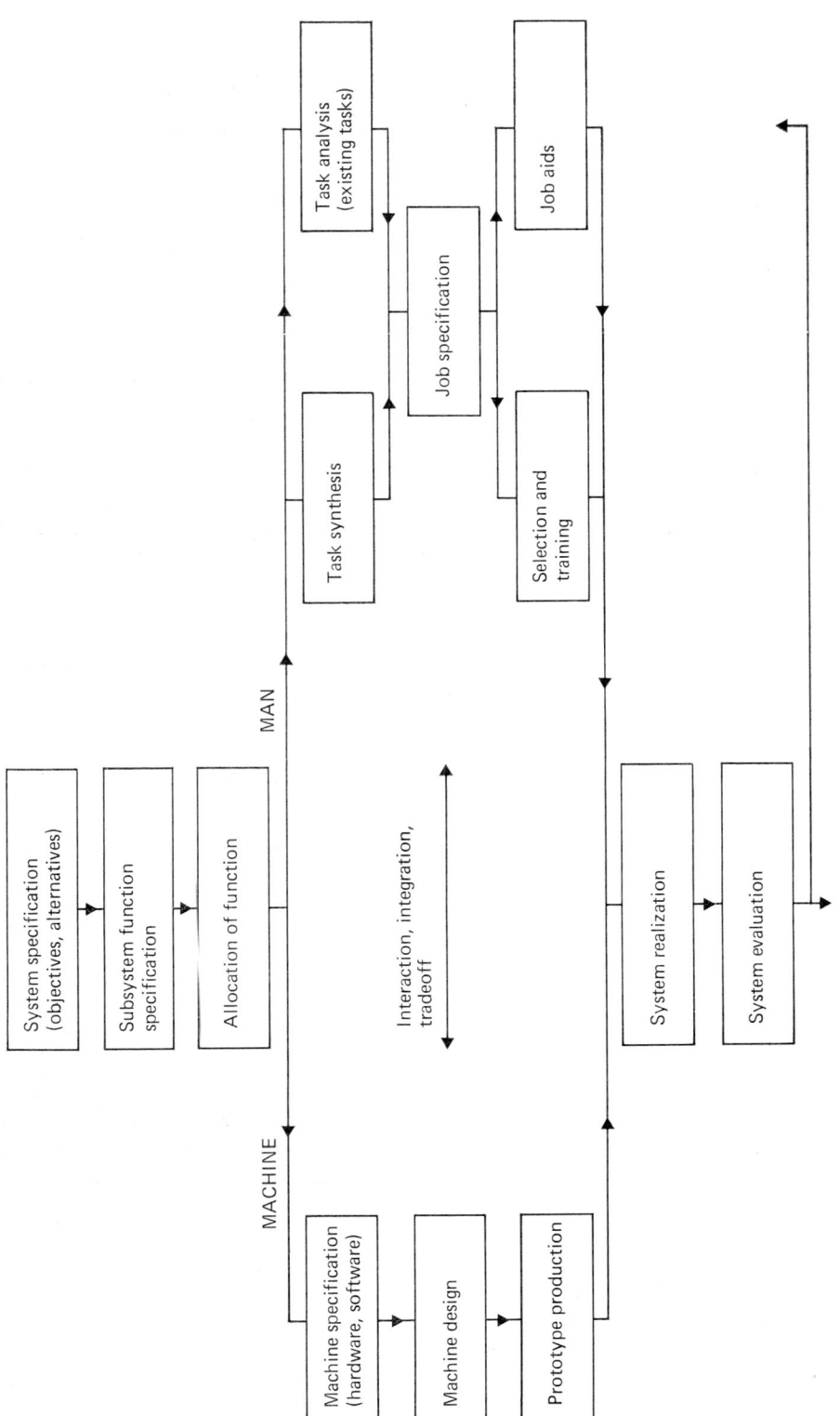

Figure 1. Human factors activities in system design.

2. Research on the Human Operator

There is now a large amount of research on the human operator. Much fundamental work has been done on the methodology of operator studies, on operator modelling, on analysis of the operator's task and on operator performance in such tasks as vigilance, tracking and decision-making.

The occupational applicability of much of this work is uncertain. In attempting to utilize results from experimental psychology the ergonomist faces much the same difficulties as those which confront the engineer who seeks to use results from the physical sciences.

In the present review the emphasis has been placed on studies which are concerned specifically with the process operator. But some brief outline of the wider context of human operator studies in general is desirable.

Some of the principal subjects of research on the human operator are listed in Table 1. This is inevitably a very limited and somewhat arbitrary selection. The aim is to give an indication of some of the main topics and leading workers in the field. The titles of the references give a more detailed impression of the work. Although some preference has been given to books rather than research papers, many classic papers are included. Similarly, although accessible material has been preferred to inaccessible, some internal reports are given, particularly where these represent pioneering work in the field; many of these reports are from organizations involved in military or aerospace work. Material on the process operator is excluded, since this is dealt with below. The table is not intended to be comprehensive: some subjects, such as work in human sciences or human factors in general, on physical environment, and on artificial intelligence, have been completely omitted. A more detailed classified bibliography is given by Edwards and Lees (1973).

Much of the early work on the human operator was industrial. In the U.S. there is the work prior to the First World War of Taylor and of Gilbreth in time study of physical tasks and in the interwar period that of Mayo at Western Electric on aspects of assembly work such as physical environment and motivation. Similarly, in the U.K. Wyatt and his collaborators at the Industrial Fatigue (later Health) Research Board carried out between the wars investigations of features such as monotony, fatigue, and rest pauses in repetitive work.

The Second World War and its immediate aftermath saw a considerable activity on both sides of the Atlantic in the area of human operator monitoring and control. In the U.K. a leading rôle was played by the Applied Psychology Unit of the Medical Research Council at Cambridge. One aspect of this work was watchkeeping, particularly on the bridge of ships and in radar and sonar operation, which gave rise to studies in vigilance, *e.g.* Mackworth, Broadbent. Another topic was gun control, which resulted in investigations of tracking, *e.g.* Craik, Tustin, North. Studies were also made of operator skill and of the effect on this of various forms of stress such as fatigue, *e.g.* Bartlett. Design of displays and controls was another subject of research, *e.g.* Murrell. The armed services have continued to be active in ergonomics studies in areas such as aircraft instrument and cockpit design through institutions such as the Royal Air Force Institute of Aviation Medicine at Farnborough.

Defence and aerospace applications were responsible for much of the work on human factors at this time in the U.S. also. Much basic work has been

Table 1. Some principal subjects of research on the human operator

Subject	Representative research or review
Information sampling and processing	G. A. Miller (1951, 1956); Hick (1952, 1953); Deininger and Fitts (1955); Quastler (1955); Crossman (1956c, 1961b); Draper (1956); North (1956); Cherry (1957a, 1957b); Kay (1957); Attneave (1959); Welford (1959); Adams and Creamer (1962); Garner (1962); Edwards (1964); Sholl (1972); Levine and Samet (1973)
Learning	Elwell and Grindley (1938); Guthrie (1952); Hilgard (1956); Deese (1958); Hovland (1960); Kay (1964); Melton (1964); Gagné (1965a); Singleton (1968); Annett (1969)
Skill	Bartlett (1948, 1951b); Mace (1950); Annett and Kay (1956, 1957); Kay (1957); Welford (1958, 1968); Crossman (1956a, 1956d, 1957); Krendel and McRuer (1960); Seymour (1966); Fitts and Posner (1967); Whitfield (1967); Bilodeau and Bilodeau (1969)
Stress, fatigue	Bartlett (1953); Conrad (1954); Garvey and Taylor (1959); J. G. Miller (1960); Appley and Trumbull (1967); Broadbent (1971); Grandjean et. al. (1971); Welford (1973)
Decision-making	von Neumann and Morgenstern (1947); Good (1950); Wald (1950); McKinsey (1952); Ward Edwards (1954, 1961, 1965); Thrall, Coombs and David (1954); Cohen and Hansel (1956); Chapanis (1957); Luce and Raiffa (1957); Newell, Shaw and Simon (1958, 1963); Williams and Hopkins (1958); Cohen (1960); Newell and Simon (1961, 1963, 1972); Rapoport (1964a); Schrenk (1964, 1969); Shelley and Bryan (1964); Luce and Suppes (1965); Ward Edwards et al. (1968); Howard (1968); North (1968); Thomas and Tou (1968); Dutton and Starbuck (1971); Vaughan and Mavor (1972); Zadeh (1973)
Diagnostic tasks	Dale (1958, 1964, 1968); Glanzer (1958); Bennett and Degan (1961); Ward Edwards (1965); Shriver, Fink and Trexler (1964); Tilley (1967); Bond (1970)
Motivation	Cofer and Appley (1964); Atkinson and Feather (1966); Haber (1966)
Performance assessment	Ericksen (1952); Summers and Ziedman (1964); Singleton, Fox and Whitfield (1971)
Task analysis	Gilbreth (1911); Taylor (1911); Maynard, Stegemartin and Schwab (1948); R. B. Miller (1953, 1963, 1967); Barnes (1958); Mager (1962); Crossman (1963); Annett and Duncan (1967); Singleton (1972)
Man-machine systems	Fitts (1951, 1962); Allen and Saul (1958); Cameron and Corkindale (1961); Flaherty (1961); Fogel (1963); Gagné (1963); Chapanis (1965, 1970); Meister and Rabideau (1965); Obermayer and Muckler (1965); Oshanin (1965); Jones (1967); Siegel and Wolf (1969); De Greene (1970a); Meister (1971); Parsons (1972)
Manual control, tracking	Tustin (1944, 1947); Craik (1947); Hick (1948); Vince (1948); Bartlett (1951a); North (1952); Poulton (1952); Birmingham and Taylor (1954); Elkind and Forgie (1959); Sweeney and Graham (1959); Crossman (1960c); Krendel and McRuer (1960); Licklider (1960); Sheridan (1960, 1966); Sinaiko (1961); Bekey (1962b); Naslin and Raoult (1963); Smith (1963); Wilde and Westcott (1963); J. W. Senders (1964); Summers and Ziedman (1964); Young and Stark (1965); Wierwille and Gagné (1966); Garner (1967); Miller and Elkind (1967); Robinson (1967); Kelley (1968); Gaines (1969); Herzog (1969); McRuer and Weir (1969); Wierenga (1969); Freedy et al. (1971); Gilstad and Fu (1971); Johannesen (1972); Rouse (1973)

Table 1.—*Continued.*

Subject	Representative research or review
Man-machine system reliability, human error	Fitts and Jones (1947); Chapanis (1951); Campbell (1958); Davis and Coiley (1959); Peters and Hussman (1959); Berry and Wulff (1960); Lincoln (1960); Cooper (1961); Kirchner (1961); Altman (1964); Meister (1964); Pickrel and MacDonald (1964); Rook (1964); Swain (1964a, 1964b, 1972, 1973b); Juran (1966); Rigby (1967); Defayolle (1968); De Greene (1970b); Favergé (1970); Singleton (1973)
Emergency situations	Fitts and Jones (1947); Ronan (1953); Rigby and Edelman (1968)
Air traffic control	Fitts (1951); Davenport and Woodson (1954); Leplat and Bisseret (1965); Hopkin (1970); Bisseret (1971); Coeterier (1971); Kirchner and Laurig (1971); Sperandio (1972)
Aircraft pilot's task	Fitts and Jones (1947); Ericksen (1952); Williams and Hopkins (1958); Simmonds (1960); Majendie (1962); Kibler (1965); Wilson (1972)
Dynamic modelling of operator	Hoehn and Saltz (1958) (fault diagnosis); Askren and Regulinski (1969) (human error); Gaines (1969) (tracking); Wierenga (1969) (flying); Baker (1970) (information processing); Towill (1973b) (learning)
Man-computer systems	Jordan (1962); G. A. Miller (1965); Mills (1967); Sackman (1967); Licklider (1968); Carbonell (1969); Nickerson (1969); Shackel (1969); Mayer (1970); Meadow (1970); Martin (1973)
Man-computer problem-solving	Rapoport (1964b); Root and Sadacca (1967); R. B. Miller (1969); Sackman (1970); Weinberg (1971); Bartlett and Smith (1973)
Displays	Sleight (1948); Murrell (1952, 1960, 1965); Birmingham and Taylor (1954); Chernikoff, Birmingham and Taylor (1955); Fogel (1955); Taylor (1957); Fogel and Dwonczyk (1958); Berbert and Kelley (1962); Kelley (1962); Fogel (1963); Wierwille (1964); Ziebolz (1964); Green (1965); Bates (1966); Poole (1966); McLane and Wolfe (1967); Gould (1968); Luxenberg and Kuehn (1968); Singleton (1969); Wolff (1970); Vartabedian (1971); Bernotat and Gärtner (1972); Monty (1973)
Vigilance, signal detection	Mackworth (1947, 1948); Broadbent (1950, 1958, 1961, 1971); V. L. Senders (1952); Hickey and Blair (1958); Wilkinson (1961); Baker (1962); Frankman and Adams (1962); Buckner and McGrath (1963); Holland (1963); Jerison and Wing (1963a); Yntema (1963); J. W. Senders (1964); Swets (1964); Baker and Ware (1966); Carbonell (1966); Sanders (1966, 1968, 1970); Čížková (1967); Smallwood (1967); Leplat (1968); Singer and Rutenfranz (1969); Smith and Lucaccini (1969); Davies and Tune (1970); Grant (1971); Tickner *et al.* (1972); Waag and Halcomb (1972
Inspection tasks	Wyatt and Langdon (1932); Mackenzie (1958); Colquhoun (1959); Drury and Addison (1973)
Controls	Ely, Thompson and Orlansky (1956); Deininger (1960, 1967); Hitt (1961); Sinaiko (1961); Jones (1962); Fogel (1963); Kolesnick and Plath (1965); Murrell (1965); Bradley (1967); Johnson (1967); Smith (1967); Conrad and Hull (1968); Alden, Daniels and Kanarick (1972); Bernotat and Gärtner (1972)
Control-display relationships	Warrick (1947); Vince (1950); Andreas (1953); Garvey and Knowles (1954); Chapanis and Lindenbaum (1959); Loveless (1959, 1962); Fogel (1963); Murrell (1965); Chapanis and Mankin (1967)
Control panels, computer consoles	V. L. Senders (1952); White, Warrick and Grether (1953); Lincoln and Auerbach (1956); Hitt *et al.* (1961); Shackel (1962); Bauer *et al.* (1966); Freund and Sadosky (1967); Bartlett and Smith (1973)

Table 1.—*Continued.*

Subject	Representative research or review
Personnel selection	Ghiselli and Brown (1955); Thorndike (1959); Mandell (1964); Guion (1965); Dunnette (1966)
Training	King (1960, 1964); Wolfle (1960); Belbin (1964); Clay (1964); Rowell and Streich (1964); Fitts (1965); Glaser (1965); Holding (1965); R. B. Miller (1965); Annett (1966); Annett and Duncan (1967); Bass and Vaughan (1968); Seymour (1968); Singleton (1968); Tilley (1969); Hartley (1972)
Organizational factors, job enrichment	Mayo (1945); Herzberg, Mausner and Snyderman (1959); Vroom (1964); Halpin (1966); Herzberg (1966); Juran (1967); Ford (1969); Swain (1973a)
Repetitive work, boredom, rest pauses, shift work	Wyatt (1927); Wyatt and Fraser (1929); Wyatt and Langdon (1937); Mayo (1945); Mott (1965); Murrell (1965); Masuda (1966); Davies (1971)

done at military establishments such as the U.S. Air Force Wright Air Development Center, Ohio, and the Naval Research Laboratory, Washington, as well as in consulting organizations such as the American Institute for Research, Pittsburgh, Dunlap and Associates, Santa Monica, and Sandia Laboratories, Albuquerque. This work has ranged over, and indeed has largely helped to define, the field of human factors, so that selection is rather invidious. Nevertheless, mention may be made of some of the early pioneering studies, particularly those relevant to process control. These include work on allocation of function in man–machine systems, *e.g.* Fitts; on task analysis, *e.g.* R. B. Miller; on vigilance, *e.g.* V. L. Senders; on displays, *e.g.* Sleight, Birmingham and Taylor, Kelley; on controls, *e.g.* Ely, Thompson and Orlansky; on control-display relationships, *e.g.* Warrick; on control panels, *e.g.* V. L. Senders; on air traffic control, *e.g.* Fitts; and on training, *e.g.* R. B. Miller.

In this field system reliability is an essential requirement. Studies on this aspect include work on human error, *e.g.* Altman, Swain; on inspection tasks, *e.g.* Rook; on fault diagnosis, *e.g.* Shriver, Fink and Trexler, Dale; on emergency situations, *e.g.* Rigby and Edelman.

The problems of large military and aerospace computer-based information systems, such as the SAGE system for the air defence of the U.S. and the N.A.S.A. space flight control centre have also stimulated studies on man–computer systems. These include work on the allocation of function between man and computer, *e.g.* Licklider; on man–computer interaction, *e.g.* Chapanis, G. A. Miller; and on man–computer problem-solving, *e.g.* Sackman.

Much has been learnt in these fields from attempts to 'automate' or 'computerize' control and other functions. In many cases severe problems have arisen and it has proved necessary to bring the man back into the system. This has led to a better understanding of the rôle of man in such systems. In many applications the most effective system, given current technology, is an operator-controlled, computer-supported system rather than a computerized one.

The demands of the large-scale, complex but critical systems which are characteristic in defence and aerospace are thus responsible for much of the initial impetus to work on human factors. These practical applications also explain the emphasis on systems criteria and on system design.

At the same time much fundamental research has been conducted into various aspects of human performance. One important area of work is the investigation of human thinking. This has many facets which include work on human information processing, e.g. Cherry; on human decision-making, e.g. Ward Edwards; and on computer problem-solving, e.g. Newell, Simon and Shaw.

Another aspect of this work is the exploration of the human learning process, e.g. Hilgard, and the application of results in this field to the training of operators.

Much of this work has been conducted in academic establishments: universities in the U.K. and the U.S. and in France and the Netherlands have been particularly active as well as research institutes in Eastern Europe.

There has also been an increasing amount of work on industrial problems. In the U.K. the immediate postwar period saw much activity in the industrial application of techniques such as work study. Considerable success was achieved in analyzing industrial skills, particularly the more 'physical' ones, and in applying the results to task synthesis, job design and training, e.g. Seymour, Singleton. This was followed by the attempt to analyze more inaccessible skills, such as those involved in control tasks, e.g. Crossman.

Inspection for quality control is another industrial task which has received some attention, e.g. Colquhoun. Similarly there have been investigations of fault diagnosis, e.g. Dale.

Attempts have also been made to improve the performance of industrial workers by attention to motivation and job satisfaction. Many of these have originated in the U.S. They range from the early work on motivation, e.g. Mayo, to the more recent work on job enrichment, e.g. Herzberg. The U.S. Air Force Zero Defects programme, e.g. Halpin, also has a large motivational content. In Japan also industry has been active in investigations of repetitive work and rest pauses, e.g. Masuda, and in encouragement of worker participation in aspects such as quality control, e.g. Juran.

Certain tasks have been studied quite intensively. In particular, there has been considerable research on two tasks critical for air safety, that of the airline pilot, e.g. Wilson, and that of the air traffic controller, e.g. Leplat and Bisseret. Both are of interest in the present context; the first because it is a control task rather similar to that of process control and the second because it is a decision-making task which may be assisted by man–computer interactive facilities.

There is, therefore, a large body of knowledge concerning human performance much of which has potential application to the problems of the process operator. Most of this has been developed outside the field of process control, though in a few instances, such as the investigation of 'non-physical' skills, e.g. Crossman, or the application of predictive displays, e.g. Ziebolz, some of the original work was in the process control area.

3. Development and Nature of the Process Operator's Job

In the period since the start of the Industrial Revolution the process operator's job has gradually changed from mainly manual labour to mainly decision-making as processes have become more mechanized and automated.

The beginning of this evolution is illustrated by the job of the gas worker, as described by Popplewell (1912) and by Thorne (1925). Many process men worked in the gas works during the winter and in the brick works during the summer, when only a skeleton crew was needed to run the gas works. The job was essentially manual work and was affected by progressive mechanization with the introduction of such devices as the ' Iron Stoker '.

Over the years, however, there has been a continual decrease in the manual work content of the operator's job, so that it is now often vestigial. The degree to which manual work is required is not necessarily a very useful means of classifying the process control task.

Much more significant is the nature of the process which is to be supervised. Increasingly the operator has become a part of the control system. And the primary function of the control system varies with the process. It may be in a chlorine cellroom the monitoring of alarm conditions; on an LD converter the combined open- and closed-loop control of the blow; on soaking pits the scheduling of ingots to the mill.

Equally important is the level of automation of the process. The three obvious stages through which process control has passed are

(1) Manual control
(2) Analogue control
(3) Computer control.

But this classification is oversimplified and even misleading. It says nothing, for example, about the degree of sophistication of the measuring instrumentation or of the information display facilities. Within analogue control it does not distinguish between systems which comprise only single-loop feedback controllers and systems which contain in addition the many types of special-purpose equipment used in particular for

(1) Measurement
(2) Information reduction
(3) Sequential control.

And it fails to bring out the quite fundamental differences within computer control: whereas some computer-based systems exercise almost complete control of the process, others leave the significant control actions to the operator, though they may provide him with an excellent tool for carrying out these actions.

Crossman (1960a) drew a distinction between control of continuous-flow production and centralized remote control. This is based on the facts that in the former the operator can visit and inspect the plant and his task is to make continuous small control adjustments, whereas in the latter he is isolated from the equipment and his task is to control sequences of large discrete changes. However, it is doubtful if this distinction is now valid; there is a large element of centralized remote control on many modern processes. Crossman also emphasized that the centralized remote control task is essentially one of decision-making in a highly artificial situation; this is very true of process control.

More detailed discussions of the influence of the type of process and of the degree of automation on the process control task have been given by J. J. de Jong (1964) and by Edwards and Lees (1971a, 1971b, 1973).

If the process control task itself is considered, a number of distinct operator functions may be identified. The following is a modification of the list given by Edwards and Lees (1973):

(1) Goal formulation
(2) Measurement
(3) Data processing and handling
(4) Monitoring
(5) Single-variable control
(6) Sequential control
(7) Other control
(8) Optimization
(9) Communication
(10) Scheduling
(11) Manual operations.

Although most process control tasks have elements of all these functions, the balance between them varies greatly with the type of plant.

The operator's task is also dependent on whether the state of the process is normal or abnormal; if the latter is the case, then he has the crucial function of fault administration. This is an increasingly important reason for including man in the control system and is a major theme of several of the papers in this collection (Crossman 1960a, Rasmussen 1968a, de Jong and Köster 1970, Duncan 1974b, Kragt and Landeweerd 1974, West and Clark 1974). Three separate stages are usually distinguished:

(1) Fault detection
(2) Fault diagnosis
(3) Fault correction.

These differences in the processes themselves, in the control problems and in the operator's task are important. The research worker needs an appreciation of all aspects of the process control task, of the factors which influence it and of the appropriate taxonomies as a guide in the selection of problems and plants for investigation and in the assessment of operator performance.

4. Studies of the Process Operator

Some of the principal studies of, or closely related to, the process operator are listed in Table 2. This list is much more extensive than that given previously (Edwards and Lees 1973). This is mainly because it includes a number of non-experimental reviews and industrial studies. Also included is a small amount of work in what might be regarded as conventional experimental psychology but in which the investigators were concerned with process operator problems. The studies described in the table as experimental mostly quote experimental results; other studies are classified as reviews or industrial studies, though many of these are based in some way on experimental work.

There are about 135 studies given in Table 2. The dates of publication of the papers in the table are shown in the histogram in Figure 2 (excluding 1974).

The peak in 1971 is partly due to the coincidence in that year of two symposia on the process operator and one on displays.

Thus an appreciable amount of work has been done on the process operator. There has been considerable progress in clearing the ground and identifying the problems. It is important, therefore, that other investigators should be aware of the work which has already been done and should define their research objectives accordingly.

The first work on the process operator appears to be the in-plant study of Hiscock (1938) on selection tests for process workers. Some desirable characteristics of the operator were proposed and tests to identify such characteristics were described.

Other early industrial work includes the in-plant studies of Pogostin (1954) and of Itelson (1961) in the U.S.S.R. on the process control task and on operator job evaluation. Details are given of the division of the operator's time between such tasks as inspection of instruments, control actions, *etc.* Arising also from job evaluation is the in-plant investigation by Kitchin and Graham (1961) on the process operator's decision-making load.

About 1960 the effect of automation on the work of the process operator began to concern government and was the subject of several investigations. Examples are the studies by Crossman (1960a) and by Welford (1960) in the U.K. and of Brenninkmeyer (1964) in the Netherlands.

Work was also sponsored on the training of process operators. This is illustrated by the work of King (1960).

The first systematic research on the process operator began with the work of Crossman, who started by studying the problem of analyzing industrial skills in which the ' cognitive ' content predominates over the ' physical ' (Crossman 1956a, 1956b, 1956c). Process control was identified as a prime example of this type of skill. Crossman and his coworkers investigated the process control task (Crossman 1958, 1960a); the manual control of slow-response systems typical of process control (Crossman and Cooke 1962); and information sampling in process control (Crossman, Cooke and Beishon 1964). This work involved the well-known ' water bath ' experiment (Crossman and Cooke 1962) and numerous plant visits including studies of process operators in a liquid oxygen plant, a board mill, and a solvents unit. Major in-plant investigations were the papermill work described in several of these papers and the liquid washing plant work done by Spencer (1962).

Decision-making in process control was studied by Beishon. His investigations included the ' water tanks ' laboratory experiment on strategy development (Beishon 1966); an in-plant study of manual control in the papermill (Beishon 1966, 1967); another in-plant investigation of manual control and scheduling in baking ovens (Beishon 1966, 1969); and a simulation study of scheduling of electric arc furnaces (Bainbridge, Beishon, Hemming and Splaine 1968).

This simulation yielded much useful data in the form of verbal protocols from the subjects. In addition to the analysis of these protocols given in the original paper, further detailed analyses have been done by Bainbridge (1968, 1969, 1972, 1974). The investigation also furnished information on the operator's use of the displays (Bainbridge 1971).

Table 2. Some studies of or work related to the process operator

Author(s)	Subject of study	Type of study
Ablitt (1969)	Reliability assessment of tasks performed by process operator	Review
Annett, Duncan, Stammers and Gray (1971)	Task analysis of and training for process control tasks	Experimental in-plant study
*Anyakora and Lees (1972a)	Detection of instrument malfunction by process operator in chemical plants	Experimental in-plant study
*Attwood (1970)	Manual control by process operator on paper-machines	Experimental laboratory and in-plant studies
Bainbridge (1968)	Decision-making by process operator in scheduling electric arc furnaces	Experimental simulation study
Bainbridge and Beishon (1968)		
*Bainbridge, Beishon, Hemming and Splaine (1968).		
Bainbridge (1969)		
Bainbridge (1971)	Use of displays by process operator in scheduling electric arc furnaces	Experimental simulation study
Bainbridge (1972)	Decision-making by process operator in scheduling electric arc furnaces	Experimental simulation study
*Bainbridge (1974)		
Beishon and Bainbridge (1964)	Evaluation of human factors aspects of control room of LD converter waste heat boilers	Industrial study
Beishon (1966)	Process control skill; manual control and decision-making by process operator in laboratory and industrial tasks	Experimental laboratory and in-plant studies
Beishon (1967)	Manual control by process operator on paper-machine	Experimental in-plant study
Beishon and Palmer (1968)	Supervision by process supervisor in paper-mill	Industrial study
*Beishon (1969)	Manual control and decision-making by process operator on baking ovens	Experimental in-plant studies
Bernard and Wujkowski (1965)	Acceptability of process computer to process operator	Industrial study
Bitticker (1971)	Process operator in computer-controlled papermill	Experimental in-plant studies

Table 2.—Continued.

Author(s)	Subject of study	Type of study
Brenninkmeyer (1964)	Process control task in 6 plants of different degrees of automation	Industrial study
Brigham and Laios (1974)	Manual control by the process operator	Experimental laboratory study
Carter (1971)	Process operator in computer-controlled refinery	Review
*Central Electricity Generating Board (1966)	Evaluation of human factors aspects of control room of nuclear reactor	Industrial study
Chadwick-Jones (1969)	Process control task in plants of different degrees of automation	Industrial study
Chemicel and Allied Products Industry Training Board (1971)	Task analysis of and training for process control tasks	Training guide
Chemical and Allied Products Industry Training Board (1972)	Education/training of process operator	Training guide
*City and Guilds Institute (1972)	Education/training of process operator	Examination syllabus
Čižková (1967)	Visual search by human operator	Experimental laboratory study
Clark (1972)	Information display for and manual control and fault administration by process operator in computer-controlled pilot plant	Experimental in-plant study
Cook and Matterson (1968)	Information useful to process operator	Handbook
Cooke (1965)	Information sampling and manual control by process operator	Experimental laboratory study
*Crawley (1968)	Allocation of function between process operator and process computer and computer graphics displays for process operator on LD converter	Industrial studies
Crawley (1971)	Simulation studies in design of man-machine interfaces for process control in steel works	Industrial studies
Cristian and Zbăganu (1964)	Decision-making by process operator in power distribution	Experimental studies
Cristian and Zbăganu (1966)		
Cristian (1967)		
Cristian (1972)		
Crossman (1958)	Effect of automation on process control task	Industrial study
*Crossman (1960a)	Process control task and skill in plants of different types	Industrial study

Table 2.—*Continued.*

Author(s)	Subject of study	Type of study
Crossman (1960b)	Evaluation of human factors aspects of control system of hot strip mill	Industrial study
Crossman and Spencer (1960) (abstract)	Process control task	Experimental laboratory and industrial studies
*Crossman and Cooke (1962)	Manual control by process operator	Experimental laboratory study
Crossman (1964a)	Effect of automation on process operator	Review
Crossman (1964b)	Process control task	Experimental laboratory and in-plant studies
Crossman (1964d)	Effect of automation on process operator	Review
*Crossman, Cooke and Beishon (1964)	Information sampling by process operator	Experimental laboratory and in-plant studies
Crossman (1965)	Process control task	Review
Cuny and Deransart (1972)	Mental models of and problem-solving by human operator	Review
Cusack (1957)	Application of human factors to process control task	Industrial study
Daniel (1965)	Control and surveillance by process operator on distillation plant	Industrial study
Daniel and Striženec (1967)	Signal decoding by process operator	Experimental laboratory study
Daniel, Florek, Košinár and Striženec (1969)	Signal decoding and conflict resolution by process operator	Experimental laboratory study
Daniel (1970a)	Mental load and arousal of process operator	Experimental laboratory study
Daniel (1971)	Performance rating of process operator	Experimental study
*Daniel, Puffler and Striženec (1971)	Mental load of process operator in four chemical plants	Experimental in-plant study
Daniel et al. (1971)	Selection tests for process operator	Experimental study
Davies (1967)	Shift work by process operator	Review
Davies (1971)	Control and surveillance tasks	Experimental laboratory study
Delacoudre (1971)	Effect of process computer on process operator	Industrial study
*Department of Labor (1970)	Task analysis of and training for process control tasks	Review and experimental in-plant study
Duncan (1972)		
*Duncan (1974a, 1974b)		
Edwards and Lees (1971a)	Historical development of process control task	Review

Table 2.—Continued.

Author(s)	Subject of study	Type of study
Edwards and Lees (1971b)	Effect of process and control system characteristics on process control task	Review
Edwards and Lees (1971c)	Information display for process operator	Review
Edwards (1973)	Human operator in advanced control systems	Review
Edwards and Lees (1973)	Man and computer in process control	Review
*Engelstad (1970)	Social and organizational functions in process control in papermill	Experimental in-plant study
Gandsey (1965)	Process computer system including process operator functions	Industrial study
Goodstein (1969, 1971)	Information display for process operator	Experimental in-plant study
Green (1969, 1970)	Reliability of process operator in alarm monitoring in control room of nuclear reactors	Experimental in-plant study
Hickling and Jones (1967)	Man-computer interaction in scheduling of steel mill	Industrial study
Hiscock (1938)	Selection tests for process operator	Experimental in-plant study
Iosif (1969)	Monitoring of instrument panel by human operator	Experimental laboratory study
Iosif (1972)	Information sampling in incident diagnosis by process operator in power stations	Experimental in-plant study
Itelson (1961)	Process control task	Industrial study
Jakeš and Striženec (1971)	Manual control by and mental models of process operator	Experimental laboratory study
Jervis and Maddock (1964)	Man-computer interaction in control of power station	Industrial study
de Jong (J. J.) (1964)	Functions performed by process operator and process computer	Review
*de Jong and Köster (1971)	Process operator in computer-controlled refinery	Review
de Jong, Oerlemans and Spaargaren (1971)	Functions of process operator in computer-controlled plant	Review
Keener (1970)	Training of process operator using process simulator	Industrial study
Kellstedt (1965)	Training of process operator using process simulator	Industrial study

Table 2.—Continued.

Author(s)	Subject of study	Type of study
Kendrick (1969)	Selection and training of process operator	Review
Ketteringham, O'Brien and Cole (1970)	Computer-aided scheduling by process operator in steel mill soaking pits	Experimental simulation study
*Ketteringham and O'Brien (1974)		
King (1960)	Training of process operator	Industrial study
*Kitchin and Graham (1961)	Decision-making and mental load of process operators in 50 chemical plants	Experimental in-plant study
Klimoski (1971)	Effect of process computer on process management	Industrial study
Kragt (1971)	Surveillance by process operator in chemical plant	Experimental in-plant study
*Kragt and Landeweerd (1974)	Manual control and surveillance by process operator	Experimental laboratory and in-plant studies
Křivolahý (1964)	Information sampling by process operator in power stations	Experimental in-plant study
Landeweerd (1968)	Manual control by process operator	Experimental laboratory study
Lees (1970)	Functions performed by process operator and process computer	Review
Lees (1973)	Human reliability assessment in process control	Review
Lees (1974a)	Design for human reliability in process control	Review
Leplat (1968)	Vigilance in control and inspection tasks	Review
Leplat and Cuny (1969)	Fault administration by and mental models of process operator in steel mill.	Industrial study
Mardon et al. (1970)	Computer-based information system in a papermill, including process operator aspects	Experimental in-plant study
*Munro, Martin and Roberts (1968)	Work load of process operator	Experimental simulation study
Murrell (1964)	Information display for process operator	Review
Offer (1970)	Man-machine communication between process operator and process computer	Review
Oshanin (1966)	Information display for process operator	Experimental laboratory study
Parish (1971)	Man-computer interaction in control of power systems	Industrial study
Pogostin (1954)	Process control task	Industrial study
Pontius, van Tassel and Field (1959)	Training of process operator on new plants	Industrial study

Table 2.—*Continued.*

Author(s)	Subject of study	Type of study
*Rasmussen (1968a)	Allocation of function between process operator and process computer, computer-based information display and alarm system for process operator on experimental nuclear reactor	Review and industrial study
Rasmussen (1968b)	Reliability of process plants and instrument systems, including human factors aspects	Review
Rasmussen (1968c)	Allocation of function between process operator and process computer, man-computer interface	Review
Rasmussen (1969)	Fault administration and identification difficulties of human operator in aircraft and nuclear reactor accidents	Review
Rasmussen (1971) Rasmussen and Jensen (1973)	Fault diagnosis by human operator	Experimental study
Rasmussen (1974)	Reliability assessment of process control systems with emphasis on human factors	Review
Savoyant (1971)	Analysis of task of process operators in granulation plant	Industrial study
Schager (1965)	Information display for process operator	Industrial study
Sell, Crossman and Box (1962)	Evaluation of human factors aspects of control system of hot strip mill	Industrial study
Sell and Pulsford (1967)	Evaluation of human factors aspects of control system of National Grid	Industrial study
Sinclair, Sell, Beishon and Bainbridge (1966)	Evaluation of human factors aspects of control room of LD converter waste heat boilers	Industrial study
Singer and Rieck (1969)	Relation between vigilance and motor activity of human operator	Experimental laboratory study
Šipoš (1971)	Relation between vigilance and personality traits of process operator	Experimental laboratory study
*Spencer (1962)	Manual control by process operator on liquid washing plant	Experimental in-plant study

Table 2.—Continued.

Author(s)	Subject of study	Type of study
Spencer and Phipps (1966)	Application of human factors to control rooms of gas and electricity distribution systems and of nuclear reactors	Review
Striženec (1966b)	Process control skill and decision-making	Review
Striženec (1967a)	Effect of remote control on process control task	Review
*Striženec (1967b)	Decision-making by process operator	Review
Striženec (1968)	Decision-making by process operator	Experimental laboratory study
Striženec (1969)	Applicability of laboratory experiments on process operator to industrial problems	Review
Striženec (1970a)	Manual control by and mental models of process operator	Experimental laboratory study
Striženec (1970b)	Manual control by and mental models of process operator	Experimental laboratory study
Strohmeyer (1970)	Man-computer interaction in startup of power station	Industrial study
Swain (1969)	Human reliability assessment in control of nuclear reactors	Review
Swain (1972)	Human reliability assessment	Review
Tavast and Mytus (1969)	Process operator in computer-controlled plant	Industrial study
*Towill (1974)	Mathematical modelling of learning process of process operator	Experimental in-plant study
Tuff (1970)	Training of process operator on computer-controlled chemical plant	Industrial study
Vander Schraaf and Strauss (1964)	Acceptability of process computer to process operator	Industrial study
*West and Clark (1974)	Information display for and manual control and fault administration by process operator in computer-controlled pilot plant	Experimental in-plant study
Whitfield (1969)	Evaluation of human factors aspects of control room of nuclear reactor	Industrial study
Yoder, Lucas and Botzum (1973)	Design for human reliability in process control	Review

Papers in this volume are marked with an *

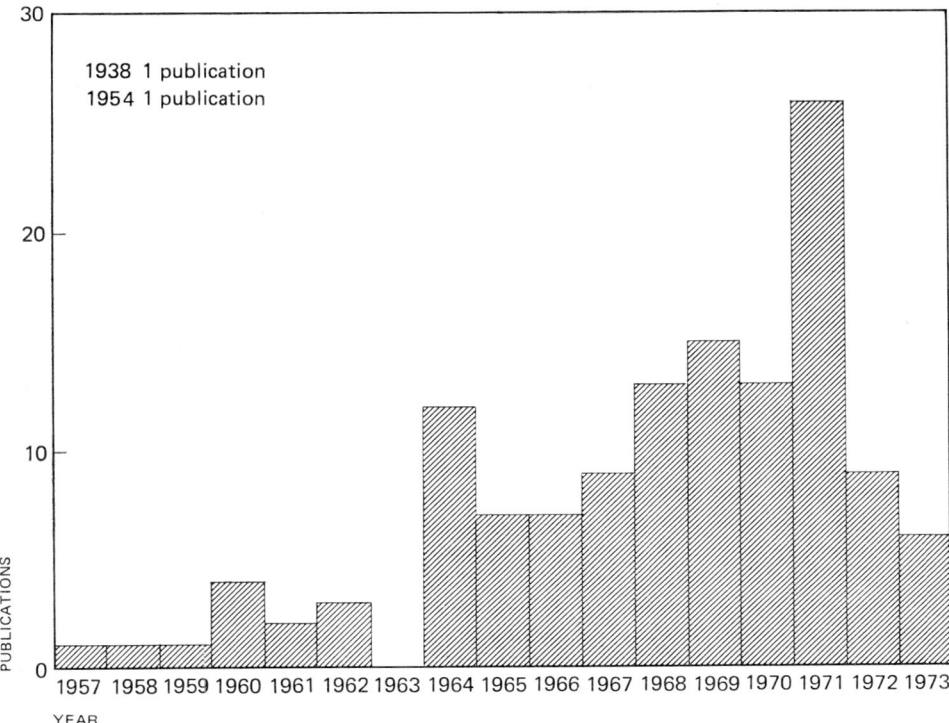

Figure 2. Development of research on the process operator.

The main object of this work on decision-making was to learn how the operator actually makes decisions. Various concepts were suggested as models of the operator's decision-making process, such as feedback control, information processing, categorization, hierarchical control. Attempts were made to write computer programs to reproduce the operator's behaviour, but although subroutines could be isolated the executive program which organizes these remained elusive.

Other studies were concerned not so much with the process operator as with industrial control rooms and control situations. These include investigations of a hot strip mill control system (Sell, Crossman and Box 1962); of an LD converter waste heat boiler control room (Sinclair, Sell, Beishon and Bainbridge 1966); of gas and electricity distribution systems and of nuclear reactors (Spencer and Phipps 1966); and of the National Grid (Sell and Pulsford 1967). Other similar evaluation studies about this time were those of the C.E.G.B. (1966) and of Whitfield (1967) on nuclear power station control rooms.

A continuing study of the process operator is also being carried out by Strížsenec and other workers in Czechoslovakia. This includes numerous investigations, usually conducted in the laboratory but using process operators, on various aspects of vigilance (Čížková 1967, Singer and Rieck 1969, Šípoš 1971); on control panel monitoring (Iosif 1969); on signal decoding (Daniel and Strížsenec 1967, Daniel, Florek, Kośinár and Strížsenec 1969); on manual control (Strížsenec 1970a, 1970b); on decision-making (Strížsenec 1966b, 1967b, 1968); and on mental models (Strížsenec 1970a, 1970b). This work also involves in-plant studies such as that on the decision-making load of the process operator (Daniel 1965, Daniel, Puffler and Striženec (1971). Other work on operator decision-making is that of Cristian and Zbăganu (Cristian and Zbăganu 1964, 1966, Cristian 1967, 1972) on the power despatcher.

Another long-term investigation is that of Leplat and coworkers in France. Although most of this work is concerned with surveillance tasks such as radar watchkeeping or inspection tasks such as quality control (Leplat 1968) and with decision-making in tasks such as air traffic control (Leplat and Bisseret 1965), it has also included work on fault administration by the process operator in a steel mill (Leplat and Cuny 1969).

The advent of the process computer has paradoxically but logically stimulated interest in the process operator. Early studies in the use of computers by operators and especially on the acceptability of the computer to the operator were conducted by Vander Schraaf and Strauss (1964) and by Bernard and Wujkowski (1965). The philosophy of control by process operator and computer has been explored by J. J. de Jong (de Jong 1964, 1965, de Jong, Oerlemans and Spaargaren 1971). The task of and information sampling by the operator in computer-controlled refinery plants under normal and abnormal conditions has been the subject of in-plant studies by de Jong and Köster (1971). The functions performed by the process computer and by the process operator have been detailed by Lees (1970). The impact of the computer on the operator's job and employment has been the object of a survey by the U.S. Department of Labor (1970).

There have been several descriptions of man–computer interactive systems in process control, such as those of Jervis and Maddock (1964) on power station control, of Hickling and Jones (1967) on steel mill scheduling, of Rasmussen (1968a, 1968c) on nuclear reactor control, of Strohmeyer (1970) on power station startup, of Mardon *et al.* (1970) on a papermill information system, and of Parish (1971) on power system control.

The British Iron and Steel Research Association (B.I.S.R.A.) has a continuing programme of work on the application of human factors to process computer systems. Crawley (1968) has described the allocation of function between man and computer in the control system for an LD converter. Extensive use is made of simulator studies in the design of the man–computer interface: an account is given by Crawley (1971). An example of this approach is the work of Ketteringham, O'Brien and Cole (Ketteringham, O'Brien and Cole 1970, Ketteringham and O'Brien 1974) on the use of a man–computer interactive game-playing facility in soaking pit scheduling.

Information display in process computer systems is important both because a simple computer console may constitute a rather poor display system and because by contrast computer graphics offer great potential for providing improved display facilities. The design of computer-driven displays on a nuclear reactor, particularly for recognition of system state, is described by Rasmussen (1968a) and by Goodstein (1969, 1971). Some computer-based predictive displays for manual control of the LD converter are described by Crawley (1968). The operator's use of both conventional panel and computer displays in manual control and fault administration on a pilot plant has been investigated by West and Clark (Clark 1972, West and Clark 1974). West (1972) has developed and tested on the pilot plant a ' status array ' for system state recognition. The use of displays for detecting malfunction of instruments and plant equipment has been discussed by Anyakora and Lees (Anyakora 1971, Anyakora and Lees 1971, 1972a).

The reliability of the control system is of increasing concern, particularly on nuclear reactors. As part of its work on the assessment of system reliability, the U.K. Atomic Energy Authority (U.K.A.E.A.) has done a considerable amount of research on operator reliability. This includes apparently unpublished work on the relative importance of human error in serious incidents (see Rasmussen 1969); investigation of operator response to alarm signals in nuclear reactor control rooms (Green 1969); and a review of methods of assessing operator reliability (Ablitt 1969). Another series of investigations is that conducted by Swain and coworkers at Sandia Laboratories in the U.S. Many of these studies, including the review by Swain (1972), are not concerned with process control, and most are listed rather in Table 1, but Swain (1969) has also discussed human error in nuclear reactor control. Rasmussen has emphasized in this context the importance of information display, particularly for state recognition, in the light of serious incidents involving human error. Anyakora and Lees (1972a) have done an in-plant investigation of detection of malfunction in instruments by the process operator. Reviews of the problems of assessment of and design for reliability in process control have been given by Lees (1973, 1974a) and by Rasmussen (1974). The importance of human factors in the areas of safety and loss prevention in the process industries has been reviewed by Yoder, Lucas and Botzum (1973).

The problem of the interpretation by the operator of the alarm signals which occur on process plants has been described by Duncan (1972, 1974b). Andow and Lees (1974) have discussed some of the principles of the design of process alarm systems.

In some plants, particularly nuclear reactors, large numbers of alarms may come up and the operator may suffer an information overload. The engineer's response to this problem has been to provide a computer-based alarm analysis facility which displays not only the alarms but the relations between them. The alarm analysis system at Oldbury nuclear power station is described by Kay (1966), by Kay and Heywood (1966) and by Patterson (1968) and that at Wylfa by Welbourne (1965, 1968). The engineering of an alarm analysis system requires considerable effort; there are also serious human factors problems, which have been discussed by Rasmussen (1968a, 1971). An assessment of the human factors aspects of the Oldbury system has been made by Whitfield (1969).

There is a small amount of more recent work in the area of selection and training. Davies (1967) made a comparative study of process operator performance as measured by the National Institute of Industrial Psychology (N.I.I.P.) selection test battery and of performance as assessed by supervisors; little correlation was found. A sustained investigation of the training of process operators including in-plant studies has been made by Annett, Duncan and coworkers (Annett, Duncan, Stammers and Gray 1971, Duncan 1972, 1974b). A central rôle is played here by the task analysis.

Process simulators are quite widely used as training aids in the process industries, particularly in conventional and nuclear power station control. General descriptions of the use of simulators for training process operators have been given by Kellstedt (1965), by Keener (1970) and by Bitticker (1971). A more detailed account is provided by Duncan (1972, 1974b).

Research has continued on manual control of processes. A persistent theme here has been the value to the operator of a ' physical understanding ' of the process. Examples of such work are that of Attwood (1970) and that of Kragt and Landeweerd (1974). Also in the area of manual control, recent work by Brigham and Laios (1974) on control of the level in the last of a series of three vessels provides some confirmation that predictive control may predominate over feedback control actions.

There is a considerable literature on the mathematical modelling of human operator performance in various tasks as Table 1 indicates. Examples in process control include the work of Crossman and Cooke (1962) on manual control, that of Crossman, Cooke and Beishon (1964) on information sampling, and that of Towill (1974) on learning process tasks.

The effect of organizational factors on the performance of process operators has been the subject of an in-plant study by Engelstad (1970). The effect of the process computer on the plant management has been studied by Constable (1971) and by Klimoski (1971).

As this brief account indicates, there has already been a substantial volume of research on the process operator. Therefore, before considering the direction which further research might take, it is appropriate to consider what the problems associated with the process operator really are and how work on the operator can contribute to meeting system objectives.

5. Problems of the Process Operator

The objective of research on the process operator must be to enable the process control system to meet its objectives more successfully. The effectiveness of the work done must eventually be judged in terms of these systems criteria. However, these criteria, which are considered in the next section, have always proved difficult to define in process control. It may, therefore, be helpful to start at a more accessible point, namely the problems associated with the process operator.

Some of these problems are listed in Table 3:

Table 3. Some problems of the process operator

Problem area	Symptom	Problem may be of concern to
Information display		
Regular instruments	Growth in number of displays and in size and cost of control room	Control system designer
Alarm system	Growth in number of alarms	Control system designer
	Lack of confidence of operator in alarm system	Plant manager
Computer console	Concern over adequacy of simple console as display-control interface	Control system designer
Operator selection	Lack of performance criteria and of associated selection tests; concern over operator's ability to handle rarely occurring but critical situations	Personnel officer

Table 3.—*Continued.*

Problem area	Symptom	Problem may be of concern to
Operator training	Lack of performance criteria; concern over training for rarely occurring but critical situations	Training officer, plant manager
Operator-computer relations	Lack of acceptance and misuse of computer by operator; poor demarcation of functions between them	Plant manager, systems engineer
Process operation	Poor overall operation (product quality, plant throughput, services usage, equipment downtime); variability of performance between shifts	Plant manager
Communication	Difficulties arising from communication, or lack of it, between operator and others	Plant manager
Human error	Lack of method or data for assessment of operator reliability	Reliability engineer
Emergency situations	Concern over operator's ability to handle emergency situations	Plant manager, reliability engineer
Job evaluation	Lack of performance criteria	Work study officer
Job satisfaction	Boredom; poor morale; decline in performance, increase in errors; high labour turnover	Plant manager, personnel officer

This table has been compiled principally from the comments made on operator problems in the literature and by control engineers and from the author's own experience rather than by discussion with all the disciplines listed in the third column of the table. The latter does, however, illustrate the wide range of jobs on which operator problems impinge.

These problems cause the plant to incur the extra costs given in Table 4:

Table 4. Some costs of defects in human factors aspects of process control systems
Additional costs associated with
  Capital equipment (plant equipment, instrumentation)
  Operation
  Maintenance
  Serious incidents
  Operator morale

The severity of a particular problem varies with the plant. But there is no doubt, for example, that problems of alarm systems, fault administration, human error and operator training are considered important in conventional and nuclear power stations and in large single-stream chemical plants.

Several factors hamper not only the solution but even the identification of these problems. One factor is the fact that the different problems are the concern of a number of different people. Another is that most of these people are engineers who are normally untrained in human factors. But almost certainly the most important factor is the difficulty of assessing process operator performance.

In addition to these existing problems, there is another which is potentially serious. This is the recruitment of process operators in the first place. So far the job of operating process plants has been relatively attractive. But it cannot be assumed that this situation will necessarily continue. And if a higher level of intelligence is demanded of operators, the problem is likely to be accentuated.

6. Systems Criteria for Process Operator Performance

In the broadest terms, the systems criteria which are applicable in process control are the economic and safe operation of the process, but these are very general goals, and it is more meaningful to break these down into subgoals, such as achievement of high throughput and high availability and avoidance of serious loss and disruption.

For these more specific criteria to be useful they need ideally to be

(1) Based on process economics

(2) Capable of being measured

(3) Affected by operator performance

(4) Usable for system improvement.

There are clearly three levels of performance criteria. Performance may be measured in terms of

(1) Process economics

(2) Process control

(3) Psychology.

The difficulty lies in relating performance at one level to that at another. It has always been a problem in process control to assess the value in terms of economic performance of a given level of control performance. In recent years the problem has arisen frequently in the guise of the difficulty of assessing the benefits of process computers. It may be noted in passing that this has not prevented a growing acceptance of computer control.

Likewise, it is not easy to relate psychological performance to process control performance. One factor here is the distinction between the part task and the whole task. Psychologists tend to deal with the separate tasks which comprise the process control task, whereas the essence of successful control performance is their coordination.

Another important factor is that it is the performance of the whole man–machine system in process control which matters. The operator's performance is only one aspect of this. The influence which the operator can exert on overall control system performance varies considerably between plants. The difficulties in this area are illustrated by the frequent lack of success of multifactor incentive schemes. The contribution of the operator to the system objectives is often obscured by the noise in the system.

Despite these problems, assessment of operator performance is important. As Crossman (1960a) points out, process operators, though relatively few in number, have control of plants which represent a large fraction of the country's capital investment.

If methods of assessing human performance in general are considered, these may be classified as follows (Edwards 1971):

(1) Direct achievement measurement

(2) Operator loading measurement

(3) Correlated function measurement.

Where it is applicable direct measurement of achievement is clearly preferable. But such measurements are often difficult to obtain and a more circuitous approach may have to be taken. In this case, measurement may be made of operator loading, *i.e.* of the ' cost ' to the operator of a given level of performance or of a correlated function, *i.e.* of an aspect of performance which is known to correlate with direct achievement; consistency in performance is a common correlated function.

In the context of process control direct achievement measurement would appear to be the most fruitful approach. There is likely to be, however, some difference of emphasis in measures of direct achievement, depending on whether the investigator's terms of reference are primarily

or
    (1) Human factors

    (2) Process control.

The differences are illustrated by the lists of functions given in Tables 5 and 6. In the first some aspects of operator performance are given expressed in human factors terms, while in the second these aspects are expressed in process control terms. Broadly speaking, the first group of performances are *means* while the second are *ends*. Or, in other words, the former only have an effect in so far as they influence the latter. Obviously there is some overlap between the two lists, notably in single-variable tracking and scheduling.

Table 5. Some aspects of process operator performance expressed in human factors terms

Vigilance, signal detection
Information sampling
Estimating averages, filtering
Categorization, quantization
Probability estimation
System state evaluation
Manual control, tracking
Sequential drills
Resource allocation, scheduling
Attention-sharing
Heuristics, strategy development
Fault diagnosis
Communication activities
Learning

Table 6. Some aspects of process operator performance expressed in process control terms

Single-variable control
Sequential control
Optimization
Scheduling
Fault detection
Fault diagnosis
Fault correction
Emergency avoidance
Emergency administration

Most of the research done on the process operator has come from workers in human factors. Inevitably they have been concerned with operator performance in terms of the established categories in human factors and the link between such performance and process control or economic criteria has remained obscure. There have been, however, several studies where a fairly direct measurement of economic performance has been made. This is the case in the study of electric arc furnace scheduling (Bainbridge, Beishon, Hemming and Splaine 1968) and in that of soaking pit scheduling (Ketteringham and O'Brien 1974). The production results obtained by Engelstad (1970) arising from organizational changes are another example. It is of interest that the first two of these investigations were both concerned with scheduling and were both simulations, while the latter was concerned with the effect on performance of broad organizational features rather than of detailed operator functions.

Some aspects of performance are more difficult to quantify economically than others and some present quite severe problems. The administration of faults and emergencies presents particular difficulty, because these are rarely occurring events and are not readily amenable to study. The use of 'accelerated' tests in this area is full of pitfalls.

Despite these problems, it is essential that research on the process operator should concern itself increasingly with systems criteria.

7. Requirements for Research on the Process Operator

7.1. *Overall Approach*

The author believes that at the present juncture the emphasis should be placed not so much on the question of which particular fields are ripe for research as on the question of how the research should be conducted. Some of the principal points which may be made concerning the overall approach to the research are as follows:

(1) There is need for quantification of industrial problems and hence of systems criteria in this area.

(2) Research should then be designed so that its effectiveness in meeting these criteria can be measured.

(3) Involvement in system design is likely to be a particularly fruitful approach to the research.

(4) Significant progress now probably requires sustained long-term investigations rather than one-off studies.

Some industrial problems and some costs arising from these were listed in Tables 3 and 4 respectively. Research is required which will quantify these problems and costs and lead to the formulation of improved systems criteria. This is a difficult area, but progress here would put work on the process operator on a much sounder footing.

More emphasis needs to be placed on research which is aimed at making design or operational improvements which can be validated in terms of systems criteria.

Probably the most effective way of conducting this research is by involvement in system design, or, to a lesser extent, in system operation. As mentioned earlier, this has been the trend in human factors generally.

Much of the research on the process operator to date has consisted of one-off studies. This type of study is likely to be less valuable in the future. Serious progress would now seem to depend on sustained and systematic long-term research involving the study of the totality of the operator's job in all its complexity and probably using sophisticated and expensive equipment.

This said, some continuing problems and some research fields in work on the process operator are now considered.

7.2. Some Continuing Problems

7.2.1. Research methodology

Some aspects of research methodology have already been discussed. Development of performance criteria and involvement in design have been emphasized.

Two long-standing questions are whether laboratory, simulation or in-plant studies are preferable and whether students or process operators should be used as subjects. The advantages and disadvantages of the different approaches have been discussed by several workers (*e.g.* Spencer 1962, Beishon 1966). Laboratory experiments allow a degree of control which is difficult to achieve in the plant situation, but tend to lack realism. Simulation represents a compromise in which, in comparison with laboratory studies, there is the same degree of control but a much higher degree of realism. However, simulation is not without its problems: the actual simulation may require considerable engineering effort and there may still be problems concerning the motivation of the subjects.

As far as the choice of subjects is concerned, students have often been used, because they tend to be more readily available and less expensive to employ and because it is possible to use enough to obtain statistically significant results. The two main problems, however, are that process control skill is only acquired over a long period and that motivation is not the same.

For these reasons, it is likely that a variety of methods will continue to be employed in investigations. But the emphasis on systems criteria in the control of industrial processes tends to favour realistic simulation or in-plant studies. In particular, it is expected that simulation will often prove to be the right compromise.

There are a number of 'objective' techniques which can be used to record what the operator does. The operator's action can be filmed. The investigator's running comments on his actions can be recorded. An eye camera or the observing response technique can be used to show information sampling by the operator.

The type of information which such methods obtain tends to be acts such as information sampling, control actions, communication.

Several investigators (Spencer 1962, Beishon 1967) have then used an activity chart in which such information is plotted together with process trends. This has proved useful principally in studying tracking tasks.

On the whole, however, the results of such 'objective' studies seem often to have been rather disappointing. Frequently the investigator has not been able to do much more than determine the fraction of time spent by the operator in certain broad classes of activity.

Investigators have therefore wished to obtain more information about the operator's thought processes. For this techniques such as the interview/questionnaire after or the verbal protocol during the working period have been used.

These methods have been used for two main purposes. One is to provide general clues to the way in which the operator thinks. This is exemplified by Rasmussen's (1971) work on fault diagnosis by operators. The other is to investigate in some detail the process of human decision-making. The work of Bainbridge (1969, 1972, 1974) illustrates this.

In the author's view there are several approaches to the methodology of studying the operator which are worth consideration:

(1) It is clear that much depends on the observer's understanding of the process control task, on his initial description of the operator's behaviour and hence on the taxonomy he is using.

(2) The verbal protocol technique may be used for purposes somewhat less ambitious than the elucidation of human thought processes. Beishon and Bainbridge (Beishon 1969, Bainbridge, Beishon, Hemming and Splaine 1968, Bainbridge 1974) have used it to identify 'subroutines' in scheduling tasks and Duncan (1974b) has obtained from it the 'operations' and fixed-sequence 'plans' in fault diagnosis tasks. In the latter work one use of the protocol was to elicit from the operator an observing response.

(3) Verbal protocol might also be exploited by training selected operators to give a description of their own behaviour in terms of the investigator's categories. Thus the subject might describe an activity such as "Sampling of trend record of variable A to confirm effect of control action taken on valve B" or a decision such as "Initial assumption, based on past experience, is that it is the instrument which is wrong".

These are rather more modest ways of using the protocol technique. The usual objections to verbal protocol apply, perhaps with even greater force, but its use may nevertheless prove justified in practice.

(4) The process computer is a very powerful tool for investigating operator activity and should be exploited. With a computer it is possible to arrange to record all displays called and all control actions taken on the computer itself. It can also record the trends of all process measurements, alarms and statuses. It therefore constitutes an extraordinarily powerful investigational tool which has not previously been available. The computer was used in this way by West and Clark (1974).

(5) The investigation of operator decision-making still appears worth while. But this should not be confined to scheduling tasks. And there is a need for additional methods of investigation to supplement verbal protocols. It has been suggested (King 1974) that the technique of linguistic analysis using fuzzy sets (Zadeh 1972) has potential in this area.

7.2.2. *Process simulation*

Process simulation may be used for several purposes. These include research on the process operator, training of the operator, and design of the man–computer interface in process control.

The advantage of simulation in research is that it permits an investigation to be more realistic than other types of laboratory study but does not involve the difficulties of experimentation on actual processes. Similar considerations apply to the use of simulators in training or design.

The simplest type of simulator is essentially only an interface which may be manipulated by the investigator/trainer. The Carmody Universal Process Trainer described by Duncan (1974b) is an example.

More sophisticated simulation requires a mathematical model of the process. Such models vary greatly in complexity. Full unsteady-state models of processes often amount to some hundreds of differential equations which require formidable computing facilities for their solution, if indeed they are soluble at all. Normally the engineer will avoid this degree of complication if he can.

Two ways in which simulation can be greatly simplified are its restriction to a model comprising only a few differential equations or to a time-interval model. In the first case, provided the number of differential equations is kept down, there is no difficulty in adding on all kinds of other features such as noise, discrete events, *etc.*, which can be used to give a high degree of realism. In the second case, the model consists almost entirely of relations between time intervals.

Scheduling simulations will normally be of the latter type. Thus the simulations of scheduling of electric arc furnaces by Bainbridge, Beishon, Hemming and Splaine (1968) and of soaking pits by Ketteringham and O'Brien (1974) fall in this category.

The degree of complexity which should be used in process simulation would appear to be a problem. It is, of course, obvious that some applications will require more detailed simulation than others. Thus general training of process operators may be conducted on a relatively simple, general-purpose simulator, but training specific to a particular plant may require a more complex simulator.

The defence and aerospace organizations make extensive use of simulators and support a whole simulation industry. Some of these simulations do involve large sets of differential equations. Analogue or hybrid computers, whose *forte* is the solution of such equations, have traditionally been used for this purpose, although digital computers are finding increasing application here also. Simulators with realistic man–machine interfaces, of which the jet aircraft trainer is one of the best known, are used for interface design and training work.

There is also a quite large number of process simulators in use. Many of these are in conventional or nuclear power stations. Typically, these are built for several purposes, such as control engineering and interface design studies as well as operator training. Many are based on large analogue computers. Some have sophisticated man–machine interfaces.

There is, therefore, considerable experience in process simulation to draw on. But very little published material has been found on questions such as the level of model complexity which is appropriate for various purposes. There appears to be a need for a specific study of simulators for process operator work.

The author believes that simulation is probably the most appropriate method of investigation for much future work on the process operator. But some degree of caution is necessary. There are important differences between a simulated and a real process situation: the motivation of the operator is one of the most important. These differences may have more effect on some tasks than others. The task of scheduling, for example, may be much less affected than that of emergency administration.

7.2.3. Mental models

The relevance to the human operator of a 'physical understanding' of the process which he controls is a well-established controversy in human factors. It is well known, for example, that a pilot may be very skilled in flying but may give a quite erroneous account of the control linkages in the aircraft.

This problem was raised in process control by Crossman and Cooke (1962) when they found that subjects who were furnished with a description of the process equipment gave performance inferior to that of subjects who were simply given details of the system response. Kragt and Landeweerd (1974) have confirmed this finding.

There has been a tendency to argue from these results that a 'physical understanding' of the process is of little use or even is a hindrance to the operator. This is surely incorrect. Knowledge of the equipment and of the responses are both types of 'physical understanding'. It just happens that in the kind of manual control task which has given rise to this discussion it is the responses which are more useful. Thus in Attwood's (1970) work the systems engineers deliberately set out to learn the responses and were then able to use this knowledge to improve performance.

Moreover, attention has been concentrated too exclusively on this type of manual control experiment to draw general conclusions. Different types of model may be expected to be useful for different tasks. In fault diagnosis, for example, a knowledge of the process equipment may be an advantage.

It is also not valid to argue on the basis of this work that education of the operator—such as that provided by the City and Guilds' Chemical Technicians course—is without value. Again, Attwood's systems engineers put their education to good use to select, obtain and use the appropriate model.

More generally, it can be said that discussion of the operator's mental models has tended sometimes to concentrate on a rather narrow definition of what constitutes a model. There are many other types of model which the operator presumably utilizes. Some of these are listed in Table 7:

Table 7. Some mental models of the process operator

Process flow diagram
Plant layout
Unit operations
Control loops
Steady-state gains
Step responses, time constants
Trend patterns
Noise patterns
System state patterns
Sequential operations
Failure probabilities
Fault patterns
Fault diagnosis strategies
Fault correction strategies

7.3. Some Research Areas

Some principal research areas are listed in Table 8:

Table 8. Some principal areas of research on the process operator

    System objectives
    Allocation of function
    Job profile
    Performance assessment
    Task analysis
    Information display
    Alarm systems
    Alarm analysis
    Manual control
    Sequential control
    Scheduling
    Emergency avoidance
      Control adjustments
      Malfunction detection
    Fault administration
      Fault detection
      Fault diagnosis
      Fault correction
    Emergency administration
    Decision-making
    Personnel selection
    Training
    Operating instructions
    Job design
    Operator error

Many of these correspond to the stages in system design shown in Figure 1. These research areas are now considered in detail.

7.3.1. System objectives

Work on the process control system must necessarily be concerned with the system objectives. Yet comprehensive specifications for such control systems are usually lacking. The outstanding exception is in the area of reliability, where increasingly there are clear specifications. While this is not perhaps a research field, it is appropriate to call attention to the need for the development of methods of specifying more clearly the requirements in process control systems.

7.3.2. Allocation of function

The allocation of function is a crucial decision in the design of a process control system. Again, this may not strictly be a subject for research, but it would undoubtedly be helpful to have some detailed case studies in advanced industrial process control systems giving an informed and reasoned approach to allocation decisions in a variety of situations.

7.3.3. Job profile

There is need for a quantitative assessment of the job profile of the process operator. Several workers (e.g. Pogostin 1954, Daniel, Puffler and Strízenec 1971) have determined the fraction of time spent by the operator on certain activities. Others (e.g. J. J. de Jong 1964, Lees 1970) have given detailed descriptions of the functions which the operator performs. Neither of these types of study constitutes an adequate profile of the operator's job. What is required is a quantitative study, using an adequate taxonomy, of operator functions which provides information on the relative importance of these functions in terms both of operator effort and of economic importance. Since there are such large variations between processes, profiles for certain broad classes of process would probably be more meaningful than a single overall profile.

7.3.4. *Performance assessment*

The assessment of operator performance is fundamental to research on the process operator. It is not enough to assess performance in human factors terms alone. It must also be assessed in terms of process control and of process economics. Much of the other research depends, in varying degrees, on the development of effective methods of performance assessment.

7.3.5. *Task analysis*

Task analysis is a crucial activity in human factors. As Figure 1 shows, logically it precedes many of the other stages of system design, such as interface design, job design and training. In practice, there is usually a degree of iteration between the stages.

A technique of task analysis has been developed by Annett, Duncan and coworkers (Annett, Duncan, Stammers and Gray 1970, Duncan 1972, 1974b). There has been some utilization by other workers (Duncan 1974c) and it would be most valuable to have feedback on the application of the method.

Since task analysis plays a central rôle and since it is a creative activity, there is scope for other work in this area. As Singleton, Easterby and Whitfield (1967) comment: " If there are enough people with the appropriate abilities doing this work, it should be possible eventually to generalize from what they are doing and thus make it possible to substitute education for experience in this field."

7.3.6. *Information display*

The operator requires information for some purpose, or rather for a variety of purposes, so that these need to be defined before information display can usefully be considered. Some of these information requirements, many of which have been discussed above, are given in Table 9.

It is only quite recently, with the availability at acceptable cost of computer-driven c.r.t.s., that a flexible display facility has become practical. Now, however, the control engineer has been provided with this very powerful display tool, but is often uncertain what to do with it. There is great scope for the development of computer-based displays for the operator.

It should be emphasized, however, that a display is only a means to an end, the end being improved performance in the execution of some operator function. The proper design of this function from the human factors aspects remains more important than the display *per se*.

The provision of displays which the operator deliberately samples with a specific aim in view is only part of the display problem. It is also important that the display system should cater both for his characteristic of acquiring information ' at a glance ' and for his requirement for information redundancy.

Table 9. Some displays for the process operator

Displays of flow and mimic diagrams
Displays of current measurements, other variables, statuses
 (other variables include indirect measurements, valve positions, *etc.*)
Displays of trends of measurements, other variables, statuses
Displays of control loop parameters
Displays of alarms
Displays of reduced data (*e.g.* histograms, quality control charts,
 statistical parameters)
Displays of system state (*e.g.* mimic diagrams, ' status array ',
 ' surface ' and polar plots)
Displays for manual control (*e.g.* predictive displays)
Displays for alarm analysis
Displays for sequential control
Displays for scheduling and game-playing
Displays for security control
Displays for protective system checking
Displays for malfunction detection
Command displays

There is, therefore, a need for the development of displays which allow the operator to obtain a rapid and effortless overall view of the state of the system. Some of the more advanced existing systems allow the operator to obtain flow or mimic diagrams and either to traverse the diagram using a rolling ball or to ' blow up ' a section of it using a separate display called up by a pushbutton or, where economics allow, a light pen. Such facilities are in use in areas such as power system control, but their use in process control has often been difficult to justify. Moreover, even these facilities do not completely compensate the operator for the loss of conventional control panel displays.

But in any case the problem is wider than this. It concerns the whole question of the additional state information which the operator requires in various situations. Thus, for example, it is argued by Rasmussen (1968a) that in a fault situation the operator needs not only alarm displays but survey displays also. In fact, he goes further and suggests a design philosophy which obliges the operator to access certain types of data only through a survey display so that he cannot avoid being aware of their context.

The operator uses displays of system state to recognize patterns. It is appropriate, therefore, to investigate such pattern recognition by the process operator. Some work on the recognition of patterns in instrument panels has been done by Duncan (1974c).

There is scope for the development of unconventional displays of system state. Two particular examples are the three-dimensional ' surface ' display described by Bowen (1967) and the polar plot devised by Wolff (1970). In the former a very large number of data points are shown as a surface so that any abnormality appears as an irregularity on the surface. In the latter a relatively small number of variables are displayed scaled in such a way that their normal values lie on the locus of a circle and abnormal values are readily distinguished. Such displays exploit the ability of the computer to process, store and display data and that of the man to recognize patterns.

It is certainly desirable that novel displays should be tried out in process control systems. But it should be recognized that not all will turn out to be as useful as was originally hoped and that some will appear to the operator to be gimmicks. While there is less danger of this if the display has been developed as part of the overall design of an operator function rather than as an end in itself, the engineer must be prepared to admit and withdraw his mistakes.

The development of appropriate displays will be greatly encouraged if there are facilities for the creation of displays as required by the engineer or even by the operator.

The nature of the display affects the control action taken by the operator. Thus, for example, the effect of displaying a variable in a binary state rather than in continuous form is likely to be to encourage ' bang-bang ' control responses. This is a relatively unexplored area in process control.

The study of displays and of the operator's response to them thus offers a rich vein of research.

7.3.7. *Alarm systems*

Alarm systems are often one of the least satisfactory aspects of process control system design. There are a number of reasons for this, including lack of a clear design philosophy, confusion between alarms and statuses, use of too many alarms, *etc.* Yet with the relative growth in the monitoring function of the operator, and indeed of the control system, the alarm system becomes increasingly important. This is therefore another field in which there is much scope for work.

7.3.8. *Alarm analysis*

When there are a large number of potential alarms, it may be desirable to provide the operator with aids to interpreting them. One objective is to assist him to relate the alarms to each other as they occur in real time by grouping together related alarms. Another more ambitious aim is to help him to work back to the prime cause of a group of alarms.

As discussed above, alarm analysis is practised on nuclear reactors. But the engineering effort required is very great. Apart from an experimental exercise by Barth and Maarleveld (1967), the technique does not appear to have been applied in the process industries. However, evidence of renewed interest in this area is the recent work of Powers and Tompkins (1973a, 1973b) and of Andow (1973) on the engineering of alarm analysis.

There are, however, serious human factors problems in alarm analysis, as Rasmussen (1968a) emphasizes. Above all, there is the difficulty that an operator will not usually accept the computer analysis of a low-probability event until he has convinced himself that the high-probability events have been excluded. This makes very stringent demands on the engineering analysis which is the basis of the method. There must therefore be some doubt how successful the technique will ultimately prove. But this is now one of the central problems in process control and the incentive to achieve either automatic or computer-assisted fault diagnosis is a very strong one.

A discussion of process alarm systems and alarm analysis is given by Andow and Lees (1974).

7.3.9. *Manual Control*

Although manual control, and in particular tracking, has been the subject of a number of investigations on the process operator, studies of performance on industrial plants have mainly been confined to papermachines. There still appears to be room for work on manual control in process systems.

Aids for manual control is an obvious area of development. The principal aid is, of course, a suitable display. Quickened displays are well established in vehicle guidance, but their relevance to process control is uncertain. Predictive model-based displays, on the other hand, have been quite widely canvassed.

Another aid which has been investigated for systems such as processes is the provision of controls with stiffness corresponding to system inertia. The stiffness is based on a model of the inertia (Herzog 1969).

The most important point, however, is that work on manual control of processes is likely to be most fruitful if it addresses itself to real problems which arise in the course of designing process control systems.

7.3.10. *Sequential control*

In many processes an important part of the operator's task is the execution of sequential operations, taking these in the broadest sense to include batch operation, semi-continuous operation, startup and shutdown, change of throughput or grade, *etc*. Yet there has been very little research concerned specifically with operator performance of such sequential control operations.

Sequential operations are often relatively complex, or at least lengthy, and are therefore an important application of the process computer. In these cases the operator is usually assigned the function of supervising the execution of the sequence by the machine.

Automation is not, however, the only means of enforcing control of sequential operations. An alternative approach is to let the operator execute the sequence, but to make use of interlocks to prevent certain actions.

In view of the importance of sequential operations this appears to be a rather neglected area.

7.3.11. *Scheduling*

The importance of scheduling as an operator function varies enormously. Sometimes it comprises virtually the whole of his job, but often it is a negligible element.

Several factors make scheduling an attractive area for research. Performance in the task is amenable to assessment. Simulation is relatively easy and motivational problems less acute than in some other functions. There is scope for man–computer interactive systems. And it is a suitable task with which to study decision-making.

It is less necessary, therefore, to urge research in this field. But certainly such work is worth while. Apart from its intrinsic value in providing guidance on the design of scheduling tasks, it may serve two other purposes: to increase understanding of operator decision-making and to furnish examples of the gain to be made from the application of human factors.

It is also of interest to define the extent to which typical industrial scheduling tasks are capable of automation, if not by operational research or other algorithmic methods then by artificial intelligence techniques akin to chess-playing. A preliminary investigation of this problem (Teja 1974) suggests that many such tasks are probably amenable to automation. It is necessary, however, that the machine have all the necessary information and in industrial systems a large proportion of such data is provided by the human operator. This situation, therefore, may well raise questions of job design.

7.3.12. *Emergency avoidance*

One of the operator's main functions on a plant is to prevent the development of situations which may become serious incidents, such as breakdowns or accidents. Although automatic protective systems are usually provided, their action tends to be limited to the rather drastic one of shutting the plant down. Such shutdowns are normally very expensive.

Incident avoidance is usually considered in terms of the recognition by the operator that an undesirable state is developing which could lead to trouble and of the formulation and execution of the multivariable control actions which can avert this. Discussions of these two aspects have been given by Rasmussen (1968a) and by de Jong and Köster (1971) respectively.

There is also another way in which the operator can contribute to the avoidance of such situations. This is the detection of incipient malfunction in the equipment, *i.e.* plant equipment or control system. This has been studied by Anyakora and Lees (1972a, 1972b).

There is considerable scope for work in both these areas.

7.3.13. *Fault administration*

As indicated earlier, fault administration can be divided into three stages:

(1) Fault detection
(2) Fault diagnosis
(3) Fault correction.

The difference between detection and diagnosis is simply that the former indicates only that something is wrong whereas the latter identifies the actual fault.

This is a most important field, and although some valuable work has been done, especially by Rasmussen (1968a), it remains wide open. In particular, there appears to be almost no work on fault correction.

7.3.14. *Emergency administration*

Emergency administration is simply fault administration under conditions of high failure penalties and hence of high stress. Typically, the stress arises from factors such as the high penalties, information overload, short available decision times. The effects of such stress are sufficiently important to warrant separate treatment of emergencies.

Although a mild level of stress tends to lead to improved performance, beyond a certain threshold, which varies widely with the individual, there is a rapid deterioration in performance. It is therefore of considerable interest to understand the factors which give rise to stress in process emergencies.

The question of the time available to the operator in relation to the time he requires to make a response is of vital importance. A few figures have been quoted. If the operator is himself to take any effective action he has about

90 seconds in a nuclear reactor trip situation (Sayers 1974) and about three minutes in the acid purification plant (Duncan 1974c). Data for other emergency situations would be valuable.

The other side of the coin is the amount of time the man needs. Studies on nuclear reactors indicate that there is a very low probability of effective response in less than 30 seconds, but a high probability in more than 60 seconds (Sayers 1974).

In this context, attention may be drawn to the phenomenon of operator indecision. It is not uncommon—a number of incidents have been related to the author—for an operator to be in possession of all the information which he requires in order to take a control action, but to be unable to bring himself to take that action. Obviously, this effect may be of crucial importance in an emergency. The prevalence of such indecisiveness is shown by the fact that it is reported even in the electric arc furnace study (Bainbridge, Beishon, Hemming and Splaine 1968) which was only a *simulation*.

As described in Section 2, there has been some work done on aircraft emergencies and it may be possible to utilize this in studying process emergencies.

7.3.15. *Decision-making*

Obviously decision-making by the process operator involves the whole gamut of human thought processes and it cannot be expected that these will be elucidated as a byproduct of work on the process operator.

Most of the research areas listed are, of course, aspects of operator decision-making in the broadest sense. But what is considered here in particular is attempts, such as that of Bainbridge, to understand human behaviour in choice situations arising in process control.

Success in this field implies the possibility of describing and reproducing such behaviour. A computer program is one type of model of operator thinking. It is also the means whereby these functions of the operator may be automated where this is appropriate. This, of course, is the sphere of artificial intelligence.

In studying operator decision-making, it is important to distinguish between the performance of inexperienced and of experienced subjects. Whereas the behaviour of the former often approximates to an algorithm, that of the latter tends to be much more subtle and elusive.

It is to be hoped that greater understanding of operator decision-making will lead to practical conclusions. The work of Rasmussen (1968a) on the human factors aspects of alarm analysis systems exemplifies this.

7.3.16. *Personnel selection*

As in so many other aspects of research on the process operator, work in both selection and training has been hampered by the lack of performance criteria.

There has been relatively little progress in personnel selection in the process control field. Although the first work on the process operator was that of Hiscock (1938) on the development of a series of selection tests, it did not include validation, and more recent work by Davies (1967) has shown little correlation between performance assessed by a selection test battery and by the judgment of supervisors.

Some guidance might be obtained from the procedures used for the selection of personnel such as pilots. The most thorough work in this area has been done by the U.S. armed forces. Such men undergo rigorous medical, intelligence and aptitude tests. These are effective in eliminating most of the completely unsuitable individuals. But this appears to be about as much as such tests achieve. At any rate, much of the selection occurs during the training process in which there is a considerable dropout rate. In general, the selection of pilots differs from that of process operators in two important respects. There is less variability in the pilot's job. And there is greater economic incentive to select effectively, since training costs are higher.

It may reasonably be argued that the process control skill is now better understood and that the attempt should be made again to develop selection tests. For what it is worth, a list is given in Table 10 of some operator abilities and characteristics which, in the light of the research described in the literature, appear on *a priori* grounds to be desirable, or at least relevant. The abilities are mostly straightforward. Learning ability, of course, has many aspects: it includes willingness to revise opinions, e.g. probability estimates, and to alter behaviour, e.g. strategies. The personal qualities given are those listed by Crossman (1960a) and his definitions are assumed.

Table 10. Some abilities and characteristics of the process operator probably relevant to selection

Abilities	*See* Table 5
Personal qualities	Responsibility
	Conscientiousness
	Reliability
	Trustworthiness
Temperament	Response to monotony
	Response to stress
Intelligence	
Education	
Motivation	
Social skills	

The relevance of intelligence has been questioned. Several points may be made. What matters is not so much to select for maximum intelligence as to match the level of intelligence to the job. Also, intelligence is not necessarily the main factor: temperament or motivation or social skills are important as well. This said, it must be added that some modern process control tasks such as those on large single-stream chemical plants do appear to make considerable demands on intelligence.

The need to match the man to the job applies, of course, to all the operator's qualities. A battery of selection tests must be suitable for effecting this match rather than for choosing a universal ideal operator.

Research on the process operator suggests that the essence of his skill is his ability ' to put it all together '. Ideally the selection procedure should test this rather than performance of the separate functions. The suggestion by Crossman (1960a) that performance in manual control of a change of operating point appears to correlate closely with process control skill is of interest in this connection.

The development of tests which eliminate certain types of individual who would be completely unsuitable as process operators can readily be envisaged. For example, in any population there is a small number of individuals who suffer disabling fits of depression, who are quite unable to adapt to shift work, who are completely incapable of handling noisy signals, or who are colour blind.

The question of the development of selection tests which discriminate more finely is more debatable. Perhaps all that need be said here is that experience in other fields is not particularly encouraging and it is probably premature to invest any significant research effort in this area.

It should not, of course, be forgotten that a considerable amount of self-selection occurs. To the extent that it does, the case for selection tests is weakened. This is a possible point of entry to work on operator selection.

7.3.17. *Training*

Training probably offers much greater scope than selection for improvement in operator performance. There is a wealth of knowledge and experience in industrial training generally. And some worthwhile progress has been made on the training of process operators.

The development of training in the U.K. is influenced by the existence of the Industrial Training Boards (I.T.Bs.). In particular, the chemical and petroleum industries are covered by the Chemical and Allied Products I.T.B. and the Petroleum I.T.B. Initially, the training boards tended to encourage general technological education but there is now a greater emphasis on specific job training. For example, the Chemical and Allied Products I.T.B.'s Training Recommendation (1971) contains Information Papers which represent outline approaches to job analysis, training needs, training programmes and fault analysis which the user should apply to his own plant, while other Information Papers, such as that on Distillation (1972), represent outline subject syllabuses. This balanced approach, involving both technological education and job training, is probably the right one.

Specific job training needs to be based on task analysis. A method of analysis has been developed by Duncan (1974b). It has already been suggested above that task analysis is sufficiently important to justify research by other practitioners also.

The method of task analysis described by Duncan is explicitly designed to oblige the analyst to consider economic criteria. Thus the level of description problem is solved by choosing as the criterion for redescription the product of the probability, p, and the cost, c, of inadequate performance. This is certainly the right approach and establishes the link between the human factors analysis and the system objectives.

Although Duncan quite rightly emphasizes that the important point about this criterion is the multiplicative nature of the relation between probability and cost of failure rather than the exact values, it may nevertheless be expected that, as progress is made in the adjacent area of loss prevention, which is very much concerned with both the probability and cost of failures, mechanical or human, it may become possible to make more informed decisions on training priorities.

Probably the greatest need in training research at present is that training work should be done, and reported, by informed and creative practitioners using an explicit method such as that described by Duncan.

Simulation is an important training technique. Unfortunately, however, although there are a number of papers on the use of process simulators for training, they are frequently not very informative on the methodology either of the training or of the simulation. Both these aspects need to be surveyed critically, relating practice in process control to that in other areas. But the greatest need is for work which demonstrates the rôle of simulation in training based on a proper task analysis and clear training objectives.

The validation of training remains a problem. Its solution depends on progress in the wider area of performance assessment.

A particular problem arises in the selection and training of operators for plants in developing countries, or even in non-industrial areas of developed countries. There appears to be an important research area here.

7.3.18. *Operating instructions*

The instructions given to the operator are extremely important. Some problems in this area are the philosophy adopted on the initiative to be left to the operator, the methodology of specifying the instructions, and the format for their presentation.

There is a close link here with task analysis. In so far as task analysis for process operators is carried out already, this tends to be in the writing of operating instructions. These can in fact be obtained directly from a task analysis—as Duncan (1974b) comments, it is only a matter of scissors and paste.

As with displays so with operating manuals there are good and bad ways of presenting the information to the operator. This is an area where professional expertise may profitably be employed.

Little appears to have been written concerning operating instructions in process control; there is need for a study.

7.3.19. *Job design*

Some of the most difficult problems in job design appear likely to develop in highly automated systems where the operator's function is primarily the monitoring and administration of fault conditions. The man is the component included by the designer to make the system self-repairing. In such cases the job is characterized by long periods of monotony interspersed with occasional bouts of intense activity.

One approach to this problem which has been suggested previously (Edwards and Lees 1973) is to accept this situation and develop those functions of the operator which are concerned with maintaining system integrity. In particular, greater involvement in malfunction detection, using computer-based displays, was suggested. Also relevant in this context is a recent report of the National Economic Development Office (N.E.D.O.) (1973) which draws attention to the involvement by process operators on the Continent in minor repair work on plants.

Another expedient which is often suggested is the introduction of some form of artificial signal to maintain operator alertness. While there are some obvious difficulties and dangers, the suggestion is often surprisingly well received by experienced managers. There may be something to be learnt here from the alerts practised in nuclear weapons systems.

Whatever approaches are taken to this problem, the publication of job design studies is to be welcomed.

7.3.20. *Operator error*

Human error or operator reliability in process control is another area on which attention is increasingly being focused. Since it interacts with almost every other aspect of system design, only a few salient points are made here. Reviews of the problem have been given by several workers (Rasmussen 1969, 1974; Edwards and Lees 1973; Lees 1973, 1974a).

A considerable amount of work in this area has been done by bodies such as the U.K. Atomic Energy Authority (*e.g.* Ablitt 1969, Green 1969). But much appears to be unpublished and further publication would be most valuable.

There is particular need for data which will help to quantify the industrial problem. Again, many data probably exist already in various firms and organizations, but are not publicly available. This is not surprising, as failures are a sensitive topic, but it is difficult to have a rational approach to system design without knowing how big the problem is.

Likewise, there is need for publication of design studies involving assessment of operator reliability in the whole process control task. Enough has been published to indicate how the probability of error in certain particular, defined tasks may be estimated, but more comprehensive studies are lacking.

At a more modest level, even the presentation of guide lines by those involved in design and assessment studies on process operator reliability would be of value.

8. Conclusions

Attention has been drawn in this paper to a number of areas of research on the process operator. However, these specific suggestions are less important than the overall approach taken in the research.

Progress in work on the process operator now depends very much on the quantitative assessment of operator performance in achievement of process control and process economics objectives.

The greatest need is for investigation of the process control task as a whole and in realistic systems. This requires a sustained programme with adequate resources. For much of the work the most appropriate systems are likely to be realistic simulators or actual plants.

It is obvious, therefore, that, for numerous reasons, industry must play an important part in such work. This is not merely a matter of encouraging external research and making plants available for experiment. It involves work by industry itself in quantifying operator problems and assessing operator performance and on human factors aspects of system design.

The purpose of this collection is to provide a necessary part of the background knowledge needed for such research on the process operator.

The author would like to thank his coeditor for many helpful discussions and comments in the course of preparing this paper.

References

Papers in this volume are marked with an *

ABLITT, J. F., 1969, A quantitative approach to the evaluation of the safety function of operators on nuclear reactors. *U.K. Atomic Energy Authority, Rep.* AHSB(S) R160.
ADAMS, J. A., 1961, Monitoring of complex visual displays. *Hum. Factors*, **3**, 213.
ADAMS, J. A. and CREAMER, L. R., 1962, Data processing capabilities of the human operator. *J. engr. Psychol.*, **1**, 150.
ALDEN, D. G., DANIELS, R. W. and KANARICK, A. F., 1972, Keyboard design and operation: a review of the major issues. *Hum. Factors*, **14**, 275.
ALEXANDER, L. T., KEPNER, C. H. and TREGOE, B. B., 1962, The effectiveness of knowledge of results in a military system training program. *J. appl. Psychol.*, **46**, 202.
ALLEN, P. S. and SAUL, E. V., 1958, An annotated bibliography of bibliographies pertinent to the design and use of machines by human operators. *Hum. Factors*, **1**(1), 26.
ALTMAN, J. W., 1964, A central store of human performance data. *Symp. on Quantification of Human Performance, Albuquerque, N. Mex.*
ANDERSON, R. C., 1965, Introduction to Part Four: Thinking and problem solving. In *Readings in the Psychology of Cognition* (Edited by R. C. ANDERSON and D. P. AUSUBEL) (New York), p. 535.
ANDOW, P. K., 1973, A method for process computer alarm analysis. *Ph.D. Thesis, Loughborough Univ. of Technology.*
ANDOW, P. K. and LEES, F. P., 1974, Process plant alarm systems: general considerations. In *Loss Prevention and Safety Promotion in the Process Industries* (Edited by C. H. BUSCHMANN) (Amsterdam: ELSEVIER), p. 299.
ANDREAS, B. G., 1953, Bibliography of perceptual motor performance under varied display control relationships. *Univ. of Rochester, N.Y., Sci. Rep.* 3.
ANDREW, A. M., 1967, To model or not to model. *Kybernetik*, **3**, 272.
ANGEL, E. S. and BEKEY, H. A., 1968, Adaptive finite-state models of manual control systems. *I.E.E.E. Trans. Man–Machine Syst.*, **MMS-9**, 15.
ANGYAL, A., 1941, *Foundations for a Science of Personality* (Harvard: HARVARD UNIV. PRESS), p. 243.
ANNETT, J. and KAY, H., 1956, Skilled performance. *Occup. Psychol.*, **30**, 112.
ANNETT, J. and KAY, H., 1957, Knowledge of results and ' skilled performance '. *Occup. Psychol.*, **31**, 69.
ANNETT, J., 1966, Training for perceptual skills. *Ergonomics*, **9**, 459.
ANNETT, J. and DUNCAN, K. D., 1967, Task analysis and training design. *Occup. Psychol.*, **41**, 211.
ANNETT, J., 1969, *Feedback and Human Behaviour* (Harmondsworth, Middlesex: PENGUIN BOOKS).
ANNETT, J., DUNCAN, K. D., STAMMERS, R. B. and GRAY, M. J., 1971, *Task Analysis.* Dept of Employment, Training Information Paper 6 (London: H.M. STATIONERY OFFICE).
ANYAKORA, S. N., 1971, Malfunction of process instruments and its detection using a process control computer. *Ph.D. Thesis, Loughborough Univ. of Technology.*
ANYAKORA, S. N., ENGEL, G. F. M. and LEES, F. P., 1971, Some data on the reliability of instruments in the chemical plant environment. *Chem. Engr., Lond.*, **255**, 396.
* ANYAKORA, S. N. and LEES, F. P., 1972a, Detection of instrument malfunction by the process operator. *Chem. Engr., Lond.*, **264**, 304.
ANYAKORA, S. N. and LEES, F. P., 1972b, Principles of the detection of malfunction using a process control computer. In *Decision, Design and the Computer* (London: INSTN. CHEM. ENGRS.), p. 6. 7.
APPLEY, M. H. and TRUMBULL, R. (eds.), 1967, *Psychological Stress* (New York: APPLETON–CENTURY–CROFTS).
ASKREN, W. B. and REGULINSKI, T. L., 1969, Quantifying human performance for reliability analysis of systems. *Hum. Factors*, **11**, 393.
ATKINSON, J. W. and FEATHER, N. T. (eds.), 1966, *A Theory of Achievement Motivation* (New York: WILEY).
ATTNEAVE, F., 1959, *Applications of Information Theory to Psychology: A Summary of Basic Concepts, Methods and Results* (New York: HOLT).
ATTWOOD, D., 1961, The use of a beta-gauge for automatic basis weight control. *Paper Technol.*, **2** (1), T19.
*ATTWOOD, D., 1970, The interaction between human and automatic control. In *Paper-Making Systems and their Control* (Edited by F. BOLAM) (London: BR. PAPER & BOARD MAKERS ASS.), p. 69.
AUSUBEL, D. P., 1968, *Educational Psychology* (New York: HOLT, RINEHART & WINSTON).

BAINBRIDGE, L., 1967, A discrete predicting controller. *Br. J. Math. Statist. Psychol.*, **20**, 31.
BAINBRIDGE, L., 1968, Maximum demand task: findings from study of a protocol. *Univ. of Reading*.
BAINBRIDGE, L. and BEISHON, R. J., 1968, The analysis of verbal protocols obtained from a continuous task. *Univ. of Bristol, Dept. of Psychol. Rep.*
* BAINBRIDGE, L., BEISHON, J., HEMMING, J. H. and SPLAINE, M., 1968, A study of real-time human decision-making using a plant simulator. *Opl. Res. Quart.*, **19**, Special Conf. Issue, p. 91.
BAINBRIDGE, L., 1969, The nature of the mental model in process control. *Man-Machine Systems, I.E.E.E. Conf. Rec.* 69C58–MMS.
BAINBRIDGE, L., 1971, The influence of display type on decision-making strategy. In *Displays, Conf. Pub. No. 80* (London: INSTN. ELEC. ENGRS.).
BAINBRIDGE, L., 1972, An analysis of a verbal protocol from a process control task. *Ph.D Thesis, Univ. of Bristol*.
* BAINBRIDGE, L., 1974, Analysis of verbal protocols from a process control task. *This volume*.
BAKER, A. V. and MCILHERAN, T. A., 1962, Unattended analog-computer pilot plant. *I.S.A. Symp.*, paper 41.2.62.
BAKER, C. H., 1962, *Man and Radar Displays* (New York: PERGAMON PRESS).
BAKER, F. G., 1967, The internal organisation of computer models of cognitive behaviour. *Behav. Sci.*, **12**, 156.
BAKER, J. D., 1970, Quantitative modelling of human performance in information systems. *Ergonomics*, **13**, 645.
BAKER, R. A. and WARE, J. R., 1966, The relationship between vigilance and monotonous work. *Ergonomics*, **9**, 109.
BALOFF, N., 1970, Startup management. *I.E.E.E. Trans. Engng. Mgmt.*, **EM-17**, 132.
BARNES, R. M., 1958, *Motion and Time Study* (New York: WILEY).
BARROW, R. and CAWLEY, D. E., 1971, Improving operator performance in a process industry. *Work Study and Mgmt. Services*, **15**, 282.
BARTH, J. and MAARLEVELD, A., 1967, Operational aspects of a d.d.c. system. In *The Application of Automation in the Process Industries* (Edited by J. M. PIRIE) (London: INSTN. CHEM. ENGRS.), p. 23.
BARTLETT, F. C., 1948, The measurement of human skill. *Occup. Psychol.*, **22**, 31 and 83.
BARTLETT, F. C., 1951a, Human control systems. *Trans. Soc. Instrum. Technol.*, **3** (3), 134.
BARTLETT, F. C., 1951b, The experimental study of skill. *Research*, **4**, 217.
BARTLETT, F. C., 1953, Psychological criteria of fatigue. In *Fatigue* (Edited by W. F. FLOYD and A. T. WELFORD) (London: H. K. LEWIS).
BARTLETT, F. C., 1958, *Thinking. An Experimental and Social Study* (London: ALLEN & UNWIN).
BARTLETT, M. W. and SMITH, L. A., 1973, Design of control and display panels using computer algorithms. *Hum. Factors*, **15**, 1.
BASS, B. M. and VAUGHAN, J. A., 1968, *Training in Industry. The Management of Learning* (Belmont, Calif.: WADSWORTH).
BATES, J., 1966, A classification of information displays. *Inf. Display*, 3(2), 47.
BAUER, R. W., CASSATT, R. K., CORONA, B. M., and WARHURST, F., 1966, Panel layout for rectilinear instruments. *Hum. Factors*, **8**, 493.
BEISHON, R. J., 1963, Analysis of control skill in operating a paper-making machine. *Ergonomics*, **6**, 301 (abstract).
BEISHON, R. J., 1964, personal communication (to E. R. F. W. Crossman).
BEISHON, R. J. and BAINBRIDGE, L., 1964, Interim report on a study of the L.D. waste-heat boiler control system at the Spencer Works of R.T.B., Newport, Mon. *Univ. of Oxford, Inst. of Explt. Psychol. Rep.*
BEISHON, R. J., 1966, A study of some aspects of mental skill in the performance of laboratory and industrial tasks. *D. Phil. Thesis, Univ. of Oxford*.
BEISHON, R. J., 1967, Problems of task description in process control. *Ergonomics*, **10**, 177.
BEISHON, R. J. and PALMER, A. W., 1968, An analysis of the activity of a paper mill supervisor. *Univ. of Bristol, Dept. of Psychol. Rep.*
* BEISHON, R. J., 1969, An analysis and simulation of an operator's behaviour in controlling continuous baking ovens. In *The Simulation of Human Behaviour* (Edited by F. BRESSON and M. DE MONTMOLLIN) (Paris: DUNOD).
BEKEY, G. A., 1962a, Sampled data models of the human operator in a control system. *Ph.D. Thesis, Univ. of California, Los Angeles, Calif*.
BEKEY, G. A., 1962b, The human operator as a sampled data system. *I.R.E. Trans. hum. Factors Electron.*, **HFE-3**, 43.
BELBIN, E., DOWNS, S. and MOORE, B., 1964, 'Unlearning' and its relationship to age. *Ergonomics*, **7**, 4.
BELBIN, R. M., 1964, *Training the Adult Worker. D.S.I.R., Problems of Progress in Industry No. 15* (London: H.M. STATIONERY OFFICE).

BENNETT, E. M. and DEGAN, J. W., 1961, The diagnostic process in men and automata. *I.R.E. Trans. hum. Factors Electron.*, **HFE-2**, 68.

BERBERT, A. G. and KELLEY, C. R., 1962, Piloting nuclear submarines with controls that look into the future. *Electronics*, June, 35.

BERGIUS, R., 1964a, Probleme und Methoden der Denkpsychologie. In *Handbuch der Psychologie, Vol. I/2* (Göttingen), p. 21.

BERGIUS, R., 1964b, Produktives Denken (Problemlösen). In *Handbuch der Psychologie, Vol. I/2* (Göttingen), p. 519.

BERNARD, J. W. and WUJKOWSKI, J. W., 1965, Direct digital control experiences in a chemical process. *I.S.A. J.*, **12(12)**, 43.

BERNOTAT, R. K. and GÄRTNER, K. P. (eds.), 1972, *Displays and Controls* (Amsterdam: SWETS & ZEITLINGER).

BERRY, P. C. and WULFF, J. J., 1960, A procedure for predicting reliability of man–machine systems. *I.R.E. Int. Conv. Rec.*, Part 10, p. 112.

BEVIS, F. W., FINNIEAR, C. and TOWILL, D. R., 1969, Prediction of operator performance during learning of repetitive tasks. *Int. J. Prod. Res.*, **8**, 293.

BEVIS, F. W., 1970, An exploratory study into industrial learning with special reference to work study standards. *M.Sc. Thesis, Univ. of Wales Inst. Sci. Technol., Cardiff.*

BILODEAU, E. A. and BILODEAU, I. M., 1969, *Principles of Skill Acquisition* (New York: ACADEMIC PRESS).

BIRMINGHAM, H. P. and TAYLOR, F. V., 1954, A design philosophy for man–machine control systems. *Proc. I.R.E.*, **42**, 1748.

BISSERET, A., 1971, Analysis of mental processes involved in air traffic control. *Ergonomics*, **14**, 565.

BITTICKER, W. R., 1971, The process operator—heart of production. In WILLIAMS, T. J., *op. cit.*, p. 96.

BLAIR, W. C. and KAUFMAN, H. M., 1959, Monitoring command control. 1, Multiple display monitoring. 2, Control display spatial arrangement. *Electric Boat Tech. Rep.* SPD-59-082.

BLOOM, B. S. (ed.), 1956, *Taxonomy of Educational Objectives* (New York: LONGMANS).

BOND, N. A., 1970, Some persistent myths about military electronics maintenance. *Hum. Factors*, **12**, 241.

BOOK, W. F., 1908, *The Psychology of Skill. Univ. of Montana Studies in Psychology, Vol. I*, republished 1925 (New York: GREGG).

BOURNE, L. E., 1970, Development of conceptual rules. *Psychol. Rev.*, **77**, 546.

BOWEN, H. M., 1967, The 'imp' in the system. *Ergonomics*, **10**, 112.

BOX, G. E. P., 1957, Evolutionary operation—a method for increasing industrial productivity. *Appl. Statistics*, **6(1)**, 3.

BRADLEY, J. V., 1967, Tactual coding of cylindrical knobs. *Hum. Factors*, **9**, 483.

BRENNINKMEYER, G., 1964, *Werken in Geautomatiseerde Fabrieken* (Amsterdam: SWETS & ZEITLINGER).

BRIGGS, G. E. and NAYLOR, J. C., 1962, The relative efficiency of several training methods as a function of transfer task complexity. *J. exptl. Psychol.*, **64**, 505.

BRIGHAM, F. R. and LAIOS, L., 1974, Operator performance in the control of a laboratory process plant. *Ergonomics, In the press.*

BROADBENT, D. E., 1950, The twenty dials test under quiet conditions. *Med. Res. Coun., Appl. Psychol. Unit, Cambridge, Rep.* APU 130/50.

BROADBENT, D. E., 1958, *Perception and Communication* (London: PERGAMON PRESS).

BROADBENT, D. E., 1961, Human arousal and efficiency in performing vigilance tasks. *Discovery*, **22**, 314.

BROADBENT, D. E., 1971, *Decision and Stress* (London: ACADEMIC PRESS).

BRUNER, J., GOODNOW, J. and AUSTIN, G., 1956, *A Study of Thinking* (New York).

BRYAN, W. L. and HARTER, N., 1899, Studies on the telegraphic language. The acquisition of a hierarchy of habits. *Psychol. Rev.*, **6**, 345.

BUCKNER, D. N. and MCGRATH, J. J. (eds.), 1963, *Vigilance. A Symposium* (New York: MCGRAW-HILL).

BUNCH, M. E., 1936, The amount of transfer in rational learning as a function of time. *J. comp. Psychol.*, **22**, 325.

CAMERON, C. and CORKINDALE, K. G., 1961, The psychologist's role in the development of man–machine systems. *Occup. Psychol.*, **35**, 65.

CAMPBELL, D. T., 1958, Systematic error on the part of human links in communication systems. *Inf. Control*, **1**, 334.

CARBONELL, J. R., 1966, A queueing model of many-instrument visual sampling. *I.E.E.E. Trans. hum. Factors Electron.*, **HFE-7**, 157.

CARBONELL, J. R., 1969, On man–computer interaction: a model and some related issues. *I.E.E.E. Trans. Syst. Sci. Cyb.*, **SSC-5**, 16.

CARTER, R. J., 1971, On-line digital control systems—the role of the process operator. In *Data Reduction, Communication and Presentation for the Process Operator* (London: INST. MEASAMT. CONTROL).
*CENTRAL ELECTRICITY GENERATING BOARD (C.E.G.B.), 1966, Study of operators information requirements at Trawsfynydd. (Cheltenham, Gloucestershire) (extract).
CHADWICK-JONES, J. K., 1969, *Automation and Behaviour. A Social Psychological Study* (New York: WILEY-INTERSCIENCE).
CHAPANIS, A., 1951, Theory and methods for analysing errors in man–machine systems. *Ann. N.Y. Acad. Sci.*, **51**, 1179.
CHAPANIS, A., 1957, A rate of making complex decisions. *Am. J. Psychol.*, **70**, 650.
CHAPANIS, A., and LINDENBAUM, L. E., 1959, A reaction time study of four control-display linkages. *Hum. Factors*, **1**(4), 8.
CHAPANIS, A., 1965, *Man–Machine Engineering* (Belmont, Calif.: WADSWORTH).
CHAPANIS, A. and MANKIN, D. A., 1967, Tests of ten control-display linkages. *Hum. Factors*, **9**, 119.
CHAPANIS, A., 1970, Relevance of physiological and psychological criteria to man–machine systems: the present state of the art. *Ergonomics*, **13**, 337.
CHEBYSHEVA, V. V., 1963, On some characteristics of the mental tasks in the work of working men. *Voprosi Psichologii*, **9**, 99.
CHEMICAL AND ALLIED PRODUCTS INDUSTRY TRAINING BOARD, 1971, Process operators. *Training Recommendation No. 12* (Staines, Middlesex). This incorporates *Information Paper No. 6*, A guide to analysis of plant training needs; *Information Paper No. 7*, A guide to operator job analysis; *Information Paper No. 8*, A guide to fault analysis; *Information Paper No. 9*, A guide to the preparation of a training programme.
CHEMICAL AND ALLIED PRODUCTS INDUSTRY TRAINING BOARD, 1972, A basic course for adult entrants with chemical process operations and an example training unit—distillation *Information Paper No. 13* (Staines, Middlesex).
CHERNIKOFF, R., BIRMINGHAM, H. P. and TAYLOR, F. V., 1955, A comparison of pursuit and compensatory tracking under conditions of aiding and no aiding. *J. exptl. Psychol.*, **49**, 55.
CHERRY, C., 1957a, *On Human Communication* (New York: M.I.T. PRESS and WILEY).
CHERRY, E. C., 1957b, On the validity of applying communication theory to experimental psychology. *Br. J. Psychol.*, **48**, 176.
CHESTNUT, H. and MAYER, R. W., 1959, *Servomechanism and Regulating System Design, Vol. I* (New York: WILEY).
*CITY AND GUILDS INSTITUTE, 1972, 086 *Chemical Technician's Certificate* (London).
ČÍŽKOVÁ, J., 1967, Effect of the quantity and complexity of visual stimuli on operator's search activity. *Studia Psychologica*, **9**, 241.
CLARK, J. A., Display for the chemical plant operator, 1972. *M.Sc. Thesis, Univ. of Manchester Inst. Sci. Technol.*
CLAY, H. M., 1960, *The Older Worker and His Job. D.S.I.R., Problems of Progress in Industry No. 7* (London: H.M. STATIONERY OFFICE).
CLAY, H. M., 1964, *Research in Relation to Operator Training. D.S.I.R.* (London: H.M. STATIONERY OFFICE).
COCHRANE, E. B., 1968, *Planning Production Costs: Using the Improvement Curve* (San Francisco, Calif.: CHANDLER PUBLISHING CO.).
COEKIN, J. A., 1969, A versatile presentation of parameters for rapid recognition of total state. *Man–Machine Systems, Vol. 4, I.E.E.E. Conf. Rec.*, 69C58–MMS, p. 4.
COETERIER, J. F., 1971, Individual strategies in ATC freedom and choice. *Ergonomics*, **14**, 579.
COFER, C. N. and APPLEY, M. H., 1964, *Motivation: Theory and Research* (New York: WILEY).
COHEN, J. and HANSEL, C. E. M., 1956, *Risk and Gambling* (London: LONGMANS).
COHEN, J., 1960, *Chance, Skill and Luck* (Harmondsworth, Middlesex: PENGUIN BOOKS).
COLQUHOUN, W. P., 1959, The effect of short rest pauses on inspection efficiency. *Ergonomics*, **2**, 367.
CONRAD, R., 1951, The study of skill by motion and time study and by psychological experiment. *Research*, **4**, 353.
CONRAD, R., 1954, Speed stress. In *Human Factors in Equipment Design* (Edited by W. F. FLOYD and A. T. WELFORD) (London: H. K. LEWIS).
CONRAD, R. and HULL, A. J., 1968, The preferred layout for numeral data entry keysets. *Ergonomics*, **11**, 165.
CONSTABLE, C. J., 1971, Managerial problems associated with computer process control. In WILLIAMS, T. J., *op. cit.*, p. 73.
COOK, J. O., 1963, Superstition in the Skinnerian. *Am. Psychologist*, **18**, 516.
COOK, T. M. and MATTERSON, K. J., 1968, *A Chemical Operatives Handbook* (Oxford: PERGAMON PRESS).
COOKE, J. E., 1964a, personal communication (to E. R. F. W. Crossman).

COOKE, J. E., 1964b, Laboratory studies of control decisions. *Ergonomics*, **7**, 364 (abstract).
COOKE, J. E., 1965, Human decisions in the control of a slow response system. *D.Phil. Thesis, Univ. of Oxford.*
COOPER, J., 1961, Human initiated failures and malfunction reporting. *I.R.E. Trans. hum. Factors Electron.*, **HFE-2**, 104.
COTTERMAN, T. E., 1959, Task classification: an approach to partially ordering information on human learning. *U.S. Air Force, Wright Air Dev. Center, Dayton, Ohio, Rep.* WADC TN 58–374.
COX, J. A. and BOREN, L. M., 1965, A study of backward chaining. *J. educ. Psychol.*, **56**, 270.
COX, R. C., 1965, Item selection techniques and evaluation of instructional objectives. *J. educ. Measamt.*, **2**, 181.
CRAIK, K. J. W., 1943, *The Nature of Explanation* (Cambridge: CAMBRIDGE UNIV. PRESS).
CRAIK, K. J. W., 1947, The theory of the human operator in control systems. *Br. J. Psychol.*, **38**, 56 and 142.
*CRAWLEY, J. E., 1968, The present and future contribution of the human operator to the control of L.D. steelmaking. *Proc. B.I.S.R.A. Symp. on Steelmaking*, p. 101.
CRAWLEY, J. E., 1971, Simulation studies of interface design. In T. J. WILLIAMS, *op. cit.*, p. 129.
CRISTIAN, G. and ZBĂGANU, G., 1964, Contributions à l'étude expérimentale de l'activité intellectuelle des opérateurs au panneau de commande. *Rev. Roum. Sci. Soc., Ser. Psychol.*, **8**, 175.
CRISTIAN, G. and ZBĂGANU, G., 1966, La solution des problèmes opératifs par des opérateurs et des dispatchers dans les conditions créées dans un laboratoire. *Manuscript*.
CRISTIAN, G., 1967, Quelques aspects concernant l'activité d'information et de décision des dispatchers énergetiques. *Rev. Roum. Sci. Soc., Ser. Psychol.*, **11**, 2.
CRISTIAN, G., 1972, Decision-making, problem-solving and creative thinking. *Studia Psychologica*, **14**, 59.
CROPPER, A. G. and EVANS, S. J. W., 1968, Ergonomics and computer display design. *Comput. Bull.*, **12**, 94.
CROSSMAN, E. R. F. W., 1956a, The measurement of perceptual load in manual operations. *Ph.D. Thesis, Univ. of Birmingham.*
CROSSMAN, E. R. F. W., 1956b, The information of the human operator in symbolic and non-symbolic control processes. In DRAPER, J., *op. cit.*
CROSSMAN, E. R. F. W., 1956c, Perception study—a complement to motion study. *Manager*, **24**, 141.
CROSSMAN, E. R. F. W., 1956d, Perceptual activity in manual work. *Research*, **9**, 42.
CROSSMAN, E. R. F. W., 1957, *The Nature and Acquisition of Industrial Skills*. *D.S.I.R.* (London: H.M. STATIONERY OFFICE).
CROSSMAN, E. R. F. W., 1958, Automation and industrial skills: A report on a field survey. *Univ. of Reading, Dept. of Psychol. Rep.*
CROSSMAN, E. R. F. W., 1959, A theory of the acquisition of speed skill. *Ergonomics*, **2**, 153.
*CROSSMAN, E. R. F. W., 1960a, *Automation and Skill*. *D.S.I.R., Problems of Progress in Industry No. 9* (London: H.M. STATIONERY OFFICE).
CROSSMAN, E. R. F. W., 1960b, Ergonomics in the steel industry—an ergonomic analysis of gauge control in a hot strip mill. *Instrum. Pract.*, **14**, 1207.
CROSSMAN, E. R. F. W., 1960c, The information capacity of the human motor system in pursuit tracking. *Quart. J. exptl. Psychol.*, **12**, 1.
CROSSMAN, E. R. F. W. and SPENCER, J., 1960, The assessment of process operator skills. *Ergonomics*, **3**, 282 (abstract).
CROSSMAN, E. R. F. W., 1961a, Fixation time, signal frequency and missed signals in a simple inspection task. *Ergonomics*, **4**, 85 (abstract).
CROSSMAN, E. R. F. W., 1961b, Information and serial order in immediate memory. In *Information Theory: Fourth London Symposium* (Edited by E. C. CHERRY) (London: BUTTERWORTH).
*CROSSMAN, E. R. F. W. and COOKE, J. E., 1962, Manual control of slow-response systems. *Int. Cong. on Human Factors in Electronics, Long Beach, Calif.*
CROSSMAN, E. R. F. W., 1963, Analysis of non-repetitive manual work. *Ergonomics*, **6**, 302.
CROSSMAN, E. R. F. W., 1964a, European experience with the changing nature of jobs due to automation. *Univ. of California, Berkeley, Calif., Hum. Factors in Technol. Res. Gp. Rep.*
CROSSMAN, E. R. F. W., 1964b, Studies on man–machine systems and on process operator skills carried out jointly by B.I.S.R.A., Reading University and Oxford University, 1959–64. *Univ. of Oxford, Inst. of Exptl. Psychol. Rep.*
CROSSMAN, E. R. F. W., 1964c, Information processes in human skill. *Br. med. Bull. (Exptl. Psychol.)*, **20**(1), 32.
CROSSMAN, E. R. F. W., 1964d, Automation et performance humaine. *Actes du Deuxième Congrès du Société de l'Ergonomie de Langue Française* (Brussels: PRESSES UNIVERSITAIRES DE BRUXELLES).

*Crossman, E. R. F. W., Cooke, J. E. and Beishon, R. J., 1964, Visual attention and the sampling of displayed information in process control. *Univ. of California, Berkeley, Calif., Hum. Factors in Technol. Res. Gp. Rep.* HFT 64–11–7.

Crossman, E. R. F. W., 1965, Fitting man into process control. *Univ. of California, Berkeley, Calif., Hum. Factors in Technol. Res. Gp. Rep.*

Cuny, X. and Deransart, P., 1972, Éléments de formalisation pour servir à l'analyse psychologique d'un travail de contrôle. *Travail Humain*, **35**, 1.

Cusack, B. L., 1957, Human engineering and direct operation labour costs in chemical plants. *Chem. Engng. Prog.*, **53** (10), 471.

Dale, H. C. A., 1958, Fault finding in electronic equipment. *Ergonomics*, **1**, 356.

Dale, H. C. A., 1964, Factors affecting the choice of strategy in searching. *Ergonomics*, **7**, 73.

Dale, H. C. A., 1968, Weighing evidence: an attempt to assess the efficiency of the human operator. *Ergonomics*, **11**, 215.

Dallimonti, R., 1972, Future operator consoles for improved decision-making and safety. *Instrum. Technol.*, **19** (8), 23.

Daniel, J., 1965, Analysis of the work of an operator in automatized production. *Studia Psychologica*, **7**, 319.

Daniel, J. and Stríženec, M., 1967, Experimental research into some aspects of the operator's activity. *Studia Psychologica*, **9**, 106 and 205.

Daniel, J., Florek, H., Košinár, V. and Stríženec, M., 1969, Investigation of an operator's characteristics by means of factorial analysis. *Studia Psychologica*, **11**, 10.

Daniel, J., 1970a, Effect of various degrees of mental load on activation level. *Studia Psychologica*, **12**, 266.

Daniel, J., 1970b, Psychologická analýza práce a profesiografia. *Zborník zo Seminára, ČSVÚP*, 1.

Daniel, J., 1971, Analysis and rating correlates of an operator's activity in automated production. *Studia Psychologica*, **13**, 252.

*Daniel, J., Puffler, M. and Stríženec, M., 1971, Analysis of operator's work at different levels of automated production. *Studia Psychologica*, **13**, 326.

Daniel, J. et al., 1971, Analýza práce operátora v automatizovanej výrobe. *Záverečná Správa ÚEP SAV*.

Davenport, W. W. and Woodson, W. E., 1954, The design of a navy air traffic control. *U.S. Navy, Electronics Lab., San Diego, Calif., Rep.* 490.

Davies, D. G., 1967, A psycho-physiological investigation of process control skill. *M.Sc. Thesis, Univ. of Aston in Birmingham.*

Davies, D. G., 1971, Human problems in shift work. *J. Iron Steel Inst.*, **209** (2), 114.

Davis, D. R., 1958, Human errors and transport accidents. *Ergonomics*, **2**, 24.

Davis, D. R. and Coiley, P. A., 1959, Accident proneness in motor vehicle drivers. *Ergonomics*, **2**, 239.

Davies, D. R. and Tune, G. S., 1970, *Human Vigilance Performance* (London: Staples Press).

Deese, J., 1958, *The Psychology of Learning* (New York: McGraw-Hill).

Defayolle, M., 1968, Approche de la fiabilité de l'opérateur humain: modèle de vulnérabilité. *Ergonomics*, **11**, 315.

De Greene, K. B. (ed.), 1970a, *Systems Psychology* (New York: McGraw-Hill).

De Greene, K. B., 1970b, Systems analysis techniques. In De Greene, K. B., *op. cit.*, p. 79.

Deininger, R. L. and Fitts, P. M., 1955, Stimulus response compatibility, information theory and perceptual motor performance. In Quastler, H., *op. cit.*

Deininger, R. L., 1960, Desirable pushbutton characteristics. *I.R.E. Trans. hum. Factors Electron.*, **HFE-1**, 24.

Deininger, R. L., 1967, Rotary dial and thumbwheel devices for manually entering sequential data. *I.E.E.E. Trans. hum. Factors Electron.*, **HFE-8**, 227.

Delacoudre, N., 1971, Tâches de surveillance et de contrôle: influence des caractéristiques de la tâche sur la genèse des incidents. *Ergonomics*, **14**, 231.

*Department of Labor, 1970, *Outlook for Computer Process Control* (Washington, D.C.).

Department of Scientific and Industrial Research (D.S.I.R.), 1956, *Automation. A Report on the Technical Trends and Their Impact on Management and Labour.* (London: H.M. Stationery Office).

Donoghue, J. A., 1967, Integrated process control at Park Gate Iron and Steel—two years after commissioning. *Steel Times*, January 20th.

Draper, J. (ed.), 1956, *The Application of Information Theory to Human Operator Problems* (London: Min. of Supply).

Drury, C. G. and Addison, J. L., 1973, An industrial study of the effects of feedback and fault density on inspection performance. *Ergonomics*, **16**, 159.

Dudley, N. A., 1955, Output patterns in repetitive tasks. *Ph.D. Thesis, Univ. of Birmingham.*

Duncan, C. P., 1959, Recent research on human problem solving. *Psychol. Bull.*, **6**, 397.

DUNCAN, K. D., 1969, Task analysis evaluated. In *La Recherche en Enseignement Programmé: Tendances Actuelles* (Paris: DUNOD).

DUNCAN, K. D., 1971a, Fading of prompts in learning sequences. *Programmed Learning*, **5**, 111.

DUNCAN, K. D., 1971b, Long-term retention and transfer of an industrial search skill. *Br. J. Psychol.*, **62**, 439.

DUNCAN, K. D., 1972, Strategies for analysis of the task. In *Strategies for Programmed Instruction: An Educational Technology* (Edited by J. HARTLEY) (London: BUTTERWORTH).

DUNCAN, K. D., 1974a, An analytical technique for industrial training. In SINGLETON, W. T. and SPURGEON, P., *op. cit.*

*DUNCAN, K. D., 1974b, Analytical techniques in training design. *This volume*.

DUNCAN, K. D., 1974c, personal communication (to F. P. Lees).

DUNCKER, K., 1945, On problem-solving. *Psychol. Monogr.*, **58** (5), ix and 113.

DUNNETTE, M. D., 1966, *Personnel Selection and Placement* (Belmont, Calif.: WADSWORTH).

DUTTON, J. M. and STARBUCK, W. H., 1971, Computer simulation models of human behavior: a history of intellectual technology. *I.E.E.E. Trans. Syst. Man Cyb.*, **SMC-1**, 128.

EDWARDS, ELWYN, 1964, *Information Transmission* (London: CHAPMAN & HALL).

EDWARDS, ELWYN, 1971, Techniques for the evaluation of human performance. In SINGLETON, W. T., FOX, J. G., and WHITFIELD, D. C., *op. cit.*

EDWARDS, ELWYN and LEES, F. P., 1971a, The development of the role of the human operator in process control. In WILLIAMS, T. J., *op. cit.*, p. 138.

EDWARDS, ELWYN and LEES, F. P., 1971b, The influence of the process characteristics on the role of the human operator in process control. In *Data Reduction, Communication and Presentation for the Process Operator* (London: INST. MEASAMT. CONTROL).

EDWARDS, ELWYN and LEES, F. P., 1971c, Information display in process control. In *Displays*, Conf. Pub. No. 80 (London: INSTN. ELEC. ENGRS).

EDWARDS, ELWYN, 1973, Ergonomics in control. *Proc. I.E.E.*, **120**, 1181.

EDWARDS, ELWYN and LEES, F. P., 1973, *Man and Computer in Process Control* (London: INSTN. CHEM. ENGRS).

EDWARDS, W., 1954, The theory of decision-making. *Psychol. Bull.*, **51**, 380.

EDWARDS, W., 1961, Behavioral decision theory. *Ann. Rev. Psychol.*, **12**, 473.

EDWARDS, W., 1965, Probabilistic information processing systems for diagnosis and action selection. In *Information System Sciences* (Edited by J. SPIEGEL and D. WALKER) (Washington, D.C.: SPARTAN BOOKS).

EDWARDS, W., LINDMAN, H. and PHILLIPS, L. D., 1965, Emerging technologies for taking decisions. In *New Directions in Psychology, Vol. II* (Edited by T. M. NEWCOMB) (New York: HOLT, RINEHART & WINSTON).

EDWARDS, W., PHILLIPS, L. D., HAYS, W. L. and GOODMAN, B. C., 1968, Probabilistic information processing systems: design and evaluation. *I.E.E.E. Trans. Syst. Sci. Cyb.*, **SSC-4**, 248.

ELKIND, J. I. and FORGIE, C. D., 1959, Characteristics of the human operator in simple manual control systems. *I.R.E. Trans. autom. Control*, **AC-4** (1), 44.

ELLIS, H. C., 1965, *The Transfer of Learning* (New York: MACMILLAN).

ELWELL, J. L. and GRINDLEY, G. C., 1938, The effect of knowledge of results on learning and performance. *Br. J. Psychol.*, **29**, 39.

ELY, J. H., THOMPSON, R. M. and ORLANSKY, J., 1956, Design of controls. In *Joint Services Human Engineering Guide to Equipment Design*, U.S. Air Force, Wright Air. Dev. Center, Dayton, Ohio, Tech. Rep. 56–172.

EMERY, F. E., 1959, Characteristics of socio-technical systems. *Tavistock Inst., London.*, Doc. 527.

EMERY, F. E. (ed.), 1969, *Systems Thinking* (Harmondsworth, Middlesex: PENGUIN BOOKS).

ENGELSTAD, P. H. with EMERY, F. E. and THORSRUD, E., 1969a, The Hunsfos experiment. *Work Research Institutes, Oslo, Rep.*

ENGELSTAD, P. H., 1969b, Sogio-teknisk analyse i prosessindustrien ved variasjons-matrise metoden. *Tidsskr. f. Samfunnsforskning*, **10**, 302.

*ENGELSTAD, P. H., 1970, A socio-technical approach to problems of process control. In *Paper-Making Systems and their Control* (Edited by F. BOLAM) (London: BR. PAPER AND BOARD MAKERS ASS.), p. 91.

ERICKSEN, S. C., 1952, A review of the literature on methods of measuring pilot proficiency. *U.S. Air Force, Hum. Resources Res. Center, Res. Bull.* 52–25.

FAVERGÉ, J. M., 1970, L'homme, agent d'infiabilité et de fiabilité du processus industriel. *Ergonomics*, **13**, 301.

FEIGENBAUM, E. A., 1961, An information processing theory of verbal learning. *Proc. Western Joint Comput. Conf.*

FIDDY, E. and JOHNSON, P. C., 1967, An approach to production control in a steelworks. *Int. Seminar on Control Systems in Metallurgical Works, Ostrava-Vlcina*.

FIEDLER, F. E., 1968, Personality and situational determinants of leadership effectiveness. In *Group Dynamics* (Edited by D. CARTWRIGHT and A. ZANDER) (London: TAVISTOCK).

FITTS, P. M. and JONES, R. E., 1947, Analysis of factors contributing to 460 'pilot error' experiences in operating aircraft controls. *U.S. Air Force, Air Matériel Command, Memo. Rep.* TSEAA–694–12.

FITTS, P. M., JONES, R. E. and MILTON, J. L., 1950, Eye movements of pilots during instrument landing approaches. *Aeronaut. Engng. Rev.*, **9**, 1.

FITTS, P. M., 1951, *Human Engineering for an Effective Air Navigation and Control System* (Washington, D.C.: NAT. RES. COUN.).

FITTS, P. M., 1962, Functions of man in complex systems. *Aerospace Engng.*, **21 (1)**, 34.

FITTS, P. M., 1965, Factors in complex skill training. In GLASER., R., *op. cit.*

FITTS, P. M. and POSNER, M. I., 1967, *Human Performance* (Belmont, Calif.: BROOKS/COLE).

FLAHERTY, B. E. (ed.), 1961, *Psychophysiological Aspects of Space Flight* (New York: COLUMBIA UNIV. PRESS).

FOGEL, L. J., 1955, A communication theory approach toward the design of aircraft instrument displays. *I.R.E. Conv. Rec.*, Part 5, p. 15.

FOGEL, L. J. and DWONCZYK, M., 1958, Anticipatory display design through the use of an analog computer. *I.R.E.-Wescon Conv. Rec.*, Part 4, p. 67.

FOGEL, L. J., 1961, Levels of intelligence in decision-making. *Ann. N.Y. Acad. Sci.*, **89(5)**, 732.

FOGEL, L. J., 1963, *Biotechnology: Concepts and Applications* (Englewood Cliffs, N.J.: PRENTICE-HALL).

FOGEL, L. J., OWENS, A. J. and WALSH, M. J., 1966, *Artificial Intelligence through Simulated Evolution* (New York: WILEY).

FOLLEY, J. D., 1964a, Development of an improved method of task analysis and beginnings of a theory of training. *U.S. Navy, Training Device Center, New York, Rep.* NAVTRADEVCEN 1218–1.

FOLLEY, J. D., 1964b, Guidelines for task analysis. *U.S. Navy, Training Device Center, New York, Rep.* NAVTRADEVCEN 1218–2.

FORD, A., WHITE, C. T. and LICHTENSTEIN, N., 1959, Analysis of eye movements during free search. *J. Opt. Soc. Am.*, **49**, 287.

FORD, R. N., 1969, *Motivation through the Work Itself* (New York: AM. MGMT. ASS.).

FRANKMANN, J. P. and ADAMS, J. A., 1962, Theories of vigilance. *Psychol. Bull.*, **59**, 259.

FREEDY, A., HULL, F. C., LUCACCINI, L. F. and LYMAN, J., 1971, A computer-based learning system for remote manipulative control. *I.E.E.E. Trans. Syst. Man Cyb.*, **SMC-1**, 356.

FREUND, L. E. and SADOSKY, T. L., 1967, Linear programming applied to optimisation of instrument panel and workplace layout. *Hum. Factors*, **9**, 295.

GAGNÉ, R. M. (ed.), 1963, *Psychological Principles in System Development* (New York: HOLT, RINEHART & WINSTON).

GAGNÉ, R. M., 1965a, *The Conditions of Learning* (New York: HOLT, RINEHART & WINSTON).

GAGNÉ, R. M., 1965b, The analysis of instructional objectives for the design of instruction. In *Teaching Machines and Programmed Learning Vol. II* (Edited by R. GLASER) (Washington: NAT. EDUC. AUTHOR.).

GAINES, B. R., 1969, Linear and nonlinear models of the human controller. *Int. J. Man–Machine Studies*, **1**, 333.

GALAKTIONOV, A. I., 1965a, Investigation of the rate of information processing by the human operator in the solution of practical problems of technical diagnostics. In OSHANIN, D. A., *op. cit.*, p. 37.

GALAKTIONOV, A. I., 1965b, The question of the quantitative assessment of complex-structured events. *Problemi Inzhenernoi Psichologii, Vol. 2* (Leningrad), p. 100.

GANDSEY, L. J., 1965, Two way communication between operator and computers. *Chem. Engng. Prog.*, **61(10)**, 93.

GARNER, K. C., 1967, Evaluation of human operator coupled dynamic systems. *Ergonomics*, **10**, 125.

GARNER, W. R., 1962, *Uncertainty and Structure as Psychological Concepts* (New York: WILEY).

GARVEY, W. D. and KNOWLES, W. B., 1954, Response time patterns associated with various display control relationships. *J. exptl. Psychol.*, **47**, 315.

GARVEY, W. D. and TAYLOR, F. V., 1959, Interactions among operator variables, system dynamics and task-induced stress. *J. appl. Psychol.*, **43**, 79.

VAN DE GEER, J. P. and JASPARS, J. M. F., 1966, Cognitive functions. *Ann. Rev. Psychol.*, **17**, 145.

GHISELLI, E. E. and BROWN, C. W., 1955, *Personnel and Industrial Psychology*, 2nd Ed. (New York: WILEY).

GILBERT, T. F., 1962, Mathetics: the technology of education. *J. Mathetics*, **1**, 7 and **2**, 7.

GILBRETH, F. B., 1911, *Motion Study* (New York: VAN NOSTRAND).

GILSTAD, D. W. and FU, K. S., 1971, Two-dimensional adaptive model of a human controller using pattern recognition techniques. *I.E.E.E. Trans. Syst. Man Cyb.*, **SMC-1**, 261.

GLANZER, R., 1958, Diagnostic skills and their evaluation. *Occup. Psychol.*, **32**, 236.

GLASER, R. (ed.), 1965, *Training, Research and Education* (New York: WILEY).

GLASER, R., 1968. *Proc. U.N.E.S.C.O. Seminar on Programmed Instruction, Varna, Bulgaria*.
GLOVER, J. H., 1966, Selection of trainees and control of their progress. *Int. J. Prod. Res.*, **5(1)**, 43.
GOOD, I. J., 1950, *Probability and the Weighing of Evidence* (New York: HAFNER).
GOODSTEIN, L. P., 1969, A process instrumentation for man–machine communication studies. *Man–Machine Systems, I.E.E.E. Conf. Rec.* 69C58–MMS.
GOODSTEIN, L. P., 1971, Operator communications in modern process plant. In *Displays, Conf. Pub. No. 80* (London: INSTN. ELEC. ENGRS.).
GOULD, J. D., 1968, Visual factors in the design of computer controlled CRT displays. *Hum. Factors*, **10**, 359.
GRANDJEAN, E. P., WOTZKA, G., SCHAAD, R. and GILGEN, A., 1971, Fatigue and stress in air traffic controllers. *Ergonomics*, **14**, 159.
GRANT, J. S., 1971, Concepts of fatigue and vigilance in relation to railway operation. *Ergonomics*, **14**, 111.
GREEN, A. E., 1969, Safety assessment of automatic and manual protective systems for reactors. *U.K. Atomic Energy Authority Rep.* AHSB(S) R172.
GREEN, A. E., 1970, Safety assessment of automatic and manual protective systems for reactors. *Instrum. Pract.*, **24**, 109.
GREEN, D., 1965, Head-up displays—the state of the art and some thought for the future. *Int. Fed. Air Line Pilots Ass. Symp.*
GUEST, G. and TOCHER, K. D., 1963, The control of steel flow. *Proc. Third Int. Conf. on Opl. Res., Oslo*.
GUEST, R. H., 1957, Job enlargement—a revolution in job design. *Personnel Administration*, **20** (March–April), 12.
GUILFORD, J. P., 1956, The structure of intellect. *Psychol. Bull.*, **4**, 267.
GUION, R., 1965, *Personnel Testing* (New York: MCGRAW-HILL).
GUTHRIE, E. R., 1952, *The Psychology of Learning* (New York: HARPER).
HABER, R. N., 1966, *Current Research in Motivation* (New York: HOLT, RINEHART & WINSTON).
HALPIN, J. F., 1966, Zero Defects in retrospect. *Ind. Qual. Control*, **22**, 669.
HARTLEY, J. and WOODS, P. M., 1968, Learning poetry backwards. *Nat. Soc. Programmed Instruction J.*, **7**, 9.
HARTLEY, J. (ed.), 1972, *Strategies for Programmed Instruction: An Educational Technology* (London: BUTTERWORTH).
HAYGOOD, R. C. and BOURNE, L. E., 1965, Attribute-and-rule-learning aspects of conceptual behaviour. *Psychol. Rev.*, **72**, 175.
HELSON, H., 1947, Adaptation level as a frame of reference for the prediction of psychophysical data. *Am. J. Psychol.*, **60**, 1.
HERBST, P. G., 1962, *Autonomous Group Functicning* (London: TAVISTOCK).
HERRMANN, T., 1964, Informationstheoretische Modell zur Darstellung der kognitiven Ordnung. In *Handbuch der Psychologie*, Vol. I/2 (Göttingen), p. 641.
HERSH, W. and SHACKEL, B., 1968, The man–computer link—A survey of existing equipment. *E.M.I. Electronics Ltd., Rep.* DMP 3145.
HERZBERG, F., MAUSNER, B. and SNYDERMAN, B., 1959, *The Motivation to Work* (New York: WILEY).
HERZBERG, F., 1966, *Work and the Nature of Man* (Cleveland, Ohio: WORLD PUBLISHING).
HERZOG, J. H., 1969, Proprioceptive cues and their influence on operator performance in manual control. *N.A.S.A. Rep.* CR-1248.
HICK, W. E., 1948, The discontinuous functioning of the human operator in pursuit tasks. *Quart. J. exptl. Psychol.*, **1**, 36.
HICK, W. E., 1952, On the rate of gain of information. *Quart. J. exptl. Psychol.*, **4**, 11.
HICK, W. E., 1953, Information theory in psychology. *Trans. I.R.E. Pf. Gp. Inf. Theory*, **PGIT-1**, 130.
HICKEY, A. E. and BLAIR, W. C., 1958, Man as a monitor. *Hum. Factors*, **1(1)**, 8.
HICKLING, B. B. and JONES, J. T., 1967, Information flow and communications in steelworks. *J. Iron Steel Inst.*, **205**, 506.
HILGARD, E. R., 1956, *Theories of Learning* (New York: APPLETON–CENTURY–CROFTS).
HISCOCK, W. G., 1938, Selection tests for chemical process workers. *Occup. Psychol.*, **12**, 178.
HITCHINGS, B., 1972, Dynamic learning curve models describing the performance of human operators on repetitive industrial tasks. *M.Eng. Thesis, Univ. of Wales Inst. Sci. Technol., Cardiff*.
HITCHINGS, B. and TOWILL, D. R., 1973, An error analysis of the time constant learning curve model. *Univ. of Wales Inst. Sci. Technol., Cardiff, Tech. Note* EP–18.
HITT, W. D., 1961, An evaluation of five different abstract coding methods. *Hum. Factors*, **3**, 120.
HITT, W. D., SCHUTZ, H. G., CHRISTNER, C. A., RAY, H. W. and COFFEY, L. J., 1961, Development of design criteria for intelligence display formats. *Hum. Factors*, **3**, 86.

HLADKÝ, A., MATOUŠEK, O. and ZASTÁVKA, Z., 1970, Algoritmisace jako metoda analýzy pracovních činností operátorů v technických systémech. *Syntéza*, 155.
HOEHN, A. J. and SALTZ, E., 1958, Mathematical models for determination of efficient troubleshooting routines. *I.R.E. Prof. Gp. Reliab. Qual. Control*, **PGRQC-13**, 1.
HOLDING, D. H., 1965, *Principles of Training* (Oxford: PERGAMON PRESS).
HOLLAND, J. G., 1958, Human vigilance. *Science*, **128**(3315), 61.
HOLLAND, J. G., 1963, Human vigilance. In BUCKNER, D. N. and MCGRATH, J. J., *op. cit.*, p. 247.
HOPKIN, V. D., 1970, Human factors in the ground control of aircraft. *N.A.S.A.,Rep.* AGARD–AG–142–70.
HOVLAND, C. I., 1938, Experimental studies in rote learning theory: III—Distribution of practice with varying speeds of syllable presentation. *J. exptl. Psychol.*, **23**, 172.
HOVLAND, C. I., 1960, Human learning and retention. In *Handbook of Experimental Psychology* (Edited by S. S. STEVENS) (New York: WILEY).
HOWARD, R. A., 1968, The foundations of decision analysis. *I.E.E.E. Trans. Syst. Sci. Cyb.*, **SSC-4**, 211.
IOSIF, G., 1969, Some relevant main problems of the control panels monitoring activity. *Studia Psychologica*, **11**, 293.
IOSIF, G., 1972, Le diagnostic des incidents par les opérateurs de centrales thermiques. *Travail Humain*, **35**, 37.
ITELSON, J. B., 1961, On the psychological characteristics of the work of the operator in continuous chemical production. *Voprosi Psichologii*, **7**, 109.
JACQUES, E., 1956, *Measurement of Responsibility* (London: TAVISTOCK).
JAGT, D. J., 1968, Your computer—an instrument maintenance tool. *Eleventh I.S.A. Nat. Symp. on Instrumentation in the Power Industry* (Pittsburgh, Pa.: INSTRUM. SOC. AM.), p. 67.
JAKEŠ, H. and STRÍŽENEC, M., 1971, Preliminary mathematical description of operators prediction in a simulated situation. *Studia Psychologica*, **13**, 138.
JENSEN, B. T., TILTON, J. R. and ANDERSON, D. N., 1961, Differential effects of knowledge of results and discussion. *Ergonomics*, **4**, 183.
JERISON, H. J. and WING, J. F., 1963a, Human vigilance and operant behaviour. *Science*, **133**(3456), 880.
JERISON, H. J. and WING, J. F., 1963b, Human vigilance and operant behaviour. In BUCKNER, D. N., and MCGRATH, J. J., *op. cit.*, p. 34.
JERVIS, M. W. and MADDOCK, P. R., 1964, Electric power station startup and control. In *Digital Computer Applications to Process Control (Int. Fed. Autom. Control Symp., Stockholm)* (Edited by W. E. MILLER) (New York: PLENUM PRESS), p. 251.
JOHANNSEN, G., 1972, Development and optimization of a nonlinear multiparameter human operator model. *I.E.E.E. Trans. Syst. Man Cyb.*, **SMC-2**, 494.
JOHN, E. R. and RIMOLDI, H. J. A., 1955, Sequential observation of complex reasoning. *Am. Psychol.*, **8**, 470 (abstract).
JOHN, E. R., 1957, Contributions to the study of the problem-solving process. *Psychol. Monogr.*, **71**(18).
JOHNSON, E. A., 1967, Touch displays: a programmed man–machine interface. *Ergonomics*, **10**, 271.
JOHNSON, K. A. and SENTER, R. J., 1965, A comparison of forward and backward chaining techniques for the teaching of verbal sequential tasks. *U.S. Air Force, Wright Patterson Air Force Base, Dayton, Ohio, Res. Rep.* AMRL–TR–65–203.
JOHNSON, P. C., 1968, Soaking pit scheduling at Guest Keen Iron and Steel Works. In *Energy Management in Iron and Steelworks, I.S.I. Pub.* No. 105 (London: IRON AND STEEL INST.).
JONES, J. C., 1967, The designing of man–machine systems. *Ergonomics*, **10**, 101.
JONES, M. R., 1962, Color coding. *Hum. Factors*, **4**, 355.
DE JONG, J. J., 1964, Basic philosophy of computer control in the processing industry. In *Digital Computer Applications to Process Control (Int. Fed. Autom. Control Symp., Stockholm)* (Edited by W. E. MILLER) (New York: PLENUM PRESS), p. 119.
DE JONG, J. J., 1965, Specific objectives in the control field. In *Automatic Control in the Chemical Process and Allied Industries* (London: SOC. CHEM. IND.).
*DE JONG, J. J. and KÖSTER, E. P., 1971, The human operator in the computer controlled refinery. *Proc. Eighth World Petrol. Cong., Moscow* (London: INST. PETROL.).
DE JONG, J. J., OERLEMANS, T. W. and SPAARGAREN, K., 1971, Technical, economic and human factors in computer control. In WILLIAMS, T. J., *op. cit.*
DE JONG, J. R., 1964, The effects of increasing skill and methods-time measurement. *Time and Motion Study*, **10** (February), 17.
JORDAN, N., 1962, Motivational problems in human-computer interactions. *Hum. Factors*, **4**, 171.
JORDAN, N., 1963, Allocation of function between man and machine in automated systems. *J. appl. Psychol.*, **47**, 161.
JURAN, J. M., 1966, Quality problems, remedies and nostrums. *Ind. Qual. Control*, **22**, 647.

JURAN, J. M., 1967, The QC Circle phenomenon. *Ind. Qual. Control*, **23**, 329.
KADOTA, T., 1968, PAC-Performance Analysis and Control. *J.I.E.*, **19**(8), 407.
KALMAN, R. E., 1960, A new approach to linear filtering and prediction problems. *Trans. A.S.M.E., J. Basic Engng.*, **82D** (March), 35.
KAMINSKI, G., 1964, Ordnungstrukturen und Ordnungsprozesse. In *Handbuch der Psychologie*, Vol. I/2 (Göttingen), p. 373.
KAY, H., 1951, Learning of a serial task by different age groups. *Quart. J. exptl. Psychol.*, **3**, 166.
KAY, H., 1957, Information theory in the understanding of skills. *Occup. Psychol.*, **31**, 10.
KAY, H., 1964, Human learning. *Br. med. Bull. (Exptl. Psychol.)*, **20**, 3.
KAY, P. C. M., 1966, On-line computer alarm analysis. *Ind. Electron.*, **4**, 50.
KAY, P. C. M. and HEYWOOD, P. W., 1966, Alarm analysis and indication at Oldbury nuclear power station. In *Automatic Control in Electricity Supply, I.E.E. Conf. Pub. No. 16* (London: INSTN. ELEC. ENGRS.), p. 295.
KEENER, E. L., 1970, Operator training with a dynamic simulation of a process. *First I.S.A. Symp. on Control Centers* (Pittsburgh, Pa.: INSTRUM. SOC. AM.), p. 90.
KELLEY, C. R., 1962, Predictor instruments look into the future. *Control Engng.*, **9**(3), 86.
KELLEY, C. R., 1967, A psychological approach to operator modeling in manual control. *Dunlap and Associates*, Santa Monica, Calif.
KELLEY, C. R., 1968, *Manual and Automatic Control* (New York: WILEY).
KELLSTEDT, C. W., 1965, A simulated boiler and control board for operating procedures training. *Eighth I.S.A. Nat. Symp. on Power Instrumentation* (Pittsburgh, Pa.: INSTRUM. SOC. AM.).
KENDRICK, P., 1969, Analytical training of operators in the process industries. *Man–Machine Systems, I.E.E.E. Conf. Rec.* 69C58–MMS.
KETTERINGHAM, P. J. A., O'BRIEN, D. and COLE, P. G., 1970, A computer-based interactive display system to aid steel plant scheduling. In *Man–Computer Interaction, Conf. Pub. No. 68* (London: INSTN. ELEC. ENGRS), p. 35.
* KETTERINGHAM, P. J. A. and O'BRIEN, D. D., 1974, Simulation study of computer-aided soaking pit scheduling. *This volume*.
KIBLER, A. W., 1965, The relevance of vigilance research to aerospace monitoring tasks. *Hum. Factors*, **7**, 93.
KING, P. J., 1974, personal communication (to F. P. Lees).
KING, S. D. M., 1960, Vocational training in view of technological change. *E.P.A. Project* 418 (Paris: EUR. PRODUCTIVITY AGENCY).
KING, S. D. M., 1964, *Training within the Organisation* (London: TAVISTOCK).
KIRCHNER, J. H. and LAURIG, W., 1971, The human operator in air traffic control systems. *Ergonomics*, **14**, 549.
KIRCHNER, W. K., 1961, The fallacy of accident proneness. *Personnel*, November.
*KITCHIN, J. B. and GRAHAM, A., 1961, Mental loading of process operators: An attempt to devise a method of analysis and assessment. *Ergonomics*, **4**, 1.
KLIMOSKI, R. J., 1971, Management information needs and the impact of the process control computer. In WILLIAMS, T. J., op. cit., p. 54.
KLIX, F. and SYDOW, H., 1966, Information processing in problem solving behaviour (Structural studies enclosing computer simulations). *Int. Cong. Psychol., General Problems of Psychol.*, Moscow, p. 126 (abstract).
KNIGHT, C. E., 1954, Managing the automatic plant. *Chem. Engng., Albany*, **61**(6), 225.
KOCHEN, M., 1961, Experimental study of hypothesis-formation by computer. In *Information Theory* (Edited by E. C. CHERRY) (London: BUTTERWORTH).
KOGAN, N. and WALLACH, M. A., 1967, Risk taking as a function of the situation, the person and the group. In *New Directions in Psychology*, Vol. III (New York: HOLT, RINEHART & WINSTON).
KOLESNICK, P. E. and PLATH, D. W., 1965, Comparison of operator performance with rotary selector, thumbwheel and digital pushbutton switches. *Autonetics*, Downey, Calif., Rep. T5-515/3111.
KOSTYUK, G. S., 1959, Questions of the psychology of thinking. *Psichologicheskaya Nauka v SSSR*, Vol. I (Moscow), p. 357.
KOZIELECKI, J., 1966, The mechanism of self-confirmation of a hypothesis in a probabilistic situation. *Int. Cong. Psychol., General Problems of Psychol.*, Moscow, p. 367 (abstract).
KRAGT, H., 1971, De operator in een chemische procesindustrie als element van het man–machine systeem. *N.V. Nederlandse Staatsmijnen/D.S.M. Geleen*.
*KRAGT, H. and LANDEWEERD, J. A., 1974, Mental skills in process control. *This volume*.
KRENDEL, E. S. and McRUER, D. T., 1960, A servomechanisms approach to skill development. *J. Franklin Inst.*, **269**, 24.
KŘIVOLAHÝ, J., 1964, Information processing in monitoring electricity works steam boilers. *Proc. Second Cong. Int. Ergonomics Ass.*, Dortmund.
LANDA, L. N., 1966, *Algorithmisation in Training* (Moscow).

LANDEWEERD, J. A., 1968, Regelvaardigheden en ergonomie. *N.V. Nederlandse Staatsmijnen/ D.S.M. Geleen.*
LEES, F. P., 1970, Functions performed by the human operator and by an on-line computer. *Chem. Engr., Lond.*, **241**, 263.
LEES, F. P., 1973, Quantification of man–machine system reliability in process control. *I.E.E.E. Trans. Reliab.*, **R-22**, 124.
LEES, F. P., 1974a, Design for man–machine system reliability in process control. In *Generic Techniques in System Reliability Assessment (N.A.T.O. Advanced Study Inst., Liverpool)* (Amsterdam: NORDHOFF).
*LEES, F. P., 1974b, Research on the process operator. *This volume.*
LEPLAT, J. and BISSERET, A., 1965, Analyse des processus de traitement de l'information chez le contrôleur de la navigation aérienne. *Bull. du C.E.R.P.*, **1-2**, 51.
LEPLAT, J., 1968, *Attention et Incertitude dans les Travaux de Surveillance et d'Inspection* (Paris: DUNOD).
LEPLAT, J. and CUNY, X., 1969, Structure of the machine and the operator's activities. *Man–Machine Systems, I.E.E.E. Conf. Rec.*, 69C58–MMS (abstract).
LEVINE, J. M. and SAMET, M. G., 1973, Information seeking with multiple sources of conflicting and unreliable information. *Hum. Factors*, **15**, 407.
LEVY, F. K., 1965, Adaptation in the production process. *Mgmt. Science*, **11** (April), 136.
LICKLIDER, J. C. R., 1960, Quasi-linear operator models in the study of manual tracking. In *Developments in Mathematical Psychology* (Edited by R. D. LUCE) (Glencoe, Ill.: FREE PRESS).
LICKLIDER, J. C. R., 1968, Man–computer communication. *Ann. Rev. Inf. Sci. Technol.*, **3**, 201.
LINCOLN, R. S. and AUERBACH, E., 1956, Spatial factors in check reading of dial groups. *J. appl. Psychol.*, **40**, 105.
LINCOLN, R. S., 1960, Human factors in attainment of reliability. *I.R.E. Trans. Reliab. Qual. Control*, **RQC-9**, 97.
LINQUIST, O. H. and GROSS, R. L., 1958, Human engineering man–machine study of weapon system. *Minneapolis-Honeywell Aero Rep.* R–ED 6094.
LOMOV, B. F., 1966, Man and technique. *Ocherki Inzhenernoi Psichologii* (Moscow).
LOVELESS, N. E., 1959, The effect of the relative position of control and display upon their direction-of-motion relationship. *Ergonomics*, **2**, 381.
LOVELESS, N. E., 1962, Direction-of-motion stereotypes: a review. *Ergonomics*, **5**, 357.
LUCE, R. D. and RAIFFA, H., 1957, *Games and Decisions. Introduction and Critical Survey* (New York: WILEY).
LUCE, R. D. and SUPPES, P., 1965, Preference, utility and subjective probability. In *Handbook of Mathematical Psychology* (Edited by R. D. LUCE, R. R. BUSH and E. GALANTER) (New York: WILEY).
LUMSDAINE, A. A., 1962, Some theoretical and practical problems in programmed instruction. In *Programmed Learning and Computer-Based Instruction* (Edited by J. E. COULSON) (New York: WILEY).
LUXENBERG, H. R. and KUEHN, R. L. (eds.), 1968, *Display Systems Engineering* (New York: MCGRAW-HILL).
MCCORMICK, E. J., 1964, *Human Factors Engineering* (New York: MCGRAW-HILL).
MACE, C. A., 1950, The analysis of human skills. *Occup. Psychol.*, **24**, 125.
MACKENZIE, R. M., 1958, On the accuracy of inspectors. *Ergonomics*, **1**, 258.
MCKINSEY, J. C. G., 1952, *Introduction to the Theory of Games* (New York: MCGRAW-HILL).
MACKWORTH, J. F. and THOMAS, E. H., 1962, A head-mounted eye marker camera. *J. Opt. Soc. Am.*, **52**, 713.
MACKWORTH, N. H., 1947, Researches on the measurement of human performance. *Ph.D. Thesis, Univ. of Cambridge.*
MACKWORTH, N. H., 1948, The breakdown of vigilance during prolonged visual search. *Quart. J. exptl. Psychol.*, **1**, 6.
MACKWORTH, N. H., 1950, Researches on the measurement of human performance. *Med. Res. Coun., Special Rep.* 268.
MCLANE, R. C. and WOLFE, J. D., 1967, Symbolic and pictorial displays for submarine control. *I.E.E.E. Trans. hum. Factors Electron.*, **HFE-8**, 148.
MCRUER, D. T. and JEX, H. R., 1967, A review of quasi-linear pilot models. *I.E.E.E. Trans. hum. Factors Electron.*, **HFE-8**, 231.
MCRUER, D. T. and WEIR, D. H., 1969, Theory of manual vehicular control. *Ergonomics*, **12**, 599.
MAGER, R. F., 1961, On the sequencing of instructional content. In *Contributions to an Educational Technology*, 1972 (Edited by I. K. DAVIES and J. HARTLEY) (London: BUTTERWORTH).
MAGER, R. F., 1962, *Preparing Objectives for Programmed Instruction* (San Francisco, Calif.: FEARON PRESS).
MAGER, R. F. and BEACH, K. M., 1967, *Developing Vocational Instruction* (Palo Alto, Calif.: FEARON PRESS).

MAJENDIE, A. M. A., 1962, Automatic landing, the role of the human pilot. *Aerospace Engng*, **21**(1), 24.
MANDELL, M. M., 1964, *The Selection Process* (New York: AM. MGMT. ASS.).
MARDON, J., BARRETT, J. E., CRIPPS, W. C., MONAHAN, R. E., CHATWIN, M. A., HOWE, B. I. and STAPLES, R.A.C., 1970, An advanced information system as a functional part of a newsprint machine. In *Paper-Making Systems and their Control* (Edited by F. BOLAM) (London: BR. PAPER & BOARD MAKERS ASS.), p. 342.
MARTIN, J., 1973, *Design of Man-Computer Dialogues* (Englewood Cliffs, N. J.: PRENTICE-HALL).
MASUDA, K., 1966, Fatigue and monotony in Japanese industry. *Studia Psychologica*, **8**, 275.
MATYUSHKIN, A. M., 1964, Features of investigation of thinking in engineering psychology. *Problemi Inzhenernoi Psichologii, Vol. I* (Leningrad), p. 153.
MATYUSHKIN, A. M., 1965, Some problems of the psychology of thinking. In *Coll. Psichologiya Myshleniya* (Moscow), p. 3.
MAYER, S. R., 1970, Trends in human factors research for military information systems. *Hum. Factors*, **12**, 177.
MAYNARD, H. B., STEGEMARTIN, G. T. and SCHWAB, J. L., 1948, *Methods-Time Measurement* (New York: MCGRAW-HILL).
MAYO, G. E., 1945, *The Social Problems of an Industrial Civilisation* (Boston, Mass.: HARVARD BUSN. SCHOOL).
MEADOW, C. T., 1970, *Man–Machine Communication* (New York: WILEY).
MECHNER, F. M. and COOK, D. A., 1964, *Behavioural Technology and Manpower Development* (New York: BASIC SYSTEMS; Paris: O.E.C.D.).
MECHNER, F. M., 1965, Science education and behaviour technology. In *Teaching Machines and Programmed Learning, Vol. II* (Edited by R. GLASER) (Washington: NAT. EDUC. AUTHOR.).
MECHNER, F. M., 1967, Behavioural analysis and instructional sequencing. In *Programmed Instruction* (Edited by C. P. LANGE) (Chicago, Ill.: NAT. SOC. STUDY EDUC.).
MEISTER, D., 1964, Methods of predicting human reliability in man–machine systems. *Hum. Factors*, **6**, 621.
MEISTER, D. and RABIDEAU, G. F., 1965, *Human Factors Evaluation in System Development* (New York: WILEY).
MEISTER, D., 1971, *Human Factors: Theory and Practice* (New York: WILEY).
MELTON, A. W. (ed.), 1964, *Categories of Human Learning* (New York: ACADEMIC PRESS).
MEREDITH, R. M. W., FLINT, A. J. and FEINSTEIN, J., 1970, An answer to the man/computer communication problems facing the steel industry. *Steel Times Ann. Rev.*
MILLER, D. C. and ELKIND, J. I., 1967, The adaptive response of the human controller to sudden changes in controlled process dynamics. *I.E.E.E. Trans. hum. Factors Electron.*, **HFE-8**, 218.
MILLER, E. E., 1963, A classification of learning tasks in conventional language. *U.S. Air Force, Wright Air Dev. Center, Dayton, Ohio, Rep.* AMRL–TDR–63–74.
MILLER, G. A., 1951, *Language and Communication* (New York: MCGRAW-HILL).
MILLER, G. A., 1956, Human memory and the storage of information. *I.R.E. Trans. Inf. Theory*, **IT-2**, 129.
MILLER, G. A., GALANTER, E. and PRIBRAM, K. H., 1960, *Plans and the Structure of Behavior* (New York: HOLT, RINEHART & WINSTON).
MILLER, G. A., 1965, Man–computer interaction. In *Communication Processes* (Edited by F. A. GELDARD) (LONDON: PERGAMON PRESS), p. 228.
MILLER, J. G., 1960, Information input overload and psychopathology. *Am. J. Psychiatry*, **116**, 695.
MILLER, R. B., 1953, A method for man–machine task analysis. *U.S. Air Force, Wright Air Dev. Center, Dayton, Ohio, Rep.* 53–137.
MILLER, R. B., 1963, Task description and analysis. In GAGNÉ, R. M., *op. cit.*
MILLER, R. B., 1965, Analysis and specification of behaviour for training. In GLASER, R., *op. cit.*
MILLER, R. B., 1967, Task taxonomy: Science or technology? *Ergonomics*, **10**, 167.
MILLER, R. B., 1969, Archtypes in man–computer problem-solving. *Ergonomics*, **12**, 559.
MILLS, R. G., 1967, Man–machine communication and problem-solving. *Ann. Rev. Inf. Sci. Technol.*, **2**, 223.
MIOLLAN, P., 1966, personal communication (to M. Striženec).
MONTY, R. A., 1973, Keeping track of sequential events: implications for design of displays. *Ergonomics*, **16**, 443.
MOTT, P. E., 1965, *Shift Work, the Social, Psychological and Physical Consequences* (Ann Arbor, Mich.: UNIV. OF MICHIGAN).
*MUNRO, H. P., MARTIN, F. W. and ROBERTS, M. C., 1968, How to use simulation techniques to determine optimum manning levels for continuous process plants. *Chem. Engr., London*, **222**, 355.
MURRELL, K. F. H., 1952, The use and arrangement of dials. *Instrum. Pract.*, **6**, 520.

MURRELL, K. F. H., 1960, A comparison of three dial shapes for check-reading instrument panels. *Ergonomics*, **3**, 231.
MURRELL, K. F. H., 1964, Visual information at the place of work. *Proc. Second Cong. Int. Ergonomics Ass., Dortmund*.
MURRELL, K. F. H., 1965, *Ergonomics: Man in his Working Environment* (London: CHAPMAN & HALL).
NASLIN, P. and RAOULT, J. G., 1963, Modèles continus et échantillonés de l'opérateur humain placé dans une boucle de commande. *Proc. Second Cong. Int. Fed. Autom. Control, Basle* (London: BUTTERWORTH).
NATIONAL ECONOMIC DEVELOPMENT OFFICE (N.E.D.C.), 1973, *Chemical Manpower in Europe* (London: H.M. STATIONERY OFFICE).
NATIONAL INSTITUTE OF INDUSTRIAL PSYCHOLOGY (N.I.I.P.), 1956, *Training Factory Workers* (London: STAPLES PRESS).
NAYLOR, J. C. and BRIGGS, G. E., 1963, Effects of task complexity and task organization on the relative efficiency of part and whole training methods. *J. exptl. Psychol.*, **65**, 217.
NEUMAN, J., 1965, Die Erfassung von Denkleistungen mit Hilfe von Markoffketten. *Zt. f. Psychol.*, **171**, 421.
VON NEUMANN, J. and MORGENSTERN, O., 1947, *Theory of Games and Economic Behaviour* (Princeton: PRINCETON UNIV. PRESS).
NEWELL, A., SHAW, J. C. and SIMON, H. A., 1958, Elements of a theory of human problem-solving. *Psychol. Rev.*, **65**, 151.
NEWELL, A. and SIMON, H. A., 1961, Computer simulation of human thinking. *Science*, **134(3495)**, 2011.
NEWELL, A. and SIMON, H. A., 1963, G.P.S., a program that simulates human thought. In *Computers and Thought* (Edited by E. FEIGENBAUM and J. FELDMAN) (New York: MCGRAW-HILL).
NEWELL, A., SHAW, J. C. and SIMON, H. A., 1963, The processes of creative thinking. In *Contemporary Approaches to Creative Thinking* (Edited by H. E. GRUBER) (New York), p. 63.
NEWELL, A. and SIMON, H. A., 1972, *Human Problem-Solving* (Englewood Cliffs, N.J.: PRENTICE-HALL).
NICKERSON, R. S., 1969, Man–computer interaction: a challenge for human factors research. *Ergonomics*, **12**, 501.
NORTH, D. W., 1968, A tutorial introduction to decision theory. *I.E.E.E. Trans. Syst. Sci. Cyb.*, **SSC-4**, 200.
NORTH, J. D., 1952, The human transfer function in servo-systems. In *Automatic and Manual Control* (Edited by A. TUSTIN) (London: BUTTERWORTH), p. 473.
NORTH, J. D., 1956, The application of communications theory to the human operator. In *Information Theory: Third London Symposium* (Edited by E. C. CHERRY) (London: METHUEN).
OBERMAYER, R. W. and MUCKLER, F. A., 1965, Modern control system theory and human control functions. *N.A.S.A. Rep.* CR–256.
OFFER, U., 1970, Verkehr Mensch-Rechner. In *Prozessrechner, Wirkungsweise und Einsatz* (Edited by A. ANKE, H. KALTENECKER and R. OETKER) (Munich: R. OLDENBOURG VERLAG).
OSHANIN, D. A. (ed.), 1965, *The Man–Machine System* (Moscow).
OSHANIN, D. A., 1966, The operative image of a controlled object in ' man-automatic ' machine systems. *Int. Cong. Psychol., General Problems of Psychol., Moscow*, p. 439 (abstract).
PARISH, C. C. M., 1971, A program system for on-line power system control. In WILLIAMS, T. J., *op. cit.*, p. 201.
PARSONS, H. M., 1972, *Man–Machine System Experiments* (Baltimore, Ma.: JOHN HOPKINS PRESS).
PATTERSON, D., 1968, Application of a computerised alarm analysis system to a nuclear power station. *Proc. I.E.E.*, **115**, 1858.
PETERS, G. A. and HUSSMAN, T. A., 1959, Human factors in reliability. *Hum. Factors*, **1(2)**, 38.
PIAGET, J., 1966, *Psychologie Inteligence* (Prague).
PICKREL, E. W. and MCDONALD, T. A., 1964, Quantification of human performance in large complex systems. *Hum. Factors*, **6**, 647.
POGOSTIN, S. Z., 1954, *Technical Norm-Setting in the Chemical Industry* (Moscow: GOSKHIMIZDAT).
PONTIUS, P. W., VAN TASSEL, P. A. and FIELD, J. H., 1959, Operator training in new plant startup. *Chem. Engng. Prog.*, **55(8)**, 38.
POOLE, H. H., 1966, *Fundamentals of Display Systems* (London: SPARTAN MACMILLAN).
POPPLEWELL, F., 1912, The gas industry. In *Seasonal Trades* (Edited by S. WEBB and A. FREEMAN) (London: CONSTABLE).
POSNER, M. I., 1965, Memory and thought in human intellectual performance. *Br. J. Psychol.*, **56**, 197.
POULTON, E. C., 1952, The basis of perceptual anticipation in tracking. *Br. J. Psychol.*, **43**, 95.

POULTON, E. C., 1957, On prediction of skilled movements. *Psychol. Bull.*, **54**, 467.
POWERS, G. J. and TOMPKINS, F. C., 1973a, Computer-aided fault tree synthesis for chemical processes. *A.I.Ch.E. Mtg., Philadelphia, Pa.*
POWERS, G. J. and TOMPKINS, F. C., 1973b, Computer-aided synthesis of fault trees for complex processing systems. In *Generic Techniques in System Reliability Assessment (N.A.T.O. Advanced Study Inst., Liverpool)* (Amsterdam: NORDHOFF).
PUSHKIN, V. N., 1959, Some questions of the psychology of the control of the production process in rail transport. *Voprosi Psichologii*, **5**, 66.
PUSHKIN, V. N., 1960, Characteristics and methods of rationalisation of the control desks of dispatchers. *Voprosi Psichologii*, **6**, 39.
PUSHKIN, V. N., 1964, On the use of chess as a model of operator thinking. *Problemi Inzhenernoi Psichologii*, Vol. 1, p. 147.
PUSHKIN, V. N., 1965, On the process of problem-solving in the course of control of complex objects. In OSHANIN, D. A., *op. cit.*, p. 37.
QUASTLER, H. (ed.), 1955, *Information Theory in Psychology. Problems and Methods* (Glencoe, Ill.: FREE PRESS).
RAPOPORT, A., 1958, Quantification of performance in a logical task with uncertainty. *Symp. on Information Theory in Biology*, New York, p. 230.
RAPOPORT, A., 1964a, Estimation of continuous subjective probability distributions in a sequential decision task. *Hum. Factors*, **6**, 433.
RAPOPORT, A., 1964b, A study of human decisions in a computer-controlled task. *J. Math. Psychol.*, **1**, 351.
*RASMUSSEN, J., 1968a, On the communication between operators and instrumentation in automatic process plants. *Atomic Energy Commission, Res. Est., Risö, Denmark, Rep.* Risö–M–686.
RASMUSSEN, J., 1968b, On the reliability of process plants and instrumentation systems. *Atomic Energy Commission, Res. Est., Risö, Denmark, Rep.* Risö–M–706.
RASMUSSEN, J., 1968c, Characteristics of the operator, automation equipment and designer in plant automation. *Atomic Energy Commission, Res. Est., Risö, Denmark, Rep.* Risö–M–808.
RASMUSSEN, J., 1969, Man–machine communication in the light of accident records. *Man–Machine Systems, I.E.E.E. Conf. Rec.* 69C58–MMS.
RASMUSSEN, J., 1971, Man as information receiver in complex tasks. In *Displays, Conf. Pub. No. 80* (London: INSTN. ELEC. ENGRS.), p. 271.
RASMUSSEN, J. and JENSEN, A., 1973, A study of mental procedures in electronic trouble-shooting. *Atomic Energy Commission, Res. Est., Risö, Denmark, Rep.* Risö–M–1582.
RASMUSSEN, J., 1974, The role of the man–machine interface in systems reliability. In *Generic Techniques in System Reliability Assessment (N.A.T.O. Advanced Study Inst., Liverpool)* (Amsterdam: NORDHOFF).
REITMAN, W. R., 1965, *Cognition and Thought. An Information Processing Approach* (New York: WILEY).
REITMAN, W. R., 1966, The study of heuristics. *Int. Cong. Psychol., General Problems of Psychol.,* Moscow, p. 362 (abstract).
RICE, A. K., 1958, *Productivity and Social Organisation: The Ahmedabad Experiment* (London: TAVISTOCK).
RIGBY, L. V., 1967, The Sandia Human Error Rate Bank (SHERB). *Sandia Laboratories, Albuquerque, N. Mex., Rep.* SC–R–67–1150.
RIGBY, L. V. and EDELMAN, D. A., 1968, A predictive scale of aircraft emergencies. *Hum. Factors*, **10**, 475.
RIMOLDI, H. J. A., 1955, A technique for the study of problem solving. *Am. Psychol.*, **8**, 469.
ROBINSON, G. H., 1967, The human controller as an adaptive, low pass filter. *Hum. Factors*, **9**, 141.
RONAN, W. W., 1953, Training for emergency procedures in multiengine aircraft. *Am. Inst. Res., Pittsburgh, Pa., Rep.* AIR–153–53–FR–44.
ROOK, L. W., 1964, Evaluation of system performance from rank order data. *Hum. Factors*, **6**, 533.
ROOT, R. T. and SADACCA, R., 1967, Man–computer communication techniques. *Hum. Factors*, **9**, 521.
ROUANET, J. and GATEAU, Y., 1964, Quelques aspects de l'utilisation du matériel électronique (entretien et programmation). *C.E.R.P., Paris, Rep.*
ROUSE, W. D., 1973, A model of the human in a cognitive prediction task. *I.E.E.E. Trans. Syst. Man Cyb.*, **SMC-3**, 473.
ROWELL, J. T. and STREICH, E. R., 1964, The SAGE system training program for the air defense command. *Hum. Factors*, **6**, 537.
RUBINSTEIN, S. L., 1960, *O myslení a spôsoboch jeho výskumu* (Bratislava).
SACKMAN, H., 1967, *Computers, System Science and Evolving Society* (New York: WILEY).
SACKMAN, H., 1970, *Man–Computer Problem-Solving* (New York: AUERBACH PUBLISHERS).

SANDERS, A. F. (ed.), 1966, *Attention and Performance*, Vol. I (Amsterdam: NORTH HOLLAND); 1968, *Vol. II*; 1970, *Vol. III*.
SAVOYANT, A., 1971, Diagnostic dans une étude de poste de l'industrie chimique. *Travail Humain*, **34**, 177.
SAYERS, B., 1974, personal communication (to F. P. Lees).
SCHAGER, A. J., 1965, The human operator and automated power plants. In *Eighth I.S.A. Nat. Power. Instrumentation Symp.* (Pittsburgh, Pa.: INSTRUM. SOC. AM), p. 4–3.
SCHRENK, L. P., 1964, Objective difficulty and input history as factors in sequential decision-making. *Hum. Factors*, **6**, 49.
SCHRENK, L. P., 1969, Aiding the decision-maker—a decision process model. *Ergonomics*, **12**, 543.
ŠEDIVÝ, A., 1966, Normovanie práce. *Základy vedeckej organizácie práce* (Bratislava), p. 262.
SELL, R. G., CROSSMAN, E. R. F. W. and BOX, A., 1962, An ergonomic method of analysis applied to hot strip mills. *Ergonomics*, **5**, 203.
SELL, R. G. and PULSFORD, H. E., 1967, The operation of the National Grid System. *Ergonomics*, **10**, 225.
SENDERS, J. W., 1955a, Tracking with intermittently illuminated displays. *U.S. Air Force, Wright Air Dev. Center, Dayton, Ohio, Tech. Rep.* 55–197.
SENDERS, J. W., 1955b, Man's capacity to use information from complex displays. In QUASTLER, H., *op. cit.*
SENDERS, J. W., 1964, The human operator as a monitor and controller of multidegree of freedom systems. *I.E.E.E. Trans. hum. Factors Electron.*, **HFE-5**, 2.
SENDERS, V. L., 1952, The effect of number of dials on qualitative reading of a multiple dial panel. *U.S. Air Force, Wright Air Dev. Center, Dayton, Ohio, Tech. Rep.* 52–182.
SEYMOUR, W. D., 1954, *Industrial Training for Manual Operations* (London: PITMAN).
SEYMOUR, W. D., 1959, *Operator Training in Industry* (London: INST. PERSONNEL MGMT.).
SEYMOUR, W. D., 1966, *Industrial Skills* (London: PITMAN).
SEYMOUR, W. D., 1968, *Skills Analysis Training* (London: PITMAN).
SHACKEL, B., 1962, Ergonomics in the design of a large computer console. *Ergonomics*, **5**, 229.
SHACKEL, B., 1969, Man–computer interaction—the contribution of the human sciences. *Ergonomics*, **12**, 485.
SHAFFER, L. H., 1965, Problem solving on a stochastic process. *Ergonomics*, **8**, 181.
SHANNON, C. E. and WEAVER, W., 1949, *The Mathematical Theory of Communication* (Urbana, Ill.: UNIV. OF ILLINOIS PRESS).
SHEARER, J. L., MURPHY, A. T. and RICHARDSON, H. H., 1967, *Introduction to System Dynamics* (Reading, Mass.: ADDISON WESLEY).
SHELLY, M. W. and BRYAN, G. L. (eds.), 1964, *Human Judgements and Optimality* (New York: WILEY).
SHERIDAN, T. B., 1960, Experimental analysis of time-variation of the human operator's transfer function. *Proc. First Cong. Int. Fed. Autom. Control, Moscow* (London: BUTTERWORTH).
SHERIDAN, T. B., 1966, Three models of preview control. *I.E.E.E. Trans. hum. Factors Electron.*, **HFE-7**, 91.
SHERIDAN, T. B., 1969, On how often the supervisor should sample. *Man–Machine Systems, I.E.E.E. Conf. Rec.* 69C58–MMS.
SHOLL, H. A., 1972, Modeling of an operator's performance in a short-term visual information processing task. *I.E.E.E. Trans. Syst. Man Cyb.*, **SMC-2**, 352.
SHRIVER, E. L., FINK, C. D. and TREXLER, R. C., 1964, FORECAST systems analysis and training methods for electronics maintenance training. *Hum. Resources Res. Office, Alexandria, Va., Res. Rep.* 13.
SIEGEL, A. I., MIEHLE, W. and FEDERMAN, P., 1964, The DEI technique for evaluating equipment systems from the information transfer point of view. *Hum. Factors*, **6**, 279.
SIEGEL, A. I. and WOLF, J. J., 1969, *Man–Machine Simulation Models* (New York: WILEY).
SIMMONDS, D. C. V., 1960, An investigation of pilot skill in an instrument flying task. *Ergonomics*, **3**, 249.
SINAIKO, H. W. (ed.), 1961, *Selected Papers on Human Factors in the Design and Use of Control Systems* (New York: DOVER PUBLICATIONS).
SINCLAIR, I. A. C., SELL, R. G., BEISHON, R. J., and BAINBRIDGE, L., 1966, Ergonomic study of an LD waste heat boiler control room. *J. Iron Steel Inst.*, **204**, 434.
SINGER, R. and RIECK, A., 1969, Relationship between motor activity and vigilance performance in an optical vigilance task. *Studia Psychologica*, **11**, 204.
SINGER, R. and RUTENFRANZ, J., 1969, Correlation between vigilance performance and probability of signal occurrence. *Studia Psychologica*, **11**, 101.
SINGLETON, W. T., 1959, The training of shoe machinists. *Ergonomics*, **2**, 148.
SINGLETON, W. T., EASTERBY, R. S. and WHITFIELD, D. C. (eds.), 1967, *The Human Operator in Complex Systems* (London: TAYLOR & FRANCIS).

Singleton, W. T., 1968, Some recent experiments on learning and their training implications. *Ergonomics*, **11**, 53.
Singleton, W. T., 1969, Display design: Principles and procedures. *Ergonomics*, **12**, 543.
Singleton, W. T., Fox, J. G. and Whitfield, D. C. (eds.), 1971, *Measurement of Man at Work* (London: Taylor & Francis).
Singleton, W. T., 1972, Total activity analysis: a different approach to work study. *Travail Humain*, **35**, 241.
Singleton, W. T., 1973, Theoretical approaches to human error. *Ergonomics*, **16**, 727.
Singleton, W. T. and Spurgeon, P. (eds.), 1974, *Measurement of Human Resources* (London: Taylor & Francis).
Šípoš, I., 1971, Operators personality traits and visual vigilance. *Studia Psychologica*, **13**, 318.
Sleight, R. B., 1948, The effect of instrument dial shape on legibility. *J. appl. Psychol.*, **32**, 170.
Smallwood, R. D., 1966, Some models for the human instrument monitor. In *An Investigation of the Visual Sampling Behaviour of Human Observation*, *N.A.S.A. Rep.* CR–434, App. I.
Smallwood, R. D., 1967. Internal models and the human instrument monitor. *I.E.E.E. Trans. hum. Factors. Electron.*, **HFE-8**, 181.
Smith, R. G., 1964, The development of training objectives. *Hum. Resources Res. Office, Alexandria, Va., Rep.*
Smith, R. H., 1963, On the limits of manual control. *I.E.E.E. Trans. hum. Factors Electron.*, **HFE-4**, 56.
Smith, R. L. and Lucaccini, L. F., 1969, Vigilance research; its application to industrial problems. *Hum. Factors*, **11**, 149.
Smith, W. A., 1967, Accuracy of manual entries in data collection devices. *J. appl. Psychol.*, **51**, 362.
*Spencer, J., 1962, An investigation of process control skill. *Occup. Psychol.*, **36**, 30.
Spencer, J. and Phipps, S. H., 1966, Ergonomics applied to distribution control systems. *Engineer, Lond.*, **222**, 259.
Sperandio, J. C., 1972, Charge de travail et regulation des processus opératoires. *Travail Humain*, **35**, 85.
Sriyananda, H. and Towill, D. R., 1973, Prediction of human operator performance. *I.E.E.E. Trans. Reliab.*, **R-22**, 148.
Staats, A. W. and Staats, C. K., 1963, *Complex Human Behavior: A Systematic Extension of Learning Principles* (New York: Holt, Rinehart & Winston).
Stachowiak, H., 1965, *Denken und Erkennen im kybernetischen Modell* (Vienna).
Stainthorp, F. P. and Searson, H. M., 1967, A program structure for DDC. In *The Application of Automation in the Process Industries* (London: Instn. Chem. Engrs.), p. 68.
Stainthorp, F. P., 1970, The computer controlled fractionating columns at U.M.I.S.T. *Br. Chem. Engng.*, **15**, 794.
Stainthorp, F. P. and West, B., 1973, Computer controlled plant startup. *Eur. Fed. Chem. Engng. Symp. on Use of Electronic Computers in Chemical Engineering*, Paris.
Stanley, J. C. and Bolton, D., 1957, *Educ. Psychol. Measamt.*, **17**, 631 (book review section).
Stolurow, L. M., 1964, A taxonomy of learning task characteristics. *U.S. Air Force, Wright Air. Dev. Center, Dayton, Ohio, Rep.* AMRL–TDR–64–2.
Stríženec, M., 1966a, *Psychológia a kybernetika* (Bratislava).
Stríženec, M., 1966b, The man–machine system: theoretical aspects of engineering psychology. *Studia Psychologica*, **8**, 132 (in Russian).
Stríženec, M., 1966c, Contemporary trends in Soviet engineering psychology. *Studia Psychologica*, **8**, 165.
Stríženec, M., 1967a, Myšlienková činnosí operátora v automatizovanej výrobe. *Psychologie v ekonomické praxi*.
*Stríženec, M., 1967b, On research into operator's thinking and decision-making. *Studia Psychologica*, **9**, 3.
Stríženec, M., 1968, Quelques aspects méthodologiques de la recherche sur les processus intellectuels de l'opérateur. *Travail Humain*, **31**, 269.
Stríženec, M., 1969, Descriptive theory of decision-making and operator's activity in automated production. *Studia Psychologica*, **11**, 81.
Stríženec, M., 1970a, Attempts to work out a more realistic model of an operator's thinking activity. *Studia Psychologica*, **12**, 164.
Stríženec, M., 1970b, Prediction of parameter changes in a simulated control system. *Studia Psychologica*, **12**, 214 and 249.
Strohmeyer, C., 1970, Application and results of digital control at Sibley station, unit No. 3. *Thirteenth I.S.A. Nat. Symp. on Instrumentation in the Power Industry* (Pittsburgh, Pa.: Instrum. Soc. Am.), p. 41.
Summers, L. G. and Ziedman, K., 1964, A study of manual control methodology, with annotated bibliography. *N.A.S.A., Rep.* CR–125.

SUVOROVA, V. V., IDASHKIN, J. V. and GADZHIEV, S. S., 1961, Experience in the psychological investigation of the activity of operators. *Voprosi Psichologii*, **7,** 47.
SWAIN, A. D., 1964a, THERP. *Sandia Laboratories, Albuquerque, N. Mex., Rep.* SC–R–64–1338.
SWAIN, A. D., 1964b, Some problems in the measurement of human performance in man–machine systems. *Hum. Factors*, **6,** 687.
SWAIN, A. D., 1969, Human reliability assessment in nuclear reactor plants. *Sandia Laboratories, Albuquerque, N. Mex., Rep.* SC–R–69–1236.
SWAIN, A. D., 1970, Development of a human error rate data bank. *Sandia Laboratories, Albuquerque, N. Mex., Rep.* SC–R–70–4286.
SWAIN, A. D., 1972, *Design Techniques for Improving Human Performance in Production* (London: INDUSTRIAL & COMMERCIAL TECHNIQUES LTD.).
SWAIN, A. D., 1973a, Design of industrial jobs a worker can and will do. *Hum. Factors*, **15,** 129.
SWAIN, A. D., 1973b, An Error-Cause Removal Programme for industry. *Hum. Factors*, **15,** 207.
SWEENEY, J. S. and GRAHAM, A., 1959, The effect of loop characteristics upon human gain. *I.R.E. Nat. Conv. Rec.*, Part 9, p. 80.
SWETS, J. A. (ed.), 1964, *Signal Detection and Recognition by Human Observers* (New York: WILEY).
TAVAST, R. and MYTUS, L., 1969, An adaptive man–computer system for a chemical plant. *Proc. Fourth Cong. Int. Fed. Autom. Control, Warsaw.*
TAYLOR, D. W. and MCNEMAR, O. W., 1955, Problem solving and thinking. *Ann. Rev. Psychol.*, **6,** 455.
TAYLOR, F. V., 1911, *The Principles of Scientific Management* (New York: HARPER).
TAYLOR, F. V., 1957, Simplifying the controller's task through display quickening. *Occup. Psychol.*, **31,** 120.
TAYLOR, L. W., 1970, How complex should a model be? *Proc. Joint Autom. Control. Conf., Atlanta, Ga.*
TAYLOR, R. V., 1963, Human engineering and psychology. In *Psychology, Vol. 5* (Edited by S. KOCH) (New York), p. 831.
TEJA, A. S., 1974, personal communication (to F. P. Lees).
THOMAS, R. E. and TOU, J. T., 1968, Evolution of heuristics by human operators in control systems. *I.E.E.E. Trans. Syst. Sci. Cyb.*, **SSC-4,** 60.
THORNDIKE, R. L., 1959, *Personnel Selection* (New York: WILEY).
THORNE, W., 1925, *My Life's Battles* (London: NEWNES).
THORSRUD, E. and EMERY, F. E., 1969, *Mot en ny bedriftsorganisasjon* (Oslo: TANUM FORLAG).
THRALL, R. M., COOMBS, C. H. and DAVID, R. L. (eds.), 1954, *Decision Processes* (New York: WILEY).
TICHOMIRÒV, O. K., 1965, The principle of selectivity in thinking. *Voprosi Psichologii*, **11,** 16.
TICHOMIROV, O. K., 1966, Experimental analysis of heuristics in man. *Int. Cong. Psychol., General Problems of Psychol., Moscow*, p. 361 (abstract).
TICKNER, A. H., POULTON, E. C., COPEMAN, A. K. and SIMMONDS, D. C. V., 1972, Monitoring 16 television screens showing little movement. *Ergonomics*, **15,** 279.
TILLEY, K. W., 1967, Fault diagnosis for maintenance personnel. *Ergonomics*, **10,** 206.
TILLEY, K. W., 1969, Developments in selection and training. *Ergonomics*, **12,** 583.
TOCHER, K. D., 1965, Review of simulation languages. *Opl. Res. Q.*, **16,** 189.
TOWILL, D. R., 1970, *Transfer Function Techniques for Control Engineers* (London: ILIFFE).
TOWILL, D. R., 1972, Cusum monitoring of operator performance during learning. *Work Study and Mgmt. Services*, **16** (January), 12.
TOWILL, D. R., 1973a, An industrial dynamics model for start-up management. *I.E.E.E. Trans. Engng. Mgmt.*, **EM-20**(2), 44.
TOWILL, D. R., 1973b, A direct method for the determination of learning curve parameters from historical data. *Int. J. Prod. Res.*, **11**(1), 97.
*TOWILL, D. R., 1974, A model for describing process operator performance. *This volume.*
TRIST, E. L., HIGGIN, G. W., MURRAY, H. and POLLOCK, A. B., 1963, *Organisational Choice* (London: TAVISTOCK).
TUFF, G. C., 1970, Computer control and the chemical process operator. *Chem. Engr., Lond.*, **241,** 260.
TUSTIN, A., 1944, An investigation of the operator's response in the manual control of a power-driven gun. *Metropolitan Vickers Electrical Co., CS Memo.* 169.
TUSTIN, A., 1947, The nature of the operator's response in manual control and its implications for controller design. *J. Inst. elec. Engrs.*, **94** Part IIA, 143.
VANDER SCHRAAF, E. and STRAUSS, W. I., 1964, Direct digital control—an emerging technology. *Oil Gas J.*, **62**(46), 167.
VARTABEDIAN, A. G., 1971, Legibility of symbols on CRT displays. *Appl. Ergonomics*, **2,** 130.
VAUGHAN, W. S. and MAVOR, A. S., 1972, Behavioural characteristics of men in the performance of some decision-making task components. *Ergonomics*, **15,** 267.

VINCE, M. A., 1948, The intermittency of control movements and the psychological refractory period. *Br. J. Psychol.*, **38**, 149.
VINCE, M. A., 1950, Learning and retention of an 'unexpected' control display relationship under stress conditions. *Med. Res. Coun., Appl. Psychol. Unit, Cambridge, Rep.* 125/50.
VROOM, V. H., 1964, *Work and Motivation* (New York: WILEY).
WAAG, W. L. and HALCOMB, C. G., 1972, Team size and decision rule in the performalce of simulated monitoring teams. *Hum. Factors*, **14**, 309.
WALD, A., 1950, *Statistical Decision Functions* (New York: WILEY).
WALKER, C. M., 1950, The problem of the repetitive job. *Harvard Business Rev.*, **28**(3), 54.
WARRICK, M. J., 1947, Direction of motion preferences in positioning indicators by means of control knobs. *Am. Psychol.*, **2**, 345.
WEINBERG, G. M., 1971, *The Psychology of Computer Programming* (New York: VAN NOSTRAND).
WELBOURNE, D., 1965, Data processing and control by a computer at Wylfa nuclear power station. In *Advances in Automatic Control* (London: INSTN. MECH. ENGRS.), p. 92.
WELBOURNE, D., 1968, Alarm analysis and display at Wylfa nuclear power station. *Proc. I.E.E.*, **115**, 1726.
WELFORD, A. T., 1958, *Ageing and Human Skill* (Oxford: OXFORD UNIV. PRESS).
WELFORD, A. T., 1959, Evidence of a single-channel decision mechanism limiting performance in a serial reaction task. *Quart. J. exptl. Psychol.*, **11**, 193.
WELFORD, A. T., 1960, *Ergonomics of Automation. D.S.I.R., Problems of Progress in Industry* No. 8 (London: H.M. STATIONERY OFFICE).
WELFORD, A. T., 1962, On the human demands of automation: mental work, conceptual models, satisfaction and training. *Proc. Fourteenth Int. Cong. Appl. Psychol., Copenhagen*, Vol. 5, p. 182.
WELFORD, A. T., 1968, *Fundamentals of Skill* (London: METHUEN).
WELFORD, A. T., 1973, Stress and performance. *Ergonomics*, **16**, 567.
WEST, B., 1972, Automatic startup of computer controlled chemical plants. *Ph.D. Thesis, Univ. of Manchester Inst. Sci. Technol.*
*WEST, B. and CLARK, J. A., 1974, Operator interaction with a computer controlled distillation column. *This volume.*
WHITE, C. T. and FORD, A., 1960, Eye movements during simulated radar search. *J. Opt. Soc. Am.*, **50**, 909.
WHITE, W. J., WARRICK, M. J. and GRETHER, W. F., 1953, Instrument reading. III, Check reading of instrument groups. *J. appl. Psychol.*, **37**, 302.
WHITFIELD, D., 1967, Human skill as a determinate of allocation of function. *Ergonomics*, **10**, 154.
WHITFIELD, D., 1969, A pilot survey of human factors aspects of power reactor safety and control. *Univ. of Aston in Birmingham, Ergonomics Dev. Unit Rep.*
WHITMAN, K. A., 1972, Computer monitoring and surveillance of process equipment. *Instrum. Technol.*, **19**(7), 50.
WIERENGA, R. D., 1969, An evaluation of a pilot model based on Kalman filtering and optimal control. *I.E.E.E. Trans. Man–Machine Syst.*, **MMS-10**, 108.
WIERWILLE, W. W., 1964, A diagrammatic classification of man–machine system displays. *Hum. Factors*, **6**, 201.
WIERWILLE, W. W. and GAGNÉ, G. A., 1966, Nonlinear and time varying dynamical models of human operators in manual control systems. *Hum. Factors*, **8**, 97.
WILDE, R. W. and WESTCOTT, J. H., 1963, The characteristics of the human operator engaged in a tracking task. *Automatica*, **1**, 5.
WILKINSON, R. T., 1961, Comparison of paced, unpaced, irregular and continuous display in watchkeeping. *Ergonomics*, **4**, 259.
WILLIAMS, A. C. and HOPKINS, C. O., 1958, Aspects of pilot decision-making. *U.S. Air Force, Wright Air Dev. Center, Dayton, Ohio, Tech. Rep.* 58–522.
WILLIAMS, P. R., HARPER, H. P. and KRONHOLM, M. B., 1967, An evaluation of an integrated V/STOL display concept. *I.E.E.E. Trans. hum. Factors Electron.*, **HFE-8**, 158.
WILLIAMS, T. J. (ed.), 1971, *Interfaces with the Process Control Computer—The Operator, Engineer and Management* (Pittsburgh, Pa.: INSTRUM. SOC. AM.).
WILLIAMS, W. L. and WHITMORE, P. G., 1959, The development and use of a performance test as a basis for comparing technicians with and without field experience and the Nike Ajax IFC maintenance technician. *Hum. Resources Res. Office, Alexandria, Va., Tech. Rep.* 52.
WILSON, J., 1972, Human factors in low weather operation of transport aircraft. *N.A.T.O. AGARD Conf. on Automation in Manned Aerospace Systems.*
WOLFF, H. S., 1970, The hospital ward—a technological desert. In *Instruments in Working Environments* (London: ADAM HILGER), p. 90.
WOLFLE, D., 1960, Training. In *Handbook of Experimental Psychology* (Edited by S. S. STEVENS) (New York: WILEY).

WOODWARD, J., 1958, *Management and Technology*. *D.S.I.R., Problems of Progress in Industry No.* 3 (London: H.M. STATIONERY OFFICE).

VON WRIGHT, J. M., 1957, An experimental study of human serial learning. *Soc. Sci. Fennica Commentationes Humanorum Litterarum*, **23**, 1.

WYATT, S., 1927, Rest pauses in industry. *Ind. Fatigue Res. Board, Rep.* 42 (London: H.M. STATIONERY OFFICE).

WYATT, S. and FRASER, J. A., 1929, The effect of monotony in work. *Ind. Fatigue Res. Board, Rep.* 56 (London: H.M. STATIONERY OFFICE).

WYATT, S. and LANGDON, J. N., 1932, Inspection processes in industry. *Ind. Health Res. Board, Rep.* 63 (London: H.M. STATIONERY OFFICE).

WYATT, S. and LANGDON, J. N., 1937, Fatigue and boredom in repetitive work. *Ind. Health Res. Board, Rep.* 77 (London: H.M. STATIONERY OFFICE).

YNTEMA, D. B., 1963, Keeping track of several things at once. *Hum. Factors*, **5**, 7.

YODER, T. A., LUCAS, R. L. and BOTZUM, G. D., 1973, The marriage of human factors and safety in industry. *Hum. Factors*, **15**, 197.

YOUNG, L. R. and STARK, L., 1965, Biological control systems—a critical review and evaluation. *N.A.S.A., Rep.* CR–190.

ZADEH, L. A., 1973, Outline of a new approach to the analysis of complex systems and decision processes. *I.E.E.E. Trans. Syst. Man Cyb.*, **SMC-3**, 28.

ZAJONC, R. B., 1965, Social facilitation. *Science*, **149** (**3681**), 269.

ZARAKOVSKY, G. M., 1966, *Psichophisiologicheskii Analiz Trudovoi Deyatelnosti* (Moscow).

ZAVALISHINA, D. N. and PUSHKIN, V. N., 1964, On the mechanisms of operator thinking. *Voprosi Psichologii*, **10**, 87.

ZIEBOLZ, H., 1964, Predictor instrumentation for selective control. *Instrum. Control Syst.*, **37(12)**, 84.

ZINCHENKO, V. P. and MAJZEL, N. I., 1964, Analysis of the activity of the operator. *Problemi Inzhenernoi Psichologii* (Leningrad), p. 7.

ZINCHENKO, V. P. *et al.*, 1964, Analysis of the activity of the human operator. In *Inzheneriya Psichologiya* (Moscow), p. 120.

Author Index

Ablitt, J. F., 396, 405, 425
Adams, J. A., 27, 389, 390
Addison, J. L., 390
Alden, D. G., 390
Alexander, L. T., 309
Allen, P. S., 389
Altman, J. W., 390, 391
Anderson, R. C., 167
Andow, P. K., 405, 418
Andreas, B. G., 390
Andrew, A. M., 157
Angel, E. S., 156
Angyal, A., 383
Annett, J., xiii, 284, 389, 391, 396, 405, 416
Anyakora, S. N., viii, xii, **238–248,** 396, 405, 420
Appley, M. H., 389
Askren, W. B., 390
Atkinson, J. W., 389
Attneave, F., 389
Attwood, D., viii, xi, **120–134**, 396, 406, 414
Auerbach, E., 390
Ausubel, D. P., 309

Bainbridge, L., viii, x, xi, xiv, **91–104,** 135, 137, 139, **146–158,** 211, 395, 396, 401, 403, 410, 412, 413, 421
Baker, A. V., 196
Baker, C. H., 390
Baker, F. G., 157
Baker, J. D., 390
Baker, R. A., 390
Baloff, N., 179, 181
Barnes, R. M., 389
Barrow, R., 178, 181
Barth, J., 418
Bartlett, F. C., 168, 388, 389
Bartlett, M. W., 390
Bass, B. M., 391
Bates, J., 390

Bauer, R. W., 390
Beach, K. M., 284
Beishon, R. J., viii, x–xii, **25–50, 79–90, 91–104,** 135, 146, 154–157, 202, 395, 396, 398, 401, 403, 406, 410–413, 421
Bekey, G. A., xi, 30, 156, 389
Belbin, E., 285, 286
Belbin, R. M., 391
Bennett, E. M., 389
Berbert, A. G., 390
Bergius, R., 167, 168
Bernard, J. W., 396, 404
Bernotat, R. K., 390
Berry, P. C., 390
Bevis, F. W., 178, 179, 181, 183–185
Bilodeau, E. A., 389
Bilodeau, I. M., 389
Birmingham, H. P., 47, 389–391
Bisseret, A., xi, 174, 390, 392, 404
Bitticker, W. R., 396, 406
Blair, W. C., 29–30, 390
Bloom, B. S., 313
Bolton, D., 313
Bond, N. A., 389
Book, W. F., 283
Boren, L. M., 289
Botzum, G. D., 402, 405
Bourne, L. E., 289, 313, 314
Bowen, H. M., 246, 248, 417
Box, A., xi, 25, 51, 120, 143, 401, 403
Box, G. E. P., 373
Bradley, J. V., 390
Brenninkmeyer, G., 395, 397
Briggs, G. E., 286
Brigham, F. R., 397, 406
Broadbent, D. E., 388–390
Brown, C. W., 391
Bruner, J., 170
Bryan, G. L., 389
Bryan, W. L., 283
Buckner, D. N., 390
Bunch, M. E., 301

Cameron, C., 389
Campbell, D. T., 390
Carbonell, J. R., 390
Carter, R. J., 397
Cawley, D. E., 178, 181
Central Electricity Generating Board, viii, xi, xiii, **348–366,** 397, 403
Chadwick-Jones, J. K., 397
Chapanis, A., xiv, 389–391
Chebysheva, V. V., 165, 166
Chemical and Allied Products Industry Training Board, 397, 423
Chernikoff, R., 390
Cherry, E. C., 389, 392
Chestnut, H., 179
City and Guilds Institute, viii, xiii, **327–347,** 397, 414
Čížková, J., 390, 397, 403
Clark, J. A., viii, xii, xiv, **206–221,** 394, 397, 402, 404, 412
Clay, H. M., 22, 391
Cochrane, E. B., 179
Coekin, J. A., 248
Coeterier, J. F., 390
Cofer, C. N., 389
Cohen, J., 389
Coiley, P. A., 390
Cole, P. G., xiv, **279–282,** 400, 404
Colquhoun, W. P., 390, 392
Conrad, R., 287, 389, 390
Constable, C. J., 406
Cook, D. A., 289
Cook, J. O., 288
Cook, T. M., 397
Cooke, J. E., viii, x–xii, **25–50, 51–66,** 90, 125, 140, 143, 146, 156, 157, 165, 172, 202, 395, 397, 398, 406, 414
Coombs, C. H., 389
Cooper, J., 390
Corkindale, K. G., 389
Cotterman, T. E., 287
Cox, J. A., 289
Cox, R. C., 313
Craik, K. J. W., 26, 30, 157, 388, 389
Crawley, J. E., viii, xii, 247, **249–259,** 397, 404
Creamer, L. R., 389
Cristian, G., xi, 165, 175, 397, 404

Cropper, A. G., 263
Crossman, E. R. F. W., vii, viii, x–xii, **1–24, 25–50, 51–66,** 67, 120, 125, 132, 135, 140, 143, 160, 165, 178, 202, 284, 286, 389, 392–395, 397, 398, 401, 403, 406, 408, 414, 422
Cuny, X., 398, 400, 404
Cusack, B. L., 398

Dale, H. C. A., 389, 391, 392
Dallimonti, R., 217
Daniel, J., viii, xi, **159–164,** 398, 403, 404, 415
Daniels, R. W., 390
Davenport, W. W., 390
David, R. L., 389
Davies, D. G., 390, 391, 398, 405, 421
Davis, D. R., 236, 390
Deese, J., 389
Defayolle, M., 390
Degan, J. W., 389
De Greene, K. B., xiv, 389, 390
Deininger, R. L., 389, 390
Delacoudre, N., 398
Department of Labor, viii, xii, **186–195,** 398, 404
Department of Scientific and Industrial Research, 1, 8
Deransart, P., 398
Donoghue, J. A., 263
Draper, J., 389
Drury, C. G., 390
Dudley, N. A., 178
Duncan, C. P., 167, 168
Duncan, K. D., viii, xiii, xiv, **283–319,** 389, 391, 394, 396, 398, 405, 412, 413, 416, 417, 421, 423, 424
Duncker, K., 168
Dunnette, M. D., 391
Dutton, J. M., 389
Dwonczyk, M., 390

Easterby, R. S., 386, 416
Edelman, D. A., 390, 391
Edwards, Elwyn, vii, xii, xiv, 206, 217, 388, 389, 393, 394, 398, 399, 408, 424, 425

Edwards, W., 98, 173, 389, 392
Elkind, J. I., 389
Ellis, H. C., 301
Elwell, J. L., 389
Ely, J. H., 390, 391
Emery, F. E., 367–369
Engel, G. F. M., 242
Engelstad, P. H., viii, xiii, **367–385,** 399, 406, 410
Ericksen, S. C., 389, 390
Evans, S. J. W., 263

Favergé, J. M., 390
Feather, N. T., 389
Feigenbaum, E. A., 60
Feinstein, J., 264
Fiddy, E., 262
Fiedler, F. E., 317
Field, J. H., 400
Fink, C. D., 389, 391
Finniear, C., 178, 179, 181, 183, 184
Fitts, P. M., 26, 27, 246, 389–391
Flaherty, B. E., 389
Flint, A. J., 264
Florek, H., 398, 403
Fogel, L. J., xiv, 157, 171, 389, 390
Folley, J. D., 284, 288
Ford, A., 27
Ford, R. N., 391
Forgie, C. D., 389
Fox, J. G., 389
Frankmann, J. P., 390
Fraser, J. A., 391
Freedy, A., 389
Freund, L. E., 390
Fu, K. S., 389

Gagné, G. A., 389
Gagné, R. M., 79, 286, 287, 298, 389
Gaines, B. R., 389, 390
Galaktionov, A. I., 165, 175
Galanter, E., 284, 317
Gandsey, L. J., 399
Garner, K. C., 389
Garner, W. R., 389
Gärtner, K. P., 390
Garvey, W. D., 389, 390
Gateau, Y., 165, 170
van de Geer, J. P., 168

Ghiselli, E. E., 391
Gilbert, T. F., 288, 289, 298
Gilbreth, F. B., 287, 388, 389
Gilstad, D. W., 389
Glanzer, R., 389
Glaser, R., 318, 391
Glover, J. H., 178, 179
Good, I. J., 389
Goodstein, L. P., 399, 404
Gould, J. D., 263, 390
Graham, A. (1), viii, xi, 26, **105–119,** 159, 165, 172, 395, 400
Graham, A. (2), 389
Grandjean, E. P., 389
Grant, J. S., 390
Gray, M. J., xiii, 396, 405, 416
Green, A. E., 399, 405, 425
Green, D., 390
Grether, W. F., 390
Grindley, G. C., 389
Gross, R. J., 30, 98
Guest, G., 262
Guest, R. H., 369
Guilford, J. P., 168
Guion, R., 391
Guthrie, E. R., 389

Haber, R. N., 389
Halcomb, C. G., 390
Halpin, J. F., 391, 392
Hansel, C. E. M., 389
Harter, N., 283
Hartley, J., 289, 391
Haygood, R. C., 289
Helson, H., 65
Hemming, J. H., viii, x, **91–104,** 395, 396, 410, 412, 413, 421
Herbst, P. G., 369
Herrmann, T., 169
Hersh, W., 263
Herzberg, F., 391, 392
Herzog, J. H., 389, 419
Heywood, P. W., 405
Hick, W. E., 30, 389
Hickey, A. E., 390
Hickling, B. B., 399, 404
Hilgard, E. R., 389, 392
Hiscock, W. G., 67, 395, 399, 421
Hitchings, B., 178, 183, 185

Hitt, W. D., 390
Hladký, A., 159
Hoehn, A. J., 390
Holding, D. H., 308, 391
Holland, J. G., 27, 390
Hopkin, V. D., 390
Hopkins, C. O., 98, 389, 390
Hovland, C. I., 290, 389
Howard, R. A., 389
Hull, A. J., 390
Hussman, T. A., 390

Iosif, G., 399, 403
Itelson, J. B., 159, 166, 395, 399

Jacques, E., 20
Jagt, D. J., 241
Jakeš, H., 399
Jaspars, J. M. F., 168
Jensen, A., 401
Jensen, B. T., 309
Jerison, H. J., 27, 390
Jervis, M. W., 399, 404
Jex, M. R., 156
Johannsen, G., 389
John, E. R., 165, 169
Johnson, E. A., 264, 390
Johnson, K. A., 289
Johnson, P. C., 262
Jones, J. C., 178, 389
Jones, J. T., 399, 404
Jones, M. R., 390
Jones, R. E., 26, 27, 390
de Jong, J. J., viii, xii, **196–205,** 247, 393, 394, 399, 404, 415, 420
de Jong, J. R., 178, 179
Jordan, N., 236, 390
Juran, J. M., 390–392

Kadota, T., 181
Kalman, R. E., 180
Kaminski, G., 167
Kanarick, A. F., 390
Kaufman, H. M., 29–30
Kay, H., 284, 285, 389
Kay, P. C. M., 405
Keener, E. L., 399, 406
Kelley, C. R., xiv, 157, 389–391
Kellstedt, C. W., 399, 406

Kendrick, P., 400
Ketteringham, P. J. A., viii, xii, xiv, **260–282,** 400, 404, 410, 413
Kibler, A. W., 390
King, P. J., 412
King, S. D. M., 22, 284, 285, 391, 395, 400
Kirchner, J. H., 390
Kirchner, W. K., 390
Kitchin, J. B., viii, xi, 26, **105–119,** 159, 165, 172, 395, 400
Klimoski, R. J., 400, 406
Klix, F., 174
Knight, C. E., 196
Kochen, M., 60
Kogan, N., 98
Kolesnick, P. E., 390
Košinár, V., 398, 403
Köster, E. P., viii, xii, **196–205,** 394, 399, 404, 420
Kostyuk, G. S., 167
Kozielecki, J., 174
Knowles, W. B., 390
Kragt, H., viii, xi, xiv, **135–145,** 394, 400, 406, 414
Krendel, E. S., 389
Křivolahý, J., 400
Kuehn, R. L., 390

Laios, L., 397, 406
Landa, L. N., 171
Landeweerd, J. A., viii, xi, xiv, **135–145,** 394, 400, 406, 414
Langdon, J. N., 390, 391
Laurig, W., 390
Lees, F. P., vii, viii, xii–xiv, 206, 217, **238–248, 386–425**
Leplat, J., xi, 174, 390, 392, 400, 404
Levine, J. M., 389
Levy, F. K., 179, 181, 182
Lichtenstein, N., 27
Licklider, J. C. R., 389–391
Lincoln, R. S., 390
Lindenbaum, L. E., 390
Linquist, O. H., 30, 98
Lomov, B. F., 174
Loveless, N. E., 390
Lucaccini, L. F., 390
Lucas, R. L., 402, 405

Luce, R. D., 389
Lumsdaine, A. A., 288
Luxenberg, H. R., 390

Maarleveld, A., 418
McCormick, E. J., xiv
McDonald, T. A., 390
Mace, C. A., 389
McGrath, J. J., 390
McIlheran, T. A., 196
Mackenzie, R. M., 390
McKinsey, J. C. G., 389
Mackworth, J. F., 26
Mackworth, N. H., 27, 28, 388, 390
McLane, R. C., 390
McNemer, O. W., 167
McRuer, D. T., 156, 389
Maddock, P. R., 399, 404
Mager, R. F., 284, 308, 389
Majendie, A. M. A., 390
Majzel, N. I., 166
Mandell, M. M., 391
Mankin, D. A., 390
Mardon, J., 400, 404
Martin, F. W., viii, xiii, **320–326,** 400
Martin, J., 390
Masuda, K., 391, 392
Matterson, K. J., 397
Matyushkin, A. M., 165, 167
Mausner, B., 391
Mavor, A. S., 389
Mayer, R. W., 179
Mayer, S. R., 390
Maynard, H. B., 389
Mayo, G. E., 388, 391, 392
Meadow, C. T., 390
Mechner, F. M., 288, 289
Meister, D., 389, 390
Melton, A. W., 389
Meredith, R. M. W., 264
Miller, D. C., 389
Miller, E. E., 287, 288
Miller, G. A., 284, 317, 389–391
Miller, J. G., 389
Miller, R. B., 286, 318, 389–391
Mills, R. G., 390
Milton, J. L., 26, 27
Miollan, P., 172
Monty, R. A., 390

Morgenstern, O., 389
Mott, P. E., 391
Muckler, F. A., 389
Munro, H. P., viii, xiii, **320–326,** 400
Murphy, A. T., 179
Murrell, K. F. H., xiv, 388, 390, 391, 400
Mytus, L., 402

Naslin, P., 389
National Economic Development Office, 424
National Institute of Industrial Psychology, 22, 405
Naylor, J. C., 286
Neuman, J., 172
von Neumann, J., 389
Newell, A., 59–60, 98, 169, 389, 392
Nickerson, R. S., 390
North, D. W., 389
North, J. D., xi, 51, 125, 388, 389

Obermayer, R. W., 389
O'Brien, D. J., viii, xii, xiv, **260–282,** 400, 404, 410, 413
Oerlemans, T. W., 399, 404
Offer, U., 400
Orlansky, J., 390, 391
Oshanin, D. A., 174, 389, 400

Palmer, A. W., 396
Parish, C. C. M., 400, 404
Parsons, H. M., 389
Patterson, D., 405
Peters, G. A., 390
Phipps, S. H., 402, 403
Piaget, J., 169
Pickrell, E. W., 390
Plath, D. W., 390
Pogostin, S. Z., 395, 400, 415
Pontius, P. W., 400
Poole, H. H., 390
Popplewell, F., 392
Posner, M. I., 98, 172, 389
Poulton, E. C., 51, 389
Powers, G. J., 418
Pribram, K. H., 284, 317
Puffler, M., viii, xi, **159–167,** 398, 404, 415

Pulsford, H. E., xi, 401, 403
Pushkin, V. N., 165, 173, 174

Quastler, H., 389

Rabideau, G. F., 389
Raiffa, H., 389
Raoult, J. G., 389
Rapoport, A., 170, 389, 390
Rasmussen, J., viii, xii, 199, 217, **222–237**, 247, 394, 401, 404, 405, 412, 417, 418, 420, 421, 425
Regulinski, T. L., 390
Reitman, W. R., 157, 158, 174
Richardson, H. H., 179
Rice, A. K., 369
Rieck, A., 401, 403
Rigby, L. V., 390, 391
Rimoldi, H. J. A., 165, 172
Robinson, G. H., 389
Roberts, M. C., viii, xiii, **320–326**, 400
Ronan, W. W., 390
Rook, L. W., 390, 391
Root, R. T., 390
Rouanet, J., 165, 170
Rouse, W. D., 389
Rowell, J. T., 391
Rubinstein, S. L., 167
Rutenfranz, J., 390

Sackman, H., 390, 391
Sadacca, R., 390
Sadosky, T. L., 390
Saltz, E., 390
Samet, M. G., 389
Sanders, A. F., 390
Saul, E. V., 389
Savoyant, A., 401
Sayers, B., 421
Schager, A. J., 401
Schrenk, L. P., 389
Schwab, J. L., 389
Searson, H. M., 207
Šedivý, A., 160
Sell, R. G., xi, 25, 51, 120, 143, 401, 403
Senders, J. W., 29–30, 37, 43–44, 199, 389, 390

Senders, V. L., 390, 391
Senter, R. J., 289
Seymour, W. D., 22, 178, 284, 285, 287, 389, 391, 392
Shackel, B., 263, 390
Shaffer, L. H., 165, 172
Shannon, C. E., 27, 29
Shaw, J. C., 59–60, 389, 392
Shearer, J. L., 179
Shelly, M. W., 389
Sheridan, T. B., xi, 51, 125, 157, 199, 389
Sholl, H. A., 389
Shriver, E. L., 308, 389, 391
Siegel, A. I., 98, 389
Simmonds, D. C. V., 390
Simon, H. A., 59–60, 98, 389, 392
Sinaiko, H. W., 389, 390
Sinclair, I. A. C., xi, 401, 403
Singer, R., 390, 401, 403
Singleton, W. T., 285, 386, 389–392, 416
Šipoš, I., 401, 403
Skinner, B. F., 27, 288
Sleight, R. B., 390, 391
Smallwood, R. D., 157, 199, 390
Smith, L. A., 390
Smith, R. G., 284
Smith, R. H., 389
Smith, R. L., 390
Smith, W. A., 390
Snyderman, B., 391
Spaargaren, K., 399, 404
Spencer, J., viii, x, 25, 39, **67–78**, 395, 398, 401–403, 411
Sperandio, J. C., 390
Splaine, M., viii, x, **91–104**, 395, 396, 410, 412, 413, 421
Sriyananda, H., 178, 183, 184
Staats, A. W., 289
Staats, C. K., 289
Stachowiak, H., 170
Stainthorp, F. P., 207, 217
Stammers, R. B., xiii, 396, 405, 416
Stanley, J. C., 313
Starbuck, W. H., 389
Stark, L., 389
Stegemartin, C. T., 389
Stolurow, L. M., 287–288

Strauss, W. I., 402, 404
Streich, E. R., 391
Střízenec, M., viii, xi, **159–164**, **165–177**, 398, 399, 402–404, 415
Strohmeyer, C., 402, 404
Summers, L. G., 389
Suppes, P., 389
Suvorova, V. V., 165
Swain, A. D., 390, 391, 402, 405
Sweeney, J. S., 389
Swets, J. A., 390
Sydow, H., 174

van Tassel, P. A., 400
Tavast, R., 402
Taylor, D. W., 167
Taylor, F. V. (1), 47, 389–391
Taylor, F. V. (2), 287, 388, 389
Taylor, L. W., 181
Taylor, R. V., 166
Teja, A. S., 419
Thomas, E. H., 26
Thomas, R. E., 389
Thompson, R. M., 390, 391
Thorndike, R. L., 391
Thorne, W., 392
Thorsrud, E., 367
Thrall, R. M., 389
Tichomorov, O. K., 166, 174
Tickner, A. H., 390
Tilley, K. W., 389, 391
Tocher, K. D., 94, 262
Tompkins, F. C., 418
Tou, J. T., 389
Towill, D. R., viii, xii, xiv, **178–185**, 390, 402, 406
Trexler, R. C., 389, 391
Trist, E. L., 369
Trumbull, R., 389
Tuff, G. C., 402
Tune, G. S., 390
Turing, A. M., 89
Tustin, A., 388, 389

Vander Schraaf, E., 402, 404
Vartabedian, A. G., 390
Vaughan, J. A., 391
Vaughan, W. S., 389

Vince, M. A., 389, 390
Vroom, V. H., 391

Waag, W. L., 390
Wald, A., 389
Walker, C. M., 369
Wallach, M. A., 98
Ware, J. R., 390
Warrick, M. J., 390, 391
Weaver, W., 27, 29
Weinberg, G. M., 390
Weir, D. H., 389
Welbourne, D., 405
Welford, A. T., 67, 135, 172, 284, 285, 389, 395
West, B., viii, xii, xiv, **206–221**, 394, 402, 404, 412
Westcott, J. H., 389
White, C. T., 27
White, W. J., 390
Whitfield, D. C., 386, 389, 402, 403, 405, 416
Whitmore, P. G., 312
Wierenga, R. D., 389, 390
Wierwille, W. W., 389, 390
Wilde, R. W., 389
Wilkinson, R. T., 390
Williams, A. C., 98, 389, 390
Williams, P. R., 236
Williams, W. L., 312
Wilson, J., 390, 392
Wing, J. F., 27, 390
Wolf, J. J., 389
Wolfe, J. D., 390
Wolff, H. S., 248, 390, 417
Wolfle, D., 391
Woodhead, A., 255
Woods, P. M., 290
Woodson, W. E., 390
Woodward, J., 2
von Wright, J. M., 285
Wujkowski, J. W., 396, 404
Wulff, J. J., 390
Wyatt, S., 388, 390, 391

Yntema, D. B., 34, 390
Yoder, T. A., 402, 405
Young, L. R., 389

Zadeh, L. A., 389, 412
Zajonc, R. B., 309
Zarakovsky, G. M., 159
Zavalishina, D. N., 173

Zbăganu, G., xi, 165, 175, 397, 404
Ziebolz, H., 390, 392
Ziedman, K., 389
Zinchenko, V. P., 165, 166, 172

Subject Index

Abilities, 303, 409, 422
Abnormal conditions (*see also* Breakdown(s), Emergencies, Fault(s), Malfunctions, Upsets), 12, 72, 135–140, 197, 202–204, 222–237, 320, 363, 394, 404
   process operator functions, 394, 404
Absenteeism, 78
Accidents, 15, 237, 347, 401, 420
Acid purification plant, viii–ix, xiii, 283–319, 396, 398, 405, 416, 423
Action-information trees, 98–100, 103
Activity charts, 36, 38, 75, 81–82, 126, 411
Activities list, 87
Activity sampling, viii–ix, 69–75, 81–84, 87, 159–161, 175, 411
Adaptation (*see also* Flexibility), 66, 318
Adaptive control, 66
Adjustment (of controls) (*see also* Control actions), 3, 5, 11–13, 23, 37–39, 51–66, 69, 120–134, 137–144, 189–191, 225, 238, 298–299, 358, 393
Aerospace systems (*see also* Aircraft, Flight –), 203, 386, 388, 391, 413
Aesthetics, 49
Age, 22, 285
Aiding
   rate a., 48
Air defence systems, 388, 391
Air mixer, viii–ix, 135–145
Air traffic control, 390, 391, 404
Air Traffic Control Centre, West Drayton, 277
Air traffic controller, xi, 174, 286, 392
Aircraft (*see also* Aerospace systems, Flight –), 26, 47–48, 51, 125, 229, 361, 392, 401, 413, 414, 421
Airline pilots, 47–48, 146, 414, 422
Alarm(s) (*see also* A. analysis, A. monitoring), 14, 20, 188, 197–198, 203, 204–205, 208, 210, 217, 219–220, 226–229, 233–235, 237, 241–242, 266, 292, 304–308, 310, 349, 352–354, 357–358, 361, 363, 393, 405, 406, 412, 415, 417, 418
   absence of a. signal not equivalent to signal of normal conditions, 197
   absolute, 241
   acknowledgment, 292, 349
   action taken by process operator, 203–204
   anticipatory features, 198
   audible, 20, 349
   design, 242, 418
   deviation, 241
   diagnosis (*see* A. analysis)
   digital printout, 210, 217, 219–220, 228, 361
   display, 227–229, 349, 417
   excessive number of, 406, 418
   false, 242, 363
   fascia, 349
   hooters, 20

   instrument, 241–242
   interpretation by process operator, 304, 310, 405
   lamps, 20, 363
   for multiple faults, 363
   new as., 363
   on nuclear reactors, 226–229, 233–235, 349, 352–354, 357–358, 363, 405, 418
   philosophy of a. systems, 205, 405, 418
   rate-of-change as., 241
   relative (*see* deviation)
   reliability, 198
   research into, lack of, 418
   scanning (*see* A. monitoring)
   during sequential operations, startup and shutdown, 226, 357, 363
   setpoint (*see* deviation)
   specific fault, failure to indicate, 304, 310
   statuses, confusion with, 363, 418
   trip as., 352–354, 357–358
   uncertainty, 197–198
Alarm analysis, xii, 226–230, 235, 248, 304–308, 310, 405, 415, 417, 418, 421
   displays, 417
   human factors in, 229–230, 405, 418, 421
      process operator's confidence, 229–230, 418
   on nuclear reactors, 226–230, 235, 405, 418
   philosophy of, 229–230, 405, 418
   by process computer, xii, 226–230, 235, 248, 405, 415, 418
   by process operator, 304–308, 310, 405
   on refinery process, 418
   work involved in, 405, 418
Alarm monitoring (*see also* M., Signal(s), Vigilance), xii, 188–192, 197–198, 225–230, 241–242, 393, 399
   by process computer, 188–192, 197–198, 226–230, 241–242
   by process operator, xii, 188–192, 197–198, 225–230, 399
   by special-purpose equipment, 226–227
Alerts, 425
Alertness (*see also* Arousal, Attention, Vigilance), 107, 108, 110, 425
   artificial signals, 425
ALGOL, 309
Algorithms (*see also* Decision trees), xiii, 158, 171, 176, 419
Alienation, 367
Allocation of function, viii–ix, xii, 135, 147, 196–197, 200–202, 205, 222–237, 246–247, 249–259, 260, 359–360, 365, 386–387, 391, 394, 397, 404, 407, 415, 418, 424
   abilities and limitations of human operator, 135, 196–197, 236, 359, 365
   in basic oxygen converter control, viii–ix, 249–259, 397, 404
   in emergencies, 359–360

in fault correction, 230–232
in fault detection, 225–226, 418
in fault diagnosis, 225–230, 418
human primacy, 391
in malfunction detection, viii–ix, 246–247
in man-computer systems, 391
motivation, xii, 200–202, 205
in nuclear reactor control, viii–ix, 222–237, 359–360
in process computer control, viii–ix, xii, 147, 222–237, 246–247, 249–259, 260, 397, 407, 418
process conditions, effect of, 197, 224–232, 359, 394
Alphanumeric symbols, 233–237
American Institute for Research, Pittsburg work on human factors, 391
Analogue control (*see* Conventional c.)
Animal behaviour, 27
'Anticipatory constraint control', 198
Anxiety, 16
Apollo system, 246
Arousal (*see also* Alertness, Attention, Vigilance), 104, 257, 398
Artificial intelligence (*see also* Cybernetics and types of A.i.), 59–60, 64–65, 91, 388, 392, 419, 421
Artificiality
of centralized remote control, 2, 15–16
of process control, 67, 145, 167, 393
Assembly work (*see also* Production lines), 2–3, 178, 181, 388
Association (in thinking), 104
Attention (*see also* Alertness, Arousal, Vigilance)
sharing, 26, 31, 39, 45, 50, 150, 201, 286, 409
Audition (*see also* Sensation), 49, 197, 223
Automated production, 1–24, 159–164
classification (Crossman), 2
centralized remote control (*q.v.*)
continuous-flow production (*q.v.*)
program machines (*q.v.*)
Automatic control, 3, 11–14
Automatic operation, 3
Automatic plant
classification (Crossman), 4
control, 4
process, 4
product, 4
size, 4
Automatic shutdown, startup (*see* Shutdown, Startup)
Automation, vii, x–xiii, 1–24, 51, 67, 79, 91, 106, 118, 125, 135, 146, 159–164, 186–195, 196, 206, 221, 222, 238, 246, 249–259, 260, 359, 368, 391, 393, 395, 397–398, 404, 419, 421, 424
effect of, vii, x–xiii, 1–24, 159–164, 186–195, 206–221, 249–259, 393, 395, 397–398
increase in monitoring, 3, 13, 424
levels of, 2–4, 159–164, 393
mental skills in, 1, 3, 7, 16, 67, 79, 91, 106, 118, 135, 146
problems in rapid a., 260

Autonomy, 367–369, 373–376, 379, 382–383
and process variability, 373, 383
Availability (*see also* Downtime, Reliability), xiii, 377, 381, 408

Backup (*see* Standby)
Baking ovens, viii–x, 79–90, 154, 395–396
Basic oxygen converters, viii–ix, xii, 249–259, 393, 397, 404
Behavioural analysis, 286, 288–290
responses, 288–290
shaping, 288
Body
anxiety symptoms, 16
Boredom, 19–20, 257, 311–312, 388, 407, 422, 424
B.P. Chemicals Ltd.
acid purification plant, 296, 305
B.P. Ltd.
Llandarcy refinery, 78
Breakdown(s) (*see also* Fault(s), Malfunctions), 3, 4, 6, 7, 10, 18, 22, 23, 45, 135, 137, 139–140, 162–164, 166, 198, 203, 217, 230, 271, 359, 373, 379, 420
avoidance, 3, 6, 7, 10, 198, 420
effects, 135, 139–140, 163, 373
partial, 164
recovery, 7, 135, 139–140, 163–164, 203, 217, 230
repair, 4, 6, 7, 18, 23, 379
'Breakdown', 135, 137, 139–140
Brick workers, 393
British Iron and Steel Research Association (B.I.S.R.A.), 50, 104, 158, 404
basic oxygen converter control system design, 249
soaking pit scheduling simulation, 260
British Steel Corporation (B.S.C.), 259, 261, 268
Normanby Park works, 255
Port Talbot works, 257
Samuel Fox and Co. Ltd., 104
United Steel Co. Ltd., 104, 158

Cakes, 79–90
Calculations
for management, 189–192
by process computer, 189–192
by process operator, 42, 108, 110, 189–192, 343–344, 355, 358
Calibration
of controls, 47, 48, 58, 64, 122–123, 215
Car drivers, 17, 146
Categorization, 42, 65, 89, 170, 403, 409
Cathode ray tubes (c.r.ts.) (*see also* Display(s), Process computer graphics), xiii, 103, 228, 231, 232–237, 255, 263–273, 279–282, 361–362, 416
touchwire, xiii, 255, 263–273, 279–282
and typewriters, 228, 232–233
Central Electricity Generating Board (C.E.G.B.)
National Grid, xi, 14, 401–403
Trawsfynydd nuclear power station, viii–ix, xi, xiii, 348–366, 397, 403

Subject Index

Centralization of control, 11, 14, 231–232, 348, 359–360
   process computer as tool for, 232
Centralized remote control, 2, 14–16, 21, 160, 165–166, 175–176
   artificiality, 2, 15–16
Change
   resistance to, 371, 379
Change in system, 203, 231–232, 247
Changeover (*see also* Sequential control, Switchover), 7, 197, 231
Chargehand, 14
Check reading, 228
Checking round, 7, 12, 14, 16, 68, 139, 198, 204, 393
Chemical analysis, 188, 337–338
Chemical and Allied Products Industry Training Board, 319, 397, 423
   Information Papers, 397, 423
Chess-playing, 174, 419
Christiana Spigerverk, Oslo
   wire-drawing plant, 367
Cine photography, 287, 411
City and Guilds Institute
   Chemical Technician certificate, viii–ix, xiii, 327–347, 397, 414
     basic science, 329–334
     chemical calculations, 343–344
     chemical industry, 346–347
     chemical plant, 334, 338–339, 342
     chemical techniques, 334–338
     control, 340–341
     environment protection, 340
     instrumentation, 333–334, 340–341, 344–346
     laboratory practice, 329–334
     safety, 327–328, 334
     supervisory studies, 346–347
     unit operations, 334, 338–339, 342
Clerks, 187
'Clock test', 28
Closed-loop control, 13, 51–66, 120–122, 143–144, 155, 213, 215, 393, 406
   computer simulation, 59–63
   use by experienced operator for fine adjustment, 58, 64
   use by inexperienced operator, 62, 143–144, 155
Coal mines, 369
Coding, 49, 228–229, 231, 298, 356, 360–361
Colour, 69, 81, 109, 385
Colour blindness, 423
Communications (*see also* Data insertion, types of C. device), 6–7, 9–10, 15, 19, 21, 23, 68, 137, 163, 176, 191, 194, 222–237, 255, 347, 348–349, 355, 358, 360, 377–378, 382–383, 394, 407, 409, 411.
   in Hunsfos experiment, 378, 382–383
   noise, 19, 360
   by process computer, 191, 194
   between process operators, 6–7, 10, 21, 163, 349, 360, 382
   between process operator and computer, 224, 232–233, 236, 255
   between process operator and laboratory, 9–10, 21, 382
   between process operator and maintenance personnel, 10, 15, 21, 304
   between process operator and management, 6–7 9–10, 21, 68, 145, 348–349, 355, 382
   rate, 68, 382
Communications centre, 379
Communication theory (*see also* Information t.), 34
Complexity in system, 171, 172, 176, 198, 203, 204, 222, 232
Computer (*see also* Process c.), 2, 14, 21, 160, 232–233, 344, 386, 390–392
Computer programmers, 170, 194
Computer-aided design, 229
Computerization, 246–247, 391
Confidence, 155, 170, 172, 228–230, 262, 407, 421
Conscientiousness, 16, 20–21, 311, 422
Consistency, 409
Consoles (*see* Operator's control panels)
Constraints (*see* Process cs.)
'Constraint value', 198–201
Continuous-flow production, 2–4, 23, 25, 160, 175, 393
Continuous work (*see also* Rest pauses), 2–4
Control (*see also* types of C.), 223
   of basis weight, 9–11, 34–39, 51, 120–126, 189
   closed-loop c. (*q.v.*)
   of composition, 5–6, 9–11, 70–75, 189–191, 194, 210–219, 249–259
   of dead-time processes, 124–134
   of flow, 5, 10–12, 70–75, 122–123, 189–191, 202–203, 339–341, 360–362
   of level, 10–11, 341, 361
   open-loop c.(*q.v.*)
   of pressure, 10–11, 109, 162, 189–191, 339, 341
   of product quality (*q.v.*)
   sampled-data, 12, 34–39, 70–75, 122, 125–127, 378
   of temperature, 11–12, 39–44, 53–64, 80–81, 109, 127–134, 140–144, 162, 189–191, 249–259, 299, 316, 339, 341, 357–359.
Control(s), 5, 10, 12, 14, 48, 76, 123, 132–133, 164, 207, 211, 215, 224, 228, 229, 231–233, 255, 263–273, 279–282, 299, 316, 349, 351–358, 360–363, 388, 390–391, 417, 419
   ambiguity, 363
   calibration (*q.v.*)
   coding, 231
   consistency, 356, 360, 362–363
   c.–c. location, 358, 360
   dedicated vs. general-purpose, 231–232, 360–361
   design, 388
   for displays, 48
   display–c. location, 123, 357–358, 360, 363
   display–c. relations, 211, 299, 316, 362, 390–391

gain (*see* calibration, sensitivity)
keyboards, 232–233, 237
knobs, 231–233
layout, 224, 231–232
light pens, 229, 232–235, 237, 417
local, 12, 123, 164, 348–349
on nuclear reactor, 349, 351
number of, 14, 231
pistol-grip switches, 363
pushbuttons, 162, 175, 233, 291, 355, 357, 362, 417
rolling balls, 417
rotary cs., 233
rotary switches, 207
sensitivity, 362
stiffness, 362, 419
strategies, effect on, 215
switches, 14, 231, 355
toggle switches, 207
touchwires, xiii, 255, 263–273, 279–282
typewriters, 132–133, 224, 232–233
unofficial cs., 5, 76
Control actions (*see also* Adjustment), xi, 5, 36, 38, 53–64, 70–75, 96, 127–134, 140–144, 146, 150–156, 161, 211–217, 411–412
frequency, 36, 38, 54, 59, 61–63, 70–75, 96, 127–134, 143–144, 146, 161, 212–213
intermittency, 150
restrictions on, 128
size, 36, 38, 54, 59, 61–63, 70–75, 96, 127–134, 143–144, 156, 212–213
switching between auto and manual, 298
Control algorithm, 57–62
Control desk, 348–351, 363–365
chair, 364
dimensions, 363–364
layout, 350–351, 363–365
Control engineer, 188, 239, 406
Control engineering, 19, 413
Control loop(s) (*see also* aspects and types of C.l.)
number of, 5, 10
Control objectives (*see also* Performance criteria, System os.)
in baking ovens, 81
in basic oxygen converters, 250, 253
in electric arc furnaces, 92
in papermill, 121–122, 373–374, 377, 383
in pilot plant, 210–211
priorities between, 92, 253, 374, 383
short- and long-term os., 253, 261
in soaking pits, 261
Control panels (*see* Ps.)
Control room (*see also* Workplace layout), xi, 14–16, 348–366, 403, 406
cost, 406
layout, 350–351
railway, 14–15
size, 350, 360, 406
window, 350, 364–365
Control room studies, viii–ix, xi, xiii, 348–366, 396–398, 401–403

Central Electricity Generating Board (C.E.G.B.), viii–ix, xi, xiii, 348–366, 397, 401–403
hot strip mill, xi, 398, 401, 403
National Grid, xi, 401–403
nuclear reactor, viii–ix, xi, xiii, 348–366, 397, 403
waste heat boiler, xi, 396, 401, 403
Control system characteristics
differences between systems nominally at same stage of evolution, 393
historical development (Lees), 393
analogue c., 11–14, 393
computer c., 393
manual c., 2–9, 393
information display, importance of, 393
measurement, importance of, 393
process operator, effect on, xii, 393, 399
special-purpose equipment, importance of, 393
Control system design, 45–49, 348, 376–378, 415
Control system designer, 45–46, 223, 227, 310, 406
Control task, x–xiii, 1–24, 197, 224, 392–394, 404
Control technician, 19, 23
Control theory, 19, 98
Control valves (*see also* Hand vs.), 11, 211, 223, 238–239, 241, 242, 244–246, 341, 360, 362, 417
display of position, 417
malfunction detection in, 238–239, 241, 244–246
Controllability, 8–9, 51, 53, 65, 67, 126, 132–133, 146, 160, 164, 172–173, 215, 378
definition, 126
manual control difficulties (Crossman), 8–9, 51, 132–133, 160
display location, 9, 132
information feedback, delays and imperfections in, 9, 51, 65, 133, 160, 164, 172–173, 378
interaction of variables, 8, 132, 146, 160, 164, 166, 172–173, 215
lags in process, 8, 9, 51, 53, 132, 146, 160, 164
measurements, lack of, 9, 132, 160, 166
visualization of process, 9, 133, 160, 164
process computer control, effect of, 189–194
Controller(s), 11–13, 19, 59–65, 66, 189–191, 194, 207–209, 223, 225, 242, 245–246, 294, 297–298, 339, 341, 393
analogue three-term, 11, 66, 207–209, 223, 242, 245–246, 294, 297–298, 393
discrete predicting, 157
Conventional control, 11–14, 159–165, 186–195, 393
Coordination
of groups, 3, 6, 11, 164, 166, 172, 178, 374, 379
Correction threshold, 73–74

Subject Index

Costs
   of human factors defects (Lees), 407
      capital equipment, 24, 407
      maintenance, 407
      operation, 6, 13–14, 51, 232, 407, 408
      operator morale, 407
      serious incidents, 51, 232, 304, 407, 408
   of human factors design studies, 260–261, 318
Cost-benefit analysis, 371
Crew size (*see* Manning)
C.r.t. (*see* Cathode ray tube)
Cues, 16, 18, 170, 296, 298
   fault diagnosis, 18
   identification of hand valves, 296
   location of instruments, 298
Cybernetics (*see also* Artificial intelligence), 165, 169–171, 177

Danish Atomic Energy Commission Research Establishment, Risö, 222
   work on process operator, 236
Data
   accuracy, importance of, 262
Data insertion, 132, 189, 191, 231–232, 276, 420
Data logging (*see also* Process log), 5–6, 12, 14, 15, 23, 68, 139, 187, 189–191, 210–211, 217, 227, 231–234, 291–292, 355, 393–394
   of faults, 233–234
   by process computer, 189–191, 210–211, 233–234
      effect of types of computer log on process operator's control behaviour, 217
   by process operator, 5–6, 12, 14, 15, 23, 68, 139, 187, 189–191, 291–292, 355, 394
   by special-purpose equipment, 190, 227, 393
Data processing and handling
   by process computer, 222–223, 226, 231, 235, 262
   by process operator, 394
Dead time (*see* Process lags)
Death, 15–16, 201
Decision-making (*see also* types of D.), vii–xi, xiii, 8, 15–16, 23, 83–90, 91–104, 114–119, 146–158, 163–164, 165–177, 223–232, 260–282, 286, 368, 382, 388–392, 395–397, 403–404, 409, 411–412, 415, 419, 421
   in baking ovens control, viii–ix, 83–90
   in chemical plant control, viii–ix, xi, 8, 114–119, 163–164, 395
   conflict resolution, 87, 168, 173, 174, 398
   decision theory, 173, 392
   in electric arc furnace scheduling, viii–ix, 91–104, 146–158, 396
   in fault administration, 230
   formulation of rules, 171
   man–computer interactive, 260–282, 390–391
   in railway power supply control, 15–16
   in soaking pit scheduling, viii–ix, xiii, 260–282
'Decision program', 64–65
   hill-climbing, 64–65
Decision trees (*see also* Algorithms), 300–308, 311–312
Defence systems (*see* Military ss.)
Department of Labor
   Outlook for Computer Process Control, viii–ix, xii, 186–195, 398, 404
Department of Scientific and Industrial Research (D.S.I.R.), 1, 78
   Human Sciences Committee, 50, 66
Depression, 423
Diagnosis (*see also* Decision-making, Fault d., Malfunction detection), 18, 23, 171, 175, 217, 226–230, 247, 286, 295, 298, 300–308, 312, 316–317, 389, 394, 399, 415, 418, 420
Dials (*see also* Display(s), Indicators, Meters), 5, 6, 7, 10, 29, 93–94, 137, 189, 191, 351, 361–362, 386
Direct digital control (d.d.c.), 207, 211
Displacement (*see also* Redundancy), 186–187
Display(s) (*see also* types of D.), 5, 10, 14–15, 16, 25–26, 31, 43–44, 45–49, 90, 93–94, 103–104, 123–124, 125, 128–131, 137, 161–164, 166, 175, 197, 204, 207–211, 217, 219–221, 224–237, 239–241, 247–248, 257–258, 260–282, 298, 299, 305, 316, 348–363, 365, 388, 390–392, 395, 396, 404–406, 412, 416–419
   accuracy, 25, 361
   aesthetics, 49
   of aircraft position, 47–48
   of alarms, 417
   for alarm analysis, 417
   alphanumeric, 228, 230
   analogue, 225, 228, 234–237, 262, 264–265, 356
   of basic oxygen converters, 257–258
   coding, 49, 228–229, 298, 356, 360–361
   command, 417
   computer-driven, 221, 224, 228–230, 232–237, 248, 257–258, 262–268, 361, 416–417
   context of information, 229, 361, 417
   of control loop parameters, 417
   of control rod position, 350–351, 355–356
   of control valve position, 123–124, 248, 417
   and decision-making, 260–282
   on demand (*see also* Observing response), 93–94, 210, 219, 262–268, 360–361
   design, 25–26, 45–49, 219–221, 224–237, 360–363, 388, 416–417
   differentiation, lack of, 49, 163
   digital, 93–94, 207, 209, 210, 219, 225, 228–229, 233–234, 248, 361
   d.–control location, 123, 357, 358, 363
   d.–control relations, 211, 299, 316, 362, 390–391
   d.–d. location, 298
   effort to access information, 31, 48, 232, 416–417

of electric arc furnaces,
    optional ds., 93–94
    permanent ds., 93–94
    teleprinter, 93–94
electronic data d. (E.D.D.), 264–270, 279–282
of engine gimbal, 248
for fault administration, 217, 417
of feedback on control actions, 231, 362
flight director, 47–48
flow diagram, 417
for game-playing, 280–282, 417
head-up, 361
hierarchical structure, 229, 262–268, 361, 365, 417
histograms, 417
identification of, 48–49, 229, 298, 360–361
illumination, effect of, 163, 364–365
' important ' ds., 137
of indirect measurements, 417
lamps (*q.v.*)
layout, 103, 137, 225, 226, 231
light tableau, 231
for malfunction detection, 239–241, 247–248, 405, 417
man–computer interactive, 262–282, 404, 417
for manual control (*see* Manual control)
means to an end, 416
of measurements (*see also* analogue, digital), 417
memorability, 48–49
mimic diagram, 14–15, 90, 93, 229, 305, 362, 417
of nuclear reactor, 233–237, 348–351, 353–357, 360–363
    count rate, 353–357
    doubling time, 353–357
    log power, 353–357
number of, 5, 10, 231, 298, 360, 406
obsolete and superfluous ds., 25, 104, 163, 217, 264, 360
and operating procedures, 103
' optimal ' ds., 103, 137
for pattern recognition, 47, 226–229, 240–241, 247–248, 416–417
phase-plane, 248
pictorial, 228–229, 358, 361
of pilot plant, 207–211
polar plot, 248, 417
power spectrum, 248
predictive, 94, 125, 230, 257–258, 262–282, 392, 404, 417
and process operator mental models, 104, 164, 166, 175
profile, 356, 358, 361
programming of, 418
quality control charts, 417
quickened, 47, 419
quickscan, 207, 226
rate-of-change ds., 49, 299, 357, 361
recorders (*q.v.*)
of reduced data, 224–237, 417
resolution (*see* scales)
restriction of, 43–44, 215, 219

scales, 49, 359, 362
for scheduling, 260–268, 417
for security control, 417
for sequential control, 231, 417
of soaking pits, 260–268
of statistical parameters, 417
of statuses, 236, 417
status array, 217, 404–405, 417
strategies, effect on, 217, 418
of submarine depth, 125
' surface plot ', 417
survey ds. (*see* system state)
symbolic, 16, 229
of system state, 207, 209, 217, 226–229, 231–237, 262–268, 298, 359, 404–405, 416–417
traditional control room, 161–164, 207, 209, 305, 351
trend (*see* Recorder(s), Trend records)
use by process operator, 104, 217, 224–229, 231–237, 239–241, 247–248, 360–363, 395, 404–405, 412, 416–417
of ' useful ' information, 104
Disruption, 408
Disturbances (*see* Process ds.)
Documentation (*see* Operating instructions)
Downtime (*see also* Availability, Reliability), 7, 51, 377, 407
Drills (*see* Emergency ds., Operating procedures)
Drivers (*see* Car ds.)
Driving (*see also* Vehicle guidance), 17, 146
Dunlap and Associates, Santa Monica
    work on human factors, 391

Ear (*see* Sensation)
Economics, 6, 13–14, 18, 24, 51, 67, 95, 197, 223, 232, 251, 254, 259, 260–261, 273–276, 291, 304, 318, 346, 370, 381, 407, 408, 410
Education, xiii, 7, 310, 312–314, 319, 347, 368, 397, 414, 422
Electric arc furnaces, viii–xi, 91–104, 146–158, 395, 396, 410, 412, 413, 421
Electrical/electronics technician, 17, 188
Electro-mechanical craftsman, 18, 23
Electronics troubleshooting, 247, 286, 312
Emergencies (*see also* Abnormal conditions, Breakdown(s), Fault(s), Malfunctions, Upsets), 3, 6, 14, 15, 111, 140, 145, 186, 190, 192, 194, 197–198, 226, 227, 291, 298, 304–308, 311, 320, 326, 359, 390–391, 405, 407, 409, 410, 413, 415, 420–421, 423
in aircraft, 421
allocation of function, 359
avoidance, 197–198, 409, 415, 420
decision-making, 420–421
fault administration, 298, 304
human error, 391, 405, 420–421
information overload, 405, 420
sequential control and shutdown, 298
simulation of, 304–305
stress, 304, 420
strategy formulation, 304–308

time available in, 111, 226, 298, 304, 420–421
time required in, 421
training for, 140, 145, 227, 304–308, 407, 423
Emergency drills, 230, 301, 327, 425
Employment
process computer control, effect of, 186–195, 404
Engineer(s) (*see also* types of E.), vii, xiii, 6, 15, 21, 23, 179, 348, 386, 405, 413
Environment (*see* Physical e., Organizational factors, Social factors)
Equipment design (*see also* Interface d.), 24, 25, 52, 310, 314, 319, 386–387.
Ergonomics (*see also* Human factors), 120–125, 348, 386, 388
Ergonomist, vii, 103, 386, 388
Error(s) (*see* Human e(s). Man–machine system reliability)
Evolutionary operation, 77, 373
Eye (*see also* Sensation)
camera, 411
fixation, 26–27, 29
movement, 27–29
Executive Routine, 84–88, 157, 403
Experience, 1, 8, 16, 23, 34, 58, 77–78, 84–88, 91, 95–97, 100–101, 104, 121, 145, 147–157, 164, 167, 178, 202, 206, 215, 220, 225, 227, 273–274, 305, 310, 317, 411, 421
characteristics of
efficient executive routine, 153–156
efficient information sampling, 104, 154–155
efficient strategies, 154–156, 215, 273–274
open-loop control, 58, 154–155
realistic objectives, 96
stored subroutines, 84–88, 100–101, 148–152, 155–156
inadequacy of, 91, 202, 227, 317
Experimentation
by process computer, 64–65
by process operator, 128, 217, 219–221, 225

Fatigue, 105, 107, 388–389
Fault(s) (*see also* Breakdown(s), Malfunctions), 12, 14, 135, 200, 203, 211, 225–230, 232, 233, 242–244, 267, 271, 292, 302, 304–308, 360, 361, 365, 414
Fault administration, viii–ix, xii, 111, 139–140, 186, 202–204, 217, 223, 225–230, 234, 298–308, 359, 394, 397, 404, 409, 410, 415, 417, 420–421
in acid purification plant, viii–ix, 298–308
displays for, 217, 225–230, 417
in nuclear reactor, viii–ix, 225–230, 359
philosophy of, 202–203, 225–230
in pilot plant, viii–ix, 217, 404
in refinery, viii–ix, 202–204
time available for, 111, 226, 298, 304, 420–421
Fault correction, viii–ix, xii, 15, 202–204, 223, 225, 230, 394, 409, 414, 415, 420

by process computer, 203, 230
in refinery, viii–ix, 202–204
Fault detection (*see also* Alarm monitoring, Malfunction d., Monitoring), viii–ix, 12, 223, 225–226, 238–248, 394, 409, 415, 420
by process computer, 226, 241–242
Fault diagnosis (*see also* Alarm analysis, D.), viii–ix, 223, 225–230, 247, 298–308, 311–312, 316–318, 340, 346, 391–392, 394, 399, 409, 412, 414, 415, 418, 420
in acid purification plant, viii–ix, 298–308
by process computer (*see* Alarm analysis)
Fault location, 12, 228, 295, 299–304, 308, 311–312, 316–318
'Feedback constraint control', 198
Feedback control (*see* Closed-loop c.)
Feedforward control, 130, 341
Flexibility (*see also* Adaptation), 2, 8, 66, 84–90, 98–104, 150–158, 196, 202, 221, 235, 247, 274–275, 284, 300–305, 311–312, 318, 360, 365, 374–376, 379, 381–384
in fault administration, 360, 365
in manual control, 66
and rules-of-thumb, 8, 202
in scheduling, 84–90, 98–104, 150–158, 274–275
training for, 300–305, 311–312, 379, 384
Flight director, 47–48
Flight emergencies, 421
Flying (*see also* Vehicle guidance), 26
Forcing functions, 51

Gain (*see* Calibration)
Games, 172–174, 419
chess, 174, 419
Hanoi tower, 172
Game theory, 172–173
Game-playing, xiii, 79, 258, 262–268, 275, 404, 417
displays for, 262–268, 417
in soaking pit scheduling, xiii, 262–268, 275, 404
Gas production and distribution, 392–393, 403
Gas workers, 392–393
Gauges (*see* Dials)
Gemini system, 247
Goal(s) (*see also* Control objectives, System objectives), 5, 7, 64–65, 85, 90, 96, 120, 122, 173, 201–202, 285, 315, 319, 367, 374, 376–377, 379, 383, 394, 408
changes in, 383
formulation, 394
priorities, 173, 202, 376–377
subgoals, 64–65, 120, 408
of subjects in simulation experiments, 96
uncertainty about, 122, 374, 383
Graphs, 47, 343, 355–356, 358
Graphics (*see* Process computer gs.)
'Green operating zone', 198–199
Group behaviour (*see also* Coordination, Motivation, Organizational factors, Shift(s), Social factors, Team(s)). 3, 140, 309, 369, 379–384

in fault administration, 140
in problem-solving, 379–384
training of gs., 309
GSP II, 92
Guns, 51, 125, 388

Hand valves, 34–36, 68, 120–124, 126, 223, 294–298, 308, 310, 314–316, 352–354
   on acid purification plant, 294–298, 308, 310, 314–316
   backlash, 122–123
   by-pass vs., 294, 296–297
   identification, 295–298, 308, 310, 314
      context, 295–297
      labelling, 297–298, 310
   for infrequent but critical duties, 223
   isolating vs., 296–297, 352–354
   on papermachine, 34–36, 120–123, 126
Hard copy, 233–234
Hardware, 223–224, 232–233, 387
Hearing, 5, 8, 222
Heuristics, 64–66, 98, 137, 140, 169, 174, 409
'Heuristic controller', 64–65
High Integrity Protective Systems (H.I.P.Ss.), 238
High reliability systems, 237, 248
Honesty, 21
Human component (*see also* H. operator, H. performance, Process operator), 51, 135, 196–197, 205, 236, 359, 365, 388–392
Human error(s) (*see also* Man–machine system reliability), 15–16, 20, 22, 31, 34, 53–56, 132, 141–143, 170, 190, 210, 214–216, 217, 219, 227, 232, 264, 276, 285, 289–290, 297–298, 310, 313–314, 356, 360–362, 390–391, 396, 399, 405, 407, 423, 425
   effects of, 15–16, 22, 31, 219, 227, 232, 297–298, 405
   e. scores, 53–56, 141–143, 210, 214–216, 313–314
   in identifying hand valves, 297–298
   and information display, 276, 362, 405
   in inserting information, 132, 276
   in manipulating controls, 264, 356
   in reading displays, 217, 219, 360, 405
   reduction by process computer, 190, 232
   reduction by training, 285, 310, 423
Human factors (*see also* Ergonomics), xiii–xiv, 120–124, 196–197, 310, 386–387, 388–391, 396–398, 404, 407–410, 423, 425
   bibliographies, xiv, 388–391
   in system design, 120–124, 196–197, 310, 386–387, 425
   texts
      general, xiv
      process control, xiv
Human operator (*see also* H. component, Process o.)
   research on, 388–392
Human performance (*see also* H. component, aspects of P.)

   capabilities and limitations of man and machine, 135, 196–197, 236, 359, 365
   laboratory vs. field studies, 178
   long-term trends, 178, 215, 220–221
   variability
      between individuals, 178
      within an individual, 178
Human sciences, 124, 386–392
Human transfer function, xi, 30, 51, 57–58, 125, 156
   inadequacy of t.f. model, 51, 57–58, 125
   sampled-data model, 30
Hunsfos papermill, 367–385
Hunting (of control loop), 53–54, 61–63, 125–131, 142–144

Illumination
   glare, 163, 364–365
Imperial Chemical Industries (I.C.I.) Ltd.
   Alkali Division, 119
   Central Work Study Department, 105
   Plastics Division, 105
Incentives, 6, 17, 22–23, 106, 374, 379–381
   multi-factor i. scheme, 22
   production bonus, 22, 374
   quality bonus, 374, 380–381
Incidents, 12, 227, 237, 420–421
Indecision, 155, 421
Indicators (*see also* Dials, Display(s), Meters), 6, 10, 12, 14, 224–225, 298, 351, 355, 358, 360–362
Indirect measurements, 103, 417
Individual differences, 7, 18, 67, 70–78, 95–97, 103, 121, 135, 155–156, 174, 178, 180, 219, 220, 225, 273–276, 303
   diagnostic tasks, 18, 303
   experience, 95–97, 121, 155–156
   information display, 103
   plant managers, 180
Industrial Democracy Project, 367
Industrial dynamics, 368–369
Industrial Fatigue (later Health) Research Board (I.F.R.B., I.H.R.B.)
   work on industrial workers, 388
Industrial problems, 1–4, 388, 392, 395, 406–410, 425
Inferred variables(*see* Indirect measurements)
Information
   acquisition, xi, 232, 416–417
   coding, 228–229
   definition, 27
   delays, 8–9, 51, 65, 69, 132–133, 160, 164, 172, 378
   entropy, 27–28, 31
   flow, 6, 10, 46, 251, 262–263, 382
   informal, 12, 252, 256, 257, 263
   peripheral, 27, 196, 257
   redundancy, 217, 239, 416
   stored, 139, 140
Information centre, 379
Information display (*see also* D(s).), viii–ix, 25–50, 145, 163–164, 172, 222–237, 393, 397, 399, 404, 406, 415, 416–418
Information load, 47, 405, 406, 418, 420

Information processing (*see also* types of I.p.), x, 1, 16, 26, 79, 91, 146, 150–152, 166, 174–175, 198, 228, 308, 389, 392, 403
  man able to accept error in i., 174
  man as single-channel component, 26, 150–152, 308
  rate dependent on format, 228
Information reduction, 172, 235, 393, 417
  by process computer, 235
  by special-purpose equipment, 393
Information requirements, 197–198, 217, 222–237, 259, 263, 348–349, 353–359
  for abnormal conditions, 197–198, 217, 225–234, 348
  for normal conditions, 197–198, 224–225
Information sampling (*see also* Monitoring, Signal(s), Vigilance), viii–x, xii, 25–50, 55–56, 104, 121, 150–153, 170, 198–202, 215, 219, 225, 228, 389, 395, 397–399, 409, 411
  accuracy required, 25, 33–34, 44, 225, 228
  aids, 47, 49
  attention-sharing, 26–27, 45, 150–152
  in change of operating point, 36–39, 41–45, 55–56, 121
  and control actions, 32–33, 36–39, 41–45, 47, 55–56, 121
  cost, 31, 41–44, 46, 48, 50
  design for optimum i.s., 25–27, 45–49
  disturbance characteristics, 29–30, 37, 39, 44–46, 48
  duration, 27, 29
  experience, effect of, 31–32, 34
  frequency, 25–34, 36–39, 41–47, 50, 198–202
  factors affecting, 44–47, 50, 198–202
  i. gain, 25, 27–28, 45, 170
  i. rate, 27–30
  interactions, 48, 198
  mental models, 29, 41, 44, 48, 104, 152–153
  memory, 34, 44, 46, 48–49, 50
  motivation, 27–29, 45–46, 200–202
  in papermachine control, viii–ix, 34–39
  penalties of inadequate i.s., 30–31, 44–45, 48, 200
  peripheral i., 27, 196, 257
  'phenomenal limit curve' (*q.v.*)
  prediction, 31, 34, 44–50, 104, 152–153, 198–201
  process characteristics, 31–32, 39, 41, 44–45
  process lags, 31–32, 39, 44
  restricted s., 43–44, 215, 219
  S. theorem (*q.v.*)
  in search tasks, 26–29
  Senders' experiments, 29–30, 37, 43–44
  signal (*q.v.*)
  in state evaluation, 31, 36–39, 46, 50, 104, 152–153, 198–201
  strategies, 27–29, 45
  time estimation, 49–50
  timers, 49
  tolerance limits, 29, 33–34, 36–37, 44–45, 46, 48, 49, 198–201
  in tracking, 30, 43, 48, 55–56, 121
  uncertainty, 30–34, 39, 41–45, 50, 197–201
    growth of, 30–34, 44–45, 199
  in water bath experiment, viii–x, 39–44, 55–56, 395
  work load, 26, 47
Information systems, 260–282, 376–379, 391, 404
Information theory (*see also* Communication t.), 27–28, 50, 169, 175
Input channels, 25, 223
Input devices (of computer) (*see* Control(s), Peripherals and types of I.d.)
Inspection (*see also* Monitoring, Vigilance), 7, 12, 16, 68, 80, 83, 108–109, 111–112, 139, 193, 198, 204, 287, 292, 390–392, 393, 404
Institute of Experimental Psychology (I.E.P.), Oxford, 25, 50, 51
Institution of Chemical Engineers
  Industrial Research Fellowship on 'Man and Computer in Process Control', vii
Instrument(s) (*see also* Malfunction detection, Measurement(s) and types of I.), 5, 10–14, 19, 166–167, 189–192, 204, 211, 217, 226–227, 238–248, 255, 290–308, 329, 333–334, 337–341, 344–346, 355, 360, 363, 377–378, 393
  analyzers, 190, 333–334, 337–338, 344–346, 393
  beta gauges, 34, 36, 39, 121–123
  bomb thermocouples, 252, 255
  chromatographs, 190, 333, 337
  critical, 248
  duplication, 241, 245, 248
  faults, xii, 12, 166–167, 191, 211, 217, 226–227, 238–248, 346, 360, 363
  flow transducers, 5, 242–243, 333, 341
  identification, 298, 316
  impulse lines, 242–243
  i. room, 350
  labelling, 297–298, 310
  level transducers, 242, 244, 341
  local gauges, 349
  noise (*q.v.*)
  pressure transducers, 5, 242, 244, 329, 341
  reliability, 167, 227, 242, 255, 355, 363
  spatial coding, 298
  special-purpose (*see* Special-purpose equipment)
  temperature transducers, 5, 242, 244, 329, 341, 354
    mercury-in-steel thermometers, 242
    resistance thermometers, 242, 329, 341
    thermocouples, 242, 329, 341, 354
  valve positioners, 242, 244, 246
  not working, 363
Instrument engineer, 188
Instrument reader, 348
Instrument technician, 17, 19, 188, 193
Integration
  in design, 387
Intelligence, 21, 311, 407, 422
Interaction
  in design, 387

Intercom, 263, 269
Interest, 21, 257–258, 309, 375, 382, 384
Interface design (*see also* Control(s), Display(s), Equipment d. and types of I.), vii–ix, xii–xiii, 91, 117, 147, 222–237, 252, 256, 412–413, 416–418
Interlocks, 231, 235, 236, 353, 419
  as alternative to automatic sequence control, 231, 419
Interpreted measurements, 122, 377–378
Interruptions, 85–86, 154–155
Interviews, viii–ix, 1, 74–76, 81, 120, 136–140, 159–161, 370, 411
Intuition, 8, 23
Inventories, 369
Iron Stoker, 393
Isolation
  physical i. not equivalent to social i., 19
Iteration
  in design, 386–387, 416

Job
  autonomy, 6, 367–369, 373–376, 379, 382–384
  gestalt, 369, 373, 378
  interest, 21, 257–258, 309, 375, 382, 384
  modification, 186–195
  potential
    for learning, 311–312, 368, 375, 384
    for promotion, 384
  social context, 384
  specialization, 368, 374–376
  variety, 368, 384
Job aids (*see also* types of J.a.), 299, 311, 387
Job description, 111, 189–193, 321, 423
  for manning simulation, 321
Job design, viii–ix, xii–xiii, 367–385, 415 416, 420, 424–425
Job evaluation, 23, 26, 106–107, 111, 193, 395
Job profile, 415–416
Job satisfaction, xiii, 7, 9, 21, 258, 367, 369, 376, 378, 379, 384, 392
  j. enlargement, 367, 369
  j. enrichment, 384, 392
  j. rotation, 379
  j. security, 7, 9, 21
Job specification, 193, 374–376, 387
Judgment, 15, 21, 173, 239, 381

Laboratory, 10, 382
  analyses, 12, 36, 38, 69, 378
  computer control in, 188, 190
Laboratory personnel, 10, 21, 187–188, 190, 374, 377–378
Labour costs, 186
Labour turnover, 21, 78, 312, 375, 407
Lamps, 15, 20, 93, 355, 362, 363
Layout (*see* Control(s), Display(s), Panels, Workplace l.)
Learning (*see also* Training), viii–ix, xii, 21, 22, 51–66, 96, 127–132, 142–144, 146, 158, 178–185, 206, 211–219, 221, 241, 283–319, 375, 378, 383, 384, 389, 392, 395, 402, 406, 409
  in acid purification plant experiments, viii–ix, 283–319
  in air mixer experiment, viii–ix, 142–144
  category-specific l., 286–287
  conceptual l., 288–289, 314
  in electric arc furnace scheduling simulation, viii–ix, 96
  fading of prompts, 286, 289–290, 299
  in groups, 309
  inhibited by lack of measurements, 378
  interest, 309
  knowledge of results, 306–308, 375, 378
  l. conditions, differences in, 288–289
  modelling of l. process, xiii–iv, xii, 178–185, 402, 406
  motivation, 21, 308–309
  in pilot plant experiment, viii–ix, xii, 206, 211–221
  by process computer, 59–66
  rate, 22, 178–185, 217–219
  retrogressive chaining, 286, 289–290
  serial l., 288–289
  strategy development, viii–ix, xii, 96, 158, 211–221, 395, 409
  transfer, 176
  in water bath experiments, viii–ix, 53–58, 127–132
Learning control (*see also* 'Decision program'), 59–66
Lighting (*see* Illumination)
'Limit value', 198–201
Line printers, 224, 228
Linguistic analysis, 412
Liquid washing plant, viii–x, 67–78, 395, 401, 411
Log (*see* Data logging, Process l.)
Logistic functions (*see* Scheduling)
Loss prevention, 7, 238, 405, 408, 423

Machine design, 387
Machine intelligence (*see* Artificial i.)
Machine minding, 3–4, 188
Machine specification, 387
Machinery, 2–3, 51, 125
Maintenance, 5–6, 10, 14, 15, 17–18, 23, 68, 120, 188, 193–194, 232, 297, 325–326, 354, 424
  by process operator, 5–6, 14, 23, 68, 325–326, 424
Maintenance personnel, 5, 10, 15, 16, 17–18, 21, 23, 68, 188, 193–194, 242, 259, 304, 374, 378–379
  on day work, 17–18, 23
  on shift work, 17–18, 23
Malfunctions (*see also* Breakdown(s), Fault(s), M. detection)
  in instruments, xii, 166–167, 191, 211, 217, 226–227, 238–248, 346, 360, 363
  in plant equipment, 12, 14, 135, 200, 203, 211, 225–230, 267, 271, 292, 302, 304, 361
Malfunction detection (*see also* Fault diagnosis), xii, 191, 217, 238–248, 346, 396, 405, 417, 420, 424

allocation of function, 246–247, 248
in control valves, 238–239, 241, 244–246
classification of checks, 245–246
definition of m., 238–239, 241, 242, 247
detection stage, 238–239, 241–242, 246, 247–248
diagnosis stage, 241, 247
displays for (*see also* Display(s)), 239–241, 247–248, 405, 417
from equipment condition, 239
from equipment performance, 239
incipient m., importance of, 238
information redundancy, 217, 239, 241, 247
by inspecting equipment, 239
in instruments (*see also* control valves, measuring instruments), 191, 238–248, 405, 420
in measuring instruments, 238–248, 346
classification of checks, 239, 241, 245
from control valve position, 239, 245
from duplicate instruments, 239, 245
from instrument behaviour, 239, 245
from other instruments, 239, 241, 245
by process computer, 238–239, 241–242, 246–248
by process operator, xii, 238–248, 405, 420
man–computer interactive, 246–248
models, use of, 226, 241–242, 245–246
noise, 239–241, 243–245, 248
by observing instruments, 239
pattern recognition, 238, 241, 247
in plant equipment, 405, 420
probabilities of m., 246
by process computer, 238–239, 241–242, 246–248
by process operator, xii, 191, 217, 238–248, 346, 405, 420, 424
experience, 239, 247
learning, 241, 247
operator's comments, 242–244, 246

Man–computer interaction, viii–ix, 206–221, 236, 390–391, 399

Man–computer interactive systems, viii–ix, xii–xiii, 222–237, 260–282, 390–392, 400, 404, 419
in process control, viii–ix, xii–xiii, 222–237, 260–282, 400, 404

Man–computer interface, 206–221, 222–237, 255–258, 262–268

Man–machine systems, 25–26, 46, 47, 51, 79, 120, 125, 177, 252, 256, 386–387, 389, 391, 397, 399

Man–machine system reliability (*see also* Human error(s)), 227, 235, 384, 405, 425

Management, 6, 7, 9–10, 15, 21–23, 26, 66, 81, 104, 268, 370, 374, 376, 378–380, 382–384, 406–407

Manipulated variables
in baking ovens, 80–81
in basic oxygen converters, 249–252
in electric arc furnaces, 94–95

in miscellaneous processes, 5, 10, 11–12, 69, 189–191
in papermachine, 34–39, 121–123
in pilot plant, 210, 213

Manipulation, 1, 17, 107, 159

Manning, 47, 91, 106, 178, 186–195, 320–326, 374
tank farm m. simulation, 320–326
trade union agreements, 374

Manpower planning, 91, 178

Manuals, 357, 363, 424

Manual actions, 5, 6, 69, 83, 106–107, 120, 163, 189, 193, 291–292, 295, 320, 393
chemical analyses, 69, 189
cleaning and oiling machines, 6, 193
hand valves (*q.v.*)
handling materials, 83, 120
maintenance (*q.v.*)
sampling, 5, 291–292, 295, 300–304, 316
shutdown (*q.v.*)
startup (*q.v.*)
threading paper machine, 193

Manual control (*see also* Human transfer function, Information sampling, Tracking, Vigilance, types of C.), vii–xiii, 5–14, 25–50, 51–66, 67–78, 79–90, 91, 104, 115, 120–134, 139, 140–144, 146, 150, 152, 155, 156–157, 160, 163–164, 166, 172–173, 186–195, 196–205, 206–221, 223, 230, 249–259, 299, 348–366, 378, 388–389, 393, 394, 395, 396–399, 402, 404, 406, 409, 414, 415, 417, 418–419, 422, 424
adaptive features, 66
of air mixer apparatus, viii–ix, 140–144
anticipatory features, 51, 52, 62, 64, 75, 87, 104, 152, 155, 213, 406
of baking ovens, viii–x, 79–90, 395, 396
of basic oxygen converters, viii–ix, 249–259
of boilers, 349
boredom (*q.v.*)
change of operating point, 6, 7, 11, 40, 53, 120, 127, 141, 160, 210, 419, 422
as criterion of c. skill, 7, 160, 422
closed-loop features, 13, 51–66, 120–122, 143–144, 155, 213, 215, 406
complexity, 5, 8, 9, 23, 115, 133, 160, 163–164, 173, 198, 210
on computer-controlled plants, viii–ix, xii–xiii, 186–195, 196–205, 206–221, 249–259, 348–366, 398, 399, 402, 404
computer simulation, 59–66
difficulties (*see* Controllability)
during controller failure, 12
displays for, 45–49, 127–133, 206–221, 257–258, 299, 361, 395, 404, 417, 419
of fast-response systems, xi, 51, 125, 146, 156–157, 388
feedback of results
delays in, 5, 8–10, 12, 36, 38, 51, 69, 115, 132–133, 160, 164, 173, 362, 378
lack of, 9, 65, 69–70, 132–133, 160, 166, 378

hunting, 53–54, 61–63, 125–131, 142–144
intermittency of human c., 150
mental models (*see* Process operator mental models)
of nuclear reactors, 349, 352–359
open-loop features, 51–66, 75, 87, 120–122, 143–144, 155, 213, 215, 406
oscillations (*see* hunting)
of papermachine, viii–xi, 34–39, 51, 120–124, 146, 395, 396, 419
partial, 249–259
of pilot plant, viii–ix, xii, 206–221, 402, 404
predictive features (*see* anticipatory features)
quickening (*q.v.*)
of rate of change, 299, 361
of slow-response systems, x, 51–66, 67–78, 79–90, 120–134, 139, 140–144, 206–221, 250–254, 257–258, 299, 361, 395
speed limitation, 189
as standby for automatic c., 12, 186, 189–192, 194, 223, 230, 259, 359, 424
during upsets and emergencies, 12, 186, 189–192, 259, 359
of water bath, viii–xi, 39–44, 51–66, 120–134, 395
Manual work, 1, 393–394
Mass production, 2–4, 7, 22
Mathematical models (*see also* Human transfer function)
   accuracy of, 268
   for basic oxygen converter control, 251, 254–255
     carbon, oxygen and temperature predictions, 254
     heat, lime and mass balances, 254
   heat and mass balances, 226, 241, 245, 254
   for instrument malfunction detection, 226, 241–242, 245–246
   for predictive displays, 258, 263, 267–268
   for simulation, 413
   for soaking pit scheduling, 263, 267–268
   steady-state, 251, 254
   unsteady-state, 255
   of water bath, 131–132
Matrix of variances, 369, 371–373, 385
Measurement(s), 5, 8–12, 31–32, 46, 50, 69–70, 81, 115, 121–123, 132–133, 160, 164, 166, 190, 199–201, 222–223, 227, 238–248, 251–258, 343–344, 361–363, 377–378, 393–394, 412, 417, 423
   in basic oxygen converters, 251–258
   basis weight, 34–39, 120–123, 189
   brightness, 377, 381, 385
   burst can detection, 350–352, 361, 363
   cake quality, 81
   carbon content, 253, 257–258
   checking, 238–248, 355
   coal quality, 192
   colour, 69, 81, 109, 385
   control rod position, 350–351, 355–356
   control valve position, 123–124, 248, 351
   count rate, 353–357, 361
   counter channel, 355–356
   current, 351
   delays in (*see also* sampled), 9–10, 115, 133, 164, 173, 362, 378
   digestion, degree of, 377
   displays (*q.v.*)
   doubling time, 353–357
   duplicate and near-duplicate, 241, 245, 248
   economics, 255, 310, 377
   errors, 343–344
   estimates, 9, 69–70, 132–133, 160, 166
   failure (*see* Malfunctions(s))
   filtering, 409
   flow, 5, 189–191, 208–216, 234, 252, 256, 294, 298, 304, 306–307, 351, 360–362
   frequency, 191
   indirect, 103, 417
   inferred (*see* indirect)
   interpreted, 122, 377–378
   iron oxide in slag, 253
   kappa number, 381, 385
   lack of, 9, 65, 69–70, 132–133, 160, 166, 378
   lance height, 251–252, 256
   level, 298, 304, 306–307, 361
   in liquid washing plant, 69
   local gauges, 9
   moisture, 10, 189, 378, 385
   noise, 31–32, 46, 48, 50, 132, 199–201, 239–242, 243–245, 248, 255, 361–362, 378, 423
   oxygen in steel, 253
   in papermill (*see also* basis weight), 189, 377–378
   period, 355
   pH, 378, 385
   physical properties, 10, 81, 377–378, 385
   power, 351–352, 353–358, 362–363
   pressure, 5, 48, 109, 189–191, 252, 256, 298, 306–307, 353, 354, 358
   by process operator (*see also* estimates, sensory), 394
   reliability, 167, 227, 242, 255, 355, 363
   sampled, 5, 10, 12, 36, 38, 51, 69, 378
   sensory, 5, 8, 10, 12, 46, 69, 81, 109, 222, 252, 256, 377–378
   smoothing (*see* filtering)
   by special-purpose equipment, 393
   speed, 189–191
   tearing strength, 377, 381
   temperature, 5, 40, 53, 80, 109, 127, 138, 189–191, 208–210, 234, 236, 252–253, 255, 256, 294, 298, 306–307, 351, 353–354, 357–359, 361, 363, 385
   thickness, 10
   voltage, 191, 351
   weight, 10, 251, 378
Mechanization, 3, 223, 392–393
Medical diagnosis, 286
Medical Research Council
   Applied Psychology Unit, Cambridge, 108, 388
Memory, 9, 16, 20, 34, 42, 48–49, 52, 58, 66, 87, 104, 108–109, 121, 170, 230–231, 268, 299, 303, 357, 358, 361
   short-term, 9, 16, 361

Memory aids, 49, 90, 122, 230–231, 268, 299, 310, 355, 357, 358, 362
   timers, 49, 355
Mental arithmetic, 108, 110
Mental effort, 106–108, 117
Mental load, xi, 8–9, 16, 42, 91, 95, 104, 105–119, 132–133, 146, 156, 159–164, 172–173, 198, 235, 395, 398, 400, 404
   automation, effect of, 118
   background l., 114, 117
   in breakdowns, 16, 163–164
   in chemical plants, 105–119
   decision-taking l. (Kitchin and Graham), xi, 114–117, 395
      complexity of factors, 9, 115, 133, 160, 163–164, 173, 198
      delays, 8, 9, 51, 53, 115, 132–133, 160, 164, 173
      interdependency of factors, 8, 115, 132, 146, 160, 163–164, 173, 198
      memory l. (see also Memory), 9, 115, 133, 160, 173, 198
      number of factors, 8, 115, 132, 172, 198
   displays, effect of, 160, 163–164
   in manning calculations, 91
   manual control difficulties (see Controllability)
   measurements, effect of, 160, 163–164
   methodology of assessment, 105–119
   in startup, 163–164
Mercury system, 247
Merit rating, 23
Meters (see also Dials, Display(s), Indicators), 14, 93–94, 209, 226, 228, 232, 305, 351, 355, 357
Method Time Measurement (MTM), 287, 321
Micromotion study, 286–288
Military systems, 125, 313, 386, 388, 391, 413, 421, 422, 425
Mimic diagrams and panels, 14–15, 90, 93, 229, 305, 362, 417
Models (see Mathematical ms., Process operator mental ms., Process operator ms.)
Monitoring (see also Alarm m., Inspection, Signal(s), Vigilance), viii–ix, xii, 3, 5, 12–14, 19–20, 23, 25–50, 69, 104, 108–109, 111, 135–140, 146, 150, 152–153, 189–192, 197–202, 222, 224–226, 234–235, 238, 249, 255, 259, 355–359, 361, 388, 393–394, 398–399, 403, 416–418, 424
   difference between m. and vigilance, 30
   intermittency of human m., 25–50, 150
   of sequential operations, 231, 355–359
Monotony (see Boredom)
Morale, 407
Motivation (see also Group behaviour, Organizational factors, Social factors), xii, 20–21, 45–46, 104, 159, 168, 200–205, 258, 308–309, 368–369, 375–376, 382–384, 388–389, 392, 407, 411, 413, 419, 422
   in allocation of function, xii, 200–205
   and decision-making, 200–205
   in fault diagnosis, 203

goal-ordering behaviour as measure of, 202, 205
incentives (q.v.)
in information sampling, 45–46, 104, 200–202, 205
information sampling behaviour as measure of, 201–202, 205
job characteristics (see also Job, Job satisfaction), 368–369
in learning, 21, 308–309
in process operator research, 411, 413, 419
of refinery operator, 200–205
rewards and sanctions, 368–369
in training, 308–309
Motor activity (see also Checking round, Manual actions), 6, 106–107, 135, 146, 159, 363, 401
Motor dynamics, 146
National Aeronautical and Space Administration (N.A.S.A.)
   flight control centre, 391
National Economic Development Office (N.E.D.O.)
   report on chemical manpower, 424
National Grid, xi, 14, 401–403
National Institute of Industrial Psychology (N.I.I.P), 405
Nobo, Trondheim
   assembly plant, 367
Noise (audible), 5, 8, 19, 222, 360, 365
Noise (signal), 31–32, 46, 48, 50, 132, 199–201, 239–242, 243–245, 248, 255, 361–362, 378, 423
Noise (system), 25, 91, 93, 171, 250, 252, 256, 408, 413
Nomenclature, 22, 356, 360
Nomograms, 251, 343, 358
Non-stop production (see Continuous-flow p.)
Normal conditions, 197–202, 224–226, 234, 349, 359, 394, 404
   process operator functions, 197–202, 224–226, 234, 394, 404
Norsk Hydro, Porsgrunn
   fertiliser plant, 367
Nuclear reactors, viii–ix, xiii, 4, 195, 222–237, 348–366, 397, 399, 401–403, 405, 407, 413, 418
Nuclear weapons, 425

Observation (of process operator), viii–ix, 1, 7, 34–39, 69–75, 81–84, 111, 120, 159–161, 197, 202, 210–211, 300–308, 411
'Observing response', 26–27, 40–42, 411–412
Older workers (see Age)
Open-loop control, 51–66, 75, 87, 120–122, 143–144, 155, 213, 215, 393, 406
   use by experienced operator, 58, 87, 143–144, 155, 215, 406
Operability (see Controllability)
Operant conditioning, 27
Operating instructions, 6, 67, 78, 118, 122, 230, 299, 316, 352–354, 357, 363, 415, 424
   and task analysis, 316, 424

Operating procedures, 6, 15, 67, 78, 84–88, 98–100, 118, 223, 231, 299, 308, 316, 352–354, 409
'Operations' (in task analysis), 291–299, 315–316, 412
Operational research, 176, 419
Operator (*see* Human o., Process o.)
Operator's control panel, xii, 189–191, 206–221, 224–237, 255, 262–268, 390, 404, 406
Optimization, 7, 13, 64–66, 74, 165–167, 172, 192, 198, 203, 223–225, 234, 359, 377, 382, 394, 409
   by process computer, 64–66, 224–225, 359
'Optimizing control', 198
Organizational factors (*see also* Group behaviour, Motivation, Social fs.), viii–ix, xiii, 118–119, 347, 367–385, 391, 392, 399, 406, 410
   followup of o. changes, 380, 383
   traditional approach to o., 376
Output devices (of computer) (*see* Display(s), Peripherals and types of O.d.)
Outstations (*see* Remote terminals)
Ovenman, 79–90
Overload, (*see also* Information load, Work load), 47, 217, 405, 418, 420
   response to, 217

Pacing, 6
Panels (*see also* Mimic diagrams and ps., Operator's control p.), xii, 93–94, 160–164, 167, 175, 189–191, 206–221, 224–237, 298, 304–305, 348–351, 360–363, 390–391, 399, 404, 406, 417
   layout, 209, 231–232, 305, 351, 360–363
   local, 349
Papermills, viii–xi, 1, 9–11, 34–39, 51, 120–134, 187, 189, 193, 367–385, 395, 396, 399, 404
Pattern recognition, 46–47, 51, 226–237, 239–241, 247–248, 255, 298, 304–308, 416–417
   in bomb thermocouple, 255
   displays for, 47, 226–237, 240–241, 247–248, 416–417
   in fault diagnosis, 308
   in instrument panels, 298, 416–417
   in malfunction detection, 239–241, 247–248
   by process computer, 247, 255
Penalties, 30–31, 44–45, 48, 51, 200, 232, 260, 304, 407, 408, 420
Perception, 8, 88, 107, 159, 163, 165–167, 287
Performance assessment, 7, 21–23, 26, 53–59, 70–75, 95–97, 106–108, 113, 127–132, 141–144, 159, 210–211, 273–276, 380–383, 398, 406, 408–410, 415, 418, 421, 424, 425
   comparison of methods, 408–410
   correlated function measurement, 408–409
   difficulties in process control, 7, 21–23, 26, 159, 406, 408–410
   direct achievement measurement, 95–97, 273–276, 380–383, 408–410
   in electric arc furnace scheduling, 95–97, 410
   operator loading measurement, 106–108, 408–409
   in papermill control, 380–383
   in pilot plant control, 210–211
   in simulations, 95–97, 273–276, 410
   in soaking pit scheduling, 273–276, 410
Performance criteria (*see also* Control objectives, System objectives),
   classification (Lees), 408
      process control, 408
      process economics, 408
      psychology, 408
   relations between, 408
Personal qualities, 7, 20–21, 118–119, 422
Personal relations (*see also* Social factors, Social skills), 16, 21, 370
Personnel officer, 406–407
Personnel selection, 1, 2, 20–22, 24, 67, 118, 145, 147, 170, 178, 195, 260, 303, 310, 311–312, 314, 319, 387, 395, 398–400, 405, 406, 407, 409, 415, 421–423, 424
   ability, 303, 311, 407, 409, 422
   in developing countries, 424
   differences between airline pilot and process operator, 422
   economics, 422
   education, 7, 422
   intelligence, 21, 311–312, 407, 422
   motivation, 20–21, 422
   in non-industrial areas, 424
   non-intellectual factors (Crossman), 20–21
      conscientiousness, 16, 20–21, 311, 422
      reliability, 20–21, 422
      responsibility, 9, 20–21, 422
      social skills, 21, 422
      trustworthiness, 21, 422
   objectives, 421–423
   performance criteria, need for, 421
   process characteristics, importance of, 195, 407
      nuclear reactors, 195
   s. tests, 21–22, 67, 395, 398, 399, 405, 406, 421–423
   self-s., 423
   simulation, 260
   supervisor's assessment, 21–22, 405, 421
   task analysis, importance of, 310, 314, 319
   temperament, 16, 20–21, 422
   during training, 422
Petroleum Industry Training Board, 423
'Phenomenal limit curve', 199–201
Physical environment (*see also* aspects of E.), 19, 364–365, 388
Pilots (*see* Airline ps.)
Pilot plant, viii–ix, xii, 206–221, 402, 404
'Plan' (in task analysis), 291–295, 299–308, 315–317, 412
   sequence, 295, 316
      fixed, 295, 316, 412
      variable, 295, 316–317
   timing, 316–317
Planning (*see also* Scheduling), 178, 376, 377
Plants
   acid purification, viii–ix, xiii, 283–319, 396, 398, 405, 416, 423

Subject Index

bakery, viii–x, 79–90, 154, 395–396
cement, 187, 190
chemical, viii–xiii, 1, 4–5, 11–12, 19, 105–119, 136–145, 159–164, 181, 187, 189–190, 193–194, 206–221, 238–248, 283–319, 393, 407, 422
electrical power
    conventional generation, 1, 4, 166, 191–192, 195, 405, 407, 413
    nuclear generation, viii–ix, xiii, 4, 195, 222–237, 348–366, 397, 399, 401–403, 405, 407, 413, 418
iron and steel, viii–xiii, 1, 17, 19, 91–104, 146–158, 181, 187–189, 191, 193–194, 249–259, 260–282, 393, 396–401
oxygen, viii–ix, 1, 4–5
papermills, viii–xi, 1, 9–11, 34–39, 51, 120–134, 187, 189, 193, 367–385, 395, 396, 399, 404
pilot p., viii–ix, xii, 206–221, 402, 404
pipelines, 196
pumping stations, 196
refineries, viii–ix, xii–xiii, 1, 4, 11–12, 14, 17–18, 67–78, 187, 190, 194, 196–205, 320–326, 397, 399
tank farm, viii–ix, xiii, 320–326, 400

Plant availability, downtime, throughput (see A., D,. T.)

Plant commissioning, 22

Plant equipment
    baking ovens, viii–x, 79–90, 154, 395–396
    basic oxygen converters, viii–ix, xii, 249–259, 393, 397, 404
    blowers, 203, 340
    boilers, xi, 4, 109, 188, 191, 230, 348–354, 363, 373–374, 378, 396
    burners, 80, 84, 203
    calendars, 120
    compressors, 4–5, 109, 340, 360
    condensers, 207–208, 292, 298, 349, 352, 354, 360
    conveyors, 80–81
    cooling towers, 236, 342
    cranes, 92–93, 269, 271–272, 277, 278, 354
    digesters, 372, 375
    distillation columns, 5, 11–12, 206–221, 292, 294, 295, 298, 304–307, 331, 336, 339, 342
    ejectors, 304, 306–307
    electric arc furnaces, viii–xi, 91–104, 146–158, 395, 396, 410, 412, 413, 421
    evaporators, 295, 298, 306–307, 310, 342
    expansion engines, 4
    fans, 236, 340, 353
    feed tanks, 304, 306–307, 354
    filters, 338, 372
    furnaces, 11–12, 203
    gas absorption columns, 11–12, 339, 342
    heat exchangers, 12, 208, 295, 302, 312, 338, 342
    Hydrapulpers, 120
    L.D. converters (see basic oxygen converters)
    liquid washers, 67–78
    papermachines, 9–11, 34–39, 120–126, 134, 374, 396, 419
    pipework, 296–298
    precipitators, 342, 352, 354
    presses, 9, 120
    pumps, 6, 11, 67, 203, 208, 211, 236, 295, 297, 304, 306–307, 310, 312, 331, 338, 340, 352, 354, 358
    reactors (chemical), 11–12, 109, 292, 295, 298, 307, 339, 342
    reactors (nuclear) (see Nuclear reactors)
    reboilers, 207–208, 295, 298, 306–307
    reflux drums, 304, 307
    screens, 372–373
    settling tanks, 67
    soaking pits, viii–ix, xii–xiii, 260–282, 393, 400, 404, 410, 413
    steam traps, 12, 341
    steel mills, viii–ix, xi, 17, 25, 181, 186–189, 191–194, 260–282, 393, 397–401, 403, 404
    storage tanks, 5, 11–12, 237, 297–298, 304, 324–326, 354, 369, 372
    trains, 14–15, 110, 261, 269, 271, 278
    trucks, 323–325
    turbines, 188, 191, 348–354, 357, 358, 362
    washing columns, 11–12

Plant foreman (see P. supervisor)

Plant manager, 6, 7, 9–10, 15, 145, 347, 376, 378–380, 383–384, 406–407

Plant services, 7, 74, 92–97, 109, 304–307, 312, 339, 347, 407
    cooling water, 312, 339, 362
    electrical power, 7, 92–97, 203, 339
    failure, 109, 203, 304–307, 312, 360
    instrument air, 109
    process water, 74, 341
    steam, 109, 207, 304, 306–307, 312, 339, 360, 362

Plant size, 4, 17, 194, 407, 422

Plant supervisor, 5, 6, 9, 11, 18, 20, 188, 204, 295, 299, 347, 374, 376, 379–380, 383–384, 396
    abolition, 20, 383–384
    automation, effect of, 20
    division of work with process operator, 376

'Polyvalent' craftsman, 18

Population stereotypes (see Ss.)

Potential correction, 238

Prediction (see also Display(s), Information sampling, Manual control, Open-loop control), 8, 44–50, 51, 62–65, 87, 94, 125, 147, 154, 157, 165–166, 198–201, 213, 230, 257–258, 262–268, 355, 392, 404, 406, 417
    of control actions, 87, 154
    of system state, 87, 154

Probabilities, 166, 170, 173, 199–201, 226–227, 229–230, 242, 246–247, 409, 418, 422
    in alarm analysis, 226–227, 229–230, 418
    in decision-making, 166, 170, 173, 226–227, 229–230, 246–247
    estimation, 166, 409, 422
    of inadequate performance (see Training)

in information sampling, 199–201
of instrument faults, 226, 242
in malfunction detection, 246–247
and motivation, 200–201
of process disturbances, 199–201
process operator's knowledge of, 199–201, 226–227, 229–230, 246–247, 414
of signals (q.v.)
Problem-solving (see also Decision-making, Strategies, types of P.), 59–60, 158, 165–177, 202–204, 260–282, 311, 379–384, 391–392, 398, 419–420
by computer, 59–60, 89, 158, 169, 203, 392, 419–420
by groups, 168, 379–384
man-computer interactive, 260–282, 391
in papermill, 379–384
Procedures (see Operating ps.)
Processes
batch, 79–90, 91–104, 249–259, 260–282, 320–326
classification (Crossman), 2–4
continuous, 1–24, 34–39, 67–78, 120–134, 135–145, 159–164, 196–205, 206–221, 222–237, 283–319, 367–385
sequential, 348–366
Process characteristics (see also Control system cs., Controllability, P. disturbances), x, 2–14, 393–394, 399, 408
of baking ovens, 79–81
of basic oxygen converters, 249–254
economic cs., 408
of liquid washing plant, 67–69
of papermachine, 34–39, 121–124
of pilot plant, 207–208, 215
process operator, effect on, x, 2–14, 393, 399
of soaking pits, 261–262
of water bath, 39–41, 53, 125–128
Process computer (see aspects of P.c.)
Process computer acceptability, 260, 396, 404, 407
Process computer control (see also Direct digital c., Surveys), vii–ix, xii, 91, 102–103, 131–133, 146–147, 186–195, 206–221, 222–237, 254–259, 260, 393, 396–402, 404–407, 408, 412, 416–421
advantages, 186–195, 222–237, 393, 416–421
differences within, 393
disappointing performance, 206, 260, 407
economics, 408
employment, effect on, 186–195
monitoring by process operator, 146, 186, 189–192, 194, 255, 259
process control task, effect on, 186–195, 393
Process computer functions (see also types of F.), 186–195, 399–400, 404
Process computer graphics (see also Cathode ray tubes, Display(s)), 103, 221, 228–237, 248, 257–258, 262–268, 361, 397, 401, 404, 416–418, 424
Process computer peripherals (see also types of P.), 224, 232–233

Process computer program, 194, 264
Process computer programmer, 194
Process computer programming, 191, 194, 224, 258, 344
Process computer systems
distributed ss., 224
Process conditions (see also Breakdown(s), Emergencies, Upsets), 197, 224
abnormal cs. (q.v.)
normal cs. (q.v.)
switchover (q.v.)
Process constraints, 29, 33–34, 37, 44–49, 84, 92, 198–203, 253, 277, 353–354
in baking ovens control, 84
in basic oxygen converter control, 253
in electric arc furnace scheduling, 92
margin from, 198, 238, 353–354
in nuclear reactor control, 353–354
in refinery control, 198–203
in soaking pit scheduling, 277
Process control, vii–xiv, 2–14, 19–24, 392–410
Process disturbances, 6, 10, 12, 14, 26, 29–30, 31, 37, 39, 40, 44–46, 48, 51, 68–69, 72, 81, 92–93, 109, 126, 132, 135, 139, 146, 190, 191, 198–202, 203, 211, 217, 225–230, 241, 249–251, 261, 267, 271, 278–279, 292, 304–307, 312, 360, 361, 373, 385
in baking ovens, 81
bandwidth, 29–30, 37, 39, 44–46, 48, 126
in basic oxygen converters, 249–251
drifting and decaying factors, 26, 31, 39, 40, 44, 45, 135, 217, 241
in electric arc furnaces, 92–93
instrument failure, 12, 191, 217, 226–227, 360
in liquid washing plant, 68–69, 72
in papermill, 51, 126, 373, 385
plant equipment failure, 135, 200, 203, 211, 217, 225–230, 267, 271, 292, 304–307, 312, 361
plant services failure, 109, 203, 304–307, 312, 360
raw materials quality, 10, 51, 135, 249–251, 373, 385
in soaking pits, 261, 278–279
in water bath, 40, 44, 132
Process lags, 8, 9, 35, 40, 51, 53, 68, 76, 77, 84, 92, 121, 124–128, 132, 139, 141, 146, 160, 164, 215, 263
in air mixer, 141
in baking ovens, 84
dead time (distance-velocity l., time delay, transmission l.), 35, 124–128, 141
exponential l. (transfer l.), 35, 40, 53, 124–128
in liquid washing plant, 68, 76, 77
in papermill, 35, 51, 121, 124–126, 146
in pilot plant, 215
in soaking pits, 263
in water bath, 40, 53, 127–128, 132
Process log (see also Data logging), 5–6, 12, 14, 15, 23, 68, 139, 187, 189–191, 291–292, 352, 355

Process models (*see* Mathematical ms.)
Process operation, 407
Process operator
    assistant os., 11, 160, 164, 166, 178, 374, 379
    importance of, 6, 13–14, 24, 51, 67, 408
    individual differences (*q.v.*)
Process operator abilities, 409, 422
Process operator activities, 5–6, 83, 159, 161, 193, 395
    in baking ovens, 83
    in chemical plants, 159, 161
    classification (Crossman), 5–6
        control, 5–6, 83, 159, 161, 193
        recording and reporting, 6, 161, 193
        routine maintenance, 6
        special procedures and drills, 6
    classification (Daniel *et al.*), 161
        communication, 161, 193
        control actions, 5–6, 83, 159, 161, 193
        logging data, 161, 193
        outdoor work, 161, 193
        rest pauses, 83, 161
        scanning instruments, 159, 161
Process operator functions (*see also* types of F.), 6, 7, 68–69, 83, 120, 160–164, 197–204, 224–232, 250–254, 292, 393–394, 398–400, 409, 416–421
    in acid purification plant, 292
    in baking ovens, 83
    in basic oxygen converters, 250–254
    in chemical plants, 160–164
    classification (Crossman), 7
        breakdown avoidance, 7, 197–198, 225–230, 394, 409, 420
        breakdown recovery, 7, 202–204, 230, 394, 409, 420–421
        changeover, 7, 197, 231–232, 394, 409, 418–419
        optimization, 7, 198, 203, 225, 394, 409
        regulation/stabilization, 7, 197–202, 224–225, 394, 409, 418–419
    classification (Lees), 394
        communication, 394, 409
        data processing and handling, 394, 409
        goal formulation, 394
        manual operations, 394
        measurement, 394
        monitoring, 394, 409, 416–418
        optimization, 7, 198, 203, 225, 394, 409
        other control, 7, 197–202, 224–225, 394, 409, 418–419
        scheduling, 394, 409, 419–420
        sequential control, 7, 231–232, 394, 409, 419
        single-variable control, 7, 197–202, 224–225, 394, 409, 418–419
    in liquid washing plant, 68–69
    in nuclear reactor, 224
    in papermill, 120
    in refinery, 197
Process operator mental activities
    classification (Crossman), 8
        deciding, 8

        familiarization with controls, 8
        perceiving, 8
        predicting, 8
        sensing, 8
    classification (Kitchin and Graham), 108–109
        alertness, 108, 110, 112
        control, 108–109, 111–112
        inspection, 108–109, 111–112
        memory, 108–109, 112
        mental arithmetic, 108, 110
        monitoring, 108–109, 111
        planning, 108, 110, 112
        state recognition, 108–109, 111
Process operator mental models (models constructed by operator), viii–xi, 8–9, 15–16, 23, 29, 31–32, 34, 41, 56, 58, 64, 66, 74, 76, 84–90, 91–104, 121, 123, 124, 128, 133, 135–145, 146–158, 160, 164, 165–177, 199–204, 224–230, 238–248, 250, 295–298, 299, 396–400, 403, 406, 414
    of acid purification plant, viii–ix, 298, 299
    action state matrix, 89–90
    of air mixer, viii–ix, 145
    of baking ovens, viii–ix, 84–90
    of basic oxygen converters, 250
    comparison of types, 414
    and complexity, 9, 133, 160
    conceptual ms. of p., 8–9, 15, 23, 41, 56, 66, 74, 136, 140–141, 145, 166, 406, 414
    control loops, 414
    critical incidents, 136–137
    and diagnostic tasks, 226–230
    dodges, knacks and wrinkles (*see also* rules-of-thumb), 74, 76
    of electric arc furnaces, viii–ix, 98–104, 146–158
    experimental studies, 91–104, 135–145, 146–158
    formation, 136, 166
    of hand valves, 123
    identification cues, 295–298
    information display, effect of content and structure, 164, 166, 175
    and information sampling, 29, 31–32, 34, 104, 152
    intuitive ms. of p., 8, 23
    of liquid washing plant, 74, 76
    logical thinking, 8, 23, 229–230
    look-up tables, 58, 64, 89, 121, 156
    'make-believe situation', 136, 140
    non-routine ms., 144–145
    operating procedures (*q.v.*)
    o.'s accounts (*see also* Verbal protocol), 74, 76, 136–140
    of papermachine, viii–ix, 123, 124, 128, 146
    patterns, 414
        displays, 248, 298
        faults, 225–230, 238–248, 414
        noise, 414
        system states, 224–230, 414
        trends, 239–241, 247, 299, 414
    'phenomenal limit curve' (*q.v.*)

'physics and chemistry', 56, 66, 140, 406, 414
plant layout, 414
probabilities
  faults, 199–201, 226–227, 229–230, 246–247, 414
p. flow diagram, 414
routines, 84–90
routine ms., 144–145
rules as ms., 8, 15–16, 23, 157, 166
rule book, 88–90
rules-of-thumb, 8, 23, 76, 202–204, 247
steady-state gains, 58, 64, 121, 414
stored information, 139, 140
strategies (q.v.)
subroutines, 84–90, 98–104, 146–158
system responses, 23, 29, 31–32, 34, 56, 66, 124, 128, 146, 299, 414
system state matrix, 29, 89–90
unit operations, 334, 414
updating, 136
of water bath, viii–ix, 56, 58, 64, 66, 128

Process operator models (models of operator constructed by investigator) (*see also* Action-information trees, Executive Routine, Human transfer function, Thought stream analysis, Time Constant M.), viii–xii, 1, 16, 25–50, 51, 56–66, 84–90, 98–103, 125, 147–158, 178–185, 317–318, 388, 402, 403, 406, 421
categorization system, 403
comparison of ms., 30, 57–58, 84–90, 98–103, 147–158
computer program, 84–88, 89, 98, 100–101, 157–158, 318, 403, 421
  Executive Routine, 84–88, 100–101, 157, 318, 403
  interrupt, 84–88, 102, 154–155
  subroutines, 84–88, 148–157, 318
control system, viii–xi, 30, 51, 56–66, 125, 156–157, 403, 406
finite state machine (FSM), 156–158
hierarchical system, 317–318, 403
information processing system, x, 1, 16, 25–50, 157–158, 403, 406
learning system, xii, 178–185, 402, 406
mathematical ms., xi–xii, 156–158
system state/action state, 89–90, 156

Process operator problems (*see also* types of P.), xii, 21–24, 311, 395, 404, 406–407
classification (Lees), 406–407
  communication, 21, 378, 407
  emergencies, 16, 311, 407
  human error, 16, 405, 407
  information display, 24, 25, 206, 406
  job evaluation, 22–23, 106–107, 407
  job satisfaction, 21, 367, 407
  operator-computer relations, 206, 262, 404, 407
  p. operation, 13–14, 21, 24, 51, 196, 311, 407
  selection, 21, 311, 406
  training, 22, 290–310, 407
costs, 21, 24, 51, 407, 420

Process operator research, vii–xiv, 24, 49–50, 65–66, 77–78, 104, 145, 158, 165–177, 205, 221, 386–425
approach, 410, 425
  design, involvement in, 410, 425
  industrial problems, quantification of, 410, 425
  industry, involvement of, 410, 425
  research programme, long-term nature of, 410–411, 425
  systems criteria, use of, 410, 425
importance of, 406–407
industry's rôle in, 410, 425
suggestions (Crossman), 24
  equipment design, 24, 145, 415–418
  information sampling, 49–50
  manual control, 65–66, 415, 418–419
  personnel selection, 24, 145, 415, 421–423
  social organization, 24
  training, 24, 145, 415, 423–424
suggestions (Lees), 414–425
  alarm analysis, 229, 415, 417
  alarm systems, 205, 229, 415, 417
  allocation of function, 205, 415
  decision-making, 104, 158, 165–177, 415, 421
  emergency administration, 205, 415, 420–421
  emergency avoidance, 205, 415, 420
  fault administration, 205, 415, 420
  fault correction 205, 230, 415, 420
  fault detection, 205, 415, 420
  fault diagnosis, 205, 229, 415, 420
  information display, 49–50, 145, 221, 226, 415–416
  job design, 415, 424–425
  job profile, 415–416
  manual control, 65–66, 415, 418–419
  operating instructions, 78, 415, 424
  operator error, 415, 425
  performance assessment, 145, 415–416
  personnel selection, 24, 145, 415, 421–423
  scheduling, 415, 419–420
  sequential control, 232, 415, 419
  system objectives, 319, 415
  task analysis, 310, 415–416
  training, 24, 145, 415, 423–424

Process operator skill (*see also* P.o. mental models, S.), x–xi, 1–24, 56, 67–78, 79, 91, 105–119, 135–145, 146, 160, 165–177, 178–185, 186, 192, 195, 217, 225, 226, 230, 300–304, 305, 308, 311–312, 392, 395, 396–397, 411, 422
acquisition
  time to acquire, 7, 77–78, 178–185, 217, 411
change of operating point as criterion of, 7, 160, 422
decision-making (q.v.)
experience (q.v.)
inaccessible, x, 7, 56, 392, 411
individual good at one aspect good at all, 7
information handling, 16

information sampling (*q.v.*)
   level of s. required, 67, 78, 195, 311–312, 422
   manual control (*q.v.*)
   mental ss., x–xi, 3, 7–8, 15–16, 23, 67, 79, 91, 105–119, 135–145, 146, 165–177, 392, 395,
   p. understanding (*see* P.o. mental models)
   retention on automated plants, 186, 192, 225, 226, 230
   specific, 7, 23
   state evaluation (*q.v.*)
   transfer, 7, 23, 56, 300–304, 305, 308
Process operator studies (*see also* Table 2, pp. 396–402), vii–xiv, 394–406
   acid purification plant, viii–ix, xiii, 283–319, 396, 398, 405, 416, 423
   air mixer, viii–ix, xi, 135–145, 400, 406, 414
   ammonia plant, 190
   atmospheric distillation plant, viii–ix, 159–164
   automation effect of, vii–xiii, 1–24, 159–164, 186–195, 206–221, 249–259, 395, 397–398
   baking ovens, viii–x, 79–90, 154, 395–396
   basic oxygen converters, viii–ix, xii, 249–259, 397, 404
   board mill, viii–ix, 9–11, 395
   British Iron and Steel Research Association ss. (*see* basic oxygen converters, electric arc furnace simulation *and* soaking pits simulation)
   catalytic cracker, 190
   cement plants, 187, 190
   Central Electricity Generating Board ss. (*see also* nuclear reactors (C.E.G.B.)), xi, 403
   chemical plants (Annett, Duncan *et al.*; Duncan), viii–ix, xiii, 283–319, 394, 396, 398, 405, 412, 413, 416, 417, 421, 423, 424
   chemical plants (Anyakora and Lees), viii–ix, xii, 238–248, 396, 405,
   chemical plants (Brenninkmeyer), 395, 397
   chemical plants (Daniel, Puffler and Stríženec), viii–ix, xi, 159–164, 398, 415
   chemical plants (Department of Labor), 187, 189–190, 194
   chemical plants (Kitchin and Graham), viii–ix, xi, 26, 105–119, 159, 165, 172, 395, 400
   chemical plants (Kragt and Landeweerd), viii–ix, xi, 135–146, 394, 400, 406, 414
   chemical plants (Towill), 181
   Danish Atomic Energy Commission Research Establishment ss. (*see* electronic equipment *and* nuclear reactors (Rasmussen))
   dates of publication, 394–403
   decision-making (*see also* baking ovens, electric arc furnace simulation, soaking pits simulation *and* verbal protocol), viii–ix, xi, 165–177, 402–403
   Department of Labor ss., viii–ix, xii, 186–195, 398, 404
   design ss., viii–ix, xii, 249–259, 260–282, 320–326, 348–366
   electric arc furnace simulation, viii–xi, 91–104, 146–158, 395, 396, 410, 412, 413, 421
   electronic equipment, 247, 401
   ethanolamine plant, 189
   granulation plant, 401
   inaccessibility of, vii
   industrial ss. (*see also* plant ss.), viii–xiii, 91–104, 222–237, 249–259, 260–282, 320–326, 396–402
   industries visited by Crossman, 1
   information sampling, viii–x, 25–50, 202, 395, 398, 406
   Institute of Experimental Psychology ss. (*see* information sampling *and* water bath (Crossman and Cooke))
   laboratory ss., viii–xii, 25–50, 51–66, 120–134, 135–145, 396–402
   L.D. converters (*see* basic oxygen converters)
   learning, viii–ix, xii, 178–185, 402, 406
   liquid washers, viii–x, 67–78, 395, 401, 411
   malfunction detection, viii–ix, xii, 238–248, 396, 405
   manual control (*see* air mixer, liquid washers, pilot plant, water bath (Attwood) *and* water bath (Crossman and Cooke))
   mental load, viii–ix, xi, 26, 105–119, 159, 165, 172, 395, 400
   mental models (*see* P.o. mental models)
   methodology of ss. (see P.o.s. methodology)
   nuclear reactors (Ablitt), 396, 405, 425
   nuclear reactors (C.E.G.B.), viii–ix, xi, xiii, 348–366, 397, 403
   nuclear reactors (Green), 399, 405, 425
   nuclear reactors (Rasmussen), viii–ix, xii, 199, 217, 222–237, 394, 401, 404, 405, 412, 417, 418, 420, 421, 425
   nuclear reactors (Whitfield), 402–403, 405
   number of, vii, 394–395, 403
   oxygen plant, viii–ix, 4–5, 395
   papermachine (Attwood), viii–ix, xi, 120–134, 396, 406, 414
   papermachine (Beishon; Crossman, Cooke and Beishon), viii–x, 25–50, 51, 146, 395, 396, 398, 406
   papermill (Beishon and Palmer), 396
   papermill (Department of Labor), 187, 189, 193
   papermill (Engelstad), viii–ix, xiii, 367–385, 399, 406, 410
   papermill (Mardon *et al.*), 400, 404
   pilot plant, viii–ix, xii, 206–221, 394, 402, 404, 412
   plant ss., viii–xiii, 1–24, 25–50, 67–78, 79–90, 105–119, 120–134, 135–145, 159–164, 178–185, 186–195, 196–205, 206–221, 238–248, 283–319, 348–366, 367–385, 396–402

polyethylene plant, viii–ix, 159–164
polymerization plant, 190
power station (Cristian and Zbăganu; Cristian), xi, 165, 175, 397, 404
power station (Department of Labor), 191–192, 195
power station (Jervis and Maddock), 399, 404
power station (Křivolahý), 400
power station (Parish), 400, 404
process computer ss., viii–ix, xii, 186–195, 196–205, 206–221, 222–237, 249–259, 260–282, 348–366, 396–402
pyrolysis plant, viii–ix, 159–164
refinery (Department of Labor), 187, 190, 194
refinery (Itelson), 159, 166, 395, 399
refinery (de Jong), 399, 404, 415
refinery (de Jong and Köster), viii–ix, xii, 196–205, 394, 399, 404, 420
refinery (Pogostin), 395, 400, 415
reviews, vii–xiv, 394–406
selection tests (Davies), 398, 405, 421
selection tests (Hiscock), 67, 395, 399, 421
separation plant (for pyrolytic gases), viii–ix, 159–164
simulation ss., viii–xiii, 91–104, 260–282, 283–319, 320–326, 396, 400
soaking pits simulation, viii–ix, xii–xiii, 260–282, 400, 404, 410, 413
solvents plant, viii–ix, 11–12, 395
steel mills
    annealing line, 191
    hot strip mill (Crossman; Sell, Crossman and Box), xi, 25, 51, 120, 143, 398, 401, 403
    hot strip mill (Department of Labor), 187, 192–194
    mill system (Hickling and Jones), 399, 404
    mill system (Leplat and Cuny), 400, 404
    rolling mill (Towill), 181
    tinning line, 191
steel works (Crawley), 397
styrene plant, 189
subjects $(q.v.)$
tank farm, viii–ix, xiii, 320–326, 400
task analysis (*see* training)
training, viii–ix, xiii, 283–319, 394, 396, 398, 405, 412, 413, 416, 417, 421, 423, 424
U.K. Atomic Energy Authority ss. (*see* nuclear reactors (Ablitt) *and* nuclear reactors (Green))
verbal protocol (*see also* electric arc furnace simulation), viii–ix, xi, 146–158, 395–396, 412
waste heat boiler, xi, 396, 401, 403
water bath (Attwood), viii–ix, xi, 120–134, 396, 406, 414
water bath (Crossman and Cooke), viii–x, 25–50, 51–66, 140, 143, 395, 398, 406, 414
water tanks (Beishon), 395–396
water vessels (Brigham and Laios), 397, 406
Process operator study methodology (*see also* Activity graphs, Interviews, P.o. activities, Questionnaires, Verbal protocol), viii–x, 1–4, 34, 43–44, 56, 57, 70–74, 77–78, 91, 94, 95–96, 104, 105–119, 128, 136, 141–144, 147, 155–156, 160, 164, 165–177, 179, 210–211, 215–221, 222, 260–261, 272, 277, 300–301, 388, 393–394, 408–413, 419, 421, 425
control system characteristics, importance of, 1–4, 222, 393–394, 412
experimentation by p.o., 128, 215, 217, 219–221
experts' judgments, 110–117, 160, 421
eye camera, 411
films, 411
graphic method, 175–176
investigator's experience, importance of, 136, 412
laboratory vs. plant ss., 77, 410, 411, 425
linguistic analysis $(q.v.)$
mental load assessment, 105–119
objective and subjective methods, 164, 411
'observing response' $(q.v.)$
performance criteria, 77, 179, 408–411, 425
physical activity assessment (*see* P.o. activities)
p. characteristics, importance of, 1–4, 393–394, 412
p. computer as investigational tool, 94, 210–211, 412
ranking methods, 117, 160, 421
simulation ss., x, 77–78, 91, 96, 104, 260–261, 412–413
statistical experimentation, 43–44, 57, 70–74, 96–97, 142–144, 300, 411
subjects
    choice of, 77–78, 95–96, 411
    experienced vs. inexperienced, 34, 77–78, 95–96, 147, 155–156, 411, 421
    instructions to, 56, 96, 141, 272, 277, 300–301
    motivation, 411, 413, 419
    number of, 77–78, 95, 220, 272, 301, 411
Product quality, 3, 7, 9–10, 23, 26, 69, 81, 84, 120, 137–140, 167, 197–201, 210, 253, 370, 373–374, 377–383, 419
Product yield, 7, 23, 198, 201, 382
Production lines (*see also* Assembly work), 2–4, 291
'Productive domain', 197, 203–204
Program, programmer, programming (*see* Computer p., Process computer p.)
Program machines (*see also* Computers), 2, 14, 21, 160
Protective systems (*see also* High Integrity P.Ss., Safety shutdown ss.), 417, 420
displays for checking, 417
Protocol (*see* Verbal p.)
Prototype production, viii–ix, 268, 365, 387

PSI apparatus, 169–170, 176
Psychologist, 1, 310, 312, 314, 386, 408
Psychology, vii, 165–177, 283–319, 403, 408
  Gestalt p., 167, 169

Quality control (*see also* Product q.), 5, 9–10, 69, 81–84, 96, 121–123, 137–140, 193, 197–201, 215, 253–254, 286, 373, 377–378, 392, 404, 417
  displays for, 417
Quantitative reading, 225
Questionnaires, viii–ix, 53, 137, 186–195, 411
Quickening (*see also* Display(s)), 47, 419

Radar, 27, 309, 388, 404
Reading(s), 225, 226, 228
  check, 228
  digital (*see also* quantitative r., Display(s)), 217, 219, 225, 228, 361
  error in taking, 217, 219, 360, 405
  quantitative, 225
Recorder(s), xii, 10–12, 47, 49, 127–131, 198–202, 207, 209, 211, 217, 219–220, 225, 228–229, 239–241, 248, 299, 339, 349, 351, 355–357, 361–363
  coarse control, use in, 219
  control performance, effect on, 127–131, 219
  displays, 240
  fault administration, use in, 217, 219
  fine control, use in, 219, 299
  information sampling from, xii, 47, 198–202
  malfunction detection, use in, 239–241, 248
  paper speed, 49
  for rate of change, 49, 299, 357, 361
  scale, 49, 362–363
Recruitment, 407
'Red operating zone', 199
Redundancy (*see also* Displacement), 20, 24, 186–187, 383–384
Refineries, viii–ix, xii–xiii, 1, 4, 11–12, 14, 17–18, 67–78, 187, 190, 194, 196–205, 320–326, 397, 399
Reliability (*see also* Availability, Downtime, High r. systems, Human error(s), Man–machine system r., R. engineering), 17, 20–21, 167, 196, 223–224, 227, 238–248, 255, 355, 363, 368, 391, 396, 399, 402, 405, 407, 415, 420–421, 422, 423, 425
  of control systems, 167, 196, 223–224, 405
  of controllers, 223, 242
  guide lines for, 425
  of instruments, 167, 227, 242, 255, 355, 363
  of plants, 17, 405, 407, 423
  of process computer, 224
  of process operator, 20–21, 196, 396, 399, 402, 405, 407, 415, 420–421, 422, 425
  r. assessment, 405, 425
  of typewriters, 232

Reliability engineer, 407
Reliability engineering, 405
Remote terminals, 194
Repetitive work, 2–3, 6, 17, 22, 23, 178, 181, 388, 391–392
Research (*see* Human operator, Process operator r.)
Research engineer, 188
Resource allocation (*see* Scheduling)
Response time, 226, 420–421
Responsibility (placed on operator), 6, 9, 15, 78, 260, 311
Responsibility (shown by operator), 2, 9, 20–21, 182, 422
Rest pauses, 6, 161, 163, 320, 325–326, 388, 391–392
  Industrial Fatigue Research Board studies, 388
Reviews (*see* Surveys)
Revision of opinion, 422
Royal Air Force
  Air Traffic Control Centre, West Drayton, 277
  Institute of Aviation Medicine, Farnborough, 388
Royal Radar Establishment (R.R.E.), Malvern
  touchwire c.r.t., 263–264
Rules-of-thumb, 8, 23, 76, 202–204, 247

Safety, 14, 22, 201, 222, 232, 250, 251, 291, 300, 327–328, 347, 350–354, 359, 405, 408, 425
  control system, 350–354
  human factors, importance of, 405, 425
  margin, 198–201, 355
Safety shutdown systems (*see also* Protective ss., High Integrity Protective Ss., Trips), 14, 139–140, 230, 304, 350–354
Sampling (of information) (*see* Information s.)
Sampling (of process materials)
  costs, 300–303, 316
  strategies, 300–304, 316
Sampling Theorem, 29–30, 37, 42–45, 126
Sandia Laboratories, Albuquerque
  work on human error, 405
  work on human factors, 391
Scales (*see* Dials)
Scheduling, viii–x, xiii, 16, 79–90, 91–104, 110, 120, 146–158, 252, 256, 260–282, 377, 394, 395–396, 399–400, 404, 409, 410, 412, 413, 415, 417, 419–420
  of baking ovens, viii–x, 79–90, 395–396
  displays for, 417
  of electric arc furnaces, viii–x, 91–104, 146–158, 395–396, 410, 412, 413
  flexibility of human operator, 85–87
  man–computer interactive, 260–282, 399–400, 404, 419
  of papermill, 120, 377
  by process computer, 260, 419–420
  of soaking pits, viii–ix, xiii, 260–282, 400, 404, 410, 413
  of steel mill, 399, 404

Secondary tasks, 6, 424
Security control
　　displays for, 417
Selection (see Personnel s.)
Self-regulation, 368–369, 371, 374
Self-repair, xii, 196, 424
Semi-Automatic Ground Environment (SAGE) system, 391
Sensation (see also types of S.), 5, 8, 76, 222
　　hearing, 5, 8, 222
　　sight, 7, 10, 12, 46, 69, 76, 81, 109, 252, 377–378
　　smell, 5, 8, 222
　　touch, 76, 419
　　vibration, 5
Sense(s) (see Sensation)
Sequential control (see also Changeover, Shutdown, Startup, Switchover), 6, 7, 11, 12, 15, 16, 53, 120, 127, 141, 160, 189–191, 193, 203, 210, 223, 231–232, 299, 316, 348–349, 352–363, 393, 394, 409, 415, 417, 419, 422
　　change of operating point, 6, 7, 11, 53, 120, 127, 141, 160, 210, 419, 422
　　displays for, 417
　　length of sequence, 231, 299
　　in nuclear reactor startup, 348–349, 352–363
　　order of sequence, 231, 299, 316
　　　　invariant, 231, 299, 316
　　　　variable, 299, 316
　　'plan' (q.v.)
　　by process computer, 189–191, 193, 231–232, 419
　　recovery from upset, 11, 203
　　by special-purpose equipment, 232, 393
　　unexpected factors, 15
Setting, 160
Sex
　　of process operator, 7
Shell U.K. Ltd.
　　Shell Haven refinery, 326
　　Stanlow refinery, 326
Shift(s) (see also Group behaviour, Team(s))
　　changeover, 77, 139–140, 225, 234, 282, 322–323
　　communications, 379
　　differences between, 70–74, 77, 180, 182, 225, 407
　　organization, 374
　　performance, 182
Shift work, 6–7, 23, 196, 311, 398, 423
Shutdown (see also Safety s. systems, Trips), 6, 12, 14, 135, 189–191, 197, 222, 224–225, 230–232, 292, 299, 304, 308, 348
　　emergency, 230–232, 420
　　by process computer, 230–232
Sickness, 6, 78, 291, 320
Sight, 7, 10, 12, 46, 69, 76, 81, 109, 252, 377–378
Signal(s) (see also Alarm monitoring, Information sampling, Monitoring, Pattern recognition, Vigilance), viii–ix, 16, 25–50, 198–201, 239–241, 409, 423
　　amplitude, 29, 37, 44–45, 46, 199

　　bandwidth, 29–30, 37, 39, 44–46, 48
　　decoding, 16, 166, 398, 403
　　detection, viii–ix, 16, 26–30, 107, 159, 409
　　discriminability, 27–28
　　estimating averages (see integration)
　　filtering, 26, 31–33, 409
　　frequency, 26–30, 37, 39, 44–46, 48, 199–200
　　information content, 27–29
　　integration, 31–32, 121–122, 409, 423
　　nature, 26–34, 199–201, 239–241
　　noise (q.v.)
　　predictability, 29–31, 34, 44–45, 46–47, 48, 199–201
　　tolerance limits, 29, 33–34, 44–45, 46, 48, 49, 198–201
Simulation (see also Simulators), viii–xiii, 59–64, 77–78, 91–104, 146–158, 169, 260–282, 320–326, 392, 395, 396–397, 400, 403, 404, 410, 412–413, 421
　　advantages, 77, 91, 104, 260, 412
　　detailed descriptions, 59–64, 91–104, 260–282, 320–326, 396–397, 400, 413
　　disadvantages, 77–78, 96, 260–261, 413
　　of electric arc furnace scheduling, viii–xi, 91–104, 146–158, 395, 396, 410, 412, 413, 421
　　of human problem-solving, 59–66, 84–90, 157–158, 169–171, 392, 403, 421
　　of manual control, 59–64
　　mathematical modelling, 413
　　motivation, 413
　　problems, 413
　　of soaking pit scheduling, viii–ix, xii–xiii, 260–282, 400, 404, 410, 413
　　of tank farm manning, viii–ix, xiii, 320–326, 400
　　time scale, 93, 272–273
　　works data, 92–93, 271–272, 321
Simulators (see also Simulation)
　　Carmody Universal Process Trainer, 305, 413
　　computer-based, 91–104, 260–282, 413
　　flight, 413
　　for interface design, 260–282, 404, 412–413
　　process, 305, 412–413
　　for process operator studies, 412–413, 425
　　for process operator training, xiii, 145, 204, 260, 299, 305–308, 399, 405–406, 412–413, 424
　　compensatory tracking, 299
　　fault diagnosis, 305–308
Single-stream plants, 407, 422
Single-variable control, 394, 409
Skill (see also Process operator s.), 1–24, 51, 56, 67, 79, 91, 103, 135, 146, 168, 283–284, 299–312, 316–317, 388–389, 392, 395, 414
　　acquisition, 283–284
　　　　time to acquire, 79
　　description, 283–284
　　diagnostic ss., 18, 23, 312
　　industrial ss., 1–24, 51, 67, 79, 91, 135, 146, 395

manual ss., 3, 67, 392, 395
meanings to industrialist and psychologist, 1
mental ss., 3, 67, 79, 91, 103, 392, 395
organization of elements of behaviour, 284, 299–300, 317
sensorimotor ss., 3, 17
social ss., 21
timing, 316–317
transfer, 7, 56, 168, 300–304, 305, 308, 310–312
variation of performance with constant outcome, 284, 299, 316–318
Smell, 5, 8, 222
Soaking pits, viii–ix, xii–xiii, 260–282, 393, 400, 404, 410, 413
Social factors (see also Group behaviour, Motivation, Organizational fs.), viii–ix, xiii, 9, 16, 19, 20–21, 168, 196, 347, 367–385, 399, 406
Social skills, 21, 422
' Socio-technical ' approach, 367–385
Software, 264, 279–282, 387
Soldering iron, 233
Sonar, 388
Sound, 5, 8, 222
Space systems (see Aerospace ss.)
Special-purpose equipment, 190, 227, 232, 393
alarm scanners, 227
data loggers, 190, 227
for information reduction, 393
for measurement, 393
for sequential control, 232, 393
for shutdown, 232
Speed, 6, 11, 15, 18, 103, 111, 146, 156, 160, 189, 226, 298, 304, 420–421
Speed skill, 146, 178, 286
Stabilization, 7, 160, 165
Standby, 12, 186, 189–192, 194, 223, 230, 259, 359, 424
Startup, 6, 11, 12, 14, 135, 163–164, 181, 188–191, 197, 206–221, 222, 224–226, 231–232, 235, 290, 292, 294–295, 299, 308, 316, 348–349, 352–363, 404
of acid purification plant, 290, 292, 294–295, 299, 308, 316
of nuclear reactor, 348–349, 352–363
special s. desk, 360
of power station, 191, 404
by process computer, 189, 231–232
of steel mill, 181, 188–189
' State ', 137–140
' STATE ', 137–140
State evaluation (see also Display(s)), 29, 104, 136, 139, 155–156, 189, 197–198, 204, 222–237, 409, 416–418, 420
process log, 189
Statuses, 412, 417, 418
alarms, confusion with, 418
Status array, 217, 404–405, 417
Stereotypes, 362–363
display-control relations, 362–363
Stocks (see Inventories)
Storage (for materials), 323–324
Storage media (for data), 233–234

Strategies (see also Decision-making), viii–ix, xii, 18, 70–74, 77, 83–90, 95–96, 103, 150–158, 165–177, 211–221, 225, 229–230, 247, 273–275, 295, 300–308, 316–317, 381–383, 395, 409, 414, 419–421, 422
in acid purification plant control, viii–ix, 295, 300–308, 316–317
in baking ovens control, viii–ix, 83–90
controls, effect of, 215
development, viii–ix, xii, 96, 158, 172, 211–221, 395, 409
long-term, 215, 217–219
short-term, 215, 217–219
in diagnostic tasks, 18, 229–230, 247, 295, 300–308, 316–317
differences between shifts, 70–74, 77, 225
in electric arc furnace scheduling, viii–ix, 95–96, 150–156
in emergencies, 300, 304–308
experience, effect of, 95–96, 155–156, 215, 273–274
in heat exchanger fault diagnosis, 295, 300–304
in information sampling (q.v.)
and mental models, 414
optimal, 295, 300–304, 317
in papermill control (see also Information sampling, Manual control), 381–383
in pilot plant control, viii–ix, xii, 211–219
in PSI apparatus, 169–170
retention, 301–304
revision, 422
in soaking pit scheduling, viii–ix, 273–275
in water bath experiment (see Manual control)
in water tanks experiment, 395
Stress (see also types of S.), 16, 100, 156, 159, 166, 230, 272, 304, 388–389, 420, 422
time s., 100, 156, 159, 272, 304, 420
Subjects, 60, 77–78, 95–96, 147, 155–156, 411
apprentices, 300
laboratory personnel, 127
normal adults, 53, 60, 63
process operators, 34, 77–78, 95–96, 147, 150, 155, 181–182, 219–220, 272, 304–305, 411
students, 41, 53, 77–78, 95–96, 141, 147, 155–156, 411
subnormal adults, 60–62
systems engineers, 128, 414
Subjective assessment, 268, 273
Subjective probability, 31, 170, 173, 175
Submarines, 125
' Subroutine ', 137
Suggestions, 382–383
Surveys
Department of Labor s., viii–ix, xii, 186–195, 398, 404
Department of Scientific and Industrial Research s., viii–x, 1–24, 395, 397
Institution of Chemical Engineers s., vii, xiv, 399
National Economic Development Office s., 424

Switchover (*see also* Changeover, Sequential control), 7, 197, 231
System(s) (*see also* Man–machine ss.)
  aided, 48
  high-order, 53
  open, 368, 376
  quickened, 47, 419
System characteristics, 368–369
Systems criteria (*see* S. objectives)
System design, xii, 310, 386–387, 391, 410, 425
  integration, 387
  interaction, 387
  iteration, 386–387, 416
  tradeoff, 310, 387
Systems engineer, 128, 194, 407, 414
Systems engineering, 386
Systems ergonomics, 386
System evaluation, xii, 260, 268, 276, 387, 424
System integrity, 424
System objectives (*see also* Control os., Performance criteria), 92, 250, 253, 319, 376–377, 379, 383, 386–387, 391, 406, 408, 410, 415, 423, 425
System realization, 387
System specification, 387
System state (*see* State evaluation)
Systems theory, 176, 368–369, 376–377

Tables, 47
Task analysis (*see also* Method Time Measurement, Micromotion study, Training, Work study), viii–ix, xii–xiii, 22, 283–319, 387, 389, 391, 396–398, 405, 415–416, 423, 424
  a. diagrams and tables, 284
  critique, 284–285, 315
  cost, c, of inadequate performance, 291, 292, 298, 300, 304, 314–315, 319, 423
  of diagnostic tasks, 300–308
  and equipment design, 310
  feedback, need for, 416, 424
  hierarchical organization, 291, 308, 317–318
  of industrial tasks, 291
    electrical maintenance, 291
    legal conveyancing, 291
    printing machine operation, 291
    production line control, 291
  level of description, 283–285, 290–291, 314–315, 423
  and operating instructions, 424
  'operations' (*q.v.*)
  performance elements, 287–288, 314, 318
  and personnel selection, 310
  'plan' (*q.v.*)
  probability, p, of inadequate performance, 291, 292, 300, 314–315, 319, 423
  progressive redescription, 290–291, 314–315, 317, 423
  t. complexity, 286
  and training, xii–xiii, 22, 283–319, 405, 416, 423–424
Task synthesis, 387, 392

Tavistock Institute of Human Relations Human Resources Centre, 367
Taxonomies, 2–9, 15–16, 20–21, 83, 105–119, 161, 193, 197, 224, 238–248, 393–394, 406–409, 414–415, 417, 420, 422
  testing of, 113–114, 116–117, 288
Team(s) (*see also* Group behaviour, Shift(s)), 3, 5, 6, 9–12, 14, 21, 24, 309, 320–326, 359–360, 382
  t. work, 3, 6, 9–12, 14, 21, 359, 382
Telephone, 14–16, 67, 263, 291, 351, 378–379
Teleprinter, 93–94, 103, 207–208, 210, 219
Temperament, 16, 20–21, 422
Terminals (for handling materials), 324
Testing, 193
Textile industry, 369
Thought (*see also* aspects of T.) x .59–66, 84–90, 98–104, 146–158, 165–177, 392, 403, 411–412, 421
  computer simulation, 59–66, 84–90, 157–158, 169–171, 392, 403, 421
  'productive thinking', 168, 170,
Thought stream analysis, 101–103
Throughput, 7, 197, 261, 273–274, 374, 408, 419
Time and motion study, 22, 287, 388
Time Constant Model (of operator performance), viii–ix, xii, 178–185, 402, 406
  choice of m., 179–182
  industrial applications, 179, 181–183
  noise and scatter, 178–180, 182–185
  parameter estimation, 180, 183–185
    Kalman filter, 180, 184–185
    least squares method, 180, 184–185
    moments method, 184–185
  performance index, 179–185
  performance plateau, 178, 182–183
  time constant, 180–184
Time lags (*see* Process ls.)
Time-sharing (*see also* Attention), 26, 31, 39, 150, 201, 217, 311, 320–326
Timers, 49, 355
Touch, 76, 419
Tracking, viii–xi, 30, 34, 43, 48, 51–66, 121–134, 146, 147, 210–215, 299, 388–389, 409, 411, 418
  compensatory, 48, 51, 147, 299
  fast, 30, 43, 51, 146
  pursuit, 30, 51
  slow, 43, 51, 146, 299
Trade unions, 347, 367, 370, 374
Tradeoff, 49, 156, 310, 387
  in design, 49, 310, 387
Traffic control (*see* Air t. c.)
Training (*see also* Learning, Simulators, Skill, Task analysis), vii–ix, xii–xiii, 1, 2, 8, 11, 22, 24, 52, 56, 66, 90, 118, 130, 136, 140, 145, 147, 168, 171, 176, 178, 186–195, 204, 210, 227, 260, 283–319, 320, 327–347, 362, 375, 379, 384, 387, 391–392, 395, 396–400, 405–406, 407, 412–413, 414, 416, 423–424
  algorithmic aids (*see also* decision trees), xiii, 171
  category-specific t., 286–287, 289–290

manual ss., 3, 67, 392, 395
meanings to industrialist and psychologist, 1
mental ss., 3, 67, 79, 91, 103, 392, 395
organization of elements of behaviour, 284, 299–300, 317
sensorimotor ss., 3, 17
social ss., 21
timing, 316–317
transfer, 7, 56, 168, 300–304, 305, 308, 310–312
variation of performance with constant outcome, 284, 299, 316–318
Smell, 5, 8, 222
Soaking pits, viii–ix, xii–xiii, 260–282, 393, 400, 404, 410, 413
Social factors (*see also* Group behaviour, Motivation, Organizational fs.), viii–ix, xiii, 9, 16, 19, 20–21, 168, 196, 347, 367–385, 399, 406
Social skills, 21, 422
' Socio-technical ' approach, 367–385
Software, 264, 279–282, 387
Soldering iron, 233
Sonar, 388
Sound, 5, 8, 222
Space systems (*see* Aerospace ss.)
Special-purpose equipment, 190, 227, 232, 393
alarm scanners, 227
data loggers, 190, 227
for information reduction, 393
for measurement, 393
for sequential control, 232, 393
for shutdown, 232
Speed, 6, 11, 15, 18, 103, 111, 146, 156, 160, 189, 226, 298, 304, 420–421
Speed skill, 146, 178, 286
Stabilization, 7, 160, 165
Standby, 12, 186, 189–192, 194, 223, 230, 259, 359, 424
Startup, 6, 11, 12, 14, 135, 163–164, 181, 188–191, 197, 206–221, 222, 224–226, 231–232, 235, 290, 292, 294–295, 299, 308, 316, 348–349, 352–363, 404
of acid purification plant, 290, 292, 294–295, 299, 308, 316
of nuclear reactor, 348–349, 352–363
special s. desk, 360
of power station, 191, 404
by process computer, 189, 231–232
of steel mill, 181, 188–189
' State ', 137–140
' STATE ', 137–140
State evaluation (*see also* Display(s)), 29, 104, 136, 139, 155–156, 189, 197–198, 204, 222–237, 409, 416–418, 420
process log, 189
Statuses, 412, 417, 418
alarms, confusion with, 418
Status array, 217, 404–405, 417
Stereotypes, 362–363
display-control relations, 362–363
Stocks (*see* Inventories)
Storage (for materials), 323–324
Storage media (for data), 233–234

Strategies (*see also* Decision-making), viii–ix, xii, 18, 70–74, 77, 83–90, 95–96, 103, 150–158, 165–177, 211–221, 225, 229–230, 247, 273–275, 295, 300–308, 316–317, 381–383, 395, 409, 414, 419–421, 422
in acid purification plant control, viii–ix, 295, 300–308, 316–317
in baking ovens control, viii–ix, 83–90
controls, effect of, 215
development, viii–ix, xii, 96, 158, 172, 211–221, 395, 409
long-term, 215, 217–219
short-term, 215, 217–219
in diagnostic tasks, 18, 229–230, 247, 295, 300–308, 316–317
differences between shifts, 70–74, 77, 225
in electric arc furnace scheduling, viii–ix, 95–96, 150–156
in emergencies, 300, 304–308
experience, effect of, 95–96, 155–156, 215, 273–274
in heat exchanger fault diagnosis, 295, 300–304
in information sampling (*q.v.*)
and mental models, 414
optimal, 295, 300–304, 317
in papermill control (*see also* Information sampling, Manual control), 381–383
in pilot plant control, viii–ix, xii, 211–219
in PSI apparatus, 169–170
retention, 301–304
revision, 422
in soaking pit scheduling, viii–ix, 273–275
in water bath experiment (*see* Manual control)
in water tanks experiment, 395
Stress (*see also* types of S.), 16, 100, 156, 159, 166, 230, 272, 304, 388–389, 420, 422
time s., 100, 156, 159, 272, 304, 420
Subjects, 60, 77–78, 95–96, 147, 155–156, 411
apprentices, 300
laboratory personnel, 127
normal adults, 53, 60, 63
process operators, 34, 77–78, 95–96, 147, 150, 155, 181–182, 219–220, 272, 304–305, 411
students, 41, 53, 77–78, 95–96, 141, 147, 155–156, 411
subnormal adults, 60–62
systems engineers, 128, 414
Subjective assessment, 268, 273
Subjective probability, 31, 170, 173, 175
Submarines, 125
' Subroutine ', 137
Suggestions, 382–383
Surveys
Department of Labor s., viii–ix, xii, 186–195, 398, 404
Department of Scientific and Industrial Research s., viii–x, 1–24, 395, 397
Institution of Chemical Engineers s., vii, xiv, 399
National Economic Development Office s., 424

Switchover (*see also* Changeover, Sequential control), 7, 197, 231
System(s) (*see also* Man–machine ss.)
    aided, 48
    high-order, 53
    open, 368, 376
    quickened, 47, 419
System characteristics, 368–369
Systems criteria (*see* S. objectives)
System design, xii, 310, 386–387, 391, 410, 425
    integration, 387
    interaction, 387
    iteration, 386–387, 416
    tradeoff, 310, 387
Systems engineer, 128, 194, 407, 414
Systems engineering, 386
Systems ergonomics, 386
System evaluation, xii, 260, 268, 276, 387, 424
System integrity, 424
System objectives (*see also* Control os., Performance criteria), 92, 250, 253, 319, 376–377, 379, 383, 386–387, 391, 406, 408, 410, 415, 423, 425
System realization, 387
System specification, 387
System state (*see* State evaluation)
Systems theory, 176, 368–369, 376–377

Tables, 47
Task analysis (*see also* Method Time Measurement, Micromotion study, Training, Work study), viii–ix, xii–xiii, 22, 283–319, 387, 389, 391, 396–398, 405, 415–416, 423, 424
    a. diagrams and tables, 284
    critique, 284–285, 315
    cost, c, of inadequate performance, 291, 292, 298, 300, 304, 314–315, 319, 423
    of diagnostic tasks, 300–308
    and equipment design, 310
    feedback, need for, 416, 424
    hierarchical organization, 291, 308, 317–318
    of industrial tasks, 291
        electrical maintenance, 291
        legal conveyancing, 291
        printing machine operation, 291
        production line control, 291
    level of description, 283–285, 290–291, 314–315, 423
    and operating instructions, 424
    ' operations ' (*q.v.*)
    performance elements, 287–288, 314, 318
    and personnel selection, 310
    ' plan '(*q.v.*)
    probability, p, of inadequate performance, 291, 292, 300, 314–315, 319, 423
    progressive redescription, 290–291, 314–315, 317, 423
    t. complexity, 286
    and training, xii–xiii, 22, 283–319, 405, 416, 423–424
Task synthesis, 387, 392

Tavistock Institute of Human Relations Human Resources Centre, 367
Taxonomies, 2–9, 15–16, 20–21, 83, 105–119, 161, 193, 197, 224, 238–248, 393–394, 406–409, 414–415, 417, 420, 422
    testing of, 113–114, 116–117, 288
Team(s) (*see also* Group behaviour, Shift(s)), 3, 5, 6, 9–12, 14, 21, 24, 309, 320–326, 359–360, 382
    t. work, 3, 6, 9–12, 14, 21, 359, 382
Telephone, 14–16, 67, 263, 291, 351, 378–379
Teleprinter, 93–94, 103, 207–208, 210, 219
Temperament, 16, 20–21, 422
Terminals (for handling materials), 324
Testing, 193
Textile industry, 369
Thought (*see also* aspects of T.) x, 59–66, 84–90, 98–104, 146–158, 165–177, 392, 403, 411–412, 421
    computer simulation, 59–66, 84–90, 157–158, 169–171, 392, 403, 421
    ' productive thinking ', 168, 170,
Thought stream analysis, 101–103
Throughput, 7, 197, 261, 273–274, 374, 408, 419
Time and motion study, 22, 287, 388
Time Constant Model (of operator performance), viii–ix, xii, 178–185, 402, 406
    choice of m., 179–182
    industrial applications, 179, 181–183
    noise and scatter, 178–180, 182–185
    parameter estimation, 180, 183–185
        Kalman filter, 180, 184–185
        least squares method, 180, 184–185
        moments method, 184–185
    performance index, 179–185
    performance plateau, 178, 182–183
    time constant, 180–184
Time lags (*see* Process ls.)
Time-sharing (*see also* Attention), 26, 31, 39, 150, 201, 217, 311, 320–326
Timers, 49, 355
Touch, 76, 419
Tracking, viii–xi, 30, 34, 43, 48, 51–66, 121–134, 146, 147, 210–215, 299, 388–389, 409, 411, 418
    compensatory, 48, 51, 147, 299
    fast, 30, 43, 51, 146
    pursuit, 30, 51
    slow, 43, 51, 146, 299
Trade unions, 347, 367, 370, 374
Tradeoff, 49, 156, 310, 387
    in design, 49, 310, 387
Traffic control (*see* Air t. c.)
Training (*see also* Learning, Simulators, Skill, Task analysis), vii–ix, xii–xiii, 1, 2, 8, 11, 22, 24, 52, 56, 66, 90, 118, 130, 136, 140, 145, 147, 168, 171, 176, 178, 186–195, 204, 210, 227, 260, 283–319, 320, 327–347, 362, 375, 379, 384, 387, 391–392, 395, 396–400, 405–406, 407, 412–413, 414, 416, 423–424
    algorithmic aids (*see also* decision trees), xiii, 171
    category-specific t., 286–287, 289–290

City and Guilds Institute
    Chemical Technician certificate, viii–ix, xiii, 327–347, 397, 414
during commissioning, 22
conceptual t., 66, 298–299
content of material, 66, 140, 286
in control panel, 210, 298, 362
cumulative part t., 285–286, 289
decision trees (see also algorithmic aids), xiii, 300–308, 311–312
Department of Labor survey, 186–195
in developing countries, 424
in diagnosis, 286, 300–308, 312
difficulties, 299, 300, 304, 308, 316
and education, xiii, 22, 312–314, 347, 423
for emergencies, 140, 145, 227, 300, 304–308, 407
errors, reduction by t., 227, 285, 310, 423
in estimating probabilities, 176
by experienced operator, 22
experienced operator's performance not optimal, 91, 317
fading of prompts, 286, 289–290, 299
feedback of results
    concurrent, 308
    terminal, 308
for flexibility (see also transfer of skill), 379, 384
followup, 22
of groups, 309
in heuristics, 176
Industry T. Boards, 423
in instrument location, 298
and job specification, 375
knowledge content, 8, 22, 295–298
lectures, 130
motivation, 308–309
in non-industrial areas, 424
objectives, 312–313, 423–424
of older workers, 22, 285
in operating procedures, 145, 308
order of presentation, xiii, 308
overlearning, 290, 298, 308
in papermill, 379
part-task t., 22, 285–286
performance criteria, need for, 424
pilot t. schemes, 308, 318
by plant supervisor, 11, 347
practice not same as instruction, 317
programmed instruction, 288
retention, 300–304, 305, 310–312
    r. curve, 301
in search strategies, 300–308
in sequential operations, 290, 299, 316
simulators, xiii, 145, 204, 260, 299, 304–308, 399, 405–406, 412–413, 424
' specialized operator t.', 22
specific control tasks, xiii, 283–319, 423
in system responses, 56, 414
and task analysis, xii–xiii, 22, 283–319, 405, 416, 423–424
time required, reduction of, 22, 285
transfer of skill, 7, 56, 168, 300–304, 305, 308, 310–312
validation, 178, 424

whole-task t., 285–286
Training officer, 283, 315, 407
Training Within Industry (T.W.I.)
    Job Breakdown, 284
Transfer lines, 4, 18, 23, 291
Trend records (see also Recorder(s)), xii, 49, 127–131, 192, 198–202, 207, 217, 219–220, 229, 234, 239–241, 248, 299, 355, 357, 361
Trips, 203, 351–355, 357–358, 360
    adjustment, 360
    by-passing, 357
Trustworthiness, 21, 422
Typewriters (see also Hard copy), 103, 224, 228, 232–233
Typewriting, 132–133, 232–233

U.K. Atomic Energy Authority (U.K.A.E.A.)
    work on process operator reliability, 405, 425
University of Manchester Institute of Science and Technology (UMIST)
    pilot plant, 206–221
Unattended plant (see Unmanned p.)
Uncertainty, 30–34, 39, 41–48, 50, 170–173, 176, 197–201
Unforeseen events (see also Emergencies), 146, 360, 365
Unmanned plant, 196, 259
Upsets (see also Abnormal conditions, Breakdown(s), Emergencies, Fault(s), Malfunctions), 136–140, 190–191, 197–204, 211, 215, 217, 220, 320
    major, 190–191, 202–204, 320
    minor, 197–202, 320
    transfer to manual control, 190–191, 220
U.S. Air Force, Wright Air Development Center, Dayton, Ohio
    work on human factors, 391
U.S. Navy, Naval Research Laboratory, Washington, D.C.
    work on human factors, 391
Utilities (see Plant services)
Utility (in decision-making), 173

Validation, 260, 268, 276, 387, 424
Values, 314, 319
Valves (see Control vs., Hand vs.)
Vehicle guidance (see also Driving, Flying), 25, 419
Verbal protocol, viii–xi, 53, 81, 95–104, 146–158, 168–169, 174, 202, 211, 305–306, 395, 411–412
    in acid purification plant study, viii–ix, 305–306
    in baking ovens study, viii–ix, 81
    in electric arc furnace simulation, viii–xi, 95–104, 395
    objections to, 148, 412
    in pilot plant study, viii–ix, 211
    in water bath experiment, viii–ix, 53
Versatility (see Flexibility)
Vibration, 5

Vigilance (*see also* Alarm monitoring, Alertness, Arousal, Attention, Inspection, Monitoring, Signal(s)), vii–ix, 8, 14, 16, 26–29, 30, 105, 108, 110, 112, 160, 388, 390–391, 397, 403, 409, 425
    difference between monitoring and v., 30
    high level of v. not required in process control, 14, 160
    maintenance by artificial signals, 425
    selective v., 16
Vision (*see also* Sensation), 17, 27, 48–49, 197, 223, 226
    peripheral, 27, 48–49, 226

Warnings (*see* Alarms)
Watchkeeping (*see also* Monitoring, Vigilance), 27, 388, 404
    radar, 27, 388, 404
    sonar, 388
Water bath, viii–xi, 39–45, 51–66, 125–134, 143, 395, 396, 398, 406, 414
Water tanks, 395
Water vessels, 406
Western Electric
    Hawthorne experiment, 392
Wolvercote papermill, 50

Work breaks (*see* Rest pauses)
Work groups, 369
Work load (*see also* Mental l.), xiii, 5–6, 14, 26, 47, 107, 163, 201, 257, 311, 320–326, 406–407, 424
    in information sampling, 26, 47
    optimization rather than minimization, 201, 257
    short periods of intense effort, 6, 163, 311, 406–407, 424
    simulation studies, xiii, 320–326
    standard ratings, 107, 321
    variability, 5–6
    w. rate, 320–321, 326
Work measurement, 17, 26, 47, 106–107
Work Research Institutes, Oslo, 367
Work situation, 225, 227
Work study, 106, 285, 347, 392
Work study officer, 407
Workplace layout (*see also* Control room), 14–15, 207, 224, 227, 231–232, 268–270, 348–351, 360–366

' Yellow operating zone ', 199, 201

Zero Defects Program, 392